Essays in Austrian Economics

by
William Barnett II
and
Walter E. Block

ISHI PRESS
INTERNATIONAL

Essays in Austrian Economics
by
William Barnett II
and Walter E. Block

second edition

First Published in 2012 by Ishi Press in New York and Tokyo

ISBN 4-87187-324-2
978-4-87187-324-6

Ishi Press International
1664 Davidson Avenue, Suite 1B
Bronx NY 10453-7877
USA
samhsloan@gmail.com

1-917-659-3397

Printed in the United States of America

Essays in Austrian Economics

Authors:

William Barnett II
Walter Block

Table of Contents:

Credits for permission to publish:

Here are the original sources of chapters that comprise this book; the authors and publisher of this book thank the initial publishers of these articles, as well as our several co-authors, for their permission to allow these publications to appear, once again, in this volume. (In a few dozen cases, where the original source listed an article as forthcoming, this has been updated to reflect a later publication. Several footnotes were removed when they were extraneous or could not be substantiated.) We also thank Nate Straight for help with formatting this book.

Chapter 1. Block, Walter and William Barnett II. 2005. "Austrian Economics, Praxeology and Intervention," *Advances in Austrian Economics*. Vol. 8, pp 87-104 (28)

Chapter 2. Block, Walter, William Barnett II and Joseph Salerno. 2006. "Relationship between wealth or income and time preference is empirical, not apodictic: critique of Rothbard and Hoppe," *Review of Austrian Economics,* Vol. 19, No. 2, pp. 69-80; http://dx.doi.org/10.1007/s11138-006-6094-8; http://www.gmu.edu/rae/archives/VOL19_1_2006/4-Block_Barnett_Salerno.pdf

Chapter 3. Barnett, William and Walter Block. 2008. "Involuntary Unemployment," *Dialogue*; Vol. 1, pp. 10-22; http://www.uni-svishtov.bg/dialog/2008/1.08.WBII.WB.pdf

Chapter 4. Block, Walter and William Barnett II. 2008. "Continuums" *Journal Etica e Politica / Ethics & Politics*, Vol. 1, pp. 151-166, June; http://www2.units.it/~etica/; http://www2.units.it/~etica/2008_1/BLOCKBARNETT.pdf

Chapter 5. Barnett, William II and Walter Block. 2008. "Economic Singularism." *Research in the History of Economic Thought & Methodology*. Vol. 26-A, pp. 15–30

Chapter 6. Barnett, William and Walter Block. 2008. "Economic categorization." *Laissez-Faire*, Issue 28, March-September; http://fce.ufm.edu/Publicaciones/LaissezFaire/

Chapter 7. Block, Walter, William Barnett II, and Stuart Wood. 2002. "Austrian Economics, Neoclassical Economics, Marketing, and Finance." *Quarterly Journal of Austrian Economics.* 5(2): 51-66. http://www.qjae.org/journals/qjae/pdf/qjae5_2_4.pdf (6)

Chapter 8. Barnett, William II and Walter Block. 2005. "On the Use and Misuse of the Laffer Curve" *Journal of Public Finance and Public Choice,* Vol. XXIV, No. 3, pp. 139-152 (14)

Chapter 9. Barnett, William II, Walter Block and Michael Saliba. 2005. "Perfect Competition: A Case of 'Market-Failure," *Corporate Ownership & Control*. Vol. 2, No. 4, Summer, pp. 70-75

Chapter 10. Barnett, William II, and Walter Block. 2005-2006. "Mises, Rothbard and Salerno on Costs." *Corporate Ownership & Control,* Winter, Vol. 3, No. 2, pp. 203-205; http://www.virtusinterpress.org/additional_files/journ_coc/issues/COC_(Volume_3_Issue_2_Winter_2005-2006_Continued).pdf

Chapter 11. Barnett, William II and Walter Block. 2006. "Spreading the Benefits of Productivity Increases: Price Increases, Decreases, or Both? A Critique of Baumol on Subsidies to the Arts" *Dialogue*. Vol. 4, pp. 38-51; http://www.uni-svishtov.bg/dialog/2006/4.06.WB.pdf

Chapter 12. Barnett, William II, and Walter Block. 2006. "Rothbard on V-shaped average and total cost curves." *Quarterly Journal of Austrian Economics*, Vol. 9, No. 3, Fall, pp. 61-66; http://mises.org/journals/qjae/pdf/qjae9_3_4.pdf

Chapter 13. Barnett, William II, Walter Block and Michael Saliba. 2007. "Predatory pricing." *Corporate Ownership & Control*, Vol. 4, No. 4, Continued – 3, Summer; pp. 401-406

Chapter 14. Barnett, William II and Walter Block. 2007. "Coase and Van Zandt on Lighthouses," *Public Finance Review*, Vol. 35, No. 6, November, pp. 710-733 (24)

Chapter 15. Barnett, William II and Walter E. Block. 2009. "Coase and Bertrand on Lighthouses," *Public Choice*; 140(1–2):1–13, http://dx.doi.org/10.1007/s11127-008-9375-x

Chapter 16. Barnett, William II, Jerry Dauterive and Walter E. Block. 2008. "Subsidy is Worse than Tax" *Icfai University Journal of Public Finance*, Vol. VI, No. 4, November, pp. 62-71

Chapter 17. Barnett, William II and Walter Block. 2004. "On the Optimum Quantity of Money," *Quarterly Journal of Austrian Economics*, Vol. 7, No. 1, pp. 39-52; http://www.mises.org/journals/qjae/pdf/qjae7_1_4.pdf (14)

Chapter 18. Barnett, William II and Walter Block. 2005. "Money: Capital Good, Consumers' Good, or (Media of) Exchange Good?" *Review of Austrian Economics.* 18 (2): 179-194; http://www.gmu.edu/rae/archives/VOL18_2_2005/4_Barnett.pdf (16)

Chapter 19. Barnett, William II and Walter Block. 2005. "In defense of fiduciary media— a comment; or, what's wrong with "clown" or play money?" *Quarterly Journal of Austrian Economics*; Vol. 8, No. 2, Summer, pp. 55-69; http://mises.org/journals/qjae/pdf/qjae8_2_4.pdf (15)

Chapter 20. Barnett, William II and Walter Block. 2005. "Professor Tullock on Austrian Business Cycle Theory," *Advances in Austrian Economics*, Vol. 8, pp. 431-443 (13)

Chapter 21. Barnett, William II and Walter Block. 2006. "On Hayekian Triangles." *Procesos De Mercado: Revista Europea De Economia Politica*; Vol. III, No. 2, Fall, pp. 39-141; http://tinyurl.com/2zkvj7; http://mises.org/journals/scholar/block18.pdf (103)

Chapter 22. Barnett, William II and Walter Block. 2006. "On exchange, monetary credit transactions, barter, time preference, interest rates, and productivity." *Etica e Politica / Ethics & Politics*; Vol. VIII, No. 2, pp. 116-126; http://www.units.it/~etica/2006_2/BARNETTBLOCK.pdf; http://www.units.it/~etica/

Chapter 23. Barnett, William II and Walter Block. 2006. "Tyler Cowen on Austrian Business Cycle Theory: A Critique." *New Perspectives on Political Economy*, Vol. 2, No. 2, pp. 26-84; http://pcpe.libinst.cz/nppe/2_2/nppe2_2_2.pdf; http://pcpe.libinst.cz/nppe/

Chapter 24. Barnett, William II and Walter Block. 2006. "Some Thoughts on Price Deflation." *New Perspectives on Political Economy*. Vol. 2, No. 1, June; pp. 1-12; http://pcpe.libinst.cz/nppe/index.php

Chapter 25. Barnett, William II and Walter Block. 2006. "On Gallaway and Vedder on Stabilization Policy" *Quarterly Journal of Austrian Economics*. Vol. 9, No. 1, spring, pp. 57-81; http://www.mises.org/journals/qjae/pdf/qjae9_1_5.pdf

Chapter 26. Block, Walter and William Barnett II. 2007. "The Austrian Tent? A Rejoinder to Gallaway and Vedder" *Corporate Ownership & Control*, Vol. 4, No. 3, p. 232-zz; http://www.virtusinterpress.org/additional_files/journ_coc/issues/COC_(Volume_4_Issue_3_Spring_2007_Continued).pdf

Chapter 27. Block, Walter, and William Barnett II. 2007. "Ron Paul and the Fed: A Rejoinder to David Frum." December 21; http://www.lewrockwell.com/block/block92.html

Chapter 28. Barnett, William II and Walter Block. 2007. "Saving and Investment: A Praxeological Approach." *New Perspectives on Political Economy*, Vol. 3, No. 2, pp. 129 – 138; http://pcpe.libinst.cz/nppe/3_2/nppe3_2_1.pdf

Chapter 29. Barnett, William II and Walter Block. 2007. "On Say's Law, Keynes's Money, and Post Keynesians," *Procesos De Mercado: Revista Europea De Economia Politica,* Vol. IV, No. 2, Fall, 139-165

Chapter 30. Barnett, William II and Walter E. Block. 2008. "On Hummel on Austrian Business Cycle Theory." *Reason Papers* Vol. 30, Fall, pp. 59-90; http://www.reasonpapers.com/pdf/30/rp_30_4.pdf

Chapter 31. Block, Walter E. and William Barnett II. 2008. "Going (back) to gold money with no government gold: blood in the streets?" *Indian Journal of Economics & Business*, Vol. 7, No. 2, pp. 185-192

Chapter 32. Barnett, William II and Walter E. Block. 2008. "Plain Old Inflation vs. Price Inflation" *Franklin Business & Law Journal;* Issue 3, pp. 139; http://www.franklinpublishing.net/franklinbusinesslaw.html

Chapter 33. Barnett, William II and Walter E. Block. 2009. "Is there a market for money, or are there markets for money? There ain't no such thing as the Supply of or the Demand for Money." *Laissez-Faire*, No. 30-31, pp. 18-22, March-September; http://fce.ufm.edu/publicaciones/laissezfaire/

Chapter 34. Block Walter and William Barnett II. 2001. "Arm the Coeds," November 10. http://www.lewrockwell.com/block/block10.html

Chapter 35. Block, Walter and William Barnett II. 2001. "Required Gun Possession the Answer to Attacks," *Loyola University New Orleans The Maroon*, November 30, p. 9; http://www.walterblock.com/wp-content/uploads/GunColumn.pdf

Chapter 36. Block, Walter and William Barnett II. 2002. "The Living Wage: What's Wrong," *Ideas on Liberty*, December, Vol. 52, No. 12, pp.23-24; http://www.fee.org/publications/the-freeman/article.asp?aid=4533 (2)

Chapter 37. Block, Walter and William Barnett II. 2003. "Voluntary Taxes: Abusive Language and Politicians," July 12. http://www.lewrockwell.com/block/block28.html

Chapter 38. Block, Walter, William Barnett II and Gene Callahan. 2005. "The Paradox of Coase as a Defender of Free Markets," *NYU Journal of Law & Liberty*, Vol. 1, No. 3, pp. 1075-1095; Reprinted in Mario Rizzo, ed. 2011. *Austrian Law and Economics;* Edward Elgar; http://thinkmarkets.wordpress.com /2011/07/29/

Chapter 39. Block, Walter and William Barnett II. 2005. "The economic case for laissez faire capitalism." *Humanomics*. Vol. 21, No. 3-4, pp. 49-62; http://tinyurl.com/ysmmrt; translated into Spanish as: "El fundamento económico del capitalismo laissez faire," *Revista de Economía y Derecho*, 2006, Vol. 3, No. 12, pp. 81-88.

Chapter 40. Block, Walter and William Barnett II. 2005. "A Positive Programme for Laissez -Faire Capitalism," *The Journal of Corporate Citizenship,* Issue 19, Autumn, pp. 31-42

Chapter 41. Block, Walter and Barnett, William II. 2006. "Rejoinder to Critics of Laissez -Faire Capitalism." *The Journal of Corporate Citizenship,* Issue 23, Fall, pp. 17-20

Chapter 42. Barnett, William and Walter Block. 2008. "Time deposits, dimensions and fraud," *Journal of Business Ethics;* www.WalterBlock.com/publications

Foreword

It is my pleasure to endorse William Barnett II and Walter Block's new book *Essays in Austrian Economics.* Like Barnett and Block, I am a lifelong student of Austrian Economics. My work on behalf of sound money and limited, frugal government has been guided by the insights of Austrian economists like Ludwig Von Misses, F.A. Hayek, and Murray Rothbard.

Barnett and Block's book reflects the depth and breath of their knowledge of Austrian Economics. However, Barnett and Block do more than demonstrate their ability to restate their predecessors' insights. Instead the authors of this work aim to build onto Austrian Economics' existing foundation, while challenging some of the accepted tenets of modern Austrian Economics. For example, Barnett and Block diverge from the earlier generations of Austrians regarding certain important (albeit highly technical) aspects of methodology and micro and macroeconomics. In this, they are following in the footsteps of Mises, Hayek, and Rothbard, each of whom never hesitated to challenge what they felt where oversights or errors in the works of the previous generations of Austrian Economists.

Only time will tell if Barnett and Block's challenges to their intellectual forebears become incorporated into the mainstream of Austrian Economics. Whatever the outcome of these internecine struggles, I am confident that future students of the Austrian school will have to contend with Barnett and Block's work. Anyone wishing to understand the economics of liberty can benefit from careful study of this book.

Dr. Ron Paul, member of Congress

Introduction

Olivier Blanchard, one of the most highly respected macroeconomists in the world[1], states in the abstract of a paper titled "The State of Macro:" (*Annual Review of Economics.* Sept. 2009. Vol. 1, pp: 209-228)[2]:

> For a long while after the explosion of macroeconomics in the 1970s, the field looked like a battlefield. Over time however, largely because facts do not go away, a largely shared vision both of fluctuations and of methodology has emerged. Not everything is fine. Like all revolutions, this one has come with the destruction of some knowledge, and suffers from extremism and herding. None of this is deadly however. The state of macro is good. The first section sets the stage with a brief review of the past. The second argues that there has been broad convergence in vision, and the third reviews the specifics. The fourth focuses on convergence in methodology. The last looks at current challenges.

Ben Bernanke, then governor of the Federal Reserve System, and currently chairman of the Board of Governors of the Federal Reserve, began a speech entitled "The Great Moderation" given at the Eastern Economics Association, February 20, 2004 as follows:

> One of the most striking features of the economic landscape over the past twenty years or so has been a substantial decline in macroeconomic volatility.... Several writers on the topic have dubbed this remarkable decline in the variability of both output and inflation "the Great Moderation." Similar declines in the volatility of output and inflation occurred at about the same time in other major industrial countries, with the recent exception of Japan, a country that has faced a distinctive set of economic problems in the past decade.

Both of these highly regarded economists are part of the broad mainstream of macroeconomics, which mainstream encompasses both left and right wing variants. The former (lead by such economists as Paul Krugman, Larry Summers, Paul Samuelson) tend to stress a mix where fiscal policy dominates monetary policy; the latter (associated with such leaders of the

---

[1] He is the Class of 1941 Professor of Economics and former chair of the economics department of MIT, a research associate of the NBER a fellow and Council member of the Econometric Society, an advisor to the Federal Reserve Banks of Boston (since 1995) and New York (since 2004), and a member of the American Academy of Sciences. Currently he is on leave from MIT, as Chief Economist , Economic Counselor and Director of the Research Department of the International Monetary Fund. A past vice president of the American Economic Association, his SSRN Author Rank by downloads is 72.

[2] First published online as a Review in Advance on May 12, 2009.

profession as Milton Friedman, Anna Schwartz, Alan Greenspan) agree to both elements, but tend to reverse the constituent elements of this "mix." This mainstream encompasses various currents such as New Classical, New Keynesian, and Real Business Cycle/DSGE that have engaged macroeconomists in theoretical debates for decades.

Nevertheless, when push came to shove with the onset of what some have referred to as our present Great Recession or even, Second Great Depression, the mainstream macroeconomists pushed aside their theoretical debates—that amounted, in our opinion, to disputations as to the number of angels that dance, simultaneously, on the head of a pin. Instead, they engaged in a search for policies to alleviate and remediate the crisis and subsequent collapse. In doing so, they all reverted to a simplistic Keynesianism aka Hydraulic Keynesianism that Joan Robinson labeled "bastard Keynesianism." (Milton Friedman was famously quoted in the December 31, 1965 edition of *Time* magazine that: "We are all Keynesians now.") This is evidenced by this statement in an article "What would Keynes have done?" in the November 28, 2008 edition of *The New York Times*, by N. Gregory Mankiw, another highly respected macroeconomist[3]:

> If you were going to turn to only one economist to understand the problems facing the economy, there is little doubt that the economist would be John Maynard Keynes. Although Keynes died more than a half-century ago, his diagnosis of recessions and depressions remains the foundation of modern macroeconomics. His insights go a long way toward explaining the challenges we now confront.

In fact, despite the "advances" of mainstream macroeconomic theory and analysis since, say, the 1960s, its policy prescriptions have not changed one whit. That is, in times of economic contractions the federal government (and foreign governments) should undertake policies to stimulate the economy, by which they mean stimulate aggregate demand or total spending. Specifically, the government should engage in massive deficit spending and "easy" monetary policy. Regarding fiscal policy, what disagreements they have among themselves revolve around the size of the deficits to be run up; how much of it should consist of increased governmental spending and how much of decreased taxes; and, the composition of such spending and tax cuts. With respect to the policies that the Federal Reserve (and foreign central banks) should engage in, such disputes are concerned merely with the size of the Fed's balance sheet and the composition of both the assets and liabilities sides thereof, as well as interest rate policies.

---

[3] He is the Robert M. Beren Professor of Economics in Harvard University's economics department, NBER research associate, Advisor to the Federal Reserve Bank of Boston and Congressional Budget Office, and former chairman of the President's Council of Economic Advisors.

The present book, in very, very sharp contrast, is not written from the mainstream perspective. It offers no governmental remedies to cure the body economic. Rather, it sees the completely unregulated economy as fully able to take care of itself. Our present (and all such past) economic doldrums are due, instead, to previous governmental interferences with the free enterprise system, which have created the very economic problems, especially massive unemployment, that government is now so miserably failing to correct. Nay, it is fairer to say, they are exacerbating the situation. (The most famous people associated with this laissez faire capitalist philosophy are Ron Paul, Friedrich A. Hayek, and Ludwig von Mises). The economic remedies proposed herein are the elimination of the central banking, fiat currency, fractional-reserve commercial banking, legal tender laws, and the embrace of private; i.e., free-market, monies, such as gold.

This Austrian perspective had many adherents in the 19th and very early 20th centuries. It was never fully implemented, but any comparison of the pre and post 1914 periods will demonstrate to those simply applying logical analysis to facts that it was far more successful than what came afterward. However, the free enterprise philosophy of Mises and Hayek was swept away at the practical level by the policies of the Hoover administration from late 1929 to early 1933, and the subsequent even more intrusive policies of the Roosevelt New Deal(s), each of which both prolonged and deepened the Great Depression, and, then, on an intellectual level, by the publication of Keynes' book in 1936.

This viewpoint has been all but frozen out of public discussion at present. There are far too many economists with a vested interest in the established modes of thought. Then, too, our perspective leaves virtually no scope at all for the battalions of bureaucrats and politicians who batten off of established institutions, such as the Fed.

As functioned under the medieval guild system, these left and right wing, not to mention middle-of-the road, Keynesians are jealous of their powers and prerogatives. They pounce on their critics as "radicals," "cultists" and "extremeists" to stifle an open airing of the failed policies they have been perpetuating on a long suffering economy for lo these many decades.

Happily, though, the publication of the present book will go some small way toward righting this imbalance. If we are to clean up our economic mess, it is important that *all* types of economic analysis, certainly including the Austrian, be included in the public conversation.

There are several "free market" schools of thought in economics. Amongst them one must count the Chicago, Virginia, Public Choice and the Austrian Schools. Although the former two are far more well-known, it is the latter which, because of its methodology, is the most radical, and yields the deepest insights into human action. The understanding so arrived at has led virtually all of those truly familiar with Austrian economics to become advocates *à outrance* of laissez faire capitalism.

Our book is based firmly within the Austrian School, and focuses most closely upon its methodology, which is its most distinct element, vis-à-vis the other economic perspectives, as well as on the micro- and macro-economic public policy subjects, on which these schools of thought take different stances.

At the present time, early 2009, many countries are experiencing the worst economic conditions seen since the Great Depression. Regardless of their various, supposedly sophisticated, but unrealistic theories, based as they are on the most simplistic of assumptions obfuscated by mathematical notation and manipulations, when it comes to macroeconomic policy to deal with the crisis, the economics profession at large has nothing to inform its policy analyses but puerile Keynesianism and thus falls back on naïve Keynesian macroeconomic so-called stimulus policies, some placing more emphasis on monetary policies and others on fiscal policies. But all are united in the belief that the cause of recessions, depressions and other nomenclature for economic panics, are due to market failure. They are due to "aggregate demand" problems, resulting from greed in an un-, or at least insufficiently, unregulated economic and financial environment, as if we actually lived in such a world. They only disagree as to the best method of ameliorating this problem.

The macroeconomic section of the present book is most relevant to these issues. It offers one of the best kept secrets of the modern day: the Austrian Business Cycle Theory (ABCT). Here, recessions and depressions are not to anything intrinsic to the market, but rather come about as the result of prior governmental meddling with the free enterprise system, typically monetary expansion through credit markets. And far from recessions being phenomena to be avoided at all costs, they actually benefit the economy: they "cleanse" away the malinvestments undertaken during the previous governmentally induced artificial boom. Nor need this "medicine" take very long to swallow. If laissez faire policies are followed, this state of the business cycle can be over very quickly.

In sharp contrast, the public policy recommendations made by most economists involve "stimulus" of one sort or another. In the Austrian view, rather than addressing the underlying economic problem, such policies are responsible for the depression in the first place, and only lengthen and deepen it if followed during a period of economic disarray.

It is our hope that the present book, merely but the tip of the iceberg of Austrian economic analysis, will do its small part in alleviating our present economic distress.

William Barnett II
Walter E. Block

Part I. Methodology

Chapter 1. Austrian Economics, Praxeology and Intervention

I. Praxeology

Praxeology is defined by Rothbard (1962, p. 64) as "The formal implication of the fact that men use means to attain various chosen ends." While men use means to attain ends in areas other than economics (e.g., war, voting) the dismal science is the only fully elaborated subdivision of praxeology. Rothbard (1962, p. 63) defines praxeological economics in contrast with "psychology (and)... the philosophy of ethics. Since all these (three) disciplines deal with the subjective decisions of individual human minds, many observers have believed that they are fundamentally identical. This is not the case at all. Psychology and ethics deal with the content of human ends; they ask, why does the man choose such and such ends, or what ends should man value? Praxeology and economics deal with any given ends and with the formal implications of the fact that men have ends and employ means to attain them."[4]

Austrian or praxeological economics is based on a few basic axioms, such as that man acts, there is scarcity, time is a constraint, there are resources, leisure is a good and work brings disutility. Coupled with the laws of logic, these axioms lead to the basic premises of economics.[5]

The method employed, then, is akin to mathematics, or logic, or geometry: deductions from premises to conclusions. The path to truth has nothing to do with empirical observations and generalizations; rather, with syllogistic reasoning.

II. What tests what?

Economics as practiced at the polar extreme from praxeology is logical positivism, or neoclassiscal economics. Here, the dismal science is not conceived of as vast latticework of deductions. It is rather modeled on the

---

[4] Material in brackets supplied by present author. For an alternative view of the relationship between economics and psychology, see Gunning, 2000.

[5] For further elaboration, see, Batemarco, 1985; Block, 1986, 1973, 1999A; Böhm-Bawerk, 1890, 1994; Bostaph, 1978; Cubeddu, 1993; Egger, 1979; Fox, 1992; Garrison, 1993; Gordon, 1986, 1993A, 1993B; Gunning, 1988, 1986; Hayek, 1955; Holcombe, 1995; Hoppe, 1989B, 1994A, 1995; de Soto, 1998B; Kirzner, 1976A, 1976C; Menger, 1960, 1981, 1985; Mises, 1978B, 1985, 1990A, 1990B; Rizzo, 1979A; Robbins, 1932; Rothbard, 1951A, 1951B, 1957, 1997B, 1997C, 1997D, 1997E, 1997G, 1997H; Selgin, 1988, 1990; Smith,1996, 1994, 1990; Witt, 1991; White, 1984.

physical sciences, where empirical observation and induction are the order of the day. States Messedaglia in this regard: "Economics is above all a science of observation and its method should be as close as possible to that of the so-called positive sciences."[6]

In mainstream economics, there is indeed room for theory. But the theory, as in the case of the physical sciences, must be tested by empirical observation. Here, econometric testing is the dog, which wags the tail of theory. In praxeology, in contrast, is found the reverse: theory is the bedrock of the enterprise, or the "dog," while very peripheral is the tail of real world facts.

Perhaps an example will better illustrate this distinction. According to virtually all practitioners, rent control has negative repercussions on the economy[7]. With a ceiling on rents, an excessive demand for rental housing develops. This leads to shortages. The incentives of entrepreneurs to invest must of necessity atrophy, since profits in every other endeavor are still uncontrolled. This means less new building of residential units, ceteris paribus. Nor do landlords of extant dwellings have as much incentive to maintain and upgrade them.[8]

But suppose someone runs an econometric regression on the relationship between this legislation and all of those incidences of housing disarray, and fails to support micro economic theory in this regard. How are we to interpret such a finding? For the Austrians, matters are simple. At best, statistical correlations (the tail of the dog) can illustrate economic theory. They can never call it (the dog itself) into question. In this particular instance, the empirical generalization failed to be compatible with apodictic (necessary and certain) economic theory, and so the former must be thrown out as unreliable.

For the logical positivists, things are different, and far more embarrassing. After checking one's figures to make sure no statistical errors were made, what must economists of this sort conclude when rent control is not associated with shortages, or inferior housing, or reduced investment, or any of its other typical correlates? They are forced by their own methodology to infer that either the supply and demand analysis which underlies the usual assumptions about this law are mistaken, or that for some reason economic law has failed to operate in this one case, or at this time, or in the particular

---

[6] Cited in Noto, Sergio, "Angelo Messdaglia and the spread of the Mengerian Methodology in Italy," 2000.

[7] Frey, et. al, 1984; Block and Walker, 1988, pp. 137-150.

[8] For more on the economic analysis of rent control, see, Arnott, and Mintz, 1987; Baird, 1980; Block, 1981, 2002C; Cragg, 1974; Downs, 1988; Grant, 1989; Johnson, 1982; Salins, 1980; Tucker, 1990.

geographical locale for which the equations were drawn. Nor will it help them to maintain that since thousands of regressions have shown rent control to be associated with housing inefficiencies, the present study must be flawed. Very much to the contrary[9], they are forced, by the laws of logic, to acquiesce in the notion that in this particular case all bets are off and economic theory cannot be relied upon. For why believe the 99% of empirical studies which show rent control in a bad light, and not the 1% which show it in a good light? As empiricists, the ultimate determination of truth is *not* the coherence of the theory, as it is for the Austrians, but instead the statistical tests performed. If they are 99% in one direction and 1% in the other, one can only deduce that economic theory is operational merely in a (overwhelming) majority of cases, or epochs, or locales, but not in all of them.

This is a rather awkward admission to make, for a discipline which wishes itself to be taken seriously as a science. Consider an analogy, from geometry. Suppose that teams of geometricians went out and measured the angles of all triangles they could find. In 99% of the cases, they found 180 degrees, but in 1% their measurements (checked and rechecked) came to a different conclusion. We would steadfastly and resolutely refuse to accept any of the minority quantifications on the ground they *must* be mistaken. Although there is not a perfect analogy between praxeology and geometry, an analogy is only a heuristic device, utilized to better explain a concept. One must not conflate an analogy with an identity. Praxeology in some few but important respects resembles geometry. Both are logical systems with real world implications.

III. Synthetic Apriori

Another way to probe the distinction between Austrian and "scientific" mainstream economics is by use of the concept of the synthetic apriori. For the logical positivists, there are two and only two kinds of statements. The first, the analytic, is apodictically true but only in the trivial sense of definition, which has nothing to do with the real world. For example, it cannot be denied that bachelors are unmarried men, or that 2+2=4, but these statements are unfalsifiable. Since nothing in reality can falsify them, they are not about the real world at all. Rather, they pertain, merely, to how we have decided to use words. They are know a priori, by their pure logic, but they avail us nothing in explaining and understanding real world events, since they are in a different universe of discourse.

The truth of the second kind of sentence is contingent, or synthetic, or applicable to the world. For example, water runs downhill, rent control reduces the quantity and quality of housing and water is composed of two

---

[9] Again, on the assumption that no statistical mistakes can be shown in the present case

parts hydrogen and one part oxygen. Information of this sort is said to be known a posteriori; that is, through experience. And further empirical data, incompatible with the first set, can always overturn it. For example, water might one day run uphill, and rent control contribute to housing betterment, and no contradiction of the laws of logic would have taken place.

Perhaps these points can be clarified in diagramatic form. Accordingly, the columns are headed by the concepts of analytic and synthetic, which depict whether application to the real world is in force: no in the former case, yes in the latter. In contrast, the rows are labeled Apriori and Aposteriori, which categorizes ways of knowing, or epistemology. Here, the former means through logic, the latter through experience. When we put the four concepts together we derive a two by two matrix: A: the analytic apriori, B: the synthetic apriori, C: the analytic aposteriori and D: the synthetic aposteriori.

	Analytic	Synthetic
Apriori	A	B
Aposteriori	C	D

There is no dispute about the status of D, ordinary empirical claims that pertain to the world and are derived from experience: the sun is yellow, the earth is round, the per capita income in the U.S. is greater than that in Cuba. Nor about A, purely definitional matters which emanate from logical considerations, whose denial would involve self contradiction and have to do with definitions and logically trivial matters: bachelors are unmarried men, 2+2=4, triangles have 180 degrees. Nor yet about C, a null category, since we do not derive matters of pure logic from experience.

The highly contentious ground is B, the synthetic aproiori. Here are statements whose denial involves self contradiction, and yet which apply to the real world. In this category we have apodictically certain undeniable knowledge of empirical reality.

It is the cornerstone of logical positivism from whence is derived the methodology of neoclassical economics, that B, too, is a null set. That is, "either a statement applies to the real world, in which it is contingent upon further empirical confirmation, and is not apodictically true; or it is necessarily so, it's denial involves self contradiction, in which case it is only trivially true, and cannot concern empirical reality." Consider this as statement "X." According to X, then, there are only two kinds of (meaningful) statements: those in category A, the trivial definitional ones, and mathematics, and D, ordinary empirical, falsifiable ones. B is a null set.

But how can we categorize statement X, itself? Into which of these four quadrants does it, itself, fall.[10] If in A, it does not involve the real world; it is purely a matter of definition, or convention, and adds nothing to our store of knowledge. It may be dismissed as "trivial." If statement X belongs in category D, we cannot know it for sure. It's denial hardly involves self contradiction. Why, then, are mainstream economists so certain of it?

Let us consider some examples of synthetic apriori statements put forth by Austrian economists, to solidify our understanding of this claim. Consider the following.

1. Man acts. This certainly applies to the real world, where we see people acting so as to render the future more desirable to them than had they not so acted. It is impossible to deny, since the very act of denial is itself an action. This means that economic action is purposive; that is, man intends to gain from bestirring himself. Teleological thinking may be illicit anthropomorphism in the hard sciences such as physics and chemistry, but not in economics, the practice of neoclassical economics to the contrary notwithstanding.

2. There is a tendency for profits to equalize in all industries, assuming away differential risk. Obviously, given that man acts so as to better his position, there will be a tendency for capital to move from lower profit opportunities (thus driving up profits there) to higher profit areas (thus reducing profits); only in equilibrium when there are no further gains available from shifting resources will this process come to a (temporary) stop. But this claim is not falsifiable, for at any given time when profits are unequal between industries, this cannot be used to deny there is a *tendency* in this direction. Even though this is apodictically true, it still applies to the real world of differing industrial profit rates.

3. All trade attains mutual benefit in the ex ante sense. Why else would two parties engage in such a commercial interaction were it not for the gain involved to each of them. This is part and parcel of acting purposefully, in order to profit, only now it involves two people engaging in a "capitalist act between consenting adults."[11] True, such attempts need not always succeed. It sometimes occurs that attempts to gain through trade are met with failure. But this is only in the ex post sense. In the ex ante sense of anticipations, mutual benefit *must* be the underlying explanation of the event. To deny this is to involve oneself in self contradiction. Nevertheless, even though this conclusion is apodictically certain, it cannot be denied that trade pertains to the real world of commerce, and that mutual gain certainly accounts for these empirical acts.

---

[10] We owe this line of criticism to Hans Hoppe.

[11] In the felicitous phraseology of Nozick, 1974, p. 163.

Chapter 2. The Relationship between Wealth or Income and Time Preference is Empirical, not Apodictic: A Critique of Rothbard and Hoppe[12]

I. Introduction: Time Preference and Wealth

It is a commonplace that individuals' time preferences decrease as they become wealthier. An interesting issue is whether this is an empirical regularity or a matter of praxeology. If it is praxeological in nature, then there could *never* arise a counterfactual. A simple thought experiment suggests that this is not the case.

Imagine an individual, A, who is 65 years of age, and not particularly well-off financially; he is a "cautious hedonist." An independent contractor, as such he has no fringe benefits other than those A provides for himself. His gross receipts from his labor were $50,000 last year. In addition, his net worth of $50,000 at the beginning of last year yielded him a cash equivalent return of $3,500. Net of FICA, Medicare, and income taxes, his available cash was $40,000. Because of a family history of long life, a desire to retire at age 67, and an expectation that social security can not be relied upon to provide much, if anything for his retirement, he spent $25,000 on consumers' goods and bought various financial assets with the other $15,000, his plan being to refrain from liquidating those assets until he retires and to reinvest any dividends and interest earned thereon. Thus only 62.5% of his available income was spent on consumers' goods. He plans to repeat the same pattern this year. The only difference is that A's cash equivalent return is expected to be $4,550, so that, after taxes and FICA and Medicare "contributions," he has $40,785, of which he intends to spend 62.5% ($25,490) on consumers goods (including that already so spent this year) and 37.5% ($15,295) on financial assets (including that already so spent this year).

A spends $1 on a lottery ticket.[13] Amazingly, he wins $100,000,000, after taxes. Now that his ship has come in, he decides to enjoy all the pleasures of life that money can buy. He puts aside $10,000,000 to provide for his old age, now figuring that his new pattern of riotous living might shorten his life span, but that, in any case, $10,000,000 will be more than

---

[12] The authors of this article wish to thank an anonymous referee of the source journal for very helpful suggestions he made regarding an earlier draft of this paper.

[13] The following is included for the sake of completeness. Because A thinks it déclassé to play the lottery, he sneaks in once a year and spends a dollar of his non-consumers' goods funds on one $1 lottery ticket. He considers this to be a financial security, and he gets no pleasure from it, directly – sort of like those people who know big business is immoral, but hold their noses and buy stocks and bonds for investment purposes. Of course, praxeologically, we know he prefers his action of spending his $1 on the lottery ticket to any other action he could have taken at the time he did; nevertheless, he does not consider it an act of consumption.

enough to provide all the purchasable pleasures relevant to him in his old age. A has no living relatives, no friends, no acquaintances, and no charities of any kind to whom he wants to leave an economic legacy. He therefore undertakes to spend the entire remaining $90,000,000 this year.[14] Therefore his ratio of expenditures on consumers' goods to available income has increased from 62.5% to, approximately, 90%. Certainly his time preference has risen with, and as a result of, the increase in his wealth.

Other people may think him profligate or a fool, but, *de gustibus non est disputandum*. To wit: although a positive rate of time preference is indeed a praxeological necessity (Mises, 1999, 488-490), the specific rate thereof, and changes in it, for any individual, are not a matter of apodictic certainty. The internal rate of discount typically falls as income rises, *ceteris paribus*, but this is a broad empirical generalization, not an apodictic claim.

Let us consider a second case in point. A man with no relatives or friends, save for one young daughter, and no life insurance, becomes terminally ill with cancer and loses his job. He receives assistance in the form of periodic money grants equal to one-half (1/2) his former wages. Also, a charitable organization, with his concurrence, takes custody of his daughter promising to maintain her in genteel poverty, taken to include a basic education. Although he has some wealth accumulated while he was healthy, he is obviously poorer than before he lost he lost his job and attendant wages. However, because he wants his daughter to be able to go to college, he does not spend any of his accumulated wealth *or even any of his periodic money grants – not a farthing-* on food or medicines, including painkillers. Rather, he allows his wealth to continue to accumulate, adding to it not only the accretions from interest and profits thereon, but also his periodic grants. Of course, he dies an agonizing death from a combination of cancer and starvation. Nevertheless, his choices bespeak his values. And his choice was to lower his purchases of consumers' goods relative to (claims against) capital goods in order to provide for his young daughter's future college education.

The point is, given his values, in the face of decreased wealth he increased his utility, relative to what it otherwise would have been, by reducing his purchases of consumers' goods in order for his daughter to be able to purchase more of a capital good (college education) in the future. These actions are only explicable if his time preference decreased when his wealth was reduced. So here we have a second example of positive, but decreasing, time preference with respect to wealth.

---

[14] So that there be no problem arising from his spending any of the money on durable consumers' goods, and therefore, having an element of provision for the future thereby, we note that A spends the entire $90,000,00 on "wine, women, and song." That is it is all spent on consumers' services and non-durable consumers' goods.

We venture to tax our readers' patience with yet a third example. We do so, first, because this is a conceptually difficult point, easy to misconstrue, and, second, because we are going to use this analytic framework as a basis for calling into question the work of two very prominent Austrian economists, and in our view we are still very far from entering that realm of negative marginal returns to numerical examples. Accordingly, here is our third attempt to put this point into "other words," the better to achieve clarity:

There is an inverse relationship between price and quantity demanded of a particular good, all other things equal, which is apodictic and can be derived from praxeological reasoning. But there is no praxeological law that specifies a determinate relationship between the size of one's income[15] and the proportion of income spent on any particular good or category of goods even at a given point in time. The reason is that value scales are autonomously determined and therefore are given data to the economist. Suppose that an individual has the following ranking of present and future goods, and let us assume that each increment of goods has a total market price of $20,000.

1st	food, clothing and shelter for family for a year
2nd	saving for child's 1st year's college tuition 15 years hence
3rd	saving for child's 2nd year's college tuition 16 years hence
4th	saving for child's 3rd year's college tuition 17 years hence
5th	saving for child's 4th year's college tuition 18 years hence
6th	lease Ferrari for a year
7th	Carribean cruise, one-month lease on Swiss ski chalet, fine wines and theater tickets for the year
8th	annual country club membership

The point is, if the individual earned $20,000 per year, then his consumption/saving ratio would be infinite and then progressively decline to .25 (=$20,000/$80,000) as his income reached $100,000 per year. As his income increased further beyond $100,000 his time preference would begin to increase until at $160,000 his consumption/saving ratio would reach 1.0 (=$80,000/$80,000). At even higher incomes this individual's time preference may either rise or fall depending on the configuration of his value scale. So, ceteris paribus, taking his value scale as given and constant, there seems to be no determinate praxeological relationship between income or wealth and time preferences. We do not deny that there is a direct praxeological relationship

[15] Rothbard (1993 [1962], pp. 350–57) calls this the "post-income" stock of money

between time preference and the pure rate of interest, and that the lower are autonomously chosen time preferences the lower is the pure interest rate, again ceteris paribus. We merely assert that there is no ceteris paribus praxeological relationship linking income or wealth to the height of the pure interest rate. This seems to be Mises'[16] position on the matter:

"The quantity of the available supply of capital goods influences neither the rate of originary interest nor the amount of further saving. Even the most plentiful supply of capital need not necessarily bring about either a lowering of the rate of originary interest or a drop in the propensity to save. The increase in capital accumulation and the per capita quota of capital invested which is a characteristic mark of economically advanced nations does not necessarily either lower the rate of originary interest or weaken the propensity of individuals to make additional savings… It is therefore impossible to formulate any praxeological theorem concerning the relation of the amount of capital available in the whole nation or to individual people on the one hand and the amount of saving or capital consumption and the height of the originary rate of interest on the other hand. The allocation of scarce resources to want-satisfaction in various periods of the future is determined by value judgments and indirectly by all those factors which constitute the individuality of the acting man (as summed up in his value scale)."

In our view, then, the graph relating an individual's time preference on the y axis, and wealth on the x axis, typically has a general downward trend, but it would not be totally unexpected to find rising portions of this curve throughout its length.

Some argue, however, that there is one exception to this general rule: at *very* low levels of income, when one is near death due to extreme poverty, then time preference rates must necessarily decline as income increases, e.g., the interest rate must rise as wealth falls to very low levels. At such a level of penury, unless the person receives food immediately, he will die. Thus, his willingness to exchange expected future consumption for present (i.e., a meal *right now*, in time to save his life) would have to be indefinitely large.

Rothbard states:

"… praxeological analysis can supply some truths about time preferences, using *ceteris paribus* assumptions. Thus, as we have seen above, each person has a time-preference schedule relating to his money stock. A lower money stock will cause a higher time-preference rate for any unit of money remaining in his possession, until finally his time-preference rate will rise to infinity when the money stock–or rather the money for consumption–is low enough. Here, one element, a man's money stock, is varied and his value scale is otherwise assumed to remain constant" (Rothbard, 1993 [1962] 380).

---

[16] Mises, 1963, pp. 533, 534, material in brackets supplied by present authors.

There is a modicum of truth in this, *if* it can be assumed that the goal of the man necessarily is to live. Unfortunately, we cannot fully rely on any such assumption. There is, after all, such a thing as suicide. A plausible counterargument to support the Rothbard hypothesis in this regard is the following: all people who act in such a manner soon die, and are no longer around to undermine this explanation. What they do no longer counts as "human action" since they are deceased. The problem with this retort, however, is that *during* the time such a person is still alive, it simply will not be true that his time preference rate will rise to infinity, or even be indefinitely large. If he is in the process of committing suicide through starvation, he would not at all be willing to give up almost anything in the future for a little bit of food, now. In fact, he would not be willing to give up anything in the future for food at present. Praxeology must account for such actions, too, no matter how abhorrent.

II. Hoppe on the relationship between income and time preference

Now that we have stated what we believe to be the true state of affairs in this regard, e.g., that time preference rates typically fall as income or wealth increases, but not necessarily so[17], it behooves us to uncover economists who have rejected this view. Otherwise, we are in danger of being (correctly) accused of beating a dead horse: insisting upon a bit of basic economic analysis with which no one disagrees. So, are there any economists of note who take a different perspective on this matter?

First out of the starting blocks on this matter is Hoppe, who states: "With real incomes rising, the effective rate of time preference falls…" (Hoppe, 1993, 119.)

To be sure, this cannot be counted as definitive support for the notion that there is a *necessary* connection between higher income and lower time preference rates, as opposed, merely, to an empirical one, but it is at least strongly suggestive of this view, in that the bare statement is not modified in any way at all[18]. Certainly, Hoppe here does not disassociate himself from the view that increased income necessarily reduces time preference rates; rather, were we to strictly interpret it, and how, better, else, to treat material of this sort, we can perhaps best say that this statement is ambiguous with regard to the two positions.

---

[17] For a fuller articulation of this view see Block (1998A).

[18] The quote continues, irrelevantly for our purposes, since we agree with the remainder of it, as follows: "(without, however, ever reaching zero or even becoming negative), adding still further increased doses of investment, and setting in motion an upward spiraling process of economic development."

What are we to make, then, of the following: "In accordance with the law of marginal utility, each individual time preference curve… slopes downward as the supply of present money increases" (Hoppe, 2001, 8).

Here, it would appear, the only possible interpretation is that it is a matter of praxeology that time preference rates decline as wealth increase. Why so? Because it is an established axiom in Austrian economics that diminishing marginal utility stems from economic principles, not psychological states[19]. Given that Hoppe likens time preference curves to marginal utility curves, and the latter *necessarily* decline in the face of increased income, it would appear to be definitive that he maintains that the same relationship also holds in the case of time preference.

On the other hand, there are reasons to believe that this is not the case, despite the foregoing. This is because Hoppe often, and continually, elsewhere modifies the seeming apodictic relationship between wealth and time preference with qualifications. He states:

"In the course of becoming an adult, an actor's initially extremely high time-preference rate *tends* to fall," (Hoppe, 2001, 4, emphasis added). This statement is only peripheral to our concerns at best, since it bespeaks not the relationship between income and time preference, but rather between age and this rate. Nevertheless, it does establish that the concept "tendency" is very much within Hoppe's lexicon; so much so that when it is not mentioned, this suggests that he sees a praxeological, not an empirical, relationship between two variables.

Next, consider this statement:

"Finally, becoming old and approaching the end of one's life, one's time-preference *tends* to rise. The marginal utility of future goods falls because there is less of a future left. Savings and investments will decrease, and consumption – including the nonreplacement of capital and durable consumer goods – will increase. This old-age effect *may* be counteracted and suspended, however" (Hoppe, 2001, 5, emphasis added).

Here, again, we find the use of the tendency qualifier as evidence of the fact that Hoppe sees the relation between wealth and internal discount rates as non-apodictic. This is strengthened by the juxtaposition of the second sentence in this quoted paragraph where this author adds no such qualifiers to his perceived relationship between marginal utility, and (implicitly) wealth. Most definitive in this surmise is the following:

---

[19] Rothbard (1993 [1962], 324) speaks of an "individual (who) has, of necessity, a diminishing marginal utility of money, so that each additional unit of money acquired ranks lower on his value scale. This is necessarily true."

"Simultaneously, the saver-investor initiates a 'process of civilization.' In generating a *tendency* toward a fall in the rate of time preference, he – an everyone directly or indirectly connected to him through a network of exchanges – matures from childhood to adulthood and from barbarism to civilization," (Hoppe, 2001, 7, emphasis added).This "tendency" would appear to be definitive: here, civilization only generates a *tendency* toward reduced time preferences, not at all a necessary move in this direction.

Elsewhere, Hoppe appears to discern a praxeological relationship in this matter: "… for with rising real incomes, the marginal utility of present money falls relatively to that of future money, and hence under the *ceteris paribus* assumption of a *given* time preference *schedule* the interest *rate* must fall" (Hoppe, 2001, 63). This is evidence that this author sees the relationship not as a tendency, but as an apodictic one, since we can rely on the time preference schedule to impart a negative impetus from rising incomes to the time preference rate only if it is everywhere a declining function. This must be necessarily so if Hoppe's conclusion is to make sense.

To summarize to this point: despite, perhaps, some slight failure to be crystal clear on this relationship, a "failure" which could easily be attributed to being concerned with other issues, and despite in one case likening this relationship to that which obtains between wealth and marginal utility, which *is* apodictic, the most reasonable conclusion is that it is unclear from the quoted passages whether or not Hoppe sees only a tendency in the negative linkage between income and personal discount rates.

If there is a certain amount of uncertainty regarding the views held by Hoppe with regard to the relationship between income and internal rates of discount in ordinary circumstances, matters are far different when it comes to taxation, and its relationship to time preference. Here, this economist clearly sees a necessary connection between more of the former and a higher rate of the latter.

States Hoppe: "… if taxation reduces one's income (which includes that derived from present consumption and leisure) and given the universal fact of time preference, that is, that human actors invariably prefer present goods over future goods (i.e., that they cannot do without continuous consumption and can engage in lengthier productions processes – more roundabout methods of production – only if a provision in the form of consumption goods has been made for the corresponding waiting period), *then it follows with logical necessity* that a person's effective rate of time preference must have been raised through this very act (the disutility of waiting must have increased), and hence that he will have to shorten the length of the structure of production as compared to the one that he otherwise would have chosen, and his output of valuable assets available at future dates accordingly will have to be lower than would be the case otherwise (Hoppe, 1993, 32, emphasis added).

Here, at last, we have a definitive statement to the effect that, it is a matter of praxeology, not an empirical generalization, that time preference rates *must* rise when incomes fall due to taxation. There is no possibility of misinterpretation in the face of so stark a claim. In the light of these remarks, we are inclined to discount, somewhat, Hoppe's previously examined "tendency" language, and impute to him the view that it is a matter of praxeology that incomes and interest rates are negatively related to one another.

III. Rothbard on the relationship between income and time preference

What are the views of Rothbard on the relationship between wealth and time preference? Given a negative relationship between them, is this an empirical generalization, from which there can be exceptions, or is it an apodictic one, from which exceptions are inconceivable? Our claim is that, as in the case of Hoppe, while there is indeed some ambiguity involved in how Rothbard answers this question, the evidence seems to point in a praxeological direction.

Based on some readings, it is possible to interpret Rothbard's views as lending support to the empirical hypothesis. He states: "Praxeology can never furnish an ultimate explanation for a man's time preference. These are psychologically determined by each person and must therefore be taken, in the final analysis, as data by economists." (Rothbard, 1993 [1962], 380).

However, Rothbard then launches into an explanation that can be interpreted in the very opposite manner on this issue. In his view: "... praxeological analysis can supply some truths about time preferences, using *ceteris paribus* assumptions. Thus, as we have seen above, each person has a time-preference schedule relating to his money stock. A lower money stock will cause a higher time-preference rate for any unit of money remaining in his possession, until finally his time-preference rate will rise to infinity when the money stock – or rather, the money for consumption – is low enough. Here, one element, a man's money stock, is varied and his value scale is otherwise assumed to remain constant" (Rothbard, 1993 [1962], 380).[20]

A difficulty with this last quote is that there is no such thing as a "time preference schedule relating to his money stock" or to anything else for that matter *apart* from his actual choices. That is, it is *not* the case that there are two separate things: an underlying schedule which can be placed in a *ceteris paribus* assumption, on the one hand, and on the other hand, actual

---

[20] This author goes on to clarify that "Actually, it is not his *money* stock that is relevant to his time preferences, but the *real* value of his money stock."

choices made. Rather, there is *only* the latter. There *is* no "schedule" out there, somewhere, with which to contrast the actual choice.

Mises offers the following analysis of this point:

"It is customary to say that acting man has a scale of wants or values in his mind when he arranges his actions. On the basis of such a scale he satisfies what is of higher value, i.e., his more urgent wants, and leaves unsatisfied what is of lower value, i.e., what is a less urgent want. There is no objection to such a presentation of the state of affairs. However, one must not forget that the scale of values or wants manifests itself only in the reality of action. These scales have no independent existence apart from the actual behavior of individuals. The only source from which our knowledge concerning these scales is derived is the observation of a man's actions. Every action is always in perfect agreement with the scale of values or wants because these scales are nothing but an instrument for the interpretation of a man's acting" (Mises, 1963 [1949], 1963, 94-95).

Precisely. The point is that Rothbard, in utilizing his *ceteris paribus* assumption of a "schedule" divorced from specific human action is in effect taking back what he had previously posited. That is, Rothbard started off his analysis with the stipulation that the negative relationship between wealth and time preference was a psychological one, not amenable to the apodictic necessity of praxeology, but then, with the help of his *ceteris paribus* assumption, reversed course and came to the very opposite conclusion. For Rothbard, as with Hoppe, the *ceteris paribus* assumption depends totally upon the fact that the relationship between internal rates of discount and income or wealth is entirely a negative one. If there are any positive sloped elements of the curve relating the two, then his conclusion could not be a valid one.

Given, however, that there are two possible interpretations of Rothbard's view pertaining to this relationship between the two variables, we shall conclude, as we did in the case of Hoppe, that there is at least some ambiguity involved, and come to no definitive conclusion on this matter.

Let us now consider Rothbard's analysis of the relationship between real money income losses that result from taxation, on the one hand, and time preference rates on the other. Our conclusion in this regard is that Rothbard is still somewhat ambiguous on this issue, but that based on a weighing of the evidence, that he, too, along with Hoppe, sees the relationship more in terms of praxeology than psychology.

While there is no "smoking gun," equivalent to Hoppe's definitive claim in this matter, Rothbard (1970, 73) draws a figure 4, depicting the relationship between time preference rates and money assets, with a negatively sloped curve.[21]. Since there are no sections of this curve with upward slopes, this most reasonably must be interpreted as implying a necessarily inverse relationship between the two variables. Rothbard then states: "The lower the level of a man's real monetary assets, the higher will his time-preference rate be (given his time-preference schedule) and the higher the proportion of his consumption to investment spending" (Rothbard, 1970, 72). The material in brackets about "given time preference schedules," could conceivably serve as a reservation to the stated conclusion. However, we are interpreting this as we have above, to indicate a curve *downward sloping throughout* which necessitates an inverse relationship between time preference and wealth.

Consider several other statements of Rothbard on this matter: "Of course, historically, there is no reason why his time preference *schedule* should remain unchanged. It is important to know, however, that, given an unchanged schedule, his relevant time preference rate will fall" (Rothbard, 1970, 380). This would appear to be very definitive, admitting of no other than a praxeological, not an empirical, interpretation.

But here is a longer rendition of the relationship, the first part of which appears to make a praxeological claim, and the second to be a matter of economic history:

"Suppose, for example, that people were certain that the world would end on a definite date in the near future. What would happen to time preferences and to the rate of interest? Men would then stop providing for future needs and stop investing in all processes of production longer than the shortest. Future goods would become almost valueless compared to present goods, time preferences for present goods would zoom, and the pure interest rate would rise almost to infinity.

"On the other hand, if people all became immortal and healthy as a result of the discovery of some new drug, time preferences would *tend* to be very much lower, there would be a great increase in investment, and the pure rate of interest would fall sharply" (Rothbard, 1970, 381-382, emphasis added).

Note the "tendency" language in the latter part of this quote, which is missing from the former. This, we contend, suggests that in the end of the world scenario Rothbard sees the relationship between wealth (and/or expectations, in this case) to be apodictic, while he sees it as a matter of economic history (Mises, 1957) in the new drug scenario.

---

[21] See, also, Hoppe (2001, 8) for a similar diagram.

IV. The views of other economists[22]

While Rothbard and Hoppe have been prominent amongst those who have mis-analyzed the relationship between time preference and wealth, they are hardly the only guilty parties.[23] This section is devoted to a critique of several other Austrian economists who have misconstrued the wealth – time preference relationship, or have come close to focusing on it, but not precisely.

a. Lewin

First, consider Lewin (1997, 7 [page on website]): "… in the actual operation of the real world economy many things will influence the degree of time preference…. Among these influences is real income or wealth. *Ceteris paribus* an increase in real income will lower the time preference rate."

There is no "tendency" language here, nor any other attempt to soften or qualify this rather definitive language. Accordingly, it is difficult to reject the supposition that this author makes the same error as Rothbard and Hoppe: he means to claim that it is an apodictic necessity, not a broad empirical generalization, for real income to vary inversely with the individual's time preference rate.

But this interpretation is highly problematic, in that, as we have seen, it is entirely logically possible for incomes to rise, and yet time preferences to increase as well. Further, it falls victim to the three numerical counter examples with which we began our analyses.

b. Fetter

What is Fetter's take on the issue at hand? He states: "The greater provision for present desires thus made possible [by exogenous increases in productivity] leads us to expect a reduction of the preference for present goods …" (Fetter, 1977, 247, material in brackets added).

---

[22] In an earlier draft of this paper, we focused on Hoppe and Rothbard, since these two, far more than any others, had dealt with the relationship between income and time preference rates. A referee of this journal called for a consideration of the views of additional economists on this matter. The difficulty is that while there are several who have touched upon the subject, they have not given it anything like a direct or full treatment, and, often, their remarks on it were peripheral to their own concerns. Hence, the paucity of commentary on the part of these authors in this section of the paper.

[23] There is an Austrian literature that addresses not the narrow issue of how changes in income affect time preference rates, but rather the more general question of the genesis of the latter. See: Block (1978A, 1990C); Bohm-Bawerk (1884); Faber (1979, 1986); Garrison (1979B, 2001); Greaves (1974); Mises (1912, 1999); Pellengahr (1986A, 1986B, 1996); Rothbard (1962, 1987).

In terms of our own present analysis, this is "neither here nor there." That is, Fetter vouchsafes us no answer regarding the question of whether the admittedly negative relationship between time preference rates on the one hand, and income, wealth or productivity, on the other, is a broad empirical generalization, a "tendency," or a necessary relationship, based on praxeological considerations.[24]

c. Garrison

Garrison (1979B, 221) cites this very page, 247, of Fetter (1977), and says of this latter author: "Fetter goes on to point out that an increase in productivity increases capital values and, hence, wealth. He suggests that to the extent that increased wealth is associated with a fall in time preference, a lower rate of discount and a lower rate of interest would result."

This is entirely unobjectionable. Unfortunately, given our present quest, we must consider this non-definitive. That is, neither Garrison, here, nor Fetter before him, reveals a position on whether the negative relationship between time preference and wealth is an empirical or a praxeological one.

Next, consider Garrison's (1988, 47, material in brackets inserted) later take on the matter: "The extent to which a particular individual discounts (the future) depends upon his own time preferences, which in turn depend upon his particular circumstances."

It must be readily admitted that there is no "smoking gun" here. There are numerous reasonable interpretations according to which Garrison would not be guilty of the error discussed in the present paper. For example, the "particular circumstances" could refer to nothing more than subjective tastes. If so, then time preferences would depend upon "particular circumstances" in much the same unobjectionable manner as preferences for ice cream depend upon them.

However, it is entirely possible that lurking in the bowels of this language is the claim that wealth and or real income would have a negative relationship with time preferences. This interpretation is strengthened by the consideration that it is awkward[25] to state that a man's preferences for ice cream depend upon his "particular circumstances." Yes, they do in that a person from a backward country not familiar with the delights of, say, Rocky Road Ice Cream, would not develop a taste for it (Hayek, 1967). But, given that the individual hails from these here parts, his tastes for ice cream flavors stems from nothing more esoteric than his own personal tastes. Similarly, it is our contention that while a man's time preference rate cannot be totally

---

[24] See also Rothbard 1977B, 1977B

[25] Given that Garrison is anything but an infelicitous writer, one possible interpretation of this "awkwardness" would be that he is committing the fallacy of seeing a necessarily negative relationship between wealth and time preference.

unrelated to his social condition, *given* its parameters, his discount of the future is entirely of his own making, as much, that is, as is his taste in ice cream or anything for that matter.

d. Kirzner.

This economist states as follows: "… physical productivity may significantly affect the level of wealth, and thus *the marginal rate of time preference"* (Kirzner, 1993, 186). But this must be unacceptable, too. It cannot be denied that physical productivity may, indeed, *will,* significantly affect the level of wealth. But that this should be taken as a definitive indication that the marginal rate of time preference will change is unwarranted. In effect, we are here objecting to the "thus" in the above quotation. That is, it does not at all logically follow that the marginal rate of time preference *need* change, even by one iota, in the face of an alteration in wealth. That it is *likely* to fall is a correct broad, and correct, empirical generalization. But that this is *necessarily* so, that it is *apodictic*, is not and cannot be established. The point is, contrary to Kirzner, and as far as praxeological considerations alone are concerned, the marginal rate of time preference may rise, fall, or stay exactly the same in the face of an increase in physical productivity and hence wealth.

V. Conclusion

Based upon our examination of the record, we derive several conclusions: When it comes to the negative relationship between time preference and wealth in the absence of taxation, while both Hoppe and Rothbard made statements to the effect that this is a matter of praxeology, they also articulate some views that might draw us to the opposite conclusion, namely, that these are only empirical tendencies based, perhaps, upon psychological considerations. However, when this relationship is explored in the context of taxation, then Hoppe is definitive, and Rothbard only somewhat less so, in maintaining that taxes, which necessarily reduce income, inevitably raise time preferences, and that this is *not* a matter of empirical generalization but rather stems from praxeological considerations.

Chapter 3. Involuntary Unemployment

Abstract

Our claim is that in the purely free enterprise system, there can be no such thing as involuntary unemployment, as long as wage demands are in accord with expected productivity, as perceived by the potential employer. Seeming counter examples are shown to violate one or more of these conditions. Nevertheless, there is great resistance on the part of professional economists to this axiomatic claim. The second part of the paper attempts to probe the cause of this resistance, and finds in praxeology, a rejection of Keynesian economics and psychological analysis, the cure for it.

I. Introduction

Our claim is that in the purely free enterprise system, there can be no such thing as involuntary unemployment, as long as wage demands are in accord with expected productivity, as perceived by the potential employer. In section II, we survey the Austrian economics literature and this question and demonstrate that seeming counter examples violate one or more of these conditions. Nevertheless, there is great resistance on the part of professional economists to this axiomatic conclusion. Section III of this paper is thus devoted to probing the cause of this resistance. We offer as explanations failure to appreciate praxeology, vestiges of Keynesianism and psychology. We conclude in section IV.

II. Involuntary unemployment?

When Mises (1998), Rockwell (2006), Rothbard (2004), Hoppe (2007) propose that there cannot be involuntary unemployment on an unhampered labor market, they simply mean that labor is a scarce good and like all scarce goods has a market-clearing price at which all sellers can find a willing buyer and conversely. On the labor market this implies that a worker is *always* employable or able to sell his labor services as long he is willing to work at a wage rate that does not exceed his *prospective* marginal revenue product to a firm, i.e. the addition to the total revenue of the firm that it *anticipates* hiring him.

Says Mises (1998, 599) in this regard:

Unemployment in the unhampered market is always voluntary. In the eyes of the unemployed man, unemployment is the minor of two evils between which he has to choose. The structure of the market may sometimes cause wage rates to drop. But, on the unhampered market, there is always for each type of labor a rate at which all those eager to work can get a job. The final wage rate is that rate at which all job-seekers get jobs and all employers as many workers as they want to hire. Its height is determined by the marginal productivity of each type of work.

In the view of Rockwell (2006):

"When we speak of unemployment, we cannot be talking about a shortage of jobs to be done. There is always work to do at some price. For that reason, there can be no such thing as involuntary unemployment in a free market. Everyone who wants to work is working and everyone who does not want to work is in that position by choice. This is a truth that follows from the universal reality of scarcity. ... There are only two reasons for unemployment: legal restrictions that forbid contracts from forming (France has plenty, and the United States does too) and price restrictions that prevent the market for labor from clearing properly (France has that too, as does the US). In other words, involuntary unemployment is always and everywhere brought about by the same cause: government restriction of the market."

And in Hoppe's analysis (2007, footnotes omitted):

"Employment will increase and wages rise so long as entrepreneurs perceive existing wages as lower than the marginal value product ... which a corresponding increment in the employment of labor can be expected to bring about. On the other hand, unemployment will result and increase so long as a person values the marginal value product attained through self-employment or the satisfactions of leisure more highly than a wage that reflects his labor services' marginal productivity. In this construction there is no logical room for such a thing as 'involuntary unemployment'."

A person is not employed, that is, not working as a hired laborer, either because he prefers leisure or because he is self-employed. In either case the person is unemployed voluntarily. But may it not be true that, on the free and unhampered market, someone is "unemployed" in the modern sense, that is, he is seeking work and cannot find a job? But such a construct raises many problems. Thus, I may be seeking a position as president of Harvard University, and this employer, for some obscure reason, may refuse to hire me for that post. We could say that I am "involuntarily unemployed," but this would distort any sensible meaning of the term.

In any wage agreement, as in any exchange on the free market, *both parties* must participate willingly in the exchange, that is, both must participate voluntarily. If half of the labor force should take it into their heads that each of them should be hired as president of Harvard, and each insists on this employment and no other, then indeed half of the labor force minus one person will be permanently and "involuntarily" unemployed. But is this, as Keynes would have it, a failure of the free market, or is it a failure of the mental processes and values of those laborers? And since this problem is clearly a failure internal to the workers themselves, we must conclude that such unemployment is "voluntary" in the realistic sense that it is the consequence of the internal mental processes and choices of those workers, even though each would "voluntarily" prefer to be president of Harvard rather than to be without work.

Rothbard (2004, 780) puts the matter very succinctly:

"... there can be no involuntary unemployment in a free market..."

The case of physically or mentally handicapped individuals does not contradict the proposition because their expected MRP may well be zero or negative in all endeavors, meaning that their labor services are not scarce.[26] Nor does the fact that an individual who is laid off from a job is not instantaneously re-employed contradict the proposition. The worker could have offered to work for a nickel an hour or some other low wage for the firm that laid him off, the local McDonald's, or doing domestic chores or errands for his neighbors and he would be re-employed in short order (assuming his expected MRP exceeded $.05 per hour). More realistically, markets are temporally separate in our world, meaning that the fact that he had to wait until the next day because labor markets do not operate at night or wait until he traveled to a prospective new employer does not contradict the proposition because where there is no market, buying and selling are necessarily absent.

Third and finally, the proposition is not falsified by the fact that prices in labor markets are never the final prices of a fictional final equilibrium or state of rest. The economy never achieves a final state of rest and a structure of final prices. This does not mean, however, that prices actually paid in real markets are not market clearing prices in the Mengerian sense. The fact that a seller withholds some of his stock of goods or a laborer decides to pass on an employment offer and keep searching because the prevailing market price does not meet his expectations is fully consistent with market-clearing and full employment in the labor market. It is a speculative and voluntary refusal to exchange that is fully consistent with a dynamic view of supply and demand curves which both include speculative elements because of uncertainty. Menger was the first to conceive an exchange equilibrium that gives rise to actual prices and wages and in which the mutual benefits of perceived exchange opportunities at a given moment are completely exhausted. He called it "points of rest"; Boehm-Bawerk, a "momentary equilibrium"; and Mises, "the plain state of rest." All three regarded this condition as a recurrent

---

[26] In such cases, we would have to modify our main contention to incorporate the possibility of negative wages. For example, if a man's expected productivity were minus $2.00 per hour, we could expect him to be employed if the employee paid the employer to work. In this regard states Bradley (unpublished): "Insull enjoyed these years despite an almost complete absence of leisure. A combination of hard work, broad skills, and smarts made Samuel a success at two jobs and family breadwinner by the time he was 18. Then in a bolt out of the blue, his day boss ended a positive performance review by firing him! A wealthy customer, it turned out, had arranged for his son to enter the business world by assuming Samuel's job and work for the experience rather than pay. The episode violated Insull's ego, which McDonald (1962, 15) described as an "untouchable area," where "even a modest affront was unforgivable and unforgettable."

and observable characteristic of all real world markets. You and the local grocery store are in a plain state of rest when you purchase and walk out with a gallon of milk, two pounds of steak, five pounds of potatoes, and two bottles of red wine, no more and no less. The precise price and quantities of these items were strictly determined by the interaction of your (concurrent buyers') maximum buying prices and the minimum selling prices (probably determined by its speculative reservation prices) of the grocery store.

III. Resistance

Why is there great resistance on the part of the economics profession to the insight that on the unhampered market, there can be no such thing as involuntary unemployment? Why do economists recoil in horror from the "specter" of zero unemployment? For example,[27] Palmer[28] refers to the "the absurd and non-Austrian view that free market unemployment is 'always voluntary.' " Our answers to these questions can only be speculative. We are, after all, addressing motive. However, there are several reasonable explanations for this state of affairs.

1. Vestiges of Keynesianism

Keynesianism has played a virulent role in the economics profession. Its central idea, that there could be an underemployment equilibrium, is a hard one, evidently, to jettison. Like a vampire, intellectually shooting this economic philosophy is not good enough: one must employ garlic, or a silver bullet, or some such,[29] lest it arise from its "killing," ghoul-like. Keynes (1936) has been "killed" over and over[30]; yet it marches on, oblivious to its own death.

To wit, one would have thought that Keynesianism would have been stopped dead in its tracks by the phenomenon of stagflation. For, the Keynesian remedy for inflation was to reduce aggregate demand; for deflation, or depression, to increase. What, then, when not one but *both* of these phenomena present themselves at the *same* time? Any economic philosophy with but a modicum of respect would have vanished into the woodwork in the face of so obvious a rejection of its basic tenets. But not, of course, Keynesianism, which has a life of its own despite being blatantly contradicted by real world experience.

---

[27] Palmer has no official credentials in economics (http://www.tomgpalmer.com /papers/cv.pdf) but frequently writes about this subject in any case.

[28] See Raico (2003), and point 4, below.

[29] The authors of the present article are located in New Orleans, the vampire capital of the universe. We brook no disagreement with our claims in this regard. Although we usually eschew argument from authority, in this one case we stand ready to employ it.

[30] For critiques of Keynes, 1936, see Butos, 2001; Garrison, 1995; Hayek, 1995, 1972; Hazlitt, 1959, 1983; Hoppe, 1992; Hutt, 1979; Rothbard, 1959, 1960; Salerno, 1992; Skousen, 1992; Smiley, 1987; Van den Hauwe, 2000.

This refusal to contemplate an equilibrium situation at other than full employment stems from this "dead from the neck up, but not below," phenomenon. This explanation may be part of the story, but it cannot constitute the complete elucidation. It can account for why many members of the profession reject the thesis, but not all. To wit, it fails to explain why Austrians, who by definition (Mises, 1998; Rothbard, 1993) adhere to praxeology, fail to grasp it.

2. Praxeology

Here, we refer to a failure to sufficiently think in praxeological[31] categories. The analysis in section II, supra, is a matter of praxeology. This means that the denial of the conclusion, that in the unhampered market there can be no such thing as involuntary unemployment, is a veritable contradiction in terms. If one buys into the premises that labor is a scarce good, the conclusion follows ineluctably. To be sure Austrians think in praxeological categories, but in this case, evidently not all of them, and not fully.

This becomes apparent when one attempts to specify conditions under which, given an unregulated free enterprise system, it would be logically *possible* for there to be involuntary unemployment. When one attempts to do so it is clear, as per our section II, that either one denies that labor is scarce, or that MRP of labor must be in the eyes of the beholder (e.g., the employer), not the worker, or that the profit maximization assumption is being violated, etc.

3. Psychology[32]

Most adults have at one time or another been fired from a job. Rarely if ever was this followed up by, within a second or two, an offer of another employment opportunity. Usually, finding another post took weeks or even months. Hence, in the mind's eye of those who reject our thesis, they, seemingly, have their own experience as a guide in this matter.

---

[31] See Block, 1973; Batemarco, 1985; Fox, 1992; Hoppe, 1989B, 1992, 1995; Mises, 1998; Rizzo, 1979A; Rothbard, 1951A, 1951B, 1957, 1971, 1973, 1976B, 1997A, 1997B, 1997D, 1997D, 1997E, 1997F, 1997G, 1997H, 1993; Selgin, 1988.

[32] Our use of psychology is compatible with Rothbard's (1997I, 218) definition of, and warning against, "Psychologizing … a common error in utility analysis. It is based on the assumption that utility analysis is a kind of 'psychology,' and that, therefore, economics must enter into psychological analysis in laying the foundation of its theoretical structure. Praxeology, the basis of economic theory, differs from psychology, however. Psychology analyzes the *how* and the *why* of people forming values. Economics, on the other hand, rests simply on the assumption of the *existence* of ends, and then deduces its valid theory from such a general assumption (footnote omitted)." This is because in the present section, strictly speaking, we are engaging in a bit of amateur psychological analysis, not economic or praxeological analysis.

It cannot be denied that in the way that ordinary people use the language, this phenomenon does exist. That is, *of course,* in the way people ordinarily speak, there is involuntary unemployment. And, for the typical economist, there is both frictional and structural unemployment, none of which can even with the wildest stretch of the imagination, be characterized as "voluntary." We know full well that as a matter of technical economics (see section II, supra), this is nonsense, and nonsense on stilts. We suggest here that there may be some sort of verbal dispute underlying these differences.

That is, words are being used differently by the contending parties. Two analogies spring readily to mind, one from physics, one from economics. From the former realm, the concept of "work" is technically defined as a "transfer of energy by a force acting to displace a body. Work is equal to the product of the force and the distance through which it produces movement."[33] This means, if it means anything, the if an object is *not* transferred through space, then, whatever else may be true, there is no work going on. But suppose a man holds two 25-pound weights with his arms extended. Sweat will immediately begin dripping from his brow. The physicist would deny that any "work" at all was going on, and yet, from an ordinary language point of view, this would be among the most excruciating types of work possible.

Now consider "indifference" from the latter realm, economics. The ordinary speaker of the English language is often indifferent between two sweaters as he reaches into his clothing drawer. He will wear whichever of them he removes from his closet. Yet, as a matter of technical economics, he *cannot* be indifferent between the two of them; he simply has no way to *demonstrate* this. Rather, the demonstration shows that, indeed, he picked sweater A, when he could have, but did not, pick B. Caplan (1999, 2001, 2003) errs in this regard, adamantly refusing to acknowledge the two different meanings of this concept[34].

A similar phenomenon seems to be operating in the present context. The psychological state of being involuntarily unemployed is being confused with technical economic considerations that vitiate against there being any involuntary unemployment at all, as a matter of praxeology. The fact that words can be legitimately used in two different contexts does not let off the hook *economists* who have been using the ordinary language concept. Qua dismal scientists, they are supposedly wedded to their profession.

4. Sheer cussedness and irrationality

In his reply to Raico, Palmer savagely attacked Hoppe -- in part because Hoppe maintains the absurd and non-Austrian view that free market unemployment is "always voluntary."

---

[33] See http://www.bartleby.com/65/wo/work.html

[34] For support of our contention w. Caplan, see Block, 1999A, 2003B; Hulsmann, 1999

Palmer and I corresponded over a year ago about another issue, but Hoppe came up. After I defended Hoppe, Palmer wrote me: "[...] who could take a self-described economist seriously when he writes that unemployment is impossible in a free market? And when he claims that that's somehow an implication of Austrian economics he adds insult to ignorance. [...] The fact is that Mr. Hoppe is an embarrassment."

In a reply to Palmer, I pointed out that Mises, in *Human Action* (Chapter XXI. work and wages, Section 4. Catallactic Unemployment, p. 599), explicitly stated: "unemployment in the unhampered market is always voluntary". Clearly Hoppe's view on unemployment is the same as Mises'. Is Mises supposed to be an embarrassment to Austrian economics too?

Palmer's reply to this? "For Mr. Hoppe it is a cult based on reading and interpreting sacred texts, the point of which is to 'master Misesian economics.' [...] I don't really give a fig about what Mises said just because it's what he said; what I care about is whether what he wrote helps me to understand the world. [...] You write, 'And it is more than an implication of Austrian economics--it is Mises' actual, express, explicit view, in his magnum opus.' If you're right, then so what? Is that an argument? If you're right about this, then Mises was wrong. Is that so hard to accept?"

Note that Palmer himself attacked Hoppe's pedigree as a free-market economist, indeed, as an Austrian economist, by citing Hoppe's allegedly absurd and non-Austrian view that involuntary unemployment is impossible on a free market. When I simply pointed out that Mises himself had the same view, I was clearly not citing Mises to prove that proposition is correct, but to show that this view is not "an embarrassment to Austrian economics," but is rather the view of one of the premiere Austrian economists. Palmer is the one who brought up pedigree; when I showed that his argument was flawed, he retreated to the charge that my citing Mises is cult-like. Need anything else be said?[35]

Well, yes, there is more to be said, at least in terms of the present paper. And it is that this claim, voluntary unemployment is impossible in the free society, is one that sticks in the craw of more than one commentator. And, noting the acidity of this interchange, this statement sticks very deeply into the craws of some commentators.

IV. Conclusion

We maintain that strictly speaking, and how else are we to speak in a scholarly publication, it is impossible for there to be any unemployment in the free economy. We have considered and rejected several arguments to the contrary, and thus rest our case.

---

[35] See Kinsella, 2003; also Kinsella, 2005.

Chapter 4. Continuums[36]

Abstract

There are continuum problems in political economy. There are no objective non-debatable solutions to any of them. All answers to them are arbitrary. Responding to these challenges is, ideally, the responsibility of courts, juries, etc.

I. Introduction

There is a plethora of problems arising in the analysis of law and political economy having in common with each other that their challenge arises from the fact that they can be placed upon a continuum. We argue that there is no real solution to this continuum problem, at least not in terms of distance, or time, or any other objective criterion. We consider physical invasions in section II. Section III is devoted to an exploration of continuums in age related issues and IV to homesteading. We conclude in section V.

II. Physical invasion

A. Crime

First consider in the regard the garden-variety issue of the (threatened) punch in the nose. If A shakes his fist right under B's nose (3 inches away from making contact) while yelling at him, in the context where this can be construed as a real threat e.g., late at night in a restaurant known for its bar-room brawls, or in a dark alley, then there is no doubt that B would be justified in taking all reasonable violent actions aimed at protecting himself. Were B to punch A first, or kick him in the crotch, or even stab or shoot him, any reasonable jury would characterize this as a defensive act, even though the first use of violent force emanated from B. That is, A's act would be considered enough of an immediate threat, a "clear and present danger," such that B's response would constitute not an invasion of another person, but rather a defense of himself.

Now suppose that the threatening fist-shaking took place not 3 inches away from its intended victim, but rather 3 miles away. Everything else remains the same (we stipulate that B has super good eyesight[37] and can perceive this threatened action). Would B be justified in resorting to deadly

---

[36] We would like to thank Gary Herbert for help on an earlier draft of this paper. All remaining errors and infelicities are our own responsibility.

[37] We are indebted to Nozick (1974) for blazing the trail with regard to imaginary inventions, abilities, situations and innovations that help shed light on philosophical puzzles.

force in order to ward off this "threat"? Not at all.[38] Even the meanest intelligence would know that this is not a real threat.

If the same action is a threat at 3 inches but not at 3 miles it follows ineluctably that at some point in between these two distances its very nature changes from the one to the other. Suppose, as a first crack at this problem we pick some such point, say, 30 yards. This means, if it means anything, that at 29 yards 11 inches it is permissible to reply to this act of fist shaking with dangerous, even deadly, force, while if it occurs at a distance of 30 yards and 1 inch, then all bets are off: if B rcsponds physically in this situation, then it is he, B, not A, the fist shaker, who is guilty of engaging in criminal behavior.

One problem with this answer is that the dividing line is so narrow: two inches in our example. Of course, mathematically, lines are not at all as wide as that; indeed, their width approaches zero. But no matter how wide, no solutions are in sight. If narrow, then there doesn't seem to be much difference between either of the end points; if very wide, e.g., in the extreme, three miles minus three inches, we arrive back at the very problem we are attempting to solve.

Another problem is that no matter what division between licit and illicit activities we choose, it is always possible to ask, "Well, if we move a small amount in one or the other of the two directions, how can that possibly make a difference." That is, in our case, if 30 yards is where the line is drawn in the sand, then why not 25 or 35 yards?; why not 29 or 31, for that matter.[39]

How, then, can we solve the problem of whether or not a response or retaliation against a threat is justified or not, given the conditions as depicted above? The only answer is that there is no answer, at least not one that admits of geographical extension. That is, no single cut off point will be both reasonable and non arbitrary.

---

[38] Barnett, 1998 discusses a death threat uttered in the context where it can only be actualized in the future, and correctly maintains that it would still be justified in killing the threatener, even though the element of clear and *present* danger is lacking. E.g., the case of the Fatwa issued against Salman Rushdie, the Indian British novelist. The difference between the two cases is that it is not clear what the man is doing who waves his fist at the "nose" of someone else from three miles away, whereas the implication of the Fatwa is all too clear. For a critical review of Barnett, 1998, see Kinsella, 1998.

[39] There are some issues in libertarian crime theory that do admit of precision. For example, that punishment shall consist of "two teeth for a tooth," and not 1.9 or 2.1 "teeth." See on this: Block, 1999B, 2002-2003, 2003A, 2004A, 2004B; Block, Barnett and Callahan, 2005; Gregory and Block, 2007; Olson, 1979; Rothbard, 1998, 88; Whitehead and Block, 2003.

What, then? The answer forthcoming from this quarter is to utilize the "reasonable man"[40] (Rothbard, 1990) standard.[41] Under ideal conditions, were a jury shown a film of exactly what happened, guilt or innocence on the part of B for retaliating or engaging in a "first strike" against A would be based upon the evaluation of the danger B faced as evaluated by 12 disinterested[42] persons.[43] This does not have at all the precision of a distance criterion, but, for all that, we maintain that it is far more satisfactory.[44]

B. International Relations

When the U.S. entered Viet Nam, the "hawks" claimed that this was only a defensive maneuver, in that the communists were intent upon conquering us, and would do so country by country, until they were poised at our jugular, having taken over every other nation in the world. Why wait until they could invade us from their bases in Mexico and Canada? Why not fight the enemy while they are still some distance away? Theirs was the "Domino Theory": once allow the enemy to gain a foothold, or, worse, to increase it, then like dominos all lined up, one falling would trigger all the others until we were undone.

---

[40] Some feminists have put forth a "reasonable woman" standard as an alternative (*Ellison v Brady, 199*, cited in McElroy, 2001, p. 38). The present authors use the word "man" in the traditional sense, to include both men and women. If women on balance are more fearful than the average human being, and men less so, then our standard would be pegged midpoint on this continuum. That of the feminists would be skewed in favor of those on the risk avoider side of the fence.

[41] "A fictional person with an ordinary degree of reason, prudence, care, foresight, or intelligence whose conduct, conclusion, or expectation in relation to a particular circumstance, or fact is used as an objective standard by which to measure or determine something (as the existence of negligence). Merriam-Webster's Dictionary of Law (1996); http://dictionary.lp.findlaw.com/scripts/results.pl?co=dictionary.lp.findlaw.com&topic=19/194efb4cb63ca323ab32d9ae9418265e

[42] Disinterested is defined by the dictionary of English (http://www.tiscali.co.uk/reference/dictionaries/english/data/d0081934.html) as follows "If you are *disinterested* in something you are impartial and do not take sides: *A disinterested observer of the scene would have wondered what all the fuss was about*. If you are *uninterested* you have no interest at all: *The player was uninterested in the public reaction to his remark. Disinterested* is often used instead of *uninterested* to mean lacking interest. This use is widely regarded as incorrect and should be avoided, especially in formal writing."

[43] We choose the number 12 for illustrative purposes only because most juries in the U.S. are composed of this many people. Were the number, instead, 9 or 25, this would not change our point in the text.

[44] But not perfectly so, since it is so subjective. We anxiously await an improved criterion. It cannot be denied, as a critic of ours stated, that "jurors' beliefs are influenced by their personal experiences, cultural, religious, political backgrounds." But this applies to *everyone*, without exception.

The "doves," in contrast, took the position that this was arrant nonsense. The fate of a small country 10,000 miles from our borders was irrelevant to our own national security. In the event, history seems to have proven the isolationists correct. The communist north overran the non-communist southern part of the country, and, instead of the dominos leading to the demise of the U.S., the ostensible beneficiary of this theory, the U.S.S.R. ended instead.

Where, then, should the U.S. draw a "line in the sand," stating so far but no further, if it is to maintain the distinction between and offensive and a defensive foreign policy? The Monroe Doctrine attempted to draw this line at the borders of North and South America. Were this criterion employed, then a take-over by the armies of Cuba or Nicaragua would be seen as serious indeed, while what goes on in Viet Nam, or on the Korean Peninsula, or between the Arabs and the Israelis would be interpreted as outside of our sphere of interests.

One difficulty with the hawkish interpretation is that any unrest, anywhere in the world, serves as a trip wire for the U.S., involving us in countries the only benefit of which is that we learn the spelling and location of out of obscure cities. Then, too, it is difficult to generalize this position. E.g., if it is really only "defensive" for the U.S. to act in such a manner, and defense is the proper prerogative of *all* nations, then countries, hundreds of them, will be continually tripping over each other in very far corners of the globe.

On the other hand, it would take a rather pacifist kind of government in the U.S. to look with equanimity at a hostile take over of the two countries which are our immediate neighbors, to our north and south, respectively.[45]

The international analogue to the "reasonable man" standard in the case of domestic crime would appear to be to adopt a reasonable Martian or Venusian standard. Suppose that an inhabitant of one of these planets were looking down upon us through a telescope powerful enough to register to movement of armies, but was disinterested enough in earthly events to be able to adopt a judicial attitude with regard to them. Would he characterize the U.S. as a world bully in the last half of the 20th century? Based only on the fact that we had stationed troops all over the third planet, and that no other country had emulated us in this regard, it is difficult to resist this notion.[46]

---

[45] However, it would be hard to deny that much of Soviet foreign policy was dedicated to the establishment of a cordon sanitaire around its own borders. What is sauce for the goose would not appear to be so for the gander, at least in some circles.

[46] For the view that there is a sharp disanalogy between individuals on the one hand and national governments on the other, see Rothbard (1984B).

Consider the following argument, regarding the above:

"… maybe if the Venusians or Martians saw what the Communists and the terrorists did to their civilian populations, maybe they would agree that somebody had to do something to prevent such crimes. If someone saw a woman being raped, would he intervene or would he ask a reasonable man what he would do before intervening?"

We do not accept this perspective. In our view it is simply not the job of the U.S. government to be the world's policeman. Nowhere in the Constitution of the U.S. is any such role articulated.[47] Of course, all men of good will would try to stop a rape in progress. But there is a disanalogy here. Suppose A hires B to be his bodyguard, and B, instead of protecting A, rushes off to stop a rape in progress across the street, leaving in danger the person he is contractually obligated to protect. Would this bodyguard be justified in running off, even, stipulating, for a good purpose, to this end? Of course not. The point is, if the bodyguard wants to stop rapes on his own time, we can all applaud him for that. But, if he does so in direction contravention to his obligations, that conclusion cannot be justified.

How does this translate into international relations? If this critic and others like him wish to stop "rapes" abroad, let them do just that. But they are not justified in bringing in the U.S. government for that role, for just as in the case of the bodyguard, this organization has an entirely different task. Let this critic and his ilk follow the path of the International Brigades, including the Abraham Lincoln Battalion aka "the Lincoln Brigade"[48] that fought in the Spanish Civil War of 1936-1939. We agree that "*somebody* had to do something to prevent such crimes." We disagree it had to be the U.S. government.

Now consider the following point that could be made by a critic:

"The authors of this paper are correct in implicitly pointing that the U.S. facing terrorists attacks may be due to past "bad" invasive foreign policy. However, one might argue that it is in the past, it's a sunk cost and nothing can be done to change the past."

---

[47] http://www.law.cornell.edu/ constitution/constitution.overview.html. Not that this should be definitive. See on this Spooner. [1870] 1966: "It is true that the theory of our Constitution is that all taxes are paid voluntarily; that our government is a mutual insurance company, voluntarily entered into by the people with each other; that each man makes a free and purely voluntary contract with all others who are parties to the Constitution, to pay so much money for so much protection, the same as he does with any other insurance company; and that he is just as free not to be protected, and not to pay tax, as he is to pay a tax, and be protected. But this theory of our government is wholly different from the practical fact. The fact is that the government, like a highwayman, says to a man: 'Your money, or your life.' And many, if not most, taxes are paid under the compulsion of that threat."

[48] http://search.eb.com/eb/article-9042576

Not so, not so. Of course, the critic is correct in his view that nothing can be done to rectify past mistakes. But, assume our *thesis* is correct. That means that *every* unnecessary and illicit action of the U.S. government[49] over and above the limited role assigned to it by the Constitution creates problems. Yes, it applies to past events, about which nothing can now be done. But, it *also* holds true for present and future such acts, which are not yet "sunk costs." That is, improper invasions *now* undertaken by the government will have negative repercussions in the future, and these can *at present* be obviated.[50]

III. Age of maturity

When does a child become an adult, for legal purposes? For some religions, confirmation can come as early as 9-13, which is, presumably, the number of years required before a person can make an informed decision on such matters. In many states of the union, a youngster can obtain a license to operate a motor vehicle when he is 14-16 years old. School leaving ages, and the age before which a work permit can be issued, are of similar vintage. The military draft kicks in at 18, the drinking age and that for sexual consent varies between 18-21, the latter of which is required for voting. No one may take the office of congressman before reaching age 30, nor may a president of the U.S. be sworn in before reaching 35.[51]

So which is it? When does a child become an adult? As with all continuum problems, the solution does not lie in objective numbers. For no matter what age is selected, it is always possible to be critical, and reasonably so, on the ground that an age 1 day older or younger would also be justified. It is always possible to point to those under this age who are more mature than some who exceed it. Surely, there are some if only a few 12 year olds who act in a more adult manner than some who have reached the age of 21.

Other criteria must instead be employed if the continuum problem is to be finessed. One such is offered by Rothbard (1998). Here, the criterion is not calendar years, but rather the type of human action, or homesteading, which is indicative of maturity. The child becomes an adult in effect when he seizes control over himself by setting up his own household. This might have to be done under the approval of a judge, but in this manner a modicum of

---

[49] This applies to *all* governments, not only that of the U.S. In our view, they *all* ought to be limited in scope.

[50] Ferguson (2000) argued in part that Britain's entry into what had been a European conflict between Germany and France escalated the conflict into The Great War (We owe this point to Bill Butos). See also Powell, (2005; we owe this cite to Tom DiLorenzo) and Taylor (1972, 1996).

[51] http://www.senate.gov/civics/constitution_item/constitution.htm

common sense is inculcated into what would otherwise be a sterile objective criterion. States Rothbard (1998, p. 103) in this regard:

"But when are we to say that this parental trustee jurisdiction over children shall come to an end? Surely any particular age (21 years, 18, or whatever) can only be completely arbitrary. The clue to the solution of this thorny question lies in the parental property rights in their home. For the child has his *full* rights of self-ownership *when he demonstrates that he has them in nature*—in short, when he leaves or "runs away" from home. Regardless of his age, we must grant to every child the absolute right to runaway and to find new foster parents who will voluntarily adopt him, or to try to exist on his own. Parents may try to persuade the runaway child to return, but it is totally impermissible enslavement and an aggression upon his right of self-ownership for them to use force to compel him to return. The absolute right to run away is the child's ultimate expression of his right of self-ownership, regardless of age."

Age plays if anything an even more dramatic role in debates involving the earliest inception of the human being. To wit, when does a fetus become a person? The pro-choice movement argues for the time of birth. The pro life faction locates the proper date at conception: the fertilized egg is a human being, since if not interfered with, that is the natural processes will result in that eventuality. This debate is so highly documented and discussed it needs no further elucidation here.[52]

In contrast, those who advocate the eviction theory in the abortion controversy (Block, 1978B, 2001B, 2004C; Block and Whitehead, 2005) offer an alternative answer to this continuum problem: whenever the fetus is viable outside of the womb, it becomes invested with the rights accorded human beings. This date would of course change as medical technology advances (McElroy, 2005). A century ago, this perspective would have given the answer offered by the pro-choice advocates: since the fetus was not viable outside of the womb until birth, it achieves human rights only at that time. A century hence, medically technology will presumably be so far advanced such that, according to this theory, the fetus at any stage of development will be invested with the same rights accorded all human beings. At these rates of improvement, each decade, at present, will subtract a few days from this point; that is, every ten years or so from now, enough advances will have made such that a fetus of, say, a week younger will be able to be supported outside the placenta, in a test tube or host mother, or some such. Thus, we arrive at a date for human life that is continually changing, and is not based upon any particular point on this continuum.

[52] For other libertarian theories pertaining to abortion, see Cobin, 1998; Long, 1993; McElroy, 2005; Rothbard, 1983C

A similar situation applies to the age at which statutory rape applies. That there must be such a law is clear; females below some cut off age point are simply incapable of engaging in consensual sexual relations. But at what level should this apply. Twelve seems far too young, and 21 too old. So is the correct age 14, 16, 18? Whichever age is picked, there will be girls younger than that who are more mature than others who are older. And what of the age of the male involved? Surely, there is a difference in physical relations between a girl who is 16 and a boy who is 17, or a man who is 45. Cut off points of this sort simply cannot be derived in any straightforward manner from the law of non-aggression. There is a need for private competing courts[53] and juries to decide such matters.

IV. Homesteading

According to libertarian theorists (Block, 1990B; Hoppe, 1993; Locke, 1948; Rothbard, 1973, 32; Rozeff, 2005) virgin territory is initially brought into a state of ownership through homesteading.[54] One mixes one's labor with the land, and in that manner comes to own it.

There are two margins for continua presented in such a scenario. On the one hand, for *how long* does the homesteading have to occur before it can be said to be completed? For one minute? Hour? Day? Week? Month? Year? The Homestead Act of 1862 required farmers to gather crops for five years[55] in a row before title devolved upon them.[56]

One principled, no continuum way to solve this issue is to hark back to agricultural rhythms. That is, the homesteading must occur for at least one growing season, in the case of farmland. After all, the goal in clearing land for this purpose is to get in a crop. If sowing alone occurs, but not reaping, it can be said that the homesteading process is not complete.

A second margin concerns the intensiveness or extensiveness of the farming that takes place, for however long it took. E.g., does there need to be one wheat plant per square inch? Foot? Yard? Acre? Mile? Indeed, stretch the extensiveness of the planting sufficiently, and homesteading devolves into claim theory, where the owner plants a flag at a point, and claims "as far

---

[53] See on this: Anderson and Hill (1979), Benson (1989, 1990), Fielding (1978), Friedman (1989), Hoppe (1993, 2001), Long (2004), Murphy (2002, 2005), Rothbard (1973, 1978A, 1978B, 1982B), Sneed (1977), Stringham, (1998-1999), Tannehills (1984), Woolridge (1970)

[54] Property titles are subsequently justified on the basis of any and all voluntary commercial and non-commercial interaction: sales, gifts, gambling, etc. See on this Nozick, 1974.

[55] http://www.nps.gov/home/homestead_act.html

[56] See Anderson and Hill, 1979, 15, for a discussion of land claims regarding gold mining.

as the eye can see" at the very least, on and up to an entire continent at the extreme.[57]

There is a way to address this problem that does not rely upon some necessarily arbitrary point along the continuum: it is to resort to common (economically efficient) practice. For example, most farming east of the Mississippi is done relatively intensively. Compared to what lies in the western part of the country, this land is irrigated, which supports intensive agriculture. West of the Mississippi, in contrast, acreage is dryer. Vegetables, bushes and trees, etc., cannot be planted as close together; it takes more pasture to support a single cow. These considerations cannot make fine distinctions, e.g., as to whether, in Iowa, the proper margin for corn is every one, two or three feet, but we can say, that whatever it is, it is more intensive than in the desert areas of Utah.[58]

V. On Buchanan and Rawls

These two authors are far from favorites of ours. We regard the former's rejection of anarchism as logically flawed, and what we consider his characterization of government as in effect a market participant as grievously mistaken.[59] As to the latter, we see his "veil of ignorance" as highly problematic, in that it focuses only on the forced transfer of money from rich to poor, and ignores such more important attributes as intelligence, beauty, sense of humor, number of hair follicles, disposition toward happiness, etc. Why not transfer these from those who have "too much" of them, and to those who have too little? Also, even with regard to money, Rawls focuses solely on the U.S. Why not include the poor from the entire world in his calculation? This would, we contend, make his redistributionist schemes far less palatable.[60]

---

[57] In the interplanetary context, one could claim an entire planet, or moon, merely by mixing one's labor with a very small part of it, provided that homesteading was interpreted in an extensive enough manner.

[58] The homesteading concerns in this section, and the question of human ownership in the previous one, are not totally unrelated. This is because people attain ownership over themselves through a process that might be described as quasi homesteading. At birth, the baby has no control over itself. Its arm and leg motions are seemingly random. After a few months, through a gradual process, growth changes occur in this regard. At this age, the parents can kiss the infant at will. But around the age of two the infant learns the word "No," and can refuse to be kissed. It is in this manner that we assert ownership over ourselves through a process of homesteading (e.g., using) our bodies.

[59] For support of these contentions, see DiLorenzo, 1990A; Block and DiLorenzo, 2000, 2001; DiLorenzo and Block, 2001; Rothbard, 1989B, 1997R.

[60] For an utter, total and complete evisceration of the views of Rawls on these matters, see Nozick (1974, 183-231).

Yet, whatever misgivings we have about the overall oeuvre of these two authors, it cannot be denied that we may learn from Rawls (1971) and Buchanan (1976, 2000) in the present context, with regard to continuums. Take Rawls first. The "veil of ignorance" is a technique employed by this author in order to place some objectivity into discussions of fairness or justice. We have rejected the implications he draws from this for income distribution. But we take the position that this can nevertheless shed light on continuums. For example, if one does not know, in advance, whether one will be shaking his fist at someone else, or, have his face subjected to the fist shaking of someone else, it may well be that a better line of demarcation between justified and unjustified fist shaking will be drawn than if one considers only one side of this issue. Or consider age of consent laws. Child molesters and parents of young children will obviously have different takes on this issue. But, if one does not know what role one will have in society, one is more likely to take a more reasonable position on the matter. Indeed, we see this as part and parcel of, and buttress for, our comments on the "reasonable man" criterion employed above. That is, the veil of ignorance can be employed to increase the "reasonableness" of man.

Buchanan's work, too, can shed light on the conundrums we have addressed in this paper.[61] One could conceivably interpret his contribution to political economy as an attempt to bridge the gap between, the centripetal forces of anarchism, as he sees them, on the one hand, and on the other hand the centrifugal forces of statism on the other. In one direction lies the Scylla of excessive individualism; anarchy is chaos, for Buchanan. In another lies the Charybdis of unwarranted centralization; if the government is too powerful, who guards us from the Leviathans? Buchanan sees the range between these two extremes as a continuum. His solution to this problem is a constitution. We need not agree with him on this to acknowledge that his analysis of continuums is not unrelated to our own.

VI. Conclusion

We have attempted to make that case that there are continuum problems[62] that beset libertarian theory. It is impossible to non-arbitrarily set precise limits in terms of age of majority, homesteading, salvage, and other important aspects of libertarian law. We conclude from this not any shortcoming in the principles of non aggression but rather the importance of private institutions in the law industry.

---

[61] See also Brubaker, 1975; Buchanan and Tullock, 1962.

[62] For other treatments of this phenomenon, see Graff, 2002; Sainsbury and Williamson, 1997; Sorensen, 2001; Varzi, 2003

Chapter 5. Economic Singularism

Abstract

What is the essence of Austrian economics? Is it praxeology? Methodology? Market process? Subjectivism? Human Action? Property rights? Information or Knowledge? Counterfactualism? The present paper does not deny that all these are important. Nevertheless, it makes the case for including singularism, too, as one of the key elements of Austrianism. We attempt to demonstrate the importance of this concept by applying it to supply and demand, indifference, and the decision between using an escalator and walking on the stairs, an issue recently debated, but not settled, by numerous economists on the internet. Our point is that Austrian Economists have emphasized deduction, individualism, subjectivism, and (at least for some) market process. But they have downplayed, virtually to the point of ignoring, singularism. This paper is dedicated to at least partially righting this imbalance.

I. Introduction[63]

There is something of an underground debate going on within Austrian economic circles. It concerns what is the best synonym for this school of thought. Here, "best" is an attempt to uncover the most accurate description of the economic strain of analysis that stems from Menger (1950[1871]). That is the first purpose of the present paper, and our attempt to answer this is the burden of section II. In section III we apply our choice for this appellation, "singularism" to supply and demand, and in IV to indifference. Section V is given over to a singularistic analysis of a challenge which has also lead a subterranean existence, this time in the neoclassical division of the economics profession: the issue of why some people stand on escalators, allowing these contraptions to carry them upward or downward, while no one treats stairs in any such manner. Specifically, we maintain, strictly speaking, it is illegitimate to even draw supply and demand curves (section III), that there are grave difficulties with indifference (section IV), and the debate concerning walking up the escalator vs. using the staircase (section V). We conclude in VI.

II. Best name

Why all the fuss over labeling? Surely it is a matter of relative unimportance what we call things? Certainly the substance of the matter is

---

[63] The authors of the present paper would like to acknowledge a debt to the editor of This Journal and two unusually active and insightful referees. The comments they made on an earlier version of this paper, and our changes in it as a result, have greatly improved both its substance and presentation. Any remaining errors of omission or commission are of course solely our responsibility.

far more important? Well, when matters are put in such a fashion, this claim can hardly be denied. However, nomenclature too, is important, particularly if it speaks to the essence of the categorization of an enterprise. For example, while it is undoubtedly an exaggeration to say that biology consists of nothing but naming things and categorizing them, this is only somewhat of an exaggeration. A great deal of biological science indeed focuses on nothing other than this. It is a matter of crucial importance whether a species is part of this or that genera, class, or phylum, for example. And chemistry is no different. Many of the insights of this science depend, intimately, on whether a given substance is to be placed in this or that part of the periodic table of elements. These are "mere" matters of nomenclature, labeling and categorization, but they are not to be dismissed by careful scientists. A similar point can also be made in economics. In the dismal science, too, scholars speak past each other if they mean different things by such terms as "capital," "interest," and "profit," etc.

So, what label should the Austrian School adopt? What term gets the closest to what it is all about? What one word or phrase comes closest to characterizing its essence? There are several obvious candidates. A prime example would be "The Praxeological School of Thought." Support for this option stems from the importance Austrians have placed on praxeology (Mises, 1998; Rothbard, 1951A, 1962; Hoppe, 1988, 1992; Selgin, 1988, Fox, 1992). Another possibility is "The Market Process School of Thought." It cannot be denied that praxeologists[64] have given a central role to the fact that the market is never in equilibrium,[65] but always, and even necessarily,[66] engaged in continual change (Kirzner, 1982; Lachmann, 1976A, 1976B, 1977; Boettke and Prychitko, 1994). We could hardly ignore "The Human Action School of Thought." This, after all, was the title of arguably Mises' (1998) most important book. Other possibilities arise, for Austrianism is a many splendored edifice, which makes numerous contributions to the profession. For example, "The Subjectivist School of Thought" (Hayek, 1979; Mises, 1998),[67] "The Methodological School of Thought" (Bostaph, 1976; Block, 1980; Hoppe, 1995; Kirzner, 1982; Lachmann, 1969; Machlup, 1978; Nozick, 1977; Rothbard, 1997D, 1997E, 1997G), since Austrians place much more emphasis on methodology than any of its competitors. Other

---

[64] Note our resort to synonyms.

[65] Some Austrians thought this element so central to their concerns that they launched a journal, unfortunately no longer publishing, entitled, Journal of Market Process.

[66] As long as there is human action, there is change. If there is no human action, there is no economics, either. Thus, as long as there is economics, there is market process.

[67] "And it is probably no exaggeration to say that every important advance in economic theory during the last hundred years was a further step in the consistent application of subjectivism" (Hayek, 1979, 52-53).

possibilities include "The Property Rights School of Thought" (Hoppe, 2004), "The Spontaneous Order School of Thought" (Klein, 2006) and the "The Information or Knowledge School of Thought" (Hayek, 1948A; Kirzner, 1973; Hoppe, 2004). If we take to heart the contribution of that gem of an article written by Hulsmann (2000A), we can characterize Austrianism as "The Counterfactual Alternative School of Thought," or perhaps "The Either Success or Error School of Thought."

As far as the "Property Rights School of Thought" title is considered, consider the following exchange (Hoppe, 2004):

Akkurt (To Hoppe): In some of your work, you emphasize that Hayek stresses the role of knowledge and ignores or neglects private property. Do you think Hayek deliberately ignored, and underemphasized the crucial place of private property? Would you describe your view of property and knowledge in an entrepreneurial economy briefly to our readers?

Hoppe: Hayek was indeed always, from his student years on, interested in psychology. He wrote an interesting book on it (Sensory Order). This may explain his special emphasis on knowledge and his relative neglect of property. For instance, Hayek wrote a famous article on the "Use of Knowledge in Society." Mises never would have written an article with that title. His title would have been the "Use of Property in Society."

The present article may be viewed as an attempt to make the case, in this sweepstakes, for Austrianism, in addition to all these other candidates, as "The Singularism School of Thought." This is not to say we think the other candidates improper, or, even, necessarily, inferior, to our own. Rather, it is to emphasize the importance of this way[68] of looking at economics, alongside all of these others. In our view, a crucially important aspect of Austrian economics is its emphasis on the fact that human action can and must be bifurcated into that which is chosen, and all of those other opportunities thereby foregone.

"Singularism" is the phrase employed by Mises (1998, 44).[69] But perhaps a more accurate word describing what we are about would be

---

[68] Alternative characterizations of Austrian economics in this vein include The Either or School of Thought, The No Third Choice School of Thought and The 0,1 School of Thought. States Hulsmann (2000A, 3): "We will argue that human choice involves a dichotomy…" We are not serious about any of these alternative characterizations of Austrian nomenclature. However, these alternatives do encapsulate the "spirit" of what praxeology is all about.

[69] http://www.mises.org/humanaction/chap2sec5.asp; chapter II, section 5. One very perceptive referee queries as to whether singularism is "a-historical" and asks "Are there others who have observed this (singularist) feature of economic theory in the past?" Our answer is that a literature search turns up very little in this regard. Mises mentions the concept on several occasions, and, to the best of our knowledge, others,

"individuation." In an earlier version of this paper we employed the term "binary economics," which is even more apt. However, it came to our attention that Kelso had already employed this term in a completely different manner,[70] so to avoid confusion we had to eschew it. Further complicating matters is that "binary" is used much as in the manner in which we previously employed it by yet other writers. State Copeland and Parsons (2004, 9): "The dismantling of 'binarisms – conceptual polarities that underlie our thinking on so many subjects – has been a salient effort of postmodern writers... We regard such enigmatic passages as symptomatic of the confusion that results when writers conflate concepts that should be kept distinct. Some 'binarisms' seem necessary for rational thought." This has several important implications, which we will explore below.

III. Supply and Demand

The market process involves buyers and sellers. Most supply and demand theory begins by developing individual's demand curves for X and aggregating them to arrive at the market demand for X. Then the individual firm's supply curve is developed, and depending on the analysis, if necessary these may be aggregated to get the market supply. Note re supply points if demand elasticity is less than - ∞ v. supply curves if demand elasticity is - ∞. It is well established mainstream theory that, save for a perfect competitor, no firm and, a fortiori, no industry, has a supply curve, but rather, only supply points, each of which depends on the demand. That is, supply is not independent of demand, nor, for that matter is demand independent of supply. In a simple, one resource (labor) model, in which a firm sells its output and buys it resource in non-perfectly competitive markets, and in which P is the inverse demand function for output and W, the inverse demand function for labor, $P = W\cdot((1+(1/e))/(1+(1/E))/MP_L$ and $W = P((1+(1/E))/(1+(1/e))\cdot MP_L$, where E is the price elasticity of demand for the output and e is the price (wage) elasticity of demand for the resource (labor), and MP_L is the marginal product of labor. Assuming, arguendo, that there are such things as supply and demand functions, save in the imaginary world of perfect competition, they are interdependent. No sooner have we said this then are we compelled to take it all back: there is no such thing as a supply or a demand *function.* Rather, a demand curve, for example, is the *maximum* price someone will pay for a given quantity. But this implies and equal to or greater than relationship, not a *function.* The latter, in contrast, implies strict equality, as in Y = f (X). In contrast Y ≥ f(X) is *not* a function. This point is obvious as soon as we consider "false" trades; i.e., trades that occur at non-market-clearing prices and non-price rationing.

---

beside the present paper who have explicitly discussed this, include only the following: Gordon (2003), Heinrich (2004).

[70] http://www.google.com/search?hl=en&q=binary+economics

In any case, once the market demand and relevant supply curves are developed, the analysis of people's and firm's/firms'[71] actions is conducted in terms of the interactions of supply and demand (S & D).

Supply and demand are "mere" pedagogical devices. Economic reality consists only in the human actor preferring (in the revealed preference sense) A over some specific not-A, say B, or B over A. Supply and demand depend essentially on the ceteris paribus assumption, but individuals know that the very act of choosing puts paid to ceteris paribus. Although this pedagogy is very useful it is only that, a pedagogical device. In the real world economic action consists *solely* in preferring A to B or B to A. There are no such things as supply and demand curves, or supply and demand, for that matter. These are merely pedagogical tools/devices intended to help us grasp the underlying reality.

There are two ways to interpret standard S & D analysis, one "objective" and one "subjective." Consider, first, the latter. In this case, the demand curve represents the different quantities of the relevant good that the buyers would be willing and able to purchase at various prices, ceteris paribus, as known by a(n omniscient) third-party. The supply curve represents the different quantities of the relevant good that the sellers' would be willing and able to offer at various prices, ceteris paribus, also as known by a(n omniscient) third-party. No matter how helpful in other regards, such analysis is also the source of important error, because it results in treating certain costs to sellers as if they are not real costs at all. These costs are the implicit revenues sellers forego when they have to reduce the prices of their goods in order to sell a larger quantity, and the explicit costs sellers incur if they have to increase the prices of their resources in order to acquire a larger quantity. These costs appear, to the omniscient, not as costs, because they "merely" represent a transfer of income from vendors to purchasers. That is, they are not viewed as costs of using resources. Taking this perspective leads many economists[72] to treat these costs, which are real to sellers, as if they should be irrelevant to them. Therefore, when the sellers themselves do not treat them as irrelevant, but, rather, take them into account in resource allocation decisions, such economists refer to the decisions so taken as

---

[71] Of course, only individuals can act; here we use the colloquialism, when we mean that some individual member of the firm acts.

[72] We need not cite a specific author on this point since it applies to *all* mainstream or neoclassical economists. There is no doubt that all of them subscribe to the familiar diagram explaining the "market failure" of "monopoly," that is, any firm facing a downward sloping demand curve. However, since a referee has called us on this point, we offer the following: Bork (1978, 107).

comprising "market failure" in the form of suboptimal resource allocations.[73] Such thinking leads to the conclusion that governmental intervention into markets cannot be ruled out on principle in virtually any case. That is, whenever either the demand curve for the good slopes downward or the supply curve of one or more relevant resources slopes upward, or both, there is a potential candidate for governmental intervention, subject only, given that intervention itself is not costless, to cost-benefit analysis of the intervention itself.

The underlying rationale is the same as that which allows mainstream economists in discussing "deadweight loss" from monopoly (i.e., downward sloping demand curves in cases where the price exceeds the average total cost over at least part of the domain of quantity) to treat the loss of profit and concomitant increase in consumers' surplus as a wash. An analogy is a case where a robber steals \$10 from a business and gives \$15 to a customer by adding \$5 of his own. The mainstream would treat this as a net gain of \$5 to the business and customer taken as a group. However, as soon as we consider the positions of the individuals, as we must as economists, we see that they are treating the \$10 of the \$15 increase in consumers' surplus that came at the expense of the business as a wash, and, of course, it is no such thing. Another way of seeing this is to consider the familiar equation for marginal revenue arrived at by taking the derivative of total revenue, PQ, with respect to Q, assuming a downward sloping demand curve; i.e., $MR = P + QdP/dQ$. Rewriting this as $P = MR - QdP/dQ$, noting that $dP/dQ < 0 \Rightarrow - QdP/dQ > 0$, we see that the vertical distance between the demand curve is divided into two parts, MR and $- QdP/dQ$. We may think of these parts, respectively, as that portion of P that the firm gets as a result of selling one additional unit at P, and the portion of P that the firm must *give up* in the form of receiving a lower P for the inframarginal units because it had to lower P in order to sell the additional unit.

The second analysis, the subjective, is asymmetrical. Although standard supply and demand analysis has the appearance of being symmetrical in that it takes into account both the (planned) behavior of the buyers (demand) and the sellers (supply), upon reflection there is an asymmetry. In fact, whether it is with respect to the buyers' or the sellers' behavior, the perspective is that of the seller. The demand curve represents the sellers' anticipation / expectation of the different quantities of the relevant good the buyers would be willing and able to purchase at various prices, ceteris paribus. The supply curve represents the different quantities of the relevant good that the sellers would be willing and able i.e., plan, to offer

---

[73] We refer, here, to the familiar "market failure" of monopoly and to the analogous one resulting from monopsony.

at various prices, ceteris paribus. That is, unlike the demand curve which represents sellers' anticipations/expectations re buyer behavior, the supply curve does not represent the buyers' anticipations/expectations re sellers' behavior. Consequently, the perspective from which both curves are viewed is that of the seller, and, is therefore, asymmetrical. This "market failure" consequent on monopsony in resource markets is analogous to that consequent on monopoly in output markets. Symmetry requires, in addition to the standard supply and demand analysis of the market for a good, an additional non-standard supply and demand analysis of the same market, along the lines sketched out above. In this latter case, the supply curve would represent the buyers' anticipations/expectations of the different quantities of the relevant good that the seller would be willing and able to offer at various prices, ceteris paribus. And, the demand curve would represent the different quantities of the relevant good that the buyers would be willing and able, i.e., plan, to buy at various prices, ceteris paribus. In contrast, the monopsonistic "market failure" argument is very much alive, though not widely used, in mainstream economics. Here, we are criticizing the use of standard supply and demand as being either from God's perspective or that of the firm, and ignoring that of the individual buyer of outputs or seller of resources, without realizing that is what is being done. Neoclassical economists sometimes try use these analytical tools to describe the case of bi-lateral monopoly in the labor market, when a union is considered to be the monopolistic seller of labor to a monopsonistic firm as buyer of labor.

IV. Indifference

Indifference curves are ubiquitous in economics. It is probably no exaggeration to say that without them, one of the most important elements of the neo-classical armory would go missing. And, yet, sad to say, were singularism economics accorded its rightful place in the profession, they would all have to be eliminated, root and branch.

For indifference is logically incompatible with singularism economics. The vision emanating from the latter source is that when choosing, the actor must pick one thing, and set to the side all other alternatives. There is simply no room for any third option, such as indifference. Nor is there any way to demonstrate, or reveal (Rothbard, 1997I) any such concept.

Austrian economics consists essentially of deducing the consequences of the apodictic truth that individuals act purposefully; that each choice consists of preferring means A to means not-A, say means B, and this is true whether the actor views A and B as means to the same end, X, or as means to different ends, X and Y respectively.

Regardless of which end the actor is pursuing, it cannot be denied that he may be wrong; e.g., he may choose A over B as a means to X and he may come think that it was a mistake – he should have chosen B, or perhaps some other means, say C, entirely, or perhaps he should have chosen some other end, say Z, and the means he thinks would have been best suited to achieving that end, say D. Moreover, two individuals may both try to achieve X, yet choose different means because of differing evaluations of the efficacy thereof. Or, they may choose different means, although they agree ion the relative efficacy of different means re differing, ends, yet they prefer different ends.

But just because error is always possible in human action does not warrant recognition of indifference in technical economics.[74] The two are entirely separate. Let us try putting this in other terms. If A gives B an X for B's Z, and B gives A a Z for B's X, then as outside commentators, economists as it were, we are entitled to infer that A and B ranked the two goods, X and Z, in inverse order.[75] When would we be able to make any such conclusion with regard to indifference? Never, that is when. If we can never deduce indifference from human action, it is as if, for economics at least, it does not exist.

Surely, there can be no mainstream intermediate microeconomics text that not only fails to mention this concept, but, even, that does not make it a central organizing tool of its entire analysis. With all the use the neoclassical economists make of this supposed tool of economic analysis, it is somewhat surprising to see so little in terms of a defense of it, or rejoinders to critiques of it. Yes, there are entire forests of trees that have been felled to *explain* indifference curves, and to *apply* them to all sorts of problems, but rare indeed is an intellectual defense of them, against criticisms made against them. The only such case we have been able to uncover written by an economist is Caplan (1999, 2001, 2003). This is neither the time nor the place to rehearse Austrian objections to the work of this particular economist.[76] At present, we are concerned, only, with the critique of indifference based on singularism. And that consists of the fact that according to singularism, *all* of human action consists of choosing one option, and setting aside all others. (Of course, the cost of the actor's choice is the value the actor thinks he is foregoing, in the form of the value he places on the next best alternative that he thinks he *would* have chosen in the absence of the actual choice). But indifference in effect sets itself up as a counter example to this necessary and essential part of the human experience. It claims that there can be two goods,

---

[74] When speaking loosely, as in ordinary language, then the word "indifference" is of course unobjectionable.

[75] For Hoppe (1995), this is a matter of praxeological necessity.

[76] For Austrian replies to Caplan, attacking the concept of indifference, and the misbegotten curves they have given rise to, see Hulsmann, 1999; Barnett, unpublished; Block, 1999A, 2003B, 2007; van Dun, unpublished. There is one other case that deserves mention in this regard. Nozick (1977), a philosopher, also weighs in on the side of indifference. For a rejoinder to him see Block (1980).

A and B, such that the person involved in choosing between them neither prefers A to B, nor B to A. Instead, he is "indifferent" between them. But he has no way, no way at all, of *demonstrating* any such preference. If he selects A, and ignores B, then he demonstrates a preference for A. If he selects B, and ignores A, then he indicates in the only manner he can that he prefers B. What *could* he do to reveal an equal preference for both, other, perhaps, than "starve to death" à la Buridan's ass? He cannot select both, for by the terms of the experiment he can choose only one; in any case he can only do one thing at a time. If he ignores both, he, again, fails to signal an unambiguous equal preference. Rather, he indicates he places greater importance on selecting *neither* of them to either one.

V. The escalator

Consider the following from a leading economist in a major research university economics department. This material appeared on the web. It was written by Professor Steve Landsburg, and it concerned his discussion of this vital issue with his colleagues at the University of Rochester. [77]

"And yet somehow last summer, we managed to spend a week in a state of collective befuddlement, obsessing over a seemingly impenetrable conundrum that came up over lunch: If people stand still on escalators, then why don't they stand still on stairs?

"It was observed early on that if you stand still on stairs, you'll never get anywhere. But for reasons I can no longer entirely reconstruct, that explanation was dismissed as overly simplistic. […]

"In other words, a step either is or is not worth the effort, and whatever calculation tells you to walk (or not) on the escalator should tell you to do exactly the same thing on the stairs.

"And so one of the world's top economics departments entered a state of near paralysis. Theories were presented, considered, and rejected; I will spare their inventors (including myself) the embarrassment of having those theories recounted here. Suffice it to say that each theory centered around one or another cockamamie reason why 'marginal analysis'—the weighing of costs and benefits associated with taking a single step—might not apply in this situation. […]

"My colleague Mark Bils figured out a way to rephrase this so that even an economist can understand it. Every producer knows that workers should spend less time with inferior machinery. Compared to an escalator, a staircase is an inferior machine, so the 'workers'—that is, the people who use

[77] For a video showing people who stand on stairs (that is precisely what a broken escalator is, see this (we owe this cite to our colleague Amy Keeler): http://www.kaneva.com/asset/assetDetails.aspx?assetId=42823&communityId=0.

the stairs—should try to minimize their time there. The way to limit your time on a staircase is to keep walking until you get to the end.

"The same argument proves, incidentally, that even if you choose to walk on the escalator, you should always walk even faster on the stairs. If you're planning to write and tell me that in fact you walk at the same speed in both venues, I'd really rather not hear about it right now.

"So what's the moral of the story? To me, the moral is that we should take seriously what we tell our students: Marginal analysis really works. If it seems not to be working, the right question is not, 'Why doesn't the marginal analysis work?' Instead, the right question is, 'How am I failing to understand the marginal analysis?' or more succinctly, 'In what way am I being stupid?' "

In fact, the whole issue is tailor-made for a singularism analysis. It was framed incorrectly by Landsburg and his colleagues[78]. To wit, there are two totally unrelated cases: being on the stairs and being on an escalator. In the former case one has to make a choice between two alternatives, walking on the stairs and reaching one's destination or standing still on the stairs and never getting to one's destination. Let us go out on a limb here and assume that the purpose of being on the stairs in the first place is to reach one's destination. Therefore, as the only way to accomplish one's purpose on the stairs is to exert the effort to walk, one always exerts the effort and walks on the stairs. In the latter case, one has to make a choice between not one but *two* alternatives, walking on the escalator and, assuming, as seems reasonable, that if one walks on an escalator one walks in the direction that the escalator is carrying one, and reaching one's destination more quickly, or standing still on the escalator and reaching one's destination less quickly. Therefore, one will walk on the escalator only in those particular situations in which he values the time saved by walking more than the effort saved by not walking. In either case he gets where he is going, which it is natural to assume is the primary objective.

Therefore we see that people "always" walk on stairs, else they won't arrive at their destinations, whereas people on an escalator always arrive at their destinations whether or not they walk, so that they only walk if and when the effort is worth it to them in order to arrive at their destination sooner. And all it took was a correct understanding and application of the concept of opportunity cost.

How does singularism come into the analysis? It contributes in several ways. First, this concept focuses our attention on the fact that human action can be reduced to a binary choice: either we do x, or we do y (non x,

---

[78] A literature review search of this issue fails to reveal any scholarly peer reviewed economics journal that has addressed this issue. Rather, the discussion has been dominated by physiometricians and physiologists concerned about caloric usage in the two modes of transportation. See on this: http://tinyurl.com/2arh6g

that is), and if y is the next best opportunity foregone to x, why then y is the opportunity cost of x, and x is our preferred choice. As can be readily seen when employing these concepts, when on a flight of steps, the only alternative to walking is to stand, and to get nowhere. (We abstract from cases where this is a goal. For example, someone is resting on the steps, or two people are having a conversation on the stairs because this is the only place they can achieve privacy.) In sharp contrast, while ensconced on the moving steps of an escalator, a man again has the *choice* of two options, but in this case *both* of which will move him to the next level: walking or standing still.

To extrapolate to an entirely different mode of vertical travel, consider the elevator. Why do people push the buttons to a different floor when they enter into this conveyance?[79] Why, to get to the desired floor of course. They, too, of course, have a second choice: to stand in the elevator and do nothing. (Again, in saying this, we ignore several possible counterexamples, concerning contemplation in the elevators, catching one's breath there, seizing a moment of privacy, as on the stairs, and, also, peculiar to the elevator, the possibility that someone else will press a button, or that the elevator is programmed to go back down to the ground floor when not otherwise engaged.) Why do the denizens of elevators typically not act so passively, but rather assertively push a button? Why, because it is their goal to ascend or descend to a different floor. This is *precisely* the story of the staircase.

Another way to see the importance of singularism for this matter is to consider a third mode of vertical transportation, the elevator. Had Landsburg and his colleagues compared and considered action in an elevator with that on an escalator and stairs perhaps they might have asked why one does not sometimes walk in elevators. This might have forced them to think in terms of singularism and arrived at the correct result. In table 1 the initial choice is among rows 3-5 in column 1 and subsequent choice is among columns 3-4 in row 2.[80]

Table 1

1	2	3	4
2		**Walk**	**Don't walk**
3	**Stairs**	Attain desired end	Do not attain desired end
4	**Escalator**	Attain desired end more quickly	Attain desired end less quickly
5	**Elevator**	Attain desired end equally quickly	Attain desired end equally quickly

[79] You will have to excuse us, gentle reader, for asking such basic questions. In our defense we can only say that Landsburg initiated the discussion. We are only trying to pick up the pieces.

[80] The concept of action is often interpreted as preferring A to B in a situation where C, or C,D… are also viable possibilities. In choosing we prefer A to B and A to C, and A to D, etc. However, the cost of choosing A is "only" the value of B, assuming we value B more than any of the other alternatives to A. That is, singularism has to do with *cost*, and only indirectly, through cost, with choice.

Surely this conclusion would have been obvious had they framed the issue correctly. Before one has chosen the mode of ascending there are two levels of choice: the mode and whether to stand still or not on/in the chosen mode. The first act/choice is to choose one mode of ascending and set the other aside. The second consists in walking or not walking. Had they concentrated on the actual individual choices/actions they would not have compared walking or not walking on stairs with walking or not walking on escalators. They would have seen that from the point of view of economics such a comparison is ambiguous.

Second, the solution to the stairs versus escalator problem is *not* marginalism, as per Landsburg. It is, rather, wait for it, singularism. Now, no Austrian can fail to appreciate marginalism. It was after all, a praxeological economist, Menger (1871), who is widely credited, along with non-Austrians Walras (1874) and Jevons (1871), for solving the diamonds-water paradox, or the paradox of value that had eluded everyone[81] before that time including the likes of Smith (1776). They did so with the insights of marginalism, a very, very valuable tool in the armament of economics, to be sure. But marginalism need not and cannot solve *every* problem. In the present case the solution is to recognize that when on a staircase, immobility of the feet will not accomplish the desired transportation, while when on an escalator, it *will*. It is only in the latter of these two cases that this alternative or opportunity cost even arises.

Having dealt with the major fallacy of Landsburg and his cohorts, let us now focus on some of their peripheral mistakes. The stairs are *not* an inferior machine to the escalator; "superiority" and "inferiority" depend, crucially, on the subjective preferences of those who use them. Possibly, this is the ranking that most people would place on these two items. But not all. Just as there are those who eschew the elevator for the stairs in order to burn calories,[82] there are others who would make a similar determination when it comes to the stairs vs. the escalator.

There is a second reason for rejecting this "solution." As we have seen, it is the stairs *and* the elevator on the one hand, that present the Landsburg "problem," and the escalator, on the other hand, that does not. Remember, this economist is trying to account for why people on stairs always walk on them, while those on escalators sometimes do and sometimes do not. Well, no one can deny that the elevator is at least the advanced technical marvel that the escalator is. Let us put this into other words, so that there can be no confusion about the issue. Landsburg attempts to explain different behavior on the two modes of vertical transportation on the ground

---

[81] The late scholastics of the School of Salamanca are an exception to this claim. See on this Woods (2005) and Chafuen (1986)

[82] The rest of us commonly refer to them as "Luddites."

that "Compared to an escalator, a staircase is an inferior machine." This account fails, in our view, because the *elevator*, easily the technological equivalent of the escalator, *also* presents this identical "problem." Yes, the escalator was invented later than the elevator, but it is by no means commonly considered and "inferior machine." If all escalators suddenly disappeared and for some reason could not be replaced, this would be an inconvenience. We would either have to climb stairs, or take elevators for short vertical trips. In sharp contrast, if all elevators were banished, high rise buildings, pretty much all of them, would become unusable. This would have dire impacts on settlement patterns, real estate values and, indeed, on our overall economy.

It is simply not true that "whatever calculation tells you to walk (or not) on the escalator should tell you to do exactly the same thing on the stairs." On the escalator you are presented with a binary choice; the singularistic insight tells us you are limited to one or the other of these: standing, and arriving at your destination more slowly, or walking, and reaching it more quickly. On the stairs you are also presented with a binary choice; the singularistic insight tells us you are limited to one or the other of these. But here, the options are very different: walking, and achieving your goal, or digging in your heels, and not doing so.

The specter of numerous economists at what are considered top-flight, research-university economics departments not being able to grasp these rather basic concepts underlying the choices available on staircases and escalators underscores even the more the importance of common sense or Austrian economics, and on an important aspect of this School of Thought, namely, singularism.

VI. Conclusion

Singularism economics may not be a household word even within the Austrian camp, but we have demonstrated the importance of looking at matters through this perspective. We claim it sheds light on supply and demand, indifference, and the escalator vs. stair case issues in a manner not available to us without this viewpoint. But more. Our argument is that this insight permeates economics, *all* of economics. It is a primordial fact that at any given time, the individual can only do A, or not A (e.g., B). Those are his *only* choices. If he engages in any one activity, he necessarily eschews his next best opportunity, B, and, a fortiori, all others. We maintain that were economists to more fully incorporate this into their analytical framework, it would become a much-improved one.

As important as we think is this concept, we do not claim more for singularism than it warrants. We claim only that it is a neglected part of our discipline that deserves greater attention than has so far been given it, and that it can indeed shed light on such issues the three discussed above.

Chapter 6. Economic categorization

Abstract

This paper is a contribution to the categorization of economics; it looks at the JEL classification of the dismal science into sub disciplines, and at schools of thought within the profession. It also focuses on praxeology, and attempts to distinguish between those elements of Austrian economics that lie at the very core of this school of thought, i.e., in its "Bull's Eye," from those which, although certainly associated with it, lie only on the periphery. We maintain that the inner elements consist of methodology, broadly conceived, and that the outer elements are implications and applications, regarding such considerations as monopoly and anti trust, law, the business cycle information and knowledge.

I. Introduction

Classification is the essence of the sciences of biology and chemistry. Without the genus and species concepts of the former, and the periodical table of elements of the latter, these disciplines would be very different enterprises. While it is of course a wild exaggeration to say that biological and chemical science consists of *no more* than cataloging, even contemplating this notion is a dramatic way of underscoring the crucial centrality of this mode of analysis to those bodies of learning.

In economics, matters are different. There is relatively little emphasis on sorting the various elements of the dismal science. However, it is our contention that taxonomy is important in this realm as well.[83] The present paper is devoted to a sorting out of the different elements of the dismal science. In section II we tackle the question of how the disciplines, and the schools of thought are to be characterized. Section III is devoted to a deconstruction of Austrian economics. In section IV we deal with an objection to our thesis. We conclude in section V.

---

[83] Rothbard (2004, ch. 13) places great emphasis on classification with regard to taxation and other violent interventions into the market. See also Lavoie (1982, 169-183) and Ikeda (1997, 245-247) in this regard. For another classificationist approach see Block and Cwik (2007).

II. Classification schemes

1. The JEL

Perhaps we do best to start with the mainstream JEL categorization in this regard. Here, the disciplines of economics are broken down as follows:

A - General Economics and Teaching
B - Schools of Economic Thought and Methodology
C - Mathematical and Quantitative Methods
D - Microeconomics
E - Macroeconomics and Monetary Economics
F - International Economics
G - Financial Economics
H - Public Economics
I - Health, Education, and Welfare
J - Labor and Demographic Economics
K - Law and Economics
L - Industrial Organization
M - Business Administration and Business Economics; Marketing; Accounting
N - Economic History
O - Economic Development, Technological Change, and Growth
P - Economic Systems
Q - Agricultural and Natural Resource Economics
R - Urban, Rural, and Regional Economics
Z - Other Special Topics

There is no controversy within the neoclassical economics world over this breakdown. This is remarkable, in that argument and debate are part and parcel of the dismal science.[84] However, Austrian economists[85] have more misgivings about this than others. Not, we hasten to say, about the very idea of breaking down the larger world of economics into its constituent elements. If there is be any chance of successfully wrestling complexity, it can only be done through a "divide and conquer" procedure: taking things a small bit at a time.

---

[84] There being none, let us offer several: this schema does not make comfortable room for experimental economics, behavioral economics, and the interdisciplinary overlap between economics and several other subject matters: biology (bio economics), and psychology (psychological economics).

[85] To be intensively discussed below. At this point let us content ourselves by saying that the Austrian school features the contributions of Menger (1950), Bohm Bawerk (1959), Mises (1998) and Rothbard (2004).

However, the JEL categorization ignores several Austrian insights. There are several leading theoreticians of this school of thought who have weighed in on this matter. Consider the following.

According to Mises (1998, 874):[86]

"Economics does not allow of any breaking up into special branches. It invariably deals with the interconnectedness of all the phenomena of action. The catallactic problems cannot become visible if one deals with each branch of production separately. It is impossible to study labor and wages without studying implicitly commodity prices, interest rates, profit and loss, money and credit, and all the other major problems. The real problems of the determination of wage rates cannot even be touched in a course on labor. There are no such things as 'economics of labor' or 'economics of agriculture.' There is only one coherent body of economics. "

In the view of Rothbard (1993, preface):[87]

"...economics has become appallingly fragmented, dissociated to such a degree that there hardly *is* an *economics* any more; instead, we find myriad bits and pieces of uncoordinated analysis. Economics has, first, been fragmented into 'applied' fields—'urban land economics,' 'agricultural economics,' 'labor economics,' 'public finance economics,' etc., each division largely heedless of the others. More grievous still has been the disintegration of what has been confined to the category of 'economic theory'. Utility theory, monopoly theory, international trade theory, etc., down to linear programming and games theory—each moves in its sharply isolated compartment, with its own hyper refined literature. Recently, growing awareness of this fragment-ation has led to vague 'interdisciplinary' admixtures with all the other 'social sciences.' Confusion has been worse confounded, with resulting invasive forays of numerous other disciplines into economics, rather than the diffusion of economics elsewhere. At any rate, it is somewhat foolhardy to attempt to integrate economics with everything else before economics has *itself* been made whole. Only then will the proper place of economics among the other disciplines become manifest."

Here is Rogge's (1979, 211-212) take on the matter:[88]

"I would be prepared to argue that the practice of breaking up this useful discipline into agricultural economics, transportation economics, development economics, labor economics, urban economics, etc., has been productive of much mischief. Behind the shield of special circumstances and special knowledge, theories have been developed and given wide acceptance

---

[86] We owe this cite to Gérard Dréan.

[87] We are indebted to David Gordon for this quote.

[88] We thank Rich Wilcke for pointing us in the direction of this quote.

that would be regarded as patently absurd if they were put as a general model; policies have been developed and urged upon society that would be recognizably catastrophic if applied generally."

Now consider some specifics. First, macroeconomics, proper macroeconomics that is, is but a branch or an implication or application of microeconomics. Austrian Business Cycle Theory is based on disaggregated[89] considerations, ideally on the choices of *individuals*, in sharp contrast to the Keynesian and monetarist schools, which sever micro from macro. The JEL system works well for these schools of thought,[90] but not for the Austrians.

Second, this applies too, to the severing of international trade from the domestic variety. For traditional economists, there is all the world of difference between the two. For the Austrians, apart from obvious institutional differences (different currencies),[91] there are none.

Third, there are other sub disciplines that do not deserve a category of their own. They constitute, merely, implications of basic economic principles. Included here would be:

H - Public Economics
I - Health, Education, and Welfare
J - Labor and Demographic Economics
K - Law and Economics
L - Industrial Organization
M - Business Administration and Business Economics; Marketing; Accounting
O - Economic Development, Technological Change, and Growth
Q - Agricultural and Natural Resource Economics
R - Urban, Rural, and Regional Economics

2. An Austrian system

What might an Austrian breakdown of this subject matter look like? This can only be speculative, since no survey of economists representative of this tradition has ever been done, but here is our estimate:

---

[89] Or at least far more disaggregated

[90] According to Milton Friedman (Ebeling 1974, 3) "... there was no such thing as 'Austrian Economics,' only good economics and bad economics." Continues Ebeling: "(This is) a rather unusual statement, because just a few weeks before he had been on public television and spent several minutes explaining the special characteristics of 'Chicago Economics.' Another argument against this view of Friedman: the widely accepted JEL system lists "B - Schools of Economic Thought and Methodology."

[91] But not trade barriers. There are numerous intra-national trade barriers: licenses, geographical limitations in countries such as Canada, etc.

A - General Economics and Teaching
B - Schools of Economic Thought and Methodology
C - Mathematical and Quantitative Methods
D - Microeconomics
- Macroeconomics and Monetary Economics
- International Economics
- Financial Economics
- Public Economics
- Health, Education, and Welfare
- Labor and Demographic Economics
- Law and Economics
- Industrial Organization
- Business Administration and Business Economics; Marketing; Accounting

E - Economic History
F - Economic Systems

It should be emphasized that we are not claiming that Austrians would object to the JEL classification per se. Economics must be broken down in some way for librarian purposes, and that seems as good way as any. The objection to this way of categorizing things lies in that academic disciplines in universities are broken down roughly in accord with this categorization, and this isolates the fields far too much.

Of course, even for purposes of presenting material to students, economic science must be broken down in *some* way. Not every course should be called plain old "economics." Specialization and division of labor must be served here as elsewhere. Thus we offer the six way categorization, A to F, that appears above.

It is an interesting question as to how a purely Austrian graduate school would organize its courses. One reason for adhering to traditional breakdowns would be to render its graduates more acceptable on the job market. But suppose for some reason this was *not* a consideration.

3. Schools of thought

Here are the schools of thought that together might be considered to comprise economics:

Austrian; Behaviorist; Cambridge, England; Cambridge, Massachusetts; Chicagoan; Classical;[92] George-ists; German Historical School; Experimental; Feminist; Fiscalist;[93] Game theory; Institutionalists; Keynesian; Lasuanne; Manchester; Marxist (socialist); Mercantilist;

---

[92] Adam Smith, Adam Ferguson, David Hume, John Stuart Mill, Marshall

[93] We are nothing if not inclusive

Monetarist; Neo-Austrian; New-Keynesians; Neo-Keynesian; Physiocrats; Post Keynesian; Pragmatists; Public Choice; Rational Expectations, Salamanca; Supply Side; Utilitarians; Walrasians.[94]

Note, these are listed in alphabetical order. On what basis, apart from the present alphabetical organization, can these be organized? Several possibilities spring to mind. One is political ideology; adherence to or opposition against laissez faire capitalism and private property rights. Let us offer three choices; pro, neutral, con. Here is how we would place each of these schools of thought into these three options:

Pro: Austrian; Chicagoan; Classical; Georgeists; Lasuanne; Manchester; Monetarist; Neo-Austrian; Physiocrats; Public Choice; Rational Expectations, Salamanca; Supply Side

Neutral: Experimental; Game theory; Utilitarians; Walrasians

Con: Behaviorist; Cambridge, England; Cambridge, Massachusetts; German Historical School; Feminist; Fiscalist; Institutionalists; Keynesian; Marxist (socialist); Mercantilist; New-Keynesians; Neo-Keynesian; Post Keynesian; Pragmatists.

We are in this section attempting to be reportorial, not confrontational. It is our expectation that adherents of these various schools of thought would agree with our assessment as to whether or not they support laissez faire capitalism with very little state participation in the economy, or prefer an economic system with a significant amount of government intervention to cure so called "market failures."[95]

Another way of organizing the economic schools of thought is on the basis of methodology. Here, there are again three options: praxeology, obscurantism and empiricism.

Praxeology: Austrian; Game theory; Neo-Austrian; Salamanca

Obscurantism: Feminist; Marxist (socialist);

Empiricism: Behaviorist; Cambridge, England; Cambridge, Massachusetts; Chicagoan; Classical; George-ists; German Historical School; Experimental; Fiscalist; Institutionalists; Keynesian; Lasuanne; Manchester; Mercantilist; Monetarist; New-Keynesians; Neo-Keynesian; Physiocrats; Post Keynesian; Pragmatists; Public Choice; Rational Expectations, Supply Side; Utilitarians; Walrasians.

---

[94] For different but overlapping schemas, see http://dmoz.org/Science/Social_Sciences/Economics/Schools_of_Thought

[95] See this literature critical of the concept of "market failure": Barnett, Block and Saliba, 2005; Block, 1983, 2003C; Cowen, 1988; De Jasay, 1989; Hoppe, 1989A; Hummel, 1990; Osterfeld, 1989; Pasour, 1981; Schmidtz, 1991; Sechrest, 2004.

Here, we have in mind the question of which is prior; which wags which: the dog or the tail. In the empirical listing we include those schools of thought we see experiments, or "reality," as the determinative factor. If for example, an econometric regression indicates that a price floor does not create a surplus, nor a price ceiling a shortage, then economists in this category would be willing to jettison basic supply and demand analysis. In the praxeological category we find dismal scientists who would tend to distrust any such empirical findings to a far greater degree than they would the economic logic underlying the analytics of supply and demand. For want of better terminology we characterize as "obscurantist" those perspectives which admit neither of logic nor empirical evidence.

III. Praxeological science, or Austrian economics.

The essence of Austrianism, its most distinctive characteristic by far, is its methodology. It is not for nothing that the best synonym for this school of thought is the Praxeological School, since praxeology is the methodology of the Austrians. There are four elements to Austrian methodology. Each is essential in that each is a necessary part, but no one, two, or even three of them is sufficient; it takes all four to be sufficient. These are, in alphabetical order: 1) deduction; 2) methodological individualism; 3) methodological singularism (to uses Mises' less than felicitous term); and, 4) methodological subjectivism (in all its aspects). These four are so closely interconnected with one another, it is impossible to tease them apart. They logically imply, and are logically implied by, each other.

Of course, there is more to Austrianism than praxeology; there are also its implications and applications. Among these are its distinctively Austrian Business Cycle Theory, its emphasis on market process, its contribution to the debate over central planning (the socialist calculation debate), its divergent (from the mainstream of the profession) perspective on monopoly, its emphasis on entrepreneurship, and its pure time preference theory of interest. But praxeology is, in effect, the centerpiece of the philosophy, the bull's eye of the target. These other albeit very important elements constitute only the surrounding areas. If the latter, somehow, vanished, the core of Austrianism would remain; it would be weakened, mightily, but it would still exist. In sharp contrast, if the core disappeared, but the periphery remained, it would no longer be Austrianism, even though it would still make a signal contribution to economics.

Rothbard (1976A, 19) uses the word "praxeology" to wit: "Praxeology is the distinctive methodology of the Austrian School." This author understands that to mean the deductive or a priori method; i.e., praxeology: deduction from apodictic truth. On the other hand, to Mises (1998, 8, 3) praxeology is not a methodology, rather it is the "general theory of human action," in which "economic or catallactic problems are embedded." What Rothbard means by praxeology is what Mises (1998, 35) refers to as "methodological apriorism," and that we in this paper refer to as deduction. Previously, we listed the four essential elements of Austrian methodology, one of which was deduction. We would have been more in keeping with Mises had we referred to the four essential elements of the method of praxeology, or of praxeological methodology, and listed them as: methodological apriorism, methodological individualism, methodological singularism, and methodological subjectivism.

IV. An objection

Boettke (2002) is of the opinion that what is unique about Austrian economics is none of these things, but, rather, "Information and Knowledge." However, his reasoning in this regard leaves something to be desired. Boettke (2002, 264) starts off his thoughts on this matter in a manner very congruent with that of the present authors (since we are in great sympathy with Rothbard on this issue): "Murray Rothbard (1962) emphasized the rejection of mathematical modeling and statistical inference as the basic tools of economics analysis. Rothbard, instead, focused on the consistent application of methodological individualism and methodological subjectivism. The defining characteristic, in other words, to Rothbard was the praxeological method— including a firm commitment to apriorism."

But then, instead of showing why Rothbard was in error, Boettke (2002, 265) cavalierly dismisses him without any criticism whatsoever: "While not disputing the arguments put forth by Rothbard … [I] suggest that perhaps Austrians ought to ground their argument for uniqueness not along methodological grounds, but instead in their analytical contributions to our understanding of the epistemic-cognitive properties of alternative institutional arrangements. It is this recognition of the contextual nature of the relevant economic knowledge that actors must work with within an economic system that represents the unique contribution of the modern Austrian school to our understanding of the price system and the market economy." In other words, Rothbard sees the uniqueness of Austrianism in praxeology. Boettke, in contrast, looks to information and knowledge for this role. But, instead of saying why Rothbard is incorrect, he contents himself with noting Rothbard's view to the contrary, and then goes on to discuss information and knowledge in this regard. We find this a most unsatisfactory state of affairs. We could follow Boettke's path; here, we would note that he sees information and knowledge as at the core of Austrian economics, and then goes on to wax eloquent about praxeology. We shall not do that. Instead, we will consider why information and knowledge are *not* the central characteristics of Austrianism.

But first, a clarification. We do not at all disagree with Boettke that a particular perspective on information and knowledge is *unique* to

Austrianism. We only decline to follow him in his view that the Austrian analysis of these matters is *central* to this school of thought.

The views of Kirzner (1973) and Hayek (1937, 1945) in particular, who are the Austrian point men on information and knowledge, are not only unique to Austrians, but clearly preferable to alternative expositions.

Let us now return to our main criticism of Boettke; that even though the Austrian analysis of information and knowledge is unique to this school of thought, and even (vastly) preferable to all alternatives, it is still not *central;* it does not lie at the very core of Austrian economics.[96] In order to demonstrate this, we offer the following two part mental experiment; take Austrian economics as it is, whatever you think it is,[97] and delete two different things from it in succession.

First, eradicate our unique perspective on information and knowledge, and along with it other elements of Austrianism associated with these phenomena, such as market process, the insight that markets are never ever in full equilibrium, etc. No doubt what remains after this radical surgery would render Austrianism a very different philosophy than before, and much an inferior product. However, it is our contention that at least with the praxeology left in, what remained would still be quintessentially *Austrian.*

Second, start again with basic Austrianism, whatever that is, and this time remove 1) deduction; 2) methodological individualism; 3) methodological singularism 4) methodological subjectivism, which together constitute the praxeological aspect of Austrianism. What would this school of thought be like absent these characteristics? There is no doubt that what would remain would still be preferable to mainstream neo classical economic analysis (it would still retain our unique perspective on information and knowledge, and along with it other elements of Austrianism associated with these phenomena, such as market process, the insight that markets are never ever in full equilibrium, etc.) but it would no longer be *Austrian.* Now, it would be an empirical economic science, acquiescing in the philosophy, ugh, of logical positivism, along with every other school of thought in the dismal science. Its findings would no longer be a matter of apodictic certainty; rather, they would be held only tentatively, subject to alteration when the product of the next econometric regression analysis becomes available.

V. Conclusion

We have argued that classification is very important, not only in the physical sciences, but also in economics. We rest our case.

---

[96] For support of this contention, see Murphy, 2003; Rockwell, 1995.

[97] Given subjectivism, it might well be at least slightly different for different practitioners.

Part II. Microeconomics

Chapter 7. Austrian Economics, Neoclassical Economics, Marketing, and Finance[98]

I. Introduction

If the neoclassical model of perfect competition were an accurate portrayal of reality, or even nearly so, there would be no need for advertising, marketing, brokering[99], or, indeed, any other institution which addresses itself to the lack of knowledge about goods or services on the part of producers or consumers[100]. But these professions patently do exist. They are alive, healthy and productive. We must conclude from this that perfect competition is a highly unrealistic model that can play little or no role in an

---

[98] Walter Block would like to thank David Kennedy, Tony Sullivan and the Board of Directors of the Earhart Foundation for financial support used to write this article. Any errors by omission or commission are solely the responsibility of the authors. Block, Barnett and Wood appreciate the efforts of two anonymous referees .

[99] With regard to the condition of "complete knowledge," Stigler (1965 pp. 258-259) maintains that brokers can exist in perfect competition: "Or let there be indefinitely many brokers in any market, and let each broker know many buyers and sellers, and also let each buyer or seller know many brokers – again we have perfect competition." This follows immediately upon his statement that: "If each seller in a market knows any *n* buyers, and each seller knows a different (but overlapping) set of buyers, then there will be perfect competition if the set of *n* buyers is large enough to exclude joint action…[hence] knowledge possessed by any one trader need not be complete; it is sufficient if the knowledge possessed by the ensemble of individuals in the market is in a sense comprehensive." However, "the" price would have to be higher if brokers are involved in order to cover the expenses thereof. Thus, it would seem that in a "perfectly competitive" market the services of brokers would be competed out of existence, as would the services of any other middleman. This is not to deny his point that no single individual need have complete knowledge directly, provided that they do so indirectly, through appropriate overlapping of sets of incomplete knowledge.

[100] Stigler (1965, 259) also maintains, contrary to the standard version of neoclassical theory, that there is a role for entrepreneurs in perfect competition: "Since entrepreneurs in a stationary economy are essentially brokers between resource owners and consumers, it is sufficient for [perfect] competition if they meet this condition. That is resource owners and consumers could dwell in ignorance of all save the bids of many entrepreneurs." We repeat the problem pointed out *supra*: "the" price would have to be higher if entrepreneurs/brokers are involved in order to cover the expenses. Therefore, it would seem that in a "perfectly competitive" market the services of entrepreneurs/brokers would be competed out of existence, as would the services of any other middleman.

understanding[101] or explication of economic reality[102]. The neoclassicals, including Stigler, take the benefits of the perfect competition model to be "predictions that will have wide empirical validity" and the provision of "normative properties that will allow us to judge the efficiency of [governmental] policies"[103]. The only "cost" of the perfect competition model they recognize is that it is unrealistic. To them, the benefits obviously outweigh the costs, and therefore the perfect competition model is and should be the dominant one in economic theory. While not denying that some of the work by economists working in the neoclassical tradition has been useful even seminal in adding to our understanding of the real world in some cases[104], we maintain that the perfect competition model is unnecessary to these developments[105]; moreover, it has wrought far more harm than good. In what follows, first we identify the both the positive and normative essences of this model. We then critique them, pointing out the real costs thereof.

II. Perfect Competition

What is perfect competition, and how does this doctrine create the difficulties outlined above? Machovec[106], locating the origin of perfect competition, states that: "...it sprang to life to satisfy Cournot's pursuit of definitional rigour, and eventually became the principal instrument of [Walras's] Elements [citation omitted]. The perfectly competitive model did not make its real debut as an analytical tool until the 1920s - after the profession had digested Frank Knight and after the influence of Alfred Marshall had waned. Until that time the way economists reasoned about the market was 'structurally different' (citation omitted)."

---

[101] As Stigler (1965, pp. 261-262) states: "We wish the definition [of perfect competition] to specify with tolerable clarity – with such clarity as the state of the science affords – a model which can be used by practitioners in a great variety of theoretical researches, so that the foundations of the science need not be debated in every extension or application of theory. We wish the definition to capture the essential general content of important markets, so the predictions drawn from the theory will have wide empirical reliability. And we wish a concept with normative properties that will allow us to judge the efficiency of policies. That the concept of perfect competition has served these varied needs as well as it has is providential."

[102] For a critique of perfect competition, see Kirzner, 1973; Mises, 1966; Armentano, 1972, 1982, 1991; Armstrong, 1982; Block, 1977A, 1982, 1994; DiLorenzo, 1997; Boudreaux, and DiLorenzo, 1992; High, 1984-1985; Hoppe, 1989D; McChesney, 1991; Rothbard, 1970; Shugart II, 1987; Smith, Jr. 1983.

[103] Stigler, 1957, p. 261-262. Material in brackets inserted by present authors.

[104] For example, Coase, 1937; Williamson, 2000; see also, Cheung, 1983; Dauterive and Sibley, 1990; for an Austrian perspective on the firm which does not rely upon perfect competition, see Machlup, 1967; Lewin, 1999; Foss, 1994; Klein, 1999.

[105] Its unrealistic assumptions are unnecessary for supply and demand analysis.

[106] Machovec, 1995, 12.

and: "… the seeds of the perfect competitor were being sown by the upcoming, mathematically-oriented members of the profession, and this is the conception which, during the 1920s came to dominate the new cerebrum of economics. The development of the perfectly competitive model can be said to have emanated from a unique seed planted in 1838 by Cournot – an atypical seed then did not even germinate until 1874 (in Walras) and finally reached maturity nearly a half century later in Knight."[107]

In subsequent years it became ubiquitous within managerial and micro economics, spreading out to a whole raft of other subdisciplines of economics such as labor, international, public policy, public finance, industrial organization, etc. It has also taken the textbook world by storm[108], making it impossible for any student to be untouched by this simplistic and misleading model.

As a positive model, the core of perfect competition is a market in which: the goods and services are homogeneous[109]; each firm is so tiny that it produces so insignificantly small a proportion of the total output that any increases in its offerings cannot effect price even by a minuscule iota[110]; and, full information is available to all market participants about all goods and services[111].

As a normative standard, the essence of the perfectly competitive model is that in equilibrium a quantity Q is produced and sold at which Q the price, P, equals the marginal revenue, MR, which equals, the marginal cost, MC, which equals the average total cost, ATC; i.e., P = MR = MC = ATC. This is held to be the normative standard because of the following.

---

[107] Machovec, 1995, p. 241.

[108] We defy the reader to unearth even one textbook that does not accord the perfectly competitive model a central position in economics, apart from Gordon, 2000.

[109] Ultimately, this implies that there can be only one good in the economy; if there are any more than one, the cloven hoof of heterogeneity seeps in.

[110] This, too, is highly problematic as it would be true only in the case where a firm produced, literally, a zero amount, and continued to do so. Consider the opposite case. Assume there is a small automobile manufacturing concern that increases its annual output from two to three units. As long as there were a negatively sloped demand curve, it is not possible for there to be a zero reduction in price.

[111] It is important to stress that the assumption of full, complete, and accurate, indeed, perfect information in a single, perfectly-competitive market would mean that no firm in that market, qua its role in that market, could in any way benefit in the slightest from the use of financial markets and institutions, or from advertising and marketing. There would be only the firm, its customers/users and its suppliers/producers of resources. No middlemen of any type allowed.

First, as P measures the marginal "social benefit" and MC the marginal "social cost,"[112] P = MC ensures that Q is the socially optimum quantity – additional units of output will be produced and sold so long as the additional benefits thereof exceed the additional costs and no unit will be produced the cost of which exceeds its benefits. Second, as MR measures the benefits to the producer (i.e., the private benefits), MR = MC ensures that Q is the privately optimum (a.k.a. the profit maximizing) quantity. Third, MC = ATC ensures Q is the optimum quantity in the sense that no other level of output could be produced at a lower per-unit cost. Fourth, P = ATC ensures that normal profits are earned – there are no above normal ("economic") profits to induce existing producers to increase the level of production or induce others to enter the market, nor are there any below normal profits (i.e., "economic" losses) to induce existing producers to decrease the level of production or to exit the market – therefore the market is in (short- and long-run) equilibrium when operating at this optimal level of output, Q. Fifth, P = MR ensures that the marginal social benefit (P) and the marginal private benefit (MR) are the same and that, therefore, there is no divergence between the condition for social optimality (P = MC) and that for private optimality (MR = MC).

It is not hard to understand how economists enamored of mathematical formalism and model building could be seduced by a model with such properties; what a standard – virtual perfection!

III. Perfect competition as a positive model

The primary critique of perfect competition as a positive model is that it is so unrealistic as to be misleading.

Its main drawback as a normative standard is that no real world firm, industry, or market can satisfy it and therefore governmental intervention to regulate the behavior of every firm, industry, and market is warranted, subject only to an analysis of each proposed intervention to insure that the benefits exceed the costs[113].

Neoclassicals use an instrumentalist defense of perfect competition as a positive model, maintaining that it is but a mere end point of the analysis,

---

[112] This ignores divergences that might arise on the supply side; i.e., so called "market failures" as a result of negative externalities. In contrast, negative externalities are a property rights problem; i.e., they arise because the legal system either does not acknowledge or enforce property rights. See Cowen, 1988

[113] This determination necessarily admits of at least some level of arbitrariness, given the essentially subjective nature of much in economics, particularly including so called cost benefit analysis. On this see Barnett II, William, 1989; Buchanan and Thirlby, 1981; Buchanan, 1969; Cordato, 1989; DiLorenzo, 1990A; Garrison, 1985A; Gunning, 1990; Kirzner, 1986; Mises, 1949, 1963, 1966; Rizzo, 1980, Rizzo (ed.), 1979B; Rothbard, 1993, 1997A, 1997Q; Schmidtchen, 1993

the analogue of an ideal gas in chemistry or a frictionless system in physics. No one expects to actually encounter the situation depicted in this model; it serves only as a useful simplification of the real world in order to facilitate analysis. One reaches a "first-cut" analysis of economic activity using the perfect competition model; then, with that understanding, more accurate progress can be made by removing the attendant less realistic simplifying assumptions. Just as the assumptions of the ideal gas must be dropped by the physicist near the condensation point in order to understand the observed phenomena involving inter-molecular attractions and condensation, so also must the simplifying assumptions of perfect competition be dropped in order to understand the observed marketing behavior.

States Stigler:

"Finally, we should notice the most common and the most important criticism of the concept of perfect competition—that it is unrealistic. This criticism has been widespread since the concept was completely formulated and underlies the warm reception which the profession gave to the doctrines of imperfect and monopolistic competition in the 1930's. One could reply to this criticism that all concepts sufficiently general and sufficiently precise to be useful in scientific analysis must be abstract: that, if a science is to deal with a large class of phenomena, clearly it cannot work with concepts that are faithfully descriptive of even one phenomenon, for then they will be grotesquely undescriptive of others. This conventional line of defense for all abstract concepts is completely valid, but there is another defense, or rather another form of this defense, that may be more persuasive.

"This second defense is that the concept of perfect competition has defeated its newer rivals in the decisive area: the day-to-day work of the economic theorist. Since the 1930's, when the rival doctrines of imperfect and monopolistic competition were in their heyday, economists have increasingly reverted to the use of the concept of perfect competition as their standard model for analysis. Today the concept of perfect competition is being used more widely by the profession in its theoretical work than at any time in the past. The vitality of the concept is strongly spoken for by this triumph.

"Of course, this is not counsel of complacency. I have cited areas in which much work must be done before important aspects of the definition of competition can be clarified. My fundamental thesis, in fact, is that hardly any important improvement in general economic theory can fail to affect the concept of competition. But it has proved to be a tough and resilient concept, and it will stay with us in recognizable form for a long time to come[114]."

In reality, the expectation is for some sort of imperfect competition, such as monopoly, duopoly, or oligopoly. In these cases there is no need to

[114] Stigler, 1965. pp. 266-267.

assume full information, and thus to assume away the possibility of marketing. States Kirzner in this regard: "It follows that, since perfect competition precludes selling effort, where advertising or other selling effort *is* in fact engaged in, this must be attributed to the monopolistic elements in the market structure."[115]

However, while imperfect competition is far more realistic than its "perfect" counterpart regarding such things as size of firm, homogeneity of goods, entry costs, etc., it is not, or, rather, need not be, as far as information is concerned. That is, it is still possible to combine the assumption of complete information with imperfect competition. For, say what you will about monopolistic competition, it remains an equilibrium model for the neoclassicals. The imperfectly competitive model is an end state theory, not one of process, and disequilibrium.[116] As such, it continues to be compatible with the assumption of full information. Thus, while advertising may be compatible with imperfect competition, this is not necessarily the case. It is still possible for advertising to be ruled out of court by the assumptions not only of perfect competition, but of imperfect competition as well, in any of its varieties.

A better tack may be the one taken by Stigler[117]. This economist posits not full knowledge of everything under the sun, as with perfect competition, but, rather, of entire probability distributions[118]. However, in this more sophisticated vein, there is no information available concerning individual events, except for the fact that they belong to a given probability distribution.

Under these assumptions, there is now room for advertising in the neoclassical world, but only of the informational variety.[119] Suppose you move to a new city and want to purchase a home. You will be very interested in ascertaining prices, quantities available, location, etc., of specific houses. Each day of search is expected to bring you lower prices, ceteris paribus, for a dwelling of a given quality, but, to put this in Stiglerian terminology, at a decreasing rate (e.g., the marginal benefit curve declines with time). On the other hand, the money costs of staying, temporarily, in a motel are constant, while the inconvenience of living out of suitcases increases as time goes on (the marginal cost curve is an increasing function of time). Eventually, the rising marginal costs meet the falling marginal gains, you end your search and finally make a purchase. You are willing to buy information through advertising, or from brokers, since in this case you save search time (by

---

[115] Kirzner, 1973, p. 164

[116] See on this Mises, 1966; Kirzner, 1963, 1973, 1975, 1979, 1985, 1986, 1989

[117] Stigler, 1961

[118] That is, nothing whatsoever is known about any given observation or occurrence, but everything is know about the universe of which is only one small sample.

[119] For a critique see Kirzner, 1973, pp. 151-180; Block, 1991C, pp. 68-79, 1997.

shifting the marginal benefit curve to the left). You gain less new information every day, which results in lower marginal savings, since with the aid of your informational mentor, you start out with more knowledge. If you had full information, an in perfect competition, the marginal benefit curve would be coincident with the Y axis, and your search time would be zero.

This is indeed an improvement on perfect competition, but the Stigler search model has drawbacks of its own. The weakness is that it covers only "name, rank and serial number" kinds of information. Advertising of this sort would impart knowledge about when the house was last roofed, the capacity of the air conditioner, or the warrantee on the boiler. But this does not even begin to scratch the surface of the full bodied robust advertising we see all around us every day, replete with Michael Jordan and Bugs Bunny, and super models hawking everything from tractors to underwear to diamonds.

Ludwig von Mises had this to say about that type of marketing:

"The consumer is not omniscient. He does not know where he can obtain at the cheapest price what he is looking for. Very often he does not even know what kind of commodity or service is suitable to remove most efficaciously the particular uneasiness he wants to remove. At best he is familiar with the market conditions of the immediate past and arranges his plans on the basis of this information. To convey to him information about the actual state of the market is the task of business propaganda.

"Business propaganda must be obtrusive and blatant. It is its aim to attract the attention of slow people, to rouse latent wishes, to entice men to substitute innovation for inert clinging to traditional routine. In order to succeed, advertising must be adjusted to the mentality of the people courted. It must suit their tastes and speak their idiom. Advertising is shrill, noisy, coarse, puffing, because the public does not react to dignified allusions. It is the bad taste of the public that forces the advertisers to display bad taste in their publicity campaigns. The art of advertising has evolved into a branch of applied psychology, a sister discipline of pedagogy.

"Like all things designed to suit the taste of the masses, advertising is repellent to people of delicate feeling. This abhorrence influences the appraisal of business propaganda. Advertising and all other methods of business propaganda are condemned as one of the most outrageous outgrowths of unlimited competition. It should be forbidden. The consumers should be instructed by impartial experts; the public schools, the 'nonpartisan' press, and cooperatives should perform this task. (emphasis added)."[120]

The point is, Stigler cannot account for anything "shrill, noisy or coarse." Yet, this describes most real world advertising. Therefore, the search model cannot explain this aspect of economic reality. Moreover, while

---

[120]Mises, 1966, p. 320.

Stigler's contribution is at least relevant for those goods and services about which the consumer starts off by being aware, it does not at all apply to those commodities about which "often he does not even know." Yet, before the advent of Mozart, or rap music, or the hula hoop, or the horseless carriage, or the personal computer, or e mail, which of us was walking about the shopping mall of the day, searching for these items? No one, of course. But this only indicates the paucity of the neoclassical explanation of this phenomenon, as compared to the Austrian.

Let us put this in other words. The weakness of the Stiglerian - University of Chicago perspective on this matter is that it applies only to goods and services for which the consumer already has a demand; namely, it is limited to that which the buyer already knows about prior to being subjected to a marketing campaign. This search model can function reasonably well with regard to items such as houses, cars and T.V. sets, which are already fully well known to the potential buyer. But unless the customer is in the act of shopping, already intending to purchase, holding off only until he determines the best deal, the Stigler model is helpless to account for his behavior. And, as such, it cannot take into account advertising, the purpose of which is not merely to inform, but to motivate.

Kirzner explains:

"What I wish to point out is simply that to treat all informational aspects of advertising exclusively as providing a separate distinct service ('information') fails utterly to perceive the crucially important role of the entrepreneur as one who brings available opportunitiesto the awareness of the consumer... But consider now the case of the man who has no inkling that a certain commodity exists. We may, of course, imagine his demand curve for this commodity once its existence has become known to him. But if we wish to discuss the commodity in its unknown state we are simply unable to talk of the consumer's demand for it. It is not that his demand curve coincides with the price axis; that he would buy none of it at any given price. It is rather that the very notion of demand has no place under these circumstances. It is non-sense to discuss the upper limit of the price this consumer is willing to pay for this unknown commodity; it is nonsense to discuss the quantity he would be prepared to purchase at a given price. These discussions refer to the eagerness with which a consumer wished to pursue perceived opportunities. With no opportunities perceived the notion of consumer demand has no meaning."[121]

IV. Perfect competition as a normative standard

Perfect competition is defended as a normative standard on the grounds of the model's optimality conditions. That is, the optimality conditions provide standards by which to gauge the performance of real

[121] Kirzner, 1973, pp. 155, 158.

world firms and markets, and thereby assist in the development and enforcement of governmental economic policies; e.g. antitrust.

"The vitality of the competitive concept in its normative role has been remarkable. One might have expected that, as economic analysis became more precise and as the range of problems to which it was applied widened, a growing list of disparities between the competitive allocation of resources and the maximum-output allocation would develop. Yet to date there have been only two major criticisms of the norm.[122] The first is that the competitive individual ignores external economies and diseconomies, which—rightly or wrongly—most economists are still content to treat as an exception to be dealt with in individual cases. The second, and more recent, criticism is that the competitive system will not provide the right amount (and possibly not the right types) of economic progress, and this is still an undocumented charge. The time may well come when the competitive concept suitable to positive analysis is not suitable to normative analysis, but it is still in the future."[123]

Because perfect competition is a normative standard, as well as a positive one, neoclassicals' defenses of perfect competition as a positive model and as a normative standard become conflated. Real world behavior is compared to perfectly competitive "behavior" with reality found wanting, thereby justifying the potential desirability of ubiquitous governmental intervention in the real world, subject only to the outcome of a cost-benefit study in each particular proposed intervention. Therefore, the comparison of perfect competition to the ideal gas and frictionless system models is a disanalogy. Unlike a ideal gas or a frictionless system, which are strictly positive models, perfect competition is a normative standard as well; e.g., it serves as the lynchpin of anti trust legislation. To the extent that a firm deviates from the strictures of this model, it is liable to become enmeshed in the machinations of the Justice Department. In contrast, no one is indicted for failure to adhere to the niceties of the ideal gas. For example, perfect competition is the lynchpin of antitrust legislation.

V. Unacknowledged problems with perfect competition

The neoclassicals rationalize and justify the use of the highly unrealistic perfect competition model on the ground that it is useful for predictions and as a standard of behavior and that the benefits of the uses outweigh the costs of unrealistic expectations. However, other costs of this model go unacknowledged. First, perfect competition is applied more widely than is appropriate, in situations where the reality is so different from the

[122] In a wider framework there have of course been criticisms of the competitive norm with respect to the ability of individuals to judge their own interests and ability of a competitive system to achieve a continuously high level of employment of resources.

[123] Stigler, 1965, p. 266.

assumptions, that not only is it not useful, save for the purpose of making the analysis mathematically tractable, but the conclusions reached are positively misleading. There is no better example to illustrate this claim than the billions of dollars that have been wasted both prosecuting and defending against anti-trust lawsuits, and the vast harm supposedly anti monopolistic laws have done to the structure of the economy[124].

Second, past generations of economists have been, and future generations are being, trained along these lines rather than in praxeology and market process analysis. The costs are the value of the alternative uses to which the resources used for such modeling would possibly be put, precluding greater progress in economic theory and history.

Third, the perfectly competitive model is embedded within the very bowels of neo classical economics. It pervades all else. It carries all before it. It completely overwhelms even "transactions costs analysis," which has also swept the economics profession like a firestorm, in terms of grip it has over the profession of economics. When business students, or those earning an MBA, are subjected to economics of the mainstream variety, they cannot help but take it in to their world view – which will tend to undermine their openness to, and ability to function in, the real world of poor information, advertising, marketing, etc.

Moreover, virtually all graduate schools of business incorporate into their core curricula courses in marketing, advertising, brokering and intermediation, financial and so on. However, also included in the business foundation are courses in economics which are invariably predicated on the neoclassical model of perfect competition. Thus, there is an inner contradiction in all such curricula: by including marketing, etc., business schools at least tacitly indicate the importance placed upon such disciplines. But by admitting a school of economics whose principal model disparages them, they take back with one hand what they have given with the other. Worse, economics (micro and managerial economics are the worst offenders in this regard) is often made a prerequisite for these other business courses. This is to add insult to injury. It is to lay in a foundation that is at loggerheads with the rest of the edifice.

When you build a house, the foundation undergirds the upper floors. These upper stories, in turn, rest upon the foundation. If there is any incompatibility between these two parts of the edifice, the entire entity is to that extent weakened. In they are incongruent with one another to a sufficient extent, the top part can even topple over.

---

[124] For the case in favor of the complete elimination of anti trust legislation, see Anderson, Block, DiLorenzo, Mercer, Snyman and Westley, 2001; Armentano, 1972, 1982, 1991; Armstrong, 1982; Block, 1977A, 1982, 1994; DiLorenzo, 1997; Boudreaux, and DiLorenzo, 1992; High, 1984-1985; McChesney, 1991; Rothbard, 1970; Shugart II, 1987; Smith, Jr. 1983.

It is much the same with regard to the offerings of the business school (and of course all other) curricula. The prerequisites, or the business core, serve much the same function with regard to these other academic offerings as does the foundation of the house to its upper stories. Indeed, this series of courses is even oft-times called the business "foundation." The student first enrolls in these required courses, and the other ones in the curriculum, those which come later, are built upon what came before. As in the case of the home, if there is any disparity between these two sets of courses, if there is a lack of "fit" between them, then the entire curriculum is less efficient that it otherwise would be. Its purpose, to confer knowledge, experience and training upon the student, and to inspire him to attain these ends on his own, are to that extent compromised.

Typically, the contributions of economics to the business core consist of microeconomics, macroeconomics, managerial economics, and statistics. The difficulty with mainstream microeconomics (this holds for managerial economics as well), is, as we have seen, that it is predicated upon the assumption of either full information about everything, or, in its more sophisticated Stiglerian manifestation, upon full knowledge about all possible probability distributions. In either case precious little scope remains for robust marketing, advertising, brokering, intermediation, financial insights, management, etc. But these, to a large part, are precisely of what the remainder of the business curriculum consist.

All graduate schools of business include a course of study of economics in their curricula. There are no exceptions known to the present authors; and, as it happens, there is in principle good and sufficient reasons for this state of affairs. For one thing, economics is itself part and parcel of business. No holder of the MBA degree, to say nothing of the D.B.A. or Ph.D. in business, can be considered fully qualified if he is ignorant of the teachings of the dismal science. For another, there are large complementarities between economics and other business disciplines such as accounting, management, finance, marketing, real estate, etc. This interdisciplinary support is a two way street: economics undergirds these other subjects, and they in turn support it[125].

Thus, all is not as well as it could be in the area of business curricula. The mainstream economic school of thought typically represented in a business school is almost totally incompatible with at least one of the other disciplines, marketing. Specifically, virtually all economists located at schools of business practice neoclassical economics; not for them the niceties of the Austrian School which emphasizes the entrepreneur, advertising, marketing, etc. To put this in another way, for the mainstream economist,

---

[125] Our emphasis in this paper, however, is in only one of these directions: that leading from economics to the other business courses.

the role of the entrepreneur virtually vanishes[126]. For the other departments in the business school in sharp contrast, the entrepreneur is crucial.

If the contribution of economics to the business foundation undercuts the very need for the advanced electives, if the former is incompatible with the latter, in what sense can it be said that the one can serve as an appropriate or relevant prerequisite for the other? Like the poorly constructed edifice, a curriculum of this sort is at best an unsteady one, and at worst continually threatens to topple over that which it is expected to support.

Our views on this matter may be summarized as follows:

"... the typical neo-Marshallian economics course is lacking in usefulness for the typical business student. In the business curriculum, one needs an economics that actually makes real references to choices made by those in business, as opposed to an economics that is so heavy in mathematical and geometric analysis that it is so rigid as to be nearly useless for someone who looks to use economics as a business tool."[127]

VI. What can be done?

What can be done to alleviate this situation? A quick and easy solution would be to eliminate microeconomics (and managerial economics) from the business curriculum. One advantage of such a plan is that it would save scarce and therefore precious academic resources. Another is that advertising and marketing courses, etc., would no longer be undermined by their ostensible foundations.

The drawback, of course, is that economics, at least ideally, can indeed contribute to the education of the business student, and significantly so. Indeed, it is probably no exaggeration to claim that the graduate business major, let alone the MBA who is completely innocent of economics, is far less prepared for a business career than either he could or should be. Without economics, the future business leader will have to do without a handle on profits, interest rates, unemployment, the business cycle, economic incentives, innovation, economic freedom, present discounted value, the list goes on and on.

A better solution, therefore, would not be to delete economics from the business curriculum entirely, but rather to eliminate only that school of thought which is incompatible with the other business disciplines. In a word, to substitute for an economics based on the simplistic assumptions of full information one that is not so puerile or unrealistic.

[126] Kirzner, 1973.

[127] This is part of a comment made by an anonymous referee to an earlier version of the present paper.

One potential candidate for this role is of course Marxism. But to substitute this variety of economics for the neoclassical would be to jump out of the frying pan and into the fire. It would be particularly unfortunate and unwarranted in an era that has seen the fall of the Berlin Wall, the collapse of the economy of the U.S.S.R., and the radical transformation of that of the People's Republic of China. This is not a promising strategy, moreover, in that Marxism is even less supportive of private business than is neoclassical economics. According to the socialist dogma, there shouldn't be any businessmen at all; the government should manage the economy.[128]

A far better candidate is the Praxeological School, or Austrian Economics. It is far more receptive to business and private enterprise than Marxism[129], and certainly exceeds neoclassical economics in this regard. In terms of the phenomenon with which we have been concerned, the assumption of full information, Austrianism is far superior to mainstream economics. For one thing, the concept of perfect competition is entirely absent from it, indeed, alien to it. Praxeologists have specifically criticized the distinction between perfect and imperfect competition. For another, Austrians have written supportively and analytically about advertising, marketing, entrepreneurship, and a whole host of concepts integral to a proper business school education.[130] A more moderate suggestion would not be to replace all neoclassical economists in business schools with Austrians, but instead to adopt an "affirmative action" program with regard to the latter. In this way at least there would be some increased representation in our nation's business colleges of a school of thought that is conducive to their overall mission[131].

Finally, because the model is so unrealistic, both economists and the discipline of economics lose credibility with businessmen and the public. It seems then that taking into account these problems, as well as those of unrealistic assumptions and a harmful standard, the costs far outweigh any benefits to be had from the perfect competition model that could not be had from supply and demand analysis without the detritus of the perfect competition assumptions.

---

[128] For an Austrian critique of socialism, Marxism and central planning, see Hayek, 1948C, 1954, 1978B; Hoppe, 1989C; Mises, 1981 (1969), 1972, 1963; Bohm-Bawerk, 1959 (1884); see particularly Part I, Chapter XII, "Exploitation Theory of Socialism-Communism"; Block, 1992; Boettke, 1993, 1990, 1994A,1994B, 1993; Boettke and Anderson, 1997; Rothbard, 1997O, 1997P

[129] This is the understatement of the century.

[130] In the interests of full disclosure, all three of the present authors are on the faculty of a business school, and support the Austrian perspective.

[131] For a particularly effective Austrian defense of advertising, combined with a critique of Galbraith's views on this subject, see Hayek, 1967

Chapter 8. On the Use and Misuse of the Laffer Curve

I. Introduction

The thesis of the present paper is that the Laffer curve has been misunderstood and hence misused by the economics profession. The implicit, and oft-times not so implicit premise of those who have utilized this model is that the optimal tax rate is that which optimizes governmental revenues. A related difficulty is that most commentators mistakenly believe that tax reductions caused budget deficits during the 1980s.

Our paper is organized as follows: in section II we discuss the misuse of the Laffer curve from a geometrical point of view; section III is devoted to a discussion of the public policy recommendations which emanate from this mistaken analysis; in section IV we introduce a new curve into the analysis, and on the basis of it call into question the geometrical analysis and public policy recommendations made in its absence. Section V is given over to a critique of the claim that during the 1980s tax reductions caused budget deficits, and we conclude in section VI.

II. The Geometry of the Laffer Curve Analysis

The Laffer curve is used to illustrate the point that, from the perspective of maximizing (total) tax revenues, sometimes income tax rates can be so high as to be counterproductive. It is a curve that relates tax revenues, R, to the average tax rate, T. The idea behind the Laffer curve is the common sense notion that if average tax rates are zero, then, by necessity, tax revenues will also be nil. At the other end of the spectrum, the revenues going to the government will also be zero if tax rates are 100%, or perhaps, something less[132], as no one will earn anything if *everything* he earns[133] will be taken away from him.

---

[132] The government's rate of income seizure need not be 100% in order to reach the situation where it derives no revenues at all. Quite possibly, this result might obtain at a slightly lower tax rate, say, between 90-99%. Here, too, the state might receive no payments, if all income earners decide to forego such activities.

[133] Although the Laffer curve concerns an income tax, the same point can be made, mutatis mutandis, for virtually any other tax, under certain interpretations, albeit with exceptions. Consider in this regard specific taxes; e.g., a head tax, a poll tax, or a tax per gallon of gasoline. At a zero rate, the IRS will of course collect nothing. But what will be the fiscal effects of a 100% tax? It is impossible even so much as to *define* such levies. Regarding ad valorem taxes, consider such a sales tax on, say, gasoline. At a zero rate of tax, it cannot be denied that nothing, again, will accrue to the "revenooers." But if this excise is raised to 100%, something easily defined in this case, it is not at all true that sales of gasoline will fall to zero, blocking government from obtaining its pound of flesh.

We defineT_0 as that minimum[134] positive T at which R falls to zero because no one has any incentive to earn an income,[135] as all, or at least too high a percentage of income is being commandeered.[136] For example, if people stop working, entirely, when the tax rate rises to 90%, then that level is defined as T_0. The maximum value T_0 can take on is of course 100%.[137]

Figure 1 depicts the Laffer curve, L. It is drawn based on: a) the fact that if $T = 0, \Rightarrow R = 0$; b) the assumption that for $T = T_0$, $0 < T_0 \leq 1$, $\therefore R = 0$; and, c) that $\forall$ T, $0 < T < T_0$, $R > 0$. Specifically, figure 1 is an example of a Laffer curve, drawn with the usual assumption that $T_0 = 1$. Note that in this figure, the region marked A tax revenues rise as a result of a boost in the tax rate, while in the region marked B, tax revenues increase as a result of a decrease in the tax rate.

The use made of this model concerns the "proper" rate of taxation. Typically, the premise of the analysis assumes that the appropriate tax rate is the rate that maximizes government revenues, T_{Rmax}. Given this, the point at issue becomes, are present tax rates higher or lower than this one? That is, in terms of figure 1 are we in region B or A? If the former, then for most commentators the public policy prescription that follows ineluctably is to lower tax rates so as to increase revenues; if the latter, then raise them, again with this same end in mind of enhancing government coffers.

III. The Public Policy Recommendations

Our claim is that the members of the economics profession who have entered the Laffer curve debate base their public policy recommendations upon

---

Throughout this paper we confine the analysis to an income tax. It should be noted that when the analysis is applied to some other types of excises, e.g., for an ad valorem sales tax on gasoline, revenues may not decline to zero until the tax rate is above 100%. Nevertheless, the value of the rate at which tax revenues declines to zero (T_0) does not affect the substance of the argument.

[134] Greater, of course, than zero.

[135] Whether by work or any other action

[136] Alternatively, T_0 may be defined as the maximum rate at which tax revenues first become zero. The minimum rate at which tax revenue goes to zero is, of course, zero. No matter which way you look at it, the reason tax revenues become zero at T_0 is that the rate has become so onerous that no one will earn an income and therefore no matter what the (positive) rate is, when multiplied by zero income it yields zero revenue.

[137] Gordon, R. (1993, p. 398) disputes the claim that tax revenues would be zero at tax rates of 100%: "Even this is not clear. Some people seem to enjoy their work so much that they might continue to work even at a tax rate of 100 percent." This, of course, ignores the fact that people without any income at all would quickly cease to exist. Fullerton (1982), who was cited by Abel and Bernanke (1992, p. 377) claimed that at that time the revenue maximizing tax rate was 79%. Based on "casual empiricism," however, this figure seems very high to the current authors.

the result that will most enhance the scope of government. If tax revenues can be maximized by low tax rates, they favor this alternative. If, on the other hand, they are convinced that the income of the state can be increased by higher tax rates, they argue in behalf of them. Consider in this regard the following statements from the authors of introductory economic textbooks[138]:

1. "The point at which the Laffer curve peaks is important because it determines whether or not tax cuts from their current rates will increase the budget deficit. If the economy ... is beyond the point of maximum revenue; tax cuts will stimulate the economy and increase revenue" (Colander, 1998, p. 449).

2. "The result [of lowering taxes]? Not very positive. Tax revenues did not increase ... " (Gottheil, 2002, p. 318; material in brackets inserted by present authors).

3. "The big debate in the 1980s was whether tax rates in the United States put the country on the upper or lower part of the (Laffer) curve in Figure 29.2. The supply-side school claimed the United States was [above the tax rate at which government revenue would be maximized] and taxes should be cut. Others argued that the United States was [below the tax rate at which government revenue would be maximized] and tax cuts would lead to lower tax revenue" (Case and Fair, 2002, p. 662; material in brackets inserted by present authors). Nor were the authors of intermediate level texts immune from this: mistake; i.e., from thinking that the optimal tax rate is that which maximizes government's revenues rather than that which maximizes the aggregate income of the members of society.

4. "The Laffer curve indicates that if the income tax rate is sufficiently high, cutting the tax rate will raise income tax revenues. Only at lower rates will tax rate reductions necessarily reduce tax revenues...The difficult problem, naturally, is determining the location of the top point of the Laffer curve." (Miller and VanHoose, 2004, 185)

5. "Whatever the theoretical possibilities, the Kemp-Roth tax cuts did not lead to an increase in government revenue. Even if we concentrate on the full-employment budget, we do not see an increase in government revenue result from the tax cuts. This excessively optimistic element in supply-side economics..." (Dornbusch and Fischer, 1987, p. 601)

---

[138] We surveyed the following introductory texts (Arnold 2001; Boyes, 2002; Case and Fair, 2002; Colander, 1998; Farmer, 2002; Gottheil, 2002; McConnell, 2002; Sexton, 2002; Tucker, 2003) and intermediate texts (Abel and Bernanke, 1992; Dornbusch and Fischer, 1987; Froyen, 1999; Gordon, R., 1993; Jansen, 1994; Miller and Van Hoose, 2001). We have chosen textbooks as our main source of information as to how economists deal with the Laffer curve since they tend to be the distillation of knowledge of the profession at any given time, with a suitable lag.

6. "But the supply side claim was stronger than a claim that a cut in income tax rates would motivate people to work more. The supply-side claim was that, despite the cut in the tax rate, total tax revenue would rise because a lot more work would be done" Dornbusch Fisher (1987, p. 599).[139]

Relying on Fullerton's (1982) claim that the tax rate that maximized government revenue at that time was 79%, and given the fact that average tax rates have never been that high, Abel and Bernanke (1992, 377) conclude that we are always on that part of the L curve where lower tax rates lead to reduced government revenues, and hence any lowering of tax rates is contraindicated.

Based on the foregoing, it is not unfair to charge that in its Laffer curve analysis the profession seems mainly interested in determining whether or not changes in tax rates will increase or decrease government revenues, with the aim of achieving the former.

IV. The Missing Curve

But this conclusion is never justified in the literature surrounding the Laffer curve[140]. Moreover, the curve, in and of itself, does not allow for a more complete analysis that focuses on some of the complexities involved. In order to remedy this weakness, we introduce a second curve, depicting the relationship between T and Y, income,[141] or the tax base.[142] In figure 2 this

---

[139] Of course, this is strictly an issue of the elasticity of Y with respect to T. ($R = T \cdot Y(T) \therefore dR/dT = T \cdot dY/dT + Y$ and $dR/dT > 0 \Rightarrow dY/Y > -dT/T$.) That is, in the region under consideration, is $dY/Y > -dT/T$? If it is then, R increases with $T < 0$; if not, then R decreases with $T < 0$. Moreover, the supply-side claim was not limited to the effects of a tax rate change on work, but included the effects on income from any and all sources.

[140] There are of course numerous attempts to justify taxation in public finance texts. For a sampling mentioned by a critic of these efforts, see Block (1989B, 1993)

[141] Income (Y), hereinafter refers to aggregate pecuniary income.

[142] The relationship between tax revenues and tax rates is a matter of great importance in the political arena. As matters currently stand, Congressional Budget Office forecasts of the expected effects on tax revenues of proposed changes in tax laws, including a fortiori, changes in tax rates, are based on the (implicit) assumption that the changes will not affect the tax base. This is referred to as "static scoring." Because under current law, any "tax cuts;" i.e., expected reductions in Federal tax revenues must be "paid for" (Moakley, 1999), the use of static scoring to forecast the effects of a proposed reduction in tax rates means that either some other tax rate has to be increased or some expenditure decreased (see Title II, Congressional Budget Act of 1974.) Given the aversion of Congress to cutting expenditures, all of which benefit one constituency or another, static scoring makes it very difficult for proposed cuts in tax rates to become law.

appears as the curve $Y = Y(T)$[143]. Without the Y curve, the Laffer curve analysis devolves into to one of ascertaining whether or not we are presently located to the left or right of the point of maximum government revenue. With the addition of the Y curve, we are in a position to gain greater insight into the advantages and disadvantages of tax policy to the government and the taxpayers.

First, let us consider the relationship between the income curve, Y, and the Laffer curve, L. It is clear that the former must everywhere lie above the latter. This is because, unless tax rates rise above 100%,[144] the government's take must necessarily be less than the GDP. In figure 2 the vertical intercept of Y is positive, at a "small" level of GDP. Here, we are implicitly assuming that government is not a necessary condition for economic performance. Rather, that without it, things will not be so chaotic that no income whatsoever will be earned by anyone;[145] instead, the tax base will be "small."[146]

The use of the assumption that underlies the Laffer curve analysis - that changes in tax rates can and do affect tax revenues – to forecast changes in tax revenues consequent on changes in tax rates is referred to as "dynamic scoring." As recently as 1999 there was an attempt to change the law to require dynamic scoring. (See HR 29, 1st Session 106th Congress.)

[143] None of the texts mentioned, supra, utilize the Y curve along with the L curve, nor mention the possibility that tax revenues might be zero at tax rates less than 100%; indeed, to the best of our knowledge no publication at all utilizes this technique, which, hence, is being introduced here for the first time.

[144] Swedish *marginal* tax rates rose above 100% during the 1970s. Tennis star Bjorn Borg was faced with paying *more* than he earned for some of his income. As a result he migrated from Sweden to Monaco; see http://www.terra.com/specials/sportsicons/borg_en.html. Ingemar Bergman the Swedish movie director also migrated to Monaco for the same reason; see http://www.neosoft.com/~pnews/issues/753/editorial.html.

[145] If we assume that without any revenue no governmental entity could exist and that in such a case conditions would be so chaotic that no one will produce any income whatsoever, then in a figure representing that situation the L and Y curves would intersect at the origin.

[146] The anarcho-capitalist contention that, absent government (i.e., tax rates and revenues are zero) not only will GDP not be zero, nor, even, "small," but will actually be maximized. In a figure illustrating that case, the Y curve would be at its maximum at $T = 0$; i.e., where it intercepted the vertical axis, and slope downward continuously until it intercepted the horizontal axis at $T = T_0 = 1$. Actually, there are several conditions required for the anarcho-capitalism. Not only must government refrain from any and all taxation, it must also desist from demanding a monopoly position; e.g., it cannot preclude entry of defense and court firms. As well, if it is to be a limited government, it cannot impose policies such as economic regulation. On this see Benson (1990), Friedman (1989), Kinsella (1995), Stringham (1998-1999).

Figure 1 is divided into two (2) regions A and B. An increase in tax rates results in an increase in tax revenues and an increase in income in region A, and a decrease in both in region B. In figure 2, region B remains the same; however, region A is subdivided into regions A1 and A2. An increase in tax rates results in an increase in governmental revenues in both of these regions; however, national income[147] increases in region A1 and decreases in region A2.

We see, then, that in region A1 both tax revenues and income rise as a result of an increase in the tax rate, whereas in region B both tax revenues and income are enhanced as a result of a decrease in the tax rate; conversely, in region A2 tax revenues increase but income decreases as a result of a boost in the tax rate or, alternatively stated, it is the region in which tax revenues decrease but income increases as a result of a fall in the tax rate.

Having addressed the behavior of the Y curve at $T = 0$, we now look at its relation with L at the other end of the diagram, where the tax rate T_0 reaches the 100% level. We note that wherever L intersects the horizontal axis, Y will do so at precisely the same point. For the intersection of L with the horizontal axis is defined as the point at which the populace no longer seeks to earn an income, given the voraciousness of the tax rate. But if no one produces anything, then, necessarily, there will be no income, Y, on the basis of which taxes are calculated. Hence, Y and L intersect the horizontal axis at precisely the same point.

Implicit in the analysis is that: a) tax revenue is equal to the product of the tax rate and income, Y; i.e., $R = T{\cdot}Y$; b) income is dependent on the tax rate; i.e., $Y = Y(T)$; c) $Y \geq 0$ at $T = 0$; d) $Y = 0$ at $T = T_0$; e) $0 < T_0 \leq 1$; and, f) $Y > 0 \ \forall \ 0 < T < T_0$.

The failure to include the Y(T) curve in the usual Laffer curve analysis makes it easy to overlook an important point. It is that the tax rate at which national income is maximized is *necessarily lower* than that at which tax revenues are maximized because the only way for tax revenues to peak (and then decline) as tax rates increase is for income to decline (in percentage terms; i.e., it is a matter of the tax rate elasticity of income) at the same (a faster) rate than that at which the tax rates increase.[148]

---

[147] We use "national income" not in some collective sense, but, rather, as the sum of individual pecuniary incomes.

[148] That is, $R_{Rmax} \Rightarrow dR/dT = Y + T{\cdot}dY/dT = 0$ and $Y, T, > 0 \Rightarrow dY/dT < 0$ at T_{Rmax}. $\therefore$ Y at T_{Ymax} > Y at T_{Rmax}. And, $Y + T{\cdot}dY/dT = 0 \Rightarrow dY/Y = - dT/T$. (It is true that $dR/dT = 0$ at $Y = T = 0$, and also at $Y = dY/dT = 0$, but these are trivial cases.)

Given that Y reaches its maximum at $T = T_{Ymax}$ (which is *necessarily* less than T_{Rmax}, the T at which L reaches its maximum), we have drawn Y in figure 2 so as to indicate that this point occurs where the tax rate is approximately 10%. What is the justification for this? This is based on the classical liberal contention that a government limited to its natural law functions of armies, courts and police[149] would require about this proportion of the GDP to properly acquit its responsibilities.[150]

It is obvious that in region A1 the government prefers a higher T as both dY/dT and $dR/dT > 0$. It is also obvious that it prefers a lower T in region B, as both dY/dT and $dR/dT < 0$.[151] Moreover, it is most reasonable to assume that that, unless the movement to higher national income from a position in either region A or B consequent on the appropriate tax rate change were to so alter the distribution of income that the majority of taxpayers ended up with lower after tax incomes, that the taxpayers as whole, although not necessarily all of them, would prefer the same adjustments in tax rates favored by the government. It is in region A2 that the conflict between the governors and the governed seems most likely to exist and to be maximized. In that region, $dY/dT < 0$ and $dR/dT > 0$. The state wants higher rates, because even though such rates will entail disincentives to production and the concomitant lower total income, the decrease in the tax base is more than offset by the increase in rates. Consequently, the government will have more of the taxpayers'[152] wealth to spend. And, mutatis mutandis, in region A2 the majority of the taxpayers would oppose the tax policy changes favored by the government. Alternatively put, at the tax rate that maximizes the state's income, the aggregate income of the members of society is not maximized, and at the tax rate at which the aggregate income of society's individuals is maximized, the state's income is not maximized.

---

[149] See Gwartney and Stroup (1993), Machan (1990), Murray (1997), Nozick (1974), Read (1964).

[150] It must be stressed that although this figure, 10%, is only an approximation, whatever the true figure would be, it most assuredly would be much lower than the current rate. Moreover, it is an average - it would rise above that level during times of war, and fall below it in times of peace.

[151] We assume that government has no objection to a higher national income if it is attendant upon an increase in governmental revenues. However, one could conceive of circumstances where that might not be the case. For example, it is possible that a less than maximal income might be distributed in a way that favored the reelection of incumbents, whereas the distribution of the maximal income might not.

[152] In a democracy, the government is, effectively, the faction that controls the machinery of government at any particular time. Although democracy has been referred to as "tyranny of the majority," typically members of a special interest group or groups that collectively only constitute a minority are able to impose their wills on the majority. For a further analysis of this issue, see Buchanan and Tullock (1971).

In region A2, the uses to which the increased revenue resulting from an increase in tax rates are put is irrelevant to Y; it decreases regardless. Consider the three possibilities; the increased R is used to: 1) finance the purchase of goods and/or services, assumed to be necessary for the provision of public goods;[153] 2) finance transfer payments; i.e., to redistribute income; and, 3) reduce a budgetary deficit or pay off existing debt.

In the first case, because the provision of additional public goods comes at the expense of national income, ceteris paribus, the gains to national income from the additional public goods must be more than offset by the losses in incomes arising from sources other than public goods, i.e., private goods.

In the second case, the redistribution of income comes at the expense of a lower average income for the entire population. Because the lower average income results despite the fact that the average income of the recipients/beneficiaries of the redistributed income increases, those from whom the redistributed funds come not only see a decline in their average incomes, but, a fortiori, a decline *greater* than the average decline in national income.

Finally, any reduction in the deficit or debt at the expense of reduced national income is suboptimal, for all that is involved is the method of financing governmental expenditures. If one method causes a reduction in national income ceteris paribus compared to another it must be inferior, and a fortiori if it involves a redistribution of income.

Note the implication of this analysis for Ricardian equivalence. In region A1, a tax rate increase that is used to finance a reduction in the deficit or debt is desirable because it increases national income, whereas in regions A2 and B, a tax rate increase that is used for this purpose is undesirable because it decreases national income. Moreover, so long as a change in the tax rate affects national income, Ricardian equivalence cannot exist.

This provides a concise explanation as to why the state is virtually always trying to raise tax rates and a large majority of taxpayers are virtually always attempting to resist such increases.

---

[153] This concept has received sharp criticism from Coase (1974B).

V. Fiscal Effects

In this section we attempt to correct the record concerning the empirical effects of lowering tax rates on tax revenues collected. In this regard, consider the following:

[1] Laffer's argument had considerable weight in President Reagan's decision to change the tax structure. In 1981, Congress passed the Kemp-Roth tax cut, which lowered tax rates. The highest marginal tax rate was cut from 70 to 50 percent. In 1986, the Tax Reform Act followed Kemp-Roth's lead, ... cutting the top marginal rate to 31 percent....

The result? Not very positive. Tax revenues did not increase, contributing to the exceptionally large budget deficits of the 1980s (Gottheil, 2002, p. 318).

[2] The evidence following the tax cuts did, however contribute to a larger budget deficit, implying that the U.S. was not on the backward bending portion of the Laffer curve" (Boyes – Melvin, 2002, p. 279).

[3] If ... the reference was to the federal income tax and the time period was the immediate short run (i.e., the year following the tax cut), the most economists felt that the economy would be on the upward-sloping part of the Laffer curve and lower income tax rates would decrease tax revenues and increase the deficit. And that is what happened in the 1980s – tax revenues fell and the budget deficit increased when tax rates were lowered from a minimum rate of about 70 percent to a maximum rate of about 36 percent (Colander, 1998, p. 450).

[4] Gordon, R (1993, p. 399) claims that in the 1980s we were on the positively sloped section of the Laffer curve based on "the fact that the U.S. entered an era of persistent deficits after the Reagan tax cuts..."

[5] "In practice, the effect of the Reagan tax cuts in 1981 was to cause an increase in the deficit..... This... does throw doubt on the idea of the supply-siders that the economy was on the wrong side of the Laffer curve (Farmer 2002, p. 96).

[6] If the economy is at any point below *m* on the curve, then tax reductions will reduce tax revenues and possibly create budget deficits. That, say critics, is exactly what happened when the Reagan administration cut Federal income tax rates by about 25 percent over a 3-year period in the early 1980s. (McConnell-Brue, 2002, p. 320)

Despite the foregoing, which can reasonably be characterized as the constituting the consensus of the profession, it is by no means true that the lowering of tax rates in the 1980s was the cause of budget deficits. These ensued, to be sure. But they came about *not* because of decreased tax revenues; rather, they were due to increased expenditures[154].

It is obvious from the data in Appendix II that the statement, "Tax revenues did not increase, contributing to the exceptionally large budget deficits of the 1980s," is factually incorrect. It is bad enough that such error is a common occurrence in the various news media; in an economics textbook written by a professional economist it is inexcusable.

Had *real* outlays remained at their 1981 level (column 9) from 1981 through 1990, instead of accumulating a deficit of $1,712 billion during that decade; i.e., an average of $171 billion per year, the debt would "only" have increased by $470 billion; i.e., an average of "only" $47 billion per year. Moreover, instead of seeing the annual deficit rise to $208 billion in 1983 and then remain above $150 billion every year for the rest of that decade, including a deficit of $221 in 1990, that matched the all time high that had been reached earlier in the decade (1986), the annual deficit would have risen to a high of "only" $149 billion. Thereafter the deficit would have declined every year until it was virtually eliminated in 1987, and then turned into a surplus of $15 billion in 1988, that would have then risen to $57 billion in both 1989 and 1990. It is true that, had real outlays remained constant, the deficit would have risen for two (2) years before starting to decline; however, there is nothing startling about the fact that people do not adjust their behavior instantly to changes in governmental policies, even tax policies.

Therefore, it is obvious that the cause of the huge and increasing deficits of the 1980s was not a decrease in tax revenues, but rather voracious federal expenditures that grew even faster than did the revenues; expenditures in 1990 were 84% higher than they had been in 1981, whereas revenues were "only" 72% higher, and this in spite of the fact that that the outlays began from a base some 13.3% higher than revenues in 1981.

---

[154] State Dornbusch and Fischer (1987, p. 601): Quite another motive than supply-side arguments also led the Reagan administration to cut tax rates, despite the high deficits that would probably result over the next few years. That was the argument that the only way to get Congress to cut government spending is to reduce the revenue it receives.

The administration believed that unless tax rates were cut, and tax revenues reduced, the Congress would continue to spend. One of the major aims of the Reagan administration was to cut government spending, and so it was willing to have deficits for some time to put pressure on the Congress to reduce spending. But this claim, too, is difficult to reconcile with the facts. As can be seen from a perusal of Appendix II, the very opposite occurred: spending *increased* from $679B to $1,252B, almost doubling.

We end this section on a positive note: an honorable mention should be given to Miller and Van Hoose (2001, pp. 240-241) who state: "The difficult problem, naturally, is determining the location of the top point of the Laffer curve. The evidence on this issue is mixed. Shortly after significant reductions in average tax rates were enacted in the early 1980s, tax revenues declined, and the deficit increased sharply. At first glance, these events seem to support the static view. The difficulty with this off-the-cuff judgment, however, is that the U.S. economy went into a sharp recession in the early 1980s even as tax rates were cut, because autonomous investment and consumption declined sharply. Even though government spending also increased in the early 1980s… these declines in private spending led to a net reduction in equilibrium real income. Consequently, the true result of the 1980s experiment with the Laffer curve is difficult to judge."[155]

This was the only analysis we encountered in our text book survey which acknowledged that ceteris might not have been paribus while tax rates were declining in the 1980s; and that emphasized the importance of the fact that government outlays might have had anything to do with resulting deficits.

VI. Summary and Conclusions

This paper has demonstrated the universal shortcoming of Laffer curve analysis: the failure to include the curve that depicts the tax base as a function of the tax rate. Such oversight focuses attention on determining the rate that would maximize tax revenues rather than on the one that would maximize aggregate income; surely, both issues are important. As a consequence, such analysis fails to point out the inherent conflict that arises between the tax payers and the recipients of the tax payments. And, it has shown that those who claim: 1) that Laffer curve analysis applied to the U.S. economy led to incorrect predictions of tax revenue increases as a result of the tax rate decreases of the 1980s; and, 2) that the deficits of the 1980s were the consequence of decreased tax rates, were factually incorrect on both counts.

---

[155] It must be noted, however, that Miller and Van Hoose fail to mention the central role that monetary policy, deployed in attempt to break the then rampant (for the US.) inflation, played in the recessions of the early 1980s.

Appendix I

Figure 1

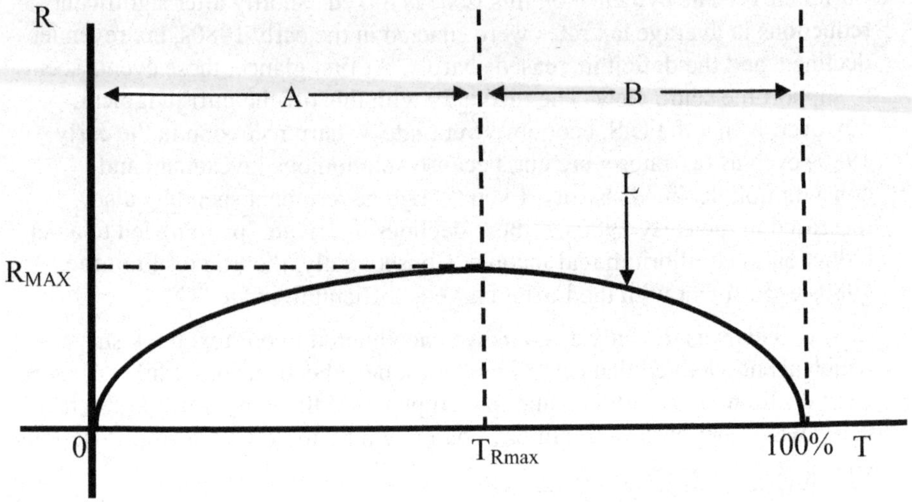

Figure 2

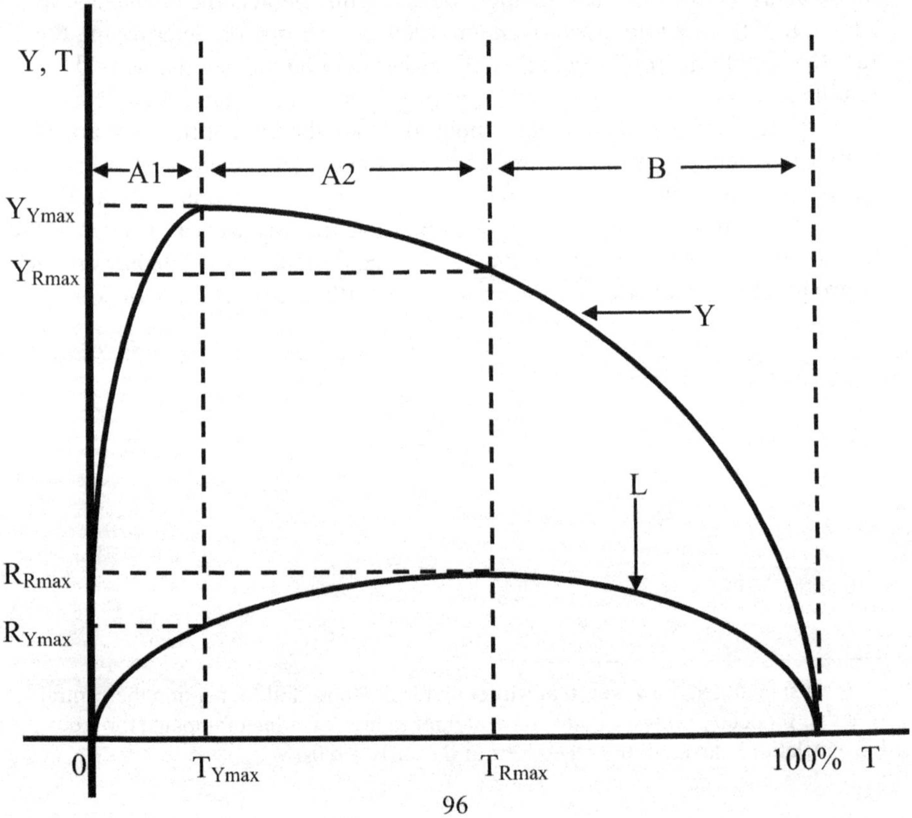

Appendix II

	1	2	3	4	5	6	7	8	9	10
	Employee taxes and "contribs."	Corporate income tax	Individual income tax	2+3	1+2+3	Receipts from all sources	Total outlays	Actual deficit (-)	Total outlays adjusted for inflation	Deficit (-) or surplus (+) if real outlays had remained constant
1981	163	61	286	347	510	599	679	-79	679	-80
1982	181	49	298	347	528	618	746	-128	722	-103
1983	186	37	289	326	512	601	808	-208	750	-149
1984	210	57	298	355	565	667	852	-186	783	-116
1985	235	61	335	396	631	734	946	-212	812	-78
1986	255	63	349	412	667	769	990	-221	834	-64
1987	273	84	393	477	750	854	1,004	-150	861	-7
1988	305	95	401	496	801	909	1,064	-155	894	+15
1989	333	103	446	549	882	991	1,144	-152	934	+57
1990	354	94	467	561	915	1,031	1,252	-221	974	+57
1981-90	2,495	704	3,562	4,266	6,761	7,773	9,485	-1,712	8,243	-470

Data in billions of dollars.

Chapter 9. Perfect Competition: A Case of "Market-Failure"[156]

I. Introduction[157]

Yes, you have read our title correctly. We show that it is not the "monopolist" of neoclassical economic theory who engenders "market failure" but rather the much beloved, from this perspective, *perfect competitors* who are guilty of this sin. If, and to the degree to which, antitrust is justified, then, in our view legal penalties should be applied not to the former but to the latter! In section II we present a graphical analysis that underlies our position; section III contains the relevant mathematics. We conclude in section IV with the explicit argument for letting loose the dogs of the Federal Trade Commission and the Antitrust Division of the Justice Department upon perfect competitors. Our main concern is the failure of mainstream economics to incorporate, properly and completely, the concept of foregone alternatives, into its analysis. The present paper is an attempt to trace out the some of the implications of this critical error for industrial organization.

II. Graphical Analysis

According to neoclassical theory, optimal allocation of resources requires that that P = MC. Regardless of the reason, anytime this condition does not hold, market failure is said to exist. Profit maximization requires that MR = MC. However, whenever the demand curve slopes downward P > MR. Therefore, given that the demand curve slopes downward and profits are maximized, market failure results, because in such cases P > MR = MC. Moreover, the market failure consists in a suboptimally low quantity of the good being produced and sold[158] because here the quantity at which P = MC is necessarily greater than that at which MR = MC.

Perfect competition is the only exception; it is the only situation in which profit maximization does not result in market failure, in the view of the neoclassicals. The reason is that in perfect competition, the demand

---

[156] We place quotes around the phrase "market failure" to indicate that, in our view, there is no such thing, in reality, as that which is depicted by this phrase. On this see Cowan, 1988; Rothbard, 1962.

[157] The word "cost" is used ambiguously in economics. On the one hand, it refers to the subjective value of the most attractive alternative foregone when choosing (i.e., opportunity cost). On the other hand, it is used synonymously with expenses, both explicit and implicit. The latter use implies that cost is objective and can be quantified, as in total cost, average cost, marginal cost, etc. Although we prefer not to use the terms cost and expense interchangeably, in this paper we will follow neoclassical tradition and do so.

[158] This suboptimally low quantity is sold at a suboptimally high price that redistributes income/wealth from sellers to buyers.

curve is perfectly elastic; i.e., P = MR and, therefore, MR – MC ⇒ P = MC. Of course, that is somewhat misleading. According to the theory, demand is perfectly elastic for the individual perfectly competitive firm, or more correctly, the firm (decision maker) thinks it is; e.g., *acts* on this basis[159]. However, the industry or market demand is not perfectly elastic; rather, regardless of the good sold by the industry, it is less than perfectly elastic. This is an instance of the fallacy of composition in that each firm thinks it could sell more without having to reduce the price it charges. It is this that gives rise to the "market failure."

Barnett and Saliba (unpublished A) demonstrate that the traditional explanation of why marginal revenue diverges from average revenue, i.e., the demand curve, is erroneous. Let us rehearse the argument. When price falls and quantity rises, a movement down and to the right on the demand curve, the firm suffers from a diminution of price on each infra-marginal unit. When this is taken into account, the result is the divergence of the marginal revenue from the average revenue or demand curve. The price decrease necessary to sell the marginal (or 1001st) unit might only be a single dollar. But if the firm is already producing 1000 units (the infra-marginal amount) then the loss is one dollar multiplied by 1000.

Certainly neoclassical analysis recognizes the existence of both explicit and implicit costs. The problem is that when price is reduced in order to sell an additional unit, thereby causing the seller to forego (some) revenue on the infra-marginal units that previously were sold for a higher price, the foregone revenue is not treated as a cost. However, it is in fact a type of implicit cost that should be added to all other implicit costs such as foregone salaries, foregone rent, forgone interest, etc. As a result, one type of implicit cost is segregated from all other implicit costs and included in neoclassical analysis as the difference between demand (price) and marginal revenue; i.e., that which must be subtracted from price in order to arrive at marginal revenue. By treating one type of implicit cost differently from all others, namely as a reduction in revenue rather than an addition to cost, a flaw is introduced into the analysis and inappropriate policy recommendations stem from this error.

The point is made by Barnett and Saliba: The key issue, then, is why in the ubiquitous cases of downward sloping demand curves neoclassical analysis finds, and a subjectivist approach does not find, a divergence between price and marginal revenue. The reason they differ on this matter is because neoclassical theory fails to treat the revenue foregone when a firm must lower its price to sell a larger quantity as an implicit cost, but, rather, deducts it from the price in order to arrive at marginal revenue. This error, the subtraction of

---

[159] For the view that "actions speak louder than words," or, that it is human action that is the basis of economics, see Mises (1966)

the foregone revenues from price to derive marginal revenue, instead of adding them to marginal cost, arises because of the failure of neoclassicists to appraise the decision situation from the subjective point of view of the seller, for whom foregone revenues are an implicit cost. Rather, they take the 'objective view point' that they assume some external observer would have.

From some point of view, perhaps that of common sense, it matters not whether an action calls for additional costs or reductions in revenue. But even from this perspective, at the very least, it is arbitrary on the part of the neoclassicals to insist that it is the latter that is in operation here, not the former. Our "strong" claim, then, is that this loss is a cost, not a reduction in revenue. Our "weak" claim, in contrast, is that the neoclassical style of describing the situation cannot be shown to be superior to our own. That is, it is a matter of indifference[160] as to which one is correct.

But we defend our strong, not our weak argument. In our view, the problem with the mainstream economist is that while he pays lip service to alternative or opportunity cost, his adherence to this doctrine is but skin deep. When push comes to shove, the neoclassical dismal scientist forgets all about it; he jettisons it without a backward glance. A loss of revenue is, if we take this doctrine seriously, a *cost*. It is an alternative foregone. As such, the differential created by the divergence between the prices at which the marginal and infra-marginal units can be sold must be added to the marginal cost curve, not subtracted from the average revenue or demand curve. It simply cannot be denied that foregone revenues are a cost to the seller. This is a direct deduction from the doctrine of alternative costs, but it has never been drawn by neo-classical economists.

Barnett and Saliba show that the traditional (neoclas-sical) marginal cost (NCMC) understates the actual, full, or complete marginal cost (CMC[161]). As they illustrate, in every case, P = MR, and therefore profit maximization (MR = CMC) coincides with optimality (P = CMC). If, then, perfect competition occurs, the allocation that results is the solution of the equation P = NCMC, and not P = CMC; thus, Q will be suboptimally *high*. That is P = CMC at a lower Q than that at which P = NCMC. Consequently, the suboptimally high perfectly competitive solution at P = NCMC is an instance of market failure. To what are we to attribute this failure of the market?

---

[160] Contrary to the neoclassical vision (Nozick, 1977; Caplan, 1999) in technical Austrian economics, there is no such thing as indifference (Rothbard, 1970, 1997I; Block, 1999A, Hulsmann, 1999). But, as a matter of common language, "indifference" is a legitimate English word, and thus must have some referent or meaning.

[161] Note every time that "***C***MC" appears the first "C" is underlined, in bold and italics typeface;; i.e., it appears as "***C***MC." This is our attempt to underscore the importance of ***complete*** marginal cost.

Among the assumptions of the perfectly competitive market are the following: each firm is so small relative to the market that it thinks, or better yet, acts as if, it has no control over the price at which it can sell its output. Therefore, it treats price as a parameter; i.e., each member of the industry is a "price-taker;" each one functions as if it can sell all it wishes to at the (parametric) market price; i.e., no one company thinks it must set price below the current market price in order to sell more; prices are known for sure, thus each seller has perfect knowledge of the current market price.

However, in fact, these (assumed) beliefs of the sellers are in conflict with reality. For a firm (industry) to be in perfectly competitive equilibrium, the firm (firms in the industry) would have to continue to hold these beliefs in the face of evidence (the behavior of the buyers and of its competitors) very much to the contrary[162]. Were this not the case, once established, the market price of a good in a perfectly competitive market would never change, regardless of alterations in buyers' and sellers' valuations of the good; i.e., there would not be any forces in the market[163] tending to eliminate shortages and surpluses as they appear. This would amount to a true case of market failure in contradistinction to alleged examples such as externalities and public goods. Of course, sellers do not hold such beliefs for long; any who do would find that competition would drive them out of the market. That is one reason why there are no perfectly competitive markets in the real world.

Therefore, because any market that exhibited market failure in the form of perfectly competitive results would be misallocating too much of "society's" scarce resources to the production and sale of that market's good, following other aspects of neoclassical reasoning, the case could be made that the firms in that industry be subject to laws analogous to anti-trust. Of course, as per another aspect of neoclassical reasoning, such laws should be enforced only if the benefits from reallocation exceed the enforcement expenses. It should be noted that, provided the (neoclassical) marginal expense curve slopes upward as do all marginal cost curves over the relevant range in reality, for any given perfectly competitive market equilibrium, the gain to be had from intervention is greater, the less elastic the market demand. That is, the more elastic the market demand, the more harm is done in terms of misallocation of resources.

---

[162] It is difficult to square this with common sense, let alone "perfect" information.

[163] Of course, the forces in the market are but the actions of normal human beings going about their business of trying to satisfy their wants. That is, frustrated buyers bid up the price in cases of shortages and frustrated sellers offer to sell at lower prices in cases of surpluses.

III. Mathematical Analysis

Let TR = P(Q)·Q and TC = C(Q), where TR is total revenue, P is price, Q is quantity, and TC is total cost. Then profit maximization requires that $P + QdP/dQ - dC/dQ = 0$. The standard formulation, then, is: $P + QdP/dQ = dC/dQ$, or MR = MC, where MR is $P + QdP/dQ$, and MC is dC/dQ. Barnett and Saliba (unpublished A) reformulated this as: $P = -QdP/dQ + dC/dQ$, where MR = P and $MC = -QdP/dQ + dC/dQ$.

The difference between the present authors and the mainstream concerns the treatment of the term QdP/dQ. Because $Q > 0$ and $dP/dQ < 0$, this term is negative. In fact it is the (per additional unit sold) foregone revenue the seller incurs because he had to lower price in order to sell the additional units. It makes no difference with respect to the profit maximizing quantity and price which formulation is used, as Q is determined as the solution to the equation: $P + QdP/dQ - dC/dQ = 0$, and P by inserting the solution value of Q into P = P(Q). Moreover, although it makes no difference to the seller whether he regards the foregone revenue as a deduction from revenue or an addition to cost, it makes a great deal of difference to the economic analyst. From the latter's point of view, foregone revenue must necessarily be a cost, a sacrificed alternative, to be added to other costs. There is simply no reason to treat *this* cost in a manner different than all others[164]. Looked at in that way, i.e., from the point of view that foregone revenue is a cost, the term $-QdP/dP$ must be added to dC/dQ to get what we have called complete marginal cost (C̲MC). Furthermore, the sale of each additional unit brings in an amount equal to its price, therefore, MR = P.

Profit maximization, then, requires that MR = C̲MC, or, because, P = MR, that P = C̲MC. Consequently, the optimal allocation of resources that occurs when P = C̲MC coincides with the profit maximizing allocation of resources that occurs at MR = C̲MC. Thus there is no divergence between the social and private optima.

---

164 A similar mistake occurs with regard to the treatment of "transactions" costs in the Chicago Law and Economics literature. Transactions costs, too, are undeserving of any particular special treatment, not enjoyed by other, more run of the mill or garden variety costs. Costs are costs are costs. For a critique of such authors as Coase (1960) and Posner (1992) who elevate the status of transactions costs above and beyond their due, see Block (1977B, 1995, 1996), Cordato (1989, 1992A, 1992B), Krecke (1996), North (1990, 1992, 2002), Stringham (2001), and Rothbard (1990). There is, however, an important difference between this debate and the one discussed in the text. Transactions cost is, at least, treated as a cost by its particular adherents. In the issue discussed in the text, however, that which is really a cost is instead dealt with in a very different manner: it is calculated as a subtraction from revenue, instead.

IV. Antitrust implications[165]

Neoclassicals argue[166] that under "monopoly" (i.e., other than perfectly competitive) conditions, production takes place at point M, whereas if social welfare is to be maximized, it must occur at point C. Therefore, there is a dead weight loss equal to AMC (the area with the vertical lines) in figure 1. In order to rescue the market from this deviation from maximum social welfare, they argue, at least theoretically, that the government must either break up the industry into numerous smaller constituent elements, socialize and run it at point C, or regulate the industry to the same end.

We maintain, in sharp contrast, that the *real* dead weight loss is not a function of "monopoly"[167]; rather, it emanates from "perfect competition." We take the position that M is the optimal point, from the social welfare point of view[168] as defended by neoclassical economics, and that the dead weight loss should be depicted not by AMC, but rather by MBC (the area with the horizontal lines). That is, perfect competitors, who occupy point C, produce *too much*, since they locate to the right of the optimal point, M, where CMC crosses the demand curve. The MR curve drops out of our analysis as shown by an MR curve illustrated by dots, not a line. The perfect competitors, in dastardly fashion, utilize *too many* of societies' resources, leaving too few for the production of other goods.

Now, if the civil penalty for monopolizing is triple damages[169], what should be the punishment for perfect "competitionizing"? Surely, it should be more severe, for it cannot be denied that it is more of an offense against the common good produce *too much,* to in effect *waste* society's resources,

---

[165] There are other good and sufficient reasons to oppose antitrust legislation. See on this Anderson, et. al. (2001), Armentano (1991), Block (1977A, 1994), Boudreaux and DiLorenzo (1992), DiLorenzo (1997), DiLorenzo and High (1988), High (1984-1985), McChesney (1991), Rothbard (1970), Shugart (1987), and Smith (1983).

[166] See Bork, 1978, Brozen, 1982, Posner, 1976, Stigler, 1968, Telser, 1987.

[167] For Austrians, "monopoly" consists solely of government grants of privileges to favored special interests, which usually take the form of restricted or prohibited entry for would be competitors. In the praxeological perspective, it matters not one whit how many firms are in an industry, since "industry" is a subjective concept, capable of being reasonably defined as widely or narrowly as one wishes. How, then, describe the situation where one firm, say, an I.B.M. or Alcoa in the mid 20th century, dominates the market for a particular type of good? As a single seller of that good, not a monopolist, since there were no laws protecting these companies from competition.

[168] For the Austrian argument in which we entirely concur that there is no such thing as social welfare, or, rather, that there is but that it obtains solely under laissez faire conditions of pure markets based on private property rights with no government interference, see Rothbard (1997I).

[169] 15 United States Code §15. http://tinyurl.com/64ztyd

than to more modestly use too few of these precious means.[170] This being so, we suggest that damages in excess of treble, say quad-, quin-, or sex-, tuple, should be assessed against all those who act as if they face a perfectly elastic demand curve.

And what is the source of such anti-social activity? It is yet another "market failure:" externalities.[171] Even though each "perfect competitor" knows he has innumerable competitors trying to sell goods identical to his, he acts as if they do not exist. Whenever the market price is above his (neoclassical, i.e., *incomplete*) marginal cost, in mechanical fashion he produces additional units. This atomistic firm acts as if it does not realize that its counterparts will *also* engage in such activities, with the consequence that when they all do, the price must inevitably fall. That is, there is no such thing as a perfectly elastic demand curve. *Over*production is the inevitable result of such "head in the sand" behavior.

---

[170] On this point, see: Barnett and Dauterive (1985, unpublished A, unpublished, B), and Barnett, Dauterive, and White (1985).

[171] In order to clarify our own position, we engage in a reductio ad absurdum argument. We do not for a moment countenance the market failure of externalities (any more than we do *any* market failure). Upon analysis, these *all* turn out to be instances of incomplete, or contradictory, or totally lacking specifications of private property rights, or the inadequate enforcement thereof. See on this (Rothbard, 1977A; Block, 1983; Cordato 1992B).

Appendix

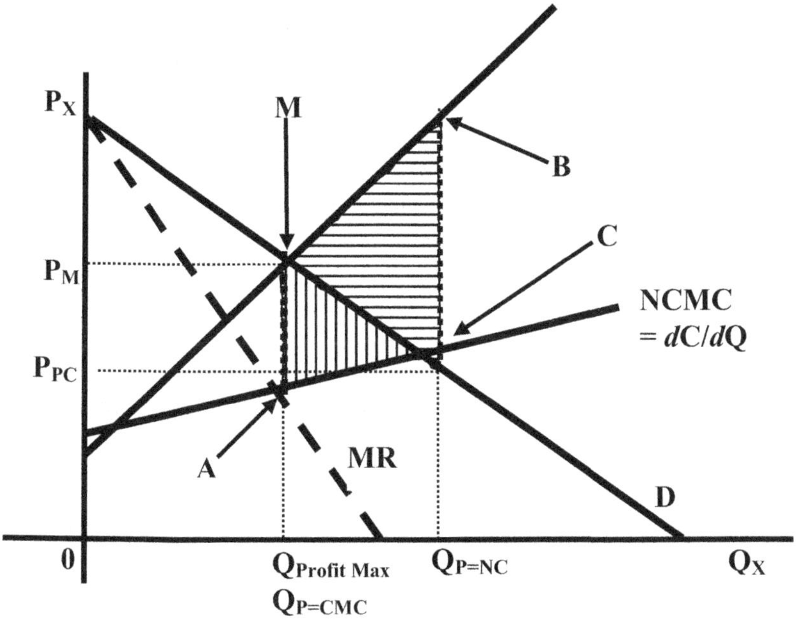

NCMC = neoclassical marginal cost   CMC = complete marginal cost
$Q_{Profit\ Max}$ = profit maximizing quantity
$Q_{P=CMC}$ = subjectivist socially optimal quantity
$Q_{P=NCMC}$ = neoclassical socially optimal quantity
P_M = "monopoly" price P_{PC} = "perfect competition" price
M = profit maximizing price-quantity point in both neoclassical analysis & subjectivist analysis,and the socially optimal point for subjectivist analysis
C = socially-optimal point in neoclassical analysis, and a socially-suboptimal point in subjectivist analysis

Chapter 10. Mises, Rothbard and Salerno on Costs

Abstract

This paper is an attempt to wrestle with the concepts of costs, causality, subjectivism, derived demand, inflation, supply and demand, and with the views of three Austrian economists on all of them: Mises, Rothbard and Salerno. In our view, in contradistinction to theirs, the choices of both buyer and sellers, in the consumer *and* producers goods markets, contribute to price determination. Our claim is that they give too short shrift to the latter markets.

Introduction

"Thus when economists, business forecasters and Alan Greenspan scrutinize indexes of input prices such as the PPI or indexes of raw commodity prices, they do so because they incorrectly believe that changes in these indexes are harbingers of future changes in general consumer prices, as if input prices determined product prices rather than the other way around" (Salerno, 2003, p. 83).

"According to Austrian theory, the value of money, which is the inverse of overall consumer prices, is determined like the individual prices of its component consumer goods by supply and demand" (Salerno, 2003, p. 83).

Let us call the first of these two statements A, and the second, B.

Each of these has something to be said in its behalf.

I. Statement A

There is a grain of truth in A. It stems from the insight of Rothbard (1970, 1993), to the effect that we value factors of production because they are necessary preconditions or causal agents, of the consumers' goods we value for their own sakes. The direction of causation of prices is, so to speak, all in a backward direction: from the final goods back to the factors of production. Or, to put this in another way, there is a *direct* demand for consumers' goods, but only a *derived* demand, from them, back to their causal agents, the factors of production.

However, Salerno goes too far. There is all the world of difference between saying two superficially similar things. First, correctly, that product prices are the dog, and input prices only the tail, in that the former comes first in the causal-genetic sense, and the latter appears only secondly in time. We do not value diamonds because diamond mines and jewelers' labor are so expensive. Rather, the very opposite is the case: diamond mines and the labor of diamond refiners are very valuable because we set such great stock on diamonds

Second, very incorrectly, that input prices play no role whatsoever in determining product prices[172]. In this vein, we contend that changes in raw commodity prices are indeed "harbingers" of future changes in general consumer prices, contrary to Salerno.

It cannot be denied that we value resources because we value the output they to the production of which they contribute. But it is an entirely different matter to say that, therefore the value of the output is the sole determinant of the value of the inputs. That would only be true if the owners of the resources themselves placed no value on the resources; i.e., if they had no reservation demand/price. Moreover, the greater the value placed on the resources by their owners, the higher will be their prices, ceteris paribus. So, we reiterate: diamond mines and the labor of diamond refiners are very valuable because we set such great stock on diamonds.

However, even if the value placed on diamonds dropped a great deal, the resource prices would rise if the demand for them to be used to produce, say, gold jewelry went up sufficiently, or if the reservation value/price of the owners increased suitably. We need to distinguish between the sources of subjective value of goods and resources and objective exchange values; i.e., prices thereof. If, tomorrow, we determined that these baubles were the spawn of the devil, and renounced them utterly, the market price of raw diamonds and labor that serve as inputs into this consumer good would drop like a stone. On the other hand, if the day after that we decided that diamond mines and jewelers were evil personified, but still valued diamonds (don't ask), the latter would still have great value.

Rothbard (1993, 118-133) articulates this perspective with a strange analysis. He shows that the price as determined by the intersection of the standard demand *and* supply curves is the same as that determined by the intersection of the *total* demand curve and the extant stock. The key here is that Rothbard adds the reservation demand[173] of the owners of the stock to

---

[172] Mises (1996, 610) makes a similar mistake when he says: "Wage rates are ultimately determined by the value which the wage earner's fellow citizens attach to his services and achievements. Labor is appraised like a commodity... because the entrepreneurs and capitalists ... are unconditionally subject to the supremacy of the consumers ..." We argue, below, that the consumers' decisions are not the only ones that play a role in this regard. In addition, the decisions of the owners of resources must be taken into account.

[173] At any price, the reservation demand is the difference between the stock and the standard quantity supplied at that price.

the standard demand to arrive at the total demand.[174] Thus when he says that price is determined solely by demand, he is including the reservation demand as well. There is nothing (logically) wrong with such a stance; the difficulty lies in the fact that when words such as demand are used with subtly different definitions than usual, errors are likely to creep in unless extra care is taken.

In the case of oil, this is like saying that an increase in demand caused the price to rise, when it was really due to a boost in the reservation demand part of the total demand. Perhaps his unusual way of looking at the matter is all right for "stock" goods because in such cases there is only one market to consider, the market for the stock, as resource markets are irrelevant. However, even in those cases, price is determined in part by standard demand and in part by reservation demand. The difference is that there are no resource prices to be affected by any changes in valuations. However, for "flow" goods it is confusing, because in their cases, both output and input markets are relevant. Here, if the total demand increases because the standard demand went up then output prices rise first and drag input prices up only afterwards. However, if total demand goes up because reservation demand increases then input prices go up first and push output prices up with a lag.

Gentle reader, please take another look at statement A. Surely that is not what Greenspan meant. It is no more correct to say that input prices determine output prices than it is to say that output prices determine input prices. Both are determined by their relative scarcities, in turn determined by the values of the relevant parties. The price of a final output is determined by the valuations placed on it by the marginal buyer and the marginal seller. The price of a resource is determined in precisely the same way: by the value placed on it by the marginal buyer and the marginal seller. In the case of an ongoing market for a flow, the seller of the output, "the firm," is also the buyer of the resources. In effect, the firm is a middleman, attempting to buy low in the relevant resource markets and sell high in the markets for its outputs. What determines the prices then are the valuations of the sellers of resources, the buyers of the outputs, and the middleman.

Consider the case, where, for whatever reason(s), the buyer(s) of a certain output value it more; i.e., the demand increases; i.e., shifts to the

---

[174] This is quite similar to standard "excess demand" analysis, where, at any price, the excess demand is the difference between the standard quantities demanded and supplied at that price. We have three cases, then. The standard case where the market price is that at which the standard demand and supply curves intersect. Rothbard's case, where the market price is that at which the total demand curve intersects the extant stock. And, the excess demand case, where the market price is that at which the excess demand curve intersects the vertical axis; i.e., at which quantity is zero.

right. Its price will be bid up. As a result it will be more profitable to produce and sell more of that good. In turn, that will lead the firm(s) to place a greater value on the relevant resources; i.e., the demand for them also rises. The firm(s) will bid up their prices. In that case, the rise in the price of the output will lead to a move in the same direction in the price of the relevant resources. Note, however, that neither the augmentation in demand for the output nor for the resources is fully determinative of their prices; rather, in both cases the prices are merely bid up from their prior levels. Both the prior output price and the prior resource prices were determined in part by the relevant supplies. And, how high the various prices will be bid up for any specific increase in valuation, and, therefore, increase in demand, by the buyers of output, will depend in part upon the relevant supply considerations; i.e., the valuations of the sellers. Thus we see that resource prices are not determined *solely* by the demand for outputs[175].

Moreover, if we consider the case where, for whatever reason(s) the seller(s) of a certain resource value it more; i.e., the supply decreases. Its price will be bid up. As a result it will be less profitable to use that resource in production and less will be sold. In turn that will lead the firm to place a greater value on the relevant output; i.e., the supply decreases. Its price will be bid up. In that case, the increase in the price of the resource will lead to a rise in the price of the relevant outputs. Note, however, that neither the decrease in supply of the resources nor the decrease in supply of the outputs is fully determinative of their prices; rather, in both cases the prices are bid up from their prior levels. However, both the prior output price and the prior resource prices were determined in part by the relevant demands. And, how high the various prices will be bid up for any specific increase in valuation, and, therefore, decrease in supply, by the sellers, will depend in part upon the relevant demand considerations; i.e., the valuations of the buyers. Thus we see that output prices are not determined solely by the supply of resources.[176]

Finally, it should be noted that both output and resource price can be affected by changes in valuations of the middleman or middlemen. If they value their own services more, they reduce the supply of output and the demand for resources, causing the prices of output to increase and of resources to decrease, thereby increasing their profit margins and profits.[177]

---

[175] Had we considered the case in which the buyer(s) of a certain output value it less, the analysis would be analogous.

[176] Had we considered the case in which the seller(s) of a certain resource value it less, the analysis would be analogous.

[177] Should they value their services less, the analysis would be analogous.

II. Statement B

Now let us consider B. This statement is completely acceptable to us. After all, it can hardly be denied that supply and demand, or rather the valuations upon which supply and demand are based, are necessary to an analysis of price.[178] It is not for nothing that if you teach a parrot to say "supply and demand" you will at one fell swoop given it a strong hint at solving virtually all economic problems. We mention B in conjunction with A not because we see anything wrong in the former. This is done, rather, in order to further impeach A.

The first thing to note about these statements is that there is a tension between them, not to say a logical inconsistency. According to A, consumer-goods prices fully determine prices of the factors of production that go into their creation. However, based on B, the prices of *all* commercial items, whether consumers' goods or capital goods, including money, are determined by supply and demand. The difficulty, here, is that the supply of the consumption good is based on the supplies of the relevant inputs. Without the latter, there is none of the former. When the former decreases (increases), so does the latter.

Another problem is that A necessarily implies that if the price of a factor of production changed dramatically, it would have *zero* effect on the final good which eventually encompasses it. For example, suppose that a bomb destroyed half the oil capacity of the world, ceteris paribus. Is there any doubt that gasoline prices, a final consumers' good, would rise? Or, posit that a frost ruins half of the entire orange crop? Can it really be doubted that the price of orange juice would catapult upward? But if these deductions are true, it is difficult to credit Salerno's claim to the effect that "they incorrectly believe that changes in these [factor price] indexes are harbingers of future changes in general consumer prices…" (material in brackets supplied by present authors). The increased oil price, in this case *would* be a harbinger of later rises in the cost of gasoline. Similarly, the increase in the price of oranges *would* foreshadow subsequent boosts in orange juice prices.

---

[178] In a barter transaction there is neither supply nor demand in the usual meaning of these terms. Supply relates to the actions of the seller(s), who give up non-money goods in order to acquire money and demand relates to the actions of buyers who give up money in order to get non-money goods. The objective exchange ratios in such transactions are money prices. Money is the only good that has no (non-trivial) money price. As such there is no market for money. Rather, there are as many markets for money as there are non-money goods that people wish to exchange for money. Thus, in a real sense there is neither a demand for, nor a supply of, money; rather, in each market there is a demand for, and supply of, the non-money good

This is not to deny that if the initial price increase was that of gasoline or of orange juice, the subsequent increase in the price of crude oil or of oranges, respectively, would stand in relation to the prior increase in the consumers' goods as effect to cause. However, this is not at all the import of Salerno's statement A.

III. Conclusion

We are in entire accord with Salerno's statement B. Indeed, enthusiastically so. Our problem is not with it, but rather with A. Nor do we deny there is a grain of truth in this problematic statement, as adumbrated by Rothbard. Our claim is that Salerno makes too much of a good thing, far too much, and is thus led into his error.

The point we are making in this article is akin to the one Rothbard (1993, 561) made against the term "consumers' sovereignty and Hutt (1940) and, who is credited with originating the term in 1934 (Rothbard, 1993, 903, n. 3). The latter talked in terms of "consumer sovereignty." Rothbard objected on the ground that this ignored the sovereignty of the producer. His "friendly amendment" to Hutt was to characterize what the latter was addressing as "individual sovereignty" not "consumer sovereignty." In like manner, we object to Salerno and Mises focusing on the consumer, only, at the expense of the producer, in general, or, in this case, the owners of the factors of production, in particular.

Chapter 11. Spreading the Benefits of Productivity Increases: Price Increases, Decreases, Both? A Critique of Baumol on Subsidies to the Arts

Abstract

This paper attempts to grapple with the market mechanism through which growth in one sector of the economy spreads to other sectors. It calls into question Baumol's argument for subsidies to the arts and by extension, to other economic areas that have not enjoyed productivity increases.

I. Introduction

Baumol's cost disease[179] is the name given to the phenomena that many services[180], tend to lag behind material goods in terms of labor productivity increases. For example, consider the efforts of those who play in string quartets or symphony orchestras. It takes just as long to play a Mozart concerto, now, as it did almost three (3) centuries ago[181]. Assuming equal talents on the part of modern and ancient musicians, there has been no technological progress in such endeavors. A similar situation presumably applies to shoe shines, haircuts, massage, music lessons, prostitution and other such "pure" services.

Therefore, the "costs" of producing them and their prices tend to rise faster than those of material goods, making them more expensive and thus we enjoy relatively fewer of them than would otherwise have been the case. Baumol used this phenomenon to argue for government funding of the arts! This is highly problematic. It is a case of confusing absolutes with relatives combined with elitism[182]. That is, with labor productivity increases, the goods produced in the sectors that experience less than average labor

---

[179] Baumol and Bowen, 1965, 1966; Baumol, Baumol and Rubinstein, 1990; see also Cowen, 1998, and Ekelund, and Ritenour, 1999. As for commentaries on the Baumol disease; on 10/11/04, Google listed 3,810 published discussions of this concept (http://www.google.com/search?q=baumol+disease; also http://www.newyorker.com/talk/content/?030707ta_talk_surowiecki; http://www.boekman.nl/summecon.html). Here are a few typical cites: http://www.cpb.nl /nl/cpbreport/2002_3/s2_1.html; http://ideas.repec.org/ p/wpa/wuwpdc/0309007.html.

[180] This applies especially to governmental services.

[181] While it cannot be denied that the complements of these services, such as air conditioning, and transportation to and from the concert hall, have vastly improved, there are even *losses* in technology in this area. For example, the shellac (or is it the glue, or the varnish, or the wood, or the workmanship?) used to manufacture the Stradivarius stringed instruments has been lost, and modern violins, cellos, etc., are in many ways *inferior* to their predecessors.

[182] Baumol and his confreres know we should want to purchase more of the performing—or other—arts than we actually support. Lacking logical consistency, they rightfully refrain from advocating state subsidies to prostitution and other such services.

productivity increases become relatively more expensive in terms of the of the goods produced in the sectors that experienced greater than average labor productivity increases. However, because of the labor productivity increases, society is now objectively wealthier, in that it can produce the same set of goods and have more leisure or with the same amount of leisure produce more of either or both goods. Then, if with labor productivity increases, the quantity of art produced goes down, it is because the substitution effect (working to decrease the quantity of art) outweighed the income/wealth effect (working to increase the quantity of art, presuming art to be a normal good). Or, if art is an inferior good, then the substitution and income/wealth effects work in the same direction (both to reduce the quantity of art)[183].

The present paper attempts to grapple with the market mechanism through which growth in one sector of the economy spreads to other sectors. It calls into question Baumol's argument for subsidies to the arts (and by extension, to other economic areas that have not enjoyed productivity increases. Section II offers an economic analysis of the uneven spread of technological progress across industries. In section III we analyze an example of this phenomenon, and conclude in section IV.

II. Economic Analysis

Increases in labor productivity do not occur simultaneously and are not of the same magnitude across industries, much less individual firms[184]. This raises the issue of how the benefits thereof are spread across the entire economy. And spread they must,[185] else the real gains in profits, wages, and remuneration to other resources consequent on the increased productivity would accrue strictly to the entrepreneurs and suppliers of resources in those specific industries. In such a case entrepreneurs and resource owners would shift resources from other uses and industries to those, thus obviating this possibility. That is, if the benefits of labor productivity improvements are not to be limited to increases in production of those self same industries, but are to result in greater production of other goods as well, then these other industries must also experience increases in real profits, wages, and/or other

[183] This is not a case of the Giffen good. There, when the price goes up (because of a decline in labor productivity) with nominal income unchanged, real income is *reduced.*

[184] We abstract from the causes of the increased labor productivity. Our analysis is invariant with regard to whether this stems from innovation, gains in mobility, education, trade, etc.

[185] Save in the case that people wish to take all of the benefits of the productivity increases in the form of (appropriately) increased quantities of the goods the production of which have been the beneficiaries of the increased productivity. For example, when the car supplanted the horse and buggy industry, logic alone did not rule out that all of the gains would have been taken in the form of improved automobile transportation.

factor compensation. Those must be at the expense of the resources in the enhanced productivity industries, in the sense that the latter's increased real profits, etc., will not be as great as if these industries received all of the benefits of the boosts in labor productivity. The original entrepreneurs and other factor owners in the initially enhanced productivity sector will not receive all the benefits in any case, for if that occurred, entrepreneurs and other resource owners would shift resources to those industries, competing away at least some of these added benefits.

The issue, then, is how the benefits are to be shared more widely.[186] Consider the following example that, though simple, illustrates the ways in which this can be done. Assume a two industry economy, X and Y, in which average labor productivity in X doubles while that in Y does not change.

1) Then, if wage rates in X are increased proportionally to the rise in average labor productivity, profits[187] and factor prices can also be boosted proportionally, in which case factor *shares* of total revenue are unaffected[188]. and all of this without an alteration in the price of X. However, for profits, etc. in Y to maintain their relative positions given the absence of labor productivity gains therein, the price of B will have to climb in the same proportion as labor productivity in X. Therefore, the appropriately weighted average price of X and B will increase, the amount depending on the relative sizes of X and Y, and the size of the productivity rise in X.

2) However, if wage rates, profits, and other factor prices in X are not increased, then the price of A will decrease in inverse proportion[189] to the increase in labor productivity in X[190]. Then, in spite of there being no rise in labor productivity in Y, wages and profits, etc. in Y can maintain their relative positions without any increase in the price of Y.

---

[186] For an interventionist perspective on this, see: Hansen (1964, 679-680).

[187] But not profit margins. The reason for this is that if the profit *margin* rises with labor productivity, that means the *share* of profits in total revenue will increases, whereas if profits rise in pari passu with labor productivity, the share of profits in total revenue will not change. On this, see appendix 1.

[188] Why proportionately? To say so smacks of neutral money, surely a fallacy. The reason is to illustrate the point that productivity gains to labor can be spread not just to labor but to all factors and profits *without* price rises if each factor's payment increases by the amount of gain in labor productivity.

[189]That is, e.g., if productivity increases by X, the price would decrease by 1 – 1/(1+X). Then for a 10% increase, X = 0.1 and the price would have to decrease by 1 – (1/1.1) = .0.1/1.1 = 0.09.

[190] Does this imply that labor is the *only* factor of production in X? The argument in favor of this position is that otherwise, the price of X would decrease, but *less* than in proportion to the increase in labor productivity in X. But the answer to this question is No, it implies that no increase in any other resource is required to increase output.

That is, if nominal factor incomes in the sector with enhanced productivity rise in response thereto, the only way the benefits of such productivity improvements can be spread to other sectors is by price increases in the latter. However, if nominal factor incomes in the sector with increased productivity do not increase, but instead, output prices are decreased, then the factors employed in other sectors can share in the benefits of the rise in productivity without the need to increase output prices. It should be noted that in the former case, productivity increases[191] can and will result in unemployment. The only exception, and this would be coincidental, would be if hoarding; i.e., people's average holding period for money, decreased, or, alternatively, unless the stock of money increased. Such an increase in the case of a commodity money would also be a fortuitous coincidence. However, with fiat money, the government/central bank might get lucky, as they are always increasing the money stock for their own purposes, in any case. This is because in order to receive the benefits of improved productivity, save in the case where all of it is taken in the form of more leisure with no increase in output, a most unlikely occurrence, output must rise. If prices do not fall in proportion to the increases in output, total expenditures must grow. Unless additions are made to the stock of money in proportion to the increase in total expenditures, or hoarding decreases, there will be a disruption in the economy involving "involuntary unemployment," until prices, including that of labor, adjust to the new amounts of output. However, if prices in the sector experiencing productivity gains decrease in proportion thereto, total expenditures would not expand. Therefore, the extant stock of money (without either being supplemented or a decrease in hoarding) would be sufficient to mediate the desired exchanges without the economy having to go through a period of adjustment in which virtually all prices and wages would have to be adjusted – a lengthy and disruptive process, as each entrepreneur searched for his optimal set of prices and wages[192].

---

[191] Such events are devoutly to be desired as the only way to increase general standards of living.

[192] Barnett and Block (2004) claim that the optimal quantity of money is the extant stock *if* it is fiat money, but is the market generated quantity if it is a commodity money. In this case, with a commodity money, if wages rise in the increased productivity sector, and wages and prices in the other sector, the market will respond partly by increasing the stock of money form non-monetary uses of gold, partly by mining and coining new gold, and partly by reducing hoarding; but this will not occur instantaneously and there would be unnecessary unemployment during the adjustment period. However, if instead, prices were decreased in the enhanced productivity sector, there would be no need to enhance the stock of money and/or decrease hoarding, so the spreading of the benefits of the productivity increases would be quicker and less disruptive of the economy, as there would be no need to adjust any wage rates and the only prices that would need to be adjusted (downward)

In sum, it is better to spread productivity increases via output price decreases than by output and factor price increases, which is the likely outcome if government does not interfere.[193] A business *in a free market* is much more likely to prefer to decrease prices of output and try to increase volume and market share than to increase wages and hold prices constant, foregoing the opportunity to use the increased productivity as a means to increase quantity and market share. Of course, in a free market, some entrepreneurs experiencing productivity increases might choose to raise wage rates while holding prices constant or, perhaps, to raise wage rates to some degree and lower prices to some extent. However, they would find either more difficult than simply lowering prices with no change in wage rates, *unless and until* the effective stock of money was increased either by reduced hoarding or by increases in the actual stock itself, either from mining and coining or from the reallocation of gold from other non-monetary uses. Entrepreneurs could be expected to learn this rather rapidly, and thus price reductions, only, would come to be the method of choice for them as they attempted to capitalize on their increased productivity.[194]

III. Empirical illustrations

There are some interesting illustrations of this phenomenon. Although one must always be cautious in making claims of this sort, it seems relatively safe to say that there has been little or no technological or other such progress in the last full century in the following fields: barbering, baby sitting, shoe shining, teaching, lawyering[195], and in several individual crafts such as hand made basket weaving, knitting, crocheting and pottery making. Little or nothing has changed in the way these callings are conducted. Great grandmother probably knitted, for example, in much the same way as does

---

would be those for products the production of which had become more efficient. The same analysis applies to a fiat money system.

[193] More generally, if there are differences in productivity gains in an economy, the only way the those gains can be shared more or less equally among those earning incomes (of various types) in different sectors is by changes in relative output prices. It is far less disruptive if these relative price changes result from price decreases than from increases. If price increases are involved, so also will be wage increases. However, wage increases should be the means by which changes in relative output are brought about, and not a means to distribute widely productivity increases.

[194] If one asks why is this not the usual course of action in modern times, the answer is the inflationary monetary policy of governments combined with less than free labor markets, especially in those industries that typically both experience the largest increases in productivity and are unionized under coercive labor laws.

[195] Objections to teaching and lawyering might possibly be sustained on the ground that computers have promoted progress in these two fields. The argument is strongest in the former case for grades kindergarten through six.

great granddaughter, now. Prostitution, table-waiting, massages, and bartending, probably, are other good examples.

The earnings in of all these cases, however, have risen remarkably since 1904. This is certainly true in terms of money wages; but even real wages are astronomical compared to their levels at the turn of the previous century[196].

Suppose this had not occurred, however. Posit, that is, that wages in terms of real earning power had remained constant in all of these fields that have not (much if at all) experienced productivity gains.[197] Would any worker have stayed in these positions under such unlikely assumptions? Not likely. Instead, there would have been a crawl up and to the left along the downward sloping demand for labor curve, based as it is on a falling marginal productivity function as the supply of labor in those fields decreased. The decline in employment in such arenas would have had one of two results: either the increased marginal productivity would have been sufficient to raise the MRP of labor and other factors to the point where incomes were sufficiently high compared to those in the enhanced productivity sectors, or, eventually, those endeavors could not have commanded any resources and those industries would vanish.

Wages, after all, do not depend solely upon the marginal revenue product in the area in which the worker is employed. The salary of the shoeshine boy is partly dependent upon the productivity in that particular job and partly a function of what he can produce in his *next best* alternative foregone. In 1904, the opportunity cost of the shoe shiner, we may suppose, was as a broom pusher. As neither of these occupations was particularly fruitful in great grandfather's time, wages in both were nothing to write home about. In 2004, the next best alternative foregone by the shoe shiner, we may suppose, is *still* as a broom pusher. But now, thanks to the modern wonders of automatic floor washing and cleaning machinery, the productivity and wages in the latter profession have radically catapulted. But the compensation for the modern shiner of shoes are still linked to that of the floor cleaner. Thus the former "free rides" on the good fortune of the latter. Or, to put this in another way, the technological progress in floor cleaning acts as a sort of "coat tails" for the man who shines our shoes. Of course, productivity increases in other, non-competing sectors also play a role in that as productivity of "suits" increases as do their real wages and thus they can afford to pay more for a

---

[196] See Scholliers (1989). For historical statistics on wages, see http://fisher.lib.virginia.edu/collections/stats/histcensus/. For statistics on teachers' wages, see http://www.uni.edu/museum/school_wages.html.

[197] This, itself, would have required an increase in nominal wages because of governmentally generated price inflation.

shine; i.e., even though the shoe shiners' marginal physical product may have increased little, if any, over the past century, his marginal revenue product has increased as his customers have been willing to pay a higher *real* price for his services. It is this combination of a decreased supply of shoe shine labor because of enhance productivity and thus wages in substitute employment opportunities and an increased demand for such services that has caused real wages in that line of employment to increase sufficiently so that one can still get a shine.

Although for the ease of explication, especially re examples, we have stated our position in terms of a two industry model, with an increase in productivity in one industry and with none in the other, the argument more properly put, though it affects neither the analysis nor conclusions, is in terms of firms *and* in terms of differential productivity gains, not all or nothing. Consider the following examples in tables 1 (scenarios 1-5) and 2 (scenarios 1, 6-8).

Scenario 1 shows two (2) industries, X and Y, identical save for the nature of their outputs. Situation 2 shows the same industries if X experiences a doubling of labor productivity (while there is no change in Y) with the benefits thereof passed on through a doubling of the wage rate and profits in X, with no increase in the price in X. This creates a shift in the relative incomes between those who earn their incomes in X and Y. Then in situation 3, in order to maintain their relative positions, the price of the output of, and the wage rate in, Y is doubled, with attendant doubling of profits. The only differences between X and Y, at this point, is that the quantity of the former has doubled to 200 units while its price is still $10.00, whereas the quantity of the latter has remained the same at 100 units, whilst its price has now doubled to $20. If consumers prefer to take the entire gain from the productivity increase in additional X, the weighted-average price increases to $13.33. In this case, the benefits of the productivity increase are spread pro rata to profit and wage incomes and between industries.

In situation 4 consumers prefer to split evenly the benefit of the productivity gain by increasing each output by the same proportion. And, in situation 5 consumers prefer to receive the benefit of the productivity gain solely in the form of more Y.

We start, again, from situation 1. Productivity again doubles in industry X (with no change in Y). This time the benefits are passed on in the form of a lower price for the output of X. Then, if consumers prefer to take the entire gain from the productivity increase in additional X, situation 6 arises, and the weighted-average price decreases to $6.67. Again, the benefits of the productivity increase are spread pro rata to profit and wage incomes and between industries.

In comparing the two (2) cases we note that in the first, output increases, the weighted average price increases, and total expenditures increase, whereas as in the second case, there is an identical increase in output, but the weighted average price decreases and total expenditures do not change at all.[198]

Situation 7 shows the situation if consumers prefer to split evenly the benefit of the productivity gain by increasing each output by the same proportion. And, situation 8 shows the situation if consumers prefer to receive the benefit of the productivity gain solely in the form of more Y.

IV. Conclusion

We have seen no justification for the Baumol "market failure" argument. This founders on two shoals. First, it is a matter of paternalism to assume that the populace should be forced to pay for more classical music and other "elite" art than it wants. The same argument may be made for rap "music" and prostitution, yet we never find any adherents of this position carrying through on such reductio ad absurda. Second, this entire issue is moot in that the productivity gains in the X industry spread throughout the entire economy into the Y industry. Thus, there is no case for any special treatment of firms in the latter, or service, sector.

---

198 Were there other resources, e.g., raw materials, energy, and machine time, that had to be doubled (or increased in some proportion less than double) in order to double the amount of output using the same amount of labor, the results would be qualitatively, though not quantitatively the same; i.e., in the first case output price would have to more than double and in the second case output price would fall, but by less than 50%.

Table 1

	industry	output	price	revenue	man-hours	wage rate	total wages	profits	weighted-average price
1	X	100.00	$10.00	$1,000.00	80.00	$10.00	$800.00	$200.00	$10.00
	Y	100.00	$10.00	$1,000.00	80.00	$10.00	$800.00	$200.00	
2	X	200.00	$10.00	$2,000.00	80.00	$20.00	$1,600.00	$400.00	$10.00
	Y	100.00	$10.00	$1,000.00	80.00	$10.00	$800.00	$200.00	
3	X	200.00	$10.00	$2,000.00	80.00	$20.00	$1,600.00	$400.00	$13.33
	Y	100.00	$20.00	$2,000.00	80.00	$20.00	$1,600.00	$400.00	
4	X	133.33	$10.00	$1,333.33	53.33	$20.00	$1066.67	$266.67	$15.00
	Y	133.33	$20.00	$2,666.67	106.67	$20.00	$2133.33	$533.33	
5	X	100.00	$10.00	$1,000.00	40.00	$20.00	$800.00	$200.00	$16.00
	Y	150.00	$20.00	$3,000.00	120.00	$20.00	$2,400.00	$600.00	

Table 2

	industry	output	price	revenue	man-hours	wage rate	total wages	profits	weighted-average price
1	X	100.00	$10.00	$1,000.00	80.00	$10.00	$800.00	$200.00	$10.00
	Y	100.00	$10.00	$1,000.00	80.00	$10.00	$800.00	$200.00	
6	X	200.00	$5.00	$1,000.00	80.00	$10.00	$800.00	$200.00	$6.67
	Y	100.00	$10.00	$1,000.00	80.00	$10.00	$800.00	$200.00	
7	X	133.33	$5.00	$666.33	53.33	$10.00	$533.33	$133.33	$7.50
	Y	133.33	$10.00	$1,333.33	106.67	$10.00	$1,066.33	$266.33	
8	X	100.00	$5.00	$500.00	40.00	$10.00	$400.00	$100.00	$8.00
	Y	150.00	$10.00	$1,500.00	120.00	$10.00	$1,200.00	$300.00	

Chapter 12. Rothbard on V shaped average and total cost curves[199]

Rothbard (1993, 638-645) refuted the important economic fallacy that excess capacity is a normal consequence of profit maximizing behavior by businesses in some industries when they are in long-run equilibrium. And, in so doing provided a manifest example of misuse of mathematics in modern economics.

According to standard theory, given a U-shaped, average-cost curve (ACC), in equilibrium, a firm whose demand is perfectly competitive will operate at the point where its horizontal demand curve is just tangent to the ACC; i.e., at the point where average cost (AC) is at its minimum.

Alternatively, a firm in an industry characterized by monopolistic competition will face a downward-sloping demand curve. In that case, again in equilibrium, the firm will operate where the demand curve is just tangent to the U-shaped ACC. However, in that case, the point of tangency will occur at lesser quantity than that at which AC is at its minimum.

Rothbard, however, puts an end to this notion, despite its vast popularity within the profession. He notes that a necessary condition for the above conclusion is that the ACC be *smooth*. As proof, he offers his famous diagram (1993, 644, fig. 72), the essential burden of which is that though the ACC curve slopes downward continuously until it reaches its minimum and then slopes upward continuously, and is in fact a graph of a continuous function, nevertheless the function is not differentiable at critical points, including especially, at its minimum. Our figure 1 accentuates this even more, drawing the ACC not in a "quasi-U" shape, but in a "V" shape. Note that in either of these cases, the downward sloping demand curve can, in contravention of the standard theory, touch[200] the ACC curve at the minimum point of the latter.

Why, in turn, the universal assumption of smoothness on the part of mainstream economists? This is because of their fetish with differentiation and integration. Unless such tools of economic analysis are used, and this certainly includes but is by no means limited to these two techniques, the feeling is widespread amongst the neoclassicals that there is something woefully wrong. However, human action occurs discretely, not in infinitesimally small steps. Mises, (1996, 118) states: "There is neither constancy nor continuity in the valuations and in the formation of exchange ratios between various commodities." Thus, the smooth curve assumptions

---

[199] The authors wish to thank an assiduous and anonymous referee for correcting several errors in an earlier draft of this paper. All remaining mistakes are of course our own responsibility.

[200] Not "be tangent to." The latter is possible only under the assumption of a smooth ACC.

promote mathematical techniques for their own sake, to the denigration of economic considerations. And it is due to the mathematical tail wagging the economic dog, and not the other way around, that we arrive at the fallacy that perfect competition[201] is needed in order to ensure location at the minimum point on the ACC, the fallacy exploded by Rothbard.

So far, so good. However, there are discontinuities, and then there are discontinuities. The difficulty here is with what the ACC in our figure 1 implies with regard to marginal cost, and the marginal cost curve (MCC). To wit, the implication is that there is a discontinuity of gargantuan proportions precisely at the minimum point of the ACC. This makes no *economic* sense.

We realize full well that Rothbard (1993) is only maintaining his position arguendo. He is not at all offering a "quasi-U" shaped, even less our own "V" shaped, ACC, on their own merits. He utilizes them, solely, as a reductio ad absurdum. Nevertheless, fair is fair. It is only proper to acknowledge this shortcoming of the diagram he utilizes to make his point, which we illustrate in our figure 1.

Consider the V-shaped AC curve in figure 1, as per the relevant equation in table 1. It is composed of two straight line segments, one with a negative, and the other with a positive, slope. The AC curve is at its minimum when Q = 10. The relevant MC curve, as per the relevant equation in table 1 lies below the AC curve and decreases continuously up to Q = 10, the Q for which AC is at its minimum. At that exact Q, the MC curve is discontinuous, jumping up above the AC curve and increasing continuously, thereafter. This means that as Q increases from zero units to 10 at which quantity AC is at its minimum: 1) MC is less than AC; 2) MC decreases continuously; and, 3) the (positive) difference between AC and MC becomes continuously greater. Then, when Q hits and continues to increase above that magic quantity, 10, for which AC is at its minimum: 1) MC experiences a discontinuous increase, so that it instantaneously becomes greater than AC; 2) MC increases continuously; and, 3) the (now negative) difference between AC and MC becomes continuously greater.

The equation for total cost (TC) from which the AC and MC were derived can be found in table 1, and the TC curve[202] is exhibited in figure 2.

---

[201] For other criticisms of the perfectly competitive model, see Barnett, Block and Saliba, 2005.

[202] We set the limit at 20 for two reasons, one practical and one theoretical. The practical reason was so that the scaling of the figures would be small enough that the essential features would show up well. The theoretical justification is that given at least one fixed resource, there is an absolute limit to the quantity that can be produced by any single firm; in this case it is 20. At that point all cost curves become perfectly inelastic, i.e., vertical.

Table 1

	For Q: $0 \leq Q \leq 10$	For Q: $10 \leq Q \leq 20$
Total cost	$40\ Q - Q^2$	$20\ Q + Q^2$
Average cost	40 - Q	20 + Q
Marginal cost	40 – 2 Q	20 + 2 Q

This is not to say that a V-shaped average cost curve cannot be drawn, nor that the equation of such a curve cannot be written; i.e., V-shaped cost curves are not erroneous as a matter of mathematics. Rather, they are implausible, to say the least, as a matter of economics.

Rothbard (1993) refuted the standard position by challenging its assumption of U-shaped cost curves by substituting for them a quasi-V-shaped cost curve. In so doing, he implicitly called into question the assumption of differentiability[203], as manifested in U-shaped cost curves. An alternative refutation, which we now propose, confronts the assumption of linear demand curves. That is, we now substitute a non-linear demand curve for the traditionally depicted one.

Consider the non-linear (third-degree polynomial) demand curve in figure 3, as per the relevant equation in table 1. This demand curve slopes downward continuously except, literally, at one point. The revenue functions were chosen such that, when placed in conjunction with the chosen U-shaped AC cost curve,[204] this one point would occur precisely at the quantity where the AC curve is at its minimum. It can be shown that: 1) for any two points on the demand curve, (P_0, Q_0), and (P_1, Q_1), $Q_1 > Q \Leftrightarrow P_1 < P_0$, that in order to sell a greater quantity the price must be reduced; and, 2) that for any $Q \neq 10$, $20\ (Q - 10)^2 + 1000 > -(Q-10)^3 + 1000$, that the demand curve lies below the AC curve, save at the one point, Q = 10, at which they are tangent[205] to each other. This, then, is a second case[206] that also refutes the neoclassical doctrine that only in perfect competition can the demand curve be tangent to the AC curve at the curve's minimum point, and therefore that save for perfectly competitive industries, all others exhibit excess capacity in equilibrium.[207]
The relevant total revenue and cost curves are in figure 4.

---

[203] On the importance and use of differentiability in mainstream economics, see Barnett (2003, 57-59).

[204] A glance at the relevant total cost curve, as given in table 2, reveals the absence of any fixed costs; however, this is as it should be, as we are considering long-run curves.

[205] Not, in this case, merely "touching" one another.

[206] We never in a million years would have thought this one up were we not inspired by the critique offered up by Rothbard. We must therefore thank him for blazing this particular path, as he has done so many others.

[207] This is not to say that every nonlinear demand curve will result in a profit-maximizing firm producing at the minimum AC in long-run equilibrium, but rather that certain specific ones would.

Table 2

	For Q: $Q \geq 0$
Total revenue	$-Q (Q - 10)^3 + 1000Q$
Average revenue	$- (Q - 10)^3 + 1000$
Marginal revenue	$-3Q (Q - 10)^2 + (Q - 10)^3 + 1000$
Total cost	$20Q (Q - 10)^2 + 1000Q$
Average cost	$20 (Q - 10)^2 + 1000$
Marginal cost	$40Q (Q - 10) + 20 (Q - 10)^2$

And just as Rothbard's (1993) refutation required rejecting standard neoclassical assumptions, so does ours. Where he rejected U-shaped cost curves in favor of quasi-V-shaped ones, we reject demand curves whose associated MR curves decline continuously in favor of those whose MR curves decline, then flatten and then decline again. However, it is quite possible, if not even probable, that both Rothbard's cost curves and our demand curves are more realistic than the respective neoclassical counterparts.

Conclusion

It will readily be appreciated that the target of the present paper, as was Rothbard's (1993), is the perversion of economics in behalf of mathematical ease and convenience, on the part of mainstream economists. Rothbard (1993) beat them at their own game. He used the very tools of the neoclassical economists to undermine their profoundly mistaken, and, as it happened, anti free enterprise conclusions. That is to say, he showed that the conclusions reached were the result of trumped up mathematics, not economics. And, by so doing further established the Austrian insight concerning the difference in correct methodology between the natural and human sciences; especially regarding the proper use of mathematics. Our contribution has been to emulate Rothbard (1993) by doing to the mainstream what he did to them, only from the demand and marginal revenue side rather from the perspective of costs and supply.

We do claim superiority over Rothbard[208] in one way. As noted above Rothbard refuted the mainstream by substituting a continuous (cost) curve, but one that was not everywhere differentiable, much less twice differentiable, for their twice-differentiable-everywhere curve. To that extent, he did not adhere fully to their "rules of the game." However, we refuted them by substituting a twice-differentiable-everywhere (demand) curve for their straight-line demand curve which, though it is differentiable everywhere, is not twice differentiable anywhere, save in the trivial sense that the derivative of a function that is a constant is zero (0). Thus we refuted them while adhering fully to their rules of the game.

---

[208] This sometimes occurs when an author stands on the shoulders of a predecessor.

Figure 1

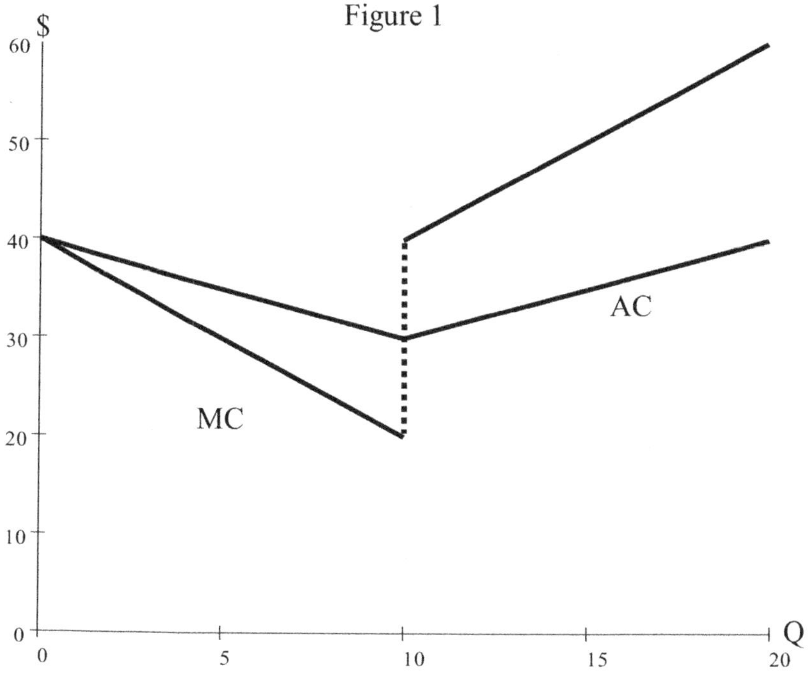

Figure 2

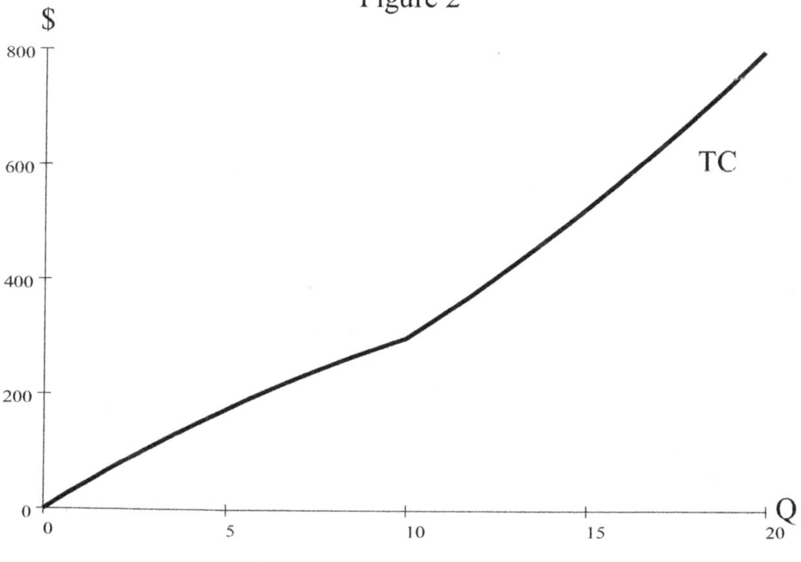

Figure 3

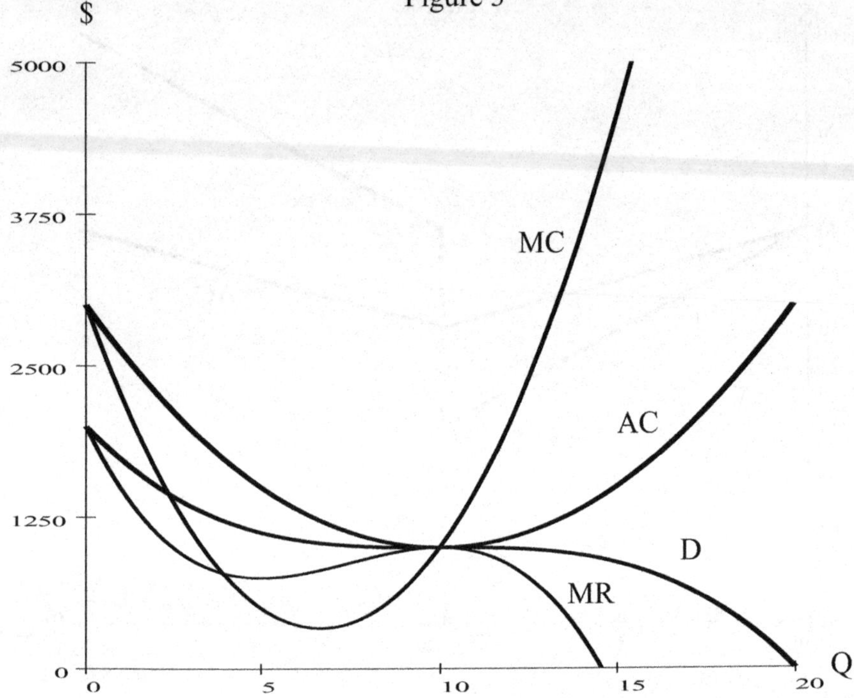

Figure 4

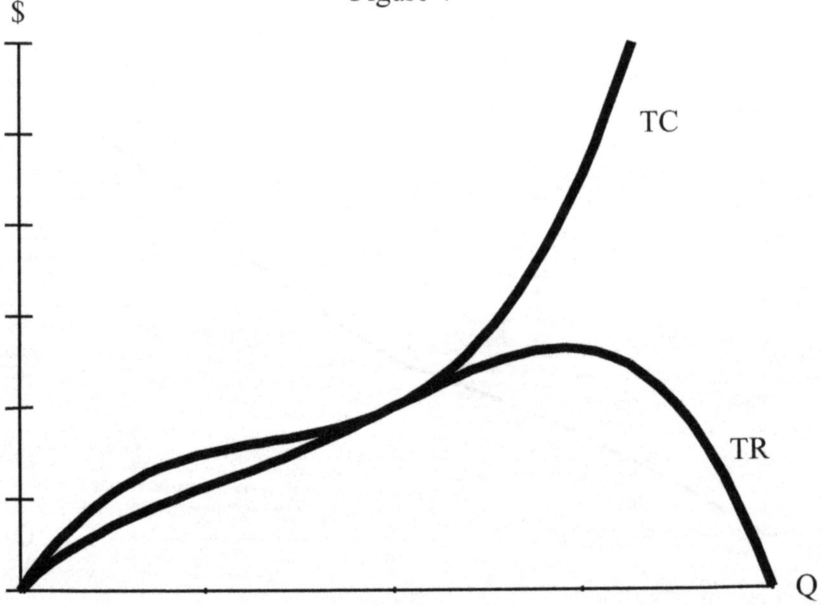

Chapter 13. Predatory Pricing

Abstract

Predatory pricing is logically impossible, because it necessarily involves pricing below cost. However, cost, properly understood as opportunity cost is subjective and is incommensurable with money prices; more important, to price below cost implies rationally choosing an alternative (selling at price) that is suboptimal, since cost is the most highly valued alternative not chosen. When critics declare that predatory pricing is to price below cost, they mean to set a price below some measure of money expenses. But this entails all kinds of problems; which concept of expense – marginal is most obvious; but also the issue of the present value of alternatives, which means discounting expected revenues and expected expenses.

Introduction

Laws against predatory pricing (PP) are a snare and a delusion. They are an internal contradiction in that "predation" implies coercion, while "pricing" at least on the market, is a necessarily voluntary activity[209]. Predatory pricing, then, is a voluntary coercive act, the economic equivalent of the square circle.

This latter internally contradictory phrase offends, only, our sense of logic. It has no practical implication for human action. Things are otherwise, however, as far as PP is concerned. An important aspect of, and a buttress to, anti trust legislation, PP is an incoherent concept which, nevertheless has strong and negative implications for public policy, resource allocation and economic freedom. When businessmen are penalized for engaging in an act that has no referent, that *cannot possibly* have a referent (since it is a self contradiction), it calls into question our entire system of law.

---

[209] That is, under the free enterprise system, people set prices only for what they own; they can only "price" their own private property, which means they can set the terms under which they are prepared to relinquish it. Since this applies to all market participants, without exception, we can conclude that pricing on the market is a mutually agreeable enterprise to all parties to a commercial interaction. In contrast, when government enters into the "pricing field" it typically either compels or prohibits sales at specified prices, or sets maximum (e.g., rent control) or minimum prices (e.g., minimum wages) in what Rothbard (19xx, 19) has called "triangular" intervention. In a free market system, prices are not set. Rather one party, buyer or seller, makes an offer to the other party. If the parties agree there is a price for that transaction; if not, then there is no price. Of course, if no transaction occurs, the process may continue with either party making a subsequent offer until the parties agree, or until one party, or both parties, decide to withdraw from the process.

Any publication that debunks the myth of predatory pricing can only be considered a welcome addition to the literature of economics. Anderson (2003) certainly qualifies in this regard. It cannot be denied that this article does yeoman work in lessening the deleterious power the PP doctrine has over the legal philosophy of our society. Indeed, it makes several important contributions to our understanding of this concept.

The foregoing notwithstanding, there were several errors, infelicities and oversights committed in Anderson (2003). Our attempt to rectify these difficulties is motivated by a desire to strengthen the case made by this author in undermining the injurious pull of the PP philosophy. It is our thought that Anderson has brought the football to the 3 year line, and we would like to help him carry it a few yards further, across the goal line. Any reinforcement of the argument against the PP thesis cannot help but make a positive contribution to our understanding of economic theory.

What, then, are the flaws in this otherwise exemplary piece of economic research? We deal with problems more or less in the order in which they appear, not necessarily in the order of importance.

I. Costs v. expenses

According to Anderson (2003, 26): ".... the costs to firm owners that are relevant are the subjective or implicit costs, which can never be determined by accountants and certainly not in the courts."

While it is true that the relevant costs to the firms' owners are subjective, and cannot be quantified, subjective and implicit are not synonymous, as he implies. This is a common error among neoclassicals, who incorrectly confuse implicit and opportunity costs. The notion of implicit (as well as explicit) "costs" is problematic. There are explicit and implicit expenses and there are opportunity costs.

Expenses are of two types: explicit and implicit. Explicit expenses are out of pocket payments for resources and are approximately the same as accounting expenses. Implicit expenses represent foregone revenues. Both explicit and implicit expenses are objective and therefore quantifiable. However, opportunity cost measures the subjective value of the next best alternative foregone when choosing, and therefore dividing opportunity cost into explicit and implicit categories makes no intuitive sense. Assuming, as many neoclassicals do, that opportunity cost and "implicit cost" are the same is also incorrect. There is such a thing as opportunity cost, but there is no such thing as implicit "cost." There are only implicit expenses.

The concept of opportunity cost is in its entirety an implicit cost, but not in the sense that neoclassicals use implicit cost. For example, when they say that total or full cost is the sum of explicit costs (i.e., accounting costs) and opportunity costs, they are using implicit cost to mean the difference between total cost and explicit cost. This is incorrect. On the other hand, since opportunity cost is the value (or benefit) foregone by choosing one alternative rather than the next best, then opportunity cost is entirely an implicit cost, since it represents value foregone. Thus, in the correct use of the terms expense and cost, opportunity cost and implicit cost are the same, whereas opportunity cost and implicit expenses are obviously not the same.

In the view of Pashigian (1998, 146): "The full price [of either good] is the market price plus the opportunity cost of consuming a good. By opportunity cost we mean the income foregone because of time used in consumption. Because you use t hours to consume each unit of X, your foregone income is wt, and so wt is the opportunity cost of time."

II. Prices

States Anderson (2003, 32): "Furthermore, within a dominant firm-competitive fringe structure, the profit maximizing price of the dominant firm is less than that of the competitive fringe."

It must be remembered here that Anderson is attempting to depict the view of mainstream economists. For Austrians, none of this can even begun to be said, since adherents of the praxeological approach do not buy into the perfectly competitive vs. the monopolistic model upon which are based Anderson's diagrams. But, if one is attempting to articulate the neoclassical vision, even if only to show its flaws, it is preferable to do this accurately.

In the present case, however, this claim of Anderson's is counter to the standard neoclassical assumption that: dominant firm maximizes profits knowing the market demand and the competitive fringe's supply, and that the competitive fringe maximizes profits acting as a "price taker," taking the price set by the dominant firm as a given.

"The only way that it would be possible for consumer prices to rise above where they were in Figure I would be for the predatory firm's costs to remain the same while the demand curve it faces has become steeper, or if the fall in factor prices had less effect than the change in demand that the new monopoly would face" Anderson (2003, 33). But that is precisely, the point. Anderson has gotten to concentrating on costs as if the primary benefit from reduced competition was to be had in factor markets rather than output markets. In fact, it is the other way around.

Let us analyze Anderson's point in two ways. First, the only way that it would be possible for consumer prices *not* to rise above where they were in Figure I would be for the predatory firm's resource prices to fall to such an extent that, while the demand curve it faces has become steeper, the effect of the falling resource prices would more than offset the combined effects of the less elastic demand and diminishing returns. Second, the only way that it would be possible for consumer prices *not* to rise above where they were in Figure 1 would be for total industry volume to increase, or at least not decrease, after the predation had eliminated the predator's competition. That is, the predator would have to expand output enough to completely cover for the output of its former competitors that would no longer be available.

He then misses the point in the very next paragraph: "This assumption [that the fall in factor prices had less effect than the change in demand and, therefore that consumer prices would increase] is based upon the premise that factor prices in this particular industry are impervious to demand, which can only be true in a constant cost industry. In the case of an increasing cost industry, however, if other competitors are eliminated and the predatory firm is not able to expand its operations to bring production to previous industry levels, then it stands to reason that factor prices will fall" Anderson (2003, 33).

There are several errors therein, from a neoclassical point of view. First, he is incorrect when he states that factor prices can be impervious to demand only in a constant cost industry. For factor prices to be impervious to demand, the demand therefore must be perfectly elastic. This never occurs in neoclassical theory for factor demand for them is the product of marginal revenue and marginal product. Now, even when they assume that the demand for the relevant output is perfectly elastic so that marginal revenue equals price, they always acknowledge diminishing returns. That is why they always have downward sloping factor demand curves even when they assume perfect competition in output markets. Second, a constant cost industry is a long run concept. It is one in which there are neither economies of diseconomies of scale. In such a case, the minimum atc for any given atc curve is the same. As costs involve both input prices and physical productivity, such an industry would require that that as inputs prices increased with the scale of the industry, physical productivity would also increase, and that in the exact degree so that the two offset each other at the minimum points of the different short-run atc curves; or, and this is their usual assumption, factor prices remain constant and physical productivity is the same at different scales, and, therefore, the minimum point every short-run atc curve occurs at the same cost. Third, he implies that predatory firm would seek to bring production to previous industry levels but might not be able to expand its operations to that level.

Of course, the predator has no desire to expand output to the previous industry level, save in the most unrealistic case that the fall in factor prices is so great as to overcome the price increasing effects both of diminishing returns and of the decreasing elasticity of demand. Fourth, if firms "are not able to expand operations to bring its production to previous industry levels," or do not seek to do so, the vastly more likely case, then industry volume will be reduced; as there is no reason to think that industry demand would have decreased, the reduced volume; i.e., the reduction in industry supply with the fixed demand will result in higher prices.[210]

Moreover, Anderson (2003, 34) maintains that: "As pointed out earlier, given the assumptions of the model, the profit-maximizing firm is not free necessarily free to charge higher prices, since its actions are limited to looking for the profit maximizing output and price. Even if the firm did manage to drive out all other competition through predatory pricing, that does not mean the firm will be *raising* prices, Figure 3 demonstrating that, indeed, prices theoretically could be *lower* after the successful predation has taken place. This solution – and it is plausible, given the assumptions of the model – clearly does not demonstrate that predatory pricing need be a menace to consumers" (footnote omitted). But the neoclassicals' concern with predatory pricing is precisely that consumers will be harmed, in that after the predation is successful, the predator will increase output insufficiently to offset the loss of output consequent on the demise of his competitors and raise prices. They fear, then, that consumers will acquire less output and pay higher prices therefore, which results they do see as a menace to consumers.

III. Post-predation "costs"

Anderson (2003, 32) also assumes that costs [for the predator] are reduced: "Thus all cost [expense] curves [for the dominant firm] are shifted to the right…."

This is correct. However, the predator will be further up the lower curves. He may face lower per unit expenses for *resources*, but he is necessarily expanding his output (how much would depend not only on his expenses, but also on the relationship between his prior demand and his new demand (the industry demand, if he drives all of the other firms out), and diminishing returns could cause his per unit expenses for *output* to increase; i.e., the "costs" he is referring to are per unit of output; these are affected by per unit expenses of resources and the productivity of the resources. With fewer firms in the industry, the assumption is that the demand for resources will decline reducing the prices thereof; however, the firm's resource productivities also will decline as it expands output. Which, if either will dominate is indeterminate in the general case.

---

[210] Technically, in neoclassical theory there is no "the" supply for an industry, or for that matter for any firm facing a downward sloping demand curve. Profit maximizing neoclassical firms are produce that quantity for which marginal revenue is equal to marginal cost, and then charge the maximum price buyers will pay for that quantity. Then, for any given mc curve, two (2) or more different mr curves can intersect it at the same quantity. As each of the mr curves is derived from a different demand curve, with a different price for the quantity at which mc = mr, the minimum price that the profit maximizing firm would be willing to sell a given quantity for depends not only on its marginal cost (as would be the case if the firm were in a perfectly competitive market), but also on the demand curve.

Anderson (2003, 32-33) claims:

"At the same time, assuming an increasing cost [expense] industry, a lack of competitors that factor prices most likely would be driven down which is why the cost [expense] curves have shifted to the right from their original positions in Figures 1 and 2."

While this may seem to be a valid approach to analyzing predatory pricing, there are a number of problems that must be discussed. First, if this is a correct scenario, one cannot claim harm to consumers at any point of the process, since the entire operation has resulted in lower prices.

This is incorrect. It is to be expected that, after the demise of his competitors, the predator would increase output. However, he certainly would not increase it sufficiently to compensate for the entire reduction in output consequent on the demise of his competitors. That means that total output of the industry would decline and that, therefore, the price would go up; i.e., there would be a reduction in industry supply and a reduction in the (industry) quantity demanded with resultant higher price. Anderson is clearly in error here. He seems to assume (in the same paragraph, unknowingly we think, that the decline in factor prices resulting from the demise of competitors would be so great, that despite diminishing returns, the predators costs would fall to such an extent that he would expand output beyond what both he and his competitors were selling previously. That is the only way that price could be lower than before he undertook the predation. Given that the predatory firm is dominant in the industry, and, therefore, the one that buys the (vast) majority of resources, the decline in prices of resources is likely to be small. Moreover, to the extent that, after the demise of its competitor, the predator firm increases its output,[211] it will require additional resources, and this even if it is more productive than the eliminated firms; e.g., dominant firm (D) was producing 100Y using 50X. The fringe firm(s) (F) were producing 20Y using 15X. After F's demise, the demand for X drops from 65x to 50 X. If D then wishes to increase output to 110Y, where it might have taken F, say 7X, to produce 10Y, it might only take D say, 6X to produce the additional 10Y. Thus, demand for X, originally 65, would fall to 50 with the demise of F, but then rise to 56 with D's increase in output. Therefore, demand would not fall as much as if there had been no response by D. Moreover, the less specialized the inputs, the less will the price fall, as they can find employment in other industries or, for labor, idleness, or for other resources, (physical) idleness.

[211] The raison d'etre of predatory pricing is, precisely, to be able to sell a larger volume and that at higher prices; i.e., it is combination of higher prices and greater quantity.

IV. Elasticity of demand and the slope of the demand curve

Moreover Anderson (2003, 32) also states: "Because other competitors are gone, we can assume (as I noted earlier) that the monopoly faces a less elastic (steeper) demand curve than it faced when other firms were in the industry." Although he is correct that the firm faces a less elastic demand curve, he equates less elastic with a steeper curve, which is not *necessarily* correct. The steepness of a curve is given by its slope, in the case of a demand curve, dP/dQ; however, the elasticity depends not only on the steepness, but also on the location; i.e., the elasticity is given by $(dQ/dP)/(Q/P)$, where the numerator is the slope of the curve that must be evaluated at the relevant point, and the denominator, which must also be evaluated at the relevant point, is, so to speak, the locator of the relevant point; i.e., it is the ratio of distance on the Q axis to that on the P axis. An example that demonstrates the incorrectness of his position is that the elasticity at any given price is the same for every straight-line demand curve that intercepts the price axis at the same point, regardless of the difference in steepness of these curves.

V. Profits

"Another point to make is that one cannot determine whether or not the profits enjoyed by the firm in Figure 3 are higher than the profits the firm was earning in Figure 1. In other words, we cannot determine *a priori*, given the assumptions of the model, if the firm's profits earned after it has eliminated its competition are more than its profits when it was an industry in which there was at least some competition between member firms" (Anderson, 2003, 33).

This is arrant incorrect. If you can't tell from his curves in figures 3 and 1 it is because one set is not superimposed upon the other or because one (or both) sets are drawn incorrectly. Of greater importance is that, according to neoclassical theory, there are two (2) possible effects of the predatory action: first, demand is increased; and, second input prices decline. Of course, it is the former that is the motivation behind predatory pricing. Consider the following scenarios.

1. No change in input prices and demand increases in such fashion that MR = ME at the same Q. In this case P will increase. With no change in input prices and the same Q, total expenses remain constant; however, with the same Q and a higher P, profits necessarily increase.

2. No change in input prices and demand increases in such fashion that MR = ME at a greater Q. In this case, the MR curve has shifted to the right. In this case, profits on the original quantity increase by an amount measured by the area between the new and old MR curves from the price axis to the original quantity. In addition profits are also increased by an amount measured by the area between the new MR curve and the ME curve from the original quantity to the new quantity.

3. Input prices[212] decrease and demand is constant. In that case the ME curve will shift down and will necessarily intersect the (original) MR at a higher Q. In that case, profits increase by an amount measured by the area under the (original) ME curve and the new ME from the price axis to the original Q. In addition profits are also increased by an amount measured by the area between the MR curve and the new ME curve from the original quantity to the new quantity.

4. Obviously, if, in addition to the decrease in input prices, demand also increased, prices would increase as a result of the demand increase and profits would go up on that account as well.

Anderson (2003, 33) also states: "It might be possible to construct graphical models in a way that demonstrates that the firm that successfully drives out its competitors through predatory pricing will also be earning more profits afterward. …However, it is important to note that such a construction would be *no less arbitrary* than the figures presented in Figures 1-3." etc.

This is incorrect. In point of fact his curves are drawn incorrectly. The avc curves in figures 1 and 2 appear to be at their respective minimums at the same q (q_m) as their atc curves; that is in each figure, the atc and avc appear to be at a minimum at the same q; however, this is only accurate for situations in which avc = atc; i.e., in which there are no fixed "costs." If there are fixed costs, then the avc hits its minimum at both a lower q and lower cost. One consequence of this is that, because the mc curves in figures 1 and 2 slope upward, as they should, and also appear to cross the relevant avc curves at their minimums, which is as it should be, they do not cross the relevant atc curves at their minimums. However, both economic theory and mathematics require that the mc curve cross the atc curve at the latter's minimum.

Once the curves are drawn correctly, with the mc, avc, and atc curves shifted downward and with the demand curve shifted upward, it is obvious that profits increase. Which, of course, is why, according to neoclassical theory, a firm might engage in predatory pricing.

Moreover, Anderson (2003, 34) states, "…even if the 'predatory' firm, after successfully engaging in predatory pricing, does practice price discrimination, it does not change the outcome of my analysis." With the decrease in elasticity of demand consequent on the elimination of

---

[212] We assume that these are variable input prices. If fixed input prices decreased, neither would the mc nor avc curves shift. Only the atc curve would shift downward. In that case, even if demand did increase with the elimination of competition, the profit maximizing price, quantity, and variable costs would remain the same. That is total revenue and variable cost would not change, and with the reduced fixed costs, profits would necessarily increase. And, if demand increased, as of course it would in the real world, profits would, a fortiori, increase.

competition, price discrimination would increase revenues even without an increase in output sold. And, given that quantity would increase, revenue would increase even more with price discrimination than without it. In any case profits would be greater with price discrimination than without it. Moreover, the added factor of price discrimination makes it even more certain that prices would be higher than before predation. Not only would factor costs have to decrease to the extent necessary to offset diminishing returns, on the one hand, and increased demand, yet less elastic demand, but it they would also have to decrease an additional amount to offset the increased revenues from the price discrimination.

VI. Equilibrium

Anderson (2003, 34) maintains that because: "...is already at an equilibrium point *from which there is on incentive to move*." He notes that at "the price the firm receives and its output level at mc = mr there are no more gains from trade" to be had.

This is only correct for neoclassical analysis in the short-run.[213] Neoclassicals recognize that in the long run a firm tries to maximize its present value. A firm can be in short-run equilibrium and still take actions that might lower its short-run profits in order to increase its expected future cash flows sufficiently to more than outweigh any short-run losses associated therewith. Of course, his point that, assuming a downward sloping demand curve (i.e., the absence of the imaginary neoclassical state of perfect competition), trading at the level where mr = mc exhausts the potential gains from exchange, as the firm sees them, is correct. In such case, the only way neoclassicals can maintain that exchanges between that quantity and the quantity at which p = mc create gains from exchange is to ignore distribution effects, as if such effects have no bearing on the economic well-being of the parties involved.

Alternatively, given factor prices, the firm's productivity, and the pre-predation structure of the market re demand, production at the quantity for which mc = mr does exhaust the potential gains from exchange from the firm's point of view. However, the primary purpose of predatory pricing is to alter the market structure in such way as to increase demand for the firms output, allowing it to both sell more and charge a higher price.

Therefore, although all short-run gains may be exhausted at mc = mr, there are long-run gains to be had from predatory pricing whose discounted expected future profits exceeds the short-run losses the firm incurs when it

---

[213] As our analysis here is with respect to per period total cash inflows and outflows, it is unnecessary to consider the elements of cash outflows. Therefore, we can ignore the neoclassical error of not discounting the (expected) marginal revenue products of the various factors in order to arrive at the factor demands.

lowers price in order to sell more and drive its competitors from the market. That is, the sum of the discounted net cash flows from operating so that mc = mr equals mr every period, is less than the expected discounted net cash flows from operating at mc > mr in the current period, or perhaps the next few periods, given that the losses in the current period are in the form of an investment designed to change the market structure in such a way that operating at mc = mr in the periods beyond those necessary to drive competitors form the market and change its structure will yield greater expected profits that will be manifested as an increased net present value of the firm.

Chapter 14. Coase and Van Zandt on Lighthouses[214]

Abstract

The issue of which, if any, goods are "public goods," is important for public policy, as mainstream economics maintains that such goods will not be provided (adequately) by free markets. Rather, if society is to have (efficient amounts of) public goods, government intervention in some form is required. Traditionally, lighthouses, along with national defense, were held up as the quintessential examples of such public goods that require governmental intervention if they are to be provided (in optimal amounts). However, this changed with Coase's celebrated 1988[1974B] article "The Lighthouse in Economics." He maintained and is widely credited with proving that, historically, the market; i.e., free enterprise, provided lighthouse services.

Our thesis is that while Van Zandt showed Coase's claim to be mistaken on the basis of this valid criticism of Coase, Van Zandt erroneously concludes that private lighthouses were *not* historically operational. The truth of the matter, we aver, is that private lighthouses were indeed historically operational, and that while Van Zandt provides evidence for this claim, he fails to recognize it as such.

Introduction

Coase maintains, and is widely credited with proving that, historically, the market provided lighthouse services for a profit. One thesis of this paper is that this is not what he actually did. Second to national defense, perhaps, the relatively lowly lighthouse is the example that has played the largest role in the mainstream economic profession's analysis of what they call public goods.[215] Neoclassical economists have used the lighthouse to underscore their claim of market failure: free enterprise is congenitally and necessarily incapable of providing (optimal amounts of) certain needed goods and services; in order to make good this lacunae, government is justified[216] in filling in the gap. Due to this tireless intellectual

---

[214] The present authors have published many papers, and thus have received many referee's reports, but never in their experience have they received two more thoughtful and thorough reactions to an earlier draft of their paper than from two referees of This Journal. We thank them for their efforts.

[215] "It is a proper office of government to build and maintain lighthouses, establish buoys, etc. for the security of navigation: for since it is impossible that the ships at sea which are benefited by a lighthouse, should be made to pay a toll on the occasion of its use, no one would build lighthouses from motives of personal interest, unless indemnified and rewarded from a compulsory levy made by the state." Mill, 1965, 968.

[216] This claim conflates normative and positive economics. Even if we were to concede *arguendo* that private individuals were unable to produce some items useful to them, it still would not logically follow that government, a legal monopolist of the

assault, virtually every economist agrees that the market had always failed, and necessarily so, to make available this service, or at least not adequately.

But then came the reaction. Coase (1988 [1974B])[217] strongly argued that history provided examples of lighthouses that *had* been supplied by private profit seeking entrepreneurs, and thus this item could not serve as an example of a public good, with all of its implied criticism of markets and support for government intervention. In his article Coase talks repeatedly of private lighthouses: lighthouses built, owned, and maintained by private interests. As a result of this article, a number of other economists have taken the position that Coase, by giving the history of, and describing, the British lighthouse system, proved that lighthouses are not a public good, as defined by neoclassicists.[218]

Since we shall maintain in the present article that Coase has indeed made the incorrect claim that the lighthouse was once a private enterprise, it is incumbent upon us to document the facts. This we do in section 2. In section 3 we provide evidence that many have been mislead by the counter-factual claim that a system of free enterprise lighthouses existed, and give an example of the improper use to which it can be put. We discuss the theory of public goods in section 4, and in section 5 offer some contrary-to-fact conditional speculations as to how a private lighthouse industry *might* have functioned, there being no evidence that it actually *did*. Section 6 considers an objection Coase might make, regarding "voluntary taxation." In section 7 we consider the views of Van Zandt and conclude in section 8.

Coase's view of the lighthouse

That Coase thought he had established the historical fact that private entrepreneurs had provided sea-going beacons on a profit-making basis is evidenced by his article to this effect. Coase correctly points out that institutions are of vital importance in economic analysis; this insight runs like a thread throughout virtually all of his writings. It is no exaggeration to say that he is an institutions man *par excellence.* Unfortunately, in this case, apparently because of his concentration on institutional detail, he overlooks[219] the critical fact that he himself provides: the revenues were extracted by the government – i.e., they were collected as a form of taxation.

---

use of force, would be *justified* in coercing people into financing these products. For that conclusion, an ethical argument is needed in the premises, one that cannot be supplied by positive economics.

[217] All further cites to Coase are to this article, by page number only. For support of the Coase position, see Barrowclough (1999), Cowen (1988), Peacock (1979) and Spulber (2002).

[218] One of the present authors (Block and Yeatts, 1999-2000) has made this mistake.

[219] For support of this claim, see Bertrand (2006), Foldvary (2003), Van Zandt (1993).

Even the Board of Trade recognized this when it stated: "Their Lordships cannot admit that is any violation of the principle of property in the reduction of a *tax* levied for public purposes, where no vested interests have been acquired in the proceeds of the *tax*; and where the tax in question is one levied upon a particular class of Your Majesty's subjects, without that class deriving any adequate advantage in return (and any excess of light *dues* beyond the amount necessary to maintain the lights is a *tax* of this character), the reduction of such a *tax* not only involves no violation of the principle of property, but is in the highest degree just and expedient" (emphases added).[220]

Coase himself quotes the Board of Trade to this effect. However, he may disagree as to whether it really was a tax. As far as Coase's history of the lighthouse is concerned, his own words refute him. There is a bit of the passing in the night problem between Coase and the typical mainstream, public-goods = market-failure, economist. The latter maintains that the neoclassical free-rider problem consists of an inability of truly-private lighthouse owners to collect sufficient revenues to warrant such an undertaking in the first place; i.e., left to its own devices, a full free enterprise system would not be able to provide (a sufficient number of) beacons at sea even though their "true value" would exceed their costs, because free-riding users would not reveal their true preferences.

In contrast Coase holds that private lighthouses can work if they are supported by "dues" (i.e., taxes), and makes his case that specific dues are superior to general taxes. He says that the average economic practitioner is mistaken regarding the relative efficiency of dues and general taxes: if dues are used some ship owner might not make a voyage that would require their payment, even though the cost of providing the spotlight to him is zero; i.e., the marginal cost of his use is nil. Coase prefers the dues/tax (i.e., user fee or tax) system to general taxes. Nevertheless, he (212) maintains, on the basis of the British experience, "a lighthouse service can be provided by private enterprise." But this is erroneous, in that extracting one's revenues by force or the threat thereof is not at all a legitimate means of engaging in "private enterprise."[221]

Specifically, Coase (212) states: "The role of government was limited to the establishment and enforcement of property rights in the lighthouse." Because, as he showed, the lighthouse owners were compensated from tolls *levied* on the ship owners, either this statement is incorrect or the property rights of a lighthouse owner includes the legal

---

[220] Report from the Select Committee on Lighthouses, in Parliament Papers, Session 1845, Vol. 9 at vi, as cited in Coase (206).

[221] Shoup (1969) has suggested that the dues/taxes discussion could be clarified if the distinction between *charges* (i.e., benefit taxes) and *taxes* (general revenues) became the standard language.

ability to tax people who benefit or, at least, can be supposed to benefit from looking at his light(house). That is, the role of government was *not* limited to the establishment and enforcement of property rights. Rather, the authorities *forced* ship owners to pay the private beacon owner for this service; these funds were *not* paid voluntarily.[222]

Coasean misinterpreters

The following are examples of what the majority of economists think Coase proved:

Coase's article is referred to as, "An important study of how what was until recently commonly cited as a public good incapable of production on the market (because consumers could not be excluded) was indeed produced through methods of exclusion (fees charged at ports)."[223] The gist of this comment is that Coase in effect overturned economists who maintain that markets cannot (adequately) function in the face of the public-goods character of the lighthouse.

"For decades, standard economic textbooks had loftily explained that lighthouses could never be supplied privately, because ships at sea benefit from the light whether or not they pay. But one day free-market economist Ronald Coase decided to do some research, and discovered that … lighthouses in Britain had in the past been supplied privately for many years. True, it was impossible to exclude non-contributors from the light of the lighthouse - but it *was* possible to exclude non-contributors from using the harbor, so the lighthouse fees were simply packaged with the harbor fees."[224]

Nothing could be further from the truth, insofar as Coase fails to distinguish between the free enterprise system, in which customers are as free to purchase a good or service as they are to pass it by, and a system wherein consumers are *forced* to pay for an item whether they wish to do so or not.

The lighthouse logo, it would appear, is a very popular one. Another organization, a think tank devoted to free enterprise, credits Coase for their lighthouse emblem: "The Independent Institute's logo was inspired by Ronald Coase's renowned … 'The Lighthouse in Economics.' Until that time, conventional wisdom from John Stuart Mill to Paul Samuelson had claimed that the lighthouse was the quintessential 'public good,' which allegedly had to be provided by government due to the inherent free-riding of those who could not be charged for the services being provided. Coase showed, however, that in Britain, 'contrary to the belief of many economists, a lighthouse service can be provided by private enterprise... The lighthouses were built, operated,

---

[222] See section VI, *infra*, on the "voluntariness" of the lighthouse fees.

[223] Included in Cowen (1988).

[224] http://freenation.org/a/f2114.html; accessed on 9/19/06

financed and owned by private individuals, who could sell a lighthouse or dispose of it by bequest. The role of the government was limited to the establishment and enforcement of property rights in the lighthouse.'"[225]

Sechrest (2003 244) says: "For many years, lighthouses were cited right along with national defense as an allegedly clear-cut example of a public good that required the involvement of government. Then Coase ... took the time to investigate the actual history of lighthouse operation in that nation where maritime issues have probably played a greater role than in any other: Great Britain. He found that the building and operating of lighthouses by private firms was quite common.... Owners of these structures gained their revenue from fees paid by ship-owners, the beneficiaries of the service."

Having seen how Coase's erroneous position regarding lighthouses has been widely accepted even by free enterprise advocates as proof that public goods such as lighthouses can be provided by private businesses, let us now consider an example of how "Coase's lighthouse" can be, and is, misused by the advocates of ever more governmental intervention to support intrusion into the market for the purpose of providing so called "global public goods."

This is from a UN web site[226] touting a book (Kaul 1999) on "global public goods." Under the caption: "The Lighthouse Story" there is an explanation of why this edifice appears: "The lighthouse on the cover is a useful icon for two reasons. First, it is a classic example of a public good: all passing ships benefit from its light, which is available to each of them undiminished regardless of their number. Second, the history of lighthouses illustrates an important message of this volume – that public goods need not be directly provided by governments. Over the centuries lighthouses have been built and operated by private investors, shipping guilds and public-private partnerships, in addition to government agencies. For more on the early history of lighthouses, we recommend Ronald Coase's article, 'The Lighthouse in Economics.'" These same web pages contain a quote from Kofi Anan, Secretary-General of the UN: "It is not beyond the power of political volition to tip the scales towards a more secure peace, greater economic well-being, social justice and environmental sustainability. But no country can achieve these global public goods on its own, and neither can the global marketplace. Thus our efforts must now focus on global public goods."

<u>The theory of public goods</u>

According to Coase (212): "The early history (of the British system) shows that contrary to the belief of many economists, a lighthouse service can be provided by private enterprise. In those days, ship-owners and shippers

---

225 http://www.independent.org/tii/tii_info/lighthse.html; accessed on 8/22/06

226 The site begins at http://www.undp.org/globalpublicgoods/text/Lighthouse/lighthouse.html; accessed on 8/22/06 and has links to the other relevant web pages.

could petition the Crown to allow a private individual to construct a lighthouse and to levy a (specified) toll on ships benefiting from it. The lighthouses were built, operated, financed and owned by private individuals… The role of the government was limited to the establishment and enforcement of property rights in the lighthouse. The charges were collected at the ports by agents for the lighthouses. The problem of enforcement was no different for them than for other suppliers of goods and services to the ship-owner."

The key word, here, is "benefiting." Note, Coase does not say, "a private individual (could) levy a toll on ships *agreeing to pay for* the lighthouse services." Rather, he states, "a private individual (could) levy a toll on ships *benefiting from* the lighthouse services." However, there is all the world of difference between "benefiting from" and "agreeing to pay for." In the latter case, we are well within the realm of the free enterprise, private property rights system. This, after all, is a paradigm case of capitalist markets. We pay you for your newspaper because we *agree* to do so. If all that were required is that we *benefit* from it, and this can be adduced *without* our assent, then the essence of a free market – voluntary interaction – has vanished in one fell swoop. For example, under this principle someone picking up and reading a discarded newspaper has benefited therefrom and should, or at least could, be forced to pay the paper company for the benefits received, as appraised by -, well, by who - the paper company, the government? Woe betide us if this principle of "free enterprise" becomes the general rule enforced by government in all such cases of benefits.

An alternative vision

According to the overwhelming majority of economists, the light-house cannot be (optimally) provided by free enterprise; so much the worse for the market. In the view of Coase, the capitalist system can indeed supply lighthouses. However, as we have seen, insofar as lighthouses are concerned, his concept of the private enterprise/free market system is unacceptable.

What, then, for the contention that this apparatus will be forthcoming in the truly free society? Without Coase's examples, we are vouchsafed no known cases of this phenomenon. However, here is a scenario in which lighthouses *could* be rendered objects of profit making. The key is to somehow make it in the interest of the ship owner to pay voluntarily for the provision of the requisite light. How might the owner of this equipment induce the captain of the boat to purchase this service?

A possibility might be for the owner to threaten to extinguish the illumination on any dark night where the only vessel in the vicinity belongs to a non-payer. How could the lighthouse firm determine who was whom out there? Perhaps in the early evening, before the time of greatest darkness, with the aid of a spy glass, this might be accomplished; the lighthouse entrepreneur would have to be very careful, lest one of his own paying customers smashes on the rocks. All clients of the lighthouse might file trip plans with him; there might be some "dark and stormy night" when none of them was scheduled to be in the vicinity.

To be sure, the non-payer need not worry, unduly, that the lights would usually be shut off when he was in the neighborhood. Often, he would be able to free ride on the efforts of others. But all it would take is one time for his craft to be placed in great danger. The sailors he hires would know this, too. Due to the extra danger to which they are subjected by this high-risk commercial behavior, the economic law of compensating differentials implies that the wages of these seamen would be higher than otherwise. It is a matter of (contrary to fact [Ferguson 1999]) economic history whether or not there would be any holdouts on the part of members of the sailing industry. It is not necessary for every last ship owner to sign on with the lighthouse owner to make the latter a commercially viable capitalist enterprise. All that is required, is that there are *enough* voluntary payments to at least defray the out-of-pocket and alternative costs of those who wish to enter this profession.

Owners must carry insurance on their ships, else they will not be able to finance them. The cargoes must be insured or no one will risk them at sea. Any ship owner trying to increase profits by avoiding payment for relevant safety services; such as lighthouses, would find themselves[227] paying more for insurance than their competitors. Their customers also would have to pay higher insurance fees when using their ships rather than those of their competitors. Therefore, any likely savings from free riding would likely be offset in the form of higher insurance fees.

Moreover, let one non-paying ship owner crash on the rocks in the absence of the light which was purposefully extinguished due to the fact that no funds were forthcoming from him, that would serve as an object lesson for all others who do not wish to avail themselves of this service. They might then well rethink their position. But this extreme scenario is by no means necessary to attain the smooth working of the system. At the very least, on those times when the lights are shut off, the captain of the vessel will have to slow down his rate of speed through the water. But "time is money,"[228] this is a costly choice, which may well, all on its own, be more expensive than voluntarily paying the lighthouse keeper.

Even if the so-called free-rider problem were to somehow preclude the commercial provision of lighthouses, the difficulty could still be solved in

---

[227] It is immaterial whether the cargo owners pay directly for cargo insurance or the ship owners pay such and pass the expense along in the form of higher shipping fees.

[228] It is a commonly held view among owners and agents that a ship is only "making money" when it is at sea. That is one reason they are continually seeking to reduce "turn-around time" in port.

the absence of government intervention through the good offices of the voluntary or charitable sector. That is, an association of boaters could chip in for lighthouse services; this would be neither governmental nor a commercial for-profit initiative. Because such actions would be voluntary they would be part of the free enterprise system, which is the concatenation of all voluntary (e.g., non statist) acts. Of course, offering this alternative might well be interpreted as an attempt to hide the free-rider problem under the rug: what would be the incentive for all boat owners to join the organization? If they would not pay the lighthouse directly, why would they fork over cash to this voluntary association? The answer is that an ideology opposed to markets that might motivate shippers to boycott the commercial enterprise, might yet allow them to join such an association. There is a sense of "belonging"[229] that might motivate those who would spurn one type of voluntary interaction to embrace yet another.

Coase does not at all agree. He refutes a version of this scenario offered by Arrow (1969 1: 47, 58): "To simplify matters, I will abstract from uncertainty so that the lighthouse keeper knows exactly when each ship will need its service… Assume further that only one ship will be within the range of the lighthouse at any moment. Then exclusion is perfectly possible; the lighthouse need only shut off its light when a nonpaying ship is coming into range." Coase (212 fn. 42) rebuts this contention as follows: "Arrow's surrealistic picture of a lighthouse keeper shutting off the light as soon as it became useful while arguing with the captain about the charge to be made (assuming that the vessel has not run on the rocks in the meantime) bears no relation to the situation faced by those responsible for lighthouse policy. In Britain, no negotiation has been required to determine individual charges[230] and no lighthouse keeper has ever turned off the light for this purpose."

The real problem with Arrow's analysis is not that it is unrealistic. Arrow explicitly acknowledges this. Rather, the difficulty is that he has abstracted from all of the important issues, those that determine whether or not this industry can be a viably profitable one. *Of course*, the provider of the beacon will threaten to or actually turn it off if he is sure there is only one boat within range, and that single party has refused to pay for this service.[231]

---

[229] Consider in this regard the recent outpouring of donations for the victims of the 911 tragedy in NYC not only from within the U.S. but also from around the world.

[230] The use of "individual charges" and the implication that a price would have to be negotiated for each instance of lighthouse service is highly problematic. Coase (197) states: "The toll varied with the lighthouse and the ships paid a toll varying with the size of the vessel, for each lighthouse passed." Certainly, negotiations would not take place on an individual-instance-of-use.

[231] We ignore any tort liability that might arise under a legal system gone haywire. In a truly free enterprise system, no such liability would arise in such a situation.

This is precisely the business strategy adopted throughout the entire economy: if you do not pay for a good or a service offered commercially, you do not get it. The problem is: How can the owner of the lighthouse be sure that only non-payers are within range of his beacon, such that he does not shut it off in the face of those who have paid him to keep it on? Or, more generally, how can this private entrepreneur collect fees for his services on a *voluntary* basis when there are those who would like to use it without paying?

Coase's answer indicates that his claim of free enterprise in the case of lighthouses is mistaken. Rather, he replies that: "no negotiation has been required to determine individual charges and no lighthouse keeper has ever turned off the light for this purpose." But this is not responsive to the point made by Arrow. The issue is not the mechanics of the negotiations, but the cost-effective ability to determine when, and the legal right to, shut off the light. Coase "refutes" a non-issue. The real concern is the extent to which an enterprise can be called free if it cannot state its intent to turn off the spigot unless it is paid, and then actually do so if the payments are not voluntary; that does not "negotiate" over its fees[232] and, can charge "customers" a fee[233] whether or not they agree to pay it.

As to the "lighthouse keeper shutting off the light as soon as it became useful while arguing with the captain about the charge to be made (assuming that the vessel has not run on the rocks in the meantime)," the issue under discussion is not that of price determination but, rather whether this service can be put on a private profit-making basis. The way Coase characterizes the matter, since the beacon is useful, it ought not to be shut off to non-payers, even if it could be, even if, that is, the owner could distinguish between customers and non-customers, as Arrow stipulates. But this denies entrepreneurship. He is not in business (solely) for benevolent reasons. He also wants to earn a profit and needs to if he is to remain one.

<u>On the voluntariness of taxes</u>

Coase was mistaken in claiming that the lighthouse industry, as he depicted it, was a free enterprise; given that the relevant payments, call them what you will – dues, or tolls, or levies, or taxes – were compulsory, this can not be reconciled with markets, where *all* commercial interaction takes place

---

[232] This latter consideration is of less importance, as it might be compatible with a private industry subject to price controls. For example, landlords under rent control cannot "negotiate" with their tenants as to rent levels, and yet this industry still has many of the earmarks of a private one. An industry is considered part of the capitalist system *to the extent* it is free to undertake these roles.

[233] Coase (213) describes Trinity House as "a private organization with public duties, but the service continued to be financed by tolls levied on ships." The very nature of "levying" is coercive; any activity involving a levy *de facto* is not part of the private marketplace.

on a strictly voluntary basis. However, there is an objection to our thesis open to Coase: these payments might ostensibly have been compulsory, but insofar as they were *requested* of the Crown by the very shippers called upon to pay them, they were, on a deeper or more profound level, really voluntary. If he succeeds in this defense, our thesis loses all validity. In this regard Coase (1988 192) states: "The method used by private individuals to avoid infringing Trinity House's statutory authority [as the only body with authority to construct lighthouse] was to obtain a patent from the Crown which empowered them to build a lighthouse and to levy tolls on ships presumed to benefit from it. The way this was done was to present a petition from ship-owners and shippers in which they said they would greatly benefit from the lighthouse and were willing to pay the toll. Signatures were, I assume, obtained in the way signatures to petitions are normally obtained, but no doubt they often represented a genuine expression of opinion. The King presumably used these grants of patents on occasion as a means of rewarding those who had served him."[234]

One might argue that since the ship-owners signed a petition stating their willingness to pay, the levies were not taxes at all, but, rather, voluntary payments for desired services rendered. However, were that true, then all that would have been necessary was a patent to build, own, and operate a light-house; there would have be no need for the patent to include a right to *levy* tolls. Moreover, even if some can be said to have paid the tax voluntarily,[235] certainly the same could not be said for others. That is, at best, Coase shows not that these levies were voluntary but only that for *some* people, e.g., the ship owners who signed the petition, these payments may have been voluntary, while for others, e.g., those who had *not* agreed to it, they were not. But in the market place, *all* consumers take part under their own steam.

It is likely that in the situation reported on by Coase, there were other things going on, apart from an attempt on the part of ship owners to promote safety. First, some shippers might have seen the obligatory fees as ways to impose a disadvantage on their competitors, who would not voluntarily agree to pay for lighthouse services under the imposed tariff rates. Second, that the King gave such patents to his favorites indicates the possible presence of monopoly pricing elements; i.e., the rates would have been above free market

---

[234] This is an odd form of "free enterprise": prospective lighthouse builders must get governmental permission to enter the business and governmental permission to levy fees on probable beneficiaries.

[235] It would be exceedingly difficult to demonstrate any such thing (Rothbard, 1997I). Suppose someone were to "voluntarily donate" some money to George Bush so that he could finance his Iraqi troop "surge." Is it beyond belief that he would be thereby attempting to curry favor with the present Republican administration, perhaps so that the IRS would go easy on him?

levels, did such exist, and therefore, the ship owners had to be forced to pay. That this privileging of some at the expense of others was later taken over by Parliament only strengthens this point.

In this interpretation, those ship owners who signed the petition were *not* volunteering to pay for lighthouse services. Rather, they were agreeing to pay the government for its service of forcing other ship owners to make payments against their will. To compel unwilling ship owners to defray part of the cost of the lighthouses, thereby providing a subsidy to the petitioners; to force added expenses onto competitors in hope of gaining a competitive advantage; to restrict entry into the industry by potential competitors; and, perhaps, in league with the lighthouse owners/monopolists to receive a kick-back from the monopoly profits to be earned.

Van Zandt

Van Zandt (1993) supports our main thesis; to wit, that Coase (1974B) was erroneous in his contention that the lighthouse constitutes a real world counterexample to the mainstream economic view that this service cannot be (adequately) provided on a market due to its public goods nature.

Van Zandt (1993 48, 56) states: "My thesis is that the term 'private enterprise' hardly captures the reality of the provision of lighthouse services. For the period Coase surveyed (Great Britain from 1513 to 1898) and both prior and subsequent periods, the government played a substantively greater role in the provision of lighthouse services than Coase's term 'private' suggests… Instead of a dichotomy between private and government provision, we might imagine a continuum between the poles of pure private provision with no government support to full governmental provision out of general revenues. In the case of lighthouses, it might include these different points: (1) private provision with no government enforcement of property or contract rights; (2) private provision with government enforcement of property and contract rights only; (3) private provision with government fixing rates, granting monopolies, and enforcing collection of specified user levies; (4) government provision from collection of specified user levies; and (5) government provision from general revenues.

In fact, the lighthouses that have existed fall into categories 3, 4, or 5…There are … no examples of lighthouses operating in the pristine 'private' world (category 2) in which the government only protected property entitlements and enforced consensual deals."[236]

---

[236] Here is Van Zandt (1993, 58) on the historical material examined in Coase (1974B): "Even within that material… there is a range of institutional structures in the provision of lighthouse services. The one structure conspicuously absent is private provision with minimal state involvement."

However, while Van Zandt (1993) does indeed put paid to the notion that Coase has shown that lighthouses operated privately, he has, in the process, committed errors of his own that should be rectified.[237] Not the least of these mistakes is that, ironically, Van Zandt's own research (1993 56) indicates that Coase was indeed *correct* in his claim that, historically, some lighthouses operated privately (i.e., they deserve to be classified in his own category (2) – "private provision with government enforcement of property and contract rights only.") The difficulty is that Van Zandt's concept of what his own category (2) really means is so clouded that he did not recognize that, in his attempt to call Coase's thesis into question, he was actually providing evidence to support it. As it happens, this discovery does not obviate our own critique of Coase, above, since if Van Zandt did not fully recognize the import of his category (2), the apparent source of Coase's error was a failure to make the distinctions Van Zandt made, thereby conflating categories 1, 2, and 3. Category 1 is a free market by any standard; category 2 is a free market by the standard of the night-watchman state; however, category 3 is not a free market by any standard. Because Coase's example fell into 3 which he conflated with 1 and 2 his error followed. For these reasons we review Coase (1974B) through the prism of Van Zandt (1993), and to focus on the weaknesses (as well as the strengths) of the latter.

Private lighthouses

Let us begin by attempting to make good on our somewhat surprising claim that there were indeed private lighthouses, so that Coase (1974B) was ultimately and paradoxically correct in his claims to this effect; 2. this "defense" of Coase is highly problematic, in that the examples he (Coase) cited to this end were invalid; 3. Van Zandt (1993) properly criticizes Coase (1974B) for misconstruing the status of lighthouses; and 4. Van Zandt (1993) himself falls into the opposite error; where Coase claimed that his examples were of private provision when they were not, Van Zandt claims that his own examples were not of private provision when they were.

Let us first consider the "smoking guns." This is the evidence adduced by Van Zandt that, *despite* his unwillingness or inability to acknowledge it as such, shows that there really were lighthouses that operated on a basis *fully compatible* with laissez faire principles. That is, it

---

[237] A referee of this Journal characterized our paper thus: "it is necessarily intriguing to publish an argument that a Nobel Prize winning economist was ultimately right, but for the wrong reasons. To add to the fun, the argument is of course that the Van Zandt criticisms that have long been viewed as debunking Coase (although ignored by free market 'acolytes' of Coase) were themselves correct, but sufficiently incomplete so as to be inadequate condemnations of the central point being made by Coase. If this sounds like a soap opera, it is. But why limit that art form to day-time television?"

shows that there really were lighthouses that operated with government doing *no more* than protecting private property and enforcing contracts, and, most emphatically, *not* forcing unwilling boat owners to pay for lighthouse services against their wills: Exhibit "A" (Van Zandt, 1993 56): "There are, however, no examples of lighthouses operating in the pristine 'private' world (category 2) in which the government only protected property entitlements and enforced consensual deals. In almost every case, the government did much more.... The only exceptions to this generalization were the lighthouses provided by religious persons or entities."

Thus, there *were* cases of truly private lighthouses. Coase's conclusion, then, is sustained; however, not by his own evidence, but rather Van Zandt's.

The obvious rejoinder to this claim of ours is that there are really three categories of economic activity: 1) governmental; 2) private for-profit; and, 3) religious/charitable, this latter completely different from either of the others. Thus, our critique of Van Zandt cannot be sustained, it will be charged. We appear to infer from his words the existence of private profit-making-business operation of lighthouses; we do so incorrectly, since Van Zandt (1993 56) supports the existence of this "third" part of the economy, the voluntary, eleemosynary sector.

There can be no doubt that for certain purposes it makes sense to divide up the economy into these three categories. Each of them is different enough from the other two to support such a tripartite distinction. Government is the only one that necessarily initiates force.[238] Market participants are the only ones who seek profits.[239] The voluntary charitable sector is the only one motivated mainly by benevolence.[240] However, our present purposes are different. We are now attempting to determine whether

---

[238] This is not to deny that *some* non governmental agents are guilty of coercion; examples: the Mafia, the Blood, the Crips. But *all* states initiate violence against their citizens; indeed, this is one of their defining characteristics (the other being that they claim a monopoly of "legitimate" violence in a given geographical area; http://en.wikipedia.org/wiki/Government)

[239] This is true in the narrow sense of monetary gain. In fact, *all* of human action is an attempt to better one's condition over what it would have been in the absence of the act (Mises, 1957).

[240] This is an empirical statement. The founders/members of many such operations do so with altruistic motives; however, as much as the capture theory of regulation explains how/why the vested interests in the regulated industry capture the regulatory process in conjunction with the political side at the expense of the consumers, quite a few charities are captured by self-interested parties who siphon off the "profits" in the form of higher than market salaries and perks. They tend to get away with this because the donors accomplish their own goals merely by donating.

or not the voluntary-charitable sector is to be placed in the public or private category. Coase (1974B) after all, claims that "his" lighthouses were an example of the latter, and the present authors, as well as Foldvary (2003), Bertrand (2006)[241] and Van Zandt (1993) maintain he did not prove his case. For these purposes, then, there can only be a two-part distinction, not a tripartite one.[242] Thus, voluntary-charitable actions must be categorized *either* as market or as governmental acts; i.e., either as voluntary or coerced. When put in so stark a manner, it is clear that the answer must be the former (Hughes, 1987, 1989, 1990). The essential criterion for distinguishing categories of human action in the present context is voluntariness v. coercion. On this basis it is obvious that private businesses and voluntary charities must be placed in the same category, while government is in the other one.

Exhibit "B" (Van Zandt, 1993 56, inserted material and emphasis added): "… in those [voluntary charitable] cases, while the government was not always involved, it is likely that similar *socially coercive* devices were used to overcome the particular problems of the lighthouse."

This is an attempt on Van Zandt's part to explain how user fees were generated without governmental coercion; i.e., how the so-called "free-rider" problem was solved. But it fails. The difficulty is that the phrase "*socially coercive* devices" is a misnomer. The devices referred to were not coercive at all. Rather, they are non-coercive forms of social pressure; e.g., being looked down upon by all and sundry, or garnering a bad reputation. This sort of thing is ubiquitous in society. The reason for instance, apart from an internal moral sense, we pay for the newspapers we pick up at the stand when the vendor has his back turned to us and there are no policeman in sight, is the fear of social opprobrium.[243] This sort of thing runs like a thread throughout virtually *all* of social interaction. To claim that this is somehow the same as governmental coercion is to render meaningless the distinction between private interaction and state compulsion.[244]

---

[241] In Barnett and Block (2009) we distinguish our views from those of this author.

[242] A similar phenomenon arises with regard to consumers and producers goods; these, together, exhaust the possibilities. In which category, then, is money to be placed? In the latter, argue Barnett and Block (2005).

[243] There is a connection between this moral sense and social sanctions. The reason one expects society to sanction certain behavior is because those acts violate that society's ethical sense.

[244] Making this distinction is not to deny that a continuum exists. The fact that we commonly distinguish between red and orange does not mean they do not meld into one another. There is a continuum between voluntary and coerced behavior. Thus, we recognize a continuum between total freedom and total lack of freedom.

Another way to put this is that these "*socially coercive* devices" are *precisely* the manner in which the market internalizes externalities.[245] Because he maintains that such sanctions would be either non-existent or insufficiently strong, Van Zandt thinks government intervention to cure "market failures" is justified. That is, without them, and the sense of morality that underlies them, people would steal anything not nailed down provided, only, they thought they could get away with it. Under such circumstances, the lion's share of the GDP would have to be devoted to protecting people's lives, liberty, and property. That we do not live in such a milieu should be obvious. But why expect it, alone, in the case of ship owners trying to evade lighthouse fees?

Exhibit "C": Van Zandt (1993 59, emphasis added) states "... the discernable historical examples ... about lonely hermits or religious orders providing lighthouse services gratis or in the hopes of contributions ... are *few and far between.*" However, *"few and far between"* means not that they did not exist, but that they *did.*[246] Since they were provided "gratis or in the hopes of contributions," does this mean they were really not part of the private sector?[247] Most emphatically not. Whether these services were provided gratis, or with the hope or expectation of voluntary contributions, the beneficiaries were not *compelled* to pay for them.

Exhibit "D" consists of yet another example of the private enterprise operation of a lighthouse, again not recognized as such by Van Zandt (1993 60-61, emphasis added), but dismissed on the spurious ground that because "social pressure" was brought to bear on users to pay for this service this in some way made them involuntary; i.e., compelled: "*Almost without fail,* these lighthouses provided by religious hermits or orders served local ports. While *they did not have the support of the government to exclude free riders,* they could call on a range of *nonlegal* social and religious sanctions to support their work. Particularly with regard to local lights, the social pressure to contribute to lights intended to protect the lives and livelihoods of family and friends *must have been great.*" But "*almost* without fail" logically

[245] Another way to deal with the so-called "free rider" problem is to internalize this externality by privatizing the ports, and the owners of these ports assigning construction and maintenance of these lighthouses, presumably within the limits of the port, edifices to their owners (see Van Zandt, 1993, p. 59). This would suffice, only, for lighting up the area under the control of the port owner.

[246] It also means that there were fewer than Van Zandt wanted, or expected, or deemed optimal, based upon subjective criteria known only to him, but that is entirely another matter.

[247] Van Zandt (1993, p. 59, ft. 38) says of the lighthouse manned by one Richard the Hermit at the Chapel of Saint Michael of Brea in Cornwell, "it is unclear whether the payments were voluntary or mandatory." So here we have yet another possible example of the market in operation in this industry.

implies that *at least some* of these lighthouses served *not* "local ports," but rather those, according to public goods theory, which would be even more difficult, if not impossible, for private interests to serve. Thus Van Zandt's contentions that, because private non-governmental lighthouses never functioned in history, Coase (1974B) was in error, stand condemned out of his (Van Zandt's) own mouth.

If these private religious order or hermit-run lighthouses *did not have the support of the government to exclude free riders*, that is all that is needed to infer the correctness of Coase's (1974B) *conclusion* to the effect that government support was not needed for this industry, in any case not more than described by category 2 ("private provision with government enforcement of property and contract rights only.") The word "*nonlegal*" in the phrase "*nonlegal* social and religious sanctions," must not be interpreted as *illegal.* Perhaps a better word choice on Van Zandt's part would have been "*alegal*" or, even better, private, if he wished to imply that these pressures were not mandated by law. But if the pressures amounted to shunning, or boycott, or refusal to offer religious services, they are certainly compatible with the operation of the free enterprise voluntary market sector.

The fact that these pressures "*must have been great*" does not lessen the claim that the operation of these lighthouses fell within the nexus of laissez faire capitalism. There is all the world of difference between the application of force, a la government, and the use of social opprobrium to rein in so called "free riders." The former is incompatible with markets, the latter is not.[248]

Exhibit "E" again supports Coase's (1974B) conclusion, albeit not his reasoning, and undermines Van Zandt's (1993 68, emphasis added) denial of this conclusion: "In 1619, Sir John Killegrew obtained a patent to build a lighthouse on Lizard Point, Cornwall. Although *the patent expressly forbade the erection of other lights in the vicinity, it did not authorize the forced levy of dues, only the collection of voluntary contributions.*" This cannot be considered a case that fully reflects markets. First of all, under free enterprise, limited to category 2, one need not seek any special permission to build anything. Governmental grants of patents, whether to build a lighthouse or for discoveries, inventions, intellectual property (Kinsella 2001) are incompatible with the capitalist order. Second, the patent in question, in

---

[248]Van Zandt (1993, p. 61, ft. 45) seems to understand this point when it comes to the operation of private turnpike roads, even those that incurred losses, but not lighthouses. He says of the former "Still, private subscribers continued to pour capital into turnpike schemes" despite the existence of "analogous … if less severe problems of exclusion." But if there is not even a question as to whether there existed private, non-governmental turnpike roads, and the two industries are "analogous," it is surprising that Van Zandt does not acknowledge the same in the case of roads.

prohibiting the erection of competing lighthouses, was incompatible with the free enterprise ethic.[249]

Public goods and excludability

Van Zandt (1993 56) appears to argue that it is lack of excludability of non-payers that has prevented private lighthouses from springing up on a profit-making basis; that this amenity thus constitutes a "public good." But as he himself concedes (1993 51, footnote omitted, emphasis added) there is an underlying cause of this state of affairs: "...international waters are free to ships of all nations, and territorial or national waters, in most nations, are public ways that *cannot* be owned or controlled by private citizens." This author goes so far down the radical path toward ocean privatization as to entertain the notion that "it might even be that the legal rule of freedom of the seas actually reduced seafaring traffic by suppressing the provision of navigational guidance so necessary for safe transport." Of *course* under the present legal regime "the lighthouse operator can make no credible threat to a passing ship that he will withhold the service unless he is paid a fee."[250] It is only due to the fact that ownership of the sea is precluded as a legal option, that "non-excludability" comes into play; it is *not* because there is anything intrinsic about water resources that is susceptible to so called market failure. If land were not allowed to be owned privately, the same difficulties would arise. "Freedom of the seas" is a recipe for, and has generated the problem of the commons with respect to water no less than the "right" to walk around wherever one pleases, without regard for property titles, is a guarantee that the tragedy of the commons will occur on land.

Indeed, the same problem *does* arise on land. The law presently prevents private individuals from owning roads and highways, too (apart from some very few private toll roads in the U.S., today). Thus, no one can have a profit making interest in providing lighthouses on land (e.g., street lights, lamp posts) either. But this difficulty, too, does not emanate from anything intrinsic to the situation. There is, after all, such a thing as private railroads, and they have no trouble in providing whatever illumination they require. Similarly, this problem does not arise in stores, shopping malls, hallways, restaurants, or, indeed, any other privately owned real estate structures. Here, too, there *might* be a problem of providing overhead lighting. Without private property, no one would have a "credible threat" to

---

[249] Van Zandt (1993, p. 68) expressly calls this provision "monopolistic." Here, in emphasizing the "express forbidding" of other lighthouses in the neighborhood, he is adopting the correct, Austrian, interpretation of monopoly and competition, and eschewing his own neoclassical interpretation.

[250] We suggest, supra, that the lighthouse owner does have at least a semi credible threat: to turn off the light whenever there are no other ships benefiting from it beside the non-payer.

withhold illumination unless one were paid. Typically, however, this service is provided as part of a package deal; the landlord provides light bulbs, and incorporates their cost into the rent. Were oceans put on a capitalist basis, this system might be employed there as well.

Van Zandt (1993 52) acknowledges that "the problem of excludability is a contingent one." That is, it depends upon the underlying institutional arrangements concerning property rights. But this means that there is no such thing as an excludability problem, or a public good, per se, and that the *only* consideration is to get these things "right." He goes so far as to state (1993 53) "Calling such things 'public goods' misses the point; they are only 'public goods' within a particular legal and technological context."

On technology, Van Zandt (1993 52-53) is of the view that "Given the nature of the good, excluding free riders can be more or less costly. But that cost depends on the existing technologies of collecting." Yes, true. But this is superficial. For technology, in turn, depends upon the level of economic freedom prevalent in a society. It is no accident that not too much new technology emanates from North Korea or Cuba. Moreover, in addition to technology, there is entrepreneurship, ignored by this author. The point is, private entrepreneurs, who have to pass the market test of profit and loss, are far more likely to develop new, cost-efficient, technologies and reduce costs for any given level of technology than are government bureaucrats owning civil "service" sinecures. Based on all of our experience with public and private enterprise, it is exceedingly likely that private lighthouse owners would figure out the most cost-efficient ways to: 1) provide lighthouse services; and, 2) collect voluntary payments for providing these services.

States Van Zandt (1993 54) regarding excludability and small numbers: "… neither requires unusual governmental involvement in the provision of lighthouse services as an a priori matter… Whether or not the service will be provided depends on whether the costs of providing it (including the costs of collecting) are exceeded by the revenues collected. And the cost of provision in turn depends on the available technology for both producing the service and collecting for it."

Our problem with this is that while it is correct as far as it goes, it does not go far enough. For the "available technology" itself will depend upon the underlying institutional arrangements. If they are based on private property and the rule of law, technology, in both respects, will be far more advanced, ceteris paribus, then if they are based on government ownership, regulation and control, and/or "the tragedy" of commons ownership. Even assuming a given level of technology, firms can be expected to lower costs of collection and production below those which prevail in government.

Small numbers

Another problem faced by would-be, private, lighthouse owners, according to Van Zandt (1993 53), is that "even if a passing ship could be identified and excluded from the service unless it entered a contract, there would be only one buyer and one seller and 'no competitive forces to drive the two into competitive equilibrium.'"[251]

But there is no such thing as a "competitive equilibrium" in the real world of human action. To think that there would be "no competitive forces" is to misunderstand the nature of competition in general, and, in particular, as would be manifest in a lighthouse situation. But this stems, solely, from a mischievous albeit ubiquitous conception of competition. According to the neoclassicals, the primary determinant of the level of competition is the number of competitors.[252] This is incorrect. The essence of competition is the attempt by a would-be seller (buyer) to entice a potential buyer (seller) to engage in an exchange. This means that the would-be seller (buyer) has to offer the potential buyer (seller) a better, from the latter's point-of-view, deal than anyone else, which includes, a fortiori, the potential buyer (seller) himself; i.e., the possibility that the potential trading partner will not view any offer as acceptable. Even if there is only one seller and buyer, each has to compete, by attempting to offer a better deal, if he is to entice the other into an exchange.

Van Zandt (1993 53-54) himself considers that lighthouse owners could, ex ante, establish and promulgate a fee schedule. In this case any opportunistic behavior by the lighthouse owner would result in a diminution of reputation that would prove costly as ships would seek alternate routes not dependent on that lighthouse. However, he suggests that "the level of traffic and the frequency of interactions" might be insufficient for the potential cost in terms of reputation to be effective. And, in this respect he also suggests the cost of such an approach might be excessively high. But this ignores entrepreneurs' constant attempts to discover and use more cost efficient methods to collect voluntary payments. He states that, as an alternative: "They [ship-owners] could...negotiate a set of fees for their ships ahead of

---

[251] The internal quotation is from: Arrow (1969).

[252] Competition is properly defined only in terms of legal entry: if it is not illegal to compete, then there can be competition even with one business in the field. The difficulty with the mainstream perspective is a reductio ad absurdum: it would render not only lighthouses "noncompetitive," it would do the same for a myriad of other goods and services. The only pharmacy in a small town would be "noncompetitive" on this basis. But each of us, indeed, is different than everyone else, and to that extent there are no "competitors" for any our services. On these grounds the lighthouse is no different than many other industries, and if so, we cannot account for its unique position.

time" (Van Zandt 1993 53). Again, he suggests that this might not be possible for "technological" reasons. But firms in the free market are adept at solving just this type of problem.

Van Zandt's instincts are sound. He (1993 53) rejects this because "it is not clear that this is a theoretically insurmountable problem." But his solution to this non-existent challenge is problematic. Based upon his flawed notion of competition he is led into embracing, of all things, price controls: "The solution would seem to be to establish a standard schedule of fees, in much the same way that supermarkets and taxis operate. The lighthouse operator could make it well known and a matter of his reputation that his charges will be announced. Thus, there is no point in bargaining with him. In addition, if he tries to deviate from the schedule, ship captains will soon realize the operator's propensity for this type of strategic behavior and make adjustments. They could either stop using the lighthouse or negotiate a set of fees for their ships ahead of time" (Van Zandt 1993 53).

But supermarkets and taxis are apples and oranges. Taxi rates are usually, if not always, set by governments, whereas the prices supermarket charge are set privately. The former is obviously a form of price controls and therefore, as we note above, problematical. The latter is not, as it is a free market practice.

Where his problem lies is with Van Zandt's concern with the "problem of small numbers" insofar as free markets are concerned. He states: "The effectiveness of this type of reputational enforcement, however, depends on the level of traffic and frequency of interactions between the lighthouse operator and ship captains. Essentially the lighthouse captain must bind himself to his schedule of fixed rates and forgo the tempting alternative of raising the price once the ship captain has chosen to run his route by the lighthouse. Particularly with respect to foreign or nonlocal vessels, it may be hard for the lighthouse operator to do this. He may not have reasonably cheap means at his disposal to announce his intention to all possible passing ships and to bind himself to follow that intention. If he cannot do this, many ships may choose to avoid the lighthouse by taking a more circuitous route. As a consequence, the lighthouse's revenues would be depressed and would threaten the economic viability of the enterprise" (Van Zandt 1993 53-54).

But the lighthouse owner does not need to reach "all possible passing ships." Of relevance is not how "many ships may choose to avoid the lighthouse," but, rather, how many choose *not* to avoid the lighthouse; i.e., how many choose to use the services of the lighthouse. There are a variety of "reasonably cheap means" to promulgate pricing policies, including word-of-mouth, in a relatively small community such as ship captains. There are also reasonably cheap means by which the lighthouse operators can bind themselves; e.g., "A binding obligation may even originate in advertisements addressed to the general public. A positive offer may be made by an advertisement or general notice in a newspaper" (17 Am Jur 2d, Contracts § 34). Therefore, Van Zandt's concerns that a free market might not work because of the alleged problem of "small numbers" are mistaken.

The role of government

Van Zandt (1993 54) points out that: "Pareto-optimal allocations of resources can occur because the ship owners and lighthouse operators are forced by market exchanges to reveal their true preferences," but that this did not occur during the historical period studied by Coase. The reason is that the ship-owners were coerced by the Crown into paying fees set by the government. A close reading of Coase (1974B) indicates that some ship-owners colluded with the lighthouse owners to obtain legislation forcing all ship-owners to pay. Obviously, the colluding ship-owners valued the service and, presumably would have been willing to voluntarily pay for it, had not they had the option of coercing others into sharing the expense.

Conclusion

Our misgivings with Coase (1974B) are that none of his examples of "private lighthouses" were cases of true free enterprise – very much to the contrary of his thesis, government forced unwilling boat owners to pay for services against their will – and yet he falsely concluded that this *was* an example of laissez faire capitalism in action. Our difficulties with Van Zandt (1993) are that *some* of the examples he employed *were indeed* cases of free enterprise in operation, and yet he falsely *denied* that they were.[253] Coase (1974B) was *correct* in his *conclusion* that private lighthouse operations took place, but his *argument* was erroneous in that he marshaled no facts in support of this correct (as it turned out) allegation. Indeed, the historical record he cited vitiates *against* his conclusion. Van Zandt (1993) was exactly on point in criticizing this error of Coase (1974B).[254] But in making the case against Coase (1974B), Van Zandt (1993) made the opposite error; failing to recognize markets of his own citation. Coase made a type I error of accepting a false positive (which turned out to be a real positive, unbeknownst to him; we know this thanks to Van Zandt's contribution). Van Zandt made a type II error: falsely rejecting a truth. He himself cited cases of lighthouse markets in operation, but failed to recognize them as such.

---

[253] Both Van Zandt and the present authors take Coase (1974B) to task for misconstruing government acts in behalf of "private" lighthouse owners as compatible with free markets. However, we, but not he, acknowledge that with the further examples put forth by Van Zandt, the Coase claim, paradoxically, turns out to be *true*, albeit based on examples supplied by Van Zandt, *not* by Coase.

[254] This was also part of the burden of our own contribution to this controversy.

Van Zandt (1993 72) concludes his essay with the remark that the modern "lighthouse is no longer in need of governmental aid to make it a viable enterprise." In our view, in contrast, he himself has provided evidence sufficient to conclude that this amenity, even in early centuries, had no need of state protection in order to survive. Surely, there were *more* lighthouses in existence than would otherwise have been the case because of governmental subsidies, protection against competitors, coercion visited upon those unwilling to pay for these services, etc. But the same could be said for *any* industry in which government enters, assuming away, arguendo, those cases where government aid boomerangs.

Chapter 15. Coase and Bertrand on Lighthouses

Abstract

Coase (1974B) failed to appreciate that the construction and maintenance of nineteenth-century lighthouses were in part financed by British taxpayers. Bertrand (2006) rightly calls him to account. While agreeing with Bertrand's conclusion, we dispute her reasoning and argue that lighthouses nevertheless could have been supplied by the private sector.

Introduction

Could lighthouse services, with the technology of the mid-19th century, be provided profitably in the absence of government action, apart from protecting private property rights and enforcing voluntary contracts signed between competent, uncoerced individuals?

Did Coase (1974B) demonstrate, that private firms did in fact make a profit by producing lighthouse services in the absence of government action, save for support of contract and property rights? If Coase did not demonstrate this, as we shall argue, *could* private for-profit firms have nevertheless provided lighthouse services? It is the burden of section two to wrestle with these important questions.

As far as most economists are concerned, Coase (1974B) proved that the market provided lighthouses on a profit-making basis. This is an important part of the history of economic thought, as the lighthouse is one of the crucial examples in the critique of markets that maintain they are unable to provide (adequate amounts of) public goods. We agree with Bertrand (2006) that Coase did not succeed in undermining this market critique. Section three is devoted to exploring our disagreements not with Bertrand's conclusions about Coase, but with her reasoning. We conclude in section four.

Coase and the lighthouse

Did Coase (1974B) succeed in showing successful market provision of lighthouse services? He did not. The examples he cited were instances of governmental, not market-based, supply. He (1974B: 206) offers the following quote from Report from the Select Committee on Lighthouses, in Parliament Papers, Session 1845, Vol. 9 at vi:

"Their Lordships cannot admit that is any violation of the principle of property in the reduction of a *tax* levied for public purposes, where no vested interests have been acquired in the proceeds of the *tax*; and where the tax in question is one levied upon a particular class of Your Majesty's subjects, without that class deriving any adequate advantage in return (and any excess of light *dues* beyond the amount necessary to maintain the lights is a *tax* of this character), the reduction of such a *tax* not only involves no violation of the principle of property, but is in the highest degree just and expedient (emphases added)."

That definitively settles the issue. A *tax, or compulsory levy,* simply is not compatible with the free enterprise system, which is predicated upon *voluntary payments.* This distinction is perhaps the most important in all of political economy, and Coase fails to make it. But, given Coase's standing in the profession, perhaps some more support for our contention would not be amiss. According to Van Zandt (1993: 48):

"My thesis is that the term 'private enterprise' hardly captures the reality of the provision of lighthouse services. For the period Coase surveyed (Great Britain from 1513 to 1898) and both prior and subsequent periods, the government played a substantively greater role in the provision of lighthouse services than Coase's term 'private' suggests… (See also Barnett and Block 2007A)."

Were there private; i.e., voluntary, lighthouse providers during this epoch? Yes. But they were *charitable* organizations, as demonstrated by Bertrand (2006). This author, however, does not recognize them as such since they were not organized on a profit-making basis. But we contend that the charitable sector of the economy is, because voluntary, as private as any other, specifically including profit-maximizing firms. There are two sectors of any economy: the violent or coercive sector and the voluntary. The former spans from government through organized crime to disorganized and/or one-off crime. The latter encompasses both actions undertaken solely either for pecuniary profit or for psychic profits (that is, subjective benefits), or those carried on for a mix of these motives. The key is not the motive for an action; rather it is the nature of the means – violent or voluntary. Therefore, that charitable organizations provided lighthouses for altruistic reasons does not alter the fact that these actions were voluntary and thus private. Some commentators lump together the activities of charitable organizations and governments and then distinguish them from those of profit-seeking firms on the basis that altruism characterizes state and charitable efforts, but not market activity. As for altruism, we adopt the Public Choice perspective that this is a component of *all* of human activity, and that governments and charitable organizations have no monopoly over it.

Next question: were there any for-profit lighthouse providers during this era in history? Our research has not been able to uncover any such. And now for the $64,000 question: *Could there have been* lighthouse services, with the technology of 1850, provided profitably in the absence of government action, over and above enforcing private property rights and voluntary contracts signed between competent, uncoerced individuals? Before answering, we note that this is a *theoretical question, calling for an analysis of a counterfactual situation.* It *cannot* be settled by resort to the historical record. And, yet, much depends upon it. For, if this question is answered in the negative, that tends to strengthen the public good argument in general, and justify including the lighthouse as an instance of this phenomenon in particular. If in the positive, the opposite tendency ensues.

Our response is positive. We suggest that *there could well have been* lighthouse services, with the technology of 1850, provided profitably in the absence of government action, (we abstract from government enforcing private property rights and voluntary contracts signed between competent, uncoerced individuals). How, then, could such entrepreneurs have excluded free riders? Several scenarios present themselves. One is moral suasion. The lighthouse entrepreneur could announce to all and sundry that the XYZ shipping line refuses to pays its fair share of costs; negative publicity would undoubtedly ensue. Or, the owners of all boats plying their trade could gather into a *voluntary* club, and together pool the resources necessary to build and operate such a venture. Yes, of course, just as cartels tend to break up over both internal and external challenges, such an arrangement might not be definitive. But, it might work in some cases where transactions costs were low, and the given trade route was used by only a few.

Escalating, the lighthouse owner has a threat that "one of these days" when weather circumstances permit, he will *turn off the light.* He will do so if with a sharp-eyed look he determines that none of his paying clients are in the vicinity of the lighthouse, but only free riders. How credible is this threat? It might not be thought too serious at first blush, since if the employees of the lighthouse firm can see the silhouettes of the ships well enough to distinguish client from non-client, then, presumably, the ship's captain can see the rocks on which the lighthouse is perched well enough to avoid them. But this is not necessarily so. It might just be that "one of these days" vision will be better in one direction than in the other, sufficient for this threat to be carried out. If the boat crashes on the rocks, a vast amount of money, and lives, will be lost; whereas, in contrast, the fees for lighthouse protection under free enterprise are likely to be far less. Then, too, once this threat is announced, the sailing ships will have to pay higher wages to their employees, to compensate them for this additional hazard. And, if, ever, the lighthouse turned off its facility and a non-paying ship perished as a result, and this were publicized, that would pretty much put paid to this ploy.[255]

But we need not rely on sharp eyes, nor the exigencies of weather conditions to see that this is indeed a credible threat. Boat owners could send

---

[255] These comments are predicated on the assumption that the lighthouse firms would not be prevented from making, and carrying out, such threats, e.g., by government safety regulations. But in a scenario of laissez faire capitalism, where government is limited to enforcing contracts, and upholding private property rights, no rules of this sort would exist.

their upcoming cruise schedules, either positive or negative, in advance, to their lighthouse provider. They would do this, one, because no one likes to see a competitor getting away with an advantage, and/or, two, because the lighthouse owner would have an incentive to give compliant shippers a reduced price. A positive notification could be of the form: "I intend to travel on such and such a date, between the hours of this and that, during which time I will need the services of your lighthouse." A negative notification might be of this form: "I do not intend to travel on such and such a date, during which time I will therefore not need the services of your lighthouse." Air pilots commonly now file flight plans; ship captains could have done so as well, even in our bygone era. For, armed with such information, the lighthouse entrepreneur would be in a position to turn off his signal when none of his clients were scheduled to use it. A mere announcement to this effect ought to quickly bring non-payers to heel.

In the long run, this "game" can only be won by the lighthouse owner, not the recalcitrant ship-owner. For, the latter has to lose only once, and it is game over. Were one of his sailing vessels to crash on the rocks due to his unwillingness to pay the fee, he would pretty much be driven out of business. Who would want to work on any of his boats ever again? In contrast, the former can "lose" every day, for years; all he needs to do is "win" just one time.

Perhaps most important would be the effects of insurance rates on shippers, ship-owners, and insurers. Shippers, for good reasons, insure their cargoes and ship-owners, their ships. Various factors affect insurance rates; e.g., the seaworthiness of the vessel; piratical activity (Leeson 2007), the hazardousness of the route. On many routes the presence of a lighthouse undoubtedly would result in lower insurance rates. It would then be in the interest of those whose ships or cargoes regularly navigate such passages to secure the services of lighthouses. The locations of lighthouses are, in general, such that the opportunity costs thereof are very low and thus the initial expense of acquiring an appropriate site would be quite small. Although the cost of building the structure might not be insignificant, nevertheless, the expected life of a well-constructed lighthouse is sufficiently long that the annual expense associated with amortizing the investment in site acquisition and construction would be relatively low. In fact, such expenses, including interest, would likely be recovered long before the economic life expired. Moreover, the type of relatively unskilled labor required to run a lighthouse was not highly remunerated. Therefore, operating expenses, including maintenance, would be almost trivial. Were the capital and operating costs spread over numerous voyages, the per-voyage expense would be cheap. Beneficiaries would find it in their interest to cooperate. No one can be sure of the details, but it seems very reasonable to think that owners or shippers or insurers, or a combination thereof, would form an organization to provide such services.

However, consider that if the ship-owners were the proprietors of the lighthouses, insurers might refuse to insure, or might charge premium rates to, ship-owners who were not part of the relevant association(s) and to those who transport with them, and shippers might use their services only at a discount, if at all. Were insurers to be the owners, insurers not part of the pertinent association(s) would find ship-owners demanding a discount, if they would insure at all; and they might refuse to carry, or carry only at a premium, cargoes insured by them. Moreover, shippers might not insure with them, or only at a discount. And, were the shippers to be the joint-venturer, ship-owners might carry their freight, if at all, at a premium, and insurers might not insure the freight, if at all, at a premium, of those not members of the appropriate organization(s).

Need any or all of these threats eliminate 100% of all possible free riders? No. There are many firms that continue to operate without being able to exclude *all* recipients of any conceivable external benefits. For example, long before government began to subsidize higher education in the United States there were thousands of such institutions sending forth educated citizens into society, benefiting not only the institutions, and the students, but society at large. In similar manner, lighthouse owners might well have been able to continue in business without deriving payments from each and every last person who benefits from their commercial undertakings.

Bertrand

Just as in marketing, so too in economic political philosophy; product differentiation is important. We now explore how our paper differs from Bertrand (2006). There are, to be sure, similarities. We agree with Bertrand (2006), along with Van Zandt (1993), that Coase (1974B) has not shown that the lighthouse has served as a real-world case of private market provision of a public good.[256] We also enthusiastically support Bertrand's (2006: 396) contention that "Coase uses the terms 'private' and 'government' too vaguely and without careful definitions."

Where do we disagree? In the following ways:

1. Bertrand (2006: 390) agrees with Van Zandt (1993), not Barnett and Block (2007A), when she states that "the 'private form (sic) Coase describes … never existed." In our view, there were "private firms" e.g., charities, that did indeed offer lighthouses.

[256] For our views on Van Zandt (1993), see Barnett, and Block (2007).

2. Bertrand (2006: 392) sees a strong parallel between Coase's work on social cost (1960) and the lighthouse (1974B). For Bertrand (2006: 392), they "fit perfectly" together. She states (2006: 393): "'The Lighthouse' could be thought of as an application of 'The Problem of Social Cost.'"

In our view, these two high-profile articles of Coase's are not at all in the same tradition. Yes, superficially, they resemble one another, in that both feature historical case studies and lawsuits. But in "The Lighthouse" Coase reaches the correct pro-market conclusion albeit for the wrong reasons: because he incorrectly maintained that lighthouses supported by governmentally coerced payments were private businesses in the relevant sense of the word "private."[257] However, in "Social Cost," although by maintaining that in cases of negative externalities, *all* costs, both those involved in using the market (transactions costs) and those involved in using government to deal with the problem, need to be considered when deciding the proper course of action, he seems to think he is promoting the market, but de facto he undermines the vary basis of the private enterprise system; to wit, the institutions of the system of private property.[258, 259] There is a second difference we see between these two Coasean articles, which is overlooked by Bertrand: we see the main error in her "Lighthouse" publication to be one of not distinguishing the voluntary from the coercive, and in his "Social Cost" the total rejection of the doctrine of private property rights.

3. Here is an assessment of Coase (1974B) by Bertrand (2006: 395, emphasis added) with which we take issue: "… Coase does not claim that lighthouse financing must always be private, but only that it *could have been* in the past, contrary to the economists' assessments." In our view, Coase (1988 [1974B]: 212) took the rather different position that "The early history shows that, contrary to the belief of many economists, a lighthouse service can be provided by private enterprise… The lighthouses were built, operated, financed, and owned by private individuals…"Bertrand (2006: 401, emphasis

---

[257] Although the profits may have gone into private pockets, the firms were not dependent upon the market for the revenues thereby raised; rather, the revenues were generated by government coercion.

[258] It would take us way too far afield to even begin to defend this very much of a minority claim. For support of it, see Block (1977B, 1995, 1996), Cordato (1989, 1992A, 1992B), Krecke (1996), North (1990, 1992, 2002), Rothbard (1982A, 1990), Stringham (2001).

[259] This is reminiscent of Keynes thinking he was saving capitalism while stating: "I, conceive, therefore, a somewhat comprehensive socialization of investment will prove the only means of securing full employment: though this need not exclude all manner of compromises and devices by which public authority will co-operate with private initiative" (Keynes 1936: 378).

added) repeats this error: "Coase *attempts to show* that the lighthouse service could have been 'private'[260] in England."

4. We part company from Bertrand (2006: 396) in her characterization of Trinity House as a "private organization." Trinity House was no more private than the Federal Reserve Banks.[261] Bertrand (2006: 399) in contrast speaks of "the public interest represented by Trinity House."

Bertrand (2006: 396-397, footnote omitted) states:

"According to Coase, property rights in lighthouses had a sole specificity. They 'were unusual only in that they stipulated the price that could be charged' (Coase 1974B: 212). Having bargained with the patentee, the King fixed the dues for each lighthouse. This point deserves more attention than Coase and Van Zandt pay to it. It recognizes the peculiarity of lighthouse service (whose marginal cost is equal to zero), and the possibility of strategic behaviour in bilateral bargaining between a shipowner [sic] and a lighthouse 'owner' (the problem raised by Arrow 1969). Price fixing avoids this bargaining and protects the user from strategic behavior on the part of the single provider."

Bertrand seems to think the only possible relation between these two parties is one of bargaining each time the ship-owner wants the lighthouse light lit. Moreover, in such a situation, strategic behavior by ship-owners is also possible. In such situations, provided the expected benefits of the service exceed the costs, the parties will find it in their own interests to evolve institutions, in this case, contracts, perhaps involving creditable commitments and the use of "hostages," to make the service viable. (Williamson1985: 163-205). But this does not at all exhaust the possible range of contracts. At the very least, it is hardly necessary to create an agreement, de novo, every time a ship-owner wants to avail himself of lighthouse services. Surely, there could also be contracts calling for monthly or annual payments. As well, the market would tend to radically reduce such strategic behavior, provided there was respect for private property and contract rights.

5. Bertrand (2006: 397) claims there is a "peculiarity of the lighthouse service … [since its] … marginal cost is equal to zero…" Cost is the value that an individual places on the most highly valued of the alternatives he thinks he is foregoing any time he acts, and as such it is necessarily subjective (Buchanan1969; Buchanan and Thirlby 1981). Bertrand has no reason to believe that they are zero at all times and places.

---

[260] We are at a loss to explain Bertrand's continual use of quote marks around the word "private" of which this is but one example.

[261] Bertrand (2006: 396, emphasis added) approvingly quotes Taylor: "'Trinity House was a *private* corporation, but performed a *public* role which would otherwise have *had* to be performed by a central government agency' (Taylor 2001: 767)."

Suppose an owner of a lighthouse takes serious objection to a would-be free rider. Who are we third-party economists to tell this property owner that he suffers no cost at this injury/insult? If nothing else, part of his cost is any revenue he considers himself to be foregoing if he turns the light on for non-payers (Barnett and Saliba, unpublished B) Secondly, even if we employ the usual "objective cost" considerations beloved of neoclassical economists, the lighthouse is still by no means unique or "peculiar." Rather, many goods for which there is less than 100% capacity utilization have a "marginal cost … equal to zero." For example, it "costs" (virtually) nothing, in this mistaken mainstream view of costs, for a theater owner to fill an empty seat, if, as is reasonable, we can ignore the additional wear and tear on the seat as trivial. Moreover, whether the marginal "objective cost" is zero depends upon the decision under consideration. Although once a lighthouse has its light lit for a storm there may be no such "costs" that arise from the use of the service by additional vessels, they may well be involved in turning the lights on in the case of a storm during the day. For this requires manning the lighthouse on a continuous basis. The operators may prefer to be elsewhere earning money during the day, as their job does not require them to be awake during the entire evening, but only to turn the light on and off at the beginning and end of the night.[262]

Bertrand takes what can be characterized as several anti market positions which seem incorrect, or at least unproven. Relying on a House of Commons report of 1834 "quoted by Coase," she (2006: 398) complains that:

"Light dues were too high in comparison with what was sufficient to maintain lighthouses and even to build and maintain new ones. The levels of dues and their modes of collection showed lack of uniformity. Contrary to Coase, the confusion which prevailed in this field at the beginning of the nineteenth century actually motivated the centralization … allowed for standardization and the constant lowering of dues."

But these were not market prices; rather, they were monopoly prices set by government. Absent market prices, there is no way to know if the prices were too high or too low. [263] Given that the prices were set by the government, and the government shared in the profits, it is a reasonable assumption that they were set above the levels which would have obtained in a free market.

---

[262] This is similar to the case of many firemen who are allowed to sleep in the firehouse while on duty and/or who have other jobs. Were they required to be awake during their entire shift they would demand higher pay.

[263] Free-market prices are neither too high nor too low, rather they are what they are. Should the profits earned by the least profitable firms be "too high" either the firms in the industry will expand or new entrants will be induced. If "too low," insufficiently profitable firms will leave the industry.

6. Bertrand (2006: 398, fn. 1) interprets problems she sees with lighthouse pricing as an indication of the "opposition between private and public interest."[264] This bespeaks an unjustified rejection of Adam Smith's "invisible hand," through which people are led to do that which is in the public good by consultation with their own private selfish interest in profit-seeking.[265] It also ignores the findings of the Public Choice school of thought (Buchanan and Tullock 1962), according to which men do not suddenly grow angel's wings when they take up "public" service.

7. Bertrand (2006: 398) takes umbrage at the fact that a "violin-maker" constructed a lighthouse. But, why not call this person an *ex* violin maker, since he is *now* involved in lighthouse construction? In any case, entrepreneurs are not properly typecast as belonging to any specific industry. Carriage makers were the first to manufacture automobiles.[266] This author, moreover (2006: 399) contradicts herself when she concedes that a "silk mercer," presumably as far removed from lighthouses as the violin maker, was responsible for a "much more solidly" built lighthouse.

8. Bertrand (2006: 399) supports governmental regulations and inspections, and sees "poor quality (as) partly due to the search for maximum profits…" But market certification institutions, such as Moody's, Standard and Poor, Underwriters Laboratories, Good Housekeeping, Consumer Union, are more reliable sources of security in products, whether for consumer or capital goods. At least they can be bankrupted in case of error.[267] Any such tendency in government "service" is greatly attenuated. The search for maximum profits leads to poor quality? Much the reverse is true.

9. Bertrand (2006: 398) states: "Several sources agree in insisting that the English lighthouse system, in the seventeenth and eighteenth

---

[264] This seems strange as on the next page she explains that; "The 'private' lighthouses had to wait until these entrepreneurs offered to share the profits with the sovereign…" Certainly this is not a case of the free market in action, where the Crown's governmental power to confer the right to build a lighthouse is exercised in the private interest of the Crown.

[265] Bertrand (2006: 399) allows this frontal attack on the invisible hand to pass without demur: "In 1580, Queen Elizabeth I refused to grant Gwen Smith the right to build a lighthouse on the Goodwin Sands. She thought his interest was only in financial gain and not in the welfare of sailors." Not us.

[266] The fact that most carriage makers failed in the auto business does not gainsay this claim.

[267] The real problem with Katrina and its aftermath was *not* that the Army Corp of Engineers and FEMA, between them, killed some 1,100 New Orleanians; it is that these organizations *still* remain in "business." Were they private, this would not be the case. See on this Stringham and Snow, 2008; D'Amico, 2008; Vuk, 2008; Dirmeyer, 2008

centuries, operated with problems." She mentions several: "it was difficult to distribute the dues to the different lighthouse owners,"[268] "complexity of the system," "inefficiency of management," "high collection costs," "wide variation in the charges for light," "lights worked poorly." But such problems do not stem from free enterprise lighthouses, but, rather, come about because lighthouses were governmentally regulated, and especially because the revenues received by for the lighthouses were coerced from the ship-owners.[269]

10. Bertrand (2006: 399) refers to several cases in which lighthouses were destroyed and rebuilt. The causes were, variously, a lighthouse "swept away by the sea in 1703" and "A fire destroyed the lighthouse in 1755." She then states: "This repeated rebuilding suggests that technical control of the quality of buildings was insufficient. Lighthouse construction, as well as maintenance, was not always closely inspected, largely owing to lack of regulations. Once again, this poor quality was partly due to the search for maximum profits, helped by collusion with the Crown." But this misunderstands the matter.

First, in a free market the construction and maintenance would have been closely supervised by the owner and/or his agents out of self-interest. There would be no need for "regulation," here understood to be governmental. Without "collusion with the Crown," the "search for maximum profits" would not have resulted in poor quality, because in a free market periods during which the light was inoperable, whether because the structure was destroyed and in the process of reconstruction, or because of poor maintenance, or because it was not lit, would undoubtedly be times during which no revenues were generated. Moreover, these two examples, some 50+ years apart seem week reeds upon which to condemn the quality of 18th century construction and maintenance. Even in the 21st century we witness the power of the sea as it destroys well-built structures. (Hurricane Katrina destroyed the Ship Island replica of the Biloxi, MS lighthouse.) And fires consume sturdy structures every day.

---

[268] Bertrand (2006: 398) approvingly quotes Taylor (2001: 756) that the "charges attracted much criticism both from merchants, who argued that high light dues inhibited foreign trade, and ship-owners who complained that in a period when shipping was 'dull and unprofitable,' the high fixed costs of light and other dues prevented them from cutting back their expenditure." Bertrand does so without noting that businessmen, including both merchants and ship owners, are known for crying poor-mouth and trying to shift costs of doing business to others.

[269] The whole issue of "public goods" and their provision as per Bertrand's discussion is reminiscent of another so-called "market failure," "natural monopolies." There, also, government is involved to the hilt, whether as provider or regulator of a "private" provider. And, there also arise problems of excessively high prices and the poor-quality services.

11. Bertrand (2006: 400) states: "Since protecting ships [by means of lighthouses] could sometimes be less profitable than plundering them [if they were wrecked], we are less confident than Coase on this matter: individual initiative alone might not be sufficient to lead to the building and maintenance of lighthouses." This greatly confuses analysis by not distinguishing among the players. Associating the honorable term "profits" with plunder misconstrues the situation. It puts dishonest earnings on a par with honest income. Regarding the protection of ships the only alternatives Bertrand considers are truly private lighthouses or intervention in the form of governmentally sponsored lighthouses. She does not consider discouraging looting by more and better efforts to: 1) prevent criminals from incapacitating or destroying lighthouses, and then looting ships; 2) catch and convict looters engaging in any of those activities; and 3) impose greater penalties for any such activities. If there are any legitimate functions of government, they are the protection of rights to life, liberty, and property. Were government to reduce the incentives for such illegal and nefarious activities by doing its job and protecting these rights, the choice would not be between more "profitable" looting and less profitable free-enterprise lighthouses, but, rather between the latter and governmentally sponsored lighthouses. The choice would then be clear: private lighthouses, because they would be built and operated to the extent they provided useful services. Poorly constructed and maintained ones, and high-cost governmentally privileged lighthouses, would not be warranted.

12. In her concluding remarks, Bertrand (2006: 401) maintains that her analysis results in qualifying Coase's conclusions in six particulars. We take issue with all of them.

12.1 "Dues for 'private' lighthouse services, collected by public officers," could only be obtained with state coercion. Her case is not proven. She merely showed that the dues *were* collected in this way, and not that revenues *could not have been* generated by voluntary payments. In fact, Bertrand (2006: 397, emphasis added) herself contradicts this point: "In the competition for Royal privileges, Sir John Clayton obtained no less than five patents, all with voluntary contributions. Among the five lighthouses built, only two were lit (in Corton) since the dues remained unpaid…We see here the *difficulty* of obtaining payment for 'private' lighthouse services…" Apparently dues were collected for the two lighthouses that were lit, else, whence did the revenues to operate them arise? Moreover, there is a difference between difficulty and impossibility. Economic reasoning would tend to draw us to the conclusion that payments were made voluntarily to the two lighthouses that were lit because they provided services worth the expense to the ship-owners, whereas payments for the services of the other three were not supported because their services were not worth while.

12.2 "Construction and maintenance of a lighthouse by a private individual were made profitable by fixing a high price, granting a monopoly, and guaranteeing the obligation of payment." Although this is true, it is misleading, for it implies that without governmental favoritism lighthouses would have been unprofitable. Arguments regularly arise that such and such an industry would go out of existence were it not for some special privilege afforded by government to it. Of course, the privileges are never removed, so the case is never exposed. Suffice it to say that in a free market any firm and industry will survive provided it generates benefits, in excess of costs, to its customers.

12.3 "Private lighthouses ended in failure and required centralization, which favoured the uniformity of the dues system, their abatement and the control of the buildings' and lights' quality…" That the system of governmentally sponsored lighthouses encountered many and growing problems should come as no surprise. The conclusion that what was required was centralization; i.e., even more control by government is, however, unwarranted. Economic analysis and the history of governmental intervention leads us to the very opposite conclusion; what was required was for the government to refrain from having anything to do with the lighthouse business, save, possibly, for enforcing property rights, contracts, etc.

12.4 "Government's role thus appears more clearly: it made the provision of the service *profitable*, but it did not make it *efficient*." Again, true, but misleading. Although it may have made it more profitable, this is not to say that it would have been unprofitable as a truly private venture, although, no doubt, profits were higher because of the requirement that they be shared with the government. (One might look at such excessive profits resulting from necessarily coercive action as a form of looting; i.e., the government joined with its privileged lighthouse gang to loot the private sector via dues extracted form ship-owners.) Misleading, also, is the idea that government made lighthouse services efficient. The implication is that fee-market services were, or would have been, inefficient, and governmental intervention was necessary to correct this problem. Actually, governmental intervention causes inefficiency in the first place.

12.5 Bertrand maintains: "However, returning to this period of history, we have encountered, almost paradoxically, all the practical elements explaining how the production of a public service, whose marginal cost is equal to zero, cannot be entrusted to exclusively private initiative." The implication is that the free market would not have provided lighthouse services, but thanks to governmental intervention, they were made available. It would be better to say: "However, returning to this period of history, we have encountered, almost paradoxically, all the practical elements (the necessity of a government patent, governmentally set prices, and mandatory profit-sharing with government) that explain how the production of any service, regardless of marginal cost, cannot be entrusted in any degree to government."

12.6 The implication is that, unfortunately the necessary governmental intervention resulted in some problems for which the only solution was more intervention. That governmental intervention resulted in more problems is to be expected. That more intervention would improve the situation is wishful thinking. As Mises (1969, 1977) teaches (see also Ikeda ,1997; Lavoie, 1982; Rothbard, 1982B, 1982C), every intervention has undesirable consequences that the political class understands as necessitating yet more intervention. Needless to say, the problems created by the subsequent interventions are always worse than those created by prior interventions, resulting in ever greater growth of government and ever more problems.

Conclusion

Contrary to the widely popular view, Coase (1974B) did *not* succeed in showing that for-profit enterprise had supplied lighthouses to the market. He confused market with government provision of these services. Bertrand (2006) *did* succeed in demonstrating this failure of Coase's, but in so doing committed a whole host of errors. The lighthouse is *not* an example of a public good; the supposed market failures of excludability and rivalrousness can be overcome by sufficiently clever entrepreneurs with credible threats against free riders. If governments were to stick to their traditional role of protector of private property rights and contracts, and not engage in compulsory safety regulations, there is good and sufficient reason to believe that markets could function in this area of the economy.

Acknowledgements

We are indebted to two unusually active, incisive and articulate anonymous referees and editors of This Journal for urging us to write much of the material in our first section, as well as for turning around the focus of an earlier version of this paper into its present direction. Their attention to detail was very thorough, to the great improvement of this paper. Needless to say, but we say it anyway, all remaining errors in this paper are solely the responsibility of the authors.

Chapter 16. Subsidy is worse than tax

Abstract

Our claim is a limited one: for strict purposes of economic welfare, subsidies are worse than taxes. This is because while taxes divert resources, necessarily, to the second best alternative, which is pretty good all things considered, subsidies come with no such guarantee. Instead, subsidies can misallocate goods, services, labor and capital to far worse alternatives still.

I. Introduction

At first blush, this is a claim that is difficult to support. Which of us, after all, would rather be taxed than subsidized? Not too many, we suspect. Businessmen and consumers continually clamor for subsidies. And while there are many who urge higher taxes, mainly for *other* people, it is the rare person who advocates that *he* be taxed to a greater extent. Yet, our thesis is the paradoxical one that subsidies are worse for economic welfare than are taxes. In section II we discuss the justification for this claim couched in algebraic terminology. In section III we offer a translation of these considerations into the King's English. Section IV is devoted to further elaboration, and V to a consideration of several objections to, and qualifications of, our thesis. We conclude in section VI.

II. The advantages of taxes over subsidies: algebraic expression

Suppose a resource, R, is used in the production of X, and prior to the government intervention the quantity of R so used is r, and the quantity of X produced is x. Consider two possibilities: 1) government imposes a tax in the market for a particular good, X; and, 2) government provides a subsidy in the market for X.

In the former case the tax will cause a reduction in the output of X, which will cause a reduction in the use of resources to produce X. Subsequent to the imposition of the tax, there is a decline in the production of X by an amount Δx and of use of resource R by Δr. Prior to the tax, the resources Δr had a value (in the production of X) to the relevant entrepreneur of $v(\Delta r, X)$. After the tax, the resources Δr are reallocated to some other use Y, with value to the relevant entrepreneur of $v(\Delta r, Y)$.[270]

In the latter case the subsidy will cause an increase in the output of X, which will cause an increase in the use of resources to produce X. Subsequent to the grant of the subsidy, there is an increase in the production of X by an amount $\Delta x'$ and of use of resource R by $\Delta r'$. Prior to the subsidy, the resources $\Delta r'$ had a value (in the production of Z) to the relevant entrepreneur

---

[270] Obviously, if the resources Δr are "idled" by their owner(s), the owner(s) is (are) the relevant entrepreneur(s).

of v(Δr′, Z). After the subsidy, the resources Δr′ are reallocated to use X, with value to the relevant entrepreneur of v(Δr′, X).[271]

The key difference between the two cases is that v(Δr, Y) is the opportunity cost of Δr, whereas there is no reason to expect that v(Δr′, X) is the opportunity cost of Δr′. Absent the tax, X was the most highly valued use of Δr at v(Δr, X), and with the tax Y is the most highly valued use of Δr at v(Δr, Y). As L = v(Δr, X) - v(Δr, Y), the loss of value resulting from the tax, is minimized. Absent the subsidy, Z was the most highly valued use of Δr at v(Δr′, Z), and with the subsidy X is the most highly valued use of Δr at v(Δr′, X). And L′ = v(Δr′, Z) - v(Δr’, X), the loss of value resulting from the subsidy, is not necessarily minimized.

III. Why subsidies are worse than taxes: verbal explanation

Suppose a farmer can plant a particular piece of his land in beans, corn, or wheat. All things considered he ranks his options in order of declining value to himself, in alphabetical order as beans, corn, and wheat, and beans. Thus he decides to plant beans. But before he begins to plant government imposes a tax on beans. He reconsiders and now decides to plant corn.

A tax decreases the activity taxed. After the tax is imposed, this activity takes place to a lesser extent than would otherwise have been the case[272] (Hulsmann, 2003). Therefore, fewer resources are used in the taxed activity than would be used absent the governmental intervention. These resources are (mis)allocated to another use – their next best use in the eyes of the owner(s) of the resource(s). That is, the resources are utilized in their second best rather than in their best use.

Consider this example regarding a tax. The best use of a parcel of farm land is for growing beans; the next best use is for growing corn. The government taxes beans such that the owner of the parcel takes it out of bean production. Of course, he then puts it to the best use remaining–growing corn.

Now consider a subsidy. A subsidy increases the activity subsidized to a higher level than would otherwise occurred.[273] Therefore, more

---

[271] Obviously, if the resources Δr had been “idle” the owner(s) thereof is (are) the relevant entrepreneur(s).

[272] It is possible that more of the taxed activity will occur after the tax than before. We say only that in this case more of this activity would have occurred in any case, and that the effect of the tax is to lower this activity below the level that would otherwise taken place.

[273] It is conceivable that there will be less of a subsidized activity after the subsidy takes effect than before hand. But this only means that ceteris paribus conditions were not upheld. If they were, then, *more* of this activity will occur than would otherwise have taken place, but for the subsidy.

resources are used in the subsidized activity than would be used absent the governmental intervention. These resources are (mis)allocated to another use; however, in this case there is no reason to expect the resources that resources are diverted from their best use to their next best use in the eyes of the owner(s) of the resource(s). That is the resources are *not* used in their second best use rather than in their best use, save by luck.

For example, the best use of a parcel of farm land is for growing beans; the next best use is for growing corn; and, growing wheat is the next most valuable use. The government subsidizes wheat such that the owner of the parcel takes it out of beans production and puts it to use growing wheat. The land has been diverted from its best use, bean production, but does not end up in its next best use, corn production; rather, it ends up in its least (of the three[3]) valuable use, wheat production.

Suppose there were 26 crops the farmer could grow: a…z. He favors them in that order; that is, a>b, b>c ….x>y, y>z. Let us generalize from the case of three choices, beans, corn and wheat, to these 26. When the tax is placed on a, the farmer moves to b, the second best option. When the subsidy applies to z, the farmer moves from a to z, the 26th best alternative. It is *only* when the subsidy is directed at b that the tax and subsidy have the same effect, namely, misallocating resources from a, the best alternative, to b, the second best. In *every* other instance, c…z, the subsidy is inferior to the tax.

IV. Further elaboration

Here, we argue by analogy, and maintain that a gift in money is more valuable than a gift in kind, with the exception of the case where the recipient of the former would have spent the money in exactly the format of the latter. This would be akin to the case where the government chooses to subsidize precisely the second best alternative, b, in the case above

An example will clarify this. Which subsidy would you prefer, gentle reader: $10,000, or this basket of goods with a market value of precisely that amount: a bicycle, a violin, a gross of beers, a hundred pounds of pretzels, 6 massages and a dozen pizzas?[274] The answer is clearly the former, unless this combination of goods and services is the exact concatenation of items on which the recipient would have spent this $10,000.

In the case of the tax vs. the subsidy, it is only in the unlikely situation when the government picks the right item to subsidize that it will be as (little) satisfactory as the tax. In like manner, in the subsidy in kind vs. the subsidy in the form of generalized purchasing power (money), it is only in the unlikely scenario when the recipient would have spent the money on the exact goods and services in the basket that the two are equally satisfactory.

---

[274] We assume that this market basket of goods can be converted to money, and then to the expenditures preferred by the recipient only at great cost.

V. Objections and qualifications

There are of course difficulties involved in claiming that X is "better" than Y. "Better in who's eyes" is the first question likely to occur to anyone familiar with Austrian subjectivist theory.[275] This is why we were careful to specify that second best, or 26th best, was always determined by the economic actor involved in the actual decision making.

Do we favor subsidies as a means toward promoting economic welfare? Given that they are exogenous, and cost the society in question nothing, manna from heaven, well, then, ok, yes; it is difficult to look gift horses in the mouth.[276] But, in any realistic scenario, the subsidies that the government disburses is first mulcted from the long suffering taxpayer. It is difficult to see why the government would better be able to spend the heard earned money of the citizen for his welfare better than can he himself.[277]

Although we have argued that in the narrow respect of resource allocation taxes are preferable to subsidies, we do not favor the latter government program either.

Obviously, it is better to be subsidized than to be taxed. The bible may state that "it is better to give than to receive," but, as a strict economic matter, truth usually lies in the opposite direction.[278] The object of these two policies is clearly wealthier under the former than the latter. This would appear to refute our thesis that a tax is preferable to a subsidy, in terms of economic welfare, and reduction of misallocations of resources.

---

[275] See on this: Barnett, 1989; Butos and Koppl, 1997; Cordato, 1989; DiLorenzo, 1990A; Garrison, 1985A; Gunning, 1990; Mises, 1998; Rizzo, 1979B; Rothbard, 1997I; Thirlby, 1981

[276] However, there is an important literature expounding on the notion that, ultimately, government subsidies are harmful to the *recipient*, whether in terms of the domestic variety ("welfare"), or the foreign version (foreign "aid.") (Scare quotes since we do not buy into the notion that either of these self serving titles is accurate.) On the former, see Anderson, G., 1987; Anderson M., 1978; Brown, 1987; Higgs, 1995; LaBletta and Block, 1999; Murray, 1984; Olasky, 1992; Rothbard, 1998; Tucker, 1984; on the latter: Alesina and Weder, 2002; Bauer, 1981, 1982, 1984, 1991; Bauer and Yamey, 1957; Castle, 1957; Loeber, 1961; McNeill, 1981; Riddell, 1987; Rothbard, 1958; Thornton, 2002; Tucker, 1997; Vance, 2000

[277] An argument contrary to the one posed in the text is commonly couched in terms of "market failure," particularly that of "public goods." A rejoinder to this would take us too far a field from our present concerns. Instead, see on this: Barnett, Block and Saliba, 2005; Block, 1983, 2003C; Cowen, 1988; De Jasay, 1989; Hoppe, 1989A; Hummel, 1990; Osterfeld, 1989; Pasour, 1981; Rothbard, 1985A; Schmidtz, 1991; Sechrest, 2004.

[278] But not always. From the fact that people voluntarily contribute to charity, we may infer (Hughes, 1988, 1990) that they prefer this act to all others they might have taken.

The problem with looking at matters in this way is that ceteris paribus conditions are not met. A subsidy enriches, a tax impoverishes; it is thus difficult to see how the latter can be preferred to the former. However, if we eradicate this element from the analysis, matters become clearer. Suppose, then, we imagine a scenario where the person taxed is later compensated so that he loses nothing from the tax, and the man who is subsidized has an amount of money later taken away from him so that he gains nothing from the subsidy. Are we then indifferent[279] to taxes and subsidies? Not a bit of it. What remains, undeniably, after this imaginary process occurs is the fact that in the tax case, resort is necessarily made to the *second best* alternative, whereas in the subsidy case, whether there are three crops or 26 alternatives, it would be an *accident* for this to take place. Only if the government subsidizes the second best alternative will this occur. But if the state chooses *any other option*, it will not.

Perhaps this insight can be further explicated by considering the impacts of different types of interventions into the market process. These may be classified in a number of manners. One way is to classify interventions according to a 2 by 2 matrix. One axis of the matrix is divided into what realm of economics the policy has an effect on, resource reallocations or income/wealth redistributions. The other axis would be arrayed so as to distinguish to object of the effect, from whether or not it could be minimized, so as to promote economic welfare.

	Effect on:	Effect-minimizable?
Reallocation of Resources	A	B
Redistribution of Income/Wealth	C	D

Let us now state our thesis in terms of this matrix. If it is a matter of the redistribution of income/wealth (C) then it is better to be subsidized than to be taxed. This is akin to the difference between being stolen from,[280] and rewarded. However, in terms of resource allocation (A), the thesis of our paper is that subsidies are inferior to taxation. Our claim, too, is that the harm of taxation can indeed be minimized (B) in that this form of wealth transfer at least allows a move from the optimal use of resources to the *second* best use of them. In contrast, if the government guesses correctly, and subsidizes the second best option, then a tax and a subsidy are equally

---

[279] For an argument that human action is incompatible with indifference in all cases, see Barnett, unpublished; Block, 2007; Hoppe, 2005; Hulsmann, 1999

[280] For support of the claim that "taxes are theft" see Chodorov, 1962; Rothbard, 1978A, 1978B, 1998; Vance, 2006, 2007

destructive of economic welfare. However, taxes necessarily have this characteristic, while subsidies do not. There are literally hundreds of thousands of things can be subsidized (and, of course, taxed). It is thus a virtually[281] impossible task for government to pick the correct item to be subsidized. Since each person will likely have a different second best alternative for his resources, the minions of the state would have to guess correctly for each and every member of society.[282]

---

[281] Is this a praxeological impossibility, as Mises (1981) characterized socialism? Or it is, merely, a practical impossibility, as Hayek (1948C) analyzed that system? We leave it to the reader to decide. For the argument that Mises and Hayek had different views on this matter, see the de-homogenization literature: Block and Garschina, 1995; Ebeling, 1992; Herbener, 1991; Rothbard, 1991A, 1997H, 1997P; Salerno, 1990A, 1990B, 1992, 1995; Stalebrink, 2004.

[282] D in this case is a null set. It cannot help in the explication of our thesis, since we are explicitly abstracting from the issue of income and wealth distribution. We focus, instead, on resource allocation.

Part III. Macroeconomics

Chapter 17. On the optimum quantity of money

Introduction

It is pretty well established within Austrian economics that the optimum quantity of money is whatever level is established at any given time. The logical implication of this claim is that any amount of the commodity that intermediates trade will do as well as any other in acquitting this task. This being the case, there is no social or even private gain to be obtained by anyone adding to the money stock.

The present paper challenges this view, but from within the praxeological tradition. That is, we shall argue that although prominent Austrian economists have indeed made this argument, they are incorrect from their own basic perspective, which is shared in full by the present authors. Our thesis, in contrast to theirs, is that "more is better," or, more strictly speaking, at the very least it is possible that additional stocks of money can make a positive contribution to economic welfare.

Given that we are making a frontal attack on economists with whom we agree on virtually all other issues[283] in the dismal science, it behooves us to be very careful in documenting the charge we are about to bring. Accordingly, we quote quite fully from several leaders of the Austrian school, in order to obviate any possible misconstruction of their position.

But before we introduce our extensive quotes from Mises and Rothbard, for these are the economists against whose views we shall be contending, let us mention a possible misinterpretation of our own position, and attempt to obviate it.

According to this possible objection, we can be accused of attributing to Mises and Rothbard the view that any amount of money in existence is an optimal quantity. That is, these two economists quite properly distinguish money from gold, even under a pure gold standard. Further, we might be interpreted as saying that it is not true that any given amount of gold in the

---

283 The authors wish to thank two referees of this Journal for their comments on an earlier version of this paper. One of these referees stated, "What the authors [that is, us] fail to realize is that Mises's and Rothbard's hostility to the increase in the quantity of money was directed at its increase *by the government*…"This, indeed, might well have been the *intention* of Mises and Rothbard. However, as we attempt to demonstrate below, these two eminent economists did not always limit themselves to this concept, but rather exceeded it.

economy at any given time is optimal. Very much to the contrary, if under free enterprise and a commodity standard gold mining occurs, and this adds to the stock of gold in contrast to money, then all is well, allocation wise.

This being the case, then, according to the critique that could be leveled at us, we are passing like ships in the night. Our correct thesis is not contradicting the correct analysis of Mises and Rothbard. Both claims can be true, since they do not contradict one another. That is, we claim that the optimal amount of gold money can possibly be increased with good effects, while Mises and Rothbard maintain that any increase in the stock of gold money is socially wasteful.

As against that, consider the following:

1. The optimal quantity of fiat money is zero[284]. However, in a fiat-money-using society, the optimal quantity of fiat money is whatever is in existence, and, from an Austrian perspective, that quantity should never be changed, either increased or decreased, save for its complete elimination in shifting to a commodity money.[285]

2. Both Mises and Rothbard distinguish money from gold in that they both see the former as a subset of the latter; i.e., gold in teeth or jewelry, or for industrial purposes, etc., is not money; gold coins are money and, at least for Rothbard[286]: "large bars of gold and silver have been used for storage or for exchange in larger transactions, while smaller, circular pieces, known as coins, are used for smaller transactions." Certainly commodity monies are included. To the extent Mises is saying that the extant quantity of fiat money should not be changed and it is socially wasteful to use scarce resources to add to the stock thereof, he is correct. However, to the extent he says that using resources (or goods in the case of conversion of the money commodity from non-monetary uses to monetary uses) to increase the supply of monetary gold, *e.g.*, any increase in the stock of gold money is socially wasteful, he is wrong in our view, as is Rothbard, who agrees with Mises on this, as we shall show.

Both are clear that using resources to add to the stock of a commodity money is socially wasteful; and both are clear that using resources to add to the stock of the money commodity is not socially wasteful provided that the increases in such stocks are not used for monetary purposes, but rather for their non-monetary (tooth and jewelry) purposes. Other than as wallpaper or for numismatic purposes, fiat money has virtually no non-monetary uses.

---

[284] Hoppe, Hulsmann and Block, 1998

[285] For Austrians, the crucial distinction is between commodity and fiat money, whereas for the mainstream it is that between real and nominal money. On the mainstream, see: Friedman, 1969, p.1.

[286] Rothbard, 1993, p. 169.

We are saying, in contradistinction to them, that it is not socially wasteful to use resources to add to the stocks of the monetary commodity regardless of whether such additions go to non-monetary or monetary uses.

In sum, neither we nor they think that, except by sheer and temporary happenstance, the quantity of gold in the economy at any point in time is the optimal quantity; however, they are saying that the quantity of gold used as money at any given time is optimal, and we are saying that, if anyone voluntarily adds to the stock of gold used as money, that alone proves[287], that the stock of monetary gold was not previously optimal. Thus, there is a real, not a semantic difference between them and us.

In section II we consider the evidence, section III is devoted to our critical analysis of Mises and Rothbard, and we conclude with section IV, in which we consider several objections to our thesis.

I. The evidence

In his magnum opus, Human Action[288], Ludwig von Mises states that

"The services money renders are conditioned by the height of its purchasing power. Nobody wants to have in his cash holding a definite number of pieces of money or a definite weight of money; he wants to keep a cash holding of a definite amount of purchasing power. As the operation of the market tends to determine the final state of money's purchasing power at a height at which the supply of and demand for money coincide, there can never be an excess or a deficiency of money. Each individual and all individuals together always enjoy fully the advantages which they can derive from indirect exchange and the use of money, no matter whether the total quantity of money is great or small. Changes in money's purchasing power generate changes in the disposition of wealth among the various members of society. From the point of view of people eager to be enriched by such changes, the supply of money may be called insufficient or excessive, and the appetite for such gains may result in policies designed to bring about cash-induced alterations in purchasing power. However, the services which money renders can be neither improved nor repaired by changing the supply of money [emphasis added]. There may appear an excess or a deficiency of money in an individual's cash holding. But such a condition can be remedied by increasing consumption or investment. (Of course, one must not fall prey to the popular confusion between the demand for money for cash holding and the appetite for wealth.) The quantity of money available in the whole economy is always sufficient to secure for everybody all that money does and can do."

---

[287] We abstract, for argument's sake, from the possibility that this accretion was mistaken.

[288] Mises, 1996, pp. 421-422.

"From the point of view of this insight one may call wasteful all expenditures incurred for increasing the quantity of money. The fact that things which could render some other useful services are employed as money [emphasis added] and thus withheld from these other employments appears as a superfluous curtailment of limited opportunities for want satisfaction…."

Murray N. Rothbard, in his treatise, Man Economy, and State[289], restates and elaborates upon this position:

"Goods are useful and scarce, and any increment in goods is a social benefit. But money is useful not directly, but only in exchanges. And we have seen that as the stock of money in society changes, the objective exchange-value of money changes inversely (though not necessarily proportionally) until the money relation is again in equilibrium. When there is less money, the exchange value of the monetary unit rises; when there is more money, the exchange value of the monetary unit falls. We conclude that there is no such thing as 'too little' or 'too much' money, that whatever the social money stock, the benefits of money are always utilized to the maximum extent [emphasis in original]. An increase in the supply of money confers no social benefit whatever [emphasis added]; it simply benefits some at the expense of others, as will be detailed further below. Similarly, a decrease in the money stock involves no social loss. For money is used only for its purchasing power in exchange, and an increase in the money stock simply dilutes the purchasing power of each monetary unit. Conversely, a fall in the money stock increases the purchasing power of each unit."

"David Hume's famous example provides a highly oversimplified view of the effects of changes in the stock of money, but in the present context it is a valid illustration of the absurdity of the belief that an increased money supply can confer a social benefit or relieve any economic scarcity. Consider the magical situation where every man awakens one morning to find that his monetary assets have doubled. Has the wealth, or the real income, of society doubled? Certainly not. In fact, the real income – the actual goods and services supplied – remains unchanged. What has changed is simply the monetary unit, which has been diluted, and the purchasing power of the monetary unit will fall enough (i.e., prices of goods will rise) to bring the new money relation into equilibrium."

"One of the most important economic laws, therefore, is: Every supply of money is always utilized to its maximum extent, and hence no social utility can be conferred by increasing the supply of money [emphasis in original]. Some writers have inferred from this law that any factors devoted to gold mining are being used unproductively, because an increased supply of gold does not confer a social benefit [emphasis added]. They

---

[289] Rothbard, 1993 (1962), pp. 670-671

deduce from this that government should restrict the amount of gold mining. These critics fail to realize, however, that gold, the money-commodity, is used not only as money but also for nonmonetary purposes, either in consumption or in production. Hence, an increase in the supply of gold, although conferring no monetary benefit, does confer a social benefit by increasing the supply of gold for direct use."

Rothbard then confuses the issue in a subsequent publication.[290]

"Thus, we see that while an increase in the money supply, like an increase in the supply of any good, lowers its price, the change *does not – unlike other goods – confer a social benefit*.... Our law – that an increase in money does not confer a social benefit – stems from its unique use as a medium of exchange.

An increase in the supply of money, then, only dilutes the effectiveness of each gold ounce; on the other hand a fall in the supply of money raises the power of each gold ounce to do its work. We come to the startling truth that *it doesn't matter what the supply of money is*. Any supply will do as well as any other supply. The free market will simply adjust by changing the purchasing power, or effectiveness of the gold-unit. There is no need to tamper with the market in order to alter the money supply it determines.

At this point, the monetary planner might object: 'All right, granting that it is pointless to increase the money supply, isn't gold mining a waste of resources? Shouldn't the government keep the money supply constant, and prohibit new mining?'

This argument might be plausible to those who hold no principled objections to government meddling, though it would not convince the determined advocate of liberty. But the objection overlooks an important pint: that gold is not only money, but is also, inevitably, a *commodity*. An increased supply of gold may not confer any *monetary* benefit, but it does confer a *non-monetary* benefit – i.e., it does increase the supply of gold used in consumption (ornaments, dental work, and the like) and I n production (industrial work). Gold mining, therefore is not a social waste.

We conclude, therefore, that determining the supply of money, like all other goods, is best left to the free market. Aside from the general moral and economic advantages of freedom over coercion, no dictated quantity of money will do the work better, and the free market will set the production of gold in accordance with its relative ability to satisfy the needs of consumers, as compared with all other productive goods." (Footnote omitted.)

---

[290] Rothbard, 1990 (1963), pp. 33-35.

II. The analysis

As is obvious from von Mises's and Rothbard's statements (see particularly those we have emphasized), both are referring to a commodity money. In what follows, we restrict our comments to such money, and assume that in the free market gold coins would evolve as the money.[291]

Consider, then, the case of gold. As it affects not the argument, let us consider only three (3) uses for gold: as money in the form of coins; as jewelry, in the form of rings, etc.; and, as electrical contacts in electronic equipment. Although the total stock of gold available to human purposes could also be increased by the discovery of gold that had been available at some time in the past but then had been lost, we ignore such examples, as the analysis is not affected in any substantive way by examining only the case where additions to the stock of gold come from mining operations.[292] We assume that newly mined gold is immediately refined and formed into bullion, and such bullion is then sold for one of the three (3) aforementioned uses.

If Mises and Rothbard are correct, then any additions to the stock of gold should be allocated only to uses as jewelry or as contacts. To allocate any to the third use, specifically, money, would be socially wasteful as it would yield no "social benefits" while there would be a cost associated with the non-use of any such gold for either of the other two (2) uses. (It must be noted that Rothbard's argument on pages 33, 34, and 35 of *What Has Government Done to Our Money* is a non sequitur. Rothbard says that an increase in the quantity of gold money confers no social benefit, that any supply will do as well as any other, and that it doesn't matter what the supply is. This is necessarily erroneous. Gold has non-monetary uses that do confer social benefits. Therefore, it does matter what the supply of money is: as little gold should be used for money as is possible and still have a quantity sufficient for it to retain the necessary characteristics a commodity must have if it is to serve as money. To use any gold beyond this bare minimum for monetary purposes deprives society of gold that could be used for socially beneficial non-monetary purposes. Moreover, given his law that additions to the stock of monetary gold do not confer a social benefit but that additions to the non-monetary stock do, it does not follow, as Rothbard says it does, that

---

[291] It is possible – even likely given historical experience -- that the free market process might yield more than one money commodity, e.g., silver or copper, but this would not affect the analysis.

[292] The stock of monetary gold could be increased by minting either newly mined gold or existing non-monetary gold into coins. If the case can be made that no newly mined gold should be monetized, it follows, a fortiori, that neither should any existing non-monetary gold be monetized, as that would require a reduction in the quantity of non-monetary gold with attendant reductions in utility therefrom, something not required if newly mined gold is used for monetary gold.

"the supply of money, like all other goods, is best left to the market. Rather, it follows that the market should determine the supply of gold for non-monetary purposes, but there should be a prohibition on socially wasteful additions to the stock of monetary gold. In other places, Rothbard recognizes that the free market always increases social welfare; e.g., "Economics, therefor, without engaging in any ethical judgment whatever, and following the scientific principles of the Unanimity Rule and Demonstrated Preference, concludes: (1) that the free market always increases social utility; and (2) that no act of government can ever increase social utility."[293]

This, however, brings us to the horns of a dilemma. Any voluntary increase in the stock of gold coins[294] from any source whatsoever, whether by minting newly mined gold into coins, or by converting gold already in use as jewelry or contacts into coins, will necessarily have one of two possible effects. Either, first, despite the fact that this will take place as a result of individuals going peaceably about their business engaging only in voluntary interactions with others, they would be utilizing scarce labor and other resources to add to the stock of money, which addition would have to be deemed by Mises and Rothbard as "socially-valueless." The difficulty, here, is that this would truly be a case of "market failure," a great bugbear of mainstream economics[295], and something that Austrians have strived mightily to show as highly problematic.[296]

Or, second, individuals would voluntarily choose not to mint additional coins from gold, whether newly mined or in use as jewelry or contacts; any additions to the stock of gold would be used only as jewelry or contacts, although gold could be reallocated between these two (2) uses.

Certainly, in the first case governmental intervention into the market to control the money stock at whatever quantity is extant not only cannot be ruled out on principle, but as a matter of fact, is implied by the analysis; after all, if Austrians (e.g., Mises and Rothbard) are calling for an unchanging stock of the monetary metal, and this is changing purely through the activity of "capitalist acts between consenting adults,"[297] it is hard to resist the notion that the state must step in to overcome this supposed market imperfection. We are thus forced to arrive at the mainstream position with respect to

---

[293] Rothbard, 1956, pp.252-253.

[294] As to why one might wish voluntarily to increase the stock of commodity money, see the argument re "the second case," p. 11, infra.

[295] It is unnecessary to document this claim, as it is practically the defining characteristic of neoclassical economics; consult any introductory or intermediate textbook -- the distillation of the thinking of most practitioners of the dismal science, for confirmation.

[296] Cowen, 1988; Hoppe, 1989A; Rothbard, 1997A, 1997B, 1997Q

[297] Nozick, 1974, p. 163

"market failures" – one must weigh the costs of governmental intervention against the benefits thereof and intervene in cases where the latter exceeds the former. Nor will it do to note that costs and benefits are subjective – neoclassical economists maintain that we can and do use expenses and revenues as measures thereof (the present authors, of course, as Austrians, stipulate that they are attempts to measure objectively that which is necessarily subjective[298]) in, for example, cases of tortious liability.[299] However, it is a certainty that neither von Mises nor Rothbard would find a voluntary minting of newly mined gold into coins to be a "market failure."

Consider the second case. One would expect that in an even relatively-free enterprise society over time there would be great increases in labor productivity and, probably, significant increases in population, the consequences of which would be vast increases in output. In such a situation, with a fixed stock of money, prices would tend to decrease continually. Eventually individuals would find that their gold, whether newly mined, or in the form of jewelry or contacts, would have such great purchasing power as money, that they would voluntarily mint gold into coins. Therefore, this scenario could not last indefinitely.

That is, in a free society, eventually individuals would decide to add to the stock of money. The only way to prevent, or at least lessen, such "socially-valueless" use of resources would be governmental intervention. In which event, see the analysis of the first case, supra.

---

[298] See on this Barnett, 1989; Buchanan and Thirlby, 1981; Buchanan, 1969; Mises, 1949, 1963, 1966; Rothbard, 1993, 1997l.

[299] Although there is no subjectivist (see ibid.) warrant for such cost benefit analysis, it is absolutely required that the courts, whether they are governmental or an anarchist dispute resolution institution, undertake it, and, *to boot*, as an everyday occurrence. Judges do this, but not as scientists, rather as laymen, economically speaking. Take the case of A who causes B to lose a part of his body. Here, the courts are forced, willy-nilly, to determine what is the cost to B of this loss. In other words, sometimes we must quantify that which is inherently non-quantifiable, based upon technical praxeological considerations. Therefore, if "we" can do it in the case of torts, why not in the case of money? This holds particularly strongly if in fact we have correctly interpreted Mises and Rothbard as logically implying (even though they would of course not explicitly accept this characterization) that this is an example of "market failure." In such a case it would make just as much sense to say "we" need to do a "cost-benefit" study to determine if, and when, additions to the stock of gold money are warranted as it does to say "we" need to do a "cost-benefit" study to determine if we have the optimal level of good X, or have correctly hit upon the true costs to B of the loss of his body part. Therefore, unless we are prepared to agree to that proposition, and accept the concept of "market failure," including as applied to gold money, it is difficult to see how the Misesian-Rothbardian position on this matter can be defended.

Moreover, the logic of the positions "[e]ach individual and all individuals together always enjoy fully the advantages which they can derive from indirect exchange and the use of money, no matter whether the total quantity of money is great or small"[300] [emphasis added] and "[w]e conclude that there is no such thing as 'too little' or 'too much' money"[301] implies that existing gold coins should be converted into use as jewelry or contacts. And, this conversion should continue so long as the benefits therefrom exceed the cost of conversion, bearing in mind that the reduction in the stock of gold money would, at some point eliminate one or more of the attributes requisite for a commodity to be money; e.g, divisibility, recognizability, portability.

Why? This stems from the fact that if we go back in time far enough[302] to reach the period of barter, right before the advent of money, there was an occasion when gold was first used to intermediate trade, not merely as a valuable commodity on its own. At that point in time, the amount of gold used for this purpose was presumably miniscule. If so, then given Mises' and Rothbard's insistence that any amount of gold money will serve as well as any other, and there is no need to expand this supply (indeed, if this somehow occurs it is equivalent to a "market failure"[303]), then it logically follows that this teeny tiny amount of gold which was first used at the dawn of the creation of money should always suffice, even unto the present day.

Thus we again arrive at a fork in the road, facing two possibilities. First, the free market is inefficient, i.e., it allocates some of the new or extant gold to a valueless use as money, when it could and should have diverted it to a valuable use in jewelry or contacts, and this after first allocating other scarce resources to mining and refining, or to the conversion, thereof. Or, second, von Mises and Rothbard are wrong. It staggers the (individualistic) mind to think that people would voluntarily commit valuable resources to the creation of socially-valueless goods.

---

300 Mises, 1996, p. 421.

301 Rothbard, M. N. 1993. *Man, Economy, and State*. Auburn, Ala.: Ludwig von Mises Institute, p. 670). Elsewhere, Rothbard modifies this position: "...once a commodity is in sufficient supply to be adopted as a money, no further increase in the quantity of money is needed. *Any* quantity of money in society is "optimal." Once a money is established, an increase in its supply confers no social benefit." (Rothbard, 1994, pp.19-20). But this obviously supports the argument that any quantity in excess of this minimum is socially wasteful, given alternative valuable uses. This supports the (false) position that a voluntary increase in gold money in a free market economy is a case of "market failure," and invites governmental intervention to correct the "problem."

302 We refer to the Austrian theory of the money regression here. See on this Mises, 1963, pp. 409-410.

303 The authors of the present paper have resolved never to employ that phrase in the absence of quotation marks.

Whence, then, the source of the value as money, if any there be, of the newly mined gold? (Its value in jewelry or contacts is obvious.)

The value of the new money would arise out of the additional transactions that would be made possible by its existence. That is, there would be transactions, previously impossible to undertake because the cost of using valuable gold to mediate such was excessive, which would now be made possible because the new monetary gold reduced the value of money at the margin. There are, at any time, a variety of potential exchanges. Some of these would create a great deal of value; others only a minute amount. The value that would be created by some potential exchanges is so small that the utility of gold in facilitating such exchanges would be less than its utility in non-monetary uses. In such cases the potential exchanges would not occur.

As to whom might be hurt by an increase in the stock of a commodity money, by the very fact that it was voluntarily minted, it is certainly not the individual(s) who voluntarily minted it (save in the case of a mistake). Nor, again, by the very fact that they accepted the new gold money voluntarily could it be any individual(s) who voluntarily accepted it. No, the individuals "harmed" by such a voluntary minting of new gold coins would be those who own gold coins at the time are those who have financial assets denominated in terms of gold coins, such assets not being indexed for changes in the value of the coins. But the same logic applies in those cases as it does in the cases of other goods as von Mises himself proved in his pathbreaking Theory of Money and Credit[304].

That additional gold money decreases the value of previously existing gold money, or assets denominated therein, is no more a problem (or whatever pejorative one wishes to use) for the free market than is any other case of an increase in a good causing a decline in the value of previously existing units thereof. The logic of seeing that as a problem is that we should never produce anything for, ultimately, all goods are substitutes for each other, and therefore, the production of any of them must reduce the value of others already extant. Moreover, if gold is voluntarily mined it is because it has value to someone. Unless we are to outlaw gold mining, it will be mined and the new gold will be put to some use. To the extent that this use is as money, the value of extant stocks of gold in other uses is not, ceteris paribus, decreased. Were the gold that otherwise would have been coined not so monetized, it would have gone into other uses which would decrease, ceteris paribus, the value of the existing stocks of gold in those other uses. Furthermore, monetary gold can always be demonetized if the owner thereof values it more in a non-monetary use.

---

304 von Mises,1912; see also Salerno, 1994

Moreover, to quote Rothbard[305] the extent that newly coined gold money becomes part of the supply of credit, unlike "bank credit expansion [that] *distorts* the market's reflection of the pattern of voluntary time preferences."

The optimum quantity of money is not, then, whatever quantity happens to exist, but rather whatever amount of gold as coins the free market process creates. As long as mine owners can unearth gold at a sufficiently low cost to make it worthwhile, and minters outbid those with other potential uses for at least some of the new gold, the money stock should be, and is, increased. Further, even in a situation where the cost of mining gold was not sufficiently low to make it worthwhile, and therefore there were no additions to the total stock of gold, if peoples' subjective values changed so that they placed a reduced value on gold in its non-monetary uses or greater value on gold in its monetary use, and therefore withdrew some of it from non-monetary uses and caused it to be converted to monetary uses, the stock of money again should be, and is, increased. In appropriately reversed circumstances, the money stock should be, and is, decreased.

We see, then, that, contrary to von Mises and Rothbard, the quantity of money available in the whole economy is not always sufficient to secure for everybody all that money does and can do. Rather, the optimum quantity of money, as with any other good, is that quantity determined in the free market process, and, contrary to Mises and Rothbard, when the free market process causes additions to be made to the stock, such additions do confer a social benefit, in the form of additional voluntary exchanges facilitated.

III. Objections

In this our concluding section, we consider several objections to our thesis, and offer replies to them.

1. "Even the teeny tiny amount of gold which first erupted onto the market as money at the close of the barter system would be sufficient to undergird all transactions. Therefore, there are no social benefits to increasing the amount of gold used for monetary purposes. One way this could occur – an "infinitesimal"[306] amount of gold sufficing for all trade – is through the intermediation of silver and copper.

But even in their absence, gold, too, could do it, even in this minute amount. This could be accomplished if that miniscule amount of gold money came to be extremely valuable, or, what is the same thing, if prices in terms of this monetary commodity were very, very low."

---

305 Rothbard,1983A[1962], p.38.

306 Infinitesimal is used herein to refer to the minimum quantity sufficient for gold to retain the necessary characteristics a commodity must have if it is to serve as money.

It is true that this infinitesimally small amount of gold could intermediate all of modern trade, but it could not do so efficiently. If it could have done so efficiently there would have been no additions to the stock of gold money as such uses have non-zero opportunity costs. That is, this may be true, in the physically possible sense; theoretically, an infinitely small mass of gold money could mediate an infinitely large number of transactions provided the prices of goods were sufficiently low in terms of gold money (e.g. all of NY, Tokyo, and London would be sold for a teeny tiny fraction of a grain of gold[307]). But, that would not happen for economic (i.e., praxeological) reasons. This is because it would not be efficient. The source of the inefficiency would be increased transactions costs and the form would be foregone exchanges of such minute value that the increased transactions costs would preclude them. Note that as the limited initial quantity of gold money were to be used to mediate an ever greater number of transactions, the value per mass unit of this monetary gold would increase toward "infinity" (imagine if all of the transactions of 2000 a. d. had been mediated by 1 kg of gold money, what each atom thereof would have to have been worth. With gold that valuable it would not pay to use it to mediate transactions that increase value only a tiny bit. Moreover, we would be back to "market failure," for, surely, as gold's monetary value increased greatly, existing non-monetary gold would be converted to, and new additions to the gold stock would be put to, monetary uses. Were this not the case, the original piece of gold money would still suffice and the entire rest of the stock could, and indeed would, be put to valuable monetary uses.

2. "This is not a praxeological issue but rather one having to do with chemistry. The correct way to interpret the benefits of increasing the amount of gold used for monetary purposes is that it saves us from undertaking heroic chemical costs. That is, with a teeny amount of gold available today, all that could be spared for even the most valuable coin would be a relatively small number of atoms, and that is beyond our technological capabilities."

Whether it is the knowledge problem or the resource cost of trying to handle such infinitesimal quantities, or both is immaterial. Can you imagine the cost of trying deal with coins of fractional-grain mass? And, yet, with gold so valuable in such small masses, most people would likely want physical possession thereof. It would no more do to keep records of transactions without physical media than it has in the past or does today.

---

[307] In the limit, the lowest possible price of a good, x, would be 1 atom of gold per x. No lower price would be physically possible, as 1 atom is the smallest possible quantity of gold.

And, imagine what would happen with an even partial run on the banks as has occurred recently in Argentina.[308]

Thus, just as it is costly to use other valuable resources to facilitate exchanges because they have alternative uses, so also with gold used in coins as money. This gold also has alternative opportunities, and its use as a resource to facilitate exchanges is not costless. Thus, gold will be used in the free market process to facilitate exchange only if, and to the extent that, such use is relatively more valuable than its alternative non-monetary uses. The source, then, of the value of additions to the stock of money is the additional value-enhancing transactions that are made economical, and occur, because the additional gold decreases the value of money at the margin and therefore it can be put to less valuable uses whether as additional less value jewelry or as a mediator of additional less valuable transactions.

3. "All this talk of chemistry, and coins with only atomic amounts of gold in them, is beside the point. It may have been relevant in a bygone era, but we now know that a gold standard can function quite adequately without, strictly speaking, placing some of this commodity in each and every single coin. Token or fiat coins can be used as an alternative, and this would obviate the need to "stretch" in effect what would be subatomic particles of gold to all modern coins, if we were limited to the amount of this metal available when first it began to be used for money."

This solves one problem, that of "stretching" a minute amount of gold to cover all coins and bullion needed for modern commerce, but only at the cost of opening up a Pandora's box. It would take us too far afield to show why this scenario would not constitute a pure or 100% gold standard. Fortunately, this work has already been done and all we need do now is cite some of it.[309]

---

[308] "Argentina has been struggling for months to prove to creditors that it can stay current on its $130 billion government debt. Fearing a default or a freeze on deposits, Argentines have been pulling their money out of banks at a rapid clip. Argentine officials say they'll use at least some of the new IMF aid to shore up the nation's financial system (emphasis added)." Druckerman, 2001.

[309] See in this regard, Block, and Garschina, 1996; Block, 1988a, 1988b, 1989A, 1999C; Cochran and Call, 1998; de Soto, 1995; Hoppe, 1990, 1994B; Hoppe, Hülsmann and Block, 1998; Hülsmann, 1996, 2000B, 2000C; Kuznetsov, 1990; Mises, 1978A, 1983, 1990C; Rashid and Samad, 1996; Rothbard, 1962, 1983B,1984A, 1985B, 1988, 1989A, 1990, 1991B, 1992B, 1997J, 1997K, 1997L, 1997M, 1997N, 1997P, 1997S; Salerno, 1987, 1982; Sechrest, 1988, 1993; Shah, 1997; Skousen, 1977, 1998; de Soto, 1998A; Thies, 1996; Vihanto, 1988.

Chapter 18. Money: Capital Good, Consumers' Good, or (Media of) Exchange Good

Abstract

Is money a producers' good or a capital good, or is it sui generus, as Mises, Rothbard, and other Austrians have maintained? We argue that all action is either consumption or production, and that exchange is but a form of production. Consequently, all goods are either consumers' goods or producers' goods; there is no third possibility. And that among these two money is a producers' good, not a consumer good.

I. Introduction

Several Austrians, Mises foremost amongst them, maintain that money is neither a capital good nor a consumers' good. It is usual to divide economic goods into the two classes of those that satisfy human needs directly and those which only satisfy them indirectly: that is consumption goods, or goods of the first order; and production goods, or goods of higher orders. The attempt to include money in either of these groups meets with insuperable difficulties. It is unnecessary to demonstrate that money is not a consumption good. It seems equally incorrect to call it a production good.

Of course, if we regard the twofold division of economic goods as exhaustive we shall have to rest content with putting money in one group or the other. This has been the position of most economists; and since it has seemed altogether impossible to call money a consumption good, there has been no alternative but to call it a production good.

This apparently arbitrary procedure has usually been given only a very cursory vindication. Roscher, for example, thought it sufficient to mention that money is 'the chief instrument of every transfer' ... (Mises, 1980, 95-96, footnote omitted)

In this paper, we argue that exchange is a form of production and, consequently, there are only two types of goods, consumers' goods and capital goods; and, that money is, then, a producers' good. The method we shall use is to quote at length from and then analyze cited material. In section II we address this topic from the perspective of "The Theory of Money and Credit" (Mises, 1980 [1912]).[310] We take issue with Rothbard (1970) on this matter in section III and in section IV focus on it using Hoppe, et. al. (1998) as a case in point. Each of these quotes is followed by our analysis and commentary. A brief summary and conclusions in section V end the paper. Throughout section II all page-number-only cites are to Mises (1980); the same applies to Rothbard (1970) in section III and Hoppe, et. al. (1998) in section IV.

---

[310] Mises (1990C [1932], 55) maintains the same position.

This is not to deny that a good that serves as money may not also be a consumers' good. A monetary good most certainly can be used for purposes of consumption. We do not at all dispute this. You can paper your wall with paper money. You can take a swim in gold and/or greenbacks (as did Scrooge McDuck of comic book fame). You can burn paper money or melt down gold and study the chemical effects of such a process. You can even light your cigar with a $20 bill. But in none of these cases are you using gold or paper bills *as* money; e.g., to facilitate trade. When you do that, money is necessarily a capital good.[311]

It must be noted that "to facilitate trade" must be understood in terms of the meaning attributed to it by relevant human mind. Consider a good, say gold coins, that is a monetary good; i.e., it serves as money, in a particular society during the time period under consideration. It may either be held by A, or A may exchange the coins with B for some non-monetary item, X. In the former case, the good is money if A holds it with the intent of exchanging it at some, perhaps as yet undetermined, point in the future, for some other, also perhaps as yet undetermined, product. That is, the coins are money in such a case, not just during the process of monetary exchange, but also during any period in which they are being held for that purpose, and as such they are capital goods. However, if A holds the coins for numismatic purposes, they are not money; rather they constitute a coin collection. And, if the coin collection is held for personal aesthetic pleasure, it constitutes a consumers' good; however, if it is held as an investment[312], e.g., a "store of value," then it is no different than any other asset held as an investment; i.e., it is a capital good. Note that this means that the monetary good; e.g., gold coins may be; 1) a consumers' good; 2) money – a capital good; or, 3) a non-money capital good. Any asset, including durable consumers' goods or even non-durable consumers' goods[313] is a store of value, and thus a capital good. If one is holding the coins as a media of exchange than they are capital goods, specifically money; if one is holding the coins for investment purposes than they are investment goods – an inventory of "junk" gold coins of an inventory of numismatically valuable gold coins.

---

[311] We thank our colleague, Stuart Wood, for this important point that he made in his commentary on our paper given at the Austrian Scholars' Conference of 2003, held at the Mises Institute in Auburn AL. Moreover, the material in the next five (5) paragraphs of the text deals with issues that arose in subsequent conversations with him, for which, also, we thank him.

[312] The same analysis applies, mutatis mutandis, if A is holding the coins for any other non-monetary purpose(s).

[313] For example, Rothbard's (1962, 7) ham sandwich in the making

In the latter case, if A, holding the coins as money, exchanges them to B for X, they are money to A. However, they may not be money to B if he intends to acquire them for numismatic purposes. In that case, B understands the exchange as a barter transaction – the trade of X for a coin collection – and the coins are not money to B.[314] Similarly, if A is holding the coins for numismatic purposes and understands the exchange as a barter transaction – exchanging his coin collection for X – the coins, even during the exchange process, are not money to A.[315]

In sum, even when used in an exchange process, the gold coins may be money to both parties, neither, party, or to only one, and that one, either, party. A good acquires its character as money depending upon the meaning attributed to it by the relevant party or parties. The question is, "What meaning is attributed to the good?" Then, in any particular historical instance in which the answer is "money," the good is necessarily a capital good.

Moreover as with other goods, the character of an item used as money can be transformed. For example, gold coins intended as money can be converted to a coin collection, in which case they are transformed from a capital good to a consumers' good; or they can be smelted and changed to an industrial use, in which case they are altered from one type of capital good to another, say electrical contacts in some piece of industrial equipment. This is in principle no different than taking scrap steel that had been part of a steel building used for industrial purposes; i.e., being used as a capital good and recycling into steel: 1) embodied in an automobile used for pleasure; i.e., converting it into a consumers' good; or, 2) embodied in a truck used for commercial purposes; i.e., converting it into a different type of capital good.

Implicit in the foregoing is that, as with other goods, the one used as money may show up, simultaneously, anywhere in the structure of production (Hayek, 1931; Rothbard, 1962), whether as a consumers' good or as a higher order good, and its location in the structure may shift from higher to lower and vice versa. However, as money it must of necessity, we contend, show up only as a higher order good. And, of course, one and the same commodity (e.g., gold) can appear-simultaneously at different places in the capital structure; i.e., the structure of production excluding the lowest; i.e., consumers' goods, order (Lachmann, 1956; Garrison, 2001). Further, it can move around in the structure from lower order to higher, and vice versa.

---

[314]The same analysis applies, mutatis mutandis, if B is acquiring the coins for any other non-monetary purpose(s).

[315] The same analysis applies, mutatis mutandis, if A was holding the coins for any other non-monetary purpose(s).

II. Mises

"In opposition to Roscher, Knies made room for money in the classification of goods by replacing the twofold division into production goods and consumption goods by a threefold division into means of production, objects of consumption, and media of exchange. His arguments on this point, which are unfortunately scanty, have hardly attracted any serious attention and have been often misunderstood. Thus, Helfferich attempts to confute Knies's proposition that a sale-and-purchase transaction is not in itself an act of production but an act of (interpersonal) transfer, by asserting that the same sort of objection might be made to the inclusion of means of transport among instruments of production on the grounds that transport is not an act of production but an act of (interlocal) transfer and that the nature of goods is no more altered by transport than by a change of ownership. (Mises, 1980, 96, footnote omitted)."

Mises maintains that Knies (1885) was right. His argument (Mises, 1980, 95-102), in essence, is that the ambiguity of the German word, *Verkehr*, led to confusion between transfers through space and interpersonal transfers and, consequently, to the confounding of money, the means of interpersonal transfers with the transportation goods, the means of transfers through space.

"The common nomenclature of the two meanings, as also their incidental confusion, may well be attributable to the fact that exchange transactions often, but by no means always, go hand in hand with acts of transport, through space and vice versa. But obviously this is no reason why science should impute an intrinsic similarity to these essentially different processes. (Mises, 1980, 97, footnote omitted)."

This is correct; however, it is a non sequitur to maintain, as Mises does, that because, on those grounds, science should not link them they should not be linked at all. Indeed, there may be, and are, other, valid grounds for such a link.

In fact, the role played by man in production always consists solely in combining his personal forces with the forces of Nature in such a way that the cooperation leads to some particular desired arrangement of material. No human act of production amounts to more than altering the position of things in space and leaving the rest to Nature. (Mises, 1980, 97, footnote omitted).

This is highly problematic. Unless "desired arrangement of material" and "altering the position of things in space" are to take on entirely trivial meanings, these statements rule out the provision of many services (e.g., the services of doctors and lawyers in conveying advice orally) as acts of production.

It is often overlooked that, among other natural qualities, the position of a thing in space has important bearings on its capacity for satisfying human wants. Things that are of perfectly identical technological composition must yet be regarded as specimens of different kinds of goods if they are not in the same place and in the same state of readiness for consumption or further production.... The only water that can quench the thirst of the traveler in the desert is the water that is on the spot, ready for consumption. (Mises, 1980, 97-98).

Mises, here, makes a most important finding: the essential aspect of a good is not its physical properties, but, rather, its "significance for satisfying human wants." Although he makes the point that, for acting man, drinking water in the desert and drinking water in a well-watered mountain district are "totally different," he does not also acknowledge that for A and B in the desert, drinking water in the desert owned by A is "totally different" from that owned by B. If A owns the water and B does not, then if B cannot meet A's price, unless B is prepared to coerce A, B must go thirsty, though A have surfeit. But, of course, coercion is outside the realm of the market – the realm of voluntary human interactions (Rothbard, 1970).

Strictly speaking, only those goods should be called goods of the first order which are already where they can immediately be consumed. All other economic goods, even if they are ready for consumption in the technological sense, must be regarded as goods of higher orders which can be transmuted into goods of the first order only by combination with the complementary good, "means of transport." Regarded in this light, means of transport are obviously production goods. (Mises, 1980, 98).

Again Mises makes clear that, "for the purposes of economics," "it is better to regard" two goods physically identical goods save for their locations them "as goods of different kinds." However, in the very next sentence he uses the phrase "where [goods] can immediately be consumed" to determine whether said items are consumers' goods. "Can," in this context, means "physically able to." However, if there is a candy bar on the desk between you and me, it can be consumed by either of us. However, assuming it is owned by one of us, it may not be consumed by the other, without permission. For the owner it is a consumers' good; for the other party it is something of a higher order that first requires neither physical transformation nor spatial relocation, but, rather, a transfer of ownership rights; i.e., exchange, for it to become a consumers' good of his. But, the transformation of a good from higher to lower order is, precisely, what is meant by production.

We have seen that transfer through space is one sort of production; and means of transport, therefore, so far as they are not consumption goods such as pleasure yachts and the like, must be included among production goods. Is this true of money as well? Are the economic services that money renders comparable with those rendered by means of transport? Not in the least. Production is quite possible without money. There is no need for money either in the isolated household or in the socialized community. Nowhere can we discover a good of the first order of which we could say that the use of money was a necessary condition of its production. (Mises, 1980, 98-99).

That money is not a capital good because it is not necessary to production is a non sequitur. That production of cooked fish was, and is, possible without the existence of steel mills does not mean they are not capital goods. Moreover, it is incorrect to say that there are no consumers' goods for the production of which "the use money is a necessary condition." It would be impossible to produce many (most?) of the goods provided by a modern capitalist economy without the use of money. Or as Mises well understood in a different context: "Our civilization is inseparably linked with our methods of calculation. It would perish if we were to abandon this most precious tool of acting" (Mises, 1966, 230). However, "Economic calculation cannot comprehend things which are not sold and bought against money" (Mises, 1996, p. 214). Therefore, we may conclude that Mises understood that, contrary to the statement, supra, even though money is not necessary for production in an underdeveloped society, it certainly is in a modern capitalist economy.

[Böhm-Bawerk's argument] leaves out of consideration the difference between transport, which consists in an alteration of the utility of things, and exchange, which constitutes a separate economic category altogether. It is illegitimate to compare the part played by money in production with that played by ships and railways (Mises, 1980, 100).

To say that transport alters the utility of goods and, implicitly, that exchange does not is incorrect. The problem is that Mises does not recognize that an exchange in the ownership rights to an article alters its utility to the individuals concerned. And, since money is that which par excellence provides exchange services it is de facto a capital good.

Every sort of economic organization needs not only a mechanism for production but also a mechanism for distributing what is produced. It will scarcely be questioned that the distribution of goods among individual consumers constitutes a part of production, and that in consequence we should include among the means of production not only the physical instruments of commerce such as stock exchanges, … account books, … but also everything that serves to maintain the legal system which is the foundation of commerce, as, for example, …. law courts … (Mises, 1980, 101).

The implication is that because the legal system is "the" foundation of commerce everything that serves to maintain it is a capital good. But, the foundation of commerce consists not of the legal system alone; money is every bit as much a foundation of commerce as are any of these other institutions correctly mentioned by Mises in this regard. Therefore, by that criterion, money is a capital good.

What prevents us nevertheless from reckoning money among these "distribution goods" and so among production goods (and incidentally the same objection applies to its inclusion among consumption goods) is the following consideration. The loss of a consumption good or production good results in a loss of human satisfaction; it makes mankind poorer. The gain of such a good results in an improvement of the human economic position; it makes mankind richer. The same cannot be said of the loss or gain of money. ... An increase in the quantity of money can no more increase the welfare of the members of a community, than a diminution of it can decrease their welfare. Regarded from this point of view, those goods that are employed as money are indeed what Adam Smith called them, "dead stock, which...produces nothing. (Mises, 1980, 101-102, footnote omitted).

The problem here is Mises' failure to see that a change in the quantity of money does affect the welfare of members of a community. Friedman (1969, 1) maintains that:

It is a common place of monetary theory that nothing is so unimportant as the quantity of money expressed in terms of nominal money units – dollars, or pounds, or pesos. The situation is very different with respect to the real quantity of money – the quantity of goods and services that the nominal quantity of money can purchase, or the number of weeks' income to which the nominal quantity of money is equal. This real quantity of money has important effects on the efficiency of operation of the economic mechanism, on how wealthy people regard themselves as being and, indeed, on how wealthy they actually are.

And, Hutt (1956, 198) states:

"Now Mises himself, and several other economists, maintain explicitly that the amount of money which individuals and firms decide to hold is determined by the marginal utility of its services. Yet for some reason they have not made the next small step needed to recognize this prospective yield (of 'utilities') which invites the holding of money, as the normal return to investment.

The prospective yield from investment in money assets consists, I suggest, (a) of a prospective *pecuniary yield*, in which case the money assets are a producers' goods; or (b) of a prospective *nonpecuniary yield* in personal convenience, in which case the money assets are consumers' goods; or (c) of a prospective "real," i.e., *nonpecuniary* speculative yield, in which case the money assets are producers' goods, whether held privately or in the course of business."

Thus, for Hutt, people hold money because it provides a yield; i.e., a benefit, to them. Moreover, Hutt (1956, 208) states that: "The mere fact, however, that a particular economic good is capable of being diluted is no proof that it is not useful or productive." Then, in a footnote, (Hutt, 1956, 208, n71) he distinguishes between "the 'number of money units' and, 'the amount of money in real terms,'" clearly implying that an increase in the "number of money units" (i.e., "nominal money") does not confer an additional yield or benefit to society, whereas an increase in "money in real terms" (i.e., "real money") does.

Barnett and Block (2004) argue that the optimum quantity of a commodity money is whatever amount is provided in a free market. They also maintain that the optimum quantity of a fiat money is the extant amount; i.e., that the amount of fiat money should be frozen. In that case, a general decline in market determined prices[316], would cause an increase in real money, which increase would be optimal in that institutional setting.[317]

However, as an economist qua economist, all that can be said is that in a commodity-money economy some individuals voluntarily add to the stock of money; e.g., by causing newly mined gold to be minted into coins. It is true that this reduces the value of the existing stock of money below what it otherwise would be, but that can no more be said to violate the rights of someone whose money holdings are so decreased in value than can the production of additional units of any other good that reduces the value of preexisting units of that good. That is, actions that are within the rights of the individuals cannot be said to improperly harm others because they cause a decline in value of the others' possessions, regardless of whether the goods in question are money or something else. In point of fact, additions to the stock of a commodity money or of the real, though not nominal, stock of fiat money provide net benefits, else they would not be made. To argue otherwise is argue that money constitutes, in effect, a case of "market failure." That is, the implicit claim here is that the free market will misallocate resources to the production of money, which resources could be put to better use elsewhere (Mises, 1996, 421- 422). Should that be the case, governmental intervention into the monetary system cannot be ruled out on logical grounds. Rather, it becomes a historical/empirical issue: do the benefits of governmental intervention outweigh the costs thereof?

Money, in fact, is indispensable in our economic order. But as an economic good it is not a physical component of the social distributive apparatus in the way that account books, prisons, or firearms are. No part of the total result of production is dependent on the collaboration of money

---

[316] Such a decline would be normal in a growing economy with a fixed stock of fiat money.

[317] See, also, Canaan (1921)

even though the use of money may be one of the fundamental principles on which the economic order is based (Mises, 1980, 102).

The problem here is the failure to see that social distributive apparatus is not solely concerned with the physical distribution of goods but also with the distribution of the rights to them. Moreover, that money is not a physical component of the social distributive apparatus (which of course it is in a commodity-money society[318]) is irrelevant; if something plays a role in transforming a good from a higher to a lower order, it is, de facto, a capital good. But that is exactly what happens in every exchange and, therefore, money, the good that facilitates exchanges is, indubitably, a capital good. Furthermore, as shown supra by Mises himself, money is essential to the production in a modern capitalist society; without it there neither would nor could be any such society.

Production goods derive their value from that of their products. Not so money; for no increase in the welfare of the members of a society can result from the availability of an additional quantity of money. The laws which govern the value of money are different from those which govern the value of production goods and from those which govern the value of consumption goods.

The argument that additions to the stock of money do not increase the welfare of the members of society social has been dealt with, supra. It is not correct to say that the laws that govern the value of money are different from those that govern the value of other goods. The value of any good is determined by the contribution it is expected to make (directly, in the case of consumers' goods or indirectly, in the case of capital goods) to the satisfaction of human wants.

In sum, because money is "the" good used in exchange, and exchange transforms goods from higher to lower order, and production is action which transforms goods from higher to lower order, money, too, is a producers' good; i.e., a capital good. That the transformations in which money is involved are not physical in nature, but, rather, are of an intangible nature – "merely" concerning ownership rights -- is irrelevant. Money is just as important, indeed, probably far more important, for the production process than any other single capital good such as steel, or cement. It would be far easier to conceive of a modern civilization without either of the latter two, than the former.

---

318 We are certainly aware of the fact that our present social arrangements do not at all feature a commodity money, or, indeed, many of the other attributes of a laissez faire economy. This point notwithstanding, we are attempting to address present realities, not, only, theoretical considerations. It cannot be denied that fiat money and central banks, for example, play very important roles in modern societies.

There is yet another series of ways in which goods can be transformed from higher to lower orders in the structure of production without moving them geographically, or changing them physically. This method, too, is thus analogous to the role played by money, in transferring items from the ownership and control of one person to another. We refer, here, to the functions of advertising, marketing, brokering, insuring and in all other ways bringing material closer to the realm of the final consumer without chemically or physically transforming it. On the somewhat superficial distinction made between selling and production costs, Kirzner had this to say:

"Every aspect of the product (including such extras as friendly service, free parking, and the like) has been produced (and the associated outlays undertaken) strictly in the belief that it would enhance the salability of the whole product. No single penny of the outlay – even those usually considered as strictly production, rather than selling, costs – can be perceived as anything but costs incurred in order to 'sell.' (Kirzner, 1973, 144)"

The point is that there is a direct analogy between activities such as advertising, marketing, brokering, etc., as intermediating agencies on the one hand, which bring goods and services out of the wilderness of the higher orders area, and into, or closer to, the more salutary-arena of consumption, and on the other hand, money, which does precisely the same thing. The purpose of products markets and capital goods is, after all, the bringing of them into fruition as items of use to consumers; they have no intrinsic value in and of themselves apart from this necessary "mission" of theirs. If the former deserve to be considered part and parcel of higher order or capital goods and services, and they do, then so does the latter.

III. Rothbard

Here is a statement from Murray Rothbard pertaining to our subject:

"We are now on the threshold of a great economic law, a truth that can hardly be overemphasized, considering the harm its neglect has caused throughout history. An increase in the supply of a producers' good increases, *ceteris paribus*, the supply of a consumers' good. An increase in the supply of a consumers' good (when there has been no decrease in the supply of another good) is demonstrably a clear *social benefit*; for someone's "real income" has increased and no one's has decreased. [Footnote omitted.]"

"Money, on the contrary, is solely useful for exchange purposes. Money, *per se*, cannot be consumed and cannot be used directly as a producers' good in the productive process. Money *per se* is therefore unproductive; it is dead stock and produces nothing. Land or capital is always in the form of some specific good, some specific productive instrument. Money always remains in someone's cash balance. (Rothbard, 1970, 670)."

An analogy arises between money and what is called a "catalyst" in the field of chemistry. Rothbard quite correctly maintains that money, per se, is not used up[319] as it is utilized in its task of facilitating trade. But the same can be said for the role of catalysts in chemical reactions. They assist in these processes, without, themselves, being used up. Yet, it would be the rare chemist who would go so far as to say that, therefore, a catalyst "*per se* is therefore unproductive."

It is much the same with money. Even on Rothbard's own grounds that money is not used up when it plays its exchange facilitating role, it hardly follows that money is therefore "dead stock and produces nothing." Very much to the contrary, the monetary commodity is a highly useful one. If, in fact, money is dead stock and produces nothing; i.e., adds no value, why would people give up valuable goods and resources to acquire it? And yet we know that they do.

Then there is the point that "money always remains in someone's cash balance." To be sure, it does. But no less could be said in behalf of any other economic good. While it is of course true that items such as steel, shoes and sugar do not enter anyone's cash balance, let alone remain there, these goods are also always under the ownership and control of someone, no matter how quickly they may travel from hand to hand in terms of turn over of property from one person to another. Thus, if (part of) the reason that Rothbard considers money "unproductive" is that it is always owned, then all other economic goods must also be "unproductive" because they also are owned.[320] But the latter position is unacceptable, as all other goods most certainly are "productive;" therefore, it cannot be maintained that money is unproductive because it is always in someone's cash balance.[321]

---

[319] Gold, of course, is subject to wear and tear as it is used, certainly in the case of jewelry and teeth fillings, but also as it passes from hand to hand in its monetary use.
[320] That is, if we accept the analogy between money always being in someone's cash balance, and economic goods always being owned by someone.
[321] This is neither the time nor the place to critically examine Rothbard's view that "An increase in the supply of money confers no social benefit whatever." See on this Barnett and Block, 2004.

IV. Hoppe et al.

Although Hoppe, Hülsmann, and Block (1998, 19-50) [322] do not directly address the issue with which we are concerned, it does arise indirectly in their discussion of money as a present good and not a future good. [323] According to Rothbard (1993 [1962], 60-61):

"Goods being directly and presently consumed are *present goods*. A *future good* is the present expectation of enjoying a consumers' good at some point in the future. A future good may be a claim on future consumers' goods or it may be a capital good, which will be transformed into a consumers' good in the future. Since a capital good is a way station (and nature-given factors are original stations) on the route to consumers' goods, capital goods and nature-given factors are both future goods."

If Rothbard is correct, as we think him to be, then money can not be a present good, as only "[g]oods being directly and presently consumed are *present goods*" (Rothbard, 1970, 59-60).- Moreover, it is no more "a claim on future consumers' goods" then it is a claim on present on future capital goods. The logical conclusion, based on Rothbard, is that it is a capital good. That is, it is a good and there are only consumers' goods and capital goods. Of course, there are claims thereto, from which these must be distinguished, but these are not the goods themselves.

However, Hoppe, Hülsmann, and Block (1998, 43) state:

"Yet money is demonstrably *not* a future good. In fact, when the money is spent - in the future - it loses all its utility for the present owner. It has utility only while and insofar as it is *not* spent, and its character as a present good stems from the omnipresent human condition of *uncertainty* [footnote omitted]."

Compare the paragraph above with the following one, in which the present authors have substantively substituted the word "inventory" for the word "money," and also non-substantively substituted "exchanged" for "spent," with the following:

---

322 The careful reader will note that Block is a co-author both of the present paper and the one now undergoing criticism in this section of it. The correct implication of this strange phenomenon is that Block has changed his mind as concerns the proper status of money as a present or future good. However, nothing said in the present paper can properly be interpreted as criticism of the main contention of Hoppe, et. al. 1998, to wit that fractional reserve banking is incompatible with the operations of a free enterprise system.

323 The purpose of Hoppe, Hülsmann, and Block is to refute the normative and positive positions of Selgin and White (1966). The conclusions of that paper stand independently of the arguments herein.

"Yet inventory is demonstrably *not* a future good. In fact, when the inventory is exchanged - in the future - it loses all its utility for the present owner. It has utility only while and insofar as it is *not* exchanged, and its character as a present good stems from the omnipresent human condition of *uncertainty.*"

This latter sentence is obviously incorrect. Inventories of any kind are not present goods; rather, it is the characteristic of being "directly and presently consumed" that makes a good a present good, and money qua money is never consumed. This applies, even, to goods that would otherwise and ordinarily be considered "consumer" goods. Suppose a person has an inventory of apples, for example. Now, apples, typically, are considered consumer, not producer goods. But with an inventory of them, this can no longer be the case. Only those apples that are consumed in any given time period can be considered consumer, not intermediate goods. The ones that are to be consumed later are at present intermediate goods[324]. We conclude that money is not a present good. Therefore, it must be a future good, and because it is a future good, it must be a capital good.[325]

To be sure, the main function of money for most people[326] is to bridge the gap between present and future, which is necessitated[327] by the

---

[324] On this point, see Rothbard, ([1962] 1993, pp. 6-8).

[325] Money is not the only good that is a claim to other goods. Properly understood any good is a claim against other goods; it is just that money is the most efficient good for the purpose of being a claim; in a commodity money world, money is also a commodity and in a paper money world, paper money is also paper. However, there are some claims that are not goods in themselves, but solely and merely claims to underlying goods; e.g. stocks and bonds. If gold coins were no longer money because people shifted to platinum coins, the gold coins would still have value as a commodity that could be traded (i.e., used as a claim against) other goods. However, if paper money were no longer money because people shifted to commodity coins the paper money would be virtually worthless, save for any collectors' value or scrap value it might have. The same can be said for the stock and bonds of a corporation the assets of which were totally destroyed. Thus a bond is not a good, but a claim to a good; only goods have value, and the bond's value is derivative from the good it is a claim against – destroy the good and you destroy the claim. The same could be said of gold coins, destroy the good (the gold coins) and you destroy the claim the gold coin constitutes against other goods. One can destroy the bond (the claim) without destroying the goods underlying it; but if you destroy the good, you destroy the value of the bond, though it may continue to exist physically. However, from an economic point to view, mere physical existence takes on a secondary role.

[326] Exceptions include misers such as Scrooge McDuck, who reveled in daily "swims" through his money bin. For a positive spin on this economic actor, see Block (1991C, 105-109).

[327] "Necessitated" might be too strong a word, since it cannot be denied that people did exist under barter.

uncertainty of the latter. If the future were known with certainty, there would be no need for money. But precisely the same state of affairs obtains with regard to inventory. There would also be no benefit in holding inventory either, were it not for this omnipresent uncertainty. Indeed, inventories of goods play much the same role in dealing with future uncertainty as do monetary holdings. Yet no one would be tempted to claim that stocks of goods whose purpose is to mediate between input and output are not higher order, or intermediate goods; no one would be tempted to categorize them as present or consumer goods.

Compare also, the following two (2) paragraphs.

"The error in classifying *money* as a future good can be revealed in a twofold manner. On the one hand, negatively, it can be shown that this assumption still leads to contradiction. In support of their thesis, Selgin and White claim that "holding *money* for later *spending*, rather than *spending it on* consumption *now,* does defer consumption to the future," implying that the holding of *money* involves the exchange of a future good (satisfaction) for a present one. In the next sentence they admit that *money* held is *spent neither* on consumer goods *nor* on producer goods. Yet they fail to notice that this implies also, as a further consequence, that holding *money* for later *spending,* rather than *spending it on* production *now,* does defer *production* (and hence *future* consumption) to the future. If the holding of *money* defers consumption and production, however, then it becomes impossible to maintain that the holder of *money* has thereby invested in a *future* good, because *there* are *no future goods—whether* consumer or producer goods—which result from the act of holding *money* and to which its holder could thus be entitled. Yet as claims to no future goods whatsoever, *money* would be worthless. By implication, if *money* is not worthless (and no one would hold *money* if it had no value), then its value must be that of a *present* good" (Hoppe et al., 1998, 43-44).

Again, a similar word substitution is employed in the next paragraph as between "money" and "inventory."

"The error in classifying *inventory* as a future good can be revealed in a twofold manner. On the one hand, negatively, it can be shown that this assumption still leads to contradiction. In support of their thesis, Selgin and White claim that "holding *inventory* for later *exchanging,* rather than *exchanging it for* consumption *now,* does defer consumption to the future," implying that the holding of *inventory* involves the exchange of a future good (satisfaction) for a present one. In the next sentence they admit that *inventory* held is *exchanged neither for* consumer goods *nor for* producer goods. Yet they fail to notice that this implies also, as a further consequence, that holding *inventory* for later *exchanging*, rather than *using it in* production *now,* does defer *production* (and hence *future* consumption) to the future. If the holding of *inventory* defers consumption and production, however, then it becomes impossible to maintain that the holder of *inventory* has thereby invested in a *future* good, because *there* are *no future goods—whether* consumer or producer goods—which result from the act of holding *inventory* and to which its holder could thus be entitled. Yet as claims to no future goods whatsoever, *inventory* would be worthless. By implication, if *inventory* is not worthless (and no one would hold *inventory* if it had no value), then its value must be that of a *present* good."

These word substitutions, again, are our attempt to illustrate the point that just because, undeniably, money is the par excellence means of dealing with doubt about future events, it by no means logically follows that it is a present good. Very much to the contrary, stocks of goods on the shelves of the retailer are also employed to this end, and no one would think to characterize them as present or consumers goods because of this fact.

An earlier example from Hoppe of a similar analysis is:

"Matters become somewhat more complex under conditions of uncertainty, with money actually in use, but the praxeological independence of money and interest remains fully intact. Under these conditions, man invariably has three instead of two alternatives as to how to allocate his current income. He must not only decide how much to allocate to the purchase of present goods and how much to future goods (i.e., how much to consume and how much to invest), but also how much to keep in cash. There are no other alternatives" (Hoppe, 1993, 119).

Compare also, the following two (2) paragraphs based upon a quote from Mises that appears in Hoppe et al. (1998, 44):

"In a system without change in which there is no uncertainty whatever about the future, nobody needs to hold *cash*. Every individual knows precisely what amount of money he will need at any future date. He is therefore in a position to lend all the funds he receives in such a way that the loans fall due on the date he will need them. (Mises 1966, 249)"

In a system without change in which there is no uncertainty whatever about the future, nobody needs to hold *inventory*. Every individual knows precisely what amount of inventory he will need at any future date. He is therefore in a position to lend all the inventory he receives in such a way that the loans fall due on the date he will need them.

Hoppe et. al. (1998, 44) also state [emphasis added]:

"The source of the utility of a consumer good is its direct and present serviceability, and the source of the utility of a producer good is its indirect future serviceability. Money, by contrast, is neither consumed nor employed in production. It is neither directly serviceable (as consumer goods are) nor indirectly useful as a way station to future consumer goods (as producer goods are). Rather, the utility of money must be that of an *indirectly* yet presently serviceable good."

However, as we have seen supra, money is a capital good. It is used in production to transform goods from higher orders to lower orders; that, precisely, is its function. That is, the entire function of money qua money is to be a more efficient means of transforming higher order goods to lower orders than barter exchange. Of course, the transformation is not physical, but rather is part and parcel of ownership. And, it most certainly is "indirectly useful as a way station to future consumer goods;" again, think of the alternative, barter. The problem seems to be thinking that transforming goods requires some physical change in the good or its location. But that is not correct.

Thus we have shown that money is not some third type of good, distinct from consumers' goods or capital goods, but, rather it is a type of capital good; moreover, it is not a present good, but, rather, a future good.

Consider the following analysis by Rothbard (1993 [1962], 6-8) of the lowly "ham sandwich" as further evidence in support of our claim regarding money as a future not a present good. In this economists view, the final good in this regard is not the creation of the sandwich by Jones' wife who "expend(s) energy in unwrapping the bread, slicing the ham placing the ham between bread slices and carrying it to Jones." No, this is only "the labor of the housewife." This, coupled with "bread in the kitchen, ham in the kitchen and a knife to slice the ham" plus time and land upon which to stand, constitute "first order producers' goods, since, in this case, these co-operate in the production of the consumers' good."

Where, then, does money figure into this idyllic picture of domestic bliss? Is it a consumers' good? Not a bit of it; rather, Rothbard informs us, "the consumers' good" in this little story is "the ham sandwich at the point of being eaten." Money is certainly not as close to this final consumption as is food-stuff at the very point of being consumed. How does it stack up, then, in comparison with the "first order producers' goods" necessary to construct this culinary delight, that is, "bread in the kitchen, ham in the kitchen and a knife to slice the ham," etc? That is, which comes first in time, in the ordinary case of putting together this concoction? Surely, the use of money is prior to any thing properly included in this category, since "bread in the kitchen, ham in the kitchen, etc." come after the purchase of them in the market.

Rothbard continues his meticulous and careful analysis by identifying "second order producers' goods" as "bread-in-retail-shop and housewife's labor in carrying it (plus the ever-present land-as-standing-room and time." Again we ask, where does money fit into this scenario, in terms of the temporal order? Clearly, if we were but to include it, as Rothbard does not, at least not this early in his magnum opus, we would have to count "bread-in-retail-shop," along with ham, lettuce and mustard in the store, as even higher order goods. This would leave money as an intermediate order production or capital good, in that it is through the intermediation of money, in between the higher and lower orders, that material in the latter is transformed into material in the former. That is, money, is a necessary concomitant of the production process in the absence of barter, and its contribution takes place somewhere in between the higher order good (bread and ham in the store, owned by the retailer) and the lower order good, bread and ham on the street, under the possession of the housewife, on its way into the kitchen.

If Rothbard is so meticulous as to consider even bread and ham in the kitchen not as a final consumption good, but rather as a first order production good, however much more strong is the case that money, which appears in this story before that stage, would be considered not only a capital good, but one of a higher order than this?

In the analysis of the present authors, see listing below, bread and ham[328] in the store is the sixth order capital good, money, which transmits these intermediate goods into the housewife's possession is the fifth, material in the grocery bag en route home is the fourth, the raw materials in the kitchen the third, the put together sandwich in the kitchen the second, and when it arrives on the plate in front of Jones, this constitutes the lowest, or first order intermediate or capital good.

- Capital or inter. goods 6. bread and ham in the store
- Capital or inter. goods 5. money and bread and ham in the process of exchange.
- Capital or inter. goods 4. bread and ham in the housewife's possession, on the street, being carried to the home.
- Capital or inter. goods 3. bread and ham in the kitchen
- Capital or inter. goods 2. ham placed on the bread in the form of a sandwich, but still located in the kitchen
- Capital or inter. goods 1. ham placed in front of Jones, in his very hands
- Consumer goods: the ham sandwich, at the very point of being eaten by Jones.

Although at first blush money might seem out of place in this list because the other items all refer to steps in the transformation of raw materials into a ham sandwich, however, to make this objection is to consider the production process from the perspective of an "engineer," not that of an economist. To the economist it is not the physical transformation that is

---

[328] "Plus etcetera" is always to be implicitly understood in all these cases.

important, but rather the value transformation; i.e., the value added. So as any of the other steps add value by advancing the work-in-process closer to its end – a consumer good being consumed – so also does the change of ownership effectuated by use of the money as a capital good in the exchange process, as per our argument in section II, supra.

V. Conclusion

Admittedly, if there are categories of action and goods other than those of consumption and production, the most likely would be exchange; then there would be a certain coherence in selecting money, out of all other possibilities, to be placed in the third grouping. However, there is simply no warrant for any such exception to the general rule that when man acts, he does so for the purpose of either consuming now and in the present, or rendering the future more to his liking than that situation which would have obtained had he not acted; that is, of increasing his store of capital or intermediate goods. There is, unfortunately for the theories of those economists we have criticized above, no third option. Money might appear to be an exception, but as we have shown, it, too, must be successfully subsumed under the rubric of one of these categories, to wit, producers' goods.

Chapter 19. In Defense of Fiduciary Media - A Comment or What's Wrong with "Monopoly" (or Play) Money?[329]

I. Introduction

In a recent issue of the *Review of Austrian Economics* George Selgin and Lawrence H. White (1996) defend their position that people should be free "...to issue and use fiduciary media of exchange" against criticisms also published in the *RAE* by Hans-Herman Hoppe (1994B), Jeśus Huerta de Soto (1995), and Jörg Guido Hülsmann (1996). Selgin and White (hereinafter, SW) write off in short order, and rightly so, monetary systems consisting of fractional-reserve banking systems based either on governmental fiat money or, a la Hayek (1978A), on fiat-type (i.e., irredeemable, non-commodity) monies. They distinguish fiduciary media bank notes and demand deposits redeemable for a commodity money (gold specie), on the one hand when they are backed less than 100% by reserves of gold specie, and on the other hand when they are backed by the full 100%. Thereafter SW commence their defense of monetary systems with fractional-reserve banking, provided they are based on gold specie money.[330] They argue that such systems are both ethically and economically defensible.[331]

Regarding ethicality, against the charge of fraud, they argue that, provided that the bank does not deceive depositors re the matter of reserves, voluntary deposit contracts involving fractional-reserve deposits are not fraudulent. The only real point of contention in the literature favoring this system appears to be whether or not depositors know full well that banks engage in fractional-reserve banking and thus whether or not banks have a duty to notify them and their assignees, and, if they do have such a duty, the particulars thereof. There is, of course, nothing exceptional about this[332].

---

[329] The present authors wish to acknowledge an intellectual debt to Hoppe, et. al. (1998). We are also very grateful to an anonymous referee of this Journal for helpful feedback and criticisms to an earlier draft of this paper.

[330] Hereinafter: 1) only systems using gold specie are considered, whether the banks are fractional-reserve or 100% reserve banks; and, 2) the term "fractional-reserve" refers only to *demand* deposits, or to bank notes redeemable in specie on demand, or to banks or banking systems that offer such notes or deposits.

[331] These are referred to by SW as legitimacy and practical-advantages arguments. Certainly they mean morality not legitimacy, as any monetary and banking system sanctioned by law is, by definition, legitimate; whether a particular such system is moral is another, and far more important, matter.

[332] For an analysis of fractional-reserve parking lots, airline overbooking, lotteries, etc., see Hoppe, et. al. 1998, pp 47-48.

With respect to the economics of the matter, they address several issues. We consider them in the following order: section II – instability; section III – resource costs savings; section IV – feasibility; and, section V – mismatching of maturities.[333] We conclude in section VI with a discussion of the possible conflation of time and demand deposits.

II. Fractional-reserve Banks are Inherently Unstable

Perhaps our most important objection to their position arises with the issue of stability. For SW, free-banking is a system, based on gold or silver specie, in which anyone could open and operate a bank, subject only to the test of the market.[334]

They assume, undoubtedly correctly, that, provided it was legal, some banks in such a system would attempt to act not as bailees (100% reserve banks), but rather as depositories (fractional-reserve banks), their obligation being limited merely to redeeming on demand, and in specie, any demand notes or deposits they had previously issued to customers. The fact that, in such a system, some individual banks, and *a fortiori*, the "system" as a whole would not, at any time, have enough specie to redeem all its obligations does not present a problem to SW. In our view, however, this is a position requiring elucidation.

Thus, putting other possible problems aside, a key objection to fractional-reserve banking is that when there are bank runs, and history provides plenty of evidence thereof, banks will fail, the banking system will shrink, if not implode, and society's payments mechanism will be damaged, causing severe damage to the system of social cooperation we know as the market, with attendant reduced levels of human want satisfactions.

SW (1996, 91-92) offer, essentially, three arguments against the problem of bank runs. First, "solvent banks are not inherently run-prone."[335]

---

[333] Actually, they treat the issue of feasibility in the section on fraud; however, it seems to us that feasibility is an economic not an ethical issue.

[334] That is, there would be no central bank or other lender of last resort, nor governmental deposit insurance, nor legal tender laws, nor any other type of governmental intervention/regulation, save for the enforcement of property rights and contracts.

[335] It is important to be clear as to the meaning of *solvent* and *insolvent* banks. Certainly by solvent (insolvent) SW do *not* mean non-bankrupt (bankrupt); i.e., a situation in which a bank's assets exceed (are less than) its liabilities, for that would be to trivialize their argument. Rather, by solvent (insolvent) they must mean either a situation in which a bank can (can not) satisfy, by paying specie, current demands to redeem its notes and demand deposits *or* a situation in which a bank is (is not) *expected* to be able to satisfy, by paying specie, anticipated future demands to redeem its banknotes and demand deposits.

Second, the market would *immediately* eliminate banks thought to be insolvent.[336] And, third, banks could insert (temporary) "option clauses" in their contracts with their customers. Let us consider these in turn.

II-1. "Solvent" Fractional-reserve Banks Are Inherently Run-prone

It cannot be denied that an interventionist fractional-reserve banking system has a number of means to deal with bank runs that are not available in a pure free-banking system. First, and most important, knowledgeable participants in the economy know full well that under Federal Deposit Insurance Corporation (FDIC) specifications, the savings of all depositors are, virtually 100%, guaranteed;[337] any bank which cannot meet its obligations, due to fractional-reserve shortcomings, is assured that the Fed stands ready and willing to print up enough new money and more, if need be, to make good on their obligations. Second, there are lender of last resort mechanisms, or purchaser (at a premium over market value) of non-(or under-)performing assets.[338] Third are "bank-libel" laws[339] prohibiting the calling in to question of the probity of a bank, and thus aiding, abetting and fomenting runs on banks.

However, none of these measures would be available for fractional-reserve notes or demand deposits in a free market.[340] The type of risk involved in potential bank runs make it impossible to insure, privately, such notes and

---

[336] "It is true that a particular bank's notes would be valued below par if market participants worried that they might not be able to redeem the notes ahead of a run on that bank. But such notes, on which the default was considered a non-negligible risk, would not continue circulating even at a discount. They would immediately be presented for redemption, and thus removed from circulation. The surviving brands of notes would be only those for which all redemption demands made in practice were expected to be met" (SW, 1996, 90). By inference, what is true for notes would also be true of deposits. Therefore, insolvent banks would be driven from the market immediately they were recognized as such and only the solvent banks would continue to operate.

[337] "On April 1, 1999, a new law raised the FDIC limits on joint accounts. Now, FDIC will cover up to $100,000 for each person listed on joint accounts at that bank. Because these limits are based on the type of ownership, not the number or type of accounts, FDIC calculates your joint-account limit by adding up your share of any accounts you own jointly at that bank (half the account total if there are two owners)…. [T]he FDIC limits apply separately to each bank where you have accounts" Lankford (1999).

[338] These means of course cause other problems, but that is an issue beyond the scope of the present paper.

[339] See Swire (1992). For the argument against laws prohibiting libel, see Rothbard (1978B,106; 1982B, 126-128) and Block (1991C, 50-53).

[340] This assumes, arguendo, that fractional-reserve banking and a free market are compatible, a claim we reject below.

deposits against default.[341] Moreover, there would be no lender of last resort (because only the state or its agent has the power to so act) as neither an individual company, nor the industry as a whole has the necessary resources.[342] Again, only a government has the wherewithal and, more important, a motive to purchase non- (or under) performing assets at a premium over market value. Finally, as there would be no bank-libel laws in a free market, the 100% reserve bank competitors of fractional-reserve banks would be able to instigate runs by advertising the essential insolvency of fractional-reserve banks, yea even to initiate runs by demanding specie for any net differential when claims were cleared with fractional-reserve banks.[343]

Therefore, whereas bank runs on fractional-reserve banks are infrequent (though not non-existent) in the presence of governmental intervention to prevent runs or stop them if they do get started, bank runs would be ubiquitous in a free market.

Against the argument that the type of risk involved in bank runs is uninsurable in a free insurance market, SW (1996, 91) argue that "*solvent*[344] banks are not inherently run-prone." The difficulty here is that, strictly speaking, *each and every* fractional-reserve bank is *immediately* "insolvent" as soon as it makes it first deposit-based loan.[345] This consideration, then, is moot. Or, to put this into other words, SW are here referring to a distinction without a difference. If *all* fractional-reserve banks are *always* and *ever* in a state of insolvency, then there can be no intelligible distinction among them

---

[341] If the potential loss from an event would affect all members of the risk class, the event is uninsurable. For example, private flood insurance is unavailable because all members of the class - parcels of property in the flood plain - will suffer losses from the same event. Therefore, the risk cannot be spread from those members of the class unfortunate enough to experience the event and consequent loss to other members of the class who do not experience the event, and therefore, do not incur a loss. If, and when, the event occurs, all members of the class experience a loss.

[342] Private deposit insurance would, in any case, only shift the "uninsurable" risk to a different level, as would be true also were private deposit insurance to be the object of reinsurance. This is true no matter how wealthy the "names" because with fractional-reserve banking, by definition, the claims, in the form of bank notes and/or deposits, to specie necessarily are in excess of the total specie in the banking system.

[343] And, that such net differences in claims would be in favor of 100 reserve banks is a virtual certainty because for any specific amount of reserves a fractional reserve bank would have more liabilities in the form of bank notes and demand deposits than a 100% reserve bank.

[344] Italics added.

[345] Such a bank may initially and thereafter make loans of any gold-coins that are part of the bank's capital without becoming insolvent. It is only when, and as soon as, it makes loans of gold coins that have been deposited into demand-deposit accounts that it becomes insolvent.

on the basis of solvency. A "solvent fractional-reserve bank," then, is no less than an oxymoron. Therefore, it is infeasible to defend their position on the basis of an "immediate" elimination of insolvent banks.

II-2. Option Clauses Naught Availeth

Now consider SW's argument that banks could preclude themselves from bank runs by stipulating in their contracts with depositors some sort of grace period. They argue that such clauses would provide "essentially solvent" banks encountering a deficiency of specie the contractual right (based on informed consent) to suspend specie redemption for a limited period of time.[346] During this grace period the bank could liquidate sufficient obligations to meet the redemption demands for specie, thus defeating runs. SW argue that (temporary) "option clauses" providing banks the contractual right (based on informed consent) to suspend specie redemption for a limited period of time would enable banks to defeat runs. In their view, solvent banks could issue notes and deposits subject to such a clause, thus giving them breathing space to liquidate sufficient assets to meet the redemption demand within the specified period

One problem with this "solution" is that all such "grace periods" and "option clauses" convert what would otherwise be a *demand* deposit (that is, money payable *on demand)* to a savings or time deposit, with just this sort of provision for a "cooling off" period. But opponents of fractional-reserve banking, such as the present authors, never denied that keeping only a fraction of outstanding balances on hand was improper for savings or time deposits, only for *demand* deposits. Thus SW's proviso avails them nothing in this debate.

Moreover, the exercise of such a clause would certainly interfere with the payments mechanism. To the extent that banks exercised such clauses, their depositors and the holders of their notes who were depending on these fiduciary media to consummate exchanges could not so do, with all the negative effects thereof; to wit: the situation in Argentina currently and in the recent past, where the government has both reduced convertibility from fiduciary media into *fiat* money[347] and, for a while, suspended all such convertibility.[348]

---

346 The exercise of such rights would involve a substantial interest penalty.

347 If fractional-reserve banking can cause such problems in a system with governmental intervention and fiat money, there can be no doubt that the difficulties would be immeasurably greater in the system SW advocate: free banking, cum legal fractional reserves, with gold backed fiduciary media and no governmental intervention in the form of note and deposit insurance, lender-of-last-resort, purchaser of distressed securities at above market prices, and bank-libel laws.

348 Granted, that there were no convertibility-suspension clauses in the Argentine situation; nevertheless, there is no reason to think that problems caused by the

We conclude this section by noting that runs would be an ubiquitous feature of a "free market economy" with a fractional-reserve banking system and that they would continuously destabilize the economy.

III. Resource Cost "Savings"

SW argue that there is a significant cost of 100% reserves. It consists of the cost of mining and storing that amount of gold needed for use as bank reserves in excess of the amount that fractional-reserve banks would have required (call this "excess gold").[349] That is, resources are not allocated optimally in a system where bank notes and demand deposits are completely backed up by gold; rather, either the resources used to mine the excess gold could have been used to produce other want-satisfying goods or, depending upon people's preferences as expressed in the market, the excess gold might have been mined anyway, but rather than being used as excess gold (undesired and unnecessary reserves), might be used to satisfy other wants (e.g., jewelry) or extant gold could be diverted from other uses to reserves. There is certainly no argument emanating from this quarter to the effect that 100% reserves are not costless; resources do have alternative uses, to be sure.[350] However, SW ignore resource costs of fractional-reserve banking save that of holding reserves of gold in excess of those required to meet demands for redemption of bank notes and demand deposits. But resource costs are not the only costs involved in fractional-reserve banking; fractional-reserve banking has been, and will continue to be a cause of the business cycle, the name we apply to a process of systematic misallocation of resources.[351] Although virtually impossible to quantify, this systematic misallocation of resources takes the form, during the false boom, of massive

---

inability to access funds would have been any less had it been because of the exercise of such clauses rather than the result of government fiat.

349 Of course, the excess gold could come from diverting extant gold from other uses rather than from mining new gold.

350 The type of monetary system, whether gold or fiat money, in conjunction with the issue of fractional-reserve, or 100% reserve, backed bank notes and demand deposits is intimately related to the issue of the optimum quantity of money. On that see: Barnett and Block, 2004.

351 With fractional reserve banking new money is lent into existence. This process does not create any new goods or resources. However, to the preexisting claims against the extant real goods and services, it adds additional claims in the form of the new fiduciary media. The spending of these new media cause the prices of the extant goods and resources to increase, but not all at the same times or by the same percentages. Therefore the structure of relative prices is distorted. Moreover, the increase in credit causes interest rates to decline, distorting the intertemporal structure of prices. Again, not all interest rates decline simultaneously or by the same degree. See on this any of the copious literature on the Austrian business cycle theory, a recent example being Garrison (2001).

misallocations of scarce capital and human resources, and during the subsequent and consequent bust, the un- and under-employment of both capital and human resources. One can look to the current and recent situations in the U.S., say 1990-2002, or Japan, say 1980-2002, to get some feel for the immense magnitude of the respective misallocations of goods and resources, and the costs thereof. Indubitably, these costs dwarf any resource costs resulting from mining and storing "excess gold reserves."

Moreover, the resource costs incurred by fractional-reserve banks, necessary to convince their clients to make and maintain demand deposits with them and to encourage the members of society-at-large to accept their deposits and/or notes in exchanges, would likely not be insignificant. In a truly just society, 100% reserve banks would be free to refuse to accept fractional-reserve notes and deposits or, if they did, to redeem them only for specie. That is, the existence of 100% reserve banks alongside fractional-reserve banks, wherein the former would demand specie for any net differential when claims were cleared with fractional-reserve banks, would force the latter to maintain very high ratios of reserves to notes and demand deposits. Therefore, resource costs savings by fractional-reserve banks from holding less than 100% reserves are very likely to be quite small. And, considering the massive misallocations of resources consequent on business cycles or bank runs, the overall resource costs of fractional-reserve banking would very likely be very much greater than that of 100%-reserve banking.

IV. Fractional-reserve Banks are Infeasible

The feasibility issue boils down to whether non-fraudulent fractional-reserve banks would have any creditors; i.e., would people knowingly accept banknotes or demand deposits from fractional-reserve banks.

Moreover, because every insolvent bank would be driven out of business immediately it became insolvent, by (SW's) definition every extant bank would necessarily be solvent. Solvent, that is, until the moment it became insolvent and was immediately driven out of business. This begs the real question as to whether "solvent" banks would be run prone – by definition any bank experiencing a run would be insolvent and any bank not experiencing a run would be solvent.

Consider what Mises (1996, 432-434) had to say about money substitutes and fiduciary media:

"Claims to a definite amount of money, payable and redeemable on demand, against a debtor about whose solvency and willingness to pay there does not prevail the slightest doubt, render to the individual all the services money can render, provided that all parties with whom he could possibly transact business are perfectly familiar with these essential qualities of the claims concerned: daily maturity as well as undoubted solvency and willingness to pay on the part of the debtor. We may call such claims *money-substitutes,* as they can fully replace money in an individual's or a firm's cash holding… A money-substitute can be embodied either in a banknote or in a demand deposit with a bank subject to check ("checkbook money" or deposit currency), provided the bank is prepared to exchange the note or the deposit daily free of charge against money proper… The main thing is that every owner of a money-substitute is perfectly certain that it can, at every instant and free of expense, be exchanged against money."

"If the debtor – the government or a bank – keeps against the whole amount of money-substitutes a 100% reserve of money proper, we call the money-substitute a *money-certificate.*"

"If the money reserve kept by the debtor against the money-substitutes issued is less than the total amount of such substitutes, we call that amount of substitutes which exceeds the reserve *fiduciary media....*" (Mises, 1996, 432-433).

Therefore, according to Mises, for demand deposits and bank notes to be money substitutes "there [must] not prevail the *slightest* doubt" about the debtor's solvency by "*all* parties with whom [the owner of the claim] could *possibly* transact business" (emphases added). Moreover, "The *main* thing is that *every* owner of a money substitute [e.g., demand deposits and bank notes] is *perfectly certain* that it can, at *every instant* and free of expense, be exchanged against money."

Certainly, only in an interventionist banking system can fiduciary media satisfy those conditions. However, we are considering a free, not a hampered, market. In such a non-interventionist banking environment there is no way that fiduciary media can meet those stringent conditions; i.e., fiduciary media would not be, nor would they be accepted as, money substitutes. That is, they would be infeasible under these circumstances.

Furthermore, the argument of SW that non-fraudulent fractional-reserve banking is feasible may be correct if by feasible we mean that people might knowingly and willingly engage in such relationships with banks at certain points in time or for relatively short periods of time.[352] However, if by

---

[352] Consider the following scenario. In an unhampered economy a fractional reserve bank (FRB) is opened alongside 100% reserve banks. In order to attract customers, it advertises that: 1) it keeps a 99% reserve against demand deposits, and therefore, for all practical purposes, its deposits are as safe as those at 100% reserve banks; and, 2) its services are less expensive than those of the 100% reserve banks, because it lends out 1% of its deposits and uses the interest thereon to reduce the prices of its services. Assuming that the FRB's calculations are correct, it attracts customers and earns a profit. This success would attract imitators, either from among the extant 100% reserve banks or from new entrants into the industry. In any case, there would still be 100% reserve banks. Necessarily, when obligations are cleared among the banks, reserves will be drained from the FRBs to the latter. And, ironically, the more

feasible we mean that such relationships are logically possible, then the SW position is untenable.[353]

For example, assume there are 1 million bushels of wheat of a certain type and grade stored in a grain elevator with a capacity of 10 million bushels. There are, then, under present non-fraudulent circumstances, without doubt, also titles, in the form of warehouse receipts,[354] to these 1 million bushels. These titles are not to specific bushels of wheat, but to the specified amount of wheat of the type and grade that was put into storage.

Now, suppose the warehouse operator were to "print up" pieces of paper that purported to be titles to another 9 million bushels of wheat of the same type and grade. But he did so under very peculiar circumstances. No (purposeful) con artist, he, he printed them up with the express willing consent of *each and every member of society*;[355] i.e., each had signed a piece of paper, stating that he was of sound mind, and consenting to the printing up of these extra titles.

What would the actual function of these extra titles to 9 million bushels of (non-existent) wheat? Suppose the original titles to be marked with an "A" and the extra titles to be marked with a "0." Not one of the owners of the 1 million bushels of wheat would have signed these

---

successful were the FRBs in attracting customers, the sooner would the clearing process drain their reserves. They would then be faced with either a continual reduction in their demand liabilities in order to maintain a constant reserve ratio of 99% as their reserves decreased, or with a reduction in the reserve ratio in order to maintain their demand liabilities in the face of the reduced reserves. In the former case, they would end up with no demand liabilities; i.e., they would no longer be FRBs; in the latter case, they would experience runs that would put them out of business.

[353] There are two issues involved here: the practical and the logical-legal. Purely on a pragmatic level, a la P.T. Barnum, there are always suckers out their waiting to be taken – at least in the short run. However, it would not take much experience with fractional-reserve banks alongside 100% reserve banks, before there would not be enough fools left to make the former system profitable. That is, were both systems allowed to function side by side, and there were no laws against libeling fractional-reserve banks as necessarily bankrupt, then there is no doubt that, purely as a practical matter, the fractional-reserve banking system would prove untenable.

In sharp contrast is the logical-legal perspective. Fractional-reserve banking is no more compatible with a private property based, anti-fraud system than is the proverbial square circle compatible with reality. No matter what the fractional-reserve bankers thought they were doing, or were trying to do, it would be praxeologically impossible for them to succeed in promoting their dubious schemes in the context of full free enterprise; at best, all they could achieve would be to create play money.

[354] Such receipts might take the form of paper documents or of entries in a computer.

[355] Spooner [1872 (1870)], then, could have no objection to these goings on.

agreements, we may be absolutely sure, if it meant the expropriation of their wheat; i.e., if the 0 titles could be redeemed for wheat. Therefore, there would be no actual transfer of wheat, attendant upon this printing of "fractional-reserve;" i.e., 0, titles to wheat. What, then, will be the actual function of these 0 titles?

It is our contention that their function, their *only possible* function, will be to serve as a sort of a joke. That is, these extra 9 million titles will serve much the same purpose as "Monopoly" money, or fake U.S. currency, which obviously is printed up not to be used as counterfeit money, but rather, in the former case, in a Parker Brothers game and, in the latter, as a joke. For example, those "$1 million bills" that are very much bigger than U.S. dollars, with a picture of a donkey or an elephant instead of a person on them, etc. The point is, there cannot be (it is logically impossible for there to be) truly operational fractional-reserve bank notes or demand deposits through any sort of agreement process as outlined above that would not be readily interpreted as a joke or as mere play money by all fully informed people.

Furthermore, Block (1988, 28-31) suggests that, because the holder of a note for which there is only a 20% reserve has only a 20% chance of redeeming it in the event of a run, such notes partake of the character of a lottery ticket and would be valued at a discount by a knowledgeable public. In sharp contrast, SW argue that if people feared they might not be able to redeem a particular bank's notes before an imminent run, the notes would be valued below par and such would not circulate, even at a discount, but rather would be presented for redemption immediately.[356] They (1996, 90) state: "The surviving brands of notes would be only those for which all redemption demands made in practice were expected to be met." That is, only "good" (our term) notes would circulate, and those at par.

We conclude this section by noting that fractional-reserve banks would be driven out of business by 100% reserve banks because fractional-reserve banks would not merely be run prone, but would actually experience runs in the normal course of events; i.e., runs on such banks would be ubiquitous. And, a few such experiences in the free market would preclude them from a regular existence as part of the banking system.[357]

---

[356] The argument applies, *mutatis mutandis*, to demand deposits.

[357] This is not to deny that occasionally fractional-reserve banks would pop up here and there, much as drop-the–pigeon and other con games make sporadic appearances until the bunko squad catches up with them or they flee town one step ahead of the law. And, similarly, such banks would last just until the runs, which would not be long in coming, began.

V. The Risk of Mismatching Asset Maturities with Demand Liabilities Not Worth Taking

SW make the case that for fractional-reserve banks demand liabilities are a form of maturity-mismatching, involving risks, and that if such risks are justified by sufficiently high (expected) returns, then the fractional-reserve banking is, in turn, warranted. If we are right, and SW wrong, about the feasibility of such banks; i.e., that they would prove infeasible, then these authors are also incorrect in this new contention because there would be no high, expected returns to offset the risk of bankruptcy consequent on chronic runs. That is, because such banks would go out of business in short order[358], they would not cause systemic risks. Alternatively, if SW are right and we wrong, and such banks would be feasible, then merely because the risks of maturity-mismatching involved in fractional-reserve banking may *seem* worth taking ex ante does not mean that that they can't or won't prove ex post to have been a mistake. The very feasibility of such banks would be incontrovertible evidence that their customers were not fully cognizant of the risks they were bearing. Moreover, considering, again, SW's statement that, "...solvent banks are not inherently run-prone," we note that it is the very mismatching of the maturities of assets and liabilities that makes fractional-reserve banks run prone. And, runs on fractional reserve banks are a cause of macro-instability in a free-market economy, in turn causing massive misallocations of resources. Thus, though the risks of maturity mismatching may seem worth taking to the fractional reserve-bankers and, perhaps, to their customers – though the latter are necessarily unaware of the risks they run personally – certainly that group, and perhaps many of the former group, as well, would be unaware of the systemic risks involved. In fact, the larger society bears the vast majority of the risk. Given the virtual certainty that runs on such banks would be chronic, the risks of massive distortions of the would-be structure of production would be realized and would far outweigh any benefits to be had from such a system.

That is, taking into account the risks of massive misallocations of resources, it is obvious that the true risks of fractional-reserve banking do not outweigh any higher expected returns.

---

[358] That is, they would go out of business in short order on the real world assumption that it takes time for market forces (e.g., bank runs) or the police power (e.g., bunko squad), to catch up with them. However, based on the assumption that all market participants are always law abiding, and that libertarian law prevails, they would *not* go out of business in "short order." Rather, they would never be started in the first place.

VI. The Conflation of Time and Demand Deposits Also Availeth Naught

Suppose the following, if only as a mental experiment. A banker sets up not a demand deposit, but rather a time deposit with a *very* short term to maturity: The time dimension for this account is very short: one (1) day. The bank would make these deposits available in either of two (2) forms: bank notes or entries in the banks' computer(s). Furthermore, in either form, these deposits would be negotiable; in the former case by transfer of the note and in the latter by time draft. Suppose additionally there were two provisions attached to such deposits: 1) at maturity they would be automatically renewed unless the customer wished to redeem them;[359] and, 2) they would be subject to an option clause that would permit the bank to postpone, for a limited period of time and with a penalty,[360] redemption for specie. Further, these terms and conditions would be promulgated to the banks' customers, and the terms would be printed both on the banks' notes and on the draft forms, which guarantees, arguendo, full knowledge to everyone about these goings on, e.g., no fraud occurs. Banks would then lend out the specie deposited in these accounts. Moreover, the term to maturity of the loan would *not* have to match that of the deposit, as this would "merely" be a case of financial intermediation. Certainly, there would be no legal mandate under free enterprise for *time* deposit banks to match the due dates for borrowers and depositors[361].

We are on record opposing fractional-reserve banking for demand deposits, not time deposits, as per se illegal. But what are we to make of these ultra short-term deposits? Although de jure they are time deposits and not demand deposits, de facto they would be appear to be excellent substitutes therefor. Certainly, some enterprises would attempt to circumvent the requirement that demand deposits be backed 100% by reserves of specie by offering such short-term time deposits to the public. Unless we are to have the state determine, by law and arbitrarily, of course, the minimum period for which a deposit must be made in order to qualify as a time deposit,

---

[359] This is the usual way that banks currently handle certificates of deposit; of course, the interest rate paid on such deposits is subject to change upon renewal.

[360] Of course the conditions under which the bank could temporarily suspend convertibility, as well as the time period and penalty, would be spelled out in detail.

[361] Suppose there were a law on the books preventing mismatching of assets and liabilities such that the term to maturity of the liability(ies) underlying an asset could, at the time the asset was created, be no longer than that of the asset. Two points must be made about such a situation. First, under this assumption, we would no longer be in the realm of "free banking. Second, the bank could set up loans analogous to these deposits; i.e., one (1) second loans that would be automatically renewed at term unless the bank demanded payment, and, so as to protect this debtor the same way the bank is protected vis-à-vis the depositor, there would be an option allowing the debtor to obtain a limited grace period (for a price of some sort; e.g., a penalty rate of interest).

such deposits would have to be considered legal time deposits. This would appear to present a problem for those of us who maintain that in a free market: 1) demand deposits would have to be backed by 100% reserves of specie; and 2) time deposits would not have to backed by *any* reserves, much less 100% reserves.

However, this is not the end of the matter, for we also maintain that even such legal, de facto, demand deposits would be unworkable for the same reasons that we maintained in section IV, supra, that de jure demand deposits would be infeasible. (Because they would be unworkable, they would amount to no more, in effect, than "clown" or play money.) We conclude then, that even based on the heroic assumption of ultra short term time deposits, the case for fractional-reserve banking still cannot be defended.

In any case, *all* time deposits, no matter how long the term to maturity at issuance, eventually reach maturity. Right before that point, they are still time deposits, but with exceedingly short time durations left until maturity. Thus, there is nothing really new in principle to this posited objection to our thesis.

VII. Fiduciary Media and Unlimited Wealth

In a monetary, in contradistinction to a barter, exchange, one party, A, is required to transfer ownership of money to the other party, B. If A gives fiduciary media in the form of demand deposits[362] or bank notes to B, then A has fulfilled his obligation. Therefore, A has paid money to B, as that is what is required in a monetary exchange. That fiduciary media are money in the normal sense of the word is obvious: money is a generally accepted medium of exchange.

Moreover, Mises (1996, 432-436) states:

"We may call such claims *money-substitutes,* as they can fully replace money in an individual's or a firm's cash holding."

"...As a rule it is not possible to ascertain whether a concrete specimen of money-substitutes is a money-certificate or a fiduciary medium...."

"A bank which does not issue fiduciary media can only grant *commodity credit,* i.e., it can only lend its own funds and the amount of money which its customers have entrusted to it. The issue of fiduciary media enlarges the bank's funds available for lending beyond these limits..."

"The fiduciary media affect the market phenomena in the same way as money does. Changes in their quantity influence the determination of money's purchasing power and of prices and – temporarily – also of the rate of interest."

---

[362] The form (e.g., bank notes) in which the transfer is effected is immaterial.

"...an increase or decrease in the quantity of fiduciary media affects the determination of money's purchasing power in the same way as do changes in the quantity of money."[363]

Therefore, money is an asset, and as such, a form of wealth. Because fiduciary media are money substitutes that "can fully replace money" and that "affect market phenomena in the same way as money," fiduciary media are a form of wealth. Thus if SW are correct that fiduciary media could exist in an otherwise free market, we would have truly reached the promised land. For fractional-reserve banks can then create *wealth* in the form of fiduciary media out of thin air, or, more precisely out of paper and ink in the case of bank notes and electromagnetic "blips" in a computer in the case of demand deposits. And, provided *all* banks expand their circulating credit,[364] with attendant fiduciary media, at the same rate, there is no limit to the expansion, because there would be no reason for anyone to cash in bank notes or deposits for specie, as everyone would have complete faith that the banks would honor every each and every demand for redemption in specie. Verily, a widow's cruse (God, 1 Kings 17: 8-16) of wealth in the form of money.

Ultimately, then, even when the partial backing is gold, and not a fiat money, fractional-reserve banking is still part and parcel of the old alchemists dream of turning base metal (in this case, read paper or "blips" in a computer) into gold.

---

[363] See also Mises (1912), Rothbard (1976B).

[364] Circulating credit is "credit granted out of the issue of fiduciary media" (Mises, 1966, 434).

Chapter 20. Professor Tullock on Austrian Business Cycle Theory

I. Introduction

In "Why the Austrians Are Wrong About Depressions," Professor Tullock (1987, 73) makes some statements that are incorrect and others which, properly interpreted, refute or, at least, fail egregiously to support, his thesis that the Austrian theory of the trade cycle is incorrect. We begin by considering one of Tullock's minor points in section II and then consider his major point in section III. In section IV we take to task Tullock (1989), also on this same topic, and conclude in section V.

II. Tullock's minor points

His: "... second nit has to do with Rothbard's apparent belief that business people never learn. One would think that business people might be misled in the first couple of runs of the Rothbard cycle and not anticipate that the low interest rate will be raised later. That they would continue unable to figure this out, however, seems unlikely. Normally, Rothbard and the other Austrians argue that entrepreneurs are well informed and make correct judgments. At the very least, one would assume that a well-informed business person interested in important matters concerned with the business would read Mises and Rothbard and, hence, anticipate the government's action" (Tullock, 1987, 73).

There are several problems with this line of reasoning. The first, which is typical of much non-Austrian analysis, is implied by Tullock when he refers to "business people" as though they are a homogeneous group. In reality, however, businessmen are a diverse lot, many, if not most, of whom have little in common save for the very fact of their *being* businessmen. Further, the composition of the group is changing continuously.

Second, given the fact that professional economists are unable to agree about the nature and cause(s) of business cycles, it is unreasonable to argue that the failure of businessmen to adopt a particular theory thereof is proof that any given theory is incorrect.

Third, Tullock seems to have adopted some form of (weak?) rational expectations theory (Salerno, 1989, p. 144). Of course, if expectations really were rational, there would be no way to explain many other economic phenomenon apart from business cycles, e.g., asset price bubbles.

Fourth, monetary-policy-induced fluctuations in interest rates are unpredictable, at least in details specific enough to be useful for many business decisions. Therefore, even when some businessmen do anticipate that an artificially low interest rate will eventually rise, they cannot *possibly* know when and by how much.

Fifth, even if a "well-informed" businessman "interested in important matters concerned with the business" who had "read Mises and Rothbard" could predict the Fed's policy actions in advance, and the effects thereof on future short-term interest rates, he would have no reliable way of predicting the effects thereof on long-term interest rates, or of the effects of interest rate changes on those variables relevant to his decisions. How can we expect businessmen to predict the Fed's actions better than professional "Fed watchers," when even they are not all of the same mind. And, how can we expect businessmen to understand the economy better than professional economists, given that the latter certainly do not agree on such matters.

Sixth, even the Fed's policy makers can't explain in detail: 1) how they make their decisions; and, what effects they expect their policies to have. Moreover, because of that, they speak in jargon, metaphors, etc. Anything but plain English; and for good reason – they avoid specificity in order to evade accountability.

Seventh, even apart from the foregoing, there is the fact that according to Austrian Business Cycle Theory (ABCT) not only is the business community in effect *fooled* into making investments which only later are shown to be mistaken, they are also *subsidized* into undertaking these profoundly misallocative activities[365]. When expansive monetary policy lowers interest rates below the levels that would otherwise have obtained, investments at the higher order stages of production come about not only as a result of the lack of information mentioned in the six points above, but *also* as a matter of pure self interest.

Suppose, arguendo, despite the completely valid six objections above, that the entire business community were well versed in the niceties of ABCT. Suppose, further, again arguendo, that none of the six objections mentioned above had any validity; that is, that all businessmen knew, full well, that they were engaging in malinvestments; and, suppose, even more heroically, that they could predict, without the possibility of failure, the exact timing of the downturn. Under these maniacally unlikely assumptions, would the ABC still take place? Yes. For as long as the extant entrepreneurs relied upon the fact that a "sucker is born every minute," they could get in while the "getting was good" and then, also, get out right before the recession began, provided, only, that there were at least some new investors who were not fully cognizant of ABCT. But this scenario is still consistent with the assumption that *all* businessmen, every last one of them, completely understood ABCT at the time of the initial monetary interference, and, despite this fact, rationally decided upon investing in the higher orders of production, even in the face of perfect knowledge that these investments were unsustainable.

---

[365] For another critic of ABCT who neglects this vitally important point, see Wagner (1999); for a rejoinder, see Block (2001A).

Consider the following analogy in this regard. Suppose that the optimal ratio of spoons and socks is one to one; that is, on average, a marginal dollars' worth of these two items yields identical utility when consumed in the ratio of one spoon for every pair of socks. Now, along comes dirigiste government with a tax on the former, and a subsidy for the latter. Arguendo, all extant businessmen know with absolute certainty that this weird policy will create misallocations, and the political realities will force government to rescind it in exactly 5 years. Will profit considerations, nevertheless, dictate fewer investments in spoon production, and more for socks? Yes, provided only that in 5 years minus one day they will be able to unload their soon to be unprofitable sock factories on people who are not now members of the business community. They would, of course, invest the proceeds in the soon to be more profitable spoon factories.

III. Tullock's major point

"[Tullock's (1987, 74)] major objection, putting it quite bluntly, is that if the process Rothbard describes did occur there would be many corporate bankruptcies and business people jumping out of the windows of office buildings, but there would be only minor transitional unemployment. In fact, measured GNP would be higher as a result."

Tullock is certainly correct about the effect of the Rothbard's process on corporate bankruptcies, though he failed to note a similar effect on personal bankruptcies. And, given the existence of a legal bankruptcy process, the more onerous it is, that is, the more protection it provides debtors at the expense of creditors, the slower the adjustment process. For a case in point, witness recent events in Indonesia[366]. (We ignore the suicides as hyperbole.)

As to the subsequent increases in interest rates having only minor, transitional effects on unemployment, several points should be made. The implication that labor markets make rapid adjustments to changes in market conditions is clearly erroneous. At best, markets for free labor are among the most slowly adjusting of free markets.[367] Moreover, labor markets are patently *not*-free. Very much to the contrary, they are among the most highly regulated of markets. And, the more intervention there is, the less rapidly will the necessary wage adjustments be made and the more severe will be the

---

[366] See, e.g., Brietzke (2001) and Muhammad (1999).

[367] Labor markets do not adjust rapidly to changes in market conditions: partly because layed-off employees frequently are uncertain as to the duration of the layoff, and thus often prefer to await anticipated recall over searching for new, possibly less desirable, employment; partly because they are not well organized; partly because of low opportunity costs (because, for example, relocation of a family in order rapidly to become reemployed after a layoff may not seem to be a very valuable alternative); and, partly because the existence of various governmental income maintenance programs has increased the viability of unemployment.

unemployment. Conversely, the less intervention, the more rapid the adjustment and the less severe the unemployment. Further, the effects vary from historical case to case, depending upon the extant institutions and the specifics of the situation. That other markets are hampered as well means that the necessary price and interest rate adjustments in those markets also will be slow, with concomitant effects on the unemployment of other resources.

As to measured GNP being higher, does an elevated measurement for this statistical aggregate constitute accurate evidence of more valuable economic activity?[368] Obviously the owners of the resources who, because of artificially low interest rates, unwittingly diverted them to sub-optimal uses; e.g., the construction of uneconomic and unneeded factories, must have had alternative uses for these resources. These alternative uses must have been considered to be of more value, else it would not have taken artificially low interest rates to divert them to their new, less valuable uses.

Moreover, measured GNP includes transactions costs in the form of the bankruptcy process; i.e., legal, accounting, etc. costs which measure the expenses of trying to rectify the mistakes of the unsustainable boom: the misallocation of resources. However, perhaps the most important problem with measurements of GNP is caused by including the value of misallocated resources at the market price at the time of the misallocation, precisely that point in time when their value in the sub-optimal use registers most highly because the market has not yet discovered that such use is a misallocation, and then failing to subtract the reduction in value from measured GNP when the discovery is finally made. That is, inflation distorts both the level and structure of prices that are used to measure the value of GNP in such ways as to artificially overstate it.

That is, there are three possibilities re measured GNP: 1) it would be higher, accurately reflecting an increase in the production of valuable goods; or, 2) it would be higher, even though valuable goods are being destroyed, and thus, if for no other reason (and there are many), because measured GNP is based, almost always, on false prices and interest rates it is a virtually useless artifact; or, 3) it would reflect, accurately, the destruction of valuable goods, in which case it would not be higher but, rather, lower. Although Tullock seems to choose the first alternative, either of the latter two would appear to be the better choice.

Let us put this into other words. Even supposing that unemployment effects will be at worst only marginal due to virtually instantaneous adjustments, still, this analysis focuses only on the tip of the iceberg of

---

[368] We assume he means *real* GDP, for certainly the process Rothbard describes is an inflationary one, which fact alone could easily account for an increase in measured nominal GNP.

problems. For, according to ABCT, unemployment is not the only, or even, necessarily, the most important negative consequence of a monetary induced artificial-boom-bust cycle. There is also that small matter of loss of productivity because of the misallocation of scarce capital goods, including not least human capital. Suppose that as a result of Fed activity 90% of the labor force were assigned to the proverbial Keynesian task of "digging ditches and then filling them up again," but that not a single solitary man were thereby unemployed (due to stipulated instantaneous labor force adjustments.) Tullock's concerns about unemployment would be assuaged in one fell swoop, but the economy as a whole would be in virtually total disarray. Now, no one is stating that the business cycle is *that* devastating. We merely content ourselves, here, with pointing out that the misallocative effects of the ABCT can be very serious indeed *even if* unemployment does not thereby increase by even one iota.

Salerno (1989) made a Herculean attempt to correct Tullock's (1987) misunderstanding of ABCT in this regard. Despite Salerno's best efforts, Tullock (1989) shows no evidence of having understood those lessons. Instead, Tullock (1989, p. 147) accuses Salerno of playing fast and loose with the definition of the word "depression." In Tullock's (1989, p. 147) view: "The standard meaning of the word "depression" is a situation in which general conditions are very bad and, most importantly, there is very high unemployment." Tullock, (1989, p. 147) is of the opinion that the misallocations created by Fed induced non-market interest rates "could not create the kind of massive unemployment we saw in 1929-33." Tullock is undoubtedly correct that *if* we posit instantaneous wage adjustments; i.e., inter alia, there are no governmental interventions in labor markets such as minimum wages, unemployment insurance, etc., then "mere" interferences with interest rates need not logically compel *any* unemployment at all, certainly not the horrendous levels of the Great Depression (they would only imply loss of capital value, as discussed above). However, the real world is not characterized by this "frictionless" system. And, despite his claims to the contrary, it is certainly conceivable that market interferences with interest rates which lead to unsustainable investments in the higher orders of the structure of production, *coupled* with interferences with downward wage adjustments, could well and actually *did* lead to massive unemployment during the Great Depression.[369]

---

[369] This is not to suggest that the Smoot-Hawley tariff and faulty Fed policy that failed to prevent a massive secondary (monetary) deflation did not also play important roles in turning what should have been, if prior history were a reliable guide, a short, sharp downturn to correct the misallocations of the 1920s, themselves the result of faulty Fed expansionary policies, into the massive, widespread prolonged depression of the 1930s. They, of course, did. See on this Rothbard (1975).

But are Austrians guilty of utilizing a stipulative definition of the word "depression?" After all, praxeologists, but no one else, would characterize as a depression (or recession) a situation without massive or indeed any unemployment, provided only (*per impossible*) that there were instantaneous adjustments in the labor market.

In our view, although the Austrian and the "man in the street" understanding of "depressions"[370] is somewhat different, the praxeologist's perspective is compatible with the essence of this phenomenon, while the alternative is not.

Suppose the government in its wisdom passed a minimum wage law pegged at $1,000 per hour. Or posit that a hurricane, more destructive than any we have before experienced, struck the U.S. Either of these would devastate the economy, bringing vast unemployment in its wake (assuming, realistically, no rational expectations, no full knowledge, and non-instantaneous adjustments). But would they constitute a "depression"? The Tullocks of the world, would, presumably, answer in the affirmative. But the Austrians would not. They, in contrast, reserve this word for massive disruptions of the economy, whether or not also characterized by "large scale unemployment," but only if there is an artificial cyclicity involved, which is patently absent in these two cases.

Although the period from the collapse of the stock market in October 1929 until the war stimulated recovery of production[371] is known as "The Great Depression," this is strictly speaking, from the point of view of Austrian analysis, a misnomer.[372] Historically, depressions referred to the sharp, but short, contraction of production and employment subsequent to an unsustainable boom, during which the economy was purged of the excesses of the boom; i.e., during which the array of relative prices was restructured to accord more closely with the preferences of consumers, with attendant reallocations of resources. By this definition, the Great Depression was a *depression plus*. That is, the fiat money/credit expansion of the 1920s caused an artificial and, therefore, unsustainable boom composed of a speculative bubble in asset prices and a massive misallocation of resources. Towards the end of 1928 or the beginning of 1929 the money/credit expansion of the 1920s ended, setting the stage for the collapse of the boom, or the cleansing

---

370 Admittedly, shared by neo classical economist such as Tullock.

371 Higgs (1992) makes the case that the economy did not recover until early 1947, some 18 months after the end of WWII and many years after the conventional dates (anywhere from 1939 to 1942, depending upon the commentator) for the end.

372 We full well recognize that the term "The Great Depression" is now so ensconced in the language that any attempt to change it would be either a hubristic venture or a Quixotic quest.

recession. The crisis occurred in October of 1929, though the "real" economy had been sliding for some six (6) months before that time. Were that the end of the story, in all likelihood the economy would have been in the recovery phase of the cycle by 1932. Instead, the economy was in the pits then, after which there was some improvement until 1937 (improvement that did not bring the economy even back to the level of 1929) despite which thereafter the economy contracted again. That is, what should have been a sharp, but short, depression turned into the Great Depression. Why?

There were several factors – each and every one of which was either a governmental policy error or the consequence of such an error. First, the Smoot-Hawley tariff that raised tariff rates to the highest level in American history was enacted and took effect in mid 1930. Second, the Fed failed to prevent massive "secondary deflation" and bank failures on an unprecedented scale that ultimately led to the "bank holiday" of 1933. Third, the government induced and coerced as necessary the cartelization of industries, and of labor in unions. Fourth, leading politicians beat the drums incessantly against allowing wages to fall, threatening, browbeating and "jawboning." All of these of these factors combined to keep money prices and wages above market clearing levels, given the collapse of the money supply; they also militated against declines in real wage rates necessary for the reemployment of labor. Fifth, terminating the gold standard domestically along with other assaults on property rights created what Higgs (1997) refers to as "regime uncertainty" which led to a loss of business confidence that in turn resulted in a reduction of business investment. These factors combined to turn what would otherwise have been the "depression of 1929 – 1932?" into the "Great Depression of 1929 – 194x."

Save for the secondary deflation, these factors may be thought of as non-monetary-induced distortions of the structure of the economy; i.e., non-monetary-induced misallocations of resources. Perhaps a better name for them, given Tullock's misunderstanding of the issue, would be *non-cyclical* governmental interventions.

According to Tullock (1987, 75) although "the interest rate" is of importance for decisions concerning expenditures on capital goods, it is "but of very little significance in deciding how much to produce in an existing factory." Certainly, however, interest rates are significant for operating decisions for those businesses that use credit to finance part of their operating expenses, e.g., payrolls, accounts receivable, and inventories. And, surely, rises in interest rates that increase such expenses tend to lead to higher prices and decreased quantities sold. The diminished volume of sales, in turn, lead to smaller orders placed by such businesses with their suppliers, including those with existing factories.

But even putting matters in this format is somewhat to do violence to economic reality. For there is no hard and fast distinction to be made between expenditures on capital goods and on all other factors of production. The key element, in determining how powerful an effect any given change in the interest rate will have on economic decision making is length of run. Other things equal, the longer the amount of time involved, the more elastic the response there will be with regard to interest rate changes. To be sure, it takes far more time to build *most* factories than to produce goods in an existing factory. But *some* factories are quickly built, and *some* products take a long time to manufacture. That is the, the key is the extent and duration of the misallocation of resources of all types – human capital, capital goods, natural resources, and, and often overlooked, scarce entrepreneurial talent – regardless of the details.

Tullock (1987, 74) then states that, as regards capital goods already existing at the time when the expansionary monetary policy is initiated, there is no reason to think either that such goods "should be particularly damaged by what has happened" or "that there is too much of [them] under the current circumstances." But does not the creation of new capital goods "damage" the value of existing capital goods? And is not the problem precisely that the new capital goods are of the wrong type, and that, although there may not be "too much" capital goods in general, there is too much of the particular types created because of the monetary expansion?

What Tullock fails to reckon with is the primordial economic fact that goods and services have substitutes and complements. Even if no extant capital good is *directly* "damaged" by misallocative investments consequent on artificially lowered interest rates, this does not mean that every extant capital good will fit in as well with other aspects of the economy compared to the situation where the government had not meddled with the economy's price signals[373]. Capital goods, contrary to Tullock's vision, are not homogeneous. They are not putty-like substances, able to be fit into, without any additional cost, any given existing capital structure. Rather, if they are to be efficiently employed, they must be created in such a manner as to fit in with the remainder of the economy. Thus, new investments must be coordinated with whatever already exists, and also with the decisions of others. And this can best be done, Tullock notwithstanding, only if market signals are not perverted by unwise governmental monetary policy.[374] The capital structure of the efficient economy is, as it were, a delicate latticework, and the Fed is like the bull in this particular china shop.

---

[373] See in this regard Salerno's (1989, p. 142) very valuable explanation of "intertemporal complementarity."

[374] See on this Lachmann (1956), Hayek (1941), Mises (1966), Rothbard (1993), Garrison (2001)

Tullock (1987, 75) next deals with that class of capital goods that were produced for those industries which, themselves, produce consumer goods, and the production of which were undertaken and completed during the period of "the artificially depressed interest rate." He thinks that, although the investors therein will lose money, the capital goods, having been already completed and therefore, being a "sunk cost", there is no reason why they "...stop being used." That is true, provided that the revenues generated therefrom cover the operating expenses with something left over to put against the overhead expenses the capital goods will be used. However, depending on the specificity of the capital goods, there may be a struggle over the control and reallocation thereof. It is impossible that during such struggles the optimal use is made of these resources.

Again, Tullock fails to take into account the interconnectedness of all capital. Yes, it cannot be denied, the *physical* manifestation of the already existing capital goods may remain largely undisturbed despite the advent of the new, misallocated, capital to come on stream. (However, the *uses* made of some of it will change.) Sunken costs are indeed sunk, as he so correctly informs us. However, the *value* of old capital goods will be attenuated by not being able optimally to work in tandem with other investments, and this is something not in Tullock's ken.

Tullock (1987, 75) also states that, as there is more of it, "... the demand for labor to work with it will be higher." But, of course, the demand for labor is derived from the demand for the goods the labor is to be used to produce, not from the supply of capital goods. He goes on to say that because there would then be increased production of the consumer goods, with sales at lower than anticipated prices," ... there should be higher living standards." To the extent that this occurs, there are indeed higher living standards, at least for many of those remaining employed. A measured rate of unemployment of say 15% would be considered by many economists evidence that the economy was bordering on, if not in, a depression; and yet, as measured, 85% of the workforce would still be employed, many of whom would benefit from the reduced prices and other conditions of the downturn.

Tullock's analysis continues along this line. His key point seems to be that malinvestments induced by monetary policy may lead to bankruptcies, but they do not cause significant unemployment. Thus although Tullock never spells out his assumptions either as to how rapidly and accurately information is transmitted in the market process or as to how rapidly people react to the new knowledge, he seems to have made a typical neoclassical assumption that markets for goods and for labor and other resources adjust very, very rapidly, if not instantaneously.

Another problem with Tullock's analysis is his (implicit) objective value theory. Thus, he critiques Rothbard's statement that in response to artificially lowered interest rates, "...businessmen react as they would react if savings had genuinely increased" by stating that if, in response to lower interest rates, more factories are being built, "...then, in fact, savings that are available for building factories must have increased" (Tullock, 1987, 74). This ignores the centrality of the concept of subjective value to sound economic analysis.

Of course, if additional factories are built, resources must be diverted to such activity from some other use, including, possibly, leisure. But this does not necessarily mean that savings, as a category of purposeful human action, have increased. It is the subjective value attached to something by the valuing mind that is important for human action and a fortiori, economic analysis. Thus the existence of the additional factories does not, ipso facto, mean that savings must have increased. Rather, it constitutes evidence of an *attempt* to increase savings. Consider the following example.

Today A has control of a volume of goods of a certain value to him. Suppose him to consume some of the goods, and not consume the rest, in an attempt to conserve and, perhaps, even increase, the value thereof for future consumption. There are various ways A could attempt to accomplish this, e.g., lending his command of resources to B. However, regardless of the method that A uses, what he is attempting to do is to shift his ability to satisfy his wants from the present into the future, by attempting to have more control of goods in the future, albeit at the cost of control at present. Should, for whatever reason, A's attempt prove unsuccessful, i.e., should he be unsuccessful in his attempt to conserve value for future consumption by preserving control of goods into the future, then his attempt to save would have *failed*.

Even without government intervention into the economy, many attempts to save would fail because of our inability to accurately foresee the future. Such failures, for the most part, are random in nature. Governmental monetary policy, however, induces, through false price signals, including false interest rates, an element of systemization in the attempts to save, and, consequently, an element of systemization in the failures of such attempts. The losses of value associated with these governmentally induced failures are referred to, at least by Austrian theorists, as "forced saving." This is an undesirable, because misleading, phrase; a more accurate but, unfortunately, more cumbersome phrase is, "forced destruction of some or all of the value of resources and/or goods because they were diverted from their most valuable use." In other words, malinvestment *is* forced saving. One manifestation of the fact that value has been destroyed in such situations is the attempt to minimize, and allocate among the different parties involved, the losses through the bankruptcy process, which process Tullock mentions several times.

IV. Tullock's (1989) reply to Salerno

Let us consider two other criticisms of ABCT presented to us by Tullock. He (1989, p. 149) speaks of a "gold inflation" during the reign of Alexander the Great, explaining that "Alexander spent the Persian emperor's gold reserve." But this is not at all "inflationary," except in the most superficial of understandings of that concept. True, if this reserve constituted a significant proportion of the gold in the hands of both the banking and non-banking public, then, when it is suddenly released, prices of goods in terms of gold would rise. But no less would apply to *any* sudden dishoarding. It is no more "inflationary" than were a bunch of misers to reach into their cookie jars and under their mattresses to abruptly spend money never before utilized in this manner. Nor, even, would the phrase "gold inflation" apply to a case where a new and significant seam of this metal found. The reason for this is that both the dishoarding and the discovery would be considered part and parcel of the market process. It would be no more "inflationary" than would be the case if one said that "burger inflation" took place after the advent of Ray Kroc.

Second, states Tullock (1989, p. 149) "It is possible to get out of an inflation without a depression." This can be understood in one of two ways.

1. "It is possible to get out of an inflation without creating unemployment." This, as we have seen, is only possible if we assume rational expectations, perfect information, instantaneous adjustment, etc. Without such heroic assumptions, it is *impossible* to get out of an inflation without unemployment.

2. "It is possible to get out of an inflation without suffering economic losses due to previous resource misallocation." This is because the prior bout of inflation necessarily misallocates resources. It is not true, as Tullock (1989, p. 149) avers, that the costs of inflation are limited to "the reduction in efficiency of the economy while the inflation is going on." To be sure, these must indeed be counted in the total tally of the costs of inflation. But the costs *also* result from the misallocations of resources in the form of durable capital and consumers' goods and of human capital that have been made and that do not cease to exist when the inflation ends. Because these misallocations do not take the form of homogeneous blobs, they can not be costlessly integrated into a different sector the structure of production, and thus constitute a very significant cost of inflation completely apart from the inefficiency correctly identified by Tullock. This economist (1989, p. 149) goes on to say that "the more severe the inflation, the easier" it is to end it without a depression. But this is surely wrong. For the greater the inflation, ceteris paribus, the more serious the misallocation it engenders. And the more serious the misallocation engendered by the inflation, the more damage it does to the economy.

V. Conclusion

In conclusion, neither has Tullock proven, nor can he prove, that Austrian business cycle theory is incorrect in this regard.

Chapter 21. On Hayekian Triangles[375]

Abstract

The triangle is an integral part of the history of economic thought. It has been used by writers such as Jevons (1871), Taussig (1896), Wicksell (1934, 1969) to illustrate and to help us understand capital theory. Since Hayek (1931) this geometrical figure has been used as a basic pedagogical device to explain the Austrian Business Cycle Theory (ABCT). The purpose of the present paper is to argue that the triangle is highly problematic, if not fatally flawed, and that if ABCT is to be made intelligible this tool of analysis must be either completely jettisoned, or heavily supplemented with a list (see below) of its shortcomings. Moreover in some ways the triangle has been responsible for the relative lack of development of ABCT for over a half century.

A triangle was first employed by Hayek (1931) to illustrate the Austrian Business Cycle Theory (ABCT).[376] Since then economists have utilized it for this purpose on numerous occasions.[377] Hayek (1935, 38-40, footnotes added) states:

---

[375] Bellante and Garrison (1988, n. 13) state: "Jevons (1970, pp. 229-36) had earlier employed a triangular construction for similar purposes. Attempting to characterize the economy's capital structure in terms of the dimensions of a triangle is what qualifies *Prices and Production* as an outline. In Hayek's more formal—and more formidable—*Pure Theory of Capital* (1941), many of the heuristic assumptions of his earlier efforts were relaxed. This volume was to serve as the basis for a more comprehensive treatment of monetary theory (Hayek, 1941, p. v-vi), but no follow-on volume was ever written."

Nevertheless, the triangle continues to be used in ABCT; moreover, Hayek's explication in that volume does not deal with most of the issues raised in this paper, and when it does, it leaves much to be desired.

[376] There had been prior uses of triangles or triangular type relationships with regard to capital theory. Jevons, 230, 231, 237, Taussig, 1896, 23; Wicksell, 1969, 113; 1934, 152, 159 used them for this purpose.

[377] This listing is by no means complete, but includes at least the following: Abrams, 1934, 25, 28; Bellante and Garrison, 1988; Block, 1998A, 154-157; Cochran and Glahe, 1999, 117; Durbin, 1933, 54; 1935, many pages; Gaitskell, 1933, 285; 292-294; Garrison, 1978, 172; 1994, 110, 112; 2001, numerous pages; 2004, 325, 338; 2005, 476, 481, 496, 498, 502, 505, and 511; Hayek, 1931, numerous pages; 1934A, 154; 1934B, 210, 214, 215, 218, 220; 1939, 10, 27; 1941, 105, 110, 117, 131 195, 197, 200, 208, 211, 213, 278, 289, 290, 363; 1948B, 23, 25, 29, 31, 33, 35; Horwitz, 2005, 21, 22; de Soto, 1998A, 34, 35; Hughes, 1997, 109; O'Driscoll, 1977, 71; Pamini, 2002, 35, 38, 45, 47, 53; Rothbard, 1962, 282, 286, 314; Salerno, 2001, 55; Skousen, 1990, many pages; 1991, 35, 86, 93, 94, 111; Snowdon, Vane, and Wynarczyk, 1994, 357; Wein Claudi, 1936, pp. 147, 149; White, 1977,

"...I find it convenient to represent successive applications of the original means of production[378] which are needed to bring forth the output of consumers' goods accruing at any moment of time, by the hypotenuse[379] of a right-angled triangle, such as the triangle [in figure 1].[380] The value of these original means of production is expressed by the vertical projection of the hypotenuse, while the horizontal dimension measured in arbitrary periods from left to right, expresses the progress of time, so that the inclination of the line representing the original means of production used means that these original means of production are expended continuously during the whole production process. The right side of the triangle represents the current output of consumers' goods. The area of the triangle thus shows the totality of the successive stages through which the several units of original means of production pass before they become ripe for consumption. It also shows the total amount of intermediate products which must exist at any moment of time in order to secure a continuous output of consumers' goods. For this reason we may conceive of this diagram not only as representing the successive stages of the production of the output of any given moment of time, but also as representing the processes of production going on simultaneously in a stationary society."

Young, 2005. Further, Macfie, 1934, 45-103 and Saulnier, 1938, 213-300, focus on the Hayekian triangle, but do not depict it. In addition, there are several authors who utilize triangle-like, or triangle-ish or quasi triangular diagrams, for purposes only indirectly related to ABCT, or, indeed, capital theory; included under this rubric are Boulding, 1966, 675 and Strigl (1934)[2000], 10. The keen reader will note that the name of one of the authors of this present paper appears on this list. It is reasonable that Menger, Bohm-Bawerk, Weiser not be included; they did not concern themselves with the business cycle. But one Austrian who devoted a lot of his thinking to this topic also cannot be found here - Mises. The authors thank Richard Ebeling for aid with this bibliography.

[378] "When I mean land and labor, I shall speak of *original means of production*" (Hayek, 1935, 36, emphasis in original).

[379] Throughout, we use the term "hypotenuse" to refer to the side opposite the right-angle in any three-sided figure in a Cartesian plane that has such an angle.

[380] We reproduce Hayek's (1935, 39) figure 1 as our H1. The authors thank Gabriella Guevara, a student at Loyola University New Orleans, for the assistance with drawing most of the diagrams in this paper. We have placed all figures in appendix 5.

In either way of interpreting it, the pecuniary value[381] of consumers' goods[382] at the moment of sale from the producer(s) to the consumer(s), C, is measured along the vertical axis. Interestingly, in the first interpretation, either time (figure 1) or stages of production (figure 2) may be measured along the horizontal axis,[383] whereas in the second, only stages of production may be measured along that axis (figure 2). The Hayekian triangle, then, is a right triangle located entirely[384] in the first quadrant of a 2-dimensional, Cartesian space

This paper is concerned only with the first interpretation, as the other necessarily involves the use of stages of production, a concept that is fatally flawed, as is explained in section 10, below.

---

[381] The output of consumers' goods at a specific point in time must be taken to mean their pecuniary value. (It certainly cannot refer to the physical output, else we encounter inherently unsolvable problems involved in attempting to aggregate heterogeneous goods. And, of course, we cannot use the subjective values of the goods, if for no other reason than that subjective values are necessarily ordinal and therefore impossible of summation.) Yet that requires that for a specific set of consumers' goods produced using the exact same production processes, the structure of production as illustrated by the triangle not be independent of the price level, however measured, or of the structure of relative prices.

[382] The triangle is used to illustrate both the production of a particular consumers' good, individually, and also the production of all consumers' goods, collectively.

[383] Because it is much more common currently to rotate the frame 90 degrees counterclockwise, as is done herein, from the way Hayek did, the quotation from Hayek immediately following this paragraph appears mutatis mutandis. Standard procedure in mathematics and science is to put the independent and dependent variables on the horizontal and vertical axes, respectively. However, economists have reversed this in the most important diagrams they use, those representing supply and demand. Hayek's placement is in keeping with this oddity of economics. Garrison (1978) was thought by some (the present authors, for example) to be the first to place time on the horizontal axis and value on the vertical in order to bring this bit of Austrian geometry into greater conformity with conventional graphical depictions, although he did have time flow from right to left in this original figure, rather than vice versa, as is standard, and as he did in subsequent work. However, a footnote must be added to this view that originality can be claimed for Garrison in this regard: for Hayek (1934B, 210, figure 1; 1941 [1975], 175, 184, 189,) and Jevons (1871, 231) before him, placed time on the horizontal axis. Thus, we can amend this bit of history of economic thought and may say instead that Garrison was the first to *consistently* use a triangle for ABCT purposes with time on the horizontal axis. If there is any person who has been most closely associated with the Hayekian triangle, it is Roger Garrison. A Google search of the phrase "Hayekian triangle" yields several pages of cites, most to his work.

[384] But see text accompanying figure 20.

The triangle may then be constructed such that one terminus of the hypotenuse is at the origin and one leg is coincident with the horizontal axis, terminating at a point, t_1, for the time at which the consumers' goods are sold. Production commences at $t = 0$ and the value of the goods in process at any time t_1, where $t_1 > 0$, is measured by the vertical distance between the t-axis and the hypotenuse, thereby illustrating that production is a process that occurs through time, and that the value of the goods in process increases during the production process until it reaches its culmination when the consumers' goods are sold at time t_1 (figure 1). The angle whose vertex is located at the origin reflects the objective rate of discount, itself based upon subjective rate of time preference; i.e., the greater the slope of the hypotenuse the higher the rate of time preference.[385] Garrison (2001, 46) states: "Alternatively stated, the slope of the hypotenuse represents value added (by time and factor input) on a continuous basis. The choice of a linear construction here over an exponential one maintains a simplicity of exposition without significant loss in any other relevant regard." This assumes that, regardless of the type of triangle used, that the value added "by time and factor input" increases with a regularity that is totally alien in the real world.

Introduction

In this paper we maintain that because of 14 fundamental problems considered below, though not necessarily in the order of importance, the "Hayekian triangle" is a faulty analytical tool. First, at the conceptual level regarding all consumers' goods collectively, the aggregative nature of the triangle is problematical. Second, again re all consumers' goods collectively, as with most other aggregative concepts in economics, there is no coherent way to construct a measure thereof. Third, more "round-aboutness" is confounded with more time consuming; i.e., a structure of production with more stages is confounded with a lengthier period of production. Fourth, the period of production inherent in a more complex structure of production is

[385] It is well understood that the straight line hypotenuse of the form $C = C_0(1+ i)t$ (figure 1) implies a lack of compounding, and a more correct figure would not be a triangle, but rather a figure in which the hypotenuse was replaced with a concave curve of the form $C = C_0((1 + i)^t-1)$ (figure 3) or $C = C_0(e^{it} - 1)$ (figure 4), as the compounding is discrete or continuous, respectively.
The slopes are given by $dC/dt = C_0(1 + i)$, $dC/dt = C_0(\ln(1 + i))(1 + i)^t$, $dC/dt = C_0 ie^{it}$, respectively, and, therefore, in each case, provided C_0, $i > 0$, the slope is either a positive constant, or it increases monotonically in t. Hayek (1934A, 153) himself was well aware of the compounding issue re the triangle and in subsequent works used a "curvilinear" triangle: "The curvilinear[2] triangle *ABC* represents, in the same way as the triangle I used in *Prices and Production*, the stock of capital belonging to processes already completed." [footnote][2]: "The reasons which make a curvilinear triangle of the kind shown in the text a more appropriate representation than the simplified form used in *Prices and Production* are probably obvious."

confounded with the period of production that exists during the transition from a less to a more complex structure of production. Fifth, the concept "stages of production" is incoherent. Sixth, the vertical axis represents the value of consumer goods, not consumption. Therefore, what is needed is not a time-structure of production, which is but one of the two types of actions, but rather a time-structure of *action*, to include both types of action; to wit: production and consumption. Seventh, the triangle can be used to account either for goods in process (or circulating capital) *or*, or for fixed capital. It cannot account for both simultaneously, a serious shortcoming as it is intended to be used to explicate the time consuming process of producing consumption goods using heterogeneous fixed capital goods at different points in the process. Eighth, re goods in process, the triangle cannot handle post- initiation-of-production infusions of resources. Ninth, when "shifting triangles" are used the time dimension is confused, and this has two baleful consequences. Tenth, the implicit assumption of differentiability regarding the hypotenuse of the triangle is anathema to Austrianism. Eleventh, the triangle model cannot incorporate leisure. Twelfth, the triangle has not been mathematized. As a consequence of these errors, the "triangle" does *not* demonstrate that which it purports to show. Thirteenth, the triangle is the wrong geometrical figure for these purposes; if one must be used, arguendo, the trapezoid is preferable. Fourteenth, the triangle ignores durable capital goods. This paper consists of 17 sections. Each of the first 14 is used to consider a different problem. The fifteenth contains a summary and the sixteenth the conclusions. The seventeenth is given over to three appendices.

1. The aggregative nature of the triangle is problematical

Central to Austrian economics is the fact that man acts in the present in an attempt to bring about a more desirable future[386] than would have obtained had he not acted. Moreover, production is a process in real, historical time through which resources are used to produce consumers' goods. In general, any particular good may be produced in more than one way, and each requires a different period of time from beginning to end. And, during any given time period, a particular good may be produced with a variety of techniques; e.g., a house may be constructed using hammers or nail guns, or both. The exact manner and sequence in which a good is produced may be referred to as its structure of production;[387] i.e., the structure of production is the configuration of the production process as it occurs through

[386] This is true whether the future that is the object of the action is immediate or remote.

[387] Rothbard (1962, 7) tells a very apropos and charming story of a ham sandwich being produced and consumed at home.

time. It consists in the application of labor, using fixed capital goods,[388] to natural resources, raw materials, and partially finished goods, in specific sequences, until completion of the last actions in the sequence, at which time the production process is completed as the finished good comes into existence.[389] Consequently, the time periods required for the production of a particular good using different structures of production, much less different goods, will differ. It is possible, then, to have different time periods of production for a given pecuniary value of sales of consumers' goods at a specific point in time. That is, a particular triangle represents but one structure of production among alternatives that could be used to produce the same value of consumers' goods at a given point in time.

In figure 5A, C_1 (t_1) and C_2 (t_2) are identical values of consumers' goods produced in ways that have different time-structures of production; to wit: C_1 (t_1) becomes available at t_1 and C_2 (t_2) at t_2. In the former case, we denote the triangle marked 1 (we label the hypotenuses throughout) and in the latter case we refer to the triangle marked 2. Note that the structure of production of 1 is shorter than that of 2, and the area[390] under 1 is less than that under 2, therefore, because the same value of consumers' goods is available in a shorter period of time, it is obviously a superior structure. That is, triangle 1 is superior to triangle 2 since the same level of consumers' goods is available sooner with 1 [C_1 (t_1)] than with 2 [C_2 (t_2)] and the sum of the present value of resources that are being, and will be, at each point in time during the production period used to produce that level of consumers' goods is lower in 1 than in 2. And, yet, the slope of triangle 1's hypotenuse

---

[388] One can think of certain production processes that do not directly use fixed capital goods, but they may safely be ignored without doing harm to the analysis. What we have in mind, here, is not a catalyst. Rather, it is a really simple process such as picking a piece of fruit (say, an apple or a banana) and eating it without using any tools. Even though a catalyst remains chemically unchanged after it works its magic, it would still be a fixed capital good.

[389] Mises (1966, 479) states: "The total expenditure of time required, i.e., working time plus maturing time, may be called the period of production."

[390] The area under the hypotenuse is proportional to the sum (over each sub-period of the total period of production) of the present value of the resources used throughout the production process of the consumers' goods. The smaller is the area, then, the lesser is the commitment of resources, in terms of present value, to the production of consumers' goods. But Hayek (1934A, 153) states "The area of the curvilinear triangles AB'C' (referring to figure 1 on his p. 154) shows the stock of capital." Note that he does not refer to the *value* of the stock of capital, nor yet, even more correctly, to the *present discounted value* of this stock of capital. See Block (1990C) for an emphasis on this latter issue. However, Hayek (1934B, 207, emphasis added) refers to "The value of the stock of capital conceived as the *discounted* value of the expected futures products..."

is necessarily *steeper* than that of triangle 2. This indicates a *higher* objective-doppelganger (the actual discount rate) of the underlying subjective, social rate of time preference for 1, vis-à-vis 2.

Alternatively, figure 5B illustrates the same point. The same value of consumers' goods, $C_1 (t_2) = C_2 (t_2)$, can be produced using either of two (2) different structures of production – one that commences on triangle 2 at 0 and the other on triangle 1 at t_1. Again, the shorter structure, triangle 1 commencing at t_1, is superior. And, the same result holds re the discount rate and rate of social time preference. Namely, that the more efficient or productive structure of production, triangle 1 in both cases, is compatible only with a *higher* rate of interest. This is not only counter intuitive, if flies in the face of standard ABCT. For, it is the *lower* time preference rate that is supposed to indicate a greater reliance on capital, and, hence, greater overall efficiency or productivity of the economy, particularly labor.

The difficulties with aggregation are well known, at least within Austrian circles.[391] How does the triangle measure up to the stringent objections leveled by praxeologists at aggregation in other areas?[392] At first glance, at least compared to the neoclassicals, pretty well. After all, the triangle distinguishes not only between consumption and production, as do all mainstream economists, but also between the different stages of production, which they most certainly do not. But this really cannot pass muster. For *each* of the stages contains a plethora of raw materials, capital goods, semi-finished products, etc. Austrian macroeconomics is properly characterized as a *microeconomic* theory of macroeconomics, but collapsing so many different things into (to be sure) separate levels in the structure of production cannot even begin to approach the usual praxeological emphasis on *individual* behavior.

---

[391] Indeed, this has been taken so far as to have created a debate between Kirzner (1976B) and Rothbard (1997K, 1997L) over whether or not even *homogeneous* data, such as money, can properly be aggregated, with the former maintaining it cannot be, and the latter that it can. In our view, the latter was correct. For support of our position, see Salerno, 1994, p. 78, fn. 8.

[392] An important element of ABCT is that it rejects, for example, the neoclassical-Keynesian practice of interpreting capital as a homogeneous blob, and labeling it "K," or some such. In sharp contrast, the Austrian theory disaggregates capital into numerous sub categories, according to its place in the structure of production. That is but one reason why ABCT is superior to macroeconomics based on neoclassical foundations.

2. There is no coherent way to construct a measure of the structure of production[393]

Consider a set of consumers' goods each with its own triangle (1 and 2 in figure 6).[394] In order to arrive at the social structure of production these must be combined in some way. Of the infinite number of possible ways, only two are reasonable prospects: one is to so arrange them that the hypotenuse of each begins at the origin (figure 7A);[395] the other is for them to be so arranged that the vertices of their right angles all coincide with that of the good whose right angle occurs at the greatest value of t (figure 7B).[396] Even a cursory examination shows that neither of these methods is capable of providing a combined figure that has a reasonable *economic* interpretation.[397] That is, there is no coherent way to combine[398] the different triangles for each consumers' good into an aggregate triangle for all consumers' goods.[399]

---

393 In our present paper, most of the examples concerning the triangle focus on the difficulties of aggregation, as they do in the present section. If we wanted to virtually double the size of the present paper, we could make every point we do regarding the shortcomings of the triangle with regard, also, to disaggregation. That is, it is no more possible to break down triangle 1+2 of figure 7C into its constituent elements found in figure 6, than it is to build up triangle 1 and triangle 2 of figure 6 into their amalgamations shown in either 7A, 7B or 7C.

394 The slope of the hypotenuse of each triangle would reflect the relevant entrepreneur's discount rate. This raises another problem; to wit: as ordinarily a multiplicity of entrepreneurs will be involved in the production of any particular consumers' good, and each may have a different discount rate, inter alia, because they face different risks, and also evaluate any given risk differently. This is true even absent considerations of compounding, the side of the figure opposite the right angle (the hypotenuse) is most unlikely to be a straight line. That is, ignoring compounding, the hypotenuse of the figure for a single good is likely to be a series of connected (straight-) line segments of different slopes (figures 6, 7A and 7B).

395 Note that in figure 7A the value of consumers' goods at t_1 consists of $C_2(t_1)$ of goods in process, and $C_{1+2}(t_1)$ - $C_2(t_1) = C_1(t_1)$ of consumers' goods at the time of sale to consumers.

396 Note that in figure 7B the value of consumers' goods at t_2 consists of $C_1(t_1)$ + $C_2(t_2) = C_{1+2}(t_2)$.

397 As will be explained in section 9, infra, in relation to a different issue, had one to choose between these two methods of superimposing triangles in the same figure, the former is the more correct way for purposes of economic analysis.

398 Even geometrically, what we have done in 7A and 7B is problematic. It was the best we can do, given geometrical limitations in depicting economic reality. To wit, note that in both 7A and 7B what is being combined with triangle 2, in order to derive the triangle we are calling 1+2 is *not* a right-angled triangle. Rather, the ordinate of 1 at every value of t is added to the ordinate of 2 point at the same value of t, in 7A, and it is added to every value of 2, at t + t_1 in 7B. The result is as if we combined a triangle with a *greater* than 90 degree (obtuse) angle (at its lower right point, precisely the

There are other ways triangles could be combined into non-triangles (see, e.g., figures 18 and 19), but we shall ignore them as irrelevant to economics. And, there are any number of ways that multiple triangles could be combined into a single triangle, 7C. Each such triangle has a length (time period of production), t_1, along the time axis, a height (value of consumers' goods at the time of sale to consumers'), $C(t_1)$ at t_1, and an area, $A = t_1C(t_1)/2$. To have any even remotely possible economic meaning, these variables would have to be related to their counterpart(s) in the original triangles. And, yet, there is no consistent way to do this. That is, it would be impossible to combine 1 and 2 in such a way that their combination had a time period equal either to that of 1, or 2, or their combined lengths, "1 + 2," *and* a height equal either to that of 1, or 2, or their combined heights, "1 + 2," *and* an area equal to either that of 1 or 2, or their combined areas, "1 + 2, " and have an economically plausible interpretation (appendix 1).

And, it should be noted that there is more than one way to produce a specific set of consumers' goods. (Hayek, 1934A, 157) puts it this way: "…any given demand for consumers' goods can lead to methods of production involving very different demands for producers' goods, and that the particular method of production chosen…."

3. Stages of production v. the period of production

The direct correlation of the number of stages of production with the duration of the production process is a commonplace in Austrian economics. For example, Garrison (2004, 324), perhaps the best-known and most highly respected Austrian macroeconomist now writing,[400] clearly equates them: "In

---

place where triangle 1 in figure 6 *is* a right triangle) by making the leg that corresponds to the one that would have been coincident with the t-axis now coincident with the hypotenuse of 2 and the obtuse angle tangent to the hypotenuse at t_1 in 7A and t_2 in 7B. The only way to avoid this, that is to maintain the right angle of triangle 1 in figure 6 when it is combined with triangle 2 (which appears in 7A and 7B exactly as it was in 6) would be to shift 1 upward vertically until its right angle was just tangent to 1's hypotenuse (dotted lines and hypotenuse 1′ in figure 7A) or to shift 1 horizontally rightward until its right angle was coincident with that of 2, at t_2, and then to shift it vertically upward until its right angle was tangent to the hypotenuse of 2 at t_2 (dotted lines and hypotenuse 1′ in figure 7B). This, of course, makes no economic sense whatever, as there would then be a vertical gap, in 7A or 7B, between the horizontal leg of 1′ and the hypotenuse of 2 the magnitude of which would have to be subtracted from the sum of the ordinates of the two hypotenuses (1′ and 2) in order to arrive at the value of C at any point on the t-axis.

[399] This is but another example of an insolvable problem arising out of an attempt to aggregate economic data.

[400] The term "Austrian macroeconomics" herein refers only to the problems considered. It should not be taken to mean that there is an Austrian economics of aggregated variables and/or their averages.

its simplest application, the two legs of this right triangle measure consumption [sic] and the corresponding time (reckoned in the number of stages of production) for an economy that has reached intertemporal equilibrium." See also, Garrison (2001, 47).

As there is no objective way to define a stage of production, unless "stage" is defined as a specific period of time,[401] there may not be a direct and consistent relationship between the number of stages and the duration of the production process. Indeed, the number of production stages may even be *inversely* related to production time.[402] Moreover, different ways to produce a particular good may involve different numbers of stages, one requiring many short stages and another requiring a few long stages. For example, figure 8A illustrates a few long stages, while 8B depicts many shorter ones.[403] Moreover, the same may be said for the relationship between stages and time in comparing the production processes of heterogeneous goods. Therefore, *nothing* may be said about the relationship between stages and time, a priori.

One bit of strong evidence for the truth of this contention is uncovered when we look clearly at the dimensions (Barnett, 2004) of the triangle, particularly, the horizontal axis. There, we find T, or time. But we also discover *stages of production* ranged in this direction. That is, a typical triangle will feature four or five production stages, each one of equal width, indicating that they all take up the same amount of time, say, one year, for each of them (figure 9A). However, there is absolutely no reason why each stage should require the same amount of time, regardless of how a stage is defined (figure 9B). Here we can see that one and the same axis is in effect being "asked" to perform two very different functions.[404] First, to measure

---

401 If so time, not stages, should be used if for no other reason than Occam's razor.

402 For more on this point see appendix 2.

403 Note that t (time), does *not* appear in our figures 2, 8A, 8B and 9. Here, instead of time, the horizontal axis depicts stages of production. On the importance of dimensions in economics, see Barnett, 2004.

404 Skousen, 1991, 93, 94, 111 is perhaps the most blatant about committing this fallacy, going so far as to label one of his axes on each of these pages: "Stages (time)." But all of those who employ the triangle are equally guilty of this logical oversight. Yet a third function given to this axis appears in Bellante and Garrison, 1988: "depth of capital structure." In a system of linear equations if the number of equations is greater or less than the number of unknowns the system is under-determined or overdetermined, respectively. In the former case there is no solution; in the latter there maybe any number of solutions or no solutions. Only if there are as many equations as there are variables is a unique solution possible. In a geometrical system, each variable is represented along an axis. Therefore, for similar reasons, one axis cannot represent two different variables – time and stages of production - much less a third, depth of capital structure, unless the three are but one in reality; i.e., unless time, stages of production, and depth of capital structure are synonyms.

time, and, second, to depict stages of production. But these are very different dimensions. Each one "deserves" a unit of its own. Just as to solve for two unknowns one needs two equations, so is it true that to perform two completely separate jobs there must be two distinguishable axes. There is only one, however, in the triangle. Is there any possible reconciliation?

Yes, if and only if time and stages of production are synonyms for each other. Then, our criticism will fall by the boards. But it simply will not do to assume, in effect, as use of the triangle de facto does, that there is no distinction at all to be made between time and stages of production. It cannot be denied that there may, in some cases, be some sort of rough correlation between the two. But to implicitly assert they are the same is incorrect from an economic perspective.

Here is another implication of the triangle as it is commonly used. Consider a given value of consumers' goods at a specific point in time. Compare multiple possible production structures each involving a different period of production: the one that results from the steeper slope (i.e., ceteris paribus, implies a *higher* social rate of discount) is the more or most desirable. Why? Ceteris paribus, the same amount of consumers' goods will be available sooner. However, this, also, is problematical. For example, in figure 5B, the hypotenuse of triangle 1 has the steeper slope, which according to standard ABCT is less desirable (it is less conducive to economic growth, because of a higher rate of time preference). And yet that triangle, 1, with a period of production, $t_2 - t_1$, has a shorter period of production (by the amount of time $t_1 - 0$) than triangle 2, with a period of production of $t_2 - 0$, which implies the very opposite. Obviously, if one can acquire the same value of consumer goods with a shorter period of production, ceteris paribus, that is more desirable.

<u>4. The period of production inherent in a more complex structure of production is confounded with the period of production that exists during the transition from a less to a more complex structure of production.</u>

The triangles are used to illustrate, inter alia, a change in the structure of production consequent upon a change in "the" interest rate. We start off with triangle 1, for illustration purposes (figure 10A). A decrease in the interest rate is shown by a new or second triangle (2) that has its vertical height (i.e., value of consumers' goods at the moment of sale to the consumers) superimposed on that of the preexisting triangle. However, 2 is of lesser height. This reflects the reduced value of consumption involved in the increased capital formation caused by the lowered interest rate, which is in turn reflected by a less steep slope of the hypotenuse (the intercept of 2 on the vertical axis, at 0, is higher than that of 1, which intersects it at a negative value). In fact, the combination of the lower vertical height and the less steep slope are drawn such that the horizontal length is increased; i.e., the hypotenuse of triangle 2 is flattened and the horizontal axis lengthened[405] compared to triangle 1.

The key to understanding the problem with all this familiar geometry is to realize that the second triangle is but a *transitory* phenomenon. In fact, changes in time preferences are manifested *not* in a desire to lengthen the period of production, but rather in a willingness to *temporarily* forego some consumption "now" in order to be able to increase consumption in the future. The temporary sacrifice is intended to be just that, temporary, and takes the form of producing relatively more capital goods[406] and relatively fewer consumers' goods,[407] *but only for a period of limited duration.* (Were this not so, what would be the *point* of saving?) During the period of sacrifice the structure of production is lengthened.

However, it is quite possible, in fact most likely, that once the necessary sacrifices have been made such that the new capital (goods) structure and concomitant period of production are in place, so that all that is required is maintenance and replacement of depreciated capital goods, the new structure will be *shortened* relative to the old; i.e., it is likely that the period is lengthened *only during the transition* from the old to the new, and that thereafter it is, ceteris paribus, *shortened.* That is, there is yet another triangle that replaces the transitory, second one (2). The "final" triangle, the one unseen until now, 3a (we are now on figure 10B), has a greater vertical height and, quite possibly, or perhaps even probably, a shorter horizontal length, 3b, than the original triangle, although 3a is the standard way of

---

[405] It is true that the shorter vertical leg and the shallower slope of 2 do not *necessarily* (mathematically) result in a longer horizontal leg. However, it is always drawn that way to illustrate the lengthened structure of production that results from the lowered interest rate. This is probably a consequence of the *assumption* that a reduction in interest rates lengthens the structure of production, instead of the correct understanding, that it alters the structure of production, in ways not necessarily predictable in terms of the length of the structure, which in any case cannot be defined in an economically meaningful and correct way.

[406] And durable consumers' goods; see Mises, 1966, 480.

[407] In fact more of both may be produced if idle (in the engineering, not economic, sense) resources, including labor, are brought into production. That is, during this boom which occurs when we move from triangle 1 to triangle 2, whether this occurs naturally, due only to the lowered time preference rates, or artificially, stemming from, say, governmental expansion of fiat currency, leisure will be reduced and idle plant and equipment brought on-line, allowing for increased production of goods at *all* stages of the structure of production.

portraying it.[408] This illustrates that as a result of the temporary increase in production of capital goods and sacrifice of consumption goods necessary thereto, the future is expected to bring a greater value of consumers' goods, and those produced possibly in a shorter period of time.[409]

In fact, if the two (2) triangles of the standard exposition are superimposed, not with their right angles coincident, but rather so that the hypotenuses intersect the time axis conterminally (figure 11), then it immediately become obvious that triangle 2 *must* be transitory. Why would 2 be preferable to 1, when from the time at which the hypotenuses intersect until the production of the consumers' goods is completed and they are sold to consumers, 1 represents a greater value than 2, especially as the important thing is the value at time of sale to consumers? As well, the goods illustrated in 1 are marketed to consumers *earlier* (t_1) than in 2 (t_2). There must be a third triangle to represent the post transition, 2, period.

Several post triangles are conceivable. That raises the issues of what these triangles look like and what, if anything, may be said regarding their ranking in terms of the quantity of goods sold to consumers and their time period of production. One possibility is that the discount rate returns to its original level after the entire transition process is completed. In that case (figure 12), 3 must overlay 1 throughout the length of the latter, and then extend even further;[410] i.e. it must extend to a point such as x, y, or z, at

---

[408] Garrison (2004, 325) recognizes that triangle 2 in figure 10B is only transitional, but thinks that the third triangle must depict: "a longer consumption [sic] leg…and a longer production-time leg…." That is, he thinks the third triangle must look like 3a on figure 10B, and can not look like 3b in that figure. It should be noted that he does not, in that place, or any other that we are aware of, use a figure that includes the third triangle.

[409] For more on this, see appendix 2.

[410] This raises an interesting issue. Can a specific structure of production be extended, or for that matter, contracted? That is, for a specific triangle can there be similar triangles? Certainly, form a purely mathematical/geometrical viewpoint they can exist. However, from the economic perspective, we understand that although the triangles are similar, in fact, each would represent a different period or structure or process of production. Then the issue is, does an x% change in the *length* of the period of production result in an x% change in the value of consumers' goods at the end of the (new) period of production? Note that although, at first blush, this issue may seem to be the same as that of scale economies, specifically, constant returns to scale, it is not. For it is one thing to ask if changing every input by x% can, or does, result in an x% increase in output. But it is an *entirely* different matter to ask about the effects of changing the time period of the structure of production, because an alteration in the time period *necessarily* implies a change in the methods of production. And it is not at all clear that one can change methods, going to a longer or shorter time period, and that output would necessarily change proportionately to the time period change. This is not to say that such a change may be ruled out on

which point the abscissa is greater than t_1, and the ordinate is greater than $C_1 1(t_1)$, indicating that the period of production has been lengthened and the value of consumers' goods at the time of sale has been increased. The reason is that it would be absurd to forego consumption during a transition phase in order to arrive at a situation in which consumption were no greater than it was before the sacrifice, $C_1(t_1)$, and even less if 3 overlays only part of 1; i.e., terminates between 0 and $C_1(t_1)$, at a point such as w.

In other words, if one is at $C_1(t_1)$ before the transition, it would make no sense to suffer the loss during the transition if one ended up only right back at $C_1(t_1)$. Even worse would be to end up at point on the hypotenuse of triangle 1, such as w, closer to the origin than $C_1(t_1)$. Now consider points x, y, and z. If any of them was the intended result of the transition, then it is preferable.

Another possibility is that the discount rate does not rise back to the pretransition level. In that case, there are three (3) possibilities: the interest rate rises above that of the transition level, but not to the pretransition level (3a in figure 13); the rate falls below that of the transition level (3c in figure 13); and, the rate remains the same as that of the transition (3b in figure 13), where 3b overlays 2, but extends beyond it). In these cases, also, the period of production would necessarily be increased,[411] else the value of consumers' goods would be less than before the transition; i.e., less than before the sacrifice. That is, we would have to end up at a point on the hypotenuse such that the ordinate was greater than $C_1(t_1)$. For example, x on 3a, y on 3b, or z on 3c, so that the value of consumers' goods is greater than $C_1(t_1)$. However, this means that the period of production would have to increase to a length greater than t_1, as each of these curves, 3a, 3b, and 3c, rises above $C_1(t_1)$ only at a later time than t_1. Moreover, the increase in consumers' goods would be less than proportional to the rise in the time period required for production. And, the lower the post-transition discount rate relative to the pre-transition rate, the smaller would be the proportion of the increase in consumers' goods to the increase in the time period of production.

---

praxeological grounds, but only that because different time structures would necessarily involve, at least to some extent, different durable capital goods, it does not seem very likely that such a result would obtain.

[411] In fact, there is a minimum increase in the time period required in order for the value of consumers' goods produced to attain the pre-transition level $C_1(t_1)$; i.e., the rise would have to be greater than $t_3 - t_1$, $t_4 - t_1$, or $t_5 - t_1$ on 3a, 3b, and 3c, respectively (figure 13). If there is an upward movement, but this minimum increase is not reached, then although the time period will have lengthened, the value of consumers' goods will be less than pre-transition. And, the lower the post-transition discount rate, the greater the required minimum augmentation in the time period.

The last possibility is that the discount rate rises above the pretransition level. In that case, there are five (5) possibilities (figure 14):

1) the period of production is shortened and the value of consumers' goods at the end of the period is reduced (v on 3) relative to that produced at the end of the pretransition period of production (j on 1);

2) the period of production is shortened and the value of consumers' goods at the end of the period is the same as that produced at the end of the pretransition period of production (w on 3);

3) the period of production is shortened and the value of consumers goods at the end of the period rises relative to that produced at the end of the pretransition period of production (x on 3);

4) the period of production returns to the same length as that of the pretransition period and the value of consumers' goods at the end of the period is increased relative to that produced at the end of the pretransition period of production (y on 3); and,

5) the period of production is lengthened and the value of consumers goods at the end of the period rises relative to that produced at the end of the pretransition period of production (z on 3). The ratio of the pecuniary value of consumers' goods to the length of the period of production is increased. And, the lower the post-transition discount rate relative to the pre-transition rate, the greater is the ratio of the pecuniary value of consumers' goods to the length of the period of production, relative to the pretransition ratio.

In this section, then, we do not so far have a criticism of the Austrian triangle per se. Everything we have said we were able to illustrate with this geometrical expression. Our criticism of "mainstream" or "classical" Austrianism has so far consisted, merely, of adding a third triangle, 3, to the analysis. That is, we would expect, that over time, the vertical height would rise, reflecting an increase in the value of consumers' goods produced, and the hypotenuse would also become steeper, reflecting the economy's ability to produce consumers' goods more quickly, both devoutly to be desired in terms of improving standards of living.

However, ideally, of course, what we really want is a "triangle" with no horizontal distance at all; it would be extended, only, in the vertical direction. That is, a "triangle" that would depict a situation in which production occurred instantaneously: one where goods were immediately available, merely upon demanding them, with no structure of production whatsoever needed for attaining these consumer goods.[412]

This new triangle 3 is but a move in that direction.

---

[412] One may speculate whether such a situation would constitute a post-scarcity world.

Such a situation is illustrated not by a three-sided geometrical structure; rather, it is depicted by a vertical line.[413] Hence, ultimately, this section of the paper not only rejects the usual Austrian triangular analysis by in effect accepting it only subject to yet a third triangle, but discards the geometry in its entirety, at least ultimately.

5. The concept of "stages of production" is confused.

Although the concept of "stages of production" is often illustrated by an example; e.g., mining, refining, manufacturing, distributing, and retailing,[414] this is not analytically satisfactory. These are but arbitrary categories. Any specific production process can be broken down into ever more discrete stages, or combined into fewer of them. The limit to the number of stages is set only by the number of individual human actions involved.[415, 416] Thus, the number of stages depends upon the judgment of the individual decision maker[417] analyst. This is not to deny that the concept may be useful in providing the flavor of production through time, but it is not analytically sound in the sense necessary to be measured along the horizontal axis of a triangle that purports to represent the structure of production from an analytical (in this case, geometrical, and, therefore, mathematical) perspective.

---

413 The height of the line would depend upon productive capacity; i.e., the quantity of resources, the state of technology, and entrepreneurial talent, after due allowance for the negative impact of governmental intervention.

414 Or, planting wheat, watering it, harvesting it, turning it into flour, baking it into bread, wholesaling and then retailing this foodstuff to consumers.

415 The relevant concept here is methodological singularism (Mises, 1966, 44-4); also Barnett and Block, 2008A.

416 Should we add at this point: plus the discrete physical/chemical/biological changes that occur, if in fact any do, between the individual human actions? This is tempting, but, strictly speaking, not logically implied by the triangle. In addition, there are good and sufficient Austrian reasons for *not* including these considerations: they are not subject to human action. Praxeology is a *subjective* discipline, and, as these chemical, etc. reactions are objective considerations, they do not fit easily, or, indeed, at all, into that world-view.

417 "It is important to realize that the period of production as well as the duration of serviceableness are categories of human action and not concepts constructed by philosophers, economists, and historians as mental tools for their interpretation of events. They are essential elements present in every act of reasoning that precedes and directs action. It is necessary to stress this point because Bohm-Bawerk, to whom economics owes the discovery of the role played by the period of production, failed to comprehend the difference" Mises (1966, 480). In effect, it is our contention that Bohm-Bawerk was not the only Austrian economist to make this error; this would include all of those who utilize the triangle without any of the reservations made in the present paper.

Further, these examples are intrinsically confusing. Consider steel in this regard. If anything "deserves" to be located in an early[418] stage of production, this item certainly does: it is the backbone of so much else, and these other productions cannot take place until the steel comes along on line. However, steel *also* occurs in *very late* orders of production. Indeed, steel may be found *throughout* the structure of production. For example, it is used pretty much at *every* stage in the production of bread, and its delivery to the final consumer. So, where does steel properly go? At an early stage of production? All though out? Moreover, things that produce steel are in turn produced by steel. For example, the rubber that goes into transportation vehicles is aided by steel, and also dependent upon steel. A similar situation applies with regard to human labor. It, too, appears at every stage. As well, things that promote the creation of human beings are in turn created by them.[419]

6. What is needed is not a time-structure of production, which is but one of the two types of actions, but rather a time-structure of *action*, to include both types of action; to wit: production and consumption.

Garrison (2001, 47- 49) recognizes this and attributes to Jevons ([1871] 1965, 231) the idea of extending the figure with a consumption right triangle that would share the vertical leg of the production triangle but whose time dimension would extend to the right, indicating that consumption of durable consumers' goods would continue, but at a declining rate, into the future; i.e., from left to right along the horizontal axis (figure 15).[420] Garrison then states: "Durable consumption goods and durable capital goods are obvious and, in some [sic][421] applications, important features of the market economy. But to include these features would be to add complexity while clouding the fundamental relationships that are captured by the simpler construction … Although the allowance for consumption time as well as production time may constitute a move in the direction of realism, there is little to be gained analytically by replacing the multistage Hayekian triangle with the Jevonsian …figure."[422] We do not at all agree.

---

[418] Not the earliest. Iron and coal go into its creation, and must come beforehand.

[419] It is no accident that Kirzner's (1963, 19) attempt to supplant (see Simpson and Kjar, unpublished) the neoclassical circular flow diagram (Stigler, 6) bears a not inconsiderable resemblance to the structure of production. The point is that if A helps in the creation of B, and the reverse is also true, then the triangle can be converted into something along the lines of a circle.

[420] These back-to-back triangles might be referred to as a "double triangle."

[421] In our view, "some" vastly understates the case as it relates to the contemporary economy, at least in the US.

[422] It should be noted that, although Jevons (1965 [1871], 231) draws his double triangle to illustrate the case of "uninvest[ment]" of durable consumers' goods, Hayek (1975 [1941], 136) draws the same figure (rotated about the horizontal axis

To exclude durable capital goods from consideration because they "would … add complexity while clouding the fundamental relationships that are captured by the simpler construction" is of course unwise. The whole purpose of the triangle is to serve as a pedagogical means to explain ABCT. And yet, for the sake of simplicity of exposition this geometrical model that ignores an absolutely essential element[423] of that same theory is employed.

Nor, at least with respect to durable capital goods, would Hayek (1935, 40-41, fn. 2) agree:

"But as soon as it is tried to use the diagrammatic representations to show the successive transfers of the intermediate products from stage to stage in exchange for money it becomes evidently impossible to treat durable goods in the same way as goods in process since it is impossible to assume that the individual services embodied in the durable goods will regularly change hands as they approach a stage nearer to the moment when they will actually be consumed. For this reason it has been necessary to abstract from the existence of durable goods so long as the assumption is made that the total stock of intermediate products as it gradually proceeds toward the end of the process of production is exchanged against money at regular intervals."

And (Hayek, 1934B, 208-209)

"It is necessary to begin by drawing a clear distinction between the two different ways in which time may be a condition to the production of the ultimate services to the consumer. This distinction between the actual time a process of production lasts and the time through which a product will give its services, to which corresponds the distinction between goods in process and durable goods, is of special importance in this connection… It seems to me, however, that in neither case will one alone of the two concepts provide a sufficient explanation, and that, in particular, the effects of changes in the data can be understood only if the relation between these two concepts is cleared up."

We think it a serious mistake to ignore either durable consumers' goods or durable capital goods for the sake of "simplification.")[424] This is

---

and then rotated 90° counterclockwise, although Hayek says it "has here been turned 90 degrees) to illustrate "disinvestment" of durable goods. As this appears in his Chapter X, *The Position of Durable Goods in the Investment Structure*, it is clear that Hayek understands this disinvestment to be with respect to durable capital goods as well as durable consumers' goods.

423 Garrison himself subtitled his magnum opus "The Macroeconomics of Capital Structure." Additionally he has often referred to ABCT as "capital-based macroeconomics." How can it make sense to exclude durable capital goods from an analysis of the structure of production?

424 One might think that for Garrison the Holy Grail is a simple set of diagrams that can be used to explicate Austrian Business Cycle Theory and that he thinks he has

not to downplay the role of goods in process. It is only to say that both goods in process *and* durable capital goods are of the essence of ABCT.

Moreover, Garrison (2001, 48) labels his production cum consumption triangle: "The structure of production (continuous input/continuous-output)." There are two (2) problems with this. First, regarding the production-triangle part of the figure, on the preceding page (47), he labels a virtually identical,[425] "continuous input-point output."[426] It seems passing odd that the same figure can be used to illustrate two (2) very different concepts of production. The second problem is that the label for the figure on page 48 that contains, also, the consumption triangle, does not refer to the nature of the consumption depicted. Consistency and clarity warrant that the figure be labeled "continuous-input/continuous (or point)-output/ continuous-consumption" and not just "continuous input/continuous-output."

Garrison (2001, 48) also states: "The notion of stages of consumption has much more limited interpretation than the corresponding stages of production. We might think of used-car lots, second-hand furniture shops, and junk shops as separating the stages." But the concept of stages of consumption is every bit as inchoate as that of stages of production, discussed supra, in section 5.

Furthermore, the idea behind the consumption triangle; i.e., that durable consumers' goods both yield their services, and decline in value over time is equally relevant to durable capital goods. This is nothing more than depreciation. And, yet, the ordinate of the hypotenuse of the standard triangle is never decreased to account for this. But this is not surprising, as the triangle is used solely illustrate the case where the only capital goods are goods in process.

In fact, then, what is required, if triangles are to be used at all, is a Jevonsian style figure (figure 15,) that represents both the time-structure of production, including depreciation of durable capital goods, and the time-structure of consumption, as *both* structures are affected by changes in interest rates, and thus *both* should be part and parcel of the ABCT. Of more importance, the triangle can be jettisoned; this would in no way affect ABCT, as the triangle is merely a pedagogical device, and therefore, this would merely affect the way in which ABCT is explicated. Moreover, it is of great

---

found it with those to be found in his book (Garrison, 2001.) However, there is a difference between simple and overly simple. Austrians understand and appreciate the complexity of the real world, especially at the "macro" level.

[425] The figures are identical, save that the figure on page 47 refers to stages labeled mining, refining, manufacturing, distributing, and retailing, in addition to early stages and late stages, whereas the figure on page 48 refers only to early and late stages.

[426] This is an excellent example of the type of confusion that arises from attempts to use the triangle.

importance that the theory itself be extended to incorporate the concept of the structure of consumption; i.e., the concept of the structure of consumption must be integrated with the concept of the structure of production into a structure of *action* that, itself, should be an essential element of ABCT.

We are all in favor of Occam's Razor. But this merely states that of two theories, both of which *equally* explain a phenomenon, the simpler one is to be preferred. In the present case, it is our contention that the Jevonsian triangle set is much to be preferred to the Hayekian.

For one thing, consumption is every bit as influenced by the interest rate as is production,[427] apart from the fact that most consumption items are of shorter duration than most producers' goods, and thus the effect is greater in the latter than in the former case. However, some consumer durables (houses in particular) remain in service for centuries, and, in the last few decades, have taken up a higher proportion of GDP than in former years, when ABCT was first being introduced. For another, institutional financial alterations over the past few decades have seen this sector of the economy take on a larger role. It is one thing to jettison so important an aspect of the economy as consumption on substantive grounds. To do so on the basis of convenience, or a misreading of Occam's Razor, is entirely another.

7. The Hayekian triangle can be used to account either for goods-in-process *or* for fixed capital. It cannot account for both simultaneously.

This is recognized, implicitly, if not explicitly, in the confusion of time and stages[428] of production (or consumption).[429] The appropriate dimension of the horizontal axis is time if we are concerned with goods in process, or stages of production if our concern is fixed capital. However, although the slope of the hypotenuse reflects the interest rate in the case of goods-in-process, there is no such relationship concerning stages of production. In the latter case, it is more appropriate to use a vertical bar

---

[427] Consider a factory and a residence that start out at the same value, and last the same 200 hundred years. It is difficult to see why the interest rate would affect them very differently at all.

[428] Some might argue that it is not possible to increase investment without increasing the number of stages of production in an economy, but that it *is* possible to increase investment without increasing the time that elapses from the beginning of production until the consumption stage. But this is erroneous. Investment can be increased without increasing the number of stages – in essence that is the difference between capital widening (same number of "stages," but each stage producing more value than before), and capital deepening (more "stages"). Figure 16A illustrates capital widening, and 16B capital deepening. For the not totally unrelated concept of "depth of capital structure," see Bellante and Garrison, 1988.

[429] See section 3, supra.

chart[430] than a triangle. Moreover, for purposes of the ABCT, stages, qua stages, are irrelevant insofar as interest rates, and changes thereof, are concerned. Rather, it is *time* that is of the essence where interest rates are concerned.

This is yet another example of "asking" one axis to do the work of representing two very different phenomena. Fixed capital, as its name implies, means preeminently machinery that "stays put" in its relevant stage of production. Assuming arguendo that this makes sense in the first place,[431] what the pro triangle Austrian economist presumably has in mind is, say, a milking machine that remains in whatever stage of production to which this process is (arbitrarily) assigned. In sharp contrast is the milk itself that gets transformed from its raw state to pasteurized to serve as inputs into ice cream, etc. Here, the good in question does not "stay put" but rather emigrates from stage to stage.

A possible objection to our argument is that it does not matter at all for the ABCT whether a given item moves around through the stages or stays in one place until it depreciates out of existence. Even were this true, this is still a flaw in the triangle, as a depiction of economic reality. But, it is not so. The presumption is that goods like milk have many more alternative uses than do milk machines, which are heavily specialized. Thus, in the downturn, the latter will have to be much more radically written down than the former.

8. In the case of goods-in-process, the triangle does not handle post-initiation-of-production infusions of resources.

That the triangle reflects the interest rate as if there were only simple; i.e., uncompounded interest, is well understood, as is the fact that a more accurate figure would replace the straight line hypotenuse[432] with a power function (figure 3) to reflect discretely compounded interest or an exponential curve (figure 4) to reflect continuously compounded interest. However, this implies that the value of the goods-in-process increases at a constant rate from the initiation of their production until the fruition of the production process in the form of consumers' goods. Historically, examples given were such as the value of grapes in the field or of uncut trees, or of

---

430 One might be tempted to assert that the triangle is merely a bar chart, with perhaps very thin bars. Strictly speaking, this is incorrect. A careful perusal of Rothbard (1962, 286) indicates that a triangle with a straight-line hypotenuse *cannot* be constructed by connecting the midpoints of the bars depicted therein. From the web (http://thesaurus.maths.org/mmkb/entry.html?action=entryById&id=2287): "A bar chart or bar graph is a way of showing information by the lengths of a set of bars. The bars are drawn horizontally or vertically."

431 We argue it does not in section 1, supra.

432 Of course, every hypotenuse is a straight line; we use the redundant term for the sake of emphasis.

wine or whiskey in casks, increasing as they matured. These had the advantage of not requiring infusions of other resources[433] once the production process had commenced, and therefore, it could be assumed that the value grew at a constant rate.[434] However, in anything but the most simple of processes such as these, post-initiation-of-production infusions of resources are the rule, not the exception. In such cases, neither a straight-line hypotenuse nor an exponential curve can accommodate such infusions of value in the form of resources.

In order to capture the effects for the triangle of infusions of resources into the goods in process, the triangle would have to be broken up into segments such that the curve, though continuous would be non-differentiable or non-smooth at the end of each segment. In fact, at each time at which there was an infusion of resources the curve would become vertical. For the length of the vertical segment is equal to the (discounted) value of the resources infused at that point. Then the triangle would look like a step function, with the horizontal parts of the steps sloped upward to the right (figure 17).

Take an example. Before the reunification of Germany, both East and West Germany, presumably, had their own separate triangles. Now, they merge. How do we illustrate this via the triangle? One way to do so would be to concoct a much larger triangle. There would be no stupendous problem with this course of action on the vertical axis; we posit, arguendo, that the value of consumption of each could be added to the other, and this would eventuate in no more insuperable problems then amalgamating consumption in any other context. However, what of the horizontal axis? Assume for simplicity that both East and West Germany have the same time preference or interest rate, and thus that the angle formed by the hypotenuse and the time axis is the same in each case. Immediately after the political union, but before economic integration occurs and causes any changes in the structure of production in either area, the structure of production of the newly united country may be depicted by simply adding these two triangles together so that the area of the one depicting the amalgamated country is equal in area to the two smaller ones.

---

433 In making this statement, we, like everyone else, implicitly ignore the continuing contributions of land, protections against criminal incursions through fences, locks, etc., not to mention the resources used after the end of that part of the process in which "nature took its course. That is, the resources necessary to process the grapes into wine and, after another period of increasing value resulting from "nature's work," the bottling and marketing of the wine, or after the timber is grown, all the resources necessary to convert timber into lumber and then incorporate, directly or indirectly, the timber into consumers' goods, the resources necessary to bottler and market distilled liquor, etc.

434 Even using such examples of relatively simple production processes, it is not at all clear that the relevant values increase at a constant rate.

Any two right triangles of whatever lengths for the legs and hypotenuse could be added vertically, which would seem to be the only way that makes sense. We can add them in such way that the hypotenuses of both intersect the time axis at the same time, 0, or so that the right angles are coincident (on the time axis). Of course, if they both have the same time dimension, the two methods yield the same result. In this case the figure is the same as that for the case of capital widening, illustrated, e.g., in figure 16A. If they have different time dimensions, then depending upon the assumptions we make, there are four (4) ways they can be added: 1) with their hypotenuses both intersecting the time axis at time 0, as illustrated in another context in figures 6, and 7B; 2) with their right angles coincident at time T, as illustrated in another context in figures 6 and 7A); 3) with neither the hypotenuses intersecting at the same point on the time axis or the right angles coincident, illustrated in figure 18, or 4), with one both begins *and* ends before the other (see figure 19). In other words, triangle 1 begins at 0 and ends at t_1; whereas triangle 2 begins at 0 and ends at t_2. However when we combine them, we do so in a way that 1 is shifted to the right so far that although it begins before 2 ends, it ends after 2 ends. Note that the part of triangle 2 that extends beyond t_1 has been shifted downward so that it is coincident with the time axis.

All of this just goes to show what nonsense is hidden, or implicit, in the triangles. The foregoing indicates yet another problem with trying to use mathematics when analyzing human action. If both the interest rate and the total (pecuniary) value of consumption; i.e., the combined height of the vertical legs, are to remain unchanged, then we must of necessity extend to the left the horizontal leg of the triangle, e.g., add stages of production *before* the zero time point (see figure 20). But this plain flat out contradicts our assumption that nothing else, economically, has changed. How can it possibly be that, at time zero, the time of unification, because of the unification, magically, new earlier stages of production somehow arise in the past? Nothing can *now* be happening in the *past*, for goodness sakes, even arguendo. Rather, right *now, before anything economically* has occurred, we must add earlier stages of production, and they must necessarily be in the past. That is, hypotenuse 1 intersects the time axis at 0, the split second in time immediately before production begins. Therefore, at 0, right now, we must add the new stages by extending the hypotenuse to the *left* of 0; i.e., into the past (hypotenuse 2). Lo and behold history is mutable; economics is no longer only forward looking; and, costs are not necessarily sunk anymore! Oh wonder of wonders! What hath the triangle wrought? From whence do these earlier stages of production spring? Basic industries, of the sort thought to occupy the leftward tip of the triangle, do not come into being automatically and instantaneously and *in the past,* and yet this is precisely what the triangle model requires in the present case.

9. Confusion of the time dimension

When multiple Hayekian triangles are constructed on the same diagram, invariably the vertical lines representing the value of consumption goods at the moment of sale to the consumer are superimposed upon each other (e.g., figures 5B, 7B, 10A, 10B, 16A, 19, 20, 21, 23, 24, 26, and 27).[435] This results in the vertices formed by the time axis and the different hypotenuses occurring at different points on the time axis. This is a backward point of view, whereas economic analysis is necessarily *forward looking.*[436] The points of coincidence should not be the vertical lines representing the value of consumers' goods. Rather, they should be coincident only at the one place that represents the point in time when each production process *begins*; i.e., they should coincide where the hypotenuse of each intersects the time axis: 0 as illustrated in figures 5A, 6, 7A, 11, 12, 13, 14, 16B, and 21 through 29. The former approach is to look backward from the time of sale of finished consumers' goods to the consumers to the time structure of production that resulted in the consumers' goods. That is fine for history, but incorrect for theory, which is *necessarily* forward looking. The latter approach looks forward from the "beginning" of the production processes.

It should now be obvious that the triangle-as-history approach results in a single *objective* triangle. That is, the specific structure of production that resulted in a particular set of consumers' goods at a certain point in time is a historical reality, regardless of whether any individual is aware of the totality

---

[435] We added the vertical lines of each triangle to the other in the previous example, but this, to the best of our knowledge, has not been done before in the published literature on the subject.

[436] Hayek himself apparently was confused on this point. Compare Hayek (1934A, 153, emphasis added):

"The curvilinear^2 triangle *ABC represents*, in the same way as the triangle I used in *Prices and Production*, the stock of capital belonging to *processes already completed*," with Hayek (1934B, 210, fn 1, emphasis added): "In both cases, however, the periods in question are *future* periods of time. In the first case the period OT_1 refers to those future moments of time at which the corresponding quantities of "labour" have to be invested in order to obtain the product at the end of the period, while in the second case it refers to the period during which the product of labour invested at its beginning, say the present, will mature." Now consider Hayek (1934B, 226), "This very widespread impression is due to the fact that the concept of the period of production has generally been interpreted in an historical, backward-looking sense. For this Böhm-Bawerk's manner of exposition is mainly responsible. But, as has been pointed out at the beginning of this article, the essential concept is not the length of the process from which current output results, but the range of periods for which the current supply of factors is being invested," and, Hayek (1934B, 227), "It is for this reason that the backward-looking interpretation of the 'period of production' will always lead to absurd conclusions."

of the facts of that structure. In contradistinction, the triangle-as-future-plan is a *subjective* triangle. Moreover, it is not *one* subjective triangle, but a group of subjective triangles, one for each entrepreneur, in the broad Misesian sense of the term. These cannot be aggregated, no way, no how! Therefore, there cannot be *a single* triangle for the entire economy in any economically meaningful sense. In fact, the very concept of *a* forward looking triangle implies complete coordination among the plans of entrepreneurs' (in the narrow sense), even if they are not coordinated with consumers' plans.

Moreover, if the former approach is to be analytically correct, no matter at what point in time the vertical lines representing the value of consumer goods' coincide, the hypotenuse must extend indefinitely to intersect the time axis only at a point in the deep recesses of human prehistory. This is so because in looking in retrospect at the process of producing a specific set of consumers' goods, we note that in reality the process began not when direct work first began on those particular goods, but rather it began at some point in antiquity.[437] For example, in retrospect, we see that a car is made with the aid of a particular, previously-produced machine, itself made with the aid of a yet another particular, previously-produced machine, etc. However, if we use the latter approach, then the point where the different triangles coincide represents the point in time when production of the set of specific consumers' goods would begin using the different processes, including the relevant, extant, resources. In that case, we see that the forward-looking, structure of production has a finite duration.

10. The assumption of differentiability regarding the hypotenuse of the triangle is anathema to Austrianism

The implicit assumption of differentiability is with respect to the linear function that forms the hypotenuse of the triangle (in the case of simple discounting), or of the exponential function (in the case of continuously compound discounting) or the power function (in the case of discrete compounding) that, respectively, form the analogs of the hypotenuse in a triangular figure. Because these functions are differentiable they are necessarily continuous,[438] a fact that renders them incompatible with

---

[437] This is reminiscent of the Austrian solution to the charge that its theory of money argues in a circle. Today's prices depend upon yesterday's, and so on. According to the money regression theorem, the circle is closed when we arrive, backwards, at the time before money was first used, e.g., to a barter system. For more on this see Mises, 1912, 97-123; Mises, 1998, 408-416, http://www.mises.org/humanaction/chap17sec4.asp. This is an insightful rejoinder to criticism of Austrian monetary theory, but it is insuperable in the present triangle case.

[438] Continuity is a necessary, but not sufficient, condition of differentiability. What else is necessary? Why isn't continuity sufficient? The missing condition is that the

praxeology.[439] Praxeology is the science of human action, and human action is discrete, not infinitesimally divisible. It is not for nothing that Austrians have long inveighed against differentiable curves[440] in economics – they are incompatible with human action. According to Mises (1996, 12): "Action therefore always involves both taking and renunciation." He (1996, 44) also states: "No less than from the action of an individual praxeology begins its investigations from the individual action," a principle he refers to as "methodological singularism."[441] Action consists, then, in discrete acts of taking and setting aside. Mises (1996, 710 emphasis added) takes note of this problem: "*Even* if we *assume* that [a good] is *perfectly divisible* and take the unit of [it] as infinitesimal…." The fact that the relevant curves of the triangle are continuous therefore is highly problematical. Utilizing them, then, is an exercise in enabling the dog of economics to become a tail, and what should be the tail of mathematics (in economics) to become the dog.

11. The triangle model cannot incorporate leisure

The height of the triangle at its maximum represents the pecuniary value of consumers' goods at the moment of sale from the producer(s) to the consumer(s). However, as it only includes the value of consumers' goods that have, in some sense, been *produced*, it does not include the value of leisure, the consumers' good par excellence. The structure of production is independent of leisure. This can hardly be correct. Can the production structure of different economies be identical if, with the same time-profile of production, each yields the same set of consumers' goods, but yet they enjoy differing

---

function must have a derivative at every point. Differentiability implies continuity, but not vice versa. Rothbard's (1993, 638-645) v-shaped cost curve is continuous, but not differentiable, because it does not have a derivative at the vertex.

[439] Rothbard (1993, 638-645) made this point very forcefully and dramatically with regard to orthodox U-shaped average cost curves. Given a downward sloping demand curve, tangency is achieved only to the left of the most efficient bottom point of average costs, seemingly implying market inefficiency. He showed that such a conclusion intimately depended upon the assumption of differentiability, which is incompatible with human action. (He did so by using a V-shaped cost curve; i.e., a curve that was continuous, but not differentiable.) However, if differentiable curves are anathema in the arena of cost curves, as they are everywhere else in economics, due to their incompatibility with human action, then the same must hold true for the case of the structure of production triangle. It, too, is a smooth curved affair, and must be rejected on that ground alone. See on this, also, Barnett and Block, 2006B.

[440] Of course, curves themselves are not differentiable, but the functions that the curves depict are, provided they are continuous over, and have a derivative at every point in, the domain.

[441] Because the dictionary (OED, 1989) definition of "singularism" is: "A philosophy which explains the phenomena of the universe from a single principle," we think this word choice infelicitous.

amounts of leisure? As leisure is a (consumers') good, the value of leisure produced[442] should be, but is not, included in the structure of production.

Is this too great an expectation to place on the triangle? It would appear not, since even so elementary a notion in economics as supply and demand is more than adequate to include leisure into the analysis. For example, the backward bending supply curve of labor (for the individual) is a case in point. In such a figure leisure is the horizontal distance between the 24-hour per day vertical line and the labor supply curve at any real wage.

It should be noted that it is possible that there are multiple structures of production that have the same period of production and the same value of consumers' goods at the end of the production process (figure 21). In that, case the hypotenuses would be different. That raises the issue of which, if any, is superior. Because the magnitude of the ordinate at any point in time (the abscissa) represents the *discounted* value of the expected consumers' goods at the end of the period of production, this is measured as the area under the curve. Therefore, the curve under which the area is smallest (2 in figure 21) represents the one with the least value of resources[443] tied up over the period of production, and, consequently it is superior.

---

[442] Leisure is "produced" by not using an actor's time in the production of other goods. As with any economic good, it is the object of action, and has a cost associated with it.

[443] Although it is not apodictically the case, in reality such a situation would, in all probability indicate that the curve with the smaller area underneath represents a structure of production with less labor and more leisure. However, the omission of leisure, an absolutely essential type of consumers' good, from the economic analysis based on the triangle, makes it impossible to determine whether any particular triangle is superior to any other. In our analysis we implicitly, and now explicitly, make the admittedly heroic assumption that the value of labor is proportional to the value of all other resources at every point in time during the production process. Therefore, the value of leisure is greater the smaller is the area under the triangle, and vice versa. Because the curves do not take into account leisure, we really cannot say anything about the value or opportunity costs of any of them. A curve might have a shorter period of production with higher a higher value of consumers' goods and a smaller area under it, and yet because leisure is a consumers' good that is absent in the analysis, we cannot draw any conclusions. That is, in the supposedly inferior curve with the higher value of resources tied-up because of a larger area under it, the resources tied–up might be almost totally non-human, so that the missing leisure is very large. Whereas, for the curve with the smaller area under it, almost all the resources might be labor, so that there is almost no leisure. Then the former, apparently less desirable curve might in fact be more desirable. That is, the failure to account for leisure makes it impossible to say anything about the superiority of one curve vis-à-vis another.

As between any two curves whose periods of production differ, but have the same value of consumers' goods at the end of the day, and which have the same areas underneath (figure 22), the one with the shorter time period (1 in figure 22) is superior, because the goods become available sooner. And, as between any two curves that have the same period of production and the same areas underneath them (figure 23), the one with the highest value of consumers' goods at the end of the period of production (2 in figure 23) is superior.

There are three other cases to be considered:

1) The value of consumers' goods at the end of the production process is the same, and either: a) the curve with shorter time period of production also has the smaller area underneath (1 in figure 24), in which case it is superior to the other; or b) the curve with the shorter period of production has a larger area underneath (1 in figure 25), in which case it is not clear, at least to the present authors, which is superior.

2) The time period of production is the same, and either: a) the curve with the higher value of consumers' goods at the end of the production process also has the smaller area underneath (2 in figure 26), in which case it is superior to the other; or b) the curve with the higher value of consumers' goods at the end of the production process has the larger area underneath (1 in figure 27), in which case it is not clear, at least to us, which is superior.

3) The area underneath the curves is the same, and either: a) the one with the higher value of consumers' goods at the end of the production process also has the shorter time period of production (2 in figure 28), in which case it is superior to the other; or b) the one with the higher value of consumers' at the end of the production process has the longer period of production (2 in figure 29), in which case it is again not clear which is superior.

It cannot be overly stressed that all this indeterminacy shows the triangle in yet again another problematic light. One would have thought that the way to answer these unanswerable questions is to resort to some sort of utilization of the concept of present discounted value. After all, the question of which is worth more, something smaller available sooner, or something greater, but only available later, is not a question totally unknown in the dismal science. That such a question cannot be answered in general by resorting to the triangle points up another weakness of this geometrical expression, for economic analysis.

<u>12. The triangle has not been mathematized</u>

It is more than passing strange that, if the structure of production can be illustrated by a triangle, it has not been mathematized. Certainly, it is not the triangle per se that is explanatory of the structure of production. In terms of the standard use of this geometrical figure, what is important is the hypotenuse, and only the hypotenuse.[444] That is, what is important is the location of each point on the hypotenuse; i.e., the coordinates of each point. Situate a Hayekian triangle (figure 1) such that the hypotenuse intersects the time axis at the origin. Then the vertical leg is unnecessary. The abscissa and ordinate represent, respectively, the elapsed time from the commencement of the production process and the (expected) value of consumers' goods at that point in time. If we assume compound discounting at a rate r, then at any time, t, $0 \leq t \leq T$ (where T is the time when the consumers' goods are sold) the value of consumers' goods, C, is given by: or $C_t = C_0((1 + r)^t - 1)$ or $C = C_0(e^{rt} - 1)$,[445] as the compounding is discrete or continuous, respectively. Certainly, one could place such an equation in a mainstream mathematical model.[446] But Austrian economists find such models sterile, as well they should. And, for the same reason, they should reject the triangle as sterile.[447]

This is not so much a criticism of the triangle per se as it is an attempt to undermine it at least in Austrian eyes, by linking it to a phenomenon they could be expected to reject out of hand: mathematical model building. Our contention is that had Hayek (1931) *not* couched ABCT in terms of the triangle, but, instead, analyzed it on the basis of the equivalent mathematical equations, while he might have made even greater inroads into mainstream economics, he would have had less effect on how *Austrians* deal with such issues.

13. The triangle is the wrong geometrical figure

The Hayekian triangle is an "optimal" one in the same sense that the traditional "cost" curves[448] of microeconomics are optimal. Those curves

---

[444] Hayek, himself (1935, 41-42, fn. 1) stated: "It is convenient to treat the quantity of intermediate products at any point of this stream as a function of time *f*(t)….In the diagrams used in the text the function *f*(t) is represented by the hypotenuse, its concrete value *f*(x + r) by the horizontal side and the integral by the area of the triangle."

[445] Note the sterility and deterministic nature of the model: the value of consumption at any point in time, t, depends only upon the value its value at some initial period, 0, and the rate of capitalization, i. That is, given the value of the goods in process at some initial time, the value grows at a constant rate until it "matures" at some later point in time when the consumers' goods are sold to consumers. This is all too suggestive of neoclassical growth models.

[446] The only adjustment necessary if the triangle intersects the time axis at a point (t_1) other than the origin, is to modify the function to shift the abscissa accordingly; i.e., $C = C_0((1 + r)^{t-1} - 1)$ or $C = C_0(e^{r(t-1)} - 1)$, as the compounding is discrete or continuous, respectively.

[447] For more on this, see appendix 3.

[448] Because costs are subjective, the term "cost" curves is a misnomer and, as a means of pedagogy, the source of much miseducation. More correct is the term "expense" curves. For more on this see: Barnett and Saliba (n.d.).

represent for any level of output of the relevant good(s) the minimum expense of production. In precisely the same manner so do Austrian triangles represent the maximum value of consumers' goods in the production process, whether at the moment of sale or in process, at any point in time. And, just as there are other, unshown, cost curves that represent less efficient; i.e., higher cost, ways of producing the same quantities of a good(s), so too are there unshown triangles that represent a smaller value of consumers' goods that could have been produced at any point in time.

A necessary implication of this is that there is an opportunity cost of the value of consumers' goods at any point in time, including 0. As an opportunity cost represents a positive value, the value of consumers' goods as represented by the height of the triangle must be positive. An alternative way to understand this point is that at 0, i.e., right now, there are extant land and labor that have positive value, if for no other reason than that they have alternative uses. A necessary consequence of either approach is that, if a two-dimensional figure is to be used to represent the complexity of the structure of production of an economy, the proper figure is an irregular trapezoid having the shape of a rectangle or square and a right triangle so constructed that one leg of the triangle is coincident with one leg side of the quadrilateral, and the right angle is to the right of the figure (figure 30).

Hayek (1934B, 213-214, see his figure 2 and accompanying text) created a three-dimensional figure that exhibited a trapezoid of the type we described above in our figure 30:

"All these apparently rather complicated relationships can be represented in a fairly simple way if we add to the former diagram, which showed only physical quantities, a third dimension, representing the relative value of these quantities. For this purpose we place the figure so far discussed, in the horizontal plane of a three-dimensional system of coordinates and measure the values attached to these quantities along the third (perpendicular) V-axis."

Hayek assumed a linear hypotenuse for the triangle in the horizontal plane; i.e., a triangle in which quantities are measured along one axis and time along the other. And then (1934B, 213):

"The value of the total quantity of "labour"[449] [footnote added by present authors] invested during the course of the process would be shown by

---

[449] "'Labour' stands here and throughout this article for an assumed uniform original factor of production. Intermediate and final products are represented in such units as are the production of a unit of such 'labour,' so that each ordinate of the curve $0L_1'$ measures the quantity of intermediate product at the respective stage of production, while the final output, obtained at the end of the period $0T_1$ is equal to T_1L_1', or the total quantity of labour applied in the course of the process" (Hayek, 1934b, 209-210).

a rectangle with the [length of the hypotenuse in the horizontal (quantity-time plane] representing the number of units of 'labour,' as a base, and …the value of a unit of 'labour,' as its height."

Because he assumed that the labor is not invested all at once, but continuously throughout the period of production, the rectangle is projected onto the time-value plane. Hayek (1934B, 214) then states:

"The value of any unit of "labour" will have to grow, while it remains invested, at the same compound rate of interest. This rate is shown by the curve T_0T_1, and the family of identical curves beginning along T_0L_1' forming together the interest surface $T_0T_1'L_1'$."

But the curve T_0T_1 in Hayek's figure 2 is but one side of a quadrilateral, $0T_0T_1'T_1$, in the time-value plane that has the shape of an irregular trapezoid formed by a rectangle as base and on top of it the leg of a curvilinear, right triangle that is parallel to the time axis coincident with the leg of the rectangle that is parallel to, but situated above, the time axis. We repeat this figure of Hayek's as our figure H2.

Thus even on its own grounds, the triangle is highly problematical. The point we are making here is not that the trapezoid is safeguarded from the criticisms we have above launched at the triangle itself. Rather, it is that *even if,* arguendo, none of these above mentioned criticisms were valid, still, the triangle would not be the appropriate geometrical figure with which ABCT can best be illustrated. Instead, it would be the trapezoid. The *only* circumstance under which the triangle itself, not the trapezoid, would suffice would be if we were to go back to the very beginning of mankind, when we had literally *nothing* in the way of tools, semi finished products. If evolution is correct, even this is impossible, since there were ape-men like creatures before our direct ancestors came upon the scene, and they could not have survived with a *zero* amount of capital, etc., as is depicted at the point where the hypotenuse hits the origin. Even if evolution is incorrect, and the bible story is true wherein Adam and Eve were abruptly cast out of the Garden of Eden, it cannot be the case that these two started out with absolutely nothing. They had, after all, some modicum of human capital, skills, etc. After all, they did eat from the Tree of Knowledge, so they had some knowledge as to how the world works. That is, from an Austrian point of view, there were always the original factors of production, labor and land, *plus* durable capital goods and semi finished consumers' goods.[450]

---

[450] A possible objection to our thesis that the trapezoid, not the triangle, is more compatible with ABCT goes as follows: "We do not need the trapezoid, the triangle will do just fine, because the latter already takes into account the phenomenon that the square part of the trapezoid is supposed to incorporate. For example, in figure H1 the original means of production are continually being added to the intermediate

14. Ignores durable capital goods

Another fundamental problem with the triangle is that, because it ignores durable capital goods, it confounds an increase in capital and capital goods with a lengthening of the capital structure. If the only capital goods one has are goods in process and the only output of final (as distinguished from finished) goods is consumers' goods, then the only way to depict an increase in capital goods during the transition phase using the triangle is to lengthen the time dimension. This is because during the transition, capital is formed by shifting resources from action in the later part of the period of production to action in the earlier part. As this occurs, fewer consumers' goods (by value) are completed and more are started, in processes of longer duration. That is, the situation changes from triangle 1 to 2, with 2 having a lower height at the point of sale to consumers (figure 31A or 31B). Now, unless the triangle is lengthened, and that by an amount large enough to more than counter the decrease in consumers' goods at the point of sale to consumers, the resultant triangle would depict fewer capital goods during the transition then before. What is never discussed when one focuses on these triangles is the fact that an increased period of production requires a new structure of production. Because we have no durable capital goods, but only consumers' goods in process, that means the only resources are the original factors of production, land and labor; thus, there must be alternative ways to produce consumers' goods using only these resources.

The inadequacy of this approach may be illustrated by introducing two new geometric figures: an irregular trapezoid (figure 32A), and another triangle (figure 32B). The trapezoid represents durable capital goods in the same way that the triangle represents goods-in-process. The ordinate of the trapezoid represents the value of the stock of capital goods at any point of time during the period of production. That it is less at t_1 than at 0 indicates that some of the capital stock depreciated during the production period. The additional triangle represents the production of new durable capital goods; i.e., investment. So as the ordinates of each of the triangles in figures 31A and 31B represent, at any time, the value of consumers' goods in process up to and including the point of sale to consumers, the ordinate of the triangle in figure 32B represents at any time, the value of capital goods in process up to and including the point of sale to businesses.

---

products. True, the intermediate products start off at zero at the top of the triangle, but this does not at all apply to the original means of production." This objection misses our point. In our view, the difficulty does *not* concern the original means of production. Rather, it involves intermediate products and durable capital goods that can *never* be literally zero, as depicted on the triangle. Even apes use sticks to get honey; even birds use twigs to build nests.

We are now in a position to see why Hayek's (1934B, 231) statement: "That anything which will tend to lengthen this investment structure of current labour will lead to increases of the quantity of capital and anything which tends to shorten it will lead to a reduction of capital, remains a point of fundamental importance" is incorrect. A reduction in the production of consumers' goods in order to form capital can now be depicted by a consumers' goods triangle (2 in figure 33A that is the same length, representing the same time period, and structure of production, but that has a smaller height than the original consumers' goods triangle (1 in figure 33A). This indicates that the same production processes are being used to produce the same set of consumers' goods only in lesser amounts, because resources have been shifted from the production of consumers' goods to production of durable capital goods.[451] At the same time the increase in the production of durable capital goods can now be depicted by a capital goods triangle (2 in figure 33B) that is the same length, representing the same period, and structure of production, but that has a greater height than the original capital goods triangle (1 in figure 33B). This indicates that the same production processes are being used to produce the same set of durable capital goods only in greater amounts, because resources have been shifted to the production of durable capital goods from production of consumers' goods.

In this section we use four (4) figures, one each for consumers' goods in process, including initial stocks thereof (34A), the stock of consumers' durable goods (34B), the stock of durable capital goods (34C), and capital goods in process, including initial stocks thereof (34D), in a consideration of some further implications for illustration of capital theory by means of 2-dimensional plane geometry.[452] If we analyze them jointly we see that at the beginning of the period of production, there are extant stocks of: 1) durable consumers' goods, CD(0) in figure 34B; 2) durable capital goods, K(0) in figure 34C; 3) consumers' goods in process, C(0) in figure 34A;[453] and, 4) capital goods in process, I(0) in figure 34D.[454] At the end of the period of production of consumers' goods there is a stock of consumers' goods at the point of sale to consumers, $C(t_1)$ in figure 34A. Also, there is a

[451] For an explication of this point see appendix 4

[452] It is important, nay, critical, to remember that the values of any variables, including the times at which the pecuniary values of goods are evaluated, are, at any and all periods or points in time post 0, *expected* values.

[453] An absence of an initial stock of consumers' goods in process could be depicted by changing the quadrilateral in figure 34A to a triangle by shifting C(0) to the origin.

[454] An absence of an initial stock of capital goods in process could be depicted by changing the quadrilateral in figure 34D to a triangle by shifting I(0) to the origin.

stock of new capital goods at the point of sale to businesses,[455] $I(t_1)$ in figure 34D. Moreover, during the period of production, 0 to t_1, because of consumption, the initial stock of durable consumers' goods has decreased from CD(0) to $CD(t_1)$ in figure 34B,[456] and, because of depreciation, the initial stock of durable capital goods has decreased from K(0) to $K(t_1)$ in figure 34C.[457]

Furthermore, the stock of consumers' durable goods extant at 0 will be consumed over the period 0 to t_3 and the consumption goods in process at 0 will be completed and sold to consumers at t_1 and consumed over the period from t_1 to t_2. The stock of capital goods extant at 0 will be depreciated over the period 0 to t_4 and the capital goods in process at 0 will completed and sold to businesses at t_5 and depreciated over the period from t_5 to t_6. A little reflection on the relationships among $t_1 - t_6$ should convince us that the triangle cannot be used to depict anything remotely relevant to a real-world, capital-using economy, especially if that world includes not only durable capital goods, but durable consumers' as well, and, a fortiori if it is supposed to illustrate an equilibrium state of some sort; e.g., an evenly rotating economy.

That is, if nothing else, for the triangle is to accommodate durable consumers' goods it is necessary that their economic lives would have to be exactly equal to the period of production of consumers' goods in order that the newly produced consumers' durables replace exactly those consumed during the period of production.[458] Did they not, the sum of the remaining units of the initial stock of durable goods plus the new production would, at t_1, either be greater than or less than the initial stock at 0. But if a single triangle cannot depict an equilibrium situation, how much less can it depict a real-world situation in a continuous state of adjustment in disequilibrium?

Moreover, the same relationship would have to exist, mutatis mutandis, between the depreciation of extant stock of durable capital goods at 0, and the production of new durable capital goods.

Finally, not only would the period of production of new consumers' goods and the period of consumption have to be identical, say t_1, and the period of production of new capital goods and the period of depreciation to be identical, say t_2, but they would have to be equal to each other. A miracle to behold! Will wonders never cease?

---

[455] This includes the case where some business(es) that produce capital goods "sell to themselves;" i.e. retain for their own use, some of the newly produced capital goods.

[456] Consumption (CN) during the period 0 to t_1 is given by $CN(t_1\text{-}0) = CD(0) - CD(t_1)$.

[457] Depreciation (D) during the period 0 to t_1 is given by $D(t_1\text{-}0) = K(0) - K(t_1)$.

[458] The only alternative would be if the durable consumers' goods were of the nature of a homogeneous or fungible stock such that depreciation would be in terms of quantity only, and not in terms of quality, in which case the economic life of the stock would have to be some exact multiple of the period of production of consumers' goods.

This section so far might be misread to indicate not that geometrical representations of ABCT are highly problematic, but that, instead, they can be saved with the judicious use of the trapezoid. Nothing could be further from the truth. The other 13 objections to this method are still in force. The burden of the present section is a more modest one: to show yet another flaw in the utilization of geometry to shed light on ABCT, not to try to salvage the triangle.

15. Summary

Hayek pioneered the use of the triangle to explain the ABCT. Subsequently, it has been widely adopted by other Austrian economists as a pedagogical device. The triangle is an aggregative concept. Because of their correct focus on the actions of individuals, Austrians are constantly on the alert for the instances of the misuse or abuse of aggregation in economic analysis.[459] The triangle, however, is one such case where they have failed either to realize that it is an aggregative concept or, in the alternative, to realize that the number and nature of the flaws render the concept highly problematic, even to the point of being detrimental.

Each individual consumers' good has, at a minimum, one structure of production, understood as the exact manner and time pattern in which any specific good is produced.[460] Associated with each such structure is a specific time sequence in which the value of specific resources enters into the production process.[461] Even if we assume that the appropriate discount rate

---

[459] It is not, however, as if Austrians reject the use of any and all aggregative concepts. Rather, in those instances where they do use them, it is because, after due consideration, they have been found to advance economic analysis and understanding. For example, they do, of course, make use of such concepts as the market demand for, and supply of, a particular (homogeneous) good, themselves aggregative concepts.

[460] The structure of production is the configuration of the production process as it occurs through time. It consists in the application of labor, using fixed capital goods, to natural resources, raw materials, and partially finished goods, in specific sequences, until completion of the last actions in the series, at which time the production process is completed as the finished good comes into existence and is placed into the hands of the consumer. For an eloquent explanation of this latter claim, see Kirzner (1973).

[461] In addition, the precise method will, except in most unusual cases that may be ignored as irrelevant, involve a set of more or less durable capital goods. Because the significant aspect of production insofar as interest rates and changes thereof are concerned is the time element, two factors are of decisive importance: the length of time during which the value of a specific resource is expected to be tied-up in the production process before it is realized through sale of the consumers' good, and the number of units of the consumers' good the resource is expected to contribute to the production of, over the expected economic life of the resource. For more on this point, see Barnett and Wood (2002, 29-30, n12).

for each process, and, therefore, each time sequence of production for the same good is identical, their time profiles can, and almost certainly do, differ; i.e., one process for producing X starting at a particular point in time in a specific economic environment will necessarily involve some differences in the nature, type, sequencing and timing of resources than that for another. Therefore, the production triangle for every production process for good X will be different from that of every other such process. Moreover, even if, per impossible, each began at the same time, t = 0, there is no reason to think that the duration of each process would necessarily be identical. The production of two different bicycles might start out concurrently; there is no guarantee they will be finished simultaneously. One might languish at the retailer long after the other is purchased. Consequently, even if each triangle were to start from the same point on the time axis, each could well end at a different point on that axis. If, then, we were to add these triangles in the value dimension at any given point we would be adding values of finished consumers' goods to the value of partially completed consumers' goods; i.e., resources, with results that are confused, to say the least. And, the problem is only magnified when we aggregate to the economy-wide level by adding not only the different production triangles for the same consumers' good, but production triangles for all other consumers' goods as well. Moreover, this problem is exacerbated because production of different goods of course commences at different times.

Further, because of the ubiquity of durable consumers goods, an analogous concept, the structure of consumption, and its attendant time sequence, is also necessary for each individual consumers' good if we are to understand the functioning of a modern economy. Again, each individual consumers' good has, at a minimum, one structure of consumption, understood as the exact manner and sequence in which any specific good is consumed.[462] Associated with each such structure is a specific time sequence during which the value of the specific consumers' good is realized.[463] Even if we assume that the appropriate discount rate for each consumers' good, and,

---

[462] The structure of consumption is the configuration of the consumption process as it occurs through time. It consists in the use of leisure, using durable and non-durable consumers' goods, in specific sequences, including periods in which the consumers' good is "idle;" i.e., not being consumed, until the economic life of the relevant consumers' good comes to an end, at which time the consumption process is completed.

[463] In addition, the precise method will, except in most unusual cases that may be ignored as irrelevant, involve a set of more or less durable consumers' goods. Because a significant aspect of consumption insofar as interest rates and changes thereof are concerned is the time element, two factors are of decisive importance: the length of time during which the value of a specific consumers' good is expected to be tied-up in the consumption process before it is entirely realized at the expiration of its economic life, and the number of times it will be utilized over its expected economic life.

therefore, each time sequence of consumption for the same good is identical, their time profiles can, and almost certainly do, differ; i.e., one process for consuming X starting at a particular point in time in a specific economic environment will necessarily involve some differences in the nature, type, sequencing and timing of complementary consumers' goods. Therefore, the consumption triangle for every consumption process for good X will be different from that of every other such process. Moreover, although each might begin at time t = 0, there is no reason to think that the duration of each process would necessarily be the same. Consequently, if each triangle were to start from the same point on the time axis, each could well end at a different point on that axis. The problem is only magnified when we aggregate to the economy-wide level by adding not only the different triangles for the same consumers' good, but consumption triangles for all other consumers' goods.

Finally, imagine the "triangle" that results from adding huge number of different production cum consumption triangles in an economy. The resultant figure, of indeterminate shape, is impossible to interpret and absolutely incomprehensible.[464]

16. Conclusions

Although the two authors agree, fully, with the critique of the triangle in ABCT offered above, they sharply differ in their assessment of its overall value and usefulness for pedagogy. They also diverge in terms of nostalgia for the triangle, on the basis of which both were first introduced to ABCT.

Here is a statement on this matter from the second listed co-author:

In the early days (Hayek, 1931, 1939, 1941, 1948B; Rothbard, 1962), this geometrical figure was utilized with time on the vertical axis, and dollars on the horizontal. Starting with Garrison (2001), this practice has been reversed. But, no matter how it has been drawn, it cannot be denied that the triangle has played a pivotal role in ABCT. And not only for illustration, heuristic or even teaching purposes. The structure of production triangle has also enabled generations of Austrians to think more clearly about macroeconomic issues.

One clear advantage of the structure of production triangle is that it tends to make ABCT more accessible to mainstream macroeconomists.[465] In

---

[464] For more on this see appendix 3.

[465] The socialist Abrams (1934, 25) stated: "This and the similar diagram that follows are taken from Prof. Hayek's 'Prices and Production.' Indeed, this whole general analysis is based upon his work. It is almost unnecessary at this date to add that no discussion of money, no matter how humble or ambitious its scope, can hope to achieve any worthwhile results unless it uses the machinery that Prof. Hayek has so brilliantly put at the disposal of English-speaking students in the last few years." Richard Ebeling supplied this quote, for which we thank him.

fact, it is no exaggeration to say that without paraphernalia of this sort, neoclassical economists, for whom geometry and mathematical expressions are veritable mother's milk, would tune out virtually completely. No one would argue that ABCT has taken the profession by storm. However, it is my claim that without putting this perspective into language most economists respect, and thus can be enticed to read, praxeology has made inroads which would otherwise have been denied to it.

A bit of evidence in support of this contention is the success of Garrison (2000), both the person and that particular book, in explicating ABCT. Another is the fact that Hayek won the Nobel Prize (in 1974), and did heavily utilize this technique (1931, 1939, 1941, 1948B), while there were others,[466] who at least some would say contributed even more to ABCT than him, who did not. I am of course not going out on a limb, very far out on one, and claiming that Hayek won this prize because of his diagrams, and that Mises failed to do so for lack of them; this is not at all my view. However, in attempting to make the positive case for the triangle in ABCT, I would be remiss did I not even mention this fact.

Another point on the credit side of the ledger for the triangle is that ABCT is rather complex. Not for praxeologists the simplicity of the Keynesian cross diagram. Sometimes, and this includes the best of us, we zig when we should zag in our explication of ABCT. The triangle is a very valuable heuristic device even for those of us who have been weaned on this theory many years ago. Even though the present paper discusses numerous difficulties with this device, and serious ones at that, I do not recommend a complete jettisoning of the triangle. When used with full knowledge of its drawbacks, it can still have some, albeit, limited, advantages.

Here is a statement on this matter from the first listed co-author:

In sum, the Hayekian triangle is not so much simple as it is simplistic, which should not come as a surprise as it is an attempt to illustrate the immeasurable complexity of a real world economy with a simple aggregative structure such as the triangle, or, in slightly more advanced mathematical terms, with a single 2-variable function. Regrettably, the Hayekian triangle is fatally flawed, and is of no use whatsoever. It should be jettisoned on the part of all serious researchers. It should be of interest only to antiquarians.

Moreover, it is fatally flawed not only regarding research, but also as a pedagogical device. I say this because, though it may assist some in understanding ABCT, bad habits are hard to break, and if future professional Austrian economists, especially those who go on to study for the Ph.D. first learn ABCT by means of the triangle, it will be that much harder for them to

[466] Mises (1912) comes to mind

develop a correct and complete understanding of the structures of production and consumption. This will hinder them as scholars and lead to a lessened interest in ABCT, resulting in a continuation of what I think has been a neglect of the theory in terms of development thereof. Furthermore, it alienates mainstream economists who, supposedly are good mathematicians,[467] and rightfully can make no sense of it. If the purpose is to attract the mainstream then the "Hayekian triangle" should be abandoned in favor what might be called the "Hayekian function." At least then they could make enough simplistic assumptions to make the function differentiable, so that they could use their favorite analytical tool – calculus – to assist them in understanding ABCT.

Thus we see that the "triangle" leaves no room for entrepreneurs, uncertainty, and the heterogeneity of the real world. But these are essential elements of Austrian economics and any theory of the business cycle that claims to be Austrian must include them; e.g., clusters of entrepreneurial mistakes. The triangle then, being an attempt to capture, mathematically, the highly complex and dynamic realm of the incalculable number of real world interactions of vast numbers of individual human beings, is absolutely incompatible with Austrian economics; it was a mistake from the beginning, and should be an abandoned.

[467] But appearances can be deceiving. For an argument that mathematical sophistication is wanting on the part of many mainstream economists, see Barnett (2003 and 2004).

17. Appendix 1

Consider two right-triangles (in the first quadrant of a Cartesian plane) 1, with legs a and b, and 2, with legs c and d, (figure 35), that are to be combined into a third, 3. Let them both have one leg (a for 1, and c for 2) along the x –axis and the other leg be parallel to the y-axis, with the hypotenuse of each having one terminus at the origin. Then the area of 1 (A1) is ab/2 and the area of 2 (A2) is cd/2, and the combined area is (ab + cd)/2. The abscissa of 3 must be either a, c, or a + c, and the ordinate either b, d, or b + d. Thus there are nine (9) possible areas for 3 (A3):

	B	d	b + d
a	A3 = ab/2	A3 = ad/2	A3 = (ab+ad)/2 OK only if a = c
c	A3 = bc/2	A3 = cd/2	A3 = (bc+cd)/2 OK only if a = c
a+c	A3 = (ab+bc)/2 OK only if b = d	A3 = (ad+cd)/2 OK only if b = d	A3= (ab+ad+bc+cd)/2 = A1+A2+(ad+bc)/2 A3 = A1+A2+(ad+bc)/2

Consider these cases numbered from left to right, then top to bottom:

1) A3 = ab/2; but ab/2 = A1; therefore unless A2 = 0; i.e., unless triangle 2 is non-existent, A3 < A1 + A2;

5) A3 = cd/2; but cd/2 = A2; therefore unless A1 = 0; i.e. unless triangle 1 is non-existent; A3 < A1 + A2;

3) and 6) A3 = (ab + ad)/2 or A3 = (ab + ad)/2; in either of these cases A3 = A1 + A2 only if a = c. That is, the period of production for triangles 1 and 2 would have to be the same;

7) and 8) A3 = (ab + bc)/2 or A3 = (ad + cd)/2; in either of these cases A3 = A1 + A2 only if c = d. That is, the value of consumers' goods at the point of sale the consumers would have to be the same;

9) A3 = (ab + ad + bc + cd)/2; but (ab+ad+bc+cd)/2 = A1 + A2 + (ad+bc)/2; therefore unless at least one (1) of a, or b, or c, or d = 0, A3 > A1 + A2. At best that would mean either triangle 1 or triangle 2 was non-existent; at worst, both;

2) or 4) A3 = ad/2 or A3 = bc/2; these are essentially the same in that A3 + A1 + A2 requires that the ratio of the period of production of the first triangle to that of the second plus the ratio of the value of consumers' goods at the time of sale to the consumers of the second triangle to that of the first must total to one (1), regardless of whether 1 or 2 is taken to be the first triangle, and the other, the second.

Thus, although mathematically possible, it is economically implausible, to say the least, that two (2) or more triangles can be combined.

Appendix 2

Perhaps the confusion concerning the relationship between stages of production and the temporal length of the production process is a consequence of the following statements by Bohm-Bawerk. Mises, Hayek, Rothbard, and Garrison.

First, Bohm-Bawerk:

"The lesson to be learned from all of these examples is quite clear. It is to the effect that roundabout methods are more fruitful than direct methods in the production of consumers' goods. And as a matter of fact, this greater fruitfulness manifests itself in two ways. Whenever a consumers' good can be produced either by direct or by indirect methods, superiority of the latter is demonstrated by the fact that the indirect method either turns out a greater quantity of product with the same quantity of labor or the same quantity of product with a smaller quantity of labor" (Bohm-Bawerk, 1959, 12).

"The disadvantage which attends the capitalist method of production consists in a *sacrifice of time*. Capitalist roundaboutness is productive but time consuming. It yields more or better consumption goods, but not until a later time" (Bohm-Bawerk, 1959, 82).

It is true that Bohm-Bawerk notes that:

"Exceptional cases may occur in which a roundabout method is not only *better* but also *quicker*... But that is not the rule. In an overwhelming majority of cases, the adoption of circuitous methods imposes conditions that require us to wait for a time and sometimes for a very long time indeed, before we obtain possession of the product in consumable form" (Bohm-Bawerk, 1959, 82).

But that is mere speculation, unsupported by analysis or data. There is no reason or a priori basis for this conjecture. Innovations often speed up the production process and even reduce the stages of production. Examples of the former are modern computers and communications technologies, and of the latter, Wal-Mart and JIT manufacturing.

And:

"It goes without saying that it is no refutation of our proposition to contend that, with the help of *previously finished* capital objects, a given product can be produced more quickly than by the direct "capitalless" method. This sort of refutation might be exemplified by the argument that a tailor needs only one day to turn out a coat with the help of a sewing machine, whereas it might require three days without that capital object. But it is obvious that the sewing by machine is only a portion – and indeed the smallest portion – of the circuitous capitalist path. The principal length of that path is covered by the making of the sewing machine. And it is equally apparent that the traversing of the entire length of the path requires a great deal more than three days" (Bohm-Bawerk, 1959, 82).

However, although it may be correct during the transition phase in which Bohm-Bawerk's "previously finished capital objects" are first produced that the period of production is lengthened, this in no way establishes that the period of production is lengthened during the *post*-transition period. Let us use his example of the production of coats. Assume it takes 100 days to produce a sewing machine. Consider three periods: pre transition, transition, and post transition. In any pre transition period of 300 days, 100 coats can be produced. During the transition of 100 days, the sewing machine is produced, but no coats are produced. In any post transition period of 200 days, 100 days can be used to produce 100 coats and the other 100 days used to produce another sewing machine. Therefore, provided a sewing machine can be used to produce at least 100 coats before it wears out, the period of production, post transition has been shortened. That is, we can produce 100 coats every 200 days for an indefinitely long (because the 200 day period allows 100 days for the production of a replacement machine, as well as the 100 days required to produce 100 coats) compared to the post transition situation in which it 100 coats required 300 days to produce.[468]

Next, Mises:

"...As acting man prefers those processes which, other things being equal, produce the products in the shortest time, only such processes are left for further action which consume more time. ...Bohm-Bawerk speaks of the higher productivity of roundabout ways of production requiring more time. It is more appropriate to speak of the higher physical productivity of production processes requiring more time.

"The higher productivity of these processes does not always consist in the fact that they produce--with the same quantity of factors of production expended--a greater quantity of products. More often it consists in the fact that they produce products which could not be produced at all in shorter periods of production. These processes are not roundabout processes. They are the shortest and quickest way to the goal chosen. If one wants to catch more fish, there is no other method available than the substitution of fishing with the aid of nets and canoes for fishing without the aid of this equipment. There is no better, shorter, and cheaper method for the production of aspirin known than that adopted by the chemical plants. If one disregards error and

[468] More generally, if D_0 and D_1 are the numbers of days it takes to produce a coat pre and post transition, respectively, and M is the number of days it takes to produce the sewing machine, then the period of production will be shortened post transition provided $C > M/(D_0 - D_1)$, where C is the number of coats that can be produced during the working life of the machine.

ignorance, there cannot be any doubt about the highest productivity and expediency of the processes chosen. If people had not considered them the most direct processes, viz., those leading by the shortest way to the end sought, they would not have adopted them (Mises 1996 [1949], 481-482, footnote omitted).

"...It is more appropriate to speak of the higher physical productivity of processes requiring more time. The higher productivity of these processes does not always consist in the fact that they produce – with the same quantity of factors of production expended – a greater quantity of products.... If one wants to catch more fish, there is no other method available than the substitution of fishing with the aid of nets and canoes for fishing without the aid of this equipment....

"...But if temporally remoter goals are aimed at, lengthening of the period of production is a necessary corollary of the venture" (Mises, 1996 [1949], 481 - 482).

Then Hayek:

"That anything which will tend to lengthen this investment structure of current labour will lead to increases of the quantity of capital and anything which tends to shorten it will lead to a reduction of capital, remains a point of fundamental importance" (Hayek, 1934B, 231).

And:

"I have already pointed out that it is an essential feature of our modern, 'capitalistic,' system of production that at any moment a far larger proportion of the available original means of production is employed to provide consumers' goods for some more or less distant future than is used for the satisfaction of immediate needs. The *raison d'être* of this way of organizing production is, of course, that by lengthening the production process we are able to obtain a greater quantity of consumers' goods out of a given quantity of original means of production" (Hayek, 1935, p. 37-38).

And:

"The thing which is of main interest for us is that any such change from a method of any given duration to a method which takes more or less time implies quite definite changes in the organization of production, or, as I shall call this particular aspect, to distinguish it from other more familiar aspects, changes in the *structure of production"* (Hayek, 1935, p. 37-38).

And:

"On the simplifying assumption that the *total* length of the of the marginal processes that are made possible by an increase in the supply of investible funds, is always greater than the total length of any process already used, this situation can be represented by the following diagram. [Present authors: This is Hayek's (1935, 138) figure 8, which we repeat as our H3] The curvilinear[1] triangle *ABC* represents, in the same way as the triangle I have used in the preceding lectures, the stock of capital belonging to the processes already completed. (The area of the curvilinear triangle *AB'C'* shows the stock of capital before the additions were begun). [footnote] 1. The reasons which make a curvilinear triangle of the kind shown in the text a more appropriate representation than the simplified form used in Lecture II are probably obvious. See p. 39" (Hayek, 1935, 137).

Now, Rothbard:

"It is obvious that the production process takes *time,* and the more complex the production process the more time must be taken" (Rothbard, 1993 [1962], 288).

Last, Garrison:

"In its simplest application, the two legs of [Hayek's] right triangle measure consumption [sic] and the corresponding production time (reckoned in the number of stages of production) for an economy that has achieved an intertemporal equilibrium. A primitive instance of this intertemporal equilibrium and of potential changes in it can be illustrated by Robinson Crusoe who for some time was content to sustain himself by catching fish with the aid of little or no fishing equipment. A greater output of fish is possible but only if Crusoe is willing to take time away from fishing in order to fashion a net and possibly a boat. Consumable output would have to fall while the production process is being enhanced. Once the new, more capital-intensive (and more time-consuming) process is completed, however, the level of output would rise above its initial level. The new intertemporal equilibrium can be depicted by a Hayekian triangle with a longer consumption [sic] leg, representing more fish, and a longer production-time leg, representing the increase in time spent maintaining the new production process" (Garrison, 2004, 324-325).

The foregoing is problematical. First, there is no mention of the meaning of the height of the triangle save that of the right leg, and that is misstated as "consumption" rather than as the pecuniary value of consumption, or, better yet, the pecuniary value of the consumption goods at the moment of sale to the consumers.

Second, in a world of heterogeneous capital goods, not to mention heterogeneous labor and natural resources, the concept of capital intensity is incoherent. Which, for example, is a more capital intensive process: a man fishing using a boat and a rod and reel or the same man fishing with a net from the shore? Or a man hunting a deer with, on the one hand, a rifle and, on the other, a shotgun. Capital intensity cannot be measured using pecuniary value, else the capital intensity can change with no change in the physical reality; nor, for the same reason, can it be measured in terms of the quantity of output. Neither can it be measured by, to coin a term, the "socially necessary" labor required to produce it.

Third, the placement of the phrase "and more time-consuming" in conjunction with its inclusion within parentheses, implies that the "new, more capital intensive" process is necessarily also "more time consuming." This is reinforced by reference to "a longer production-time leg" of the Hayekian triangle. We offer a counter-factual example; references are to table 1.

Crusoe works eight (8) hours a day to catch one fish by hand. The other 16 hours constitute leisure. (See day 1.) This an ERE or steady state equilibrium.[469] It takes him eight (8) hours of fishing by hand to catch one fish, a total of eight (8) hours of work of any and all kinds to catch one fish, and thus 128 calendar days to catch 16 fish.

It takes eight (8) hours to make a net without any tools. Although a net becomes weaker and weaker with every hour of use, it will still hold fish, until after 64 hours of use it breaks completely apart and becomes useless.

One day, Crusoe spends eight (8) hours during which he weaves a net from scratch to completion, but makes no change in his leisure.[470] Of course, he goes hungry that day. (See day 2A.) Alternatively, he spends eight (8) hours making a net from scratch to completion, fishes by hand for eight (8) hours, and reduces his leisure by eight (8) hours. In this case, he catches a fish and does not go hungry. (See day 2B.) Either of these is a transition day, after which he faces a new set of alternatives, and no longer concerns us.

Now what happens? Consider three such alternatives, each of which is an ERE or steady state equilibrium and which we compare with the initial such condition. In the first, day 3A, he maintains his original level of leisure, 16 hours per day, spends[471] 7.11^{+} hours per day fishing with the net, and 0.88^{+} hours per day making a replacement net. Therefore, his total hours of work also remain the same, though the nature of the work differs in part. In this situation, he is able to continuously replace his net as it wears out, and catch 1.77777^{+} fish per day. Therefore, it takes him four (4) of fishing with a net to catch one fish, a total of four and one-half hours (4.5) hours of work of any and all kinds to catch one fish, and 9 calendar days to catch 16 fish.

In the second scenario, day 3B, he spends four (4) hours per day fishing with the net in order to maintain his original quantity (1) of fish caught per day and 0.5 hours per day making a replacement net; his leisure increases to 19.5 hours per day. Therefore, his total hours of work decrease

---

[469] It is a basic tenet of Austrian economics that no such state of affairs can characterize economic reality.

[470] The eight (8) hours is, of course, socially-necessary-labor time. ☺

[471] The superscript + sign indicates a repeated decimal.

to four and one-half per day, though the nature of the work differs in part. In this situation, also, he is able to continuously replace his net as it wears out. Therefore, it takes him four (4) hours of fishing with a net to catch one fish, a total of four and one-half hours (4.5) hours of work of any and all kinds to catch one fish, and 16 calendar days to catch 16 fish.

In the last situation, day 3C, he wishes to enjoy the benefits of his improved productivity partly in the form of increased fish and partly in the form of increased leisure. He chooses to spend 6 hours a day fishing with a net and catching 1.5 fish and three-quarters of an hour making a replacement net; and, he enjoys17¼ hours of leisure. Therefore, it takes him four (4) of fishing with a net to catch one fish, a total of four and one-half hours (4.5) hours of work of any and all kinds to catch one fish, and 10⅔ calendar days to catch 16 fish.

It is obvious that, however we look at it, the structure of production on day three (3) has been *shortened* relative to that on day one (1). That is, though the structure of production was lengthened during the transition period [day two (2)] from day one (1) to day three (3), even to the point of being "infinitely," or better yet, undefinably long in the case of day 2, thereafter it has been "permanently" shortened. However, on day three (3) there are two (2) stages of production; to wit: working on a replacement net and fishing with the extant net; whereas, on day one (1) there is only one (1) stage of production – fishing by hand. Therefore, not only is there no necessary direct relationship between the number of stages of production and the time structure of production, but they may even be *inversely* related.

Q.E.D.

Appendix 3

Table 1

1	2	3	4	5	6	7	8	9	10	11	12	13	**14**	15	16
Day	leisure (hrs per calendar day) L	labor fishing without net (hrs per calendar day)	labor fishing with net (hrs per day)	labor making net (hrs per day)	total labor (hrs per day)	capital goods produced (nets per day)	stock of finished capital goods (nets)	depreciation		consumer goods produced per day (fish/day)	consumption = goods & leisure (fish & leisure hours per day)	Stages of production (#)	**time structure of production to produce 16 fish** (man-hours; work days	labor per fish (hours fishing/ fish)	labor per fish ((hours fishing/ + hours making net)/fish)
								(nets per hour of fishing)	(nets per calendar day)						
					1+2 +3						1&2			3/11 or 4/11	6/11
1	16 L	8 h	0 H	0 M	8 W	0 N	0 N	0 N	0 N	1 F	1 F & 16 L	1	128 h;16 D	8 h/F	8W/F
2A	16 L	0 h	0 H	8 M	8 W	1 N	0 N	0 N	0 N	0 F	0 F & 16 L	1	–	–	–
2B	8 L	8 h	0 H	8 M	16 W	1 N	0 N	0 N	0 N	1 F	1 F & 16 L	2	–	8 h/F	16W/F
3A	16 L	0 h	7.11$^+$ H	0.88$^+$M	8 W	1/9 N	1 N	1/64 N	1/9 N	1.77$^+$ F	1.77$^+$F&16L		64 H; 9 D	4 H/F	4.5W/F
3B	19.5 L	0 h	4 H	0.5 M	4½W	1/16 N	1 N	1/64 N	1/16 N	1 F	1 F & 20 L	2	64 H; 16 D	4 H/F	4.5W/F
3C	17¼ L	0 h	6 H	0.75 M	6¾W	0.75 N	1 N	1/64 N	3/32 N	1.5 F	1.5 F&17¼L	2	64 H; 10⅔ D	4 H/F	4.5W/F

Appendix 4

In this appendix we eschew "plain old" plane geometry for analytical geometry. We also ignore the incompatibility of differentiable functions with praxeology. We assume that the discount rate, r, is the same for all goods and that there is *no* compounding.

Let:

C_i = the ith consumers' good;

C_{it} = the expected (at time t = 0) pecuniary value of a quantity of consumers' good i at time t, to include the expected value of the partially completed units of that consumers' good at time t;

$C_{i0} = P_i Q_{i0} \; \forall \; i$;

P_i = the expected price of unit of C_i at time of sale;

Q_{i0} = the quantity of the ith consumers' good at time production of that particular good commences, to include the expected value of the partially completed units at the moment;

$Q_{i0} = Q_0 \; \forall \; i$; and,

r = the relevant rate of discount for C.

Based on the standard Hayekian triangle, consider the production structure of an economy producing four (4) consumers' goods, $C_1, \ldots C_4$, assuming production commences at time t = 0; and,

Let:

$0 < \tau_i < T; \; \forall \; i$;

$C_{1t} = C_{10}(1+r)t$; $0 \leq t \leq T$, where 0 and T are times at which production of C_1 commences and C_1 is sold, respectively;

$C_{2t} = C_{20}(1+r)t$; $0 \leq t \leq \tau_h$, where 0 and τ_h are times at which production of C_2 commences and C_2 is sold, respectively;

$C_{3t} = C_{30}(1+r)(t - \tau_i)$; $\tau_i \leq t \leq T$, where τ_i and T are times at which production of C_3 commences and C_3 is sold, respectively; and,

$C_{4t} = C_{40}(1+r)(t - \tau_j)$; $\tau_j \leq t \leq \tau_k$, where τ_j and τ_k are times at which production of C_4 commences and C_4 is sold, respectively.

There are 24 possible temporal orders of τ_j, τ_i, τ_h, and τ_k, and thus 24 possible figures of the function $C_t = \sum C_{it}$, 1 = 1,…, 4. For illustrative purposes, we choose but one (1): $\tau_j < \tau_i < \tau_h < \tau_k$. Then:

$$\sum C_{it},\ 1,..,4, = \quad \begin{array}{l} C_t = (P_1 + P_2)Q_0\,(1 + r)t \\ C_t = (P_1 + P_2)Q_0(1{+}r)t + P_4Q_0(1 + i)(t - \tau_j) \\ C_t = (P_1 + P_2)Q_0(1{+}r)t + P_4Q_0(1 + i)(t - \tau_j) + P_3Q_0(1 + i)(t - \tau_i) \\ C_t = P_1Q_0(1 + r)t + P_4Q_0(1 + r)(t - \tau_j) + P_3Q_0(1 + r)(t - \tau_i) \\ C_t = P_1Q_0(1{+}r)t + P_3)Q_0(1{+}r)(t - \tau_i) \end{array}$$

That is the function for the "hypotenuse" of a somewhat more realistic "triangle," and that is depicted in figure 31.

Consider, now, the implications of this model. The value of consumers' goods depends only on: 1) the quantity thereof at the time production of each such good commences Q_0; 2) the price each such good is expected (at time = 0) to command at the moment of sale to the consumers, P_i; 3) the rate of interest, r; and, 4) the time elapsed between the initiation of production of each good and its sale to consumers, or if it has not yet been completed and sold, the time of interest; i.e., t, T and the various τs. This is very mechanistic, reminiscent of mainstream growth models.[472]

The equation of the hypotenuse of the triangle 1 (in figure 33A) is given by: $C_1(t_1) = V_1(0)(i + i_1)t_1$, [or, if one wants compound interest, either $C_1(t_1) = V_1(0\,)((1 + i)^{t1} - 1)$ or $C_1(t_1) = V_1(0)(e^{it1} - 1)$, as the interest is compounded discretely or continuously], where $C_1(t_1)$ is the value of consumers' goods at the time of sale to consumers, t_1, $V_1(0)$ is the initial value of resources used in the production process represented by triangle 1, and i_1 is the discount rate relevant to triangle 1. The same notation is used, mutatis mutandis, for triangle 2.

As $V_1(0)$ is denominated in value terms, we may write $V_1(0) = R_1(0)X_1(0)$, where $R_1(0)$ and $X_1(0)$, represent, for triangle 1, the price per unit of resources and the initial quantity of resources at time 0, respectively. Similarly for triangle 2, we may write $V_2(0) = R_2(0)X_2(0)$, with analogous meaning. Then, $C_1(t_1) = R_1(0)X_1(0)(i + i_1)t_1$ and $C2(t_1) = R_2(0)X_2(0)(i + i_2)t_1$. Moreover, as $C_1(t_1)$ is also denominated in value terms we may write $C_1(t_1) = P_1(t_1)Q_1(t_1)$, where $P_1(t_1)$is the price of consumers' goods at the time of sale to consumers' and $Q_1(t_1)$ is the quantity of consumers' goods sold at that time. Similarly, for triangle 2, $C_2(t_1) = P_2(t_1)Q_2(t_1)$.

---

[472] On this see virtually any model in Barrow and Sala-i-Martin (1998).

Compare these two (2) triangles 1 and 2; the hypotenuse of each originates at time 0, when the abscissa is 0, just as production commences, and terminates at the time, t_1, when the consumers' goods are sold to consumers; i.e., when the abscissa is t_1. Thus both have the same period of production. However, let the value of consumers' goods at the time of sale to the consumers, $C_1(t_1)$ and $C_2(t_1)$, for 1 and 2, respectively, differ.

Regardless of which functional form we use, one (1) of the triangles will lie above the other throughout their range. Let 1 be that triangle; i.e., $C_1(t_1) > C_2(t_1)$. The only possible causes for this difference are either $R_1(0) \neq R_2(0)$ or $X_1(0) \neq X_2(0)$ or $i_1 \neq i_2$, or some combination thereof.

The essence of ABCT is an unsustainable distortion of the structure of production; i.e., an unsustainable misallocation of resources, brought about by a governmental-policy-induced lending of money into existence and attendant reduction, ceteris paribus, in interest rates. Therefore, because the triangle is used to explain ABCT, we take the cause of the morphing of triangle 1 into 2 to be a decrease in the discount rate; i.e., $i_1 > i_2$. However, that can not be the sole cause, for it means that the quantities of resources at 0 is the same for both triangles; i.e., $X_1(0) = X_2(0)$. But as the period of production and thus the structure of production are also the same, the quantity of consumers' goods must also be the same; that is = $Q_1(t_1) = Q_2(t_2)$. But this is incompatible with ABCT as there is no shift in resource use from consumers' to capital goods, nor is there a decrease in the quantity of consumers' goods produced.

Therefore, something else besides the discount rate must have changed if the story illustrated by the triangles in figure 33A is to be compatible with ABCT. And, it must be the quantity of resources used and the output of consumers' goods, both of which must have decreased; i.e., $X_1(0) > X_2(0)$ and $Q_1(t_1) > Q_2(t_1)$. The reduced discount rate signals a decrease in time preferences manifested as a fall in demand for consumers' goods and an increase in demand for producers' goods. In order for production to shift in accord therewith, the demand for resources on the part of the capital goods industries must increase and that stemming from the consumers' goods industries must fall. However, It is quite probable that the former will occur before the latter, and as a consequence, prices of resources will rise; i.e., $R_1(0) < R_2(0)$. Nevertheless, the combined effects must be such that any increase in prices is more than offset by fall in interest rates and the decrease in the use of resources for the production of consumers' goods. This is depicted in figure 33A by the morphing of triangle 1 into 2.

Appendix 5

Figure 1

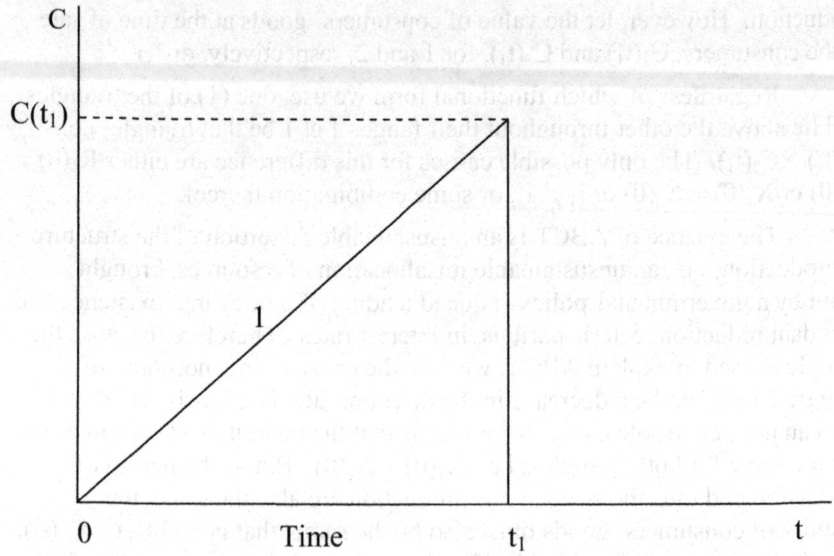

Figure 2

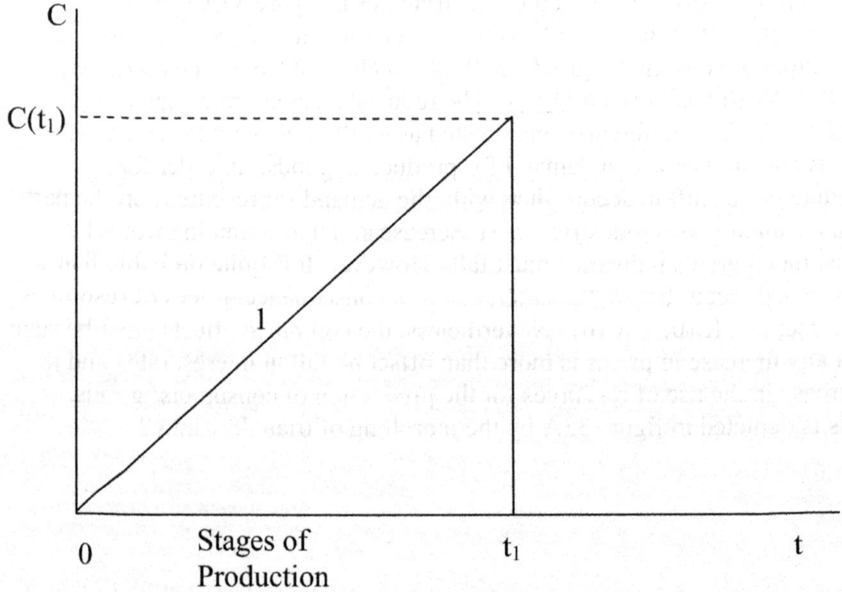

Figure 3

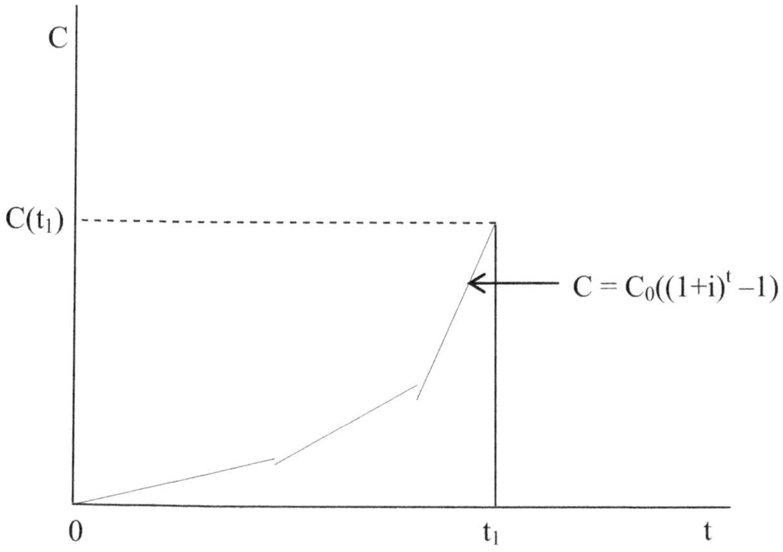

Figure 4

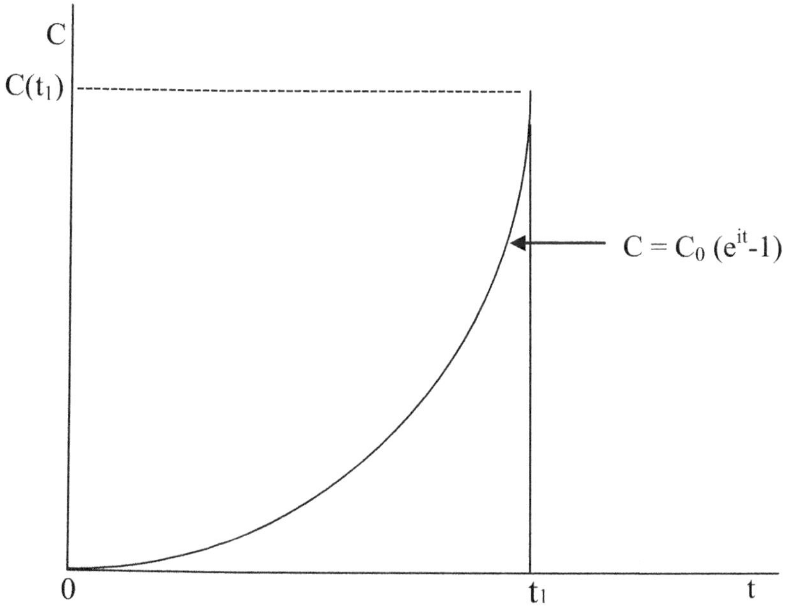

Figure 5A

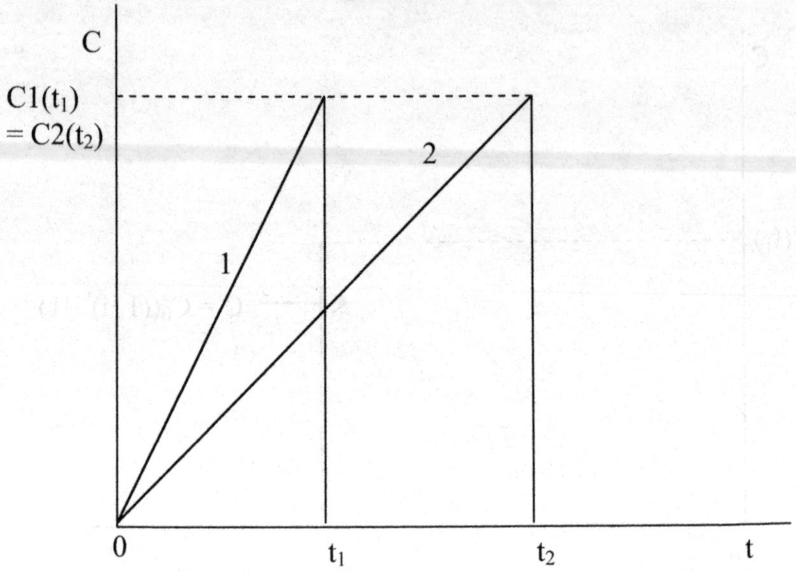

Figure 5B

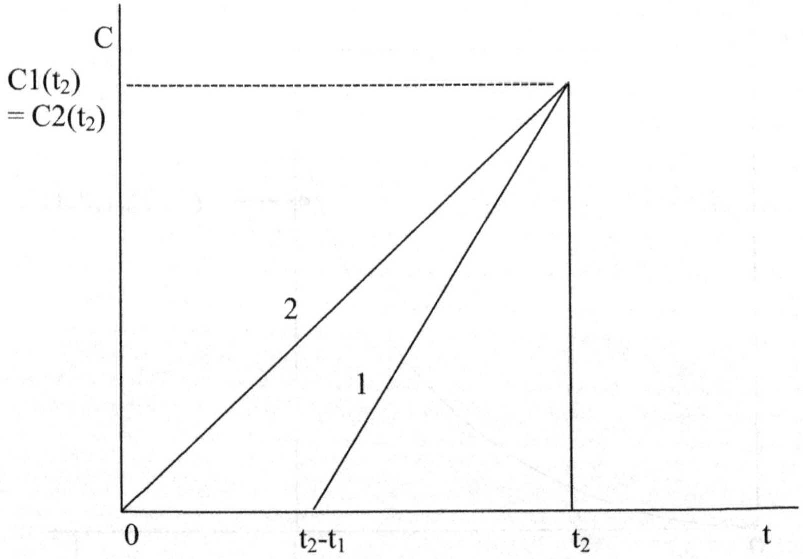

Figure 6

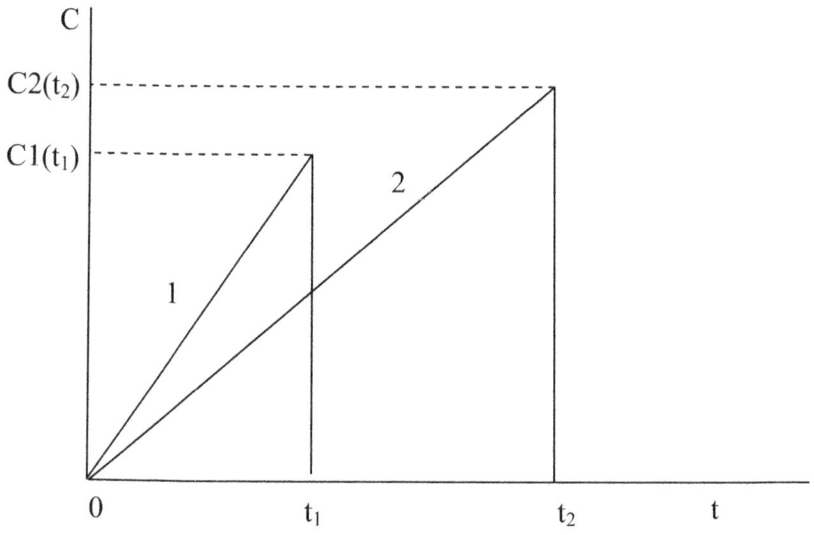

Figure 7A

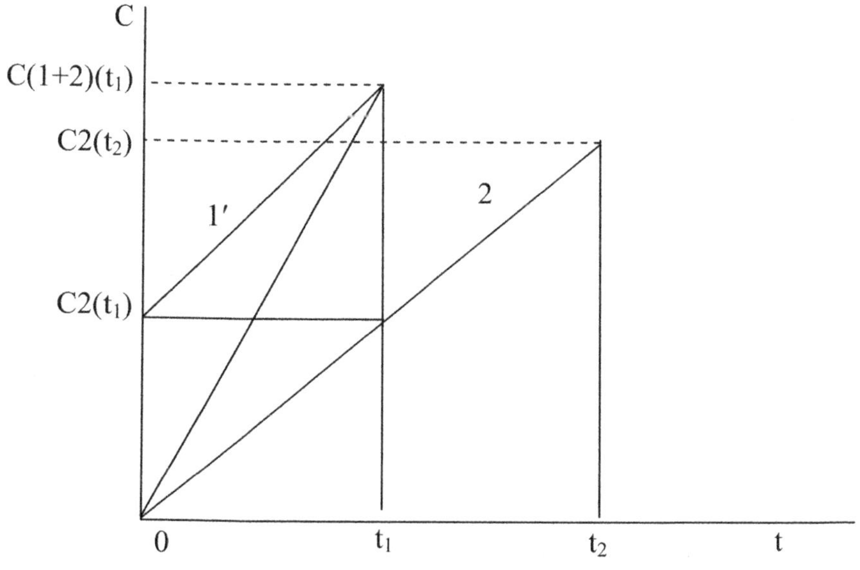

Figure 7B

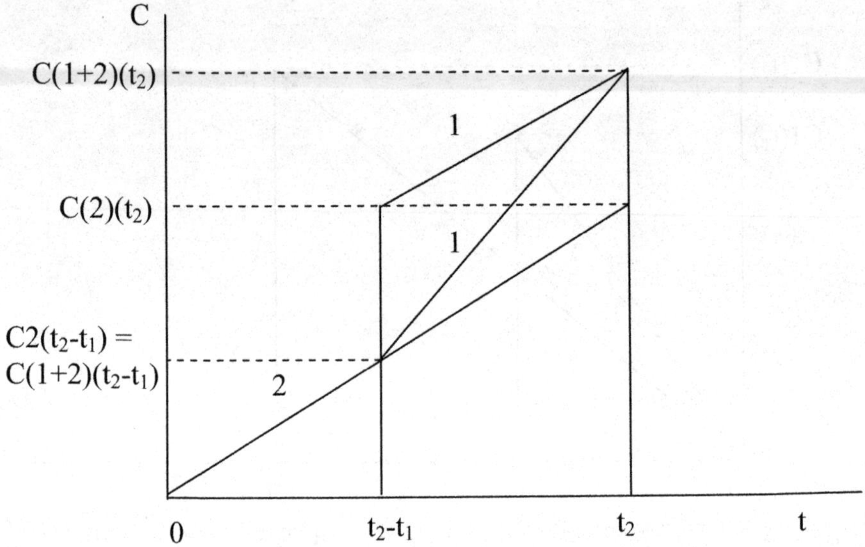

Figure 7C

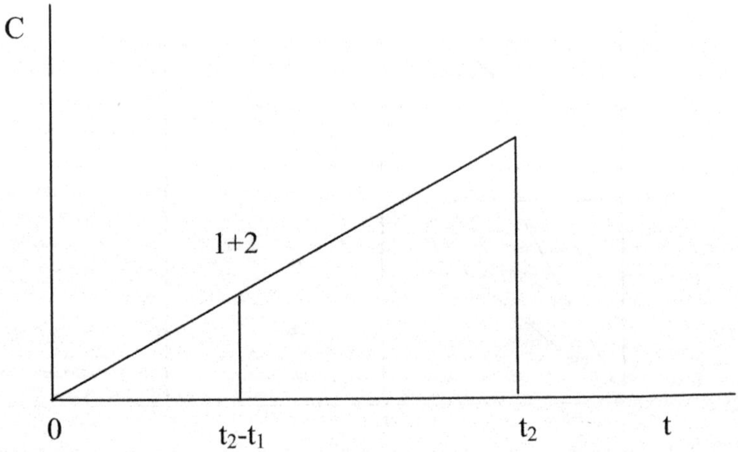

Figure 8A

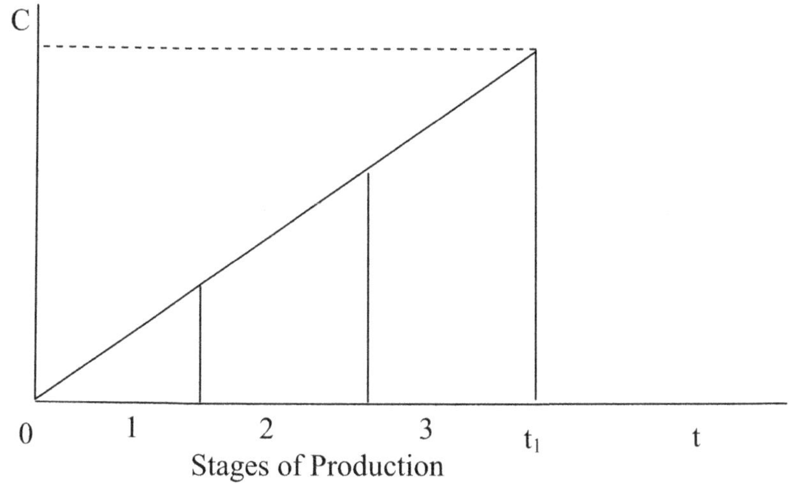

Figure 8B

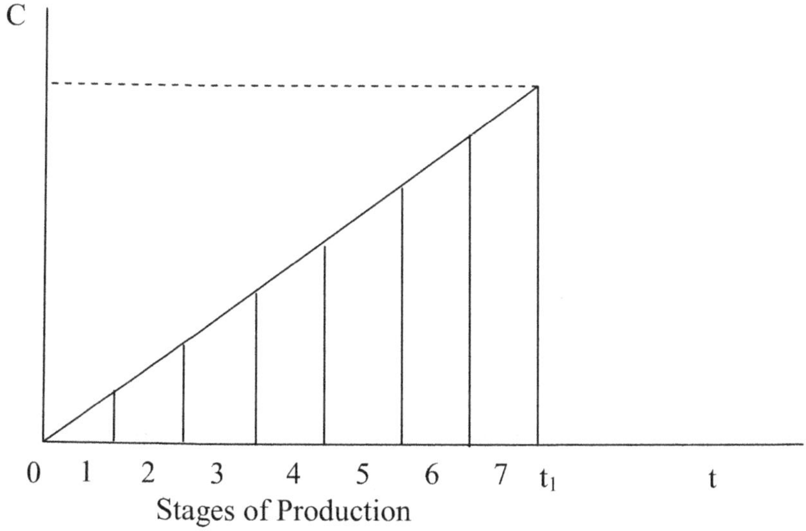

Figure 9A

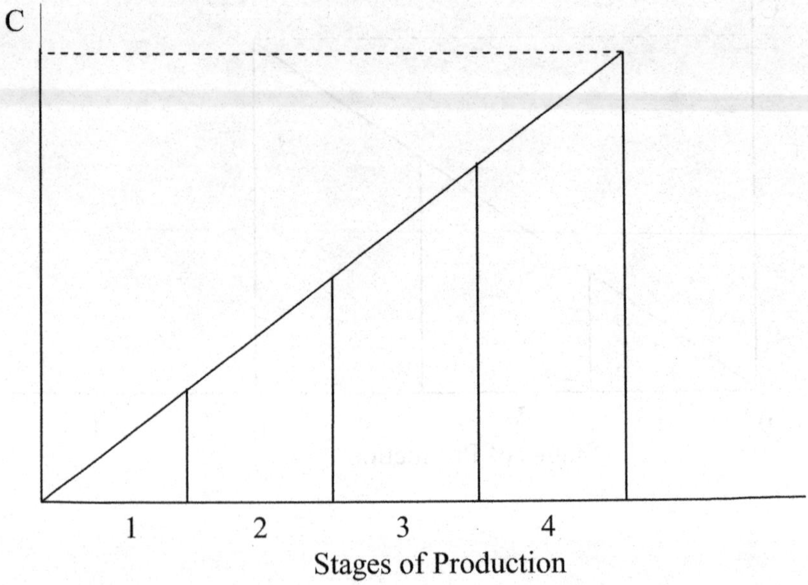

Figure 9B

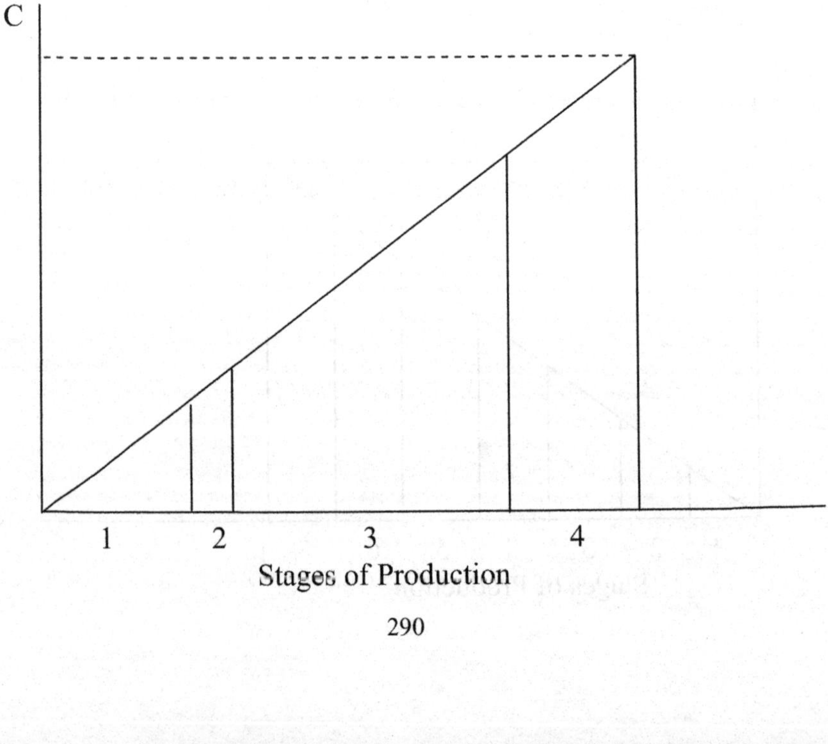

Figure 10 A

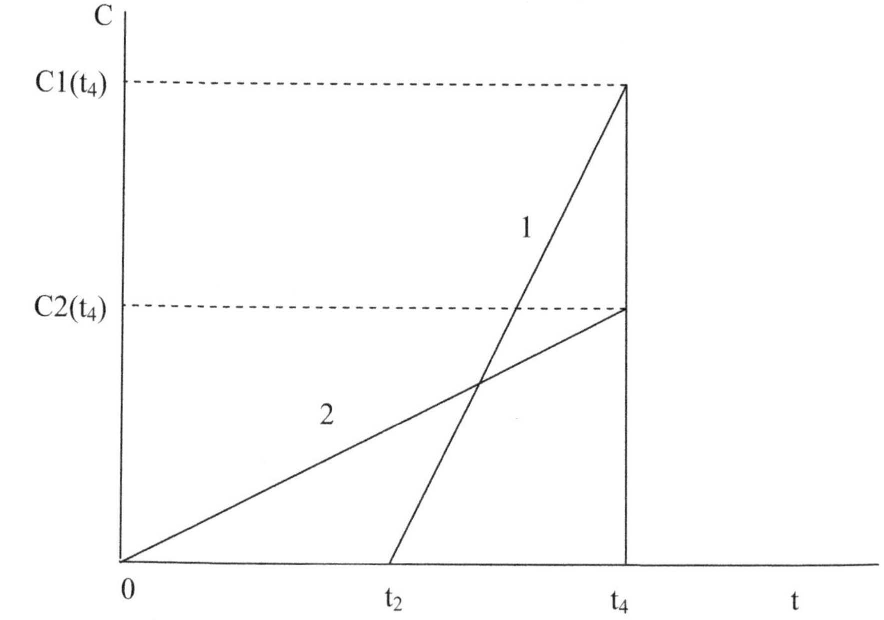

Figure 10 B

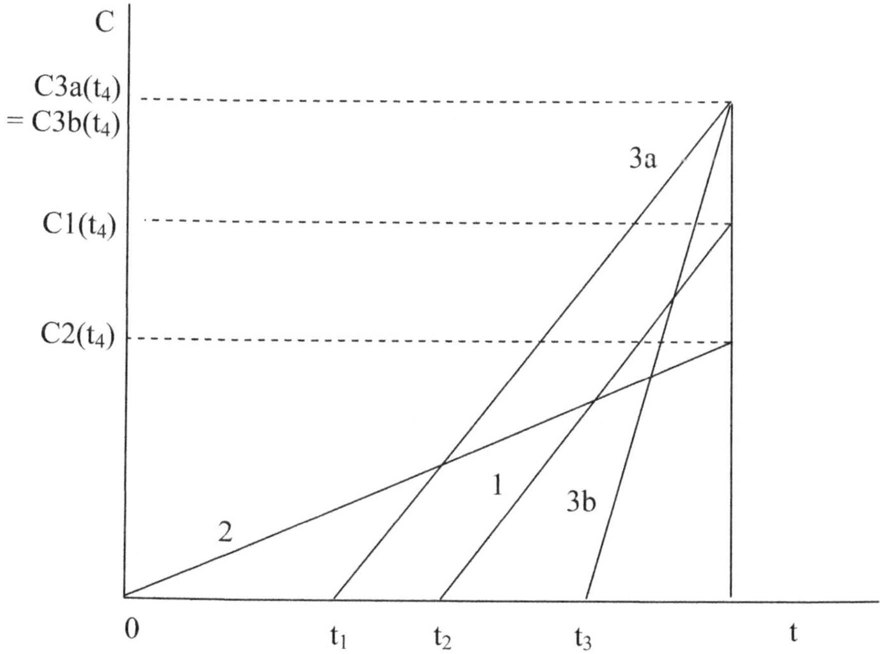

Figure 11

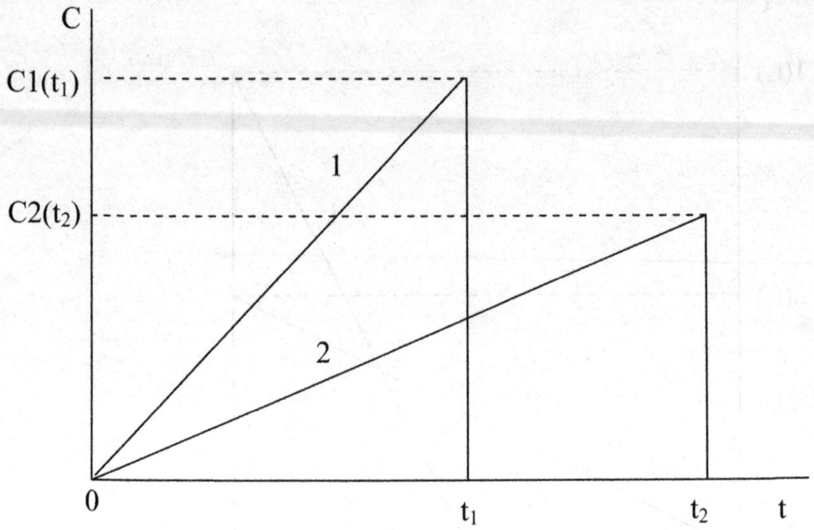

Figure 12

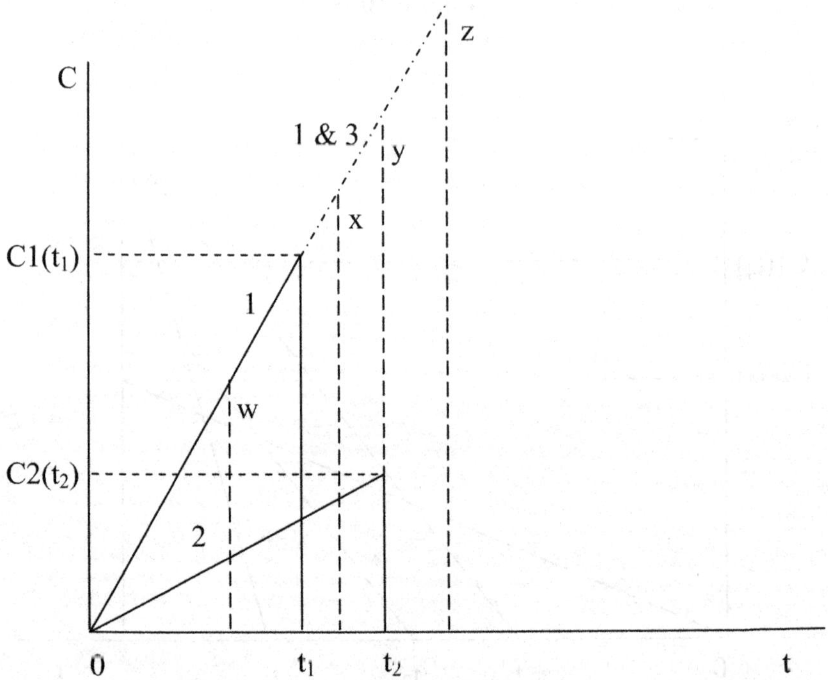

Figure 13

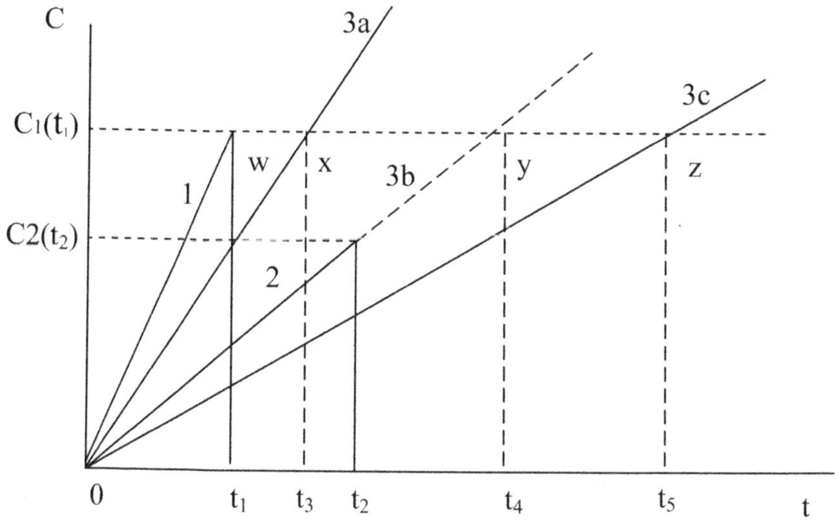

Figure 14

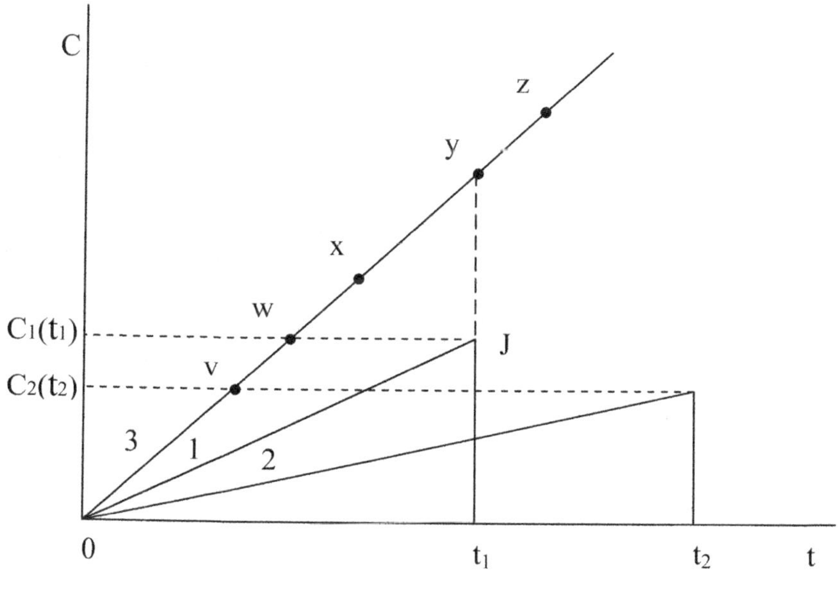

Figure 15

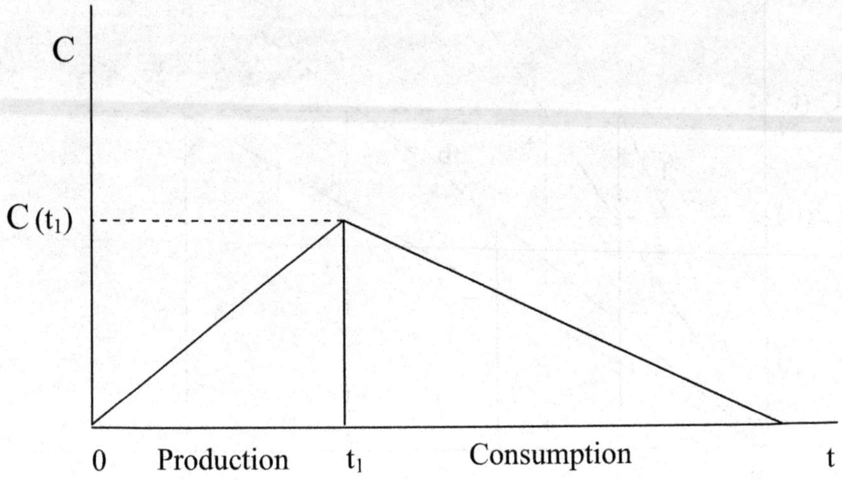

Figure 16A

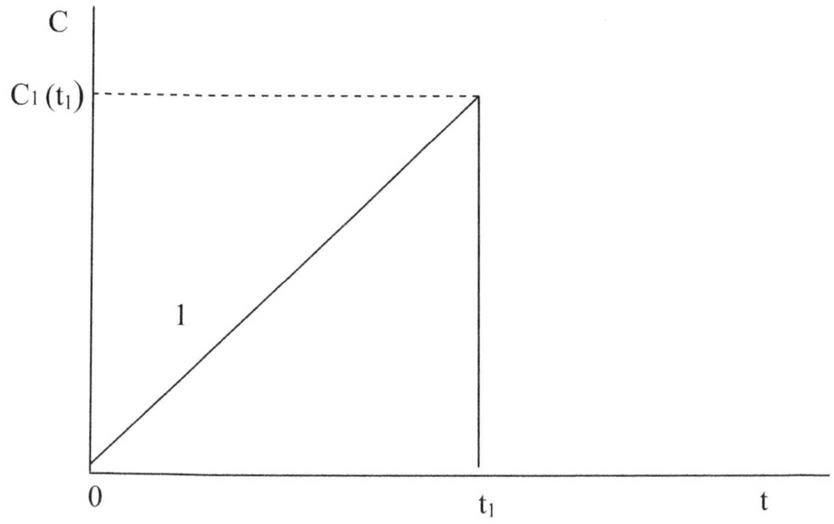

Figure 16B

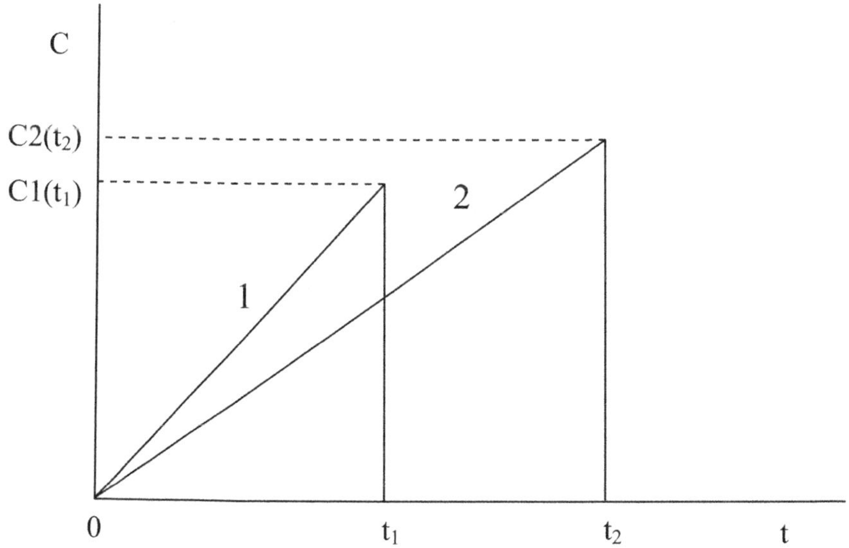

Standard Capital Deepening

Figure 17

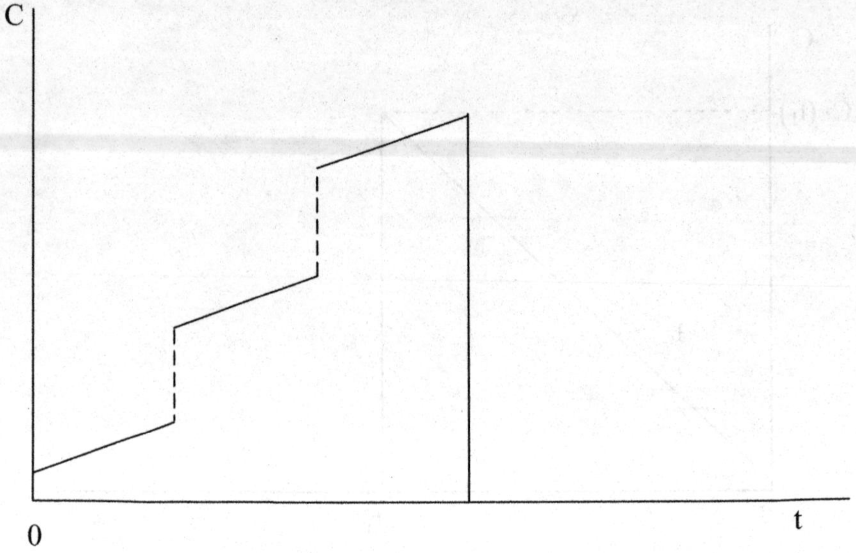

Figure 18

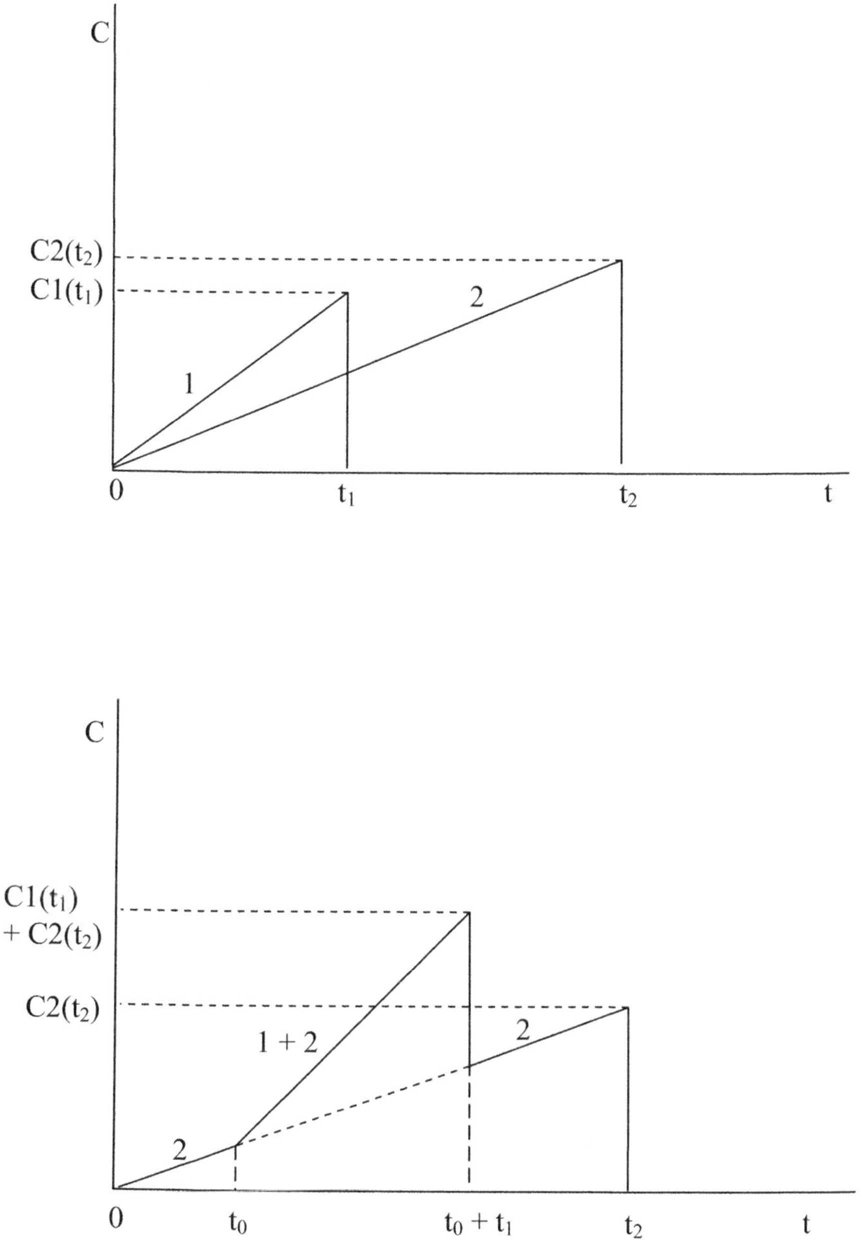

Figure 19

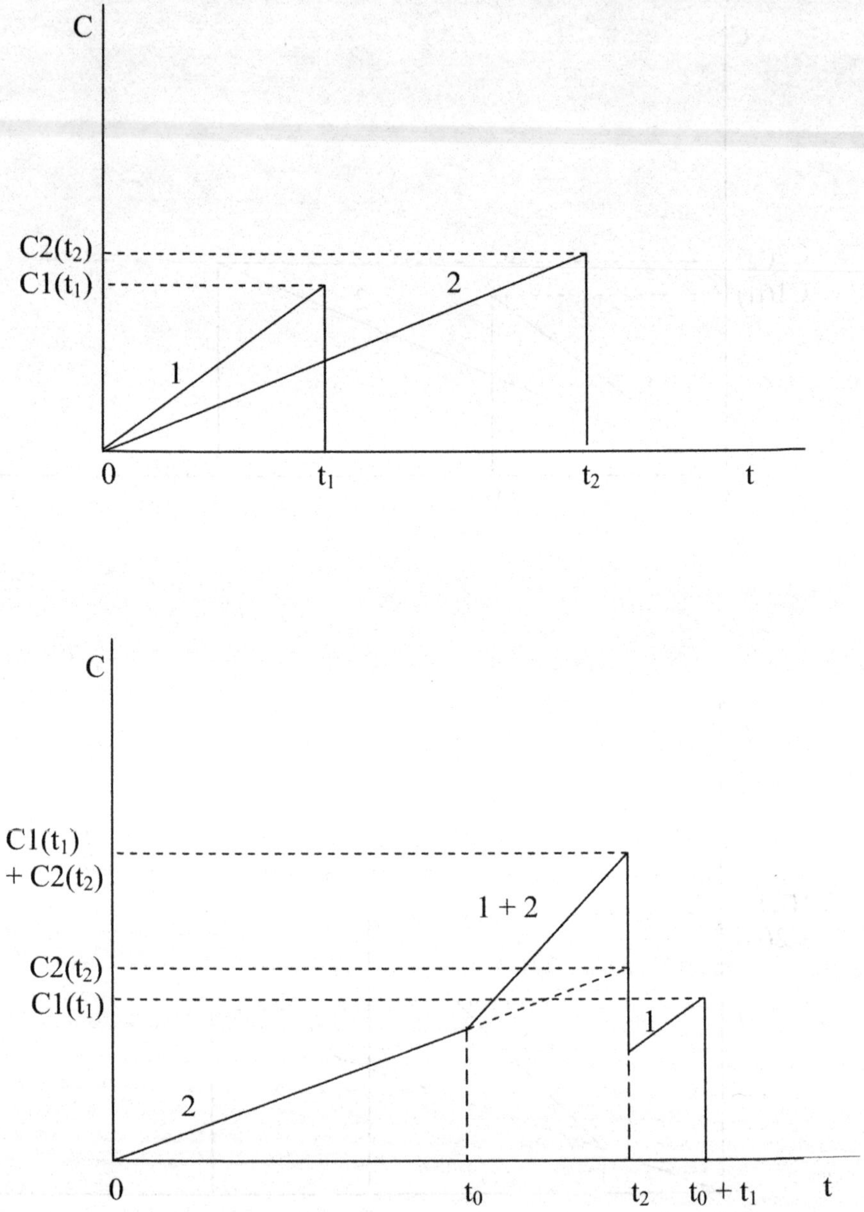

Figure 20

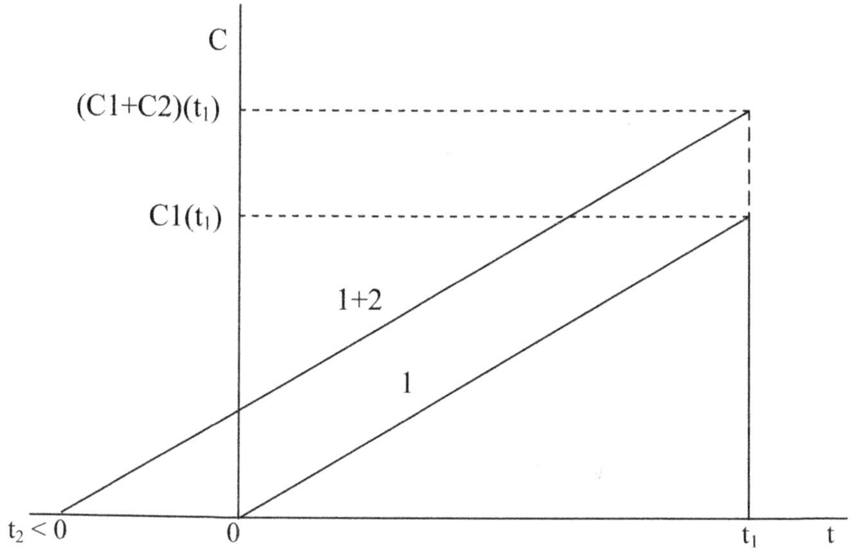

Figure 21

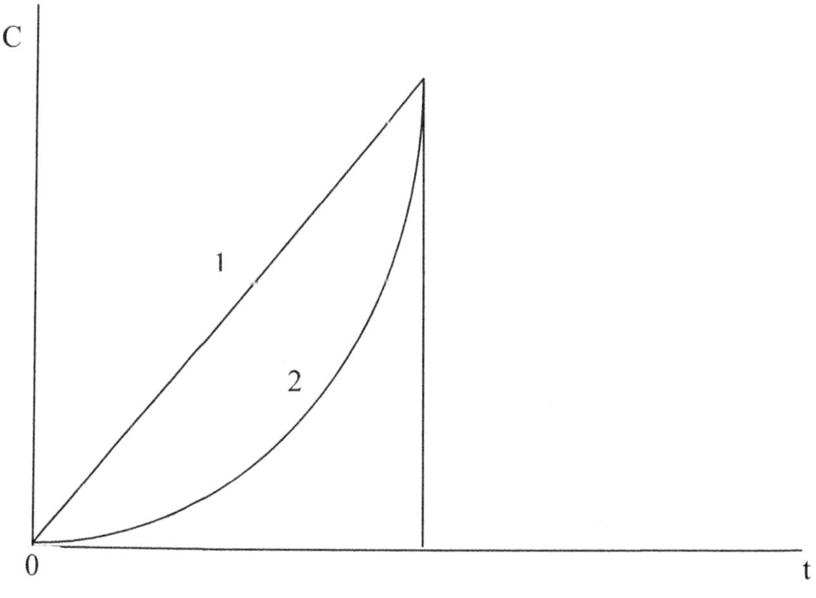

0

Figure 22

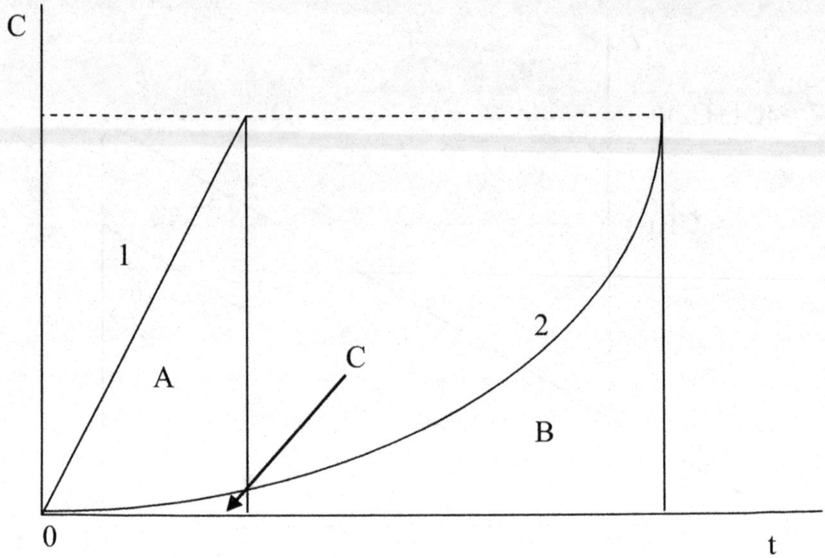

Area A = Area B

Figure 23

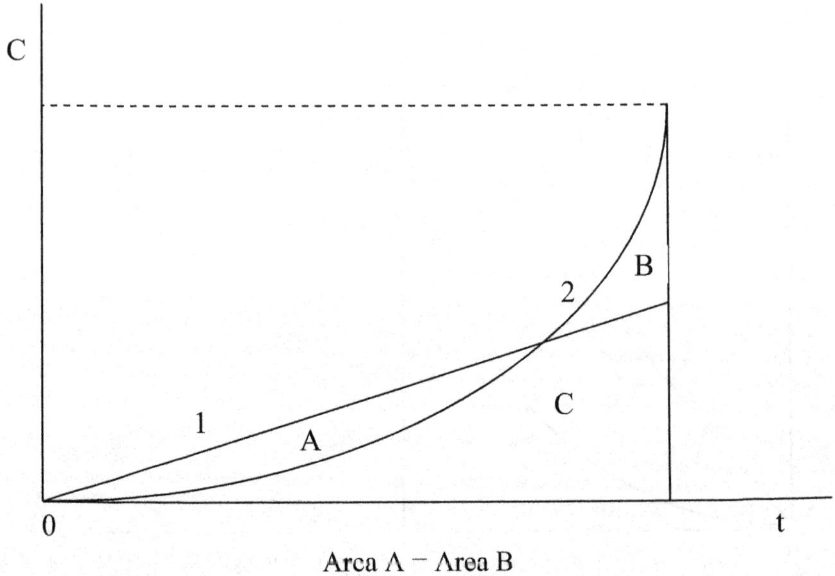

Area A = Area B

Figure 24

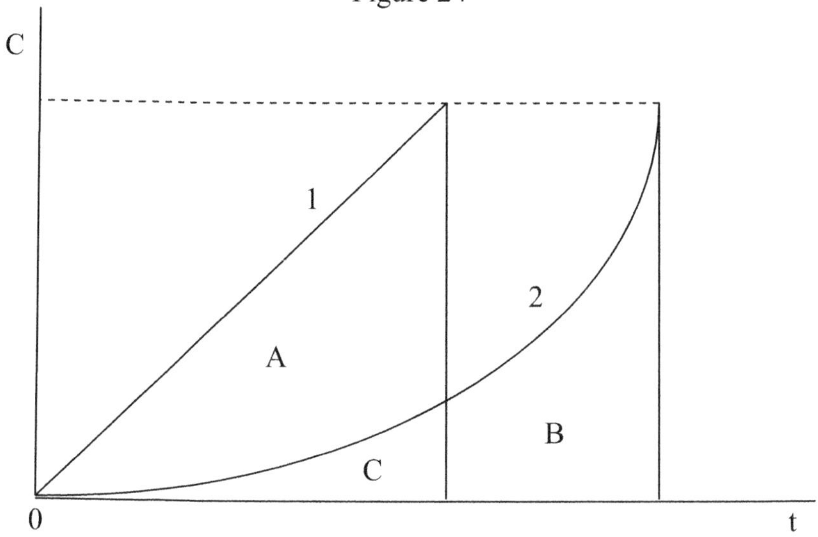

Area A > Area B

Figure 25

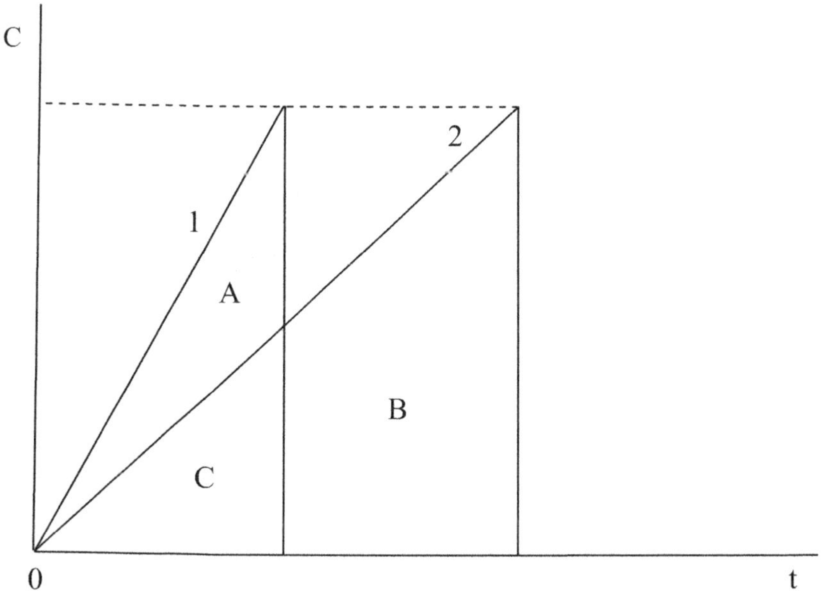

Area A < Area B

Figure 26

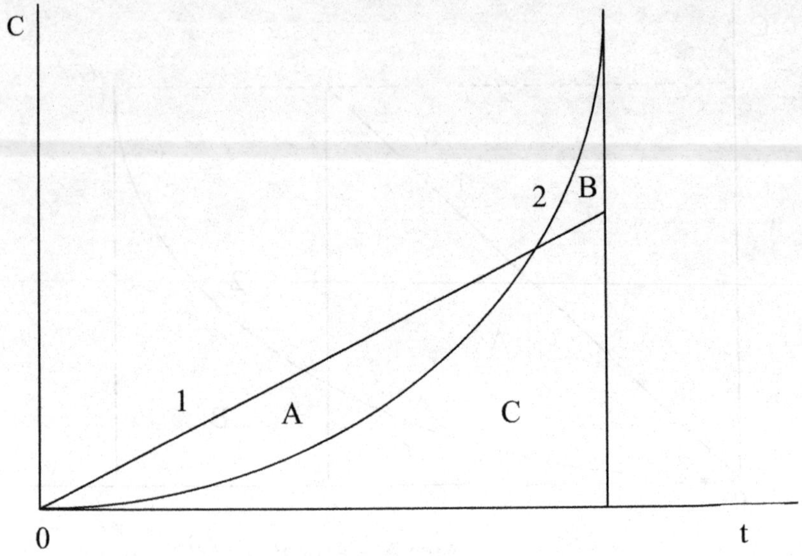

Area A > Area B

Figure 27

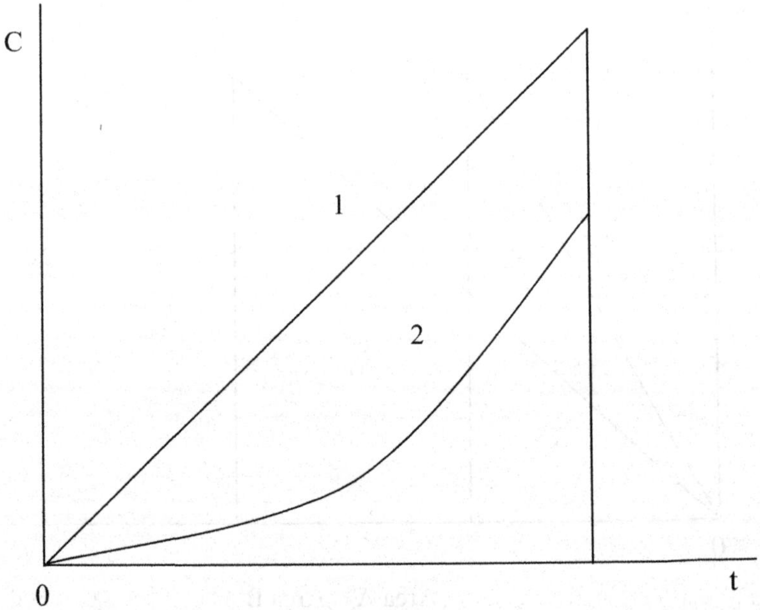

Figure 28

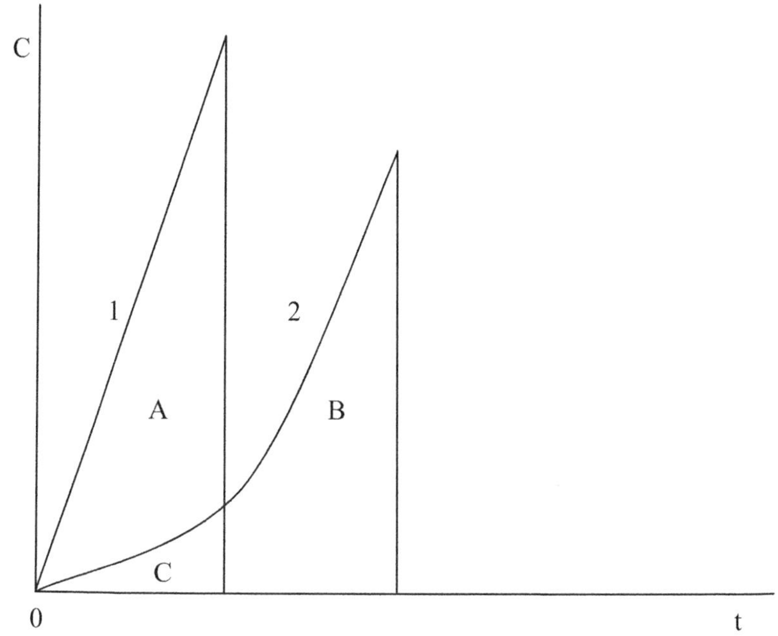

Area A = Area B

Figure 29

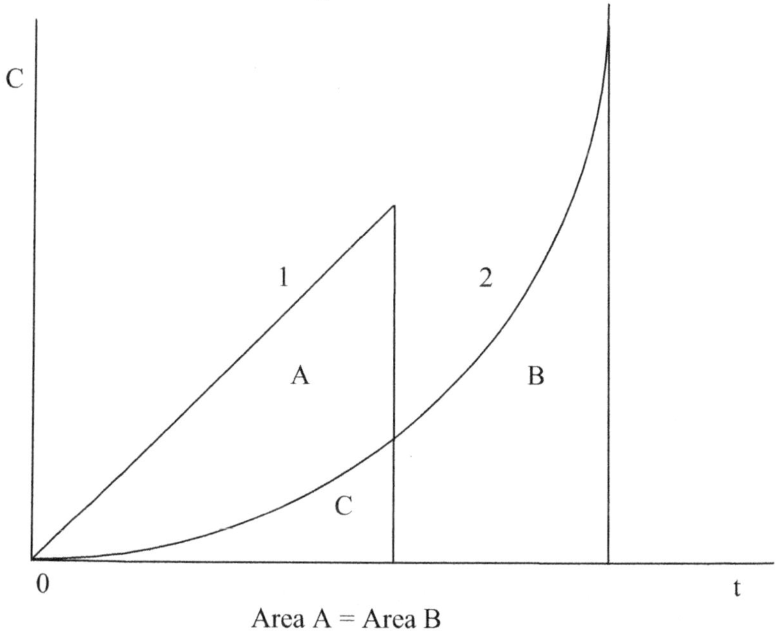

Area A = Area B

Figure 30

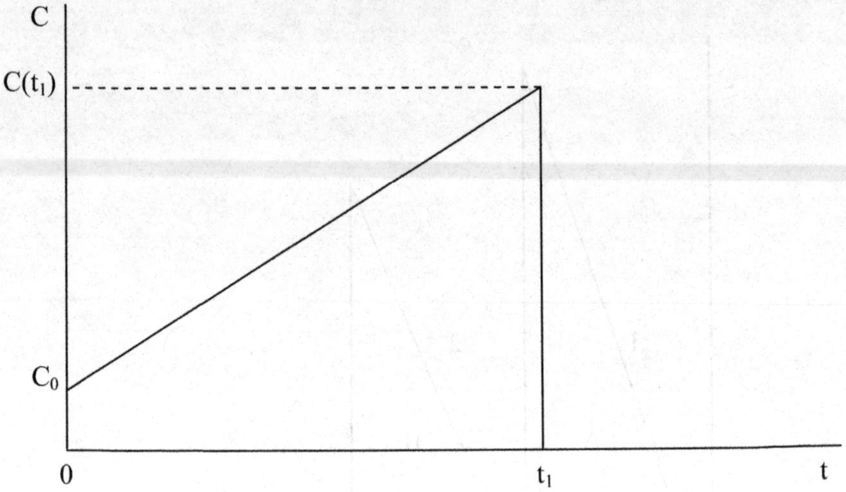

Figure 31

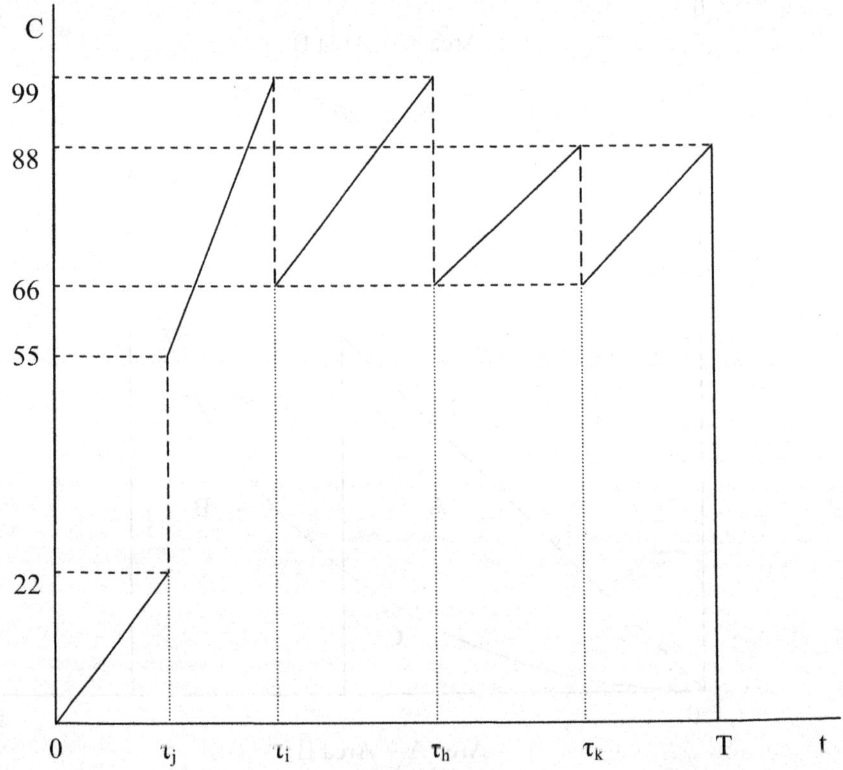

Figure 31A

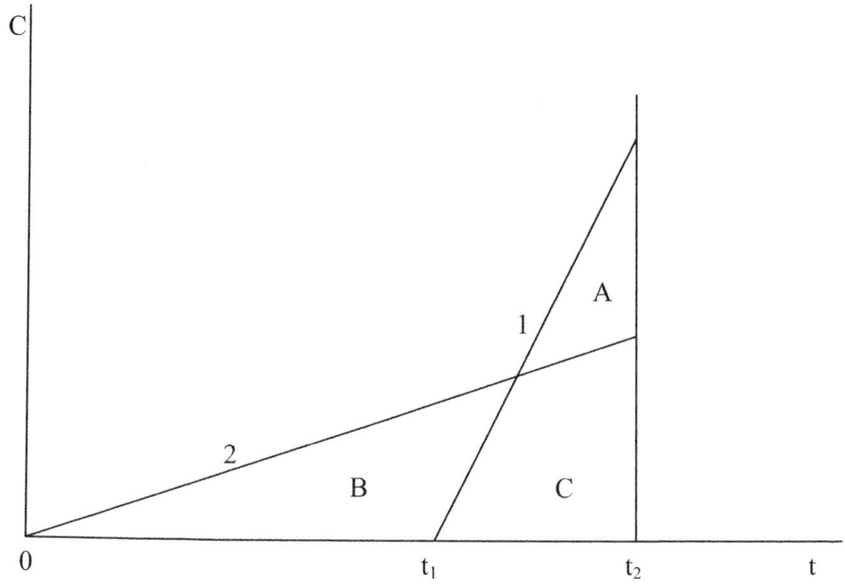

Area A < Area B

Figure 31B

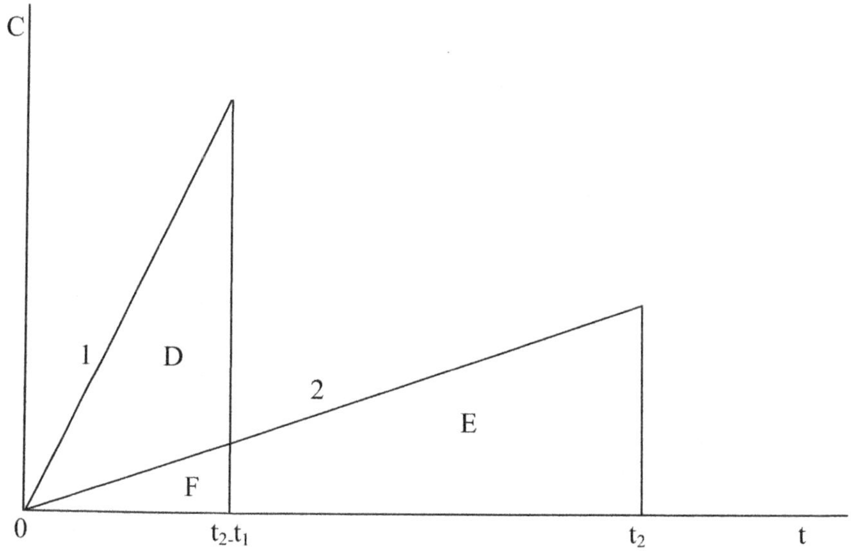

Area D < Area E

Figure 32A

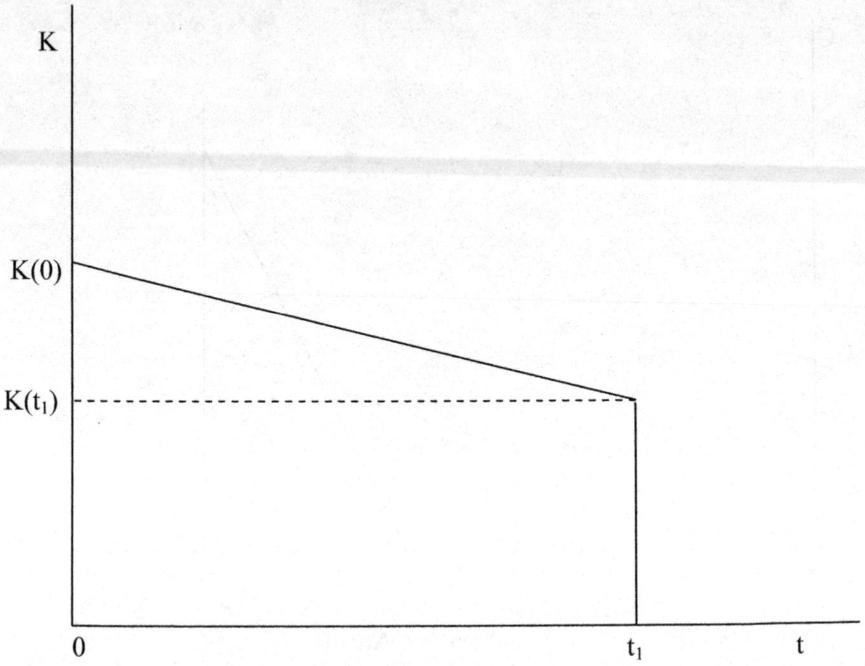

Figure 32B

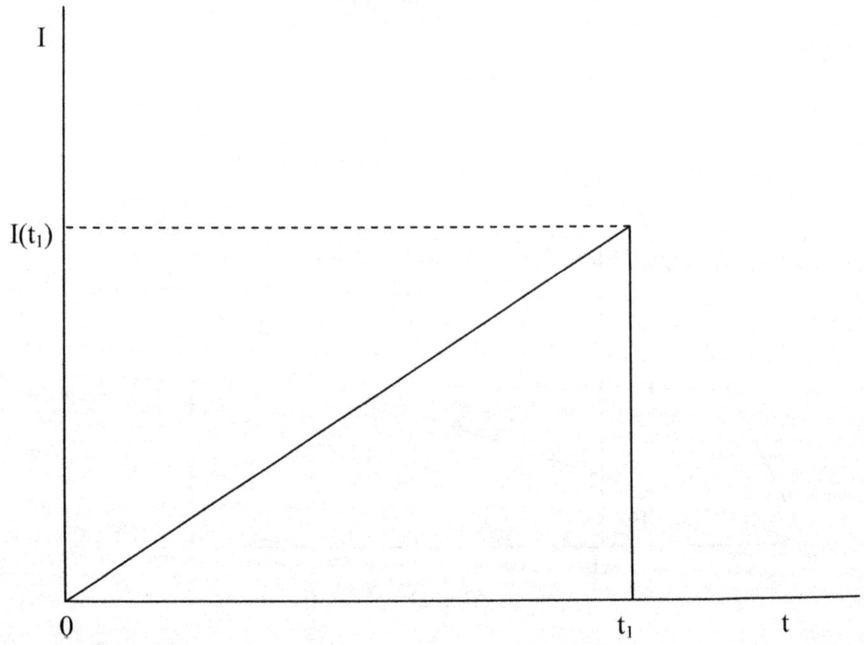

Figure 33A

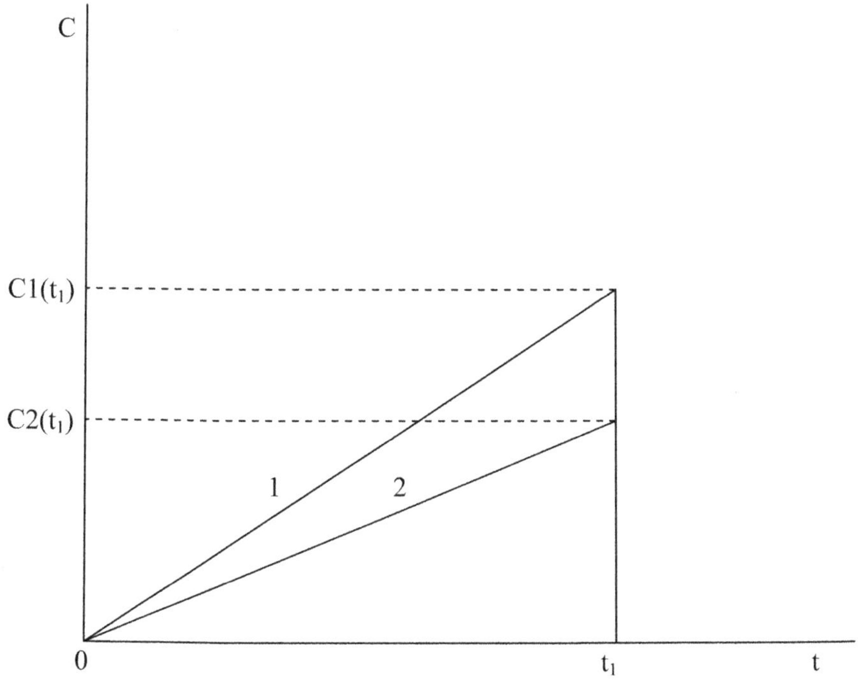

Figure 33B

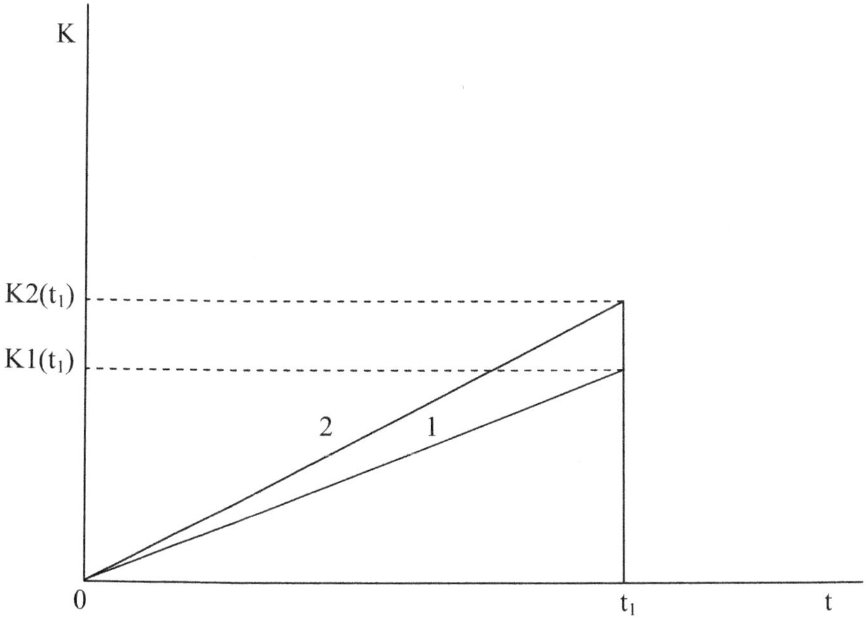

Figure 34A

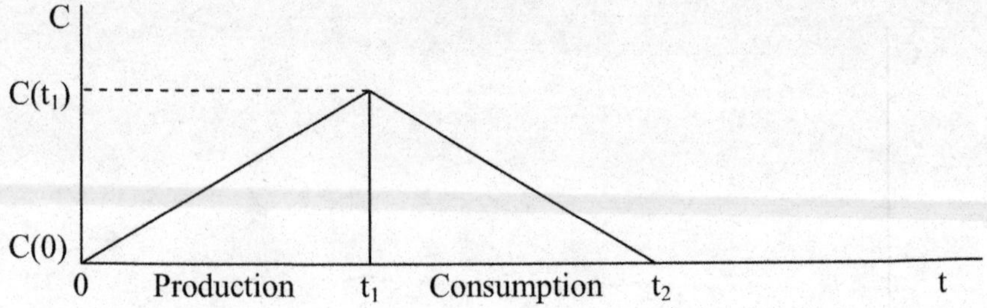

Figure 34B

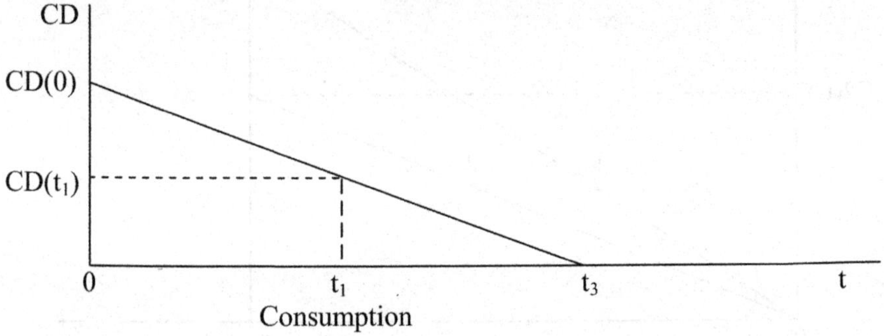

Figure 34C

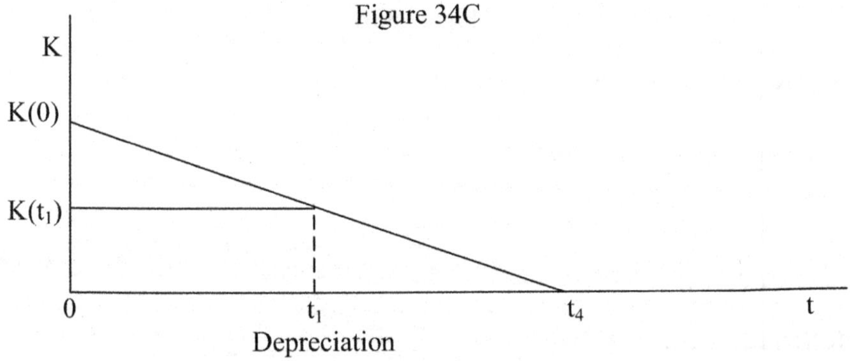

Figure 34D

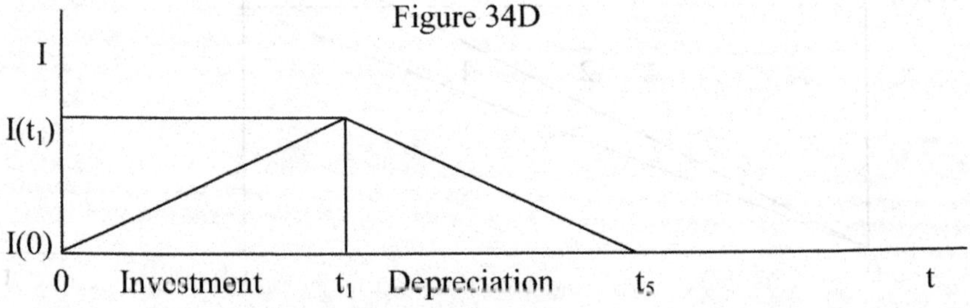

Figure 35

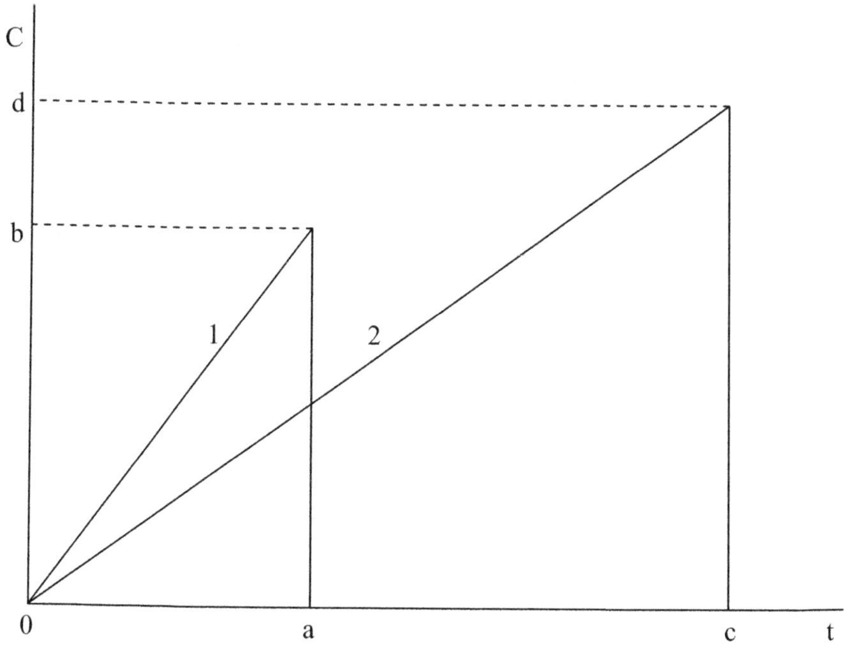

Figure H1 (Source: See Hayek, 1935, 39)

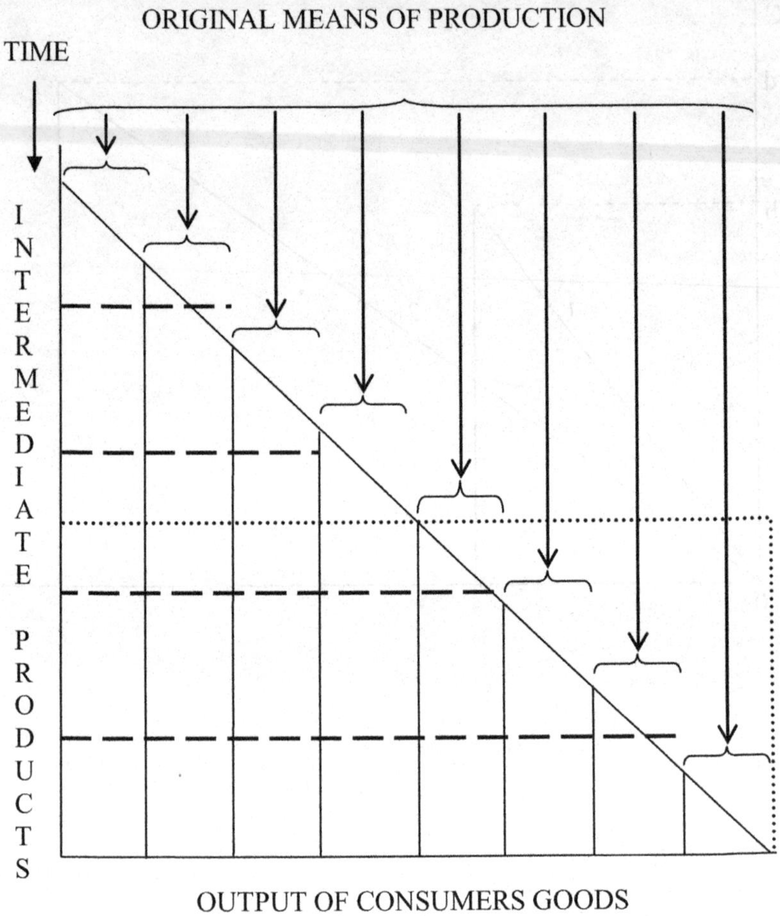

Figure H2

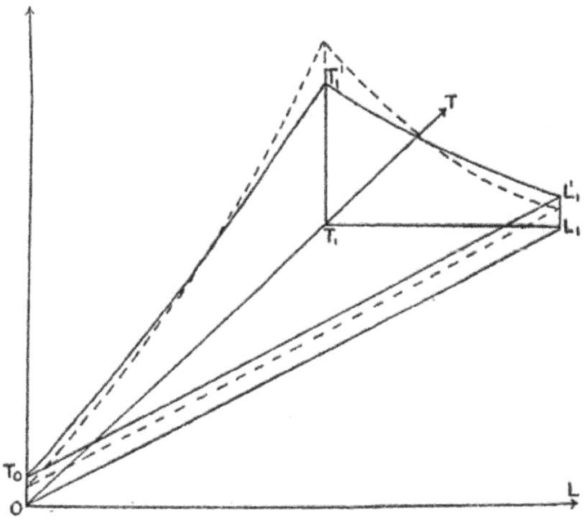

Figure H3

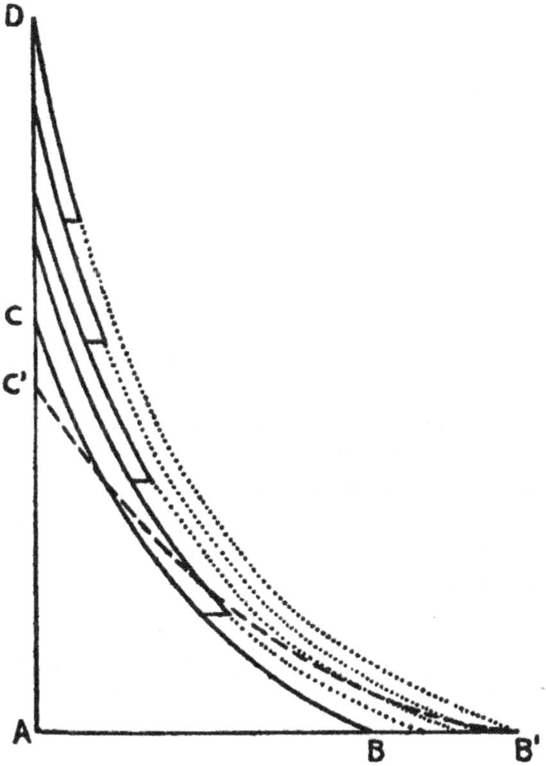

Chapter 22. On exchange, monetary credit transactions, barter, time preference, interest rates, and productivity[473]

Abstract

We attempt in this paper to tie together several basic insights of praxeology, and several that are not at all that basic. These include the following: that gains from exchange are subjective; that this applies to profits and interest; that credit transactions can occur under barter; that interest arises from time preference even under a pure time preference theory of interest; and that productivity can, under disequilibrium conditions, affect the various rates of interest.

I. Introduction

It is a common place of economics that all parties to a voluntary exchange expect[474] to be made better off or gain thereby.[475] Such gains are always subjective. A voluntarily exchanges X with B for Y. That A(B) values Y(X) more than X(Y) is obvious. It is equally true that the gain from exchange for A(B) is the difference between the greater value he places on

---

[473] The authors thank Lew Rockwell, Steve Berger and the Mises Institute for financial support in the aftermath of Hurricane Katrina.

[474] Whether either or both parties' retrospective evaluation of the exchange will yield a gain will only be known after it has occurred. Moreover, the ex post evaluation of either or both parties may change, and that more than once, and this is particularly likely to happen if the exchange involves durable assets, and the more durable they are the higher is the probability of this occurring.

[475] What is less commonly accepted, though equally true, is that all parties to an involuntary; i.e., coerced, exchange also expect to be made better off thereby. For example, if A threatens to kill B unless B hands over his money to A, which he would not do were there no threat, and B complies, then it is not only A who is made better off by the coerced exchange, but B also is better off according to his, B's, own evaluation of the exchange, else B would not hand over his money. That is, praxeologically speaking, all action consists in preferring (demonstrably through action) X to Y, or vice versa. B, in this case prefers to acquiesce to A's demand; i.e., give up his money in the hope that A will not kill him, then to not hand over his money with the fear that A will carry out his threat and kill B.

There are two reasons it is a common place to say that the coerced party is made worse off by a coerced exchange: 1) because the coerced party, himself, thinks so, else he would not have to be coerced; and, 2) because we as a society do not think that the coercing party has the moral or legal right, in contradistinction to the physical power, to confront the other party with the proffered choice. Thus, A has every right to "force" B to choose between the options: give me your money and you will receive, say, Z (which Z A has every right to exchange for B's money) or you will not receive Z. (Note, B is forced to make a choice once A makes the offer.) On the other hand A has no right at all to force B to choose between the options: your money or your life.

Y(X) compared to the lesser value he places on X(Y). But as these values are subjective to the individuals involved, they are not measurable or, a fortiori, commensurable. That is, both A and B expect to gain from the exchange, but there is no way to measure these gains, even by the parties themselves. For example, suppose B offers A the choice between Y or Z for X. A would be willing to trade X for either Y or Z, but in actuality chooses Y. Then in A's mind the gain he received from exchanging X for Y was expected to be greater than the gain he thought he would have received had he exchanged the X for Z. However, there is no valid way for A to say that his expected gain from trading for Y is n times greater than, or greater by an amount, m, than his expected gain from trading for Z. And, this is so because his values are subjective and, therefore, non-quantifiable; and, there can be no n times anything, or greater by m than, without quantification. All gains from exchange are, then, necessarily subjective and non-quantifiable (Rothbard, 1997, pp. 225-227). In cases of monetary exchange, these gains may be referred to as buyers' and sellers' gains (from exchange).

However, such gains may cast an (admittedly-necessarily imperfect) image in the objective world. The literature refers to the images in the objective realm of buyers' and sellers' gains as consumers' and producers' surplus, respectively. They are "measured" in monetary terms, and are equal in those terms to the area under the demand curve and above the actual market price, and to the area above the supply curve and below the actual market price. It is interesting to note that in the cases of these two types of exchanges, specific names have been assigned to the producers' surplus; to wit, in sales[476] by businesses, the producers' gains are known as profits, and in credit transactions involving the loan of money at one point in time in return for the promise of (re)payment of money at some future date, the creditors' gains are known as interest.

In this paper we address several implications of exchange. Section II is devoted to an examination of monetary credit transactions. Section III addresses credit transactions under barter, section IV analyses the objectivity of interest rates, section V deals with different types of interest rates, and section VI looks at the relationship between productivity and interest rates. We conclude in section VII.

II. Monetary credit transactions

Let us consider the phenomena of monetary credit transactions in a little more depth. Credit transactions are exchanges that are different from other transactions in that the latter take the form of X, now, for Y, now, whereas the former take the form of \$X, now, for \$Y, later. However, in that

---

476 The very use of the term "sales" necessarily implies that the sale is an exchange of goods for money, and not a trade of goods for goods.

all parties expect to gain therefrom, credit transactions are no different from other exchanges. In fact, for Mises (1966, 194), every action is an exchange in the sense of an attempt to exchange a less desired situation for a more desired one. Trades between or among individuals are but a subset of the totality of commercial interactions that also includes every action by every individual that is not an exchange with one or more other individuals. Therefore, all expected and actual gains from exchange arise from time preference.[477]

It is no exaggeration to claim that all macroeconomic issues must pass what is in effect a microeconomic litmus test. This is a necessary condition if macroeconomics is ever to attain a microeconomic foundation. If gains ex ante are a necessary concomitant of microeconomic purchases such as $1 for a newspaper, then this must be equally true in the macroeconomic sphere. For example, it is a logical contradiction for borrowing and lending not to adhere to these principles. And a similar analysis holds for the ex post situation of exchange, whether at a point in time (microeconomics) or over time (macroeconomics). Phelps (1970) and Aghion (2003) may be credited with attempting this integration, but it is our contention that only the Austrians have succeeded in it.

Says Rothbard (1981) in this regard of Mises (1912):

"Whereas general 'micro' theory was founded in analysis of individual action, and constructed market phenomena from these building blocks of individual choice, monetary theory was still 'holistic,' dealing in aggregates far removed from real choice. Hence, the total separation of the micro and macro spheres. While all other economic phenomena were explained as emerging from individual action, the supply of money was taken as a given external to the market, and supply was thought to impinge mechanistically on an abstraction called 'the price level.' Gone was the analysis of individual choice that illuminated the 'micro' area. The two spheres were analyzed totally separately, and on very different foundations. This book performed the mighty feat of integrating monetary with micro theory, of building monetary theory upon the individualistic foundations of general economic analysis."[478]

Similarly, monetary phenomena must pass the "barter" test. That is, before a phenomenon may be said to be monetary, we must first determine if it could exist in a barter economy. If it could, it is not a monetary phenomenon. If not, then money is of the essence, and it is a monetary phenomenon.

---

477 Because the term "time preference" is ambiguous, we shall use two terms: "narrow time preference" and "broad time preference." The difference is explained in the appendix.

478 See also Hayek, 1945.

For example, Friedman has famously stated:

"It follows that [price] inflation is always and everywhere a monetary phenomenon, in the sense that it cannot occur without a more rapid increase in the quantity of money than in output. There are, of course, many possible reasons for monetary growth--gold discoveries, the manner in which government spending is financed, and even the manner in which private spending is financed." (http://www.britannica.com/nobel/macro/5004_32.html)

One need not agree with Friedman's entire statement to accept that price "inflation is always and everywhere a monetary phenomenon." This is easy to understand. Price inflation requires that prices in general rise, but this is impossible in a barter economy. Let there be n goods, A_i, i = 1, …, n. Then, because there is no money, there can be no money prices, only barter-exchange ratios. Consider an exchange chosen at random, between, say A_j and A_k. Let the current exchange ratio between them be nA_j for one A_k; then the barter price of one A_k is nA_j: i.e., nA_j / A_k, and the barter price of one A_j is $(1/n)A_k$. Let the barter-exchange ratio change to $(n+\Delta n)A_j$ for one A_k, $\Delta n > 0$. Then the barter price of one A_k is nA_j: i.e., $(n+\Delta n)A_j / A_k$, and the barter price of one A_j is $(1/(n+m))A_k$. And, the increase in the barter price of A_k is $(\Delta n/n)\%$ and the decrease in barter price of A_j is $(-\Delta n/(n+\Delta n))\%$. In other words, in barter exchange, for every barter price increase there is necessarily an offsetting barter price decrease and, therefore, there cannot, as a matter of mathematical necessity, be a general rise in barter prices.

III. Credit transactions under barter

There can be credit transactions under barter as well as in a monetary economy.[479] Therefore, there are creditors' gains from exchange in barter

[479] Economies are usually classified as barter or monetary. Seemingly, there are three types of economies, at least conceptually: pure barter, pure monetary, and mixed. A pure barter is economy is one in which there is *no* indirect exchange, save because of error. That is, all transactions take the form of X for Y, with no intention on the part of either party to then further exchange what was received for anything else. Of course, it might well be that after the initial trade conditions change in such a way that one or both of the parties decides to further exchange that which was received initially. At the opposite end of the spectrum, a pure monetary economy is one in which every exchange is indirect. That is, every exchange takes the form for X for M (the monetary good), or vice versa, M for X. Finally, a "mixed" economy is one in which some exchanges are direct and some indirect. In reality, save for the absolutely most primitive, probably all actual economies are mixed. In such cases, the decision whether to refer to a particular economy as barter or monetary is subjective and depends, undoubtedly, upon the relative share of each type. However, these three alternatives can be reduced, conceptually, to just two: barter and monetary exchange, with the real world mixed system merely an amalgamation of these two more basic categories.

economies.[480] However, save in the case where X today is lent in return for the promise of more (or even less) X at some time in the future, there is no interest and, a fortiori, no interest rate. That is, because interest is the objective image of the creditors' gain, and in the case where X today is lent in return for Y at some time in the future, because X and Y are incommensurable, there can be no measure of the objective gain.[481]

In credit transactions involving money, now, for money, later, the interest is objective and measurable, and interest rates can be calculated. The past master in Austrian economics in terms of tracing out how the merely subjective can engender objective prices is undoubtedly Menger (1950). His analysis is in terms of consumer/producer goods such as horses and bushels of wheat, but, given our determination to apply the same insights to macro as to microeconomics, there is no reason not to extrapolate this to borrowing and lending, and interest rates.

IV. Objective interest rates

In credit transactions involving money now for money later, the interest is objective and measurable, and interest rates can be calculated. For example, \$100 now, for \$110 one year from today. The interest is measurable \$110 (principal and interest) - \$100 (principal) = \$10 (interest). And, it is objective in that everyone who is numerate will agree on the matter.[482] Similarly with the interest rate, calculated as \$10 / \$100 = 10% (per annum).

---

[480] Creditors' gain is used instead of buyers' or sellers' gains because in a barter economy the terms buyers and sellers are ambiguous. In a monetary economy, if one wished to refer to gains of the creditor in terms of buyers' or sellers' gains, the term buyers' gain is the appropriate one, as the creditor is the one who can be said to have purchased, either in the initial sale or in a resale by a prior owner, a promise from the borrower for by paying for it with money, now.

[481] The one conceptual exception to this, which is totally irrelevant to reality, is the case of an ERE with n-goods, in which all n(n-1)!/2 relative prices are fixed, in which case even though every transaction be indirect, any good may be used as a numéraire, thereby making commensurable that which in reality is not.

[482] We are dealing here with nominal values. Real interest and real interest rates; i.e., inflation adjusted interest and interest rates, are another matter, whether ex ante or ex post. In the former ex ante, case, they are subjective because they depend upon expectations of inflation, and these are subjective for two reasons: 1) the goods that are relevant to the seller of an IOU are virtually certain to differ from those relevant to the buyer of an IOU; and, 2) even if, mirabile dictu, they have exactly the same stock of goods, including human capital, and allocate their resources identically, unless they also have indistinguishable expectations regarding the courses the various prices of these goods and those they intend to demand, their expectations of inflation, and thus their expectations as to the amount of interest and the interest rate involved with any specific IOU, will differ. In the latter ex post, case, the first of these factors, the difference in pertinent goods, also plays its role. However, as

V. Types of interest rates

Consider the rate of interest. Mises (1996, 524-550) distinguishes the originary from the market rate of interest, both of which exist in the evenly rotating economy (ERE) and in the real world. Originary interest depends solely on present preference and the originary rate of interest depends solely on time preference,[483] whereas the market rate of interest depends not only on time preference, but also on returns to the lender qua entrepreneur for the risks of default and of price changes. Because, in the ERE, there are no risks of default or of inflation or deflation: "There prevails in the whole system only one rate of interest. The rate of interest on loans coincides with the rate of originary interest as manifested in the ratio of prices of present and of future goods" (Mises, 1996, 538).

However, this is only a first approximation of the truth. Insofar as the market rates of interest are concerned, whether in the ERE or the real world, the quantum of interest and the rate of interest must also take into account the expenses involved in acquiring the other resources (i.e., other than the money lent), of the creditor, qua entrepreneur; e.g., for a bank, the services of loan officers, desks, office space, etc.[484] Additionally, a measure of profit for the creditor qua entrepreneur must be included, though this element is relevant only in the real world and not in the ERE, as of course no profits could exist in the latter.

Moreover, there is no reason to think that "market rates" should include, in addition to originary interest, only returns to the lender qua entrepreneur for risk bearing and a measure of profit. Why should they not incorporate, also, returns to the lender qua entrepreneur from these other sources; e.g., specifically, for his contributions to the realization of gains from *increases* in productivity? Of course this element, also, is irrelevant in the ERE, as there would be no changes in productivity. Furthermore, it should be noted that with regard to profits, the other objective image of a gain from exchange that has been assigned its own name, according to

---

expectations are not relevant, the second factor, differing expectations, plays no part. There is, nevertheless, a (different) second factor: unless each party has exactly the same historical data re the relevant prices and computes historical inflation the same way, they will disagree as to the historical rate of inflation re the relevant goods.

[483] In addition to time preference, the other condition necessary for interest – that the credit transaction be in terms of commensurables – would necessarily be met in the ERE as no objective exchange ratio would ever undergo alteration; e.g., there is no risk either of default or of inflation/deflation. Because of the very nature of the ERE, whatever amount of interest pertained to any point in time or time period would pertain at every other point in time or time period of equal duration.

[484] We are indebted to Michael Saliba for this important point concerning the expenses of the creditor.

Greaves (1990, 40) Mises recognizes uncertainty re future consumer demand, changes in productivity,[485] the time consuming nature of production, and differences in entrepreneurial foresight.

VI. Productivity and interest rates

As with all other gains, the phenomenon of creditors' returns arises from exchange. As interest is but the objective image of creditors' gains from exchange, interest also and necessarily arises because of time preference; that is, without time preference there would be no credit transactions and therefore, no creditors' gains from exchange or interest.

In the non-ERE situation, one of the factors that can affect the quantum of interest and interest rate of a specific credit transaction is *an increase*[486] *in* productivity. For example, imagine an entrepreneur willing to offer r% for funds to acquire a set of resources, R, to produce X. He then foresees an opportunity to acquire a set of resources, S, to produce Y, where he expects the use of S to produce Y to be more profitable than the use of R to produce X. In that case he would be willing to offer s% (>r%) in order to acquire the resources, R, thereby bidding up the "price of credit;" i.e., the interest rate. Of course, he would also have to offer a higher prices[487] for the resources in S, in order to bid them away from their current uses. That is, the gains from the increased productivity would be manifested by increased prices for the resources *and* a higher interest rate.

However, we stress that this latter would be a transitory phenomenon. As other entrepreneurs attempted to earn greater profits by competing to acquire resources of the type in S, or suitable substitutes, and produce Y, or substitutes therefor, more and more of the gains from the increased productivity would end up redounding to the benefit of the resource owners, in the form of higher prices paid for them, and to the benefit of the purchasers of Y. At the same time, profits would decrease below the level initially earned by the entrepreneur who first perceived and acted on the S/Y opportunity. Consequently, he would not be willing to pay as high an interest rate as he had previously, and, consequently, the interest rate would decrease.

---

[485] "The ceaseless changes in the demand for and supply of the various human and physical factors of production, which constantly create new opportunities *for better adjusting production to anticipated future consume wants*" (Greaves, 1990, 40, emphasis added).

[486] What about a *decrease* in productivity? The same analysis would hold, mutatis mutandis, again given the absence of ERE conditions.

[487] This discussion could be in terms of higher rental rates for the services of the resources instead of higher prices for their outright purchase, or some combination thereof. However, it would make no difference as higher rental rates would result in higher prices, and vice versa.

Assuming no change in the other relevant data, preeminently time preference rates, competition over time would bid up the prices of the resources in S, and down the price of Y, so that the entire benefits from the increased productivity were received by the relevant resource owners and purchasers of the good. With all of the gains thus absorbed, there would be none left for the entrepreneur in the form of "above normal" profits, nor any to be paid by the entrepreneur to lenders in the form of higher interest rates. So as profits would fall back to "normal" so also would interest rates fall back to their prior levels. Therefore, as noted above, the effects of productivity increases on interest rates are transitory, lasting only during the adjustment period. Once the market is fully adjusted to such changes the effects on interest rates are eliminated.[488]

We see, then, that with an unchanged rate of time preference,[489] an entrepreneur would be willing to offer a higher rate of interest to borrow funds to acquire resources for invest in a project expected to be more productive than one expected to be less productive, until competition bids away the profit opportunity at which time he is no longer willing to pay the higher rate of interest.

Therefore, though time preference is, and productivity is not, essential to, i.e., a necessary condition for, the existence of interest (Bohm Bawerk, 1959, 73-120, 290-308; Mises, 1998, 524-532; Rothbard, 2004, 297-301, 313-332) nevertheless changes in productivity can and do affect market rates of interest.

In sum, the originary rate of interest is a pure time preference phenomenon. Therefore, the theory of interest is a pure time preference theory. Bohm Bawerk, 1959, 73-120, 290-308; Mises, 1998, 524-532; Rothbard, 2004, 297-301, 313-332). However, market rates of interest, whether in the ERE or in the real world are affected by other factors.

These include changes in productivity and the expenses incurred in acquiring collaborating factors necessary to the functioning of the credit business. They affect market interest rates in the ERE as well as the real world, whereas others, risks of default and of (unanticipated) inflation or deflation, and entrepreneurial profits are non-existent in the ERE, but are relevant in the real world.

---

[488] Of course, in the real world productivity is continuously changing so that the market is never fully adjusted, with consequent effects on interest rates.

[489] It could be argued that becoming aware of the opportunity to use S to produce Y decreased the entrepreneurs' future orientedness; however, to do so would be to trivialize the concept of time preference and, in the process define away the possibility of productivity affecting the rate of time preference.

VII. Conclusion

If macroeconomics is to be placed on a microeconomic basis, praxeology must be employed. If so, then the ex ante and ex post analysis commonly applied to spot markets (necessary gains to both parties in the former case) must also be employed in exchanges at different times, namely, borrowing and lending. The pure time preference theory of interest is of course a staple of Austrian economics. However, in non-ERE conditions, e.g., the real world, it is no violation of praxeology to say that other influences impact the rate of interest; certainly, productivity changes can be one of these phenomena.

Appendix

Mises (1996, 483-484) describes the phenomenon known as time preference as: "Satisfaction of a want in the nearer future is, other things being equal, preferred to that in the farther distant future;" and, "The very act of gratifying a desire implies that gratification at the present instant is preferred to that at a later instant." That is, time preference is the preference for the satisfaction of a *specific* want sooner rather than later, ceteris paribus, or, alternatively stated, time preference is the preference for gratification of a *specific* desire presently rather than later, ceteris paribus. Because it is concerned with specific wants or desires, ceteris paribus, it takes the form of: $A_0 > A_1$, where A, regardless of subscript, stands for the satisfaction of the exact same specific want or the gratification of the exact same specific desire, and the subscript refers to the point in time of such satisfaction or gratification, where 1 is later in time than 0, and > means "is preferred to."

Chapter 23. Tyler Cowen on Austrian Business Cycle Theory: A Critique

Abstract

Cowen (1997) criticizes Austrian Business Cycle Theory (ABCT) on eight grounds: 1. systematic errors; 2. inflation volatility; 3. confusion of inflation and savings; 4. confusion of inflation and investment; 5. real vs. nominal rates of interest; 6. interest rate information; 7. investor interpretation of interest rates; 8. validation of inflationary investments. The present paper rejects all of these claims, and defends ABCT against them.

I. Introduction

In recent years, there have been several criticisms of Austrian Business Cycle Theory (ABCT). These include Hummel (1979), Tullock (1987, 1989), Cowen (1997), and Wagner (2000). Replies have been made to Hummel by Block and Barnett (Barnett and Block, 2008B); to Tullock (1987) by Salerno (1989); to Tullock (1987 and 1989) by Barnett and Block (2005A); and, to Wagner by Block (2001A). The present paper is devoted to an analysis and rejoinder to Cowen's (1997) particular critique of ABCT.

This critique of ABCT is contained in Cowen (1997, Ch. 4), where he argues that ABCT fails for the eight (8) following reasons: 1. systematic errors; 2. inflation volatility; 3. confusion of inflation and savings; 4. confusion of inflation and investment; 5. real vs. nominal rates of interest; 6. interest rate information; 7. investor interpretation of interest rates; 8. validation of inflationary investments. Following section II, in which we offer a general perspective, the remainder of our paper is organized along the same lines. Our method shall be to quote liberally from Cowen (1997), and then offer specific criticisms.[490] We conclude in section IX.

II. An Austrian perspective

Assume that, initially, the allocation of cheese and chalk was in its optimal ratio, say, 1:1. Then, government, in its infinite wisdom decides that the proper allocation between these two items is *not* the one that stems from posited unchanging consumer preferences, but rather 2:1 in favor of cheese.

With the truly heroic assumption of *full* information, we all know *exactly* how long this subsidy will last. Suppose this to be for one year; after that, we return to laissez faire capitalism, where things like this are simply not done. Would anyone now reallocate some investment from the chalk industry to cheese? The answer depends upon the expected profitability of

[490] Cowen (1997, 16, 102-104) compares ABCT with his "risk-based" theory. It should be noted that he uses the term "risk" in the standard probabilistic way, and that true uncertainty of the type experience in the real world does not play a part therein.

the reallocation. Obviously it is yes if: 1) the resources we are talking about are non-specific to either industry; and, 2) the costs (if there be any) of reallocation, including resources complementary to the reallocated capital goods, from chalk to cheese and then back is zero, or at least less than the expected increase in revenue[491] to be had from the temporary reallocation. If, instead, the resources under consideration were absolutely specific to cheese, the answer is neither so obvious nor unambiguous. Of course, it still depends upon the expected profitability, but that is now a more complex matter, involving future periods beyond that of the temporary, one-year intervention, as well as the expected economic life of the diverted resources. The following factors[492] would, ceteris paribus, make the reallocation profitable:

1) A higher discount rate, as that would reduce the present value of any cash flows in the post-first-year periods, lessening such offsets to the first year gains.

2) A longer economic life of the diverted resources, as this will reduce the cost of producing cheese not only in the first year, but in the later years, also. (This assumes that the resources diverted to the production of cheese, though specific to the production thereof, are not used in Leontief-type; i.e., fixed proportions production processes, and thus do not become redundant when the production of cheese is scaled back, but rather that they then substitute for other resources that would have been used. That is, because of the existence of the diverted resources, the optimal mix of inputs with which to produce cheese has changed reducing the need, at any level of output, for investments complementary to the diverted ones.)

3) The higher the cost of the complementary resources made unnecessary for the production of cheese in later years because of the diverted resources.

4) The smaller the increase in quantity, and the lower the price, of the additional resources (necessitated by the shortfall of fixed capital because of the diverted resources) necessary to produce chalk in accord with the optimal ratio, post intervention.

Now assume, instead of a subsidy, that interest rates were pushed down below the level that would otherwise have obtained, based on the time preferences of the public, by similar governmental policies (e.g., by the

---

[491] That is, if the total revenue from cheese and chalk combined would be greater than without the reallocation.

[492] This is but a partial list; e.g., we do not inquire into depreciation of preexisting fixed resources used in the production of either good, or to what extent the diverted resources were gross or net investment, nor do we consider the issue of heterogeneity of fixed resources with the new ones being superior to the old.

central bank flooding the credit market). After that, we again return to laissez faire capitalism, where things like this are simply not done.

Would the pattern of investment, or for that matter, expenditures on consumers' goods, be any different than they would have been in the absence of this governmental interference with the economy? Certainly there are specific circumstances where there would be differences. It is easiest to see this in the case of consumers' goods. Some individuals might buy furniture, major appliances, or expensive consumers' electronics, and even automobiles on credit, even if they were to go into debt for more than a year, if the monthly payments in the first year were sufficiently decreased. That is, the lower interest rates, even though only for a year, do reduce the costs of buying on credit. This would be sufficient to induce consumers at, and some near, the margin to make such purchases.[493]

What is true for consumers is no less true for businesses. A decrease in interest rates reduces the cost of investing in interest-rate-sensitive projects. Such undertakings produce capital goods whose contributions to the production of consumers' goods occur a relatively long time before the pecuniary value of the consumers' goods are realized;[494] and/or very durable capital goods whose contribution to the production take place over relatively long periods of time; and/or very expensive capital goods the purchases of which are financed by means of credit.[495] In all these cases, lower interest rates can be expected to have a disproportionately positive effect upon their profitability.

What we are saying is that there is no difference in principle between inter-temporal misallocations of resources stemming from statist interferences with markets such as cheese and chalk and intra-temporal ones. *Both* misallocate resources, even under heroic assumptions about information.

---

[493] A simple example: Joe rates his alternatives, A, B, C, D ….., such that A and B are the top two, with A > B, where B is the purchase of a boat (Z), that he expects to have an economic life of 20 years, with monthly payments of $1,000 for the next five years. Then, because of Fed policy, Joe has a new alternative, C, where C is the purchase of the same boat, Z, with monthly payments of $500 for the first year and $1,000 for the next four years. Although Joe previously preferred A to B, he now prefers C to A.

[494] From the point of view of the producers, this realization occurs when the goods are first sold to consumers, because it is the revenue from these sales that, ultimately, pays for the resources used to produce the goods. To the extent that the revenues are insufficient to cover the resource payments, either the firms' owners, or its creditors, including its suppliers of resources, incur a loss.

[495] The latter type of goods are those for which credit is normally a complement; i.e., although they may be purchased without credit, because they are so expensive, they are usually purchased on credit and thus credit is a complement to these items.

And, both do so for the same reason: intervention, in order to have any effect must alter the set of alternatives available to the decision maker thereby inducing him to act differently than he otherwise would have. This is a praxeological claim, not a contingent one.

But, if the government is to "succeed" in ruining market coordination, again under these assumptions, then at least some entrepreneurs (or households) must be led by the invisible hand of profit seeking to act as they would not have otherwise done, to misallocate resources in the first place. That is, if all far-seeing businessmen refuse to act differently than they otherwise would in the face of these governmental programs, either of them, the intra-temporal one between chalk and cheese, *or* the inter-temporal one between different capital-goods projects, then, the state *could not* render markets inefficient.[496] In fact, the whole purpose and result of intervention is to alter people's behaviors. And, in the cases where it wants to "stimulate" the economy, the government will continue to lower rates until a response is forthcoming.[497]

---

[496] Suppose under laissez faire our political masters suddenly institute a minimum wage law of $0.01 per hour (assume that no one has a marginal revenue product of less than $1.00 per hour), or maximum hours legislation of 200 hours per week (there are fewer hours in the week than that). Will any of this "bite?" It will, if these enactments demonstrate to market participants that government has gone off the rails and embraced economic fascism. For example, Higgs (1997, 563-564) maintains that the dearth of private investment in the U.S.A. from 1935-1940 was the result of FDR's policies in the "Second New Deal" that undermined confidence in the security of property rights.

[497] And, not to worry about a "liquidity trap," for as the then, and now former Vice-chairman of the Board of Governors of the Federal Reserve System, ex Chairman of the President's Council of Economic Advisors, and current Chairman of the Board of Governors, Ben S. "Benny the Printer" Bernanke (2002) stated: "Indeed, under a fiat (that is, paper) money system, a government (in practice, the central bank in cooperation with other agencies) should always be able to generate increased nominal spending and inflation, even when the short-term nominal interest rate is at zero." A liquidity trap is said to occur when the relevant interest rate is so low that the "demand for money" is infinite. Of course, there is no such thing as the demand for money; rather there are as many different demands for money as there are goods, including resources and financial assets, for sale for money. What must be meant by that term is, then, an infinite supply of notes by potential borrowers will be offered at "the" interest rate. Of course, not all potential borrowers are equally credit worthy, and thus the risk-adjusted interest rate decreases as additional loans are made at the same nominal rate to borrowers who are ever-less creditworthy. If expectations as to the future course of prices are important in understanding credit markets and their impacts on economic activity, so too are the differing degrees of credit worthiness among borrowers. Thus the only real liquidity trap that could occur would not arise from the demand-side (supply of notes) of a credit market, but, rather, from the

From this perspective, there will be no "holding of the bag" phenomenon in operation. Critics of ABCT typically maintain that according to its premises, if entrepreneurs are far sighted enough, they will not make misallocative business decisions in response to inter-temporal governmental mismanagement. They will refrain, out of the fear that if they do, then, when the crunch comes and government stops its program, they will be stuck with an investment they would not otherwise have made. Nor will there be any yokel or greenhorn who will bail them out, since *all* market participants are in this model assumed to have full, complete and total information.

Of course, these assumptions are outlandish. There is nothing anything like full information available in the real world. Not only has an appreciation for ABCT not taken over the business community,[498] it has not even done so within the profession of economics.[499] That being the case, there should be little real fear that government cannot create an ABC. We are arguing here, on the basis of contrary to fact conditionals. The present authors maintain that ABCT is so incisive and powerful an explanation that it would operate *even in* this heady non-existent world. That is, *even if* all market participants were not only fully cognizant of ABCT, but were also fully and totally informed about the decisions of the central bankers and, in addition, all consumers and firms, ABCT would *still* be correct. We claim it is an underestimate of ABCT to posit that inter-temporal misallocation due to money creation and funneling through the credit market works *only* through lack of information. Moreover, in reality, many businesses and industries are well aware of the "Too big to fail" syndrome.[500] The point is that in the real

---

supply-side (demand for notes), when potential creditors refuse to make any more loans because the "real" risk-adjusted interest rate is too low. This can occur in the case of banks regardless of the quantity of excess reserves in the banking system, when, because of the increased risk of default on marginal loans, they are perceived to be unprofitable, and so are not made. This seems to have been the case in the U.S.A during part of the Great Depression (Hall and Ferguson, 1998, 148-149).

[498] Understatement of the century.

[499] Another understatement of the century ☺.

[500] For example, in their applied work, many Austrians maintain the following. The immense monetary expansion of the 1990s, especially in the latter half of that decade caused the massive stock market bubble. The Fed, fearing inflation, engaged in monetary tightening in 1999. That policy was the *proximate*, but not the ultimate, cause of the bursting of the bubble. The manifestation of this bubble in the "real" sector was the vast, but unwarranted, expansion of infrastructure and equipment in and for, and the huge misallocation of human resources to, the information / communication/technology sector. Then, in an attempt to stave off a severe downturn in the "real" economy and that great bugbear of mainstream economists, price deflation, in the wake of the collapse of the stock market, the Fed began reflating money/credit. That led to the next bubble, the current (2005- 6) one, that also *must* burst. (So as there were various symptoms of the stock market bubble, so

world the idea of full (or complete or perfect) information is absurd. However, sometimes decision makers do have sufficient information to know that activities they might undertake in response to a Fed engineered money/credit expansion, with consequent reductions in interest rates, will, in all likelihood, prove unprofitable if the Fed reverses itself, causing interest rates to rise, even to the point of bankrupting them. Nevertheless, they may rationally undertake such activities hoping to make big profits before the Fed changes its policy, fully expecting the Treasury to bail them out and, indirectly, also rescue their creditors, if they prove to have been mistaken. Of course, they are able to become so highly leveraged because their creditors also fully expect such bailouts. Consequently, even if they know and understand ABCT, and even if they know that, without the possibility of a bailout, they would not engage in certain activities, nevertheless they *do* engage in them.

Let us attempt to put this into other words, so important is this point. The ABCT is a theory about how people's actions are affected (changed) by a particular type of governmental intervention. Even in a world of perfect competition (we assume, arguendo, that this concept is a coherent one), were new fiat money to be lent into existence there would necessarily be a distortion in the structure of prices that would change the sets of alternatives individuals face, and thus have real effects. The perfectly competitive model beloved of neoclassical economics includes, of course, perfect information. But the relevant information is about current and past prices and quantities of goods, assets, and resources, and about monetary policy: the Fed's pattern of increasing money/credit, and the period before the policy reverts. But even perfect competition cannot include information about the future. That would bring us to the world of science fiction, or magic.

---

also are there symptoms of a real estate bubble.) Had the Fed not reflated, there neither would nor could have been this real estate bubble. All of which brings us to the point at hand. Although the Fed must bear the ultimate blame for the real estate boom, there is enough blame to spread around to other parties that aided and abetted them. (We use them, rather than it, in keeping with the Austrian understanding that it is only individual people who act, not nonhuman "its.") Inter alios, and probably most important, were the folks at Fannie Mae and Freddie Mac. They facilitated the real estate boom in a variety of ways. But what is relevant here is that in so doing they both expanded their balance sheets immensely, and did so by vastly increasing their leverage, which they were able to do to the extent they did only because they, and everyone else, understand their debt to be guaranteed by the U.S. Treasury, if not legally, then morally and practically – a major case of moral hazard, though not of the same magnitude as that involved in Social Security and Medicare. That is, they have become "To big to fail." They know it and so does everyone else. And, what is true of Fannie and Freddie, now, was true in the past for various corporations, banks, and even a city (e.g., Chrysler, Continental Illinois, and New York City, respectively).

Injection effects and their consequent distribution effects, are such that the economy would be tilted in favor of interest-rate-sensitive goods and their producers; i.e., there would be an ABC, though milder, because of the perfect competitive (PC) assumptions.[501] That is, the effect of a money / credit expansion in a perfectly-competitive world would be a misallocation of resources that reduces people-in-general's well-being. From God's point of view, people "in general" would be better off if, in response to the Fed's attempt to expand money/credit through open market operations, no one would sell securities to it; or if, when they tried to use discount rate policy, no bank would borrow any more reserves than they otherwise would have; or, if, when they lowered the reserve ratio, banks just held excess reserves and made no additional loans. However, because of changed incentives resulting from the Fed's policy, and consequent injection and distribution effects, some people are presented with alternatives superior to those extant. They respond and thus, though, people-as-a-whole are worse off, not all are; some find they are better off because of the Fed's [502] actions.[503]

---

[501] Of relevance here are Barnett and Wood, 2002; and Barnett and Block, 2007B, which concentrates on all interest-rate-sensitive goods, rather than traditional ABCT that focuses on the Hayekian triangle (Barnett and Block, 2006C), and "higher-order" goods.

[502] There is another problem with the use of these unrealistic, imaginary, worlds (in contradistinction to sane imaginary worlds; e.g., the type free-market entrepreneurs imagine in trying to decide the best uses of resources). Consider a world of perfect competition and efficient markets, all-round, with attendant absurd assumptions about information. Suppose the government (Fed) to announce a policy of increasing the money supply by purchasing specific quantities of 90-day T-bills at specific times for the next year, after which there would be no further purchases. Assume, also, that everyone knows the correct, economic model of the economy; i.e., how the economy works, and that they use this knowledge plus the information about monetary policy to form (obviously, rational) expectations. But how could this be? Such a system would have inherent contradictions built into it.

In order for the Fed to execute its monetary policy, it would have bid up the price of the T-bills in order to purchase them, causing the nominal interest rates thereon to decrease. However, the increased money supply would cause inflation immediately, not with a lag, because of all the "perfect" conditions (PC). Again, because of the PC, expectations of price-inflation would immediately increase to the correct "level." Even were the creditor (the Fed, as the buyer of the T-bills) willing to take a loss by bidding up the price of the T-bills and thereby accepting a lower yield thereon, other, rational, profit maximizing "agents" would not be. In fact, they would know that the prices of these T-bills (and other, fixed-income, securities) should fall thereby driving up the expected, nominal, rates of interest on them, so that the expected, real, rates of interest would not decrease.

Therefore, as the Fed tried to buy the T-bills, putting upward pressure on their prices, the entire stock of extant T-bills would be offered to them. In order to keep

Cowen (1997, 79) quotes Rothbard (1975, 19, emphasis added by present authors) to the effect that "… businessmen were *misled* by bank credit inflation to invest too much in higher-order capital goods…" and then criticizes him on the ground that with full information, such cluster of errors are impossible. But Rothbard was writing in the real world context of (far) less than full information.[504] Were this analysis to be applied to the unrealistic full information of the critics of ABCT, then Rothbard's "mislead" would have to be replaced with "induced," or "subsidized."[505]

---

their prices from falling, the Fed would have to buy the entire stock, and not just of T-bills, but of all other assets, real, as well as financial, else all of their prices would fall so that their nominal yields would increase to offset the correctly-expected- by-all, and thus immediate, price inflation. (Side note: Such PC requires, then, not just that expectations about "level of prices" be correct, but that expectations about the course of very individual price be correct.)

As the purpose of the monetary policy is, ostensibly, to stimulate the economy, else why do it? (Of course the real answer is to enrich the government, and the banks and other financial institutions – really the politicians, bureaucrats and other government employees, and the owners and employees of financial institutions). But certainly, given a PC world, such policy could not possibly bring about the ostensible, desired end.

503 Creating machines or other factors that fit into the higher orders of the structure of production does not necessarily imply that the investment will last for a longer time-period. How long it lasts can, within limits of course, be tailored to suit. All that is required for higher order capital investment is that the new material is complementary to other goods and services which function in that arena of the economy.

504 Whatever that means. We are writing, arguendo, as if the concept of "full information" is a completely coherent one. It is not. The difficulties with it are legion. The only things it is possible to have "full information" about are historical facts including, in some sense, "present facts." One can *know* nothing of the future, save what one expects about it, including; e.g., what one expects (not on the basis of thymology, but, rather because that is what someone has said he will do) others to do.

505 Cowen (1997, 77) states: "The postulated entrepreneurial mistakes in the traditional Austrian theory, which are systematic, violate the rational expectations hypothesis. Entrepreneurs with rational expectations will sometimes choose unprofitable term-lengths for investment, but they will not err systematically towards excessive term-length. This is precisely the error made by Wagner (2000). For a rejoinder, see Block (2001A). Cowen (1997, 8), states "the rational expectations assumption serves as a tool of analytical organization, rather than as a descriptive assumption about the real world. Rational expectations models help us trace which economic results can be generated without assuming systematic forecasting errors and which cannot. Whenever we wish to specify a coordination problem, rational expectations theory requires us to justify, or at least outline, the underlying informational asymmetries. I view the rational expectations assumptions as a useful form of discipline. Rational expectations does not rule out significant marketplace errors, but it does require us to specify the source of these errors in some explicit

Similarly, Cowen (1997, 78, emphasis, and material in brackets added by present authors) claims "For the [ABC] theory to hold, entrepreneurs must be *fooled* by incorrect price signals emanating from the interest rate." Again, the same reply is in order: in the real world of vastly imperfect foresight and governmental intervention, there are two sources of systematic entrepreneurial errors: imperfect foresight and governmentally-distorted incentives. In fact, in the real world either of these alone is sufficient to cause such errors. Thus, in the imaginary one concocted by Cowen, "fooled" would have to be changed to "encouraged" or "provoked," as, by assumption, the former cause is not allowed.

1) Systematic errors

States Cowen (1997, 81): "The Austrian claim postulates systematic entrepreneurial errors in the most costly direction. Entrepreneurs do not merely err in their choice of term-length; entrepreneurs choose excessive investment term-length when confronted with inflation. More specifically, the theory does not allow entrepreneurs to overestimate the dangers of an inflationary boom by keeping investment term-length too short. Excessive caution may be just as likely as excessive boldness."

First, in order for entrepreneurs to misestimate, whether over or under, the effects of an inflationary boom, they must perceive there to be one. However, although "inflation is always and everywhere a monetary phenomenon" (Friedman, 1992, 262), the way the term is used differs. When Cowen refers to entrepreneurs misestimating the dangers of inflation, it is

---

informational asymmetry." This is incorrect. This is a way of claiming that, although it is not a good assumption about the real world, it is still a useful assumption – akin to Friedman's (1953) methodology, except instead of asking if a model predicts well, using the assumption for "discipline" purposes. Cowen's (1997, 8) definition of rational expectations is in terms of an individual's expectations. In his footnote 3, p.9, he attempts to finesse the problem he has created. Moreover, he assumes risk, not uncertainty. The key is the assumption of no systematic errors. First, the idea "Even if the idea of a population mean is not well defined, individual forecasts may, on average, still hit the mean of the observed sample," makes no sense unless the sample is defined. So, exactly what events constitute the sample?" Most (all other?) rational expectations models quantify the concept; e.g., Snowdon, et al., p 190. The idea of rational expectations is highly problematic. Consider, if we believe in cause and effect, then the causes of the stock market meltdown in 2000 preceded the effect, the meltdown itself. If individuals' expectations are rational, how is it that so many made mistakes? Of course, the systematic entrepreneurial "cluster" of errors of ABCT violate the assumption of rational expectations – that is a strength of ABCT. The very concept of rational expectations is irrational in the sense of comporting with reality, though its use is compatible with the advancement of modern academic macroeconomists, whereas the assumptions of ABCT are consistent with reality.

obvious he uses the term to mean an increase in the general level of prices, not, as Austrians do, an increase in the money supply. This is an important point, for as Friedman (1968, 15) has maintained, there is a long and variable lag between the onset of an increase in the stock of money and its attendant effects on the general level of prices. However, because the new money is lent into existence its effects are felt sooner in the credit markets; i.e., interest rates, usually short-term rates, are affected first. Entrepreneurs do not, as a rule, follow changes in the stock of money.[506] Thus, by the time the price inflation is perceived by them, they will already have responded to the changed interest rates, both because of a lack of information and because of altered incentives.[507]

In this our author demonstrates that his command of economic theory is not all that it could be. We must reject this facile equation of caution with lower orders of capital goods (or consumer goods) and boldness with higher orders. Nothing could be further from the truth. Neither capital goods nor consumer goods, neither higher nor lower orders of the former, are

---

[506] Even were they to attempt to do so, they would find themselves in a quandary: of which monetary aggregate should they follow the statistics? M1? M2? M3? MZM? Remember that it was not that long ago that MZM did not exist, and, there were such things as M9 and L (for liquidity).

[507] Cowen (1997, 8-9) maintains that the rational expectations assumption disciplines his thinking by forcing him to consider the sources of "asymmetrical" information. However, insofar as ABCT is concerned with expectations, it is with expectations that prove to be incorrect. He maintains one has to identify the source of such "asymmetrical" information, as if symmetrical information were the normal course of events. Regardless, even if information were symmetrical, in the real world expectations would not always prove to be correct. The real issues are the sources and magnitudes of the expectational errors. As noted above, it is the long and variable lags between changes in the money stock and their effects on prices, as well as the injection and distribution effects, that are the sources of these errors. (Even without this source, people would still make expectational errors because they are human.) These errors tend to be systematic because the increases in the money stock affect interest rates and the prices of financial assets before they affect other prices. Of course, the magnitude of these errors depends upon the size of the increase in the money supply. It should be noted that, in a hyperinflation, when everyone is sensitized to inflation, the lags tend to be shorter. As to rational expectations, if it is to mean merely that a decision maker makes the best forecasts he can based on all the information available to him, while allowing for his forecasts to be affected by his emotions, and admitting of systematic errors, Austrians would have no problem with that. However, as soon as rational expectations is taken to mean no systematic forecasting errors, Austrians must part ways, as there is no praxeological reason to think that such errors are not made, and there is plenty of real world evidence that they are; e.g., the winner's curse in auctions, including mergers and acquisitions involving other than consumers' goods; and, gambling to win, as opposed to for pleasure, against the house.

intrinsically more risky[508] than the other. The mistake stems from Cowen's assumption that the further away from final sale of the consumer good, the more things can go wrong, and therefore, the more risky it is. But this is to confuse the micro with the macro; the total with the marginal. Yes, if you compare *all* of capital goods orders with but the lowest of them, *then* what Cowen says has a modicum of sense. Surely there is more that can go wrong, and thus lead to bankruptcy, when you compare more things with fewer. But when we compare any *one* stage of production, with *any* other, high or low, this no longer holds. For, if each stage of production takes the exact same single year to complete, the *investment of any one man* has the *same* length of run as that of any other. For example, A invests in something that is 12 years away from consumption, and gets out one year later, when it is now 11 years away. In contrast, B invests in something that is 2 years away from consumption, and gets out one year later, when it is now 1 year away. Each of them invests for the same identical 12 months. It is unclear why Cowen would consider A's investment "longer" than B's, unless he is under the sway of the confusion we attribute to him. If Cowen were correct, then corner grocery stores, or greasy spoons, would rarely go broke since they are so close in time to final consumption, and by that fact alone were safer harbors for cash. Not at all. Indeed, if there were any truth to this contention, the tendency of the market would be to *lower* profitability there, so as to render the expected return on investment equal in all regions of the structure of production.

Let us argue by analogy. Suppose someone to have claimed that high priced items (Mercedes, Rolex, diamonds, lobster) were more risky to

---

[508] Cowan (1997, 16) states: "The focus on investment risk defines the context for the business cycle theory of this chapter [Ch.2 A Risk-based Theory in Real terms]. Real business cycle theories focus on the risk or volatility induced by technology shocks. Traditional Austrian theories identify the risks created by distortionary monetary policies by the central bank. Neo-Keynesian theories, although they view risk in implicit terms, concentrate their attention on the risk of non-clearing markets. In contrast to these theories, I [Cowen] focus on the risks that investments will not match consumer demands, and thus will decline in value. Technology shocks, monetary policy, and non-market-clearing prices all may constitute particular causes of supply/demand mismatches, and in this sense a risk-based theory does not contradict the options listed. None the less I focus on the initial willingness of entrepreneurs to accept vulnerable positions with regard to shocks in general, rather than on a single kind of shock."

Cowen thinks that because his theory "focus[es] on the risks that investments will not match consumer demands it "contrast[s]" with "traditional Austrian theories" because the latter identify the risks created by distortionary monetary policies." However, according to "traditional" ABCT the risks created by distortionary monetary policies are *precisely* the risks that investments will not match consumer preferences. This is standard ABCT, and has been ever since it was first enunciated (in however rudimentary form) in 1912 by Mises (1912 [1971], 362).

produce and sell than lower priced ones (Ladas, Timex, bread, corn). It would be relatively easy to see the fallacy: you can lose just as much money manufacturing a Chevy as a Rolls Royce. This is a confusion of big and small ticket items with high and low risk. There is some plausibility here (it costs more to produce any one Mercedes than any one Lada), but this is only superficial. If there *were* any bias in this direction, it would soon enough be incorporated by markets.

Cowen (1997, 81) asks: What happens if entrepreneurs take lower interest rates resulting from increased savings to be a sign of price inflation, which they consider risky, and are inflation-risk averse." His answer is that they would shift from long-term investments to short-term investments. But this is an absurd assumption. Professional economists, maintaining different models of reality, don't agree on the causes of lower interest rates in specific cases. And, Cowen ignores the incentive effect thereof. It is much like saying, Suppose an entrepreneur is afraid of inflation and responds to an increase in the price of his products by reducing production. There is no reason to think that, in the real world, entrepreneurs take lower interest rates to be a sign of inflation. This happens only in Cowen's "mirror image" world – the mirror he used must be Alice's, for his mirror image world bears as much resemblance to the real world as hers did.

We of course agree with Cowen that, ceteris paribus there is more "risk" in long-term investment projects than in short-term projects.[509] But this is irrelevant. We need both. Moreover, merely because an investment project is relevant to an early stage of a production process does not mean that it is a long-term investment. In fact, it may be a short-term investment for an investor who is not invested in the rest of the process. And, this is true even if the project is relevant to a stage of the larger process that occurs long before the process reaches fruition in the form of consumers' goods. It is also true even if the project involves durable (capital) goods that will contribute to the production of many "batches" of consumers' goods over an extended period of time.

For example, consider the manufacturer who makes drilling pipe for oil exploration and needs to finance his purchases of steel pipe. He is concerned with the short-term interest rate and is not going to reduce his borrowings to purchase an inventory of steel pipe when interest rates decline. This is obvious when we see people increase their purchases of stocks, especially on margin, and borrow to purchase real estate by selling adjustable

---

[509] Are we contradicting ourselves? We just said that a rose is a rose is a rose: a one year investment is a one year investment is a one year investment, and it does not matter where, in the structure of production it is. But there is a significant difference between a one year investment and a ten year investment, no matter where each enters the production process

rate notes, when short-term rates decline. That is, investors are concerned not with "the period of production," of some project they invest in, but, rather, they are concerned with "the period for which they are invested" in that project.

Cowen zigs where he should be zagging. He (1997, 81) invents a "mirror image" of ABCT where when interest rates fall, entrepreneurs attribute this to inflation, when in reality it is the result of increased savings. He castigates Austrians for not addressing "why the mirror image scenario is less plausible than the case they emphasize." We have a similar complaint about Cowen and other neoclassical critics of Austrianism: why do they not address the issue we are now making up that calls for entrepreneurs to avoid profit making "unicorn" ventures in favor of those that bring losses? The answer to both is that they have not been addressed because they have just been manufactured out of the whole cloth and are silly to boot. Any firm embracing losing unicorn ventures vis-à-vis profit making ones will soon enough be consigned to the dustbin of economics.

Entrepreneurs who act as Cowen would have them do will incur losses and will be weeded out by the market process. The challenge Austrians have faced and met is to explain why the ordinary profit and loss considerations do not preclude the cluster of errors attendant upon the governmental intervention considered in ABCT. The answer of praxeologists is that in the less than full information world firms have no way of distinguishing a fall in interest rates which emanates from increased savings (a greater orientation to the future) from one that is a result of central bank meddling with credit markets. In the imaginary full information model, we note that it is no longer a cluster of errors which accounts for the structure of production being bent out of shape, but rather purposeful human action to this same end, taking advantage of government subsidies.

Another difficulty with Cowen's (1997, 82) analysis is his expectation that the marginal entrepreneur would be "risk averse." This of course is not a matter of praxeology, but rather of economic history. Nevertheless, it is more than passing curious that he would rely so heavily on the owners of firms not being risk takers. One would have thought that this would be the expected situation. After all, to set up a business is intrinsically a risky endeavor.

As per Mises (1998), every action is risky, but some are riskier than others, at least if we consider not just the potential for loss, but also the relevant magnitudes. Also, and certainly to the extent that managers are playing with other people's money, there is a principal-agent problem. It seems certain that agents, who in many cases make the decisions for the owners, and thus are in some sense the entrepreneurs, are more likely to engage in risky behavior. If Cowen thinks that agent-entrepreneurs are risk averse, how does he explain such things as the S&L debacle of the '80s, and the various ventures undertaken with governmental funding or implicit guarantees; e.g., Fannie Mae and Freddie Mac; and Enron, etc.?

States Cowen (1997, 82, fn. 7): "The original Austrian theory, for reasons not fully explicated by its advocates, associates the move from long-term investments to short-term investments with an economic bust. Within the same framework, entrepreneurial moves from short-term to long-term investments cause an economic boom…"

Contrary to Cowen, these are points well articulated in the ABCT literature.[510] But we should clarify. These are not any old "moves" from one to another; very much to the contrary, they stem from governmental incursions into the economy. If entrepreneurs are shifting from long to short or vice versa in response to changing consumer time preferences, then there is no boom or bust at all.

Perhaps it is his insistence on rational expectations that causes him to frame changes in the stock of money in terms of information, rather than incentives. Cowen, apparently, does not see that governmental monetary policy can alter incentives in ways that lead to an unsustainable boom.

2) Inflation volatility[511]

According to Cowen (1997, 83): "The economic volatility associated with inflation provides one reason why entrepreneurs might respond to monetary shocks by decreasing rather than increasing long-term investment."

We agree with Cowen that governmental inflationary policy adds to price volatility, and that this, in turn, renders all decision-making less certain. And, that this has a systematic effect on the structure of production because the more interest-rate-sensitive goods are more risky than those less sensitive. What Cowen gets wrong, or ignores, is the temporal sequence of events. It is only some time after the increase in money/credit has driven interest rates below what they otherwise would have been that the effects are felt on prices;

---

[510] See, for example, Hayek (1935) and Rothbard (1963 [1975]).

[511] Cowen (1997) is guilty of a sin common enough among economists, but not serious scientists: a failure to define his terms. Thus, "volatility" makes its first appearance on page 36: "…and, increases in uncertainty or economic volatility." From the context, and material on page 26, it seems that Cowen either views uncertainty and volatility as the same thing or, at least, assumes a very high degree of correlation between them. But, surely, uncertainty and volatility are not the same thing. In that case, it is incumbent upon him to tell us what he means by this word "volatility." Although it would seem that volatility causes uncertainty, there is no reason to think that uncertainty causes volatility. In fact, an increase in uncertainty might well reduce volatility by inducing people to engage in less risky behavior, risky behavior being itself a cause of volatility.

that inflation is felt. It is at *that* point that lenders and borrowers start to build inflation expectations, both as to levels and as to volatility, into their thinking. This causes the former to demand, and the latter to be willing to agree to offer or supply, an inflation premium in the form of higher rates of interest.

Of course, part of the increase in rates is an attempt to reestablish the real rate that had decreased when the nominal rates declined before the inflation expectations changed. But part of the increase is an attempt to boost real rates because of the perceived rise in risk attendant upon expected higher rates of inflation with the concomitant increased risk that results from the fact that an incorrect forecast of any percentage leads to a greater mistake in absolute terms the greater the actual rate turns out to be. For example, if someone expected inflation to be 3% and at the same time realized he might be mistaken, and if he thought he might be off by as much as 33⅓%, then if he entered a credit contract at 3% as a lender (borrower) and inflation turned out to be at the high (low) end of his range, 4% (2%), his real rate is 1% less (greater) than he expected, and he is worse off by 1%. Alternatively, if he expected the rate of inflation to be 30% and, again, realized he might be mistaken, and if he thought, again, that he might be off by as much as 33⅓%, then if he entered a credit contract at 30% as a lender (borrower) and inflation turned out to be at the high (low) end of his range, 40% (20%), his real rate is 10% less (greater) than he expected, and he is worse off by 10%.

Certainly, the potential for a greater loss at higher expected rates is sufficient to cause an increase in the rates demanded by lenders, and, as a consequence, a reduction in the total pecuniary value of loans contracted. At the higher rates, fewer creditworthy borrowers are willing to take out loans, and lenders become, at least at some point, more demanding in terms of the creditworthiness of borrowers. This leads to a contraction of credit. This is what Austrians refer to as the crisis: it ends the unsustainable boom and precedes the bust. What Cowen (1997, 83) seems to have missed is the timing, when he states: "The economic volatility associated with inflation provides one reason why entrepreneurs might respond to monetary shocks by decreasing rather than increasing long-term investment." This is correct, but misleading as it ignores the time element. He implies that the price inflation is concurrent with the monetary shock, which, of course, it is not; rather the inflation, and hence the "economic volatility associated" therewith, occurs later, and therefore, so does the decrease in long-term investment. But according to Austrian economists that, inter alia, is precisely what happens when the boom set off by the monetary shock can no longer be sustained. Of course, during the interim, the monetary shocks drive down real and nominal interest rates misleading entrepreneurs into increasing investment.

Here is another way of seeing this point. Consider what happens when the Fed engages in open market operations to increase the supply of money/credit. The Fed buys T-Bills from A, setting in motion a portfolio adjustment process that will eventually affect the yields on all assets. Ceteris paribus, if the interest rate falls, this disproportionately impacts the higher orders more than the lower, in a positive direction. A lower interest rate raises all present discounted values of future income streams, but much more so the further away in time from completion they are. For example, at 12% the present discounted value of a dollar receivable 1 year from now is $0.8933, whereas at 3% it is $0.971, a percentage increase of only 8.7%. However, at 12% the present discounted value of a dollar receivable 10 years from now is $0.322, whereas at 3% it is $0.744, a percentage increase of 131%. That is, a decrease in the yield on an asset with one year to maturity from 12% to 3% increases the capital value by 8.7%, whereas the same decrease yield on asset identical in very way, save that it has 10 years to maturity, would increase its capital value by 131%. Even if we consider that only the first period discount rate for longer-term investments decreases (i.e., if the portfolio substitution process has no effect on yields beyond the first period), the ratio of the present values of long term to short term investments increases, however minimal that rise may be, and therefore, a policy induced decrease in the short rate would disproportionately stimulate long term investments.

This is not the end of the matter for the transmission mechanism posited by Cowen is also problematic. He states (1997, 83): "An increase in economic volatility decreases the reliability of current information and induces entrepreneurs to shy away from long-term projects… Entrepreneurs will be less inclined to make long-term commitments, and will be more inclined to move to short-term assets, such as cash or T-Bills. Inflation therefore may lead to an immediate contraction of long-term investment." Again, this is but ABCT, provided the volatility is the result of higher and more variable rates of inflation that occur as the unsustainable boom matures and turns into the crisis.

Cowen here becomes in effect a sort of Johnny one-note. If government inflates, this increases volatility; all the risk avoiding entrepreneurs pull in their horns, fearful of the long term, and pile on, instead, for the immediate run. However, if government *deflates,* this, too, will boost instability and precariousness. Given the same kind of business firms (we must hold ceteris paribus conditions, must we not?) this, *too*, will exacerbate unpredictability, to the same end: a rise in risk avoidance, which for Cowen automatically translates into short run investments at the cost of long run ones.[512]

---

[512] However, Cowen (1997, 82) contradicts himself on this matter when he says "… excessive entrepreneurial optimism does not imply a systematic distortion in the direction of excess long long-term investment. Entrepreneurs can be overly optimistic about the prospects for short-term investment as well, even in the presence of monetary inflation."

The shift from long-term to short-term investments in response either to inflation or to deflation is, for Cowen, but a possibility; investments could also shift from short term to long term, or, we assume, not shift at all, in response to inflation or to deflation. Were one to accept that point of view, the effects of monetary policy could not be expected to be systematic.[513] Rather, not just the details, but the very general course of the effects of monetary policy would depend upon the specifics of any situation. This would include the effects upon inflationary expectations and the resultant increase in risk, regardless of whether the policy were expansionary or contractionary.[514] Truly, then, the only possible way for the policy makers to achieve their goals would be either blind luck, or else to turn discretionary policy making over to Super Economist; i.e., Allen "the Man" Greenspan. Mere mortal economists would be unable, absent pure luck, to fathom the complexities of the real world sufficiently to gear policy to the desired ends.

But this is nonsense on stilts. Here we have two opposite effects: central bank imposed inflation, and then central bank imposed deflation. Thanks to the increased volatility of each, both of them pervert the structure of production in the identical direction. Such a situation would not, of course, render ABCT incorrect; only inapplicable to the real world. One way out of this quandary is to suppose that government's inflationary policy was *not* "volatile." Unless we define any and all statist interference with the economy in this manner,[515] this should be possible to accomplish. For example, it could be a gradual process, with no sharp spikes (in either direction.) Or, we may suppose that the central bank has long been inflating at the same steady

---

[513] This harks back to the views of the German Historical School, against whom the early Austrians reacted. If there are no systematic effects of policy, there are no economic laws, only historical occurrences.

[514] There are two effects of monetary deflation on risk that tend to counteract each other: that felt first tends to increase risk as the change in the pattern and level of prices elevates uncertainty; that felt second, as prices fall and the risk of a given percentage forecast error declines, decreases risk. And, though the former tends to dominate when the deflation begins, the latter tends to govern as time passes. It should be noted that Cowen's theory concerns a fiat monetary system. So too our analysis. In such a system, the optimal quantity of fiat money is the extant amount (Barnett and Block, 2004), save during a transition, were there to be one, to a commodity money. As the authorities are terrified by a price deflation and know how to defeat one (see Bernanke, 2002), actual price deflation seems to be ruled out. Therefore, and in any case, deflation and deflationary policies are used herein to refer to a decrease in price inflation and a slowing of the growth of money/credit. This seems to be in keeping with Cowen's meanings.

[515] Something with which the present authors, we admit, have some sympathy.

rate,[516] and either continues to do so, or, at worst, alters this in teeny tiny steps. Another alternative is for the central bank to announce its nefarious plans in advance. As well, we could return to our heroic assumption of full information on the part of everyone. Any of these ways ought to put paid to Cowen's claim not that ABCT is incorrect, but that it is irrelevant to the real world, in that central bank inflation may not lengthen the structure of production, due to the fact that *any* of its actions are volatile, which, in turn, may lead to a truncation of the structure of production due to risk avoidance.

3) Confusion of inflation and savings

Neoclassical economists like Cowen have long sought after the Holy Grail of constants in economics. Previously thwarted and disappointed at all turns, Cowen now sees this in savings rates. We are informed by him (1997, 84) that according to ABCT,

"Entrepreneurs confuse nominal money supply growth with increases in private saving… To the extent that private saving is either stable or predictable, the postulated monetary misperception will not occur. In the limit, a totally stable rate of private savings implies that entrepreneurs will never associate real interest rate moves with changes in the savings rate…. Yet empirical macroeconomists traditionally have found savings to be one of the most stable variables over time…"

There are problems here. "Most stable" is a far cry from completely stable and thus totally predictable. Due to that little matter of human free will, there *can be* no such thing as a constant in economics (Mises, 1998, 55-56).

Assume, arguendo, per impossible, that the relation between savings and *income* was rigid, while not so with regard to the interest rate. In such a case, Cowen's criticism would also be rendered impotent.

Again, Cowen focuses only on the cluster of error phenomenon, ignoring the subsidization aspect of inflationary monetary policy. *Even if* entrepreneurs were *never* fooled by compromised market signals, they would *still* have an incentive to pervert the structure of production, as we have seen, in response to governmental financial mismanagement.

Cowen (1997, 84) takes the position that "Unstable private saving implies that misperceptions of the savings rate will cause business cycles even in the absence of distortive monetary polity." Not so, not so. The ABC refers to *systematic* variations in employment and productivity, etc., not to random changes. In Cowen's lexicon, *there would always be* a business cycle, due to ordinary changes in market decision-making. But, surely, if the business cycle is *always* with us, and necessarily so, then there is no such

[516] Perhaps they have adopted Friedman's (1997) "3% rule." See also Simons (1936). For a critique of the latter, see Block, 2002A.

thing as a business cycle in the first place. For words and phrases are supposed to distinguish presence or absence of their referent. This would no longer be the case for Cowen. It is as if he were to have said, "Human beings are always sick." Then, we would have to distinguish two kinds of "sickness": the ordinary type we now have, from this new overarching sickness. Similarly, if we are *always* in a business cycle, we shall have to distinguish real ones of the sort we have experienced in the past from this new type. It is unclear what intellectual progress is made by such grammatical legerdemain.

Moreover, though Cowen says that, as a matter of empirical fact, savings are stable, yet the savings rate in the U.S. has declined dramatically in recent decades,[517] and currently is a matter of great concern to economists.

Finally, Cowen (1997, 84) makes a critical mistake, one often made by some Austrians as well. Cowen purports to have a more realistic theory than ABCT. However, when he states that: "Entrepreneurs confuse nominal money supply growth with increases in private savings," and then goes on to examine the "plausibility of such a confusion," he departs from the real world. It is true that Austrians do sometimes speak that way,[518] however, it is misleading. In fact, entrepreneurs do *not* think about "private savings" or "money supply growth." Rather, the "signal extraction problem" arises because entrepreneurs when faced with lower interest rates cannot determine the cause. (And, as noted above, even if they could, some would still find it profitable to alter their behavior as per ABCT).

An important aspect of this is that interest rates are *not* determined by the interplay of saving and investment. This way of thinking arises because of macroeconomic; i.e. aggregative, analysis. Interest rates are initially set in credit markets and even in the absence of them, if there were no saving and investment at all, there could *still* be positive interest rates. For example, if there were no investment, but A and B engaged in a credit transaction the purpose of which was solely consumption by the borrower, there would be an interest rate set for the credit transaction. In this case there would be no investment and no saving, as the saving of the lender would be offset by the dissaving of the borrower, yet there would be an interest rate. If entrepreneurs were interested in the causes of a decline in interest rates they would not think in terms of the behavior of savers or of investors re interest

---

[517] See, for example the chart at: http://research.stlouisfed.org/fred2/series/PSAVERT/112/Max.

[518] For example, Rothbard (1963, 18): "Businessmen, in short, are mislead by bank inflation into believing that the supply of saved funds is greater than it really is."

rates,[519] rather they would think in terms of demanders and suppliers of credit, and they would not limit their thinking to the domestic private sector, but would include the governments at all levels, and foreign borrowers and lenders, both private and governmental, including supernational organizations as well.

So yes, there is a signal extraction problem in that investors (and other borrowers, for that matter) cannot discern whether lower interest rates are the result of a rise in saving, an increase in the money supply, or a combination of both. But more important, it is *irrelevant* to them, as individual decision makers, save in a world of perfect competition, efficient markets, and rational expectations. Neither is the entrepreneur, qua entrepreneur, a macroeconomist, nor is he interested in macroeconomics, save as macroeconomic phenomena affect the profitability of his current ventures and/or the expected profitability of future projects. So what macroeconomic phenomena are of importance to him? Not "the" interest rate or interest rates in general, but the particular interest rate(s) he must pay if he wishes to borrow. Not "the" exchange rate or exchange rates in general, but specific exchange rates of currencies he exchanges, if any. Not "the" wage rate or wage rates in general, but the precise wage rate(s) he must pay. Not some economy-wide measure of productivity and changes thereof, but the productivity, and changes, if any, the productivity of his own operations.

We suspect that Cowen, himself, in deciding whether to finance a new, or refinance his old, residence, or for that matter, investments in other real estate, because of a lowered interest rate does not take into consideration the reason(s) for the lowered rate. Is it possible that Cowen, himself, with his understanding of macroeconomics and thus no signal extraction problem, yet alters his behavior when interest rates are reduced because of an increase in the supply of money/credit?

<u>4) Confusion of inflation and investment</u>

Cowen's next attack on ABCT is that it conflates shifts in supply (savings) with demand (investment). He (1997, 85) states: "The Austrian claim assumes that entrepreneurs attribute a lower real interest rate to a shift in the supply curve for loanable funds rather than to a shift in the demand curve. The Austrian literature, however, does not address why one kind of confusion might be more likely than the other. At least three factors may lower real interest rates: higher non-inflationary savings, inflationary injections into the loanable funds market, and declines in investment demand. The Austrian claim implicitly assumes entrepreneurs confuse the

---

[519] This is not to suggest that entrepreneurs are not concerned with the investments of their competitors or suppliers, but that preoccupation is not with respect to the effects of such behavior on interest rates.

first and second of these causes, and does not consider the alternative possibility of a confusion between the second and third causes."

There are several difficulties here. Consider that there are four sets of interest rates that are worthy of concern:

1) Nominal market rates of interest: actual rates of interest at which credit transactions take place. All parties to a credit transaction face the same nominal market rates of interest

2) Real market rates of interest: nominal market rates of interest adjusted for expectations of inflation/deflation. Parties to a credit transaction face the same real market rates of interest only if they have the same expectations about inflation/deflation.

3) Nominal natural rates of interest: nominal market rates of interest that would exist absent governmental intervention re the stock of money and supplies of credit.

4) Real natural rates of interest: nominal natural rates of interest adjusted for expectations of inflation/deflation.

Note: Because expectations of inflation are the same whether we are considering market or natural rates, real natural rates differ from nominal natural rates by the same amounts as real market rates differ from nominal market rates.

Artificial increases in credit result in lower real and nominal market interest rates, not natural ones, creating a divergence between them. It is this divergence between the market rates on the one hand, and the natural rates on the other, that causes the problem.

More basic and more important, there is an *identity* between real savings and real investment (Barnett and Block, 2007B).[520] Untold confusion has arisen in economics because of the failure to distinguish between real and financial savings and/or investment. That Cowen does not appreciate this merely demonstrates that he is in thrall to an "academic scribbler"[521] of the past, Keynes. For this latter worthy, the two are not at all connected. But this is not at all the case.

The problem with Cowen's analysis of a shift to the left of the "investment-demand curve" in the loanable-funds analysis he uses, has to do with the basics of human action. It is easy to understand why either the

---

[520] Untold confusion has arisen in economics because of the failure to distinguish between real and financial savings and/or investment.

[521] Keynes (1936, p. 383) stated: "Practical men, who believe themselves to be quite exempt from intellectual influences, are usually the slaves of some defunct economist. Madmen in authority, who hear voices in the air, are distilling their frenzy from some academic scribbler of a few years back."

"supply curve of saving," and/or the supply of money/credit, in the context of "loanable-funds-market" analysis might shift outward/downward. The former would stem from an increase in the strength of preferences by consumers given the same income or a rise in income with the same strength of preferences, or a boost in both; the latter would be the result of expansionary money/credit policy. In either case, thymology can give reasons for such behavior. Consider, on the other hand, why "demand for investment" in the context of "loanable-funds-market" analysis might shift inward/downward. There are no preferences that directly affect it. Rather, such a change would always be induced. It would not be an exogenous alteration but, rather, endogenous. Therefore, the burden is on Cowen to explain the causes of the downward/inward shift – it cannot merely be posited. This smacks of Keynes' "animal spirits." In fact, changes in investment are induced by a prior change in some other variable; they cannot be as, some changes in consumption are, direct consequences of altered preferences, though, of course, they could be indirect consequences of changed preferences. As we teach our students, the demand for resources is a derived demand; we do not demand resources, qua resources, for themselves, but for how they can assist in the production, directly or indirectly, of consumers' goods.

A shift to the supply curve of savings, though it does cause a reallocation of resources, does not cause a misallocation of resources. The same would be true if the demand curve for investment shifted to the left. Though in both cases, the use of supply and demand is incorrect. There is no supply of saving or demand for investment. There are demands for, and supplies of, various types of capital goods. These demands constitute "the" real demand for investment and these supplies constitute "the" real supply of investment. But in those markets the price is not "the" interest rate, but, rather, the price of the specific good; e.g., $x/ ton of steel or $Z/welding machine. Though, in fact, it is the specific acts of producing new capital goods (and durable consumers' goods) that, at one and the same time, constitute both saving and investment. The markets where these goods are exchanged are just that – markets; i.e., processes in which goods are exchanged – in these cases, new capital goods. Or, if one is considering "saving" in the context of "loanable funds market" analysis, then the supply of saving is about financial saving. In that case, the supply of saving is but a demand for non-money financial assets, whether debt (including deposit 'receipts' or other forms of "IOUs" such as notes or bonds) or equity certificates. These are more accurately portrayed as markets for financial assets; i.e., the demand and supply of financial assets, than as markets for loanable funds. In any case, it is in these markets for financial assets, including deposits, that interest rates emerge as the exchange ratios of such transactions. Thus, as per above, interest rates are not determined by saving and investment. This is not to say that that plans to produce consumers' goods (both durable and non-durable, including services and labor, and capital goods) as well as plans to consume and supply or withhold resources, including natural resources, do not affect interest rates; they do. It is just that these rates are set in markets for financial assets. Moreover, other factors enter into the equation as well.

5) Real vs. nominal rates of interest

Cowen (1997) makes two claims in this section, one of which is correctly attributed to the praxeological school, and the second not. He finds no fault with the first, but does with regard to the second. Cowen is here guilty of setting up a straw man, and then (partially, as we will see below) knocking it down.

According to Cowen (1997, 88, material in brackets inserted by present authors): "First, the lower real rate [of interest] increases the relative present value of long-term projects. Second, the lower real rate provides a signal about the composition of future demands. In other words, entrepreneurs expect demand to be high for the outputs of long-term projects, and expect demand to be relatively low for the outputs of shorter-term projects."

It cannot be denied both that Austrians make the first of these two claims, and that it is correct. Indeed, this is an essential aspect of ABCT. Increased investment flows to interest sensitive products[522] in response to a lower real rate of interest, precisely because the latter has a differential effect on long and short-term investments, raising the value of both, but disproportionately the former. As Cowen does not call this into question, we move to his second contention.

For one thing, it is by no means clear that this is a legitimate "Austrian claim" (1997, 88). A cite to the praxeological literature on his part would have been very helpful at this point. For another, the phrase "outputs of long-term projects" is ambiguous. Is the "long term project" a consumer durable, such as a house, piano or car, or is it an investment good, such as a cement factory or steel mill? There are several reasons for making this inquiry. First, in some cases it takes a long time to produce a consumer good that is consumed very quickly. For example, some 5 years of growth and development of a coffee tree must initially take place before the product is ready for market (http://kaffee.netfirms.com/Coffee/CoffeeProduction.html), after which the time taken to consume it is brief. In other cases, the production time can be trivial, e.g., picking up a gold nugget right off the ground, but that self same consumer good might serve for decades or even centuries. Second, our author (1997, 88) also makes use of the phrase "long term outputs": "Lower real interest rates will not induce entrepreneurs to conclude that demand for long-term outputs has risen…" What, then, is the

[522] These are traditionally called the higher orders of the structure of production.

relationship between "outputs of long term projects" on the one hand and "long term outputs" on the other? Synonyms, possibly? We are vouchsafed no clarification. Nor does his (1997, 88) discussion of consumer durables shed any light on this mystery: "Real interest rates do have significant predictive power for the demand for debt-financed consumer durables, such as homes and automobiles." Rather, this opens up even more mischaracterizations of the praxeological position. For if there is one thing that Austrians *eschew* it is all things related to prediction, "predictive power" certainly included. Says Mises (1998, 117-118) on this issue:

As Mises (1998, 117-118) stated:

"Praxeological knowledge makes it possible to predict with apodictic certainty the outcome of various modes of action. But, of course, such prediction can never imply anything regarding quantitative matters. Quantitative problems are in the field of human action open [p. 118] to no other elucidation than that by understanding.

"We can predict, as will be shown later, that--other things being equal--a fall in the demand for *a* will result in a drop in the price of *a*. But we cannot predict the extent of this drop. This question can be answered only by understanding.

"The fundamental deficiency implied in every quantitative approach to economic problems consists in the neglect of the fact that there are no constant relations between what are called economic dimensions. There is neither constancy nor continuity in the valuations and in the formation of exchange ratios between various commodities. Every new datum brings about a reshuffling of the whole price structure. Understanding, by trying to grasp what is going on in the minds of the men concerned, can approach the problem of forecasting future conditions. We may call its methods unsatisfactory and the positivists may arrogantly scorn it. But such arbitrary judgments must not and cannot obscure the fact that understanding is the only appropriate method of dealing with the uncertainty of future conditions."

Here are two statements of Cowen (1997, 88):

"The Austrian claim requires that entrepreneurs use interest rates to forecast the content of consumer demand. Following a decline in real interest rates, long-term investment rises for two distinct reasons, according to the Austrian claim. First, the lower real rate [of interest] increases the relative present value of long-term projects. Second, the lower real rate provides a signal about the composition of future demands. In other words, entrepreneurs expect demand to be high for the outputs of long-term projects, and expect demand to be relatively low for the outputs of shorter-term projects."

And: "Lower real interest rates will not induce entrepreneurs to conclude that demand for long-term outputs has risen…."

Here is our reaction. First, Austrians do not claim that entrepreneurs use interest rates to forecast consumer demand. As is explained below, a decline in interest rates causes changes in consumers' demands in the present to which entrepreneurs respond by increasing the quantities supplied of those goods experiencing the increased current demand. Second, as to using interest rates to forecast consumers' future demands, the analysis of this point requires development of some other matters.

Cowen uses the terms, "long-term projects," "the outputs of long-term projects," "long-term outputs," and "the outputs of shorter-term projects." These phrases are problematical, to say the least. He does not define them, yet their meanings are, at best, ambiguous. What is a "long-term project?" A "shorter-term project?" Because he refers to "the outputs of long-term projects" and "the outputs of shorter-term projects," and outputs result from production processes, it would seem that "long term projects" and "short term projects" are production process that take, from beginning to end, a long time or short time, respectively. And, from the context, "long-term outputs" seems to be synonymous with "the outputs of long-term projects." The only other meaning that may reasonably be assigned to the former term is "durable goods," and that certainly cannot also be the meaning of "the outputs of long-term projects," as many outputs of long-term projects are not very durable at all; e.g., gasoline. Moreover, the term "durable goods" is a commonplace in economics that he could have been expected to use had that been his intended meaning. So we assume that the two terms are synonyms, and ask what they mean. As "the outputs of long-term projects" is a less confusing term, we shall examine it. We ask, then, what do the outputs of different, long-term projects, on the one hand, and of different, shorter-term projects on the other, necessarily have in common? More specifically, what common characteristics do the former have, and what common characteristics do the latter have, that causes the demands for the former to be more responsive to changes in real interest rates than the demands for the latter. In fact, other than the length of the production processes themselves, there does not seem to be any common characteristics among members of either group. And, although the supplies of the goods in the different groups may respond differently to changes in real interest rate, there is no reason for their demands to do so.

Therefore, a far better term to use than "long-term projects" is "interest-rate-sensitive goods." And second, as we shall see below, it is the demand for interest-rate-sensitive goods, not the outputs of shorter-term projects, that entrepreneurs expect to increase relatively (not necessarily be high) and the demand for interest-rate-insensitive goods, not the outputs of shorter-term projects) that they expect to decrease (not necessarily be low).

Therefore, in order to analyze these statements we must first come to grips with exactly which types of goods are the ones for which the demand is stimulated by declines in real interest rates. There are three types of such goods, all of which may be referred to as interest-rate-sensitive goods.[523] These are goods the quantity demanded of which is relatively responsive to changes in the relevant interest rates. There are two ways that interest rates affect the demand for such goods, one direct and the other indirect. In the former, the demand for these goods increases when interest rates decrease, because their future values are discounted less and thus their present values increase. In the latter, the demand for these goods rises because the price of a complementary good, credit, falls.

There are, then, three characteristics of a good, any one of which may be sufficient to make it interest-rate sensitive. The first two are both time aspects, which are a matter of degree. These two affect demand directly. The third is "credit complementarity," which is also a matter of degree; i.e., the extent to which credit is necessary (or at least the optimal) method of financing purchases of a specific good. Every good may be considered to have two time aspects, which we, designate PT (for period of time) and DR (for durability). Consider, first, capital goods. The value of an individual capital good is tied up in the production process until it is realized in the form of sale to the consumer of the consumer good(s) it was used, directly or indirectly, to produce. This value depends upon the period of time from the application of the capital good in the production, directly or indirectly, of a specific individual consumer good, until that specific individual consumer good is sold to the consumer. This is the PT aspect. The value of the same capital good also depends upon the time period during which it contributes, directly or indirectly, to the production of different individual consumers' goods. This is the DR aspect.

Consider, for example, a stick of dynamite used on 1/1/2005 to blast free a piece of marble which is used solely for the production of one sculpture. This sculpture requires five years of work by the sculptor, and ends up being sold to a collector on 1/1/2010. Note that all of the "work" done by the capital good (the dynamite) was done instantaneously on 1/1/2005, but the value of that work was not realized until 1/1/2010; therefore that value was tied up in the production process for five years; i.e., PT is 5 years. And, as the dynamite contributed to the production of only one consumers' good, its durability aspect may be said to be zero years; i.e. DR is 0 years.

Next, consider a cash register used at the point of sale at a retail store. In this case, the capital good does its "work" with respect to any specific individual consumer good virtually instantaneously, as did the

[523] The more interest-rate-elastic is the demand for a good, the greater is its interest-rate sensitivity.

dynamite, but now, unlike in the case of the dynamite, this "work" is tied up in the production of a specific individual consumer good only momentarily; i.e., for the brief time necessary to consummate the transaction. Thus its period of time aspect is virtually zero; i.e., PT is 0 years. However, and unlike the case of the dynamite, which could be used but once, and contributed to the production of but one consumers' good, the cash register can be used over and over again in the production process; i.e., in the production[524] of many individual consumer goods. If the cash register is expected to be used for, say, 10 years, then its durability aspect is 10 years; i.e., DR is 10 years.

This example has contrasted the extremes; that is, two capital goods, for each of which one of the time aspects is zero or nearly so). Of course, for a vast number of capital goods, neither time aspect is zero.

The greater is PT, the earlier is entry of the capital good into the production process. Because there is not necessarily a one-to-one correlation between steps – or, stages – in a production process and PT, it is incorrect to say that as between two capital goods, one with a larger, and one with a smaller, PT, the former is of higher order than the latter.[525] However, as between two such goods, one with a larger, and one with a smaller, DR, it is *correct* to say that the former is more durable than the latter.[526] We may also consider that a capital good has a composite time aspect, T, such that T depends on both DR and PT in such fashion that, ceteris paribus, the greater is either (or both), the greater is T; i.e., the earlier a capital good enters into the production process and/or the more durable it is, the larger is T.

---

[524] In our view, selling the good (or for that matter marketing it) is as much "production" of it as what is usually considered manufacturing. That is, the cash register is as much a part of producing as a sweater as is the cotton that goes into it, or the sewing machine that assembles it. See on this Kirzner (1973).

[525] A possible objection: This does not sound right. Surely, the bigger the PT, the earlier the stage of production? The logic here is that the orders of goods (or stages of production) are really ordinal; i.e., first stage/order, second stage/order, etc, whereas the time period is cardinal.

[526] Another possible objection: This sounds correct, alright, but too correct: that is, merely tautological. Our reply: in the standard ABCT literature there is no discussion of the durability issue, only of the time period/stages (orders) issue. According to Barnett and Block (2007B) the stages/orders approach is invalid because what is of interest is interest rate sensitivity, which is related to time (cardinal) but not stages/orders (ordinal). And there is no necessary consistency between stages/orders and time; i.e., one process might involve many temporally short stages/orders and another a few lengthy stages/orders. Interest rate sensitivity is also affected by durability (cardinal). However, in this case there is no parallel ordinal setup; i.e., nothing similar to stages/orders.

The time aspect is important for consumer goods also. However, in their case there is only one time aspect, the durable (DR). That is, as consumer goods are intended to satisfy wants directly, the only time element of concern is their durability. Thus for consumer goods, the composite time aspect, T, depends solely on DR, and is such that the greater is DR the greater is T.

In addition to the time aspects, there is another factor that makes a good sensitive to interest rates. These are goods, whether capital or consumers', the purchases of which are financed by credit. Although these are usually goods that are relatively expensive, they need not be. Moreover, although most purchases of goods with large Ts are financed by means of credit, the purchases of some purchases of goods with small Ts are also financed by means of credit; e.g., some people use credit to finance vacations.

And, before we consider Cowen's second claim another thing that must be examined is the process of by which the supply of money/credit is expanded. The expansion process begins when the FED buys something, say 90-day T-bills,[527] in the "open market," bidding up the price and lowering the yield as it does so. This sets in motion what may be viewed as two different paths of activity.

The first is the direct, portfolio-adjustment process. The sellers of the T-bills receive deposits; i.e., money, at commercial banks.[528] These sellers then find themselves with "too much money;" a larger share of their assets held in the form of deposit/money than they think best. As they look for more desirable, substitute, assets for this money they are most likely to look to other (than 90-day T-bills) short-term, low-risk, securities, to replace the ones they sold to the FED. Some may prefer to extend the maturity rather than take on higher (default) risk. They might purchase, e.g., 180-day T-bills. Others, with different preferences might buy high-grade, 90-day commercial paper, instead. Yet others may prefer neither to accept greater default risk, nor to extend the maturity of their portfolios. In such cases, they may prefer to take on some exchange risk, buying say 90-day £-denominated securities issued by the U.K. In any case, as the portfolio-adjustment process proceeds, it affects securities that are more and more risky, and that have longer and longer terms to maturity.[529] As these securities are purchased, their prices are bid up and

---

[527] It is true that the FED is not constrained to operate in the short end of term structure, but that is its standard operating procedure. And, this assumption is conservative re the ABCT, in that operations in the longer end of the term structure have a more direct and greater effect on long-term yields.

[528] Thus, the FED has "monetized" part of the U.S. Government's debt.

[529] The term to maturity of a financial security or, more broadly, the economic life of any good, resource, or asset, is subjective as it depends on the estimation of the individual concerned – the owner and prospective owners. However, some financial assets also have an objective-in-some-sense term-to-maturity; e.g., a security that

their yields fall. As to foreign securities, in order to purchase them, the appropriate foreign currency must first be purchased.[530, 531] And, some of the excess money will, later, if not sooner, spill over into markets for real assets, especially real estate, bidding up the prices and lowering the yields on these assets and goods, as well. Therefore, we see that the inflationary effects of expansive money/credit policies affect long-term financial and real assets, as well as short-term financial assets and goods.[532]

---

purports to mature in 90 days. Equities, for accounting purposes, are treated as perpetuities, and therefore as long-term securities; however, as with any other thing of economic value, from the economic point of view, equities may be considered by relevant parties to be short term. This is not unrelated to Keynes' (1936) point that that from an aggregative point of view an economy's liquidity is fixed in the short run and changes only slowly over time, but that individuals are concerned with the liquidity of their own portfolios, not that of the "social portfolio." Thus attempts by individuals to increase their own liquidity by selling securities and holding "money" do not alter the social liquidity, but only drive down the prices, an increase the yields, of such assets.

[530] We ignore, here, American depository receipts, though a consideration of them would not alter our analysis.

[531] Re the international aspects, three possibilities arise. First, the U.S. government might try to hold the exchange rate fixed. In that case, it would merely be offsetting part of its expansion of the supply of money/credit. Moreover, it would, in that case be maintaining the dollar in an overvalued condition re the relevant foreign currencies, which would lead to continuing balance of payments deficits, continuing surpluses of $ in the foreign exchange markets, and a continuing need to purchase the U.S. dollar (USD) in those markets, if the exchange rate is to remain fixed. Second, one or more foreign governments may wish to maintain the USD in an overvalued condition. The usual reason for this is that governments follow mercantilist policies that go by the name of "export led development," as they try to grow their domestic economies through production of goods for sale, with those sales stimulated by "under pricing" their goods on world markets by means of their undervalued currencies. In such cases, the foreign governments must buy up the surplus dollars in the foreign exchange markets. Essentially, there are four ways they can do this: 1) inflate their own money supplies and use the new money to buy the USD; 2) borrow some of their own domestic money and use it to buy the USD; 3) raise tax collections, either by increases in the tax base, or by increasing tax rates (It is most likely that such interventionist regimes are in the inelastic range of the tax revenue curve; i.e., that range where an increase in the tax-rate "price" would lead to a less than proportional decline the tax-base "quantity" and, thus tax revenues would increase as the rate was raised.). Nevertheless, for a variety of reasons, they are most unlikely to lower rates in an attempt to raise revenues, and thus this method of raising funds for the purpose of intervening in the foreign exchange market is most unlikely to succeed; and, 4) engage in exchange controls. Each of these methods is undesirable in terms of their longer-term, if not also, the short-term, effects on their domestic economies.

[532] Let us discuss the concept of inflation. Most think of price inflation only in terms of the prices and, where appropriate, the rental rates, whether actual or imputed, of

consumers' goods and services, and, perhaps some also include the prices of goods-in-process and newly produced capital goods. However, such concepts exclude a vast number of prices involving immense quantities of other goods that are relevant for understanding economics, especially business cycles. These other prices include exchange rates, the prices of foreign currencies. When the government in conjunction with the banking system expands the supply of money/credit, it creates a situation in which there is "too much money." As is well understood, when individuals have too much of something they try to get rid of the excess, normally by exchanging it for something of which they have a dearth. In the case of excess money, this means spending it. But as the quantity of anything increases, its per-unit value decreases relatively to what it otherwise would have been. And, as we know from basic economic theory, the money will be spent on different goods until its value at the margin tends to be the same relative to every good. Now this will not happen immediately; once the structure of prices has been disturbed by the injection of new money, it will take some time to reestablish a structure appropriate to the new quantity of money. Nevertheless this will tend to happen. In fact, usually when the injections of new money begin the first markets affected are those for financial assets, including foreign moneys. While the prices of these assets are bid up in the initial stages of a monetary inflation, it usually takes some time before the prices of real assets and goods begin to rise in any significant way. This early period is not seen by most as inflationary. In fact, most take the increased prices of financial assets as a positive sign about the condition and direction of the economy, not realizing that these are inflationary price increases. They are price-inflationary in that they are higher prices for the same financial assets; these price increases would not be price-inflationary only if the value of these financial assets had risen for some "legitimate" way; e.g., the risk involved re future cash flows decreased or future cash flows, adjusted for expected inflation, were expected to increase. As "printing" money cannot increase the wealth of a society; else if it could we could end poverty and enrich everyone very quickly and virtually costlessly, there is no reason for the value of the claims to that wealth; i.e., the financial assets, to increase in value. Therefore, the increases in their prices, taken as a whole, are unwarranted; i.e., price-inflationary. Similarly, when the prices of foreign monies are bid up, that also is price inflationary as we must pay more for the same assets. The only way that would not be price inflationary would be if the assets, the foreign monies, became more valuable; i.e., if the prices of foreign goods and assets denominated in terms of foreign monies fell so that even though we would have to pay a higher price per unit of the foreign money each unit of that money would be able to buy more goods and assets, such that the net effect would be a wash. Only at some remove in time does the excess money begin to have a significant effect in terms of the prices of (domestic) real assets and goods. A useful metaphor is that money is like water in that so as water seeks its own level, in all channels through which it flows, so the value of money of money seeks its own level in (spending) channels through which it flows. The upshot is that when we understand price inflations to be a phenomena that affect the prices of *everything*, we realize that they commence at the same time that their causes, monetary inflations.

It should also be noted that the quantities supplied of longer-term financial assets in response to increases in the demand tend to respond more slowly than do the quantities supplied of shorter-term financial assets, goods, resources, and real assets, in response to increases the demand for them.

The second occurs as banks invest the excess reserves created in the initial monetization of U.S. governmental debt. If the banks invest by purchasing U.S. governmental securities or preexisting private sector securities, they pay for such purchases by increasing the deposits/money of the sellers; i.e., they do so as did the Fed monetized part of the U.S. Government's debt, or in the case of private securities, the banks monetize private sector debt. This would then become part of; i.e., expand, the portfolio-adjustment process discussed supra. If instead, they buy new governmental or private sector securities, that are being sold in order to refinance existing and preexisting debt, whether maturing or not, then the effects will be felt in the portfolio-adjustment process discussed above. However, to the extent that the preexisting securities are not owned by the banks and are quite similar in characteristics to the new securities, as is likely to be the case, the effects on the portfolio-adjustment process are likely to be trivial. If, however, the banks own the preexisting securities, this will have virtually no effect on the expansion process, as it amounts merely to substituting the new securities for the preexisting ones in the banks' portfolios, without affecting the quantities their excess reserves. The banks' investments have a more direct effect on the economy when they take the form of the purchase of newly-created governmental or private-sector securities that are not used to finance the purchase of preexisting securities. In the case in which it is governmental securities that are purchased, the newly created money will be used to finance the government's current deficit. In that eventuality, there is no way to know which goods would not have been purchased by the government had it avoided deficit financing by reducing its purchases of goods, or what goods would not have been purchased by the private sector had it avoided deficit financing by reducing transfer payments or increasing tax revenues.

It is a different matter when it comes to banks investing their excess reserves by creating new money and using it to purchase newly-created, private-sector securities. In that case as the process of money/credit creation continues until there are no, or virtually no, excess reserves, we may make reasonable forecasts of how the new money will affect, directly or indirectly, the structure of purchases in the economy, and thus the course of changes in production.

With this introduction, let us now consider Cowen's claims. Regarding the first, he is correct when he says, "...the lower real rate (of interest) increases the relative present value of long-term projects," provided by long term projects he means not just those with relatively large PTs, but, rather, all projects with relatively large Ts, including consumers' goods whose large Ts are the consequence of their DRs. We must point out that although these provisos clarify his statement, it is still incomplete as it fails to account for those goods that are interest-rate-sensitive because credit is a complement in their purchase.

The problems with his second claim, "…the lower real rate provides a signal about the composition of future demands. In other words, entrepreneurs expect demand to be high for the outputs of long-term projects, and expect demand to be relatively low for the outputs of shorter-term projects" are much more serious."

Austrians do not claim that lower real interest rates provide signals about the composition of [consumers'] *future* demands. Rather, lower real interest rates cause changes in consumers' *current* demands. Specifically, demands for consumers' goods with high values of T increase, both absolutely and relative to those with low T values. In particular, the demands for built-to-order, new, single-family residences rise. And, as is well understood, that boosts the demands for such "big-ticket" items as major house-hold appliances and furniture. Moreover, the demands for these latter types of goods increase independently of the rise in demands for new, single-family residences, as the lower real interest rates induce some people replace older furniture and appliances. Then there is the issue of personal transportation. The lower real interest rates also induce some people to purchase new vehicles. These types of goods all have high T values.

Furthermore, to the extent that the expansion of money/credit lowers the real interest rates on revolving credit, debt service charges decrease. This induces some consumers to borrow additional money, as they can now afford more loans in terms of their debt service loads. In addition to the aforementioned types of consumers' goods, this increased purchasing capacity may be used to buy various other goods. Many, perhaps even most, of these items have low T values, but that is irrelevant in that entrepreneurs respond to the actual increases in demands, both for those goods with low, and those goods with high, T values. Businessmen do not have to use changes in real interest rates to forecast alterations in the composition of demands for consumers' goods. What they must do is respond to the changes in demand consequent on the lowered real interest rates.[533]

Now consider demands for some new capital goods with high values of T, say office buildings. An entrepreneur does not have to know that lower

---

[533] And, with respect to the crises and busts, the role played the expansion of the quantity supplied of these high-T-value, consumers' goods, is that when real interest rates rise, demands for these types of goods decline, both absolutely and relative to consumers' goods with low T values. Moreover, increased debt-service expenses cause a decline in the demands for consumers' goods in general.

interest rates suggest increased future demands for the relevant consumers' goods; i.e., the consumers' goods to the production of which the workers in the office building will contribute. In fact, different firms with offices in the same building may be involved in different industries spanning the entire time structure of production for early to late entry in the production processes of the economy. Even individual firms may be engaged in activities that range from early entry to late. Yet none of that need concern the entrepreneur. He merely needs to recalculate the present value of his ownership interest, assuming the same expected net cash flows, but using whatever lower discount rate he thinks appropriate given the decline in real interest rates. Of course, he may wish to increase his projected net cash flows as the economy would be expanding. Only if he thought the lower real interest rates would, for some reason, cause a decrease in his net cash flows would he expect the present value of his office building to decrease, and then only if the expected decrease in net cash flows were expected were of sufficient magnitude to offset the decrease in his discount rate.

But, as with office buildings, it is also the case with other capital goods such as industrial and commercial real estate, including investor owned residential properties,[534] especially multi-family apartment and condominium buildings and developments, and "plant," in general, as well as much equipment. That is, without any change in expected net cash flows, the present value of plants, in general, and much equipment, increases. Of course, the present values increase even more if the lowered real interest rates lead to forecasts of rising net cash flows. These enhancements in present values stimulate demands for more plant and equipment, as projects that formerly were seen as marginal, now appear profitable.

What of entrepreneurs not given to present values analysis? Many, particularly smaller, entrepreneurs may merely view interest as an "expense of doing business." For them, the lower real interest rates are seen to reduce their interest expenses of financing production; e.g., payrolls and inventories, thereby increasing profit margins, and inducing them to *expand* operations. Some of them will be induced to expand operations by purchasing new plant and equipment; i.e., goods with high values of T, now viewed as cheaper because the interest expense involved in financing such purchases would be lower. This effect is probably quite large when it comes to contractors building residential properties on speculation.

---

[534] Although apartment buildings are viewed as capital goods by their landlords, yet the apartments themselves are viewed as consumers' goods by their renters, and, given that the renters enjoy some of the rights of owners – the rights to use and exclude others from using – it is more correct to refer to both the renters and landlords as owners of different sticks in the bundle of rights.

We see then, that ABCT neither claims, nor relies upon, interest rate signals re future demands. Rather this theory depends upon claims that changes in interest rates affect current demands, and that there is a pattern to these effects. That is, the demands for goods, whether consumers' or capital, with relatively high values of T increase, both absolutely and relative to goods with lower values of T.

Speaking of misunderstandings of Austrianism, this is only the tip of the iceberg for our author. Consider in this regard the following (Cowen, 1997, 88-90, emphasis added by present authors): "The Austrian claim postulates not only that the interest-elasticity of investment decisions is *high*..." "The Austrian claim ... specifies ... that consumption demand ... will be *strong* in the relatively distant future." "The Austrian claim ... requires that *significant* changes in the intertemporal distribution of consumption be correlated with observable changes in the real interest rate. For a change in the real interest rate to *significantly* alter expected project profitability through demand side effects, interest rate changes must imply relatively *large* shifts in expected demand across time. If the real interest rate is low today, consumption in some future period must then be *especially high.* This *prediction* ..." "Success of the Austrian claim ... requires that signals about aggregate expenditure flows play a *large* role in determining the success of investment *forecasts*..."

In all of these cases Cowen interprets Austrians making definitive statements about the *strength* of various effects; e.g., "high," "strong," "significant" and "large role." But for this school of thought there are no constants in human action. Economic actors have free will, and are thus able to choose *differently* each time, even when confronted with similar, or, if possible, *identical* data. Austrians *reject* transitivity, as some sort of handcuff for human action. A man may prefer A>B and B>C, but when faced with options A and C, pick the latter. Irrational? Not at all. For the first choice, between A and B took place at time T1, between B and C at time T2, and A versus C at time T3. Only the decision maker may say that he prefers A to B, and thus the opportunity cost of A is the subjective value of B to the decision maker. The rest of the world only knows that the decision maker prefers A to every other alternative *he* perceived, some of which might not have been perceived by anyone else, and other "alternatives" perceived by others may not have been perceived by the decision maker. People can, and do, change their minds; they can make different decisions at different points of time, even, sometimes, when the time span between them is very short.[535]

---

[535] For example, Joe gets up at 6:00 a.m. and prefers exercising to showering; at 6:15 a.m., he prefers showering to eating breakfast; and at 6:30 a.m. he prefers eating breakfast to exercising. Lo and behold, transitive preferences in the space of ½ hour. So much for indifference curves, etc.

And, a similar analysis applies to *prediction.* Free will, also, renders impossible prediction of the future. It cannot be denied, of course, that entrepreneurs engage in such acts every day; indeed, they sink or swim on the basis of how well they acquit themselves of such tasks. Those who do so as economists, cannot be Austrians. Cowen would do well to consider Mises (1957), where he explains the difference between theory and history and the use made by Austrian economists of supplementary assumptions. We can legitimately use *pattern prediction*; i.e., qualitative, not quantitative, predictions based on theory and the ceteris paribus assumption.

As Austrian economists we can for example predict, with the assumption (explicit or implicit of ceteris paribus), that if gasoline prices go to $5.00/gallon, the volume sold in the U.S will decline, though by how much we can have no idea, although we could use history, verstehen, experience, to help us get some idea of a ball park range.

As Mises (1998, 117-118) stated:

"Praxeological knowledge makes it possible to predict with apodictic certainty the outcome of various modes of action. But, of course, such prediction can never imply anything regarding quantitative matters. Quantitative problems are in the field of human action open [p. 118] to no other elucidation than that by understanding. We can predict, as will be shown later, that--other things being equal--a fall in the demand for *a* will result in a drop in the price of *a*. But we cannot predict the extent of this drop. This question can be answered only by understanding.

"The fundamental deficiency implied in every quantitative approach to economic problems consists in the neglect of the fact that there are no constant relations between what are called economic dimensions. There is neither constancy nor continuity in the valuations and in the formation of exchange ratios between various commodities. Every new datum brings about a reshuffling of the whole price structure. Understanding, by trying to grasp what is going on in the minds of the men concerned, can approach the problem of forecasting future conditions. We may call its methods unsatisfactory and the positivists may arrogantly scorn it. But such arbitrary judgments must not and cannot obscure the fact that understanding is the only appropriate method of dealing with the uncertainty of future conditions."

Cowen (1997, 89) makes the claim that "Real interest rates do not signal which particular goods will be in high demand at a given point in time." But no Austrian worthy of his salt ever claimed that interest rate changes could distinguish between demand for peas and carrots, or canoes and row-boats. However, when it comes to consumer durables such as houses, cars, violins, versus immediately used consumer goods such as coffee, orange juice, tissue paper, the interest rate most certainly does have differential implications. A higher rate favors the latter, and a lower, the former.

Cowen (1997, 89) characterizes it as "ironic" that the Austrians, who eschew aggregation, and criticize it when it appears in other macroeconomic theories, are themselves guilty of this sin in ABCT. This is because "... within the Austrian theory itself, the real interest rate, at most, signals the distribution of aggregate demand over time; the real interest rate does not signal how that demand will be distributed across particular products once that time period arrives." But there is aggregation, and then there is aggregation. The mainstream economics profession sees capital as a homogeneous blob. Neoclassical economists even have a name (or at any rate a letter) for it, all of it: "K." For Austrians, in very sharp contrast, capital goods are heterogeneous, consisting of fixed "plant and equipment" of various degrees of specificity and also of goods-in-process of varying specific kinds. For Cowen, unless an interest rate change has different implications for, say, steel than it has for coal, or tea vis-à-vis potatoes, the school of thought engaging in the analysis is guilty of excessive aggregation. This only illustrates once again that Austrianism constitutes a "golden mean" between extremist theories that lie on both sides of it (Garrison, 1982.)

Cowen (1997, 90-91, fn. included) states:

To the extent investors have naïve expectations, they do not fully anticipate the forthcoming effects of money supply growth. Incipient price inflation will not raise nominal interest rates through a Fisher effect. Future price increases will arrive unexpectedly, and *ex post* real rates of interest will be lower than currently observed nominal rates would indicate. In other words, entrepreneurs will have overestimated forthcoming real rates of interest on borrowing. *Ex post* real borrowing rates will be especially low, perhaps even negative.

Investments financed with medium- to long-term debt will reap an unexpected windfall from the arrival of unexpected inflation. Entrepreneurs, by initially overestimating the real rates of interest that will prevail, will have been reluctant to borrow money. To that extent, entrepreneurs will choose too little short-term investment. Real vs. nominal confusions thus counteract the traditional Austrian claim, which suggests that entrepreneurs choose too much long-term investment.[536]

It is hard to overestimate the confusion that caused by his use of "naïve expectations," which Cowen (1997, 77) defines as: "entrepreneurs underestimate the probability that monetary inflation is responsible for observed changes in the economic data" that he assumes ABCT is based

[536]Austrian economists have recognized the possibility of a Fisher effect from almost the beginning of their work in monetary (Mises, 1978A, pp. 93-4), but have not considered whether imperfect Fisher effects might counteract traditional Austrian business cycle theory.

on. What is truly naïve is his assumption of rational expectations, which he (1997, 8) defines as: "Individual economic forecasts are efficient and unbiased; subjective probability distributions for an economic variable correspond to the true distribution. As a result, individual forecasting errors are serially uncorrelated over time." And, implicit is his assumption that, insofar as expectations are concerned, only rational expectations are not naïve.

It is not, then, that "investors do not fully anticipate the forthcoming effects of money supply growth," in the sense Cowen means; i.e., under-estimating the effects re inflation. Instead, it is that they misestimate the effects first by underestimating them, and then by overestimating them, and not because they exhibit naiveté in the process of forming their expectations. Rather, these are the results of the human condition; i.e., of people operating in the flawed, real world, that necessitates having to make decisions when not even one market is perfectly competitive, much less all markets, and when not even one financial market is efficient, much less all such markets; and, of expectations formed by flawed human beings based in part upon their (bounded) rationality and in part upon their emotions. Alternatively put, Cowen's "naïve expectations," which he attributes to ABCT, has nothing to do with ABCT properly understood.

Cowen's (1997, 90-91) claim that, "Incipient price inflation will not raise interest rates through a Fisher effect" is misleading. When the expansion of the supply of money/credit commences, investors, for the most part, do underestimate the price-inflationary effects re goods (especially as the initial form of price inflation – increases in the prices of financial assets - is taken as a positive sign) that will come at some point in the not too near future (as per Milton Friedman's long and variable lags). It is *this* that causes expected real interest rates to decline with attendant effects on both the level and structure of demand.

However, after some time, the price-inflation, insofar as goods and resources are concerned, commences.[537] Unless the expansion of the supply of money/credit was huge, when these price effects start they will be relatively minor,[538] and entrepreneurs are likely to continue to underestimate them, thereby maintaining real interest rates at reduced levels. It is only as the monetary/credit expansion continues that these price effects become significant. At that point, the Fisher effect comes into play as lenders demand higher inflation premiums. And, having been burned once by earning real

---

[537] The price inflation begins re financial assets at the same time as the monetary inflation commences.

[538] As praxeologists, of course, we could not make any such statement, for this science deals not in amounts, only directions. However, the present paper includes elements of theory and applications; i.e., it is not *pure* praxeology. We make this claim, then, not as an apodictic one, but rather as an empirical statement.

interest rates below what they had anticipated, thereby reducing their capital below what they had expected it to be, they tend to become more cautious and conservative, concerned more with preserving their capital, then earning high returns; i.e., they become more risk averse. This causes them to refuse to lend to less creditworthy would-be borrowers, and to tend to overestimate future, price inflation, thereby demanding inflation premiums that not only cause expected real interest rates to increase more than would otherwise be the case, but to rise to levels in excess of those prevailing before the monetary/credit expansion.

So, yes, Cowen's analysis is correct when he claims that "Incipient price inflation will not raise nominal interest rates through a Fisher effect. Future price increases will arrive unexpectedly, and *ex post* real rates of interest will be lower than currently observed nominal rates would indicate. In other words, entrepreneurs will have overestimated forthcoming real rates of interest on borrowing. *Ex post* real borrowing rates will be especially low, perhaps even negative," but this is only true for the period from the commencement of the monetary inflation until the increases in the prices of real goods and assets becomes significant. It is not correct from that point on, although Cowen implies that it holds throughout, if not the entire cycle, at least throughout the boom phase.

Again, his statement that, "Entrepreneurs, by initially overestimating the real rates of interest that will prevail, will have been reluctant to borrow money. To that extent, entrepreneurs will choose too little short-term investment. Real vs. nominal confusions thus counteract the traditional Austrian claim, which suggests that entrepreneurs choose too much long-term investment," is misleading, if not incorrect.

Although much more could be said about these statements, we focus on the claim that, "Entrepreneurs, by initially overestimating the real rates of interest that will prevail, will have been reluctant to borrow money. To that extent, entrepreneurs will choose too little short-term investment. Real vs. nominal confusions thus counteract the traditional Austrian claim, which suggests that entrepreneurs choose too much long-term investment."

Cowen is correct that entrepreneurs initially overestimate the "real rates of interest that will prevail." The reason this is the case is that the same, beginning-of the period, underestimations of future, price inflation that cause decreases in the expected, real, rates of interest, also cause the real rates of interest realized at the end of the period to be less than those (same underestimates of) expected, real, rates of interest.[539]

[539] The initiation of money/credit expansions causes both a decrease in nominal market interest rates and an underestimation of future price inflation. This combination results in reductions in the expected, real market rates of interest.

However, it is not correct that, because the realized, end-of-period, real rates of interest prove to be less even than the underestimates thereof, "entrepreneurs will choose too little short-term investment," because they "will have been reluctant to borrow money." That is, that borrower-entrepreneurs' overestimations of the real rate of interest will cause them to borrow less than they would have had their estimates been correct; i.e., had their estimates been lower than they actually were. The problem is that although Cowen considers the actions of those entrepreneurs who are borrowers, he fails to take into account the actions of those entrepreneurs who are lenders. The period under consideration is the early stages of monetary inflations. There is no reason to think that lender-entrepreneurs' expectations of price inflation differ systematically from those borrower-entrepreneurs during those time-periods. Therefore, lender-entrepreneurs' overestimations of the real rate of interest cause them to lend *more* than they would have had their estimates been correct; i.e., had their estimates been lower than they actually were. Thus, there is no reason to think that, had expectations as to the real rate of interest been correct all around, investment would have been any different than it would have been with the widespread incorrect expectations. Although entrepreneur-borrowers would have desired to borrow more, entrepreneur-lenders would not have been willing to accommodate them. And, in that case, entrepreneurs would not, then, "choose too little short-term investment." Thus Cowen's claim that, "Real vs. nominal confusions thus counteract the traditional Austrian claim, which suggests that entrepreneurs choose too much long-term investment," is incorrect.

<u>6) Interest rate information</u>

In this section Cowen (1997, 91) makes two kinds of charges.

First, that Austrians are wrong in that they out rationally expect "even some rational expectations theorists." He makes this criticism because of his position that "the Austrian claim therefore requires the relative insignificance of the real vs. nominal signal extraction problems" and "when it comes to real vs. nominal variables, the Austrian claim implicitly attributes information-processing skills to agents that even some rational expectations theorists, such as Lucas, do not." As we explained the relative unimportance

---

However, the, decreased, expected, real market rates of interest, ex ante, prove, ex post to be higher than the realized, real, rates of interest; i.e. the expected, real rates, of interest decline, but, viewed ex post, they prove to have been incorrect in that they did not decline as much as they should have.

An interesting point is that, although these insufficient declines are the result of the (ex ante) underestimations of the price inflation for the period under consideration, the problem could not be solved by correct, necessarily ex ante, estimations, in the sense that, had the estimations of expected, price inflation been correct to begin with, the problem would not even have arisen.

of this particular "signal extraction problem" for ABCT,[540] we must reject this claim of Cowen.

Second, Cowen maintains in effect that even if ABCT is true, which of course in his view it is not, there are mitigating factors that weaken its effect. To wit, there is a "counteraction" or "offsetting" phenomenon, whereby some aspects of ABCT cancel out others.

States this author (1997, 90-91):

"Real vs. nominal mistakes counteract the tendency for chosen investments to be excessively long term, and raise the likelihood of investments which are insufficiently long term… As long as the inflation continues, the real vs. nominal confusion counteracts the permanent vs. temporary confusion. If unperceived inflation continues, so will the unexpectedly low realizations of real interest rates… If entrepreneurs come to anticipate the inflation, or if the inflation stops, the real vs. nominal confusion ceases. In those cases, however, the other signal extraction problems disappear as well, limiting malinvestment… one signal extraction problem offers a kind of insurance against another signal extraction problem. Entrepreneurs underestimate the rate of money growth and conclude that a lower real interest rate is permanent when in fact it is temporary…. An error of this nature, however, will be partially remedied by the decline in borrowing costs brought on by unexpected inflation. The two postulated errors tend to offset each other."

There are problems here. This criticism incorrectly multiplies factors. It says, in effect, that X "counteracts" or "offsets" Y when X and Y are merely but different aspects of the same thing. For example, consider "Real vs. nominal mistakes counteract the tendency for chosen investments to be excessively long term, and raise the likelihood of investments which are insufficiently long term." Focus on a confusion between real and nominal interest rates, of the sort where the entrepreneur is either fooled into over (e.g., mal) investing in the higher orders of the structure of production and/or subsidized into doing so. This does not at all "counteract the tendency for chosen investments to be excessively long term," it *is* the tendency for chosen investments to be excessively long term. How, then, can one and the same thing counteract itself? Eating sweets and fatty foods leads to weight gain. The one inevitably follows the other. They are biologically connected with one another; that is, it is a law of nutrition that this be the case. The one can hardly "counteract" or "offset" the other. Similarly, real vs. nominal

---

[540] That is, some entrepreneurs would find it profitable to reallocate resources in response to a monetary shock even though from the perspective of the all-knowing economist such reallocations will prove to be misallocations from the point of view of society-as-a-whole.

interest mistakes, in ABCT, lead to excessively long term malinvestments. The one inevitably follows the other. They are economically connected; e.g., according to the tenets of ABCT. Again, one can hardly "counteract" or "offset" the other.

The problem arises in large part from Cowen's use of the concept of "long-term investments" instead of the correct concept – interest-rate-sensitive goods. This makes it virtually impossible to analyze his claim (Cowen, 1997, 90-91, footnote omitted) that, "Real vs. nominal confusions thus counteract the traditional Austrian claim, which suggests that entrepreneurs choose too much long-term investment." His uses of the phrase "real vs. nominal confusions" are, themselves, confusing. Certainly he does not mean that entrepreneurs do not understand the difference between real interest rates and nominal interest rates (interest rates being the relevant variables in this part of his work). In fact, the only reasonable meaning that may be assigned to our author's phrases is that entrepreneurs' ex ante estimates of expected, price inflation prove to be erroneous, ex post. However, such errors or mistakes do not "counteract the traditional Austrian claim." Rather, they are an important, though not the sole, *cause*, of the Austrian claim."

This is not, as he states, that entrepreneurs choose too much long-term investment, but rather that there is mal-production, especially in the form of excess production of *interest-rate-sensitive* goods. Because as explained, supra, even if we assume arguendo, per impossible, that an expansion of money/credit would lower actual nominal interest rates in the face of correct expectations as to the course of price inflation, the lowered actual nominal interest rates would be sufficient to cause a misallocation of resources in the direction of interest-rate-sensitive goods. Therefore, that (because of mis-estimations of expected, price inflation) expected real interest rates also decline reinforces, not counteracts, the effect of the decline in the actual nominal interest rates.

7) Investor interpretation of interest rates

In this section, Cowen maintains that there are "offsetting" or "counteracting" effects which render ABCT impotent. Only now, the factors at issue are the long- and short-term real rates of interest, not the phenomena mentioned above. He (1997, 92) states: "Monetary inflation tends to lower short-term real rates more than it lowers long-term real rates; the resulting signals limit entrepreneurial tendencies to malinvest."

The problem, here, is the ambiguity involved with the phrase "limit entrepreneurial tendencies to malinvest." If what Cowen means is that demands for interest-rate-sensitive goods do not increase as much as they would if expected long-term real interest rates declined as much as do expected short-term real interest rates, then he is correct, but his phrasing is misleading. If he means that because the short-term real rates decline more than do the long-term rates, "shorter-term projects" become more attractive than "longer-term projects," then, in general, he is incorrect. What he neglects to consider is that, ceteris paribus, the longer the expected stream of net cash flows, the greater will be the increase in the present value for a given decrease in the discount rate. This "economic life effect" is very powerful. Therefore, even though when a money/credit expansion begins, and both the actual nominal, and expected real, short-term interest rates decline more than do their long-term counterparts, the present values of the expected longer streams will increase more than those of the expected shorter streams,[541] whether the real or nominal interest rates are used to do the discounting.

Our author (1997, 93) also takes another crack at ABCT in this section by reiterating his objection to it on the ground that "Banks generally will not be fooled about current monetary policy – banks themselves receive the new inflationary monetary reserves. Under the Austrian claim, *someone* – at the very least the new money recipients – must know inflation has taken place rather than an increase in private savings." This is unexceptionable if he means that banks (and, for that matter, anyone else who is paying attention) is aware of the Fed's stated monetary policy.[542]

But, the "must" is entirely unsustainable. First, as Cowen (1997, 94) himself acknowledges, it is the rare "investor who understands the Austrian theory." When professional economists either ignore ABCT entirely, or reject it with derision,[543] it is difficult to see how knowledge of it can percolate into the investment community.[544] Moreover, because most bankers, as most economists, are not Austrians, even were they to realize when the receipt of reserves was an injection of new money, this would not affect their operations. This is so because to the extent that their investments are short term, they are able to raise the rates they charge when price-inflation materializes; and, as to longer-term investments, banks frequently package mortgages[545] into Mortgage-Backed Securities, including

---

[541] One can make up examples where Cowen would be correct. But the combinations of relatively large differences in the declines between the short- and long-term rates, and relatively small differences between what are considered to be short- and long-term projects that are required to achieve Cowen's result are most unrealistic.

[542] In the current era of the Fed, the stated policy takes the form of a target for the Federal funds rate.

[543] For example, Yeager (1986, 378) said: "I want to support modern Austrianism by helping rid it of an embarrassing excrescence." ABCT was what he was referring to as an "embarrassing excrescence."

[544] We speculate, however, that knowledge about, and appreciation for, ABCT is more prevalent among professional investors than in academia, since the latter do not directly and financially suffer from erroneous opinions as do the former.

[545] Actually these are notes, usually made in connection with residential properties, secured by mortgages.

Collateralized Mortgage Obligations, which they then sell, earning the originations fees and, sometimes, fees for servicing them.

Second, it is exceedingly likely that even bankers, all-knowing creatures that they are, will be "fooled" about monetary polity. Cowen's great trust in them is hard to reconcile with their failure to know if we are in a trough or a peak in the business cycle at any given time, let alone a quarter or more into the past. How often does the National Bureau of Economic Research revise its estimates as to the pattern of business? It is an everyday occurrence (http://www.nber.org/). If experts at that august institution are "fooled," then it is more than likely this applies to everyone else as well. Moreover, open market operations are conducted only between the Fed and "primary dealers,"[546] (and/ or their customers).[547] Any funds transfers are made between the Fed and these dealers' (or their customers') clearing banks. Thus, banks in general have no knowledge of specific open market operations, whether as to the value of transactions[548] or the nature thereof.

This holds true for temporary ones, involving repurchase agreements or reverse "repos," or permanent ones involving outright purchases or sales, or the specific portions of the term structure involved. Therefore, only ex post can banks be aware of the nature of the reserves they receive – preexisting reserves or reserves newly created. Ordinarily, unless a bank receives reserves directly from the Fed, either for the account of a primary dealer or a customer of a primary dealer, it has no idea whether the reserves are newly created or not.

Third, as we have argued above, *even if,* arguendo, *no one* is "fooled," still, the extra money flowing into the credit market will *subsidize* entrepreneurs into making unsustainable investments in the higher orders of production.

---

[546] At present there are but 22 of them: ABN AMRO Bank, N.V., New York Branch; BNP Paribas Securities Corp.; Banc of America Securities LLC; Barclays Capital Inc.; Bear, Stearns & Co., Inc.; CIBC World Markets Corp.; Citigroup Global Markets Inc.; Countrywide Securities Corporation; Credit Suisse First Boston LLC; Daiwa Securities America Inc.; Deutsche Bank Securities Inc.; Dresdner Kleinwort Wasserstein Securities LLC.; Goldman, Sachs & Co.; Greenwich Capital Markets, Inc.; HSBC Securities (USA) Inc.; J. P. Morgan Securities Inc.; Lehman Brothers Inc.; Merrill Lynch Government Securities Inc.; Mizuho Securities USA Inc.; Morgan Stanley & Co. Incorporated; Nomura Securities International, Inc.; UBS Securities LLC. See on this http://www.ny.frb.org/markets/pridealers_current.html

[547] Some are conducted with foreign official and international institutions.

[548] When it enters the open market, the trading desk of the NY Fed does not reveal the value of the intended transactions.

8) Validation of inflationary investments

Here, Cowen (1997, 94) argues that "Even if an initial burst of money growth increases the term-length of investment, it remains an open question whether these new investments are necessarily malinvestments."[549] But it is not really an "open question," for he (1997, 94) also says: "Constant rates of nominal money growth, or nominal money rules, may sustain the new long-term projects to some degree."

Our author (1997, 94) considers two cases; first, "an initial burst of unexpected inflation, followed by maintenance of that inflation rate for the foreseeable future."

Let us quote Cowen at length on this, to ensure there are no misunderstandings that arise from such a source[550]. He (1997, 95) says:

"I see 'the natural rate of interest' as an incomplete concept; the more important relation is whether investors' expectations are consistent with forthcoming market demands and supplies. In Austrian models the interest rate *always* clears the market for loanable funds. In that sense the market rate is always a 'natural' rate or an 'equilibrium' rate. If expectations are sufficiently sophisticated, this real interest rate will not induce disequilibrium, even if it has been lowered by monetary inflation. If entrepreneurs know that inflation caused the lower real rate, they do not necessarily respond with malinvestments. They can simply borrow the new funds and make safe, short-term investments. I am not suggesting that entrepreneurs always see through inflation, but the example shows that we cannot blame the level of the interest rate *per se.* Intertemporal discoordination arises, not when interest rates are at 'incorrect' levels, but when entrepreneurs misinterpret the information contained in interest rates and other market signals. Inflation may increase the likelihood of incorrect forecasts, but business cycle theory should focus on the derived expectational errors, rather than assuming that any inflation-induced interest rate movement necessarily creates distortions of a particular kind."

There are problems here.

In his reliance on "sufficiently sophisticated expectations," again Cowen relies upon a virtually all-knowing economic actor. In this, he takes the side of the socialists in the Austrian vs. Socialist Calculation Debate,[551] only he substitutes his new brand of omniscient entrepreneur for the central

---

549 As throughout, Cowen does not make clear exactly what type of investments these are.

550 Had Cowen quoted from, or more fully cited the Austrians he criticizes, his misinterpretations of them might well have been fewer.

551 For the opposite view: Boettke, 1991, 1993; Gordon, 1990; Hoppe, 1989C, 1991, 1996; Keizer, 1987; Klein, 1996; Lavoie, 1981; Mises, 1975, 1981; Rothbard, 1976C, 1991A, 1997O; Salerno, 1990B, 1995

planner. The relevant Austrian insight in this calculation debate is that it is *only* (accurate) market signals that give us even a hope and a prayer of attaining rational economic calculation. The entrepreneur is not a magician.[552] Be his expectations ever so "sophisticated," he simply cannot be relied upon to ferret out optimal savings, investment, time preference rates, structure of production, etc. With all the possible sources of error, the entrepreneur requires market price signals, and accurate ones at that, if his calculations are not to lead to substantial misallocations of resources and concomitant losses. Cowen writes as if a modern complex economy is somehow equivalent to that of a Robinson Crusoe – Friday scenario, or perhaps that of the Swiss Family Robinson, with fewer than a dozen economic actors all told. Then, and only then, can the economy limp along, or, perhaps, even thrive, as Cowen would have it, in the absence of market price and interest rate signals. "See through inflation," indeed.

Cowen seems to have great faith in the power of rational expectations. It is as if by invoking the term "rational expectations," or in this instance, "sufficiently sophisticated expectations," monetary inflation, regardless of its effect on the real rate of interest, cannot cause a misallocation of resources. But he hoists himself on his own petard. For, if, as he assumes, "expectations are sufficiently sophisticated," then of course, "this real interest rate will not induce disequilibrium, even if it has been lowered by monetary inflation." But the reason is not, as he thinks, because: "If entrepreneurs know that [monetary] inflation caused the lower real rate, they do not necessarily respond with malinvestments." No, the reason is that if they know the real interest rate was lowered by monetary inflation they know an impossibility. That is, with the ability to form such sophisticated expectations, as soon as the monetary inflation begins, they will discern the price inflation to follow,[553] and, in response, drive nominal rates up by the amount of the expected price inflation, thereby maintaining the real interest rates at their "natural" levels; i.e., at the levels that would have prevailed in the absence of the monetary inflation. Therefore, there would be no malinvestments because the monetary inflation would not have caused a decrease (or increase) in real interest rates.

---

[552] Still less so, of course, is the central planner – at least the former but not the latter benefits from the weeding out process of capitalism. Entrepreneurs who misread prices, or act in defiance of them, are disproportionately likely to lose profits, and ultimately be drawn into bankruptcy. The ones who remain are less likely to exhibit this calculational error.

[553] Of course, with such sophisticated expectations, the inflation would follow instantaneously.

Cowen (1997, 95) also maintains that: "Intertemporal discoordination arises, not when interest rates are at 'incorrect'[554] levels, but when entrepreneurs misinterpret the information contained in interest rates and other market signals." Of course, if an entrepreneur misinterprets correct market signals he will cause intertemporal discoordination. But entrepreneurs who do so are soon driven from the market and, therefore, such errors do not cause business cycles. Rather, it is when, and because, "interest rates are at 'incorrect' levels," that sufficient entrepreneurial errors arise to cause massive intertemporal discoordination; i.e., business cycles.

Now to his second point. How does the analysis change for Cowen under the assumption of constant monetary growth? He starts off this section of his work on a high note, exhibiting, but for one single word, a correct understanding of ABCT. He says (1997, 96-97, emphasis added by present authors):

Proponents of the Austrian claim offer a primary argument why constant rates of money growth may not sustain new investments. Once the new inflationary funds spread through the economy, old spending/saving patterns will reassert themselves. Banks channeled the entirety of the inflationary burst into the loanable funds market, but the recipients of the invested funds *probably* will not save the entirety of their new income. These fund recipients will demand goods and services in accordance with their previously expressed market-place demands. The Austrians argue consumers will demand goods and services consistent with the pre inflation structure of production, rather than with the post-inflation structure.

The problematic one word is of course "probably." If this were eliminated from the above quote, Cowen might have been saved his subsequent misinterpretations of ABCT. For the latter is predicated upon different round recipients of the new inflationary money revealing different time preferences, or, in Cowen's (1997, 97) Keynesian expression of this phenomenon, "marginal propensities to consume."[555]

But ABCT makes the ceteris paribus assumption, and takes it seriously. *Of course* if the market participants magically change their time orientation in precisely the manner that will justify the new structure of production based upon the inflation, then there will be no ABC. But *why* should we expect the people to change their savings - consumption choices in the right direction (e.g., more of the former, less of the latter), neither over or under shooting that precise additional amount necessary if the decisions of the entrepreneurs, based upon the inflation, are to be proved correct? Cowen

[554] We find the quote marks around this word highly problematical. In implies that there is no such thing as a correct level, even in principle.
[555] For a critique of this concept, see Hazlitt (1959, 49, 98-134, 429)

is speaking of a dream world, fashioned, expressly, to undermine ABCT. Well, we "concede." If such a world were actually to exist, ABCT would not be able to explain it.

If, somehow, magically, people can be induced to change their time preferences, after the fact so to speak, so as to ensure that what previously appeared to be a malinvestment was no longer that, then ABCT would not be wrong, but the ABC would be nullified. And thus ABCT would not *apply* to such a situation. In other words, assume the following. We are now at equilibrium with an interest rate of 5%. The government pumps money into the credit market, lowering the interest rate to 2%. Entrepreneurs lengthen the structure of production by reallocating resources to higher (earlier) orders of goods. It looks as if the ABC is in the process of getting started, because it appears as if this reallocation of resources, will prove to be a malinvestment. That is, we expect it soon to be discovered that the people are back at the same old lemonade stand, saving and investing and consuming as if their time preferences, which give rise to the old interest rate of 5%, have not changed. Whereupon a miracle occurs. Cowen waves his magic wand, and, mirabile dictu, time preferences fall, and with them the interest rate, to, you'll never guess what, yes, precisely 2%. Thus, the reallocation of resources prove in fact not to be misallocations/malinvestments, but rather to be warranted by these new lower time preferences.

But there is simply no reason to suppose this to be a realistic model of the actual world. Nor can we acquiesce in Cowen's notion that the banks, as the "first-round fund recipients" of the new inflationary money will act, *qua consumers* any differently than anyone else, to wit, second, third, etc., round recipients of the new monies.[556] Bankers, to be sure, can be relied upon to act differently than non-bankers in their professional capacities. There is, after all, such a thing as specialization and the division of labor. But we need not assume that this is necessarily so for bankers in their capacity as consumers. Indeed, ceteris paribus methodology *requires* us to posit that this is *not* the case.

Cowen would have a more accurate picture of ABCT in his mind if he assumed, arguendo, that each and every economic actor had precisely the *same* time preference orientation, and that it did not change by one iota in response to his constant money growth scenario.

States this author (1997, 97) however: "Entrepreneurs can avoid being fooled if they recognize that expenditure patterns do not remain constant across differing rounds of received funds." But no advocate of ABCT ever made any such claim. Rather, the usual assumption in this school of thought is that the very likely different spending patterns of the people in

[556] The banks, qua first round recipients, are producers, not consumers.

the different rounds would not be *systematic*. Cowen, here, is creating a straw man and then attempting to knock it down. His attempt fails. *Even if* entrepreneurs "realize that latter-round recipients of the newly spent funds need not allocate those funds in the same manner as the first-round recipients" (1997, 97) this would *still not* undermine the Austrians' finding that artificially lowering interest rates through inflation will entice entrepreneurs to malinvest, and that these placements would be unsustainable once the *unchanged* time preference rates of the populace again registered.

Cowen (1997, 97-98, footnotes added) maintains that:

The Austrian claim implies that for one kind of forecast – inferring the spending and saving preferences of latter-round fund recipients – fixed positive rates of money growth may increase the volatility of the environment. Several hypotheses attempt to explain why this signal extraction problem might become worse; each hypothesis is plausible, but none is necessarily compelling. In each case the validity of the Austrian claim relies on the postulation of yet another set of signal extraction problems.

"One hypothesis notes that inflation disrupts the link between the rate of interest on loanable funds and consumers' intertemporal marginal rate of substitution. Investors no longer have access to a price signal which directly expresses the intertemporal marginal rate of substitution on non-inflationary funds. Positive rates of money growth create a wedge between the savings rates of first-round recipient of funds and latter-round funds recipients. Price signals reflect marginal rates of saving – those of bank shareholders – which are not representative of the economy as a whole."[557, 558]

At this point we must distinguish between preferences in the praxeological sense and preferences in the thymological sense. Properly understood, an individual, on the basis of his "thymological preferences," chooses from among only those alternatives of which he is aware. A monetary inflation that changes the set of alternatives perceived by an individual may cause him to change his behavior. In that case, monetary inflation is the cause of a change in his "praxeological preferences," as revealed by his actions; i.e., his preferences in the praxeological sense. But there is absolutely no reason to think that this would change his "thymological preferences." Therefore, it is necessarily true that the marginal rates of savings, as manifested by praxeological preferences, of first-round recipients are different

---

[557] Surely, Cowen is referring to the preferences of banks' depositors and borrowers, as well as their shareholders; i.e., owners. It is the joint interactions of these people that affect the quantity and quality of bank credit and interest rates.

[558] The relevant preferences are praxeological, not thymological, and, as praxeological preferences are only manifested in action, such preferences are necessarily marginal.

from those of latter-round recipients; i.e., "not representative of the economy as a whole."[559] And, it is precisely those praxeological preferences that are relevant in this context.[560] Of course, individuals' praxeological preferences are not the same either because their thymological preferences are different, or because they have different perceptions of the sets of available alternatives. Regarding this point of Cowen, it matters not one whit whether one or both of factors is responsible for the divergences in praxeological preferences.

This argument suffices to defeat Cowen's point, in that we have shown that the first of his three plausible, but not compelling, hypotheses, is in fact compelling. Therefore, based on Occam's Razor, we do not address the other two hypotheses.

Cowen (1997, 99) concedes that "Entrepreneurs will sometimes forecast the real effect of inflation incorrectly, and will sometimes choose unsustainable long-term investments." What he fails to acknowledge is that this is the "cluster of errors" of ABCT (Rothbard, 1963). It is not, merely, that "sometimes" entrepreneurs misallocate investment resources. Very much to the contrary, they do this *all the time*. That is, entrepreneurial error is a constant and continual occurrence; it takes place *every day*. And, these errors are in *all* directions: sometimes in the direction of excessively "long-term investments," sometimes in the direction of excessively "short-term investments." Even when they get this aspect correct, there are still numerous other errors possible: purchasing factors that are not complementary to what already exists, misunderstanding changing consumer tastes, etc.

If that were all there was to the matter, the weeding out process of profit and loss would soon enough put paid to their mistakes. That is, there is a word for entrepreneurs who err excessively: "bankrupt." Thus, at any given time, absent government subsidies to the contrary, we can posit that the entrepreneurs now active are the best the population can support. True, they still commit errors, but minimally, at least compared to other institutional arrangements. The real problem is not that there are errors, but that sometimes they are *systematic*; that there is a *cluster* of them, and preponderantly in one direction. That this should be the case calls for *explanation* and only ABCT has been so far able to account for this phenomenon.

---

[559] One might note that: 1) it is probably only people who have bought into modern, mainstream macroeconomics with its use of representative agents and utility functions (a non-praxeological concept) who would even think it worth mentioning that different people have different preferences; and, 2) that only one so schooled, who having mentioned it, would suggest that though "plausible" it is not "necessarily compelling."

[560] Of course, when Austrian economists speak of the misallocation of resources that occurs during the business cycle, that misallocation is re thymological preferences, as there can never be a misallocation re praxeological preferences.

When one student misses a question on an exam, it is his fault. When the entire class does so, poor students but good ones too, then we cannot rule out the hypothesis that it is the fault of the professor. A similar consideration applies here. When one or a few entrepreneurs misallocate resources in the direction of more interest-rate-sensitive goods, it is their fault and they pay a penalty. When most or all investors do so, it is by no means clear they are to blame. Here, the economy in general suffers. In such a case, we look seriously at the possibility that they were systematically mislead. And who or what is the possible culprit? Why, it is false signals in the form of non market prices and rates of interest, according to ABCT. And these in turn come to us courtesy of the monetary/credit inflation engendered by government in conjunction with the banking system.

Consider now Cowen's (1997, 100) charge: "Under the Austrian claim, only those entrepreneurs who make new investments during an inflationary boom will misallocate resources; previously invested resources should not become unprofitable."

But this is clearly wrong. Let us argue here by analogy. Assume a market in equilibrium,[561] whereupon government somehow contrives matters so that there soon are greater investments in pencils than there otherwise would have been but for this intervention. The producers of these new superfluous (from the point of view of unchanging consumer tastes) writing implements will lose money. But what of the previous firms in the industry, the marginal one earning normal profits and the infra marginal ones earning economic profits at the outset of our little mental experiment? According to the "logic" employed by Cowen, they would be safe. After all, these "previously invested resources" should not become unprofitable; "only investments made within a particular time frame should become unprofitable" (Cowen, 1997, 100), and the "particular time" is *after* the governmental intervention into the pencil market.

But a moment's reflection will convince us that "pencils are pencils are pencils."[562] The market little knows, and distinguishes, if anything, less, between properly (before government promotion of excessive pencils) and improperly (after) invested pencil resources. It is an equal opportunity destroyer of profits in this industry, given that there are too many pencils available. That is, given the increase in the supply, the prices of pencils will decline. Consider the firms, new or old, that made the new investments in pencil production. Some of their sales can be explained by an increase in the quantity demanded of pencils resulting from the decreased prices, but some

[561] We appreciate Garrison's (2001) emphasis on the point that economics must explain not only the boom bust cycle, but also the possibility that the economy ever avoids these two alternatives.

[562] We are speaking her thymologically, not praxeologically

could be expected to come at the expense of firms that did not make new investments. Additionally, competition for resources in the pencil industry will rise. The combination of these factors will put a squeeze on profits in the industry, and not only for those firms that did not engage in new investment.

Moreover, if, as is to be expected, prices of pencils decline, firms in other industries will find that their sales are affected. And, those that have to compete for resources with the pencil industry find the prices that they have to pay higher for those resources.

Now return to macro theory. The same considerations apply. *Not* "only those entrepreneurs who make new investments during an inflationary boom" will suffer losses. *All* of those who misallocate resources will suffer. This includes both those who before, by stipulation, were investing correctly, and those, who, again by stipulation, were not (they were either fooled or subsidized into making these investments). To further mix our metaphors, a rising tide raises all boats.

Therefore, it is clearly incorrect to argue that "previously invested resources should not become unprofitable."[563]

III. Conclusion

We have thoroughly discussed Cowen's (1997) numerous critiques of ABCT. We have not seen our way clear to agreeing that any of them call for revision of this theory. However, we are indeed and nevertheless very grateful to this author on several grounds. First, his commentary shows great familiarity with the Austrian analytical apparatus; there was thus very little of "ships passing in the night" in our disagreements with him. To the contrary, we have achieved real disagreement, something not to be spurned in intellectual debate. Second, the thoroughness and yes, severity of his criticism, have forced us to a deeper appreciation of ABCT than otherwise we would have had.

---

[563] Given that Cowen's point, were it correct, would apply to excess investment regardless of the cause, examples that prove it to be incorrect occur with great regularity. Consider the investments in retailing that become unprofitable because of new Wal-Mart stores. However, if one desires examples arising specifically because of a monetary induced decrease in interest rates, there are the declines in profitability of older office and apartment buildings when new structures of those types arise precisely because of such lowered interest rates.

Chapter 24. Some Thoughts on Price Deflation[564]

I. Introduction

Price deflation has long been a bugaboo of economics; cordially hated, reviled and feared by practically everyone. There is some justice in these sentiments when the price deflation comes about as a result of government action. However, there is no warrant for them when they stem from the freely made economic decisions of the masses of economic actors. Then, price deflation is not only not problematic, it is a positive virtue. In section II of this paper we discuss money as a productive capital good, and demonstrate that this quality can be enhanced by deflation. Section III is devoted to an analysis of deflation, looking at it on the basis of three (3) different assumptions: 1. Full free enterprise in money; 2. Quasi free enterprise: free banking; and 3. Fiat currency. We conclude in section IV.

II. Money as capital good

It seems curious that virtually all economists are concerned about P-deflation and that the news, information and opinion media seem to consider it either a disaster in itself, or a prelude thereto. As has been noted by others, mainstream economists have a fear of P-deflation that leads such as Governor Bernanke of the Federal Reserve System to state:

"Thus, as I have stressed already, prevention of [p-] deflation remains preferable to having to cure it. If we do fall into [p-] deflation, however, we can take comfort that the logic of the printing press example must assert itself, and sufficient injections of money will ultimately always reverse a [p-] deflation (Bernanke, 2002)[565]."

---

[564] Today "inflation" and "deflation" are commonly used to refer to increases and decreases, respectively, in the general level of prices. Formerly, they were used to refer to increases and decreases in the stock of money. Even that was problematic, as some restricted the term to increases and decreases in the stock of non-commodity media of exchange. Therefore, throughout we shall use the terms "P-inflation" and "P-deflation" to refer to changes in the general level of prices. When referring to changes in the money stock, we will make explicit which concept is relevant.

[565] Stated Rudolf Havenstein, the head of the German Reichsbank in 1923: "The wholly extraordinary depreciation of the mark has naturally created a rapidly increasing demand for additional currency, which the Reichsbank has not always been able fully to satisfy. A simplified production of notes of large denominations enabled us to bring ever greater amounts into circulation. But these enormous sums are barely adequate to cover the vastly increased demand for the means of payment, which has just recently attained absolutely fantastic level, especially as a result of the extraordinary increases in wages and salaries. The running of the Reichsbank's note-printing organization, which has become absolutely enormous, is making the most extreme demands upon our personnel" (Ringer, 1969, 96; in Rothbard, 1983B, 73).

Money is a capital good (Barnett and Block, 2005B). It is a commonplace in economics that the more productive is a capital good the better it is. As the essence of money is that it is a generally accepted medium of exchange and means of final payment,[566] the more productive a money is in terms of this function, the better the capital good it is. This leads us to the issue of the productivity of money.

"Productivity" is used in four different senses: subjective value productivity, pecuniary value productivity, and productivity with respect to the quantity and quality of output. Consider, first, subjective value productivity. The actions that are relevant to money qua money are exchanges. The purpose of every voluntary exchange is to improve the expected well-being of each party thereto relative to what he thinks it would have been if he were to have done something else.[567] That is, the purpose is to create subjective value or utility. However, as all we can do is ordinally rank alternatives, there is no way to measure value productivity; i.e., all the actor may say is: "I prefer A to B." He may not say: "I prefer A twice (or any other multiple) as much as B." Therefore, in terms of productivity all that may be said is that action A is more productive than action B, and there is no way to say that A is twice (or some other multiple) as productive as B. This concept is irrelevant for our discussion.

---

[566] Most economists usually define money in terms of its essential function as a generally accepted medium of exchange. Because they are guaranteed by financial institutions, a very large number of individuals' personal notes are more or less generally accepted in exchange for goods and services. It is therefore necessary to include a second essential function of money – as a of means of final payment - in order to distinguish it from such notes. We realize that because money is a medium of exchange, some maintain that when an economic actor gives ups goods in return for money, in an important sense the exchange is not final, and therefore the money does not constitute final payment, because the money is intended to later be exchanged for other goods. Nevertheless, though that may be the intent of the seller of goods who receives money in exchange therefore, the buyer who pays in money has completed his part of the exchange, and the seller has no recourse against him; to wit: if immediately after the sale, the exchange value of the money fell to zero because, for whatever reason, no one wanted it anymore, the seller would have no recourse against the buyer, or, for that matter, anyone else. This is most easily seen, when money is a commodity; e.g., gold. It is obvious that no one accepting gold coins in an exchange for goods would have any recourse against the buyer should, for whatever reason, the value of gold coins fall to zero immediately thereafter (for the claim that property rights can only apply to things themselves, and not their value, see Hoppe and Block, 2002).

[567] Every involuntary exchange creates subjective value in the ex ante sense for every coercing party thereto, and destroys subjective value for every coerced party, not relative to the coerced options, but relative to those that would have existed absent coercion. See on this Rothbard (1997I).

Pecuniary value productivity is the ratio of the pecuniary value of the output to that of the relevant inputs. For money, this is the ratio of the pecuniary value of the non-money goods whose exchange is mediated in a given period of time to the amount of money stock involved in those transactions.[568] Note that a change in pecuniary value productivity could be the result of a change in prices not completely offset by changes in transactions. Because of this, the concept of value productivity is also unsatisfactory for our purposes.

Quality of output productivity is the quality of a given output relative to the inputs used to produce it. This concept is also unsatisfactory for our purposes, in that, in addition to being subjective[569] (similar to subjective value productivity), it also has the same defect as pecuniary value productivity. Note that a change in quality productivity could be the result of changes in quality not completely offset by changes in transactions. Moreover, changes in quality as they affect productivity do so by affecting prices. Because of this, the concept of quality productivity is unsatisfactory for our purposes.

This brings us full circle to the productivity of money – the quantity of exchanges mediated by a given stock of money, ceteris paribus. That is, the greater the quantity of exchanges mediated by a given stock of money, the more productive is money.

---

[568] Consider the quantity equation of money: MV = PQ = Y as per mainstream economics. M is the stock of money, V is the average (transactions) velocity of the stock of money, P is the average price of a transaction, T is the total number of transactions in a given period of time, and Y is the pecuniary value of those transactions. Then, the value productivity of money is V (=PQ/M). Thus, an increase in value productivity would allow, in the same period of time, the same pecuniary value of transactions to be executed with a smaller amount of capital in the form of money, or the same amount of capital in the form of money to mediate a greater pecuniary value of transactions. Austrians economists eschew the use of mathematics as unsuitable for the study of human action. However, this does not preclude them from considering the concept of the value productivity of money. Thus, an increase in value productivity would allow an individual, in the same period of time, the same pecuniary value of transactions to be executed with a smaller amount of capital in the form of money, or the same amount of capital in the form of money to mediate a greater pecuniary value of transactions.

[569] Although there are, depending on the specific good involved, various objective measures of the quality of an output, including even exchange, still, ultimately quality is subjective. Thus, e.g., even if we consider the quality of an exchange to be related so that there would be some objective measure of that aspect of quality, nevertheless, quality is, fully considered, subjective. Is it possible that there could be an inverse relationship in operation here? Yes. This could come about if some market participants desired to prolong the exchange process because, say, of an attraction to the other party[ies]).

In sum, the productivity of the specific capital goods that constitute money is the quantity of transactions that are mediated in a particular period of time with a given stock of money. The productivity of money, in that sense, changes only if during that particular time period, ceteris paribus: 1) individuals (or firms) change their average holding periods of money in such ways that they do not offset each other, with productivity increasing (decreasing) with decreases (increases) in the holding periods; or 2) the prices of goods change in such ways that they do not offset each other, with productivity increasing (decreasing) with decreases (increases) in prices.

Therefore, ceteris paribus, P-deflation increases the productivity of the capital goods that comprise money, and thus is greatly to be desired[570].

III. Deflation in three different contexts

Milton Friedman (1992, 262) has famously said that, "[Price] inflation is always and everywhere a monetary phenomenon."[571] The corollary is, "[Price] deflation, also, is everywhere a monetary phenomenon." In fact, the very concepts of inflation and deflation are nonsensical in a barter economy. And, this is true regardless of whether inflation and deflation are taken to refer to changes in the general level of prices (or, what is the same, alterations in the purchasing power of money) or in the stock of money.[572]

Before proceeding, it is interesting to ask why one should be interested in monetary deflation, or for that matter, monetary inflation. Certainly in a world of perfect helicopter money[573] neither M-inflation nor deflation[574] should be of concern. The reason is that perfectly-anticipated helicopter-borne changes in the money supply would have absolutely no effects on *any* real variable, including subjective ones. Then, the only impact of monetary inflation or deflation would be to cause price inflation or

---

[570] Other defenses of deflation, Rockwell, 2003; Rothbard, 1976B, 1991B; and Salerno, 2003, 2004B

[571] For Austrians, the crucial distinction is between commodity and fiat money, whereas for the mainstream it is that between real and nominal money. On the latter, see: Friedman, M. 1969, 1.

[572] The term "money" is used ambiguously, also, in order to avoid confusion, herein it is taken to mean a generally, though not necessarily universally, accepted medium of exchange and means of final payment.

[573] Of course, in the real world perfect helicopter money is impossible, if for no other reason than that real resources would have to be diverted to the production of the new paper money, or storage or destruction of withdrawn money, not to mention the real resources devoted to adjusting the records of nominal values.

[574] We assume that just as the helicopters can disburse money in such fashion that its effects are perfectly neutral, they can also withdraw it with the same lack of effect on real variables. For a critique of the claim that neutral money can exist in the real world, however, see Cochran (2004), Mises (1998), and, Shostak (2003, 2004).

deflation, respectively; i.e., only nominal variables would be affected. However, it is precisely because real-world monetary inflation and deflation do cause real effects, both distributional and with respect to the allocation of resources,[575] as well as causing booms with attendant crises and busts in the former cases and exacerbating busts in the latter case, that they are of interest.

Although there are and have been many different monetary arrangements or systems, only three (3) are considered herein.

1. Full free enterprise in money

Consider, first, a market, commodity money with 100% reserve requirements for demand deposits and banknotes, with no governmental intervention re money and banking, save to enforce the 100% reserve requirement and other contractual obligations, should such prove necessary. Barnett and Block (2004, 48) make the case that: "The optimum quantity of money is … whatever amount of gold as coins the free-market process creates." That is, if the voluntary actions of individuals resulted in a monetary deflation, that would be optimal as it would indicate they had chosen to divert some of the scarce monetary commodity to more valuable non-monetary uses.

In such a situation, the only way the monetary commodity would not be so reallocated would be if governmental intervention prevented it. Obviously, such intrusion would lead to sub-optimality. Moreover, in such a system price deflation could result from monetary deflation, increased hoarding of money, or increased production. Assuming that neither the monetary deflation, nor the increased hoarding, nor the increased production[576] was the result of govern-mental intervention, the price deflation would come about as the result of an adjustment of the structure and level of prices to accord with individuals' preferences, precisely what would be expected to occur in a free enterprise economy.

All of which is to say that, from an economic point of view, any deflation, or, for that matter, inflation, whether monetary or price, that results from the voluntary choices of individuals is optimal, and any that results from governmental interference is suboptimal (Rothbard, 1997I).

---

[575] This is the main insight of Austrian Business Cycle Theory. On this see Rothbard (1963), Garrison (2001), Cochran (2004).

[576] It might seem strange to think that deflation consequent on any increase in production might be sub-optimal; however, of the production were the result of governmental intervention, say taxation on leisure and direct subsidization of production, output of goods might be sub-optimally high, leisure sub-optimally low.

2. Quasi free enterprise: free banking

Second, posit a market commodity money with free banking in the sense that there is no legal reserve requirement for either demand deposits or banknotes, and without any government intervention re money and banking, save for the enforcement of any contractual obligations, should that prove necessary[577]. Assuming, arguendo, that competition would not eliminate any banks choosing to hold only fractional reserves, and also that people would voluntarily accept the fractionally-backed banknotes and checkable deposits as money, the only relevant difference between this situation and the previous one is the possibility of a deflation in the form of a decrease in the sum of banknotes, checkable deposits, and commodity money not held as reserves by the banks.

The same thing can be said in this case as in the previous one. From an economic point of view, any deflation, or, for that matter, inflation, whether monetary or price, that results from the voluntary choices of individuals is optimal, and any that results from governmental intervention is suboptimal.

3. Fiat currency

The third system is one of inconvertible paper money issued by the government, or by a central bank that has been given monopoly powers re the issue of banknotes, with such banknotes having the quality of legal tender, and a regulated, fractional-reserve banking system. Banks may hold reserves in the form either of banknotes or deposits at the central bank. Two versions of this latter system are considered, one in which the central bank can act as lender-of-last-resort and/or the government provides deposit insurance, and the other in which it can do neither.

Barnett and Block (2004, 40) state:

"The optimal quantity of fiat money is zero (Hoppe, Hülsmann, and Block, 1998, 1–50). However, in a fiat-money-using society, the optimal quantity of fiat money is whatever is in existence, and, from an Austrian perspective, that quantity should never be changed, either increased or decreased, save for its complete elimination in shifting to a commodity money."

The reason for this position is straightforward. Any change in the stock of money involves injection and distribution effects, and attendant resource reallocations. Because such effects and reallocations are costly, fiat-money inflation is never warranted. Moreover, the only justifiable reasons for fiat-money deflation are: 1) if it is part and parcel of a process to reinstate a commodity money; or, 2) if it would rectify the injustices brought about both

---

577 I assume, arguendo, that such free banking is non-fraudulent by virtue of fully informed parties. On this, see Selgin and White (1996, 85-92). For a critique of this position, see Hoppe, et al. (1998).

by the introduction of the fiat money system and by subsequent monetary inflation. However, as this last is an impossible task, if for no other reason than a lack of relevant knowledge (Hayek, 1945), only the former remains as a legitimate purpose. Fiat money deflation, merely to reduce the amount of fiat money, without eliminating it entirely, is not warranted because not only would it not remedy past injustices, it would add to them new ones in the form of injection and distribution effects, and consequent misallocations of resources. In such a system, optimal monetary policy would require that the stock of fiat money remain constant, literally in perpetuity. And, in that case, any price deflation, or, for that matter, inflation, resulting from the otherwise voluntary actions of individuals would be optimal; and, any consequent on governmental intervention would be sub-optimal.

The importance of this distinction cannot possibly be overstated. There are two very different kinds of deflation. The first is that which ensues as the result of the decisions of the millions upon millions of people who together constitute the market. They decide, for their own reasons, to increase their demands for cash balances. Naturally, if the amount of money in circulation is fixed, they cannot all, at least initially, succeed in obtaining this goal. But as each economic actor makes this attempt, the "magic of the market" moves them in this direction. For the attempt to achieve greater cash implies that people are now more likely to sell what they own and to hold on to whatever cash they already have. If everyone does this at around the same time, prices will fall below the level that would otherwise have obtained[578]. At reduced prices, the real value of the extant money stock rises, thus allowing the market participants to attain their purposes.

Deflation emanating from this source is not only non objectionable, it is part and parcel of the market process. To oppose it is to oppose the free decision making on the part of the masses of people in the pursuit of their economic goals. There is nothing whatsoever to fear from general price falls occurring as a result. This is not a "market failure," nor untoward in any manner shape or form.

Deflation that occurs as the result of government[579] intervention is entirely a different matter. Here, it is not at all the case that the deflation stems from the voluntary decisions of all. Rather, it is the result of the actions of a few monetary central planners. Since this is not a result of markets, it

---

[578] For the view that economic analysis is largely a matter of counter factual reasoning, see Hulsmann (2003).

[579] According to Friedman and Schwartz (1965) the great depression came about after then Fed chairman Benjamin Strong died, and his successors presided over the fall of the money stock by about one third in a matter of mere months. For an alternative explanation of this event see Rothbard (1963).

cannot constitute a "market failure" (Cowan, 1988); rather, it is a "government failure" (DiLorenzo, 2002).

IV. Conclusion

Deflation sounds horrible to most economists because it evokes the image of the Great Depression during which there was massive deflation.

But we have demonstrated the case to the contrary: it enhances the value of money, and is harmless, as these matters go, under three widely differing assumptions, as long as it emanates from the private decision making of market participants, and does not stem from government intervention into the economy.

Chapter 25. On Gallaway and Vedder on Stabilization Policy*

In a recent article Gallaway and Vedder (G&V) (2000, 31-32)[580] state that their "...arguments can be summarized with the ... propositions:

> (1) All major macroeconomic paradigms have as their centerpiece the productivity-adjusted real wage rate.
>
> (2) The productivity – adjusted real wage rate has the property of being a trendless stationary time series.
>
> (3) Variations in the productivity-adjusted real wage are of two broad types: (a) Exogenous shocks and (b) An endogenous recoordinating mechanism.
>
> (4) The exogenous shocks are random in character and generate cycles in the productivity-adjusted real wage rate (and unemployment and economic growth) in the fashion suggested by Slutsky (1927 and 1937).
>
> (5) The endogenous recoordinating dampens the amplitude of these cycles, reducing the variance in the productivity-adjusted real wage rate in the United States by 42% over the period 1959.1 through 1996.2
>
> (6) Consequently, short-term economic forecasting is a rather dubious proposition.
>
> (7) *Ex post* attempts at implementing stabilization policy are *destabilizing*, not stabilizing.
>
> (8) Therefore, the notion of short-run contracyclical macroeconomic policymaking is an exercise in futility."

---

* It is customary at this point to thank anonymous referee(s) for their contribution to the improvement of the paper, stating that all remaining errors that somehow got by him are the responsibility of the authors. We do not at all question this convention. But to limit ourselves to such a traditional statement in the present case would be to do the present referee a vast injustice. For this referee went way over and above the usual call of duty: his report consisted of eight pages of single spaced type, with not a wasted word; every substantive paragraph, without exception, was pithy, informative and helpful to us. Many are the errors that no longer appear in the present version of the paper thanks to his Herculean efforts. In addition, he has asked us to expand and elaborate upon additional points, also to the great benefit of this paper. We are very, very grateful to him.

[580] The ideas in G&V (2000) are largely a reprise of those in G&V (1987) and Vedder and Gallaway (V&G) (1997).

Certainly, their proposition 1, properly understood, and propositions 6-8 do not come as a surprise to Austrian economists.[581] However, what sets Austrians apart from mainstream economists is methodology and consequent analyses. Part I contains an analysis of their methods, which are found wanting. Although G&V "tip their hats" to Austrian economics, in Part II we challenge their claim that their analysis is compatible therewith. We conclude in section III.

I. Methodology

I. 1. Excessive aggregation[582]

G&V's models are highly aggregated. They use the money wage (W), general price level (P), real output of goods and services (Q), and [total] employment (L) to construct the real wage ($w_r = W/P$) and the average product of labor (Q/L), hereinafter AP_L (i.e., $AP_L = Q/L$), and, in turn, "the productivity adjusted real wage for labor in the economy" ($ARW = w_r/AP_L$). This latter, the ARW, is the central concept in their paper. Virtually their entire contribution revolves around deviations of the ARW from its "natural" or "normal" or "equilibrium" value.

Their use of artificially constructed, highly aggregated variables such as "the money wage," "the general price level," "the real wage rate," "real output of goods and services," "[total] employment," and "the average product of labor," negates the Austrian project from the start, as it precludes any analysis involving changes in relative prices and wages, their attendant changes in allocation of resources and resource productivities, and resulting changes in the composition of output. This problem is not unrelated to that of the analysis done with these variables.

---

[581] This refers to mainstream-type "counter-cyclical policies." It is not to deny that there are policies not commonly regarded as counter-cyclical that should be undertaken immediately on their own merits regardless of whether there is a cycle, or that may be useful in mitigating the downturn if there is cycle, regardless of the stage. Such policies include inter alia, elimination of anticompetitive regulations. For more on this, see section II – 8, infra.

[582] G&V's fn. 2 is tacit acknowledgment of the aggregation problem when they note that Austrians are "more oriented toward considerations of the structure of wages rather than their overall level." However, after then maintaining that both the level and structure are important, they then proceed to ignore the structure of wages entirely. Their rationalization for this is a quote from Mises (1966, 578). Certainly, Mises himself did not think in terms of aggregates, whether of wages are any other economic phenomena. Rather, the distortion in the *structure*, not level, of wages and prices was, to Mises (2000, 75), "the main source of the social consequences of inflation." Moreover, it is not at all clear that wage rates in the passage G&V single out refer to nominal-wage, and not real-wage, rates.

However, in what follows, the problems involved with aggregation are ignored, arguendo, and we follow G&V (2000) in their use of aggregate variables and analysis in order to demonstrate the difficulties with their presentation even when we abstract from this problem. G&V analyze the ARW in three models: Keynesian, Classical, and Austrian.

I. 2. Models

I. 2. A. Keynesian

G&V (2000, 20) begin with a "pure" Keynesian model in which (1) $L = f(AD)$, where L is employment and AD is aggregate demand.[583] They define AD as PQ and invoke Keynes's suggestion that the money wage, W, should be the unit of account, transforming the right-hand-side of (1) into (2) $AD = PQ/W$.[584] They then assume a linear form for (1), yielding (3) $L = b(PQ/W)$,[585] which they convert to (4) $W/P = b(Q/L) = bAP_L$, with no justification given for the linear form, though there is a rationale available, as will be shown below. Moreover, the same reasoning makes clear that $0 < b < 1$, although G&V do not vouchsafe us this information.[586]

Rewriting (3) or (4) yields $P = W/bAP_L$. G&V state that: "…within the pure Keynesian framework, money wage rates are assumed to be rigid, which, holding the average productivity of labor constant,[587] leaves only the price level as a variable that may adjust or be adjusted to alter levels of employment." However, this is incorrect. There are only four terms in the

---

[583] Of course, Keynes' concept of aggregate demand is quite different from that of standard or modern economics, where demand, Q, aggregate or otherwise, is in terms of real phenomena. For Keynes, the aggregate demand function, $D = f(N)$, is in term of nominals, not reals, with "D be[ing] the proceeds entrepreneurs expect to receive from the employment of N men…." (Keynes, 1936, 25).

[584] It should be noted that this converts Keynes's nominal aggregate demand function, denominated in monetary units, say dollars ($), into a real aggregate demand function, denominated in labor units, say man-hours (man-hrs). Let output be denominated in units of X, some composite good; P be the price level in terms of $ per unit of X, $/X; and, W be the wage rate in $ per man-hour, $/man-hr. Then for Keynes, aggregate demand is PQ, and its units are ($/X)(X) = $; whereas for G&V, aggregate demand is PQ/W, and its units are ($/X)(X)/($/man-hr) = man-hr. For these two concepts to be equivalent, there must be a constant relationship between the quantity of employment and the monetary value of output. This necessitates that the real-wage rate be constant, but with W assumed constant that requires that P also must be a constant.

[585] "b" is implicitly assumed to be constant.

[586] In this equation "b" is the fraction of the average product of labor that labor receives as real wages, the rest going for interest, rent, and profits. The absolute maximum b could take on would be 1, if labor got the entire amount of output; in any case it has to be greater than 0, or else labor gets nothing and starves to death.

[587] However, though a constant AP_L means that the ratio of Q to L is constant, the levels of Q and L are indeterminate.

relevant equation, however written; to wit: W, P, b, and AP_L. Because three of them (W, AP_L, and b) are assumed constant, the fourth, P, necessarily is also. Therefore, P may *not* "adjust or be adjusted to alter levels of employment," or anything else for that matter.[588]

Moreover, the key equation, (3) $L = b\,(PQ/W)$, in V&G's Keynesian framework is but the standard Keynesian/Post-Keynesian markup pricing model,[589] where price is taken to be a markup, m ($m > 1$), over unit labor expense, U; i.e., $P = mU$.[590] U, in turn, is equal to W divided by the AP_L; therefore, $P = mW/AP_L$. This equation may be rewritten as $W/P = (1/m)\,AP_L$. This is G&V's (4) with $m = 1/b$,[591] or as $L = (1/m)\,(PQ/W)$ which is G&V's (3), again, with $m = 1/b$.[592]

If prices are, or if they are assumed to be, a constant markup over unit labor expense; i.e., if m in the equation $P = m\,(W/AP_L)$ is constant, then G&V's result that ARW, the ratio of the real wage to the AP_L, is constant, must hold; i.e., $ARW = b = 1/m$. And, a fortiori, if, for whatever reason, at some point in time $ARW \neq b = 1/m$, and, as G&V assume, m, W, and AP_L are constant, then *of course* only P can adjust to eliminate the disequilibrium. That is, in their Keynesian model ARW is a constant because the model is in reality a constant-markup-over-unit-labor-cost pricing model in which the markup, b, is a "parametric value;" i.e., a constant.

Moreover, if what G&V mean is that in a *disequilibrium situation* (i.e., $P \neq W/bAP_L$),[593] given the assumption that every term on the right-hand-side is constant, so that the entire right-hand-side is constant, only P can adjust to alter levels of employment, they are certainly correct, mathematically. If $A \neq B$, and B cannot change, then the only way that A and B can become equal is for A to adjust. However, we are entitled to ask, from the perspective of economics, if at some point in time $A = B$, and surely it must have in the case in hand, then how does it come about that $A \neq B$? That is, if we start with $P = W/bAP_L$, where W/bAP_L is a constant, we must be told how we arrive at a point where $P \neq W/bAP_L$; i.e., how it came to be that P became either too low or too high? But this issue is ignored by G&V, and probably with good reason. Perhaps it is because in this model, it is virtually impossible for P to

---

588 We thank a very thorough and insightful referee for this point.

589 Snowdon et al. (1994, 372).

590 A markup of 1 sets $P = U$ with nothing left for the complementary resources or profits, therefore, $m > 1$.

591 Note that, given $m = 1/b$, the constraints $m > 1$ and $0 < b < 1$ are identical.

592 This equation may be interpreted as either the demand for labor or an aggregate supply curve.

593 It should be noted that in a disequilibrium situation, the link between G&V's real model and Keynes's nominal model is broken, as the link is dependent on a constant real-wage rate

change from an initial equilibrium value: P does not change in response to a change in W, as the latter is constant; nor does P change in response to b, as that also is constant; nor does P change in response to a change in AP_L, as that also is constant; nor does P change in response to a change of equal proportion (necessitated by the assumption that AP_L is constant) in both Q an L. We are left to wonder how given the assumptions of the model it could ever be in disequilibrium. Furthermore, given the assumptions of the model, $P \neq W/bAP_L$ cannot be some sort of unemployment equilibrium, else (2), (3), and (4) are not equations, and should not have been written with equal signs.

I. 2. B. Classical

G&V (2000, 20-21) build their classical model by utilizing a Cobb-Douglas production function, (5) $Q = A\,K^a\,L^{(1-a)}$, where Q is as before, and K and L are "capital and labor inputs, respectively."[594] Then they convert from real to monetary values of output: (6) $PQ = PAK^aL^{(1-a)}$. Next these authors take the partial derivative[595] with respect to L, to arrive at the [value of] the marginal product of labor: (7) $\partial PQ/\partial L = P(1\text{-}a)(Q/L)$. Whereupon because of the classical assumption "that the money wages will be equal to the money version of the marginal product of labor" (the value of the marginal product under competitive conditions)[596] they (G&V, 2000, 21) set up (8), $W = P(1\text{-}a)(Q/L) = P(1\text{-}a)AP_L$ and (9) $W/P = (1\text{-}a)(AP_L)$. Finally, they offer us (10), $w_r/(AP_L) = 1\text{-}a$ or $w_r/AP_L = ARW = 1\text{-}a$.

Because, as with b, G&V (2000, 21) assume a to be a parametric value, (4) and (9) are equivalent. That is, the Keynesian ARW = b and the classical ARW = 1-a, though arrived at differently, are mathematically the same. The difference is that, with a, b, and AP_L, held constant in both models, but W held constant only in the Keynesian model, in the classical world it is possible for W and P to get misaligned, in which case either or both can adjust, whereas in G&V's Keynesian model P is necessarily a constant, also, and nothing can get misaligned. However, if somehow, P did become misaligned, only P could adjust.

---

[594] Their production function is written aK^aL^{1-a}. This obviously is a typo, so we have rewritten it AK^aL^{1-a}.

[595] Although they say that they differentiate with respect to L, actually they partially differentiate, treating a, A, and K as constants. Moreover, they implicitly assume "perfect competition" in the real world, because they treat P as a constant. Had they taken the partial derivative without assuming perfect competition, the result would have been the marginal revenue product, $(P+Q\partial P/\partial Q)(1\text{-}a)(Q/L)$; i.e., $MR(1\text{-}a)(Q/L)$ instead of their $P(1\text{-}a)(Q/L)$.

[596] By "competitive conditions" they mean perfect competition as per the mainstream concept thereof. They also imply perfect competition in the labor, as well as the output, market, else they would have set the "money version of the marginal product of labor" equal to $W + L\partial W/\partial L$; i.e., the marginal factor expense

I. 2. C. Austrian

As to the Austrian version of the ARW, G&V (2000, 22) state that:

"By contrast, the Austrian perspective places greater emphasis on the elements of market process, exploring the way in which discoordination of markets occur and how markets respond to discoordination. In general, Austrians are more interested in expression (10) when it reads (11) w_r/AP_L [= ARW] $\neq$ 1-a."[597] [Footnote added.] Certainly the former statement is correct. However, the latter is misleading, to say the least. On this, see section II, infra, especially subsection 4.

I. 3. Reality v. perfect competition and average v. marginal productivity; Cobb-Douglas (CD) v. constant elasticity of substitution (CES); and dimensional analysis[598]

I. 3. A. Reality v. perfect competition and average v. marginal productivity

But certainly this model, though in keeping with Keynesianism, is not consistent with either classical or Austrian thinking. Let us derive (9) – or (10), which, save for a change in symbols, is identical to (9) – in a different, yet more standard, way. Let p be profits. Then p = PQ - WL - rK, where r is the rental price on capital inputs.

First maximize p with respect to L assuming, as G&V do, perfect competition in all markets, and then maximize without this special assumption.[599] Maximization of p requires that we set $\partial p/\partial L = 0$, and solve. With P and W constant, $\partial p/\partial L = P\partial Q/\partial L - W = 0$, or $w_r/MP_L = 1$. Therefore, G&V's ARW = $w_r/AP_L = (MP_L/AP_L)$; i.e., their definition of the ARW *requires* that it be equal to MP_L/AP_L, which is the output elasticity of labor (ε_L).

Next, maximizing p with respect to L *without* assuming perfect competition yields: $\partial p/\partial L = (P + Q\partial P/\partial Q)(\partial Q/\partial L) - (W + L\partial W/\partial L) = 0$; or, $(MR)(MP_L) = MFE_L$, where MR is "aggregate marginal revenue," MP_L is the "aggregate marginal product of labor," and MFE_L, the "aggregate marginal factor expense of labor." Then, $(MFE_L/MR))/(MP_L) = 1 =$ ARP. This is "the correct equation" for the (productivity) Adjusted Real Wage. That is, the appropriate ARW is the ratio of marginal factor expense of labor to the

[597] In the published version (11) is actually given as $w_r \neq$ 1-a, not $w_r/AP_L \neq$ 1-a. This is obviously a typo. Moreover, these authors somehow infer from this that Austrians would be interested in their eq. (11): $w_r/AP_L = (1\text{-a})$. One wonders what Mises and Rothbard would have made of this curious claim.

[598] The mathematics supporting this section may be found at: http://www.mises.org/journals/scholar/Barnettblock.pdf

[599] Of course, it is both a theoretical truth *and* an empirical fact, that markets, whether individual or aggregated, are not perfectly competitive. Had G&V allowed P and W to fluctuate, as they maintain they *do* fluctuate to adjust the labor market to equilibrium, their eq. (10) would have been, instead: $(MFE_L/MR)/AP_L$ = 1-a.

marginal revenue of output, relative to the marginal product of labor, not the real wage relative to the average product of labor. And, as is to be expected in economics the relevant relationships involve *marginals*, not *averages.*

To make the correct equation comparable to G&V's equation, we must convert from $(MFE_L/MR)/MP_L$ to w_r/AP_L. This results in: $w_r/AP_L = ((1+1/E)/(1+1/e))(\varepsilon_L)$, where e is the elasticity of labor supply with respect to the (nominal) wage rate, E is the elasticity of output demand with respect to the price thereof, and ε_L is the output elasticity of labor. This is quite a different relationship than the ARW= ε_L formulated and posited by G&V.

Indeed, instead of setting ARW = w_r/AP_L they should have set ARW = w_r/MP_L. However, in order to estimate a model based on the MP_L one needs data thereon, whereas to estimate G&V's model "all" one requires is data on the AP_L, which, according to V&G (1997, 32) are "readily available."

I. 3. B. CD v. CES

Even if we accept arguendo G&V's (implicit) assumption of perfect competition, their results still depend critically on another assumption: that the economy as a whole can be characterized by a one good-two resources, CD production function.[600]

G&V use a constant-returns-to-scale, CD function, $Q = AK^aL^{(1-a)}$. In this case, the $MP_L = \partial Q/\partial L = (1 - a)AK^aL^{-a}$ and the $AP_L = AK^aL^{-a}$. Therefore, $MP_L = (1 - a)AP_L$. Consequently, profit maximization requires $w_r = (1\text{-}a)AP_L$. G&V then rearrange terms to arrive at $w_r/AP_L = 1\text{-}a$. or ARW =1-a. The point is, this constitutes no more than a special case based upon their implicit assumptions of perfect competition and a one good-two resources CD production function. G&V's analysis depends critically on these assumptions. Specifically, they appear to have chosen the CD function because the $MP_L = AP_L$ multiplied by the exponent of the labor term.[601]

Consider, next, the results had G&V used, with their AP_L based ARW, a different commonly used function, say the constant-elasticity of-substitution (CES) function, in its simplest form: $Q = (cK^{-\alpha} + (1\text{-}c)L^{-\alpha})^{-1/\alpha}$, $\alpha > -1$, $0 < c < 1$. Then, $MP_L = AP_L/((c/(1\text{-}c))(L/K)^{\alpha} + 1) \Rightarrow$ ARW = $(1\text{-}c)/(c(L/K)^{\alpha} + (1\text{-}c))$. Compare that with G&V's CD based ARW, ARW = 1-a. For these two formulations to have the same equilibrium values, the capital to labor ratio (K/L)[602] must be a constant such that:

---

[600] It is hard to imagine a model more in conflict with Austrian methodology.

[601] Although G&V chose the exponents of K and L, a and 1-a, respectively, such that the production function is one of constant-returns-to-scale, this result holds for any exponents of K and L, say a and b, where $a > 0$, $b > 0$.

[602] Of course, such a ratio is inherently confused, and incapable of being measured, much less be expected to be constant. This is but one manifestation of the aggregation problem; i.e., in this case, the impossibility of aggregating heterogeneous capital and

$K/L = ((c - ac)/(a - ac))^{1/\alpha}$. Therefore, even if at some point the equilibrium values of the CD and CES ARWs were identical; i.e., $(1\text{-}a) = (1\text{-}c)/(c(L/K)^{\alpha} + (1\text{-}c))$, a change in K/L would cause them to diverge. Whether, then, they deviate, and if so, to what extent, is an empirical matter depending upon the specific values of a, c, α, and K/L, which given the limits on the parameters ($0 < a, c < 1$; $\alpha > -1$) are potentially large. Therefore, there is no way of knowing this, save on the basis of consistent, empirical estimates.[603]

Moreover, the correct, general formulation of the ARW[604] is equal to the afore-shown ratio involving the price elasticity of demand for output, the wage elasticity of supply for labor, and the output elasticity of labor; i.e., $((1+1/E)/(1+1/e))(\varepsilon_L)$. There is no reason to expect any of these elasticities to be constant, or a fortiori, for the ratio involving them to be constant.

Therefore, we conclude that the appropriate real wage-productivity relationship is the ratio of the real wage to the marginal product of labor; to wit: $w_r/MP_L = (1+1/E)/(1+1/e)$, and that this ratio would be constant for any reasonably long time period only by coincidence.

I. 3. C. Dimensions

Regardless of the production function used, the mathematics is untenable as soon as dimensions are introduced. For example, using G&V's CD function, $Q = AK^aL^{1-a}$, if we measure Q in units of widgets per year (wid/yr), K in units machine-hours per year (cap-hr/yr), and L in units of man-hours per year (man-hr/yr) then attaching the units (in brackets) to the variables, yields: $Q[wid/yr] = A(K[cap\text{-}hr/yr])^a (L[man\text{-}hr/yr])^{1-a}$. Note that the exponent a attaches not just to the magnitude of K, but also to its units.

But as $1 > a > 0$, say $a = 0.5$, the units of K are the square root of the ratio of machine-hours to time. Similarly, for L the units are the square root of the ratio of man-hours to time. And, the units of A are the ratio of widgets

---

labor inputs. On the other hand, if one tries to measure them in monetary terms, then the problem manifests itself in that the monetary value of the physical inputs can alter without any change in the inputs; i.e., the measured value of the inputs diverges without any transformation in the outputs.

603 On the issue of consistent estimates, and also the magnitudes involved, see Huang and Whalley (2003, 3): "This study includes a section on skilled unskilled labour substitution elasticities. While Abrego and Whalley use an elasticity estimate of 1.25, behind this is a key table in Hamermesh reporting 19 estimates. 5 of these are of the wrong sign, 1 is below 0.3 and 2 are above 5. While 1.25 may be a defensible central tendency value for their purposes, how best to use this additional information in their model procedures is not clear, as also is whether one can make useful statements as to the likelihood of certain model outcomes in light of this range of estimates" (emphasis added), and also Table 1 (Huang and Whalley, 2003, 13-14) and accompanying text.

604 This assumes the ARW is defined as w_r/APL, as per G&V.

to the product of the square roots of machine hours and man hours.[605] Surely, all this is intellectually unacceptable.[606]

It availeth naught to reply that production functions are merely symbolic.[607] That is: If 5 men using 5 hammers can produce 45 widgets, writing "45 widgets = 5 men + 5 hammers" is just symbolic and one can't take the incommensurability of the three units seriously. The reason it naught availeth is that soi-disant (mathematical) economists do not use equations in the manner suggested above; i.e., as a form of shorthand. No, they put such ideas in forms they can and do use mathematically.

There would be no problem if economists used mathematical notation solely in symbolic fashion, save for potential confusion by numerate people who had not been initiated into economists' ways of using mathematical forms solely in a symbolic way and who came across some economics involving the use of mathematics as shorthand. That, however, is not the case. Rather, such formulations are subjected to various mathematical operations. One very relevant example is G&V (2000, 21): "Differentiating (6) [$PQ = PAK^{a}L^{(1-a)}$] with respect to L to produce the marginal product of labor produces (7) $dPQ/dL = P(1-a)(Q/L)$." And, truthfully, were that the worst offense, one might be tempted to look the other way. However, it is not, so one should not.

In sum, G&V's attempt to establish their regression equations based on a constant relationship between the real wage and the AP_L, in turn based upon the concept of perfect competition in all markets and a CD aggregate production function is unjustified.

I. 4. Disequilibrium real-wage rates and implications of perfectly inelastic labor supply

This issue arises because of this statement by G&V (2000, 24):[608]

"Given the ... statistical relationship between variations in the ARW term and employment, unemployment, and ... rates of growth in ... output, the variations of the ARW ... are quite meaningful. Higher levels of ARW are associated with higher unemployment and lower rates of economic growth (Vedder and Gallaway 1997, app. B)."

[605] In a more general CD function, one without constant returns to scale; i.e., one in which the exponents of K and L do not sum to one (1), the units become even more problematic.

[606] On this, see Barnett (2003A, 59-60; 2004).

[607] Again, we thank a very thoughtful referee for raising this issue.

[608] As G&V (2000) explicitly refer to, and rely on, V&G (1997) some of our analysis concerns the latter.

V&G (1997, 31) state: "neoclassical and Austrian economists essentially believed that unemployment varies directly with" the ARW.[609] V&G (1997, 31-32, 313) assert an inverse relationship between the ARW and unemployment. The model they develop is:

(1) $D_L = f(w_r)$; (2) $S_L = S_0$;[610] and, (3) $S_0 = D_L = f(w_r)$.

Eq. (3) determines the equilibrium real-wage rate, w_r^* and level of employment, N^*, at which there is an equilibrium level of unemployment, U^*. w_r is the actual real-wage rate and U is the actual level of unemployment. If $w_r \neq w_r^*$, then $U \neq U^*$. "A rise in prices lowers real-wage rates, *enabling* employers to hire workers whose marginal product previously was lower than the real wage they would have commanded. Thus unemployment falls below U^* and $(U - U^*)$ becomes negative" (V&G, 1997, 314, emphasis added).[611]

---

[609] G&V (2000, 22) similarly links the "classical perception of the macroeconomy and the Austrian view."

[610] We note that V&G (1997, 313) assume that: "…the supply of labor (S_L) [is] a fixed proportion of the population; i.e., perfectly inelastic… For purposes of simplifying the analysis, we will assume an invariant population over time." The former assumption may be unobjectionable, but surely, in a work that uses 37½ years of quarterly data, a period in which the population increased ≈85 million or ≈50% from less than 180 million to more than 265 million, the latter is unacceptable. V&G's perfectly-inelastic labor supply puts us in a Henry Georgian situation re labor, not raw land, thus we offer "a modest proposal:" eliminate the income tax, et al., in favor of a single tax on labor.

[611] One can model a labor market such that in disequilibrium the difference between the actual and natural rates of unemployment is negative; i.e., the actual rate is less than the equilibrium rate. For example, by making the demand for labor dependent upon the actual real wage and the supply of labor dependent upon the expected real wage; however, such a model requires, at a minimum, in addition to variables for the actual, nominal wage and actual price level, an expected, nominal-wage variable. V&G have no such variable – in fact, expectations do not appear in their model at all. A model can be constructed without an explicit labor market, in which U can be less than U^*, but this entails including a variable for expectations re either price level or inflation. Again, V&G have no such variables.

V&G (1997, 314) state: "A rise in prices lowers real wage rates, enabling employers to hire workers whose marginal product previously was lower than the real wage they would have commanded. Thus unemployment falls below U*, and (U – U*) becomes negative." However, although employers may wish to hire more workers (an increase in the quantity demanded), G&V have provided no reason why more workers would be willing to work (an increase in the quantity supplied) in the face of a decrease in the real-wage rate. In a standard labor market, as in any standard supply and demand model, the quantity exchanged is at most the equilibrium quantity. At any real wage greater than or less than the equilibrium real wage, the quantity exchanged is less than would be exchanged at equilibrium, being equal to the either the quantity demanded or the quantity supplied, respectively. The quantity is determined by the lesser of the quantity demanded or the quantity supplied. Therefore,

Furthermore, "[k]eeping in mind our assumption of a fixed supply of labor, we may write (13) "$U - U^* = f(w_r^*) - f(w_r) = f(w_r^* - w_r)$ where (14) $d(U - U^*)/d(w_r^* - w_r) < 0$" (V&G, 1997, 315).[612]

If, as V&G assume, the supply of labor is perfectly inelastic, for real-wage rates at or above the equilibrium level, no change in their analysis is necessary. However, the decrease in the volume of employment and attendant increase in the amount of unemployment would be less, ceteris paribus, with a perfectly inelastic supply of labor than in the normal case of an upward-sloping supply curve of labor.[613] However, when the real-wage rate is below the equilibrium rate, employers may *desire* to employ more labor, but most emphatically they are not *able* to do so, or at least not in a society of free men. Therefore, there would be no change whatsoever in the levels of employment or unemployment when compared with their respective rates at the equilibrium real-wage. And, of course, this means that eq. (14), $d(U - U^*)/d(w_r^* - w_r) < 0$ is incorrect, or, at least, incomplete, in that it only applies if $w_r \geq w_r^*$.

I. 5. The lack of clear documentation of data sources

Because G&V (2000) did not directly provide the source(s) of their data, we assume that it was the same as in their book (V&G, 1997). However, in trying to figure out if the money-wage rate included in the ARW took into account non-wage compensation, which, of course, it should, we were led to Table B.1, in V&G, 1997, 324-327. Although they provide the data used, they do not offer adequate citations to the sources thereof, or at least not sufficiently for a non-specialist. The sources are cited as: "U.S. Department of Labor, U.S. Department of Commerce, and authors' calculations" (V&G, 1997, 327). Because the only wage-type variable in the table is "Compensation per Hour," and not "Wages per Hour," we assume that the compensation variable includes more than wages and, therefore, that the money-wage rates they used to calculate ARW included non-wage compensation as well.

G&V's model, contrary to their statements about it, does not allow for a decrease in the actual unemployment rate below the natural rate.

[612] This is an odd formulation as, other than the function $f(x) = x$, we are unaware of any function such that $f(a) - f(b) = f(a - b)$. However, this is obviously not a relevant function for the matter at hand. Again, had dimensions/units been clearly specified (Barnett, 2004) it is likely this problem would have been avoided.

[613] In a normal market with an upward-sloping, labor-supply curve, regardless of whether the real-wage rate is above or below the equilibrium rate, actual employment will *always and necessarily* be less than equilibrium employment.

Finally, $\%\Delta ARW_t = f(ARW_{t-1} - \overline{\mathbf{ARW}})$,[614] [eq. (12)], is critical. It says that the percentage change in the ARW from period t-1 to period t is a function of the divergence between the ARW in period t-1 and natural or trend value of the ARW. G&V estimate a linear form of (12):

$$(12')\ \%\Delta ARW_t = \alpha + \beta\ (ARW_{t-1} - \overline{\mathbf{ARW}}) + \varepsilon_i.^{615}$$

Although they never tell us how to calculate $\overline{\mathbf{ARW}}$, it must be done in order to estimate (12'). Assuming that a bar over a variable has the standard meaning, the mean value of the variable, this presents a problem from the point of view of Austrian economics. This school of thought is based upon praxeology – the study of human action. To make sense, we must understand (12) to mean that a divergence between the ARW in period t-1 and the equilibrium or natural value thereof means that the labor market is in a state of discoordination. That is, in retrospect, some individuals consider their behavior to have been suboptimal and make adjustments thereof. Specifically, because the ARW in t-1 was too high or too low, interpreted to mean above or below, respectively, the natural ARW, the economic actors made suboptimal decisions. Assume, as G&V do, that AP_L is constant; this means that entrepreneurs have to adjust w_r, either by adjusting either W or P, or some combination of both. Therefore peoples' behavior is affected by the value of $\overline{\mathbf{ARW}}$. However, this is anti-praxeological.

Consider, their model uses quarterly data from 1959.1 through 1996.2, some 150 quarters.[616] Let us number them from 1 (1959.1) to 150 (1996.2). Consider now the implications for human action of eq. (12), picking a data point at random, for example, 100. Then, eq. (12) reads:

$$(12)\ \%\Delta ARW_{100} = \alpha + \beta(ARW_{99} - \overline{\mathbf{ARW}})$$

However $\overline{\mathbf{ARW}} = (\Sigma\ ARW_t)/150$, t = 1 150. Therefore, people are basing their decisions in period 100 on an average value that depends on information (ARW_t, t = 100-150) that that is not yet available! And this is true for every period from 1 through 150, as even when people are acting during period 150, they are only creating data for that period. It will not be fully available until period 151. It is simply impossible to reconcile this procedure with Austrian or indeed with any rational economics.

The argument might be made that we have misinterpreted $\overline{\mathbf{ARW}}$,

---

[614] In their eq. (12) G&V write ARW_{tt-1} – ARW. We assume that the absence of a bar over ARW is a typo.

[615] Eq. (12′) is not in their paper, but it is implicit, as it is the equation that must have been estimated to arrive at (13).

[616] They assume the stock of capital goods is constant, and then use data for 37½ years!

that in fact $\overline{\mathbf{ARW}} \neq (\Sigma\ ARW_t)/150$, t = 1-150, but, rather, that in considering deviations from the average, we use not the average for the entire period, but the average value of the ARW from the beginning up to and including the period for which we are calculating the deviation, i.e., $\overline{\mathbf{ARW}} = (\Sigma\ ARW_t)/T$, t = 1…T, where T is the period whose deviation is being calculated, or, perhaps, the immediately prior period. If so, then a different, but no less fatal, problem arises. In that case the calculated value of the independent variable $(ARW_{t-1} - \overline{\mathbf{ARW}})$ depends critically upon the length of the time series used, a theoretically arbitrary length, though, perhaps not arbitrary from the point of view of data availability. Let us use our previous example, but assume that they had had used only 100 data points, from 1 (1971.3) to 100 (1996.2).

Using the same randomly chosen data point, formerly #100, now #50; (1983.4 in either case) the calculated value of the independent variable then becomes $ARW_{1983.4} - \overline{\mathbf{ARW}}_{1971.3\text{-}1983.3}$ in the case of 100 data points and $ARW_{1983.4} - \overline{\mathbf{ARW}}_{1959.1\text{-}1983.3}$ in the case of 150 data points. Moreover, not only will the value of the independent variable vary with the number of data points, but so, in consequence, will that of the dependent variable. That is, the strength of their "simple endogenous recoordinating mechanism for the macroeconomy (12) $\%\Delta ARW_t = f(ARW_{t-1} - \overline{\mathbf{ARW}})$," where $\overline{\mathbf{ARW}}$ is the "'normal' or 'natural' or 'equilibrium' value for ARW," depends on the period for which $\overline{\mathbf{ARW}}$ is calculated.

(G&V, 2003, 24) imply this choice is unimportant because: "In the data set under consideration, the initial value of ARW is 99.92 (1992 = 100) and the terminal value is 100.63. In between, the maximum value is 104.14 (in 1980.2) and the minimum is 96.24 (in 1965.4). This indicates a time series that is essentially trendless with a variation of approximately four percent, plus or minus, about its mean value (= 99.72). This is quite consistent with the notion of an underlying normal or equilibrium value. A unit root test of this data series reveals that it is a stationary series."

This is problematical for two reasons. First, the price, wage and productivity data used to calculate ARW and, a fortiori, $\overline{\mathbf{ARW}}$, is suspect. Second, according to their model, if $ARW \neq \overline{\mathbf{ARW}}$ then it will revert, and the greater the deviation the stronger the response. However, the only factor that affects the rate of reversion is the deviation of the actual ARW from the mean ARW, and time. This (implicitly) assumes there are no sectoral differences in adjustment speeds or, if such exist, that sectoral weights do not change over time. Such assumptions are highly unrealistic, from the Austrian or any other perspective. Finally, $\overline{\mathbf{ARW}}$, is an *average of averages*. Such aggregated measures and most especially any supposed relationship between their values as cause, and human action as effects, is certainly incongruous with Austrian economics

I. 7. Exogenous shocks: Inherent in the data or artifacts of the calculations

In a section on "The Sources of Discoordination," G&V suggest three possibilities: 1) an endogenous "mechanism;"[617] 2) systematic exogenous shocks; and, 3) random exogenous shocks. They then "attempt to identify the nature of the changes in the ARW variable." "[G&V] begin by defining a simple endogenous recoordinating mechanism for the macroeconomy: (12) %ΔARWt = f(ARWt-1 -ARW), which is to argue that this period's percentage change in ARW is systematically related to last period's deviation from the 'normal,' or 'natural,' or 'equilibrium' value for ARW, denoted by ARW." They then convert it to a linear form and estimate the parameters to arrive at:

$$(13)\ \%\Delta\,\mathbf{A\hat{R}Wt} = -0.007 - 0.135(ARW_{t-1} - \overline{\mathbf{ARW}}).$$[618]

They provide regression statistics, including $R^2 = 0.067$ and a t-value of 3.24 for the independent variable. They then state: "Clearly, there is a statistically significant endogenous adjustment mechanism. However, it accounts for only a small proportion of the variation in percentage changes in the ARW measure and the value of the regression parameter that describes it seems, at first glance, to be small. More will be said about this later."

They then go on to use this equation in their derivation of (16) $\%\Delta ARW_x = \%\Delta ARW_a + 0.135(ARW_{t-1} - \overline{\mathbf{ARW}})$. (16) is the basis for an extensive discussion which leads to their (G&V, 2000, 31) proposition: "(4) The exogenous shocks are random in character and generate cycles in the productivity-adjusted real wage rate (and unemployment and economic growth) in the fashion suggested by Slutsky (1927 and 1937)."

Unfortunately, their discussion and proposition are based on a derivation that is unsatisfactory. Specifically, (G&V, 2000, 24) assume: 1) an endogenous recoordinating mechanism and exogenous shocks; 2) "that the [endogenous recoordinating] mechanism described in (13) represents the *sole* source of endogenous variation in movements in ARW;" and, 3) that because "the constant term in 13 is not significantly different from zero," it may be disregarded.

---

[617] Because Austrian economists understand economics to be about purposeful human action, the use of terms such as "mechanism" are best avoided, as their use tends to divert our attention from the actions of individuals to a search for some type of mechanical process, particularly one that can be expressed in a mathematical model, which can then serve as the basis for statistical estimation of the relevant parameters, themselves assumed to be constants, of which there are none in the real world of human action. No doubt "process" would have been a better choice for a paper that purports to have an Austrian flavor.

[618] That there is no standard symbol over %ΔARWt to indicate that it is an estimated value is surely an oversight, therefore we have inserted a caret or "hat" (^) where appropriate.

The concept of exogenous shocks is reasonable in certain contexts. However, when dealing with the entire economy it makes much less sense. One is entitled to ask what sort of shock(s) might be exogenous to the whole economy? Moreover, G&V (2000, 21-22) assume that when the entire economy is discoordinated, manifested by variations in ARW, the essence of the full adjustment mechanism for the whole economy is captured in one eq. (13), which mechanism, by their own admission is "simple," taking the form of a predetermined, invariant response "that systematically relates this period's percentage change in ARW to last period's deviation from the 'normal,' or 'natural," or 'equilibrium' value for ARW" (G&V, 2000, 24).[619]

Consider now their derivation, annotated, and the consequences thereof. The key is to see that they have used three different symbols for the same variable. No doubt this was inadvertent, nevertheless it is critical to understanding the results of their statistical analysis. For G&V, $\%\Delta ARW_n$, $\%\Delta ARW_t$, and $\%\Delta ARW_a$ are one and the same. It is obvious that the former two are the same when we note that their eq. 15 arises from substituting the right-hand-side of eq. 13, $-0.135(ARW_{t-1} - \overline{\mathbf{ARW}})$ (their estimate of $\%\Delta ARW_t$) for $\%\Delta ARW_n$ in eq. 14. Note that the right hand side of eq. 13 is actually $-0.007 - 0.135(ARW_{t-1} - \overline{\mathbf{ARW}})$, but they drop the constant term -0.007 because it is not "significantly" different from zero.[620]

That $\%\Delta ARW_a = \%\Delta ARW_t$ may be understood through examination of eq.16, itself a rearrangement of the terms in eq. 15. The values of ΔARW_x are calculated.[621] Eq.16, $\%\Delta ARW_x = \%\Delta ARW_a + 0.135(ARW_{t-1} - \overline{\mathbf{ARW}})$, was used for this purpose. As we know the data used for $(ARW_{t-1} - \overline{\mathbf{ARW}})$, the only question is that of the data used for $\%\Delta ARW_a$. The answer is clear, the only data they had was that for $\%\Delta ARW_t$, the *actual* data for each time period, t, which must be what they used; i.e., $\%\Delta ARW_a = \%\Delta ARW_t$. The actual value of ARW_t is equal to its estimated value plus the error term; i.e., $\%\Delta ARW_t = \%\Delta\, \mathbf{A\hat{R}Wt} + e_t$. Therefore, $\%\Delta ARW_a = -0.007 - 0.135(ARW_{t-1} - \overline{\mathbf{ARW}}) + e_t$. If we then substitute $-0.007 - 0.135(ARW_{t-1} - \overline{\mathbf{ARW}}) + e_t$ for $\%\Delta ARW_a$ in eq.16, that equation reads: $\%\Delta ARW_x = -0.007 - 0.135(ARW_{t-1} - \overline{\mathbf{ARW}}) + e_t + 0.135(ARW_{t-1} - \overline{\mathbf{ARW}})$, or, $\%\Delta ARW_x = e_t$.

---

[619] The specific mechanism is very unAustrian because of its deterministic nature.

[620] The use of "insignificant" in this context is infelicitous. We say that because the context is statistical analysis, and in that context significance refers to the probability that the estimated parameter is different from the hypothesized value. Because the t-statistic they provide for the constant term is 0.11, they may mean that the estimated value of the constant terms is not statistically significant from the hypothesized value, (implicitly) zero. Or, they may mean that the difference between the estimated value and zero is a very small number; to wit 0.007.

[621] "Using the calculated values of the exogenous component in the adjusted real wage..." (G&V, 2000, 25).

That is, in *computing* the value of $\%\Delta ARW_x$ as the difference between the actual and estimated values of $\%\Delta ARW_t$, they calculated the error term and labeled it the percentage change in the exogenous element. They plot this data series in their figure 1, and state: "The visual pattern is suggestive of a 'white noise' series with a zero mean. This is confirmed by a correllogram analysis" (G&V, 2000, 25). Of course, it looks like "white noise." They plotted the data for a variable assumed to be random, with zero mean and constant variance;[622] i.e., the data for the error term from an OLS regression. Is it any wonder, therefore, that the "graphic representation of this data series … is suggestive of 'white noise'?" What would have been noteworthy would have been if the plot did *not* look like white noise. Certainly, then, their calculations re the exogenous part of variations in the ARW cannot support G&V's (2000, 31) conclusions.

Because the analysis in the section "The Sources of Discoordination" subsequent to eq. (16), as well as in the subsequent section, "The Impact on Contra-Cyclical Macro-economic Policy," is dependent on the calculations of $\%\Delta ARW_x$, there is no reason to analyze it.

II. Incompatibility with Austrian economics

G&V identify their own work with that of Austrianism, despite the fact that it is patently no such thing. Let us consider a few such instances[623], and demonstrate that they are mistaken not only in this regard, but also substantively erroneous in some of these cases.

II. 1. Relative-wage rates and unemployment

According to their model, provided the *average* real-wage rate is "correct," no misalignment of relative money-wage rates or of relative real-wage rates can cause unemployment. Certainly, this is not compatible with Austrian economics.

II. 2. "Money wage rates don't matter."

G&V (2000, 19) maintain that "Keynes set the spiritual tone for the next half-century with his remark, 'It can only be a foolish person who would prefer a flexible wage policy to a flexible money policy' (1936, p.268) [which] translate[d] into the notion that 'money wages don't matter.'"

---

[622] As G&V did not mention the estimation technique used, we assume they employed the standard regression method, OLS, and that the data are such that the assumptions of that statistical model regarding the error term hold; i.e., that the error term is a randomly distributed variable of zero mean and constant variance.

[623] Apart from these gratuitous citations of Austrians, there is nothing in G&V (2000) that would be at all remarkable were it to appear in the *American Economic Review* or any other such mainstream scholarly periodical, or, for that matter, the *Journal of Post Keynesian Economics*.

They then purport to "Contrast these views with those of Ludwig von Mises (1998, 577-78),"[624] obviously intended as a representative of the Austrian viewpoint:

"[it is] vain to justify a new credit expansion by referring to unused capacity, unsold … stocks and unemployed workers… The belief of the advocates of credit expansion and inflation that abstention from further … expansion and inflation ... would perpetuate the depression is utterly false. The remedies these authors suggest … would merely upset the process of recovery" [footnote omitted].

But this quote of Mises' they cite has little or nothing to do with wages, whether they "matter" or not. This is more than passing curious, in that they *could* have cited Mises (1998, 577) to the following effect just a few pages away: "If commodities cannot be sold and workers cannot find jobs, the reason can only be that the prices and wages asked are too high."

II. 3. Dissimilarities with Mises

G&V (2000, 20) offer the following as the main thesis of their article: "This fundamental disagreement between what would become the mainstream view with respect to macroeconomic policy and Mises is the focus of this article." An examination of G&V (2000), compared to any of the writings of Mises will demonstrate the falsity of this claim: The former relies heavily on mathematical argumentation[625] and equations,[626] which, for the Austrian, could only be relevant for economic history, not theory, as it is for G&V. A more thorough reading of G&V, as for example that offered in Part I of this present paper, will show in greater depth the sheer enormity of the intellectual chasm between these two sets of authors.

II. 4. G&V on the similarities between classical and Austrian macroeconomics and equilibrium

In the view of G&V (2000, 22, material in brackets inserted): "Both [classical and Austrian views on macroeconomics] are rooted in the marginalist tradition and both entertain the possible existence of a unique equilibrium position given appropriate *ceteris paribus* conditions."

However, this is somewhat misleading. First, terminology. The "classical period," insofar as microeconomics is concerned, is widely believed to end with the marginal and subjectivist revolutions usually dated 1870 or

---

[624] Minor typo: G&V's (2000, 19) cite of Mises (1998, 577-78[sic]) should be Mises (1998, 580), instead.

[625] And that in quite simple form which captures none of the complexity of the real economy that is so central to Austrian economics.

[626] There are no fewer than 17 equations in 15 short pages, but this sort of "reasoning" is virtually unprecedented in the publications of Mises or other Austrians.

there about; however, with respect to macroeconomics, the classical period is thought, at least by Keynes, to end with the Keynesian revolution usually dated around 1936. Second, "macroeconomics" refers to economic analysis that involves in a fundamental way relationships among aggregated variables. Certainly, before 1890, there really was no "classical perception of the macro-economy" in any meaningful sense.[627] Therefore, the period of "classical macroeconomics" was roughly four and one-half (4 ½) decades in length, from roughly 1890-1936. (This is not to deny the development of a variety of ideas as to how the overall economy functioned during that period and prior thereto.) Thus, it is questionable whether the term "macroeconomics" is appropriate pre-Keynes.[628]

Second the neoclassical microeconomics which dominated that period was thoroughly grounded in marginalism. So also was Austrian theory, including the Austrian theory of the cycle, that can be said to date from Mises *Theorie des Geldes und der Umlaufsmittel* in 1912 (trans. as: *The Theory of Money and Credit* (Mises, 1981 [1912]). However, it is at best questionable to what extent the various pre-Keynesian analyses of cycles can be said to be grounded in marginalism,[629] though this and similar claims seem to have arisen because of Keynes's (1936, 5-7) largely successful attempt in the General Theory to define *a* simplistic pre-Keynesian "macrotheory;" i.e., to set up a straw man as a foil for his theory. To wit [bold emphasis added]:

"**The** classical theory of employment – supposedly simple and obvious – has been based, I think, on two fundamental postulates, though practically without discussion, namely:

I. ***The*** *wage is equal to the marginal product of labour...*

II. ***The*** *utility of* ***the*** *wage when a given volume of labor is employed is equal to the marginal disutility of that amount of employment.*"

However, even though such analysis is "marginalist" in some sense, it is not marginalist from the Austrian perspective. That is, it is some sort of analysis of the relationships among aggregate variables at their margins. But, relationships, at the margin or otherwise, among aggregate variables are alien to praxeological economics.

---

627 Keynes (1936, 7), for example, said that, "...Professor Pigou's *Theory of Unemployment*[is] the only detailed account of the classical theory of employment which exists" [footnote omitted].

628 According to the OED, "macro-economic" and "macro-dynamic" were first used in 1939 (OED 1) and 1933 (OED 2), respectively. http://dictionary.oed.com/cgi/entry/00299035, http://dictionary.oed.com/cgi/entry/00299033.

629 Many were based on such concepts as overproduction, underconsumption, the denial of "Say's Law of Markets" and/or the "Equation of Exchange' and the "Quantity Theory of Money" (Schumpeter, 1954, 738-750, 1074-1135).

Third, this statement is highly problematic as it misconstrues the different positions re equilibrium within Austrianism itself, as well as in classical economics. There are two positions on this issue within what might be called the broad Austrian camp. The more popular one, exemplified by the writings of, among others, Mises (1998, 245-251) and Rothbard (1962, 467), is that the notion of equilibrium, or the "evenly rotating economy" is merely a heuristic device, an attempt to hold fast onto *ceteris paribus* conditions, the better to be able to make sense of a complex world. Yes, in this vision, there are always forces pushing markets in the direction of equilibrium, but no one (apart from a neoclassical) seriously contemplates ever reaching such a state of affairs. But, in this perspective, the concept does have some positive value, and not only for introducing sophomores to the problems attendant upon price ceilings and floors. In contrast, in what might be called the minority Austrian view (e.g., Lachmann, 1976B) the equilibrium concept is not only not of positive benefit, it is actually an impediment to clear thinking.

In sharp contrast to these Austrian views, the pre-Keynesian tradition, whether the partial equilibrium of Marshall or the general equilibrium of Walras, what is true or not true in equi-librium states is of the keenest interest. Their methodology is predicated to a surprisingly large degree upon this claim, as are their public policy recommendations[630]. And, this holds in spades for modern mainstream macroeconomics; e.g., real business cycles and New Keynesianism.

II. 5. G&V on the similarities between classical and Austrian market adjustment mechanisms

Consider the views of G&V (2000, 22) on market adjustment mechanisms:

"Where does the Austrian perception of the macroeconomy fit in this paradigmatic description? We begin by noting that there are similarities between the classical perception of the macroeconomy and the Austrian view. Both are rooted in the marginalist tradition and both entertain the possible existence of a unique equilibrium position given appropriate *ceteris paribus* condition. However, they differ in one critical point, the nature of the adjustment toward … equilibrium. The classical view is susceptible to being interpreted as arguing for instantaneous adjustment to equilibrium (Boettke 1997). In fact it is often characterized in this fashion, perhaps unfairly. Such a depiction leads to the rather obvious point that business cycle fluctuations, especially of the magnitude of the Great Depression of the 1930s, are

---

[630] In particular, the (limited) support given by the mainstream economists to anti trust legislation is strongly related to their view that the real world rarely attains the characteristics of their perfectly competitive equilibrium model. Any deviation between the two serves as a presumptive case for "competition" legislation.

evidence of the shortcomings of the classical model, and by implication, market adjustment mechanisms in general."

"By contrast, the Austrian perspective places greater emphasis on the elements of the market process, exploring the ways in which discoordination of markets occur and how markets respond to that discoordination. In general, Austrians are more interested in (10) when it reads (11) $w_r/AP_L \neq (1\text{-}a)$."

It is difficult to find support in Boettke (1997) for G&V's statement that "the classical view is susceptible to being interpreted as arguing for instantaneous adjustment to equilibrium."[631] Moreover, it seems that these authors have spilled ink merely to say that Austrians prefer $w_r/AP_L \neq (1\text{-}a)$ to the classicals' $w_r/AP_L = (1\text{-}a)$. In fact, all of this seems designed to justify their eq. (12) $\%\Delta\ ARW_t = f(ARW_{t-1} - \overline{\mathbf{ARW}})$ and (13) $\%\Delta\ \hat{\mathbf{ARW}}\mathbf{t} = -0.007 - 0.135(ARW_{t-1} - \overline{\mathbf{ARW}})$.[632]

The obvious retort to this claim is that the Great Depression was hardly characterized by a legal regime that allowed for free markets at all, let alone "market adjustment mechanisms in general." After all, this was the decade of the Smoot Hawley tariff, price supports for agriculture, as well as the cartelization of industries (NRA) and labor (NLRA) to maintain prices and wages, respectively, the CCC, WPA, PWA, and a host of other "alphabet soup" agencies, and many other accoutrements of what became known under FDR as the "New Deal." That is, it is a myth that because the Great Depression continued on for at least a decade[633] the market system failed; in reality the market process was not allowed to function.

---

[631] Boettke (1997, 49) did state: "For involuntary unemployment to be a myth, the New Classical economists posited economic actors who adjusted their behavior so quickly (for all practical purposes, instantly) that equilibrium would be achieved at all points." However, there is a world of difference between the classicals and the New Classicals, and, surely, G&V were not referring to the New Classicals in the quoted statement.

[632] The caret is missing from the LHS of G&V's eq. (13); we assume that this was an oversight. In the same equation, G&V have a bar over ARW_{t-1} as well as over ARW. As the average of a single value is identically itself, i.e., $\sum ARW_{t-1}/1 = ARW_{t-1}$, $\overline{\mathbf{ARW}}_{t-1}$ makes no sense, we assume this is a typo.

[633] Higgs (1997, 563) maintains that: "In light of the foregoing observations, we may justifiably adopt the following chronology: Great Depression, 1930 to 1940; transition to the war economy, 1940 to 1941; war-command economy, 1942 to 1945; demobilization, reconversion, and decontrol (the true Great Escape [from the Great Depression], 1945 to 1946; postwar prosperity, 1946 and beyond."

II. 6. Wage levels

Here is footnote 2 of G&V (2000, 22):

"It might be objected that Austrians are more oriented toward considerations of the structure of wages rather than their overall level.... However, both are important. Mises recognizes the significance of the level of wages in *Human Action* (1966, p. 578) when he remarks: 'Out of the collapse of the boom there is only one way out [sic].... Wage rates must drop.' See also Rothbard (1983A) regarding the role of wage levels in the Great Depression."

G&V have misconstrued the views of Mises on this issue. Compare the truncated quote of Mises in their footnote with what he actually said (we italicize what G&V left out of this quote, to demonstrate the enormous importance of the context dropped by these authors):

"Out of the collapse of the boom there is only one way *back to a state of affairs in which progressive accumulation of capital safeguards a steady improvement of material well being: new saving must accumulate the capital goods needed for a harmonious equipment of all branches of production with the capital required. One must provide the capital goods lacking in those branches which were unduly neglected in the boom.* Wage rates must drop; *people must restrict their consumption temporarily until the capital wasted by malinvestments is restored. Those who dislike these hardships of the readjustment period must abstain in time from credit expansion"* (Mises, 1998, 575-576).

Based upon the mangled G&V quote one would think that Mises would support their focus on average wage rates, when this was really no part of his intention. Mises was concerned primarily with relative prices. Moreover, *if, arguendo,* we interpret Mises in the manner to which G&V wish us to, he was only speaking roughly. It is simply not true that *all* wage rates must drop. Very much to the contrary, during the cleansing bust phase of the depression, *only* those wage rates in the higher or earlier or more interest rate sensitive orders of production (a concept that appears nowhere in G&V, and yet is highly relevant to their concerns) must drop. This is because there was *over* investment in these areas of the economy, which need to be written down or off. However, and this cannot possibly be overemphasized, wage rates must *increase*, at least relatively, in the lower or later or less interest rate sensitive orders of production, because, previously, during the boom, they were decreased, at least relatively. We must never forget that the Austrian Theory of the Business Cycle is *neither* an overinvest-ment nor yet an under-investment theory; rather, it is a *mal*investment theory. But the malinvestments take the form of *over* investment in the capital goods sector (this is why not only must wages fall there, but so must other prices) and *under* investment in the lower orders of production, preeminently in non durable consumer goods (this is why not only must wages *rise* there, but so must other prices).

And what of Rothbard? G&V (2000, 22, n.2) purport to find support by him for their distinctively non-Austrian views, when they aver in this context: "See also Rothbard (1963) for a discussion of the role of wage levels in the Great Depression?" We do not think so. Rothbard (1983A [1963], 238) supportively offers the position of Hugh Bancroft, publisher of Barron's: "… it was particularly necessary for wage rates to decline in the producer goods' industries in view of the great decline in prices there." Elsewhere (1983A, 51) Rothbard states: "Business as we have pointed out, depends for its profitability on price *differentials* between factor and selling prices, not upon general price levels." Because a wage is a price, we see that Rothbard, in contradistinction to G&V, was concerned with wage rates relative to other prices and not with their levels.[634]

II. 7. Exogenous or endogenous

In Keynes' vision of the economy, the source of the business cycle is instability in invest-ment. "*Any* fluctuation in investment not offset by a corresponding change in the propensity to consume will, of course, result in a fluctuation in employment" (Keynes, 1936, 314). Further, "But I suggest that a more typical, and often the predominant, explanation of the crisis is, not primarily a rise in the rate of interest, but a sudden collapse in the marginal efficiency of capital" (Keynes, 1936, 315). For Keynes, the downturn is caused by a "market failure:" the collapse of investment demand because of a sudden deflation of businessmen's "animal spirits," themselves irrational to begin with. Only government intervention, appropriate both as to type and magnitude, can save the day. Austrians, in contrast, see the bust as the necessary consequence of the false boom, itself stemming from prior inflationary monetary policy, that interfered with market signals, pre-eminently the interest rate. For them, there is no other way to explain the cluster of entrepreneurial errors that constitute the business cycle. To the question, "Why do entrepreneurs, whose very survival and prosperity is predicated upon successful anticipation of prices, act like lemmings rushing into the sea in the depression?" only the Austrians answer that they operate on the basis of market signals, and these are perverted by governmental monetary policy.[635]

---

[634] Rothbard (1963, 154-155) is concerned with wages in *manufacturing*, a proxy for the higher, earlier or more interest rate sensitive orders of production, not with *all* wages, or the wage *level*.

[635] Cycles are misallocations of resources caused by inaccurate calculations (of expected profits) based on "dishonest prices," themselves a consequence of "dishonest money" that is lent into existence during a governmental policy induced monetary-credit expansion. Thanks to Tony Deden who stated, at the 9th Austrian Scholars Conference in March, 2003: "[You] cannot have honest accounting if you have dishonest money."

How do G&V (2000, 27) deal with this issue? In their view, there are two "sources of stability. One, of course, is the modest, but important, recoordinating mechanism we have described. The second is less evident, but certainly significant. It takes the form of a phenom-enon articulated by Slutsky in the 1920s. In a paper published in Moscow (1927) he demonstrated that random perturbations in a basic data series are capable of generating cycles in the data" (footnote omitted). Say what you will about this theory, one thing is certain, it is *not* an Austrian perspective. But further, it is a highly problematic one, as it does not even address itself to the structure of production or interest rate sensitivity, essential elements of the Austrian Business Cycle Theory (ABCT). Nor does it even broach the cluster of errors phenomenon, much less answer it.

II. 8. Contracyclical macroeconomic policy-making is an exercise in futility

According to point 8 of G&V (2000, 32), "… the notion of short run contracyclical macroeconomic policy making is an exercise in futility."

At first glance, there are good and sufficient reasons for taking this stance. Rothbard (undated, 25-26) himself has stated: "What is the governmental role in the cure of depression? … what the government should do, according to the Misesian analysis of the depression, is absolutely nothing. It should only from the point of view of economic health and ending the depression as quickly as possible, maintain a strict hands off, '*laissez faire'* policy. Anything it does will delay and obstruct the adjustment process of the market."

It is hard to see how the public policy advice could be more definitive. And yet, let us take another look at the matter, for it is our contention that Rothbard is, as are G&V, incorrect in this assessment, and is corrected by no less an expert than, paradoxically, Rothbard himself. For he *also* says (undated, 26) after giving a long list of things government should not do[636]: "The government must do nothing to encourage consumption, and it must not increase its own expenditures, for this will further increase the social consumption/investment ratio. In fact, cutting the government budget will improve the ratio. What the economy needs is not more consumption spending but more saving in order to validate some of the excessive investments in the boom."

That is, Rothbard in effect contradicts himself. First he maintains the state should do "absolutely nothing"; then, that it should reduce its budget, which is certainly doing *something.* Rothbard is too much of a libertarian to call for the state to *do* anything other than cutting back its scope of activity, but surely to do this is to *act.* Reading in between the lines of Rothbard

---

636 It should not inflate, prop up failing businesses, promote wage increases or prohibit decreases through law.

(undated), we may infer that were government to subsidize saving and penalize consumption, he would not think it all to the bad, insofar as this is *precisely* the medicine implied by ABCT for the cure of the depression.

Of course, whether or not the state could *succeed* in any such operation is greatly to be doubted, given the wealth of libertarian, Austrian and even Public Choice analysis to the contrary. The point is, arguendo, that *if* credence could be placed in central planning, which it most certainly cannot, then, at least, this would be the direction indicated for intervention, at least insofar as interventions intended to directly to affect saving and/or consumption are concerned. Moreover, cutting governmental expenditures, cutting tax rates, and reducing or eliminating anticompetitive regulations would also hasten the recovery.[637]

II. 9. The centrality of the productivity-adjusted real wage

G&V (2000, 31) maintain: "All major macroeconomic paradigms have as their centerpiece the productivity-adjusted real wage." But either Austrian economics is not a major macroeconomic paradigm or else this proposition is false. The essence of ABCT is an unsustainable misallocation of resources induced by a fiat credit expansion; it is not at all the productivity-adjusted real wage. This term *never* even appears in either *Human Action* or *Man, Economy, and State.* Nor is there an entry for "real wage(s)" in the index of either of these treatises. Further, one looks in vain in the index of Garrison's (2001) book on ABCT for either "productivity" or "real wage(s)." Certainly, then, this concept is not central to ABCT. Of course, that may merely mean that ABCT is not a major macroeconomic paradigm.

III. Conclusion

In their very last paragraph they (G&V, 2000, 32) state: "... it is clear that Mises's vision of the nature of the macroeconomy is substantiated by our findings." We totally disagree.

Austrians ought not to get involved with aggregation, simple / simplistic math models, and nonsensical statistical models/estimations. The very few valid points in G&V can be made without these. "While it is, no doubt, possible to construct economic aggregates and to test them empirically in such a way that their conclusions appear consistent with the general vision of Mises, this is a method that is entirely and profoundly antithetical to his conception of economics." These are the words of our super referee.

There may be a (very weak and limited) sense in which G&V can be interpreted as compatible with Austrianism, apart from the foregoing. They

[637] It should be noted that Keynesians would agree that cutting tax rates would be countercyclical in a downturn, they would not agree that cutting governmental expenditures in the same circumstances would be countercyclical; rather, they would think such a policy would exacerbate the downturn.

mention Austrians in their paper.[638] But this simply is not good enough. Mere lip service paid to a few leaders is not sufficient to warrant membership in a distinct school of thought. It is as if an atheist were to mention "God," and "explain" how his position on morals is compatible with His moral code, and, on that basis, a religious order were to seize upon such a statement as indicating the atheist to be a believer.

There was a period of time during which the very existence of the Austrian school was threatened by a dearth of followers (Rockwell, 1995). Did such a possibility constitute a legitimate excuse for this sort of thing in those dark days of Austrianism? That question calls for tactical and strategic insights, to say nothing of an ethical analysis. Were Austrians under those conditions to accept as praxeological that which is patently no such thing, it would constitute a sort of intellectual fraud. Whether it would have been worth doing, were this the *only* way to keep the tradition alive, is a question beyond the scope of the present paper.

The Austrian school is now so well established that it ought to be well beyond any temptation to characterize as Austrian obviously mainstream work that merely condescends to mention its name and some of its leading lights. Nevertheless, that is exactly the case regarding G&V. We conclude that there is every need for a paper such as this present one, which strips away the supposed veneer of Austrianism from a publication which is no such thing.

[638] They also discuss marginalism. But this is hardly unique to Austrians. There are three economists typically credited (The Concise Encyclopedia of Economics) with the birth of this idea: Menger, Jevons, and Walras. The first was indeed an Austrian; but the others most certainly were not

Chapter 26. The Austrian Tent? A Rejoinder to Gallaway and Vedder

How do neoclassical economists reply to Austrian critiques of their work? Typically, although to be sure there are exceptions, they ignore them.[639] That is, the former move mountains in an effort to avoid the arguments of the latter. Sometimes this occurs even when neoclassicals explicitly reply to Austrian critiques.

A case in point is Gallaway and Vedder (2006). Ostensibly written as a critique of Barnett and Block (2006A), this "Reply" manages to ignore every substantive criticism leveled at them by their critics. Instead, it focuses on a point irrelevant to the substantive issues, but an interesting one for all that.

What are the specifics? Barnett and Block (2006A) took to task Gallaway and Vedder[640] (1987, 1997 and 2000). Here are the criticisms launched by the former at the latter (Barnett and Block, 2006A, 58):

"... what sets Austrians apart from mainstream economists is methodology.... It is thus with the methods and analysis of G&V that we take issue. To that end we pursue in part I six strands: 1) excessive aggregation,the meaning of 'the *wage rate*,' and the 'adjusted real wage;' 2) average v. marginal productivity and reality v. perfect competition; 3) consequences for unemployment of disequilibrium real-wage rates in the labor market and implications of perfectly inelastic labor supply; 4) the lack of clear documentation of data sources; 5) statistics, and 'normal' or 'natural' values; and, 6) exogenous shocks: inherent in the data or artifacts of the calculations. In part II we address some further questions concerning the classification status of G&V (2000) and claim that despite its 'tipping of the hat' in the direction of Austrian economics, it cannot be properly categorized as compatible with that school of thought."

In other words, our *main* focus in B&B (2006) was in our part I (pp. 58-72), where we challenged them on substantive issues. Since they claimed to be Austrians we considered that claim in our part II (pp. 72-79). But even here in this second section of our paper we (B&B, 2006, 72) charged G&V with being "substantively erroneous."

And what is the response of G&V (2006)? It is to completely ignore our substantive criticisms, every last one of them, and to focus, instead, on our characterization of them as mainstream economists, not Austrians.[641] So

[639] Block, Westley and Padilla (forthcoming) lists some 100 instances where the two schools of thought have tangled.

[640] Hence, B&B and G&V

[641] Despite rejecting this claim, we do take kindly to it. After all, if neoclassicals are falsely claiming adherence to praxeological principles, this is surely a sign of success for Austrian economics.

be it. If they implicitly accept our substantive criticisms by not replying to them in their "Reply,"[642] we are happy to acknowledge this concession. Let us, then, consider the points they do make.

They (G&V, 2006, 67) are concerned about the "economic taxonomy" in which we have categorized them. One defense of their Austrian "bona fides" is that they have "proceeded in good faith (G&V, 2006, 68)." But good faith is neither a sufficient nor necessary condition for being properly classified as an Austrian.

Another defense is the letter written to them (G&V, 2006, 68) by Murray N. Rothbard, dated 11/21/83, accepting a paper of theirs for publication in the *Review of Austrian Economics* (G&V, 1987). We repeat it here:

"One criticism, for example is that Mises' insight that unemployment is caused by excessively high wage rates in not uniquely Austrian, and it not essential to Austrian business cycle theory. Since it is part of Austrian theory, however, and since Mises was one of the few people hammering away at this, your reference to Mises is perfectly justified (also, business cycle theory is not all there is to Austrian economics.)"

This Rothbard letter is mentioned (G&V, 2006, 68) to rebut our claim (B&B, 2006, 76, 80) that G&V (2006) "mangled" a Mises quote, and "condescended" to Austrians. But this letter simply cannot bear the weight G&V place upon it. Yes, to be sure, the "insight that unemployment is caused by excessively high wage rates is not uniquely Austrian" is true. It is also true that "Mises was one of the few people hammering away at this," which makes it an Austrian concern, albeit not uniquely so. On this matter, all Austrians and many if not most neo-classicals overlap.[643] But so what? B&B (2006) didn't even come close to criticizing any of the publications of G&V on *this* particular ground. Merely because we did indeed take G&V to task for "mangling" and "condescending" does not mean we take issue with these authors on *everything* they ever said, let alone regarding this particular point.

The *core* of Austrian business cycle theory (ABCT), it cannot be denied, does indeed concern things like "monetary creation, interest rates and capital theory" (G&V, 2006, 68). Of course, unions, and minimum wage laws create unemployment, as do subsidies such as unemployment

---

642 G&V (2006, 67) state: "We do not want to destroy a lot a (sic) trees in a detailed line-by-line defense of our position…" However, contrary to GV, it would not take too many trees to reply substantively; QJ isn't a mass circulation journal. If they were so worried about trees, or, more to the point, precious and severely limited pages of one of the few refereed journal open to Austrian ideas, why waste so many of them on avoiding our substantive criticisms?

643 Card and Krueger (1994) would certainly be an exception at least with respect to low-wage jobs.

"insurance," and, yes, some of these phenomena played a role in the events of the 1930s. But this still does not render them *central* to ABCT, or, indeed, even related to it. The Smoot-Hawley tariff also was instrumental in playing havoc with our economy during this epoch. But, surely, no one would go so far as to claim that protectionism is the essence of ABCT; or, even, that tariffs are part of the ABCT story.[644] Thus, G&V (2006, 68, emphasis added) are wrong in their contention that "*any* action … that lead (sic) prices of factors of production to deviate from their 'natural' level determined by human action, sets the stage ultimately for a boom and bust condition that we call 'business cycles.'" Perhaps that is a neoclassical view, but it is certainly not an Austrian one. Certainly, governmental intervention that mandates the blending of ethanol with gasoline, thereby distorting various relative prices; e.g., increasing those of ethanol and corn, cause misallocations of resources, but no Austrian would expect such regulations to give rise to a business cycle.

According to G&V (2006, 68-69), "In their analysis, Barnett and Block imply that at one point in time, say 1995 and earlier, Austrians were a relatively small tenuously established group that perhaps had to take a 'big tent' approach to defining Austrian economics for strategic reasons, but at the present time, the school is large and growing, and such expediencies are no longer needed." In other words, we Austrians tolerated the likes of G&V in the early days, but, now that we no longer need them, it is time for the old "heave ho." This is an interesting hypothesis, and perhaps one that G&V would care to test empirically, but none of it can be reconciled with what we actually said in B&B. Instead, we called it no less than an "intellectual fraud" (B&B, 2006, 80) to do any such thing, and this offense is a timeless one.

State G&V (2006, 69): "Being somewhat libertarian inclined, we have always been uncomfortable with being identified by group characteristics." Not only do these authors not understand Austrianism, this applies to their comprehension of libertarianism as well. Group characteristics that apply to G&V include white, male, economists, professors, of a certain age, etc.[645] How and why libertarianism would mitigate against anyone, including themselves, ascribing such characteristics to them must surely be a mystery.

We, too, "have no desire to engage in a prolonged debate on" (G&V, 2006, 69) whether and to what extent these authors are Austrians. That much, at least, is clear. "Fellow travelers" will do quite nicely in describing them. However, we had indeed hoped for a reaction to our *substantive* economic points. In this, alas, we remain disappointed.

---

[644] It is true that barriers to trade can slow down the adjustment process during the post-crisis bust.

[645] Come to think of it, if we may be so bold, these characteristics also apply to the present authors.

Chapter 27. Ron Paul and the Fed: A Rejoinder to David Frum.

According to David Frum:

"Ron Paul … is best known for his vehemently isolationist foreign policy views. But his core supporters also thrill to his self-taught monetary views, which amount to a rejection of everything taught by modern economists from Alfred Marshall to Milton Friedman.

"… Paul (has) not the faintest idea of what (he) is talking about. The problem is not that (his) answers are wrong – that can happen to anyone. The problem is that (he does not) understand the questions, and (is) too lazy or too arrogant to learn."

There is more wrong here than you can shake a stick at. Let us list the errors.

Congressman Paul is *not* an isolationist; rather, he is a *non-interventionist.* He has repeated this over and over again, but, evidently, Frum has still not caught on. An isolationist wants to, well, *isolate* our country from all others. Dr. Paul desires nothing of the sort. Rather, he wants the U.S. to be fully involved in world affairs. He seeks cultural, social and economic relationships with members of all other nations. He only rejects the imposition of our values on others at the point of a gun; that is, he opposes *interventionism.* In this he may be out of step with the other candidates for the Republican nomination, but not at all with our founding fathers:

"My ardent desire is, and my aim has been...to comply strictly with all our engagements foreign and domestic; but to keep the United States free from political connections with every other Country. To see that they may be independent of all, and under the influence of none. In a word, I want an American character, that the powers of Europe may be convinced we act for ourselves and not for others; this, in my judgment, is the only way to be respected abroad and happy at home." – George Washington (letter to Patrick Henry, 9 October 1775) Reference: *The Writings of George Washington, Fitzpatrick*, ed., vol. 34 (335)

"Peace, commerce and honest friendship with all nations – entangling alliances with none, I deem [one of] the essential principles of our government, and consequently [one of] those which ought to shape its administration." – Thomas Jefferson: 1st Inaugural Address, 1801. ME 3:321

"But [the United States] goes not abroad, in search of monsters to destroy. She is the well-wisher to the freedom and independence of all. She is the champion and vindicator only of her own.

"She will commend the general cause by the countenance of her voice, and the benignant sympathy of her example. She well knows that by once enlisting under other banners than her own, were they even the banners of foreign independence, she would involve herself beyond the power of extrication, in all the wars of interest and intrigue, of individual avarice, envy, and ambition, which assume the colors and usurp the standard of freedom. The fundamental maxims of her policy would insensibly change from liberty to force.... She might become the dictatress of the world. She would be no longer the ruler of her own spirit...." *When John Quincy Adams served as U. S. Secretary of State, he delivered this speech to the U.S. House of Representatives on July 4, 1821, in celebration of American Independence Day.*

Nor is Dr. Paul opposed to our imperialist venture in Iraq merely "because what we are doing in Iraq isn't working." He opposes this since such policies are incompatible with the views of the founding fathers, with the Constitution, and because no one from On High has appointed us to be the policeman of the world. In any case, whether something "works" or not depends entirely upon one's goal. The present debacle in that tormented country is "working" just fine, thank you, for the likes of Bechtel and Halliburton.

His monetary views are not at all "self-taught." He readily admits he stands on the shoulders of giants in this regard, members of the Austrian School of Economics, preeminently, Ludwig von Mises and Murray Rothbard. However, even if Frum was correct on this and Paul's economic views were self-taught, that at least implies he has *learned* some of the dismal science, unlike many of his fellow congressmen, and even some journalists (hint, hint, Frum). Moreover he is actually a many times published author on this subject.

Alfred Marshall (1842–1924) is hardly a "modern economist."

"Lazy?" "Arrogant?" Sounds more like the author of these words than Ron Paul. The congressman from Texas, who is now crisscrossing the country giving speeches at a rate that would exhaust a much younger man, may be the most well-read member of the House of Representatives. Okay, okay, to say that is to damn with faint praise. Let us put it in these terms then; were he not a politician, *and* a doctor, *his published research in economics* would alone falsify Frum's charge.

This "indictment" constitutes nothing more than name-calling. Frum does not mention even *one* specific error made by Paul. He contents himself with the material quoted above.

Despite the glee with which we have pointed out these errors, the main focus of the present essay, however, concerns the oft made charge that Mr. Paul is "kooky" in his criticism of the Fed. After all, this monetary institution has been around since 1913, almost 100 years. Is it not irresponsible to advocate its demise?

Well, no. Very much to the contrary, Ron Paul's plan to abolish the Fed is the essence of monetary soundness. And this for several reasons. Under the control of this "venerable" institution, inflation has soared.

According to the inflation calculator, "What cost **$100.00** in 1913 would cost $**2014.81** in 2006. Also, if you were to buy exactly the same products in 2006 and 1913, they would cost you $**100.00** and $**4.96** respectively." In other words, under the aegis of the Fed, every $1.00 under its control is now worth slightly less than $.05, or a nickel.

Let us compare this with a similar 93-year time period before the creation of the Fed. This calculation shows that "What cost **$100.00** in 1820 would cost $**63.02** in 1913. Also, if you were to buy exactly the same products in 1913 and 1820, they would cost you $**100.00** and **$158.69** respectively." In other words, the dollar held its value to a far greater degree under the relatively more free market situation before the advent of the Fed. (Indeed, it was worth *more* at the end of that period than at its beginning.) What is so "kooky" about ridding ourselves of an institution that debauches the currency to such a degree, particularly when the free enterprise system has shown money not only need not lose its value but can actually increase in purchasing power?

Far from "ironing out" the business cycle, under the watch of the Fed it has been exacerbated.

But is not Frum correct in asserting that Paul is "out of touch" with the respectable mainstream of the economics profession, as represented by Milton Friedman. Yes, this cannot be denied. Just as Dr. Paul is "out of touch" with the mainstream media, so is this true in terms of what passes for the community of "expert" economists.

Milton Friedman, although linked in the public mind as the chief exemplar of free enterprise, was actually no such thing. Rothbard shows that his claim as a leading spokesman for liberty and the marketplace is highly overblown. This is a conclusion that emerges from this exchange as well: Friedman and Block, 2006. Further, Prof. Friedman is particularly weak in the monetary arena as an exemplar of capitalism.

Here is an interesting quote from Milton Friedman, which is very much apropos to our present concerns:

Major premise: Socialism is a failure. Even lifelong Communists now accept this proposition. Wherever socialism has been tried, it has proved unable to deliver the goods, either in the material form of a high standard of living or in the immaterial form of human freedom.

Minor premise: Capitalism is a success. Economies that have used capitalism – free private markets – as their principal means of organizing economic activity have proved capable of combining widely shared prosperity and a high measure of human freedom. A private market system has proved to be a necessary though not a sufficient condition for prosperity and freedom.

Conclusion: The U.S. needs more socialism. An obvious non sequitur, yet there is no denying that many apparently reasonable people – including most members of Congress and of the Bush administration – accept all three propositions simultaneously.

This, we readily admit, is a *brilliant* way to put matters. It is not for nothing that this economist has a wide reputation as a defender of private property rights and free enterprise. The only problem with it is that it applies to Friedman himself, certainly in the field of monetary economics.

For the Fed is to money as is the central planner to the entire economy. In other words, unpalatable and uncharitable as it sounds, for much of his career Milton Freidman was a monetary socialist. What, after all, is the case in favor of governmental monopolization of the money supply? It is no stronger for state control over education, or retirement funds, or health or welfare, or the post office or, indeed, much if anything else. And, a case can easily be made that money is more important than any of these other things. After all, it constitutes the very lifeblood of the entire economy, upon which all of these other things intimately depend. That is, without an economy, we need not "worry" about education, the post office, food, etc. And without money, there is only barter; a modern economic system is precluded.

There are those who wish to consign this crucial institution to the tender mercies of the government. Ron Paul, happily, is not one of them. For this he is forced to bear the howls and outrage from economic illiterates such as David Frum, and, yes, Milton Friedman, at least for long stretches of his career. (At least the latter has written voluminously on this matter; the former confines himself to sneers.)

The advantage of the gold standard, vis-à-vis fiat currency supplied by government is that the state cannot inflate the former. Thus, it functions, at least relatively, as a veritable Rock of Gibraltar. In fact, had we remained on a gold standard we would have been far better off than at present. Any example illustrating this claim would be an underestimate of the benefits of free market money for if we had remained on the gold standard, there would be a lot more gold today than there now is. The extra demand for it would have led to more exploration and development, better technologies for extracting gold from ore, and more substitution from non-monetary uses, and the complementary use of other commodities as money. Nevertheless, we offer the following: 1 oz gold was worth approximately $20 in 1913 and today about $800, so it takes approximately 40 times more dollars to buy an ounce of gold at present.

In this regard states J. H. Huebert: "And with the subprime mortgage meltdown and the dollar's value collapsing, another of Dr. Paul's campaign issues is gaining traction – his desire to abolish the Federal Reserve, an unaccountable, privately owned bankers' bank that inflates the money supply.

This makes the dollars in your pocket, your savings, and your investments worth less and less each year as the politically favored recipients of the Fed's new money profit at ordinary Americans' expense. The other candidates, who have benefited from the status quo, ignore the issue, but Ron Paul has been fearless; clips of him grilling Fed Chairman Ben Bernanke at congressional hearings have been a surprise hit on YouTube."

But Frum's case is far worse than all this would indicate. We have mentioned above that the Frumster was correct in at least one of his allegations: for many years, Milton Friedman was indeed a bitter opponent of the gold standard, in opposition to Ron Paul's position on the matter. However, Friedman was a "second thoughtster" on this matter, as demonstrated by Richard Ebeling. This economist demonstrates that toward the end of his career, Friedman came to support, if not in full, and enthusiastically, then at least in great part, Ron Paul's views on monetary institutions.

Let us allow Friedman to speak for himself on this matter, courtesy of Ebeling's research:

"Most of my own work dealing with public policy has had the same character of proceeding as if I were addressing governmental officials selflessly dedicated to the public interest. I have attempted to persuade the Federal Reserve System that it was doing the wrong thing and it ought to adopt a different policy. This time was ill spent because the public-interest characterization of government, is basically flawed.... We do not regard a businessman as selflessly devoted to the public interest. We think of a businessman as in business to improve his own welfare, to serve his own interest.... Why should we regard government officials differently? They too aim to serve their own interest, and in government as in business we must try to set up institutions under which individuals who intend only their own gain are led by an invisible hand to serve the public interest. The Federal Reserve System puts a great deal of power in the hands of a few people and it is so constructed that it has been in their self-interest to pursue a policy which, I believe, has been very harmful for the public rather than helpful.... Clearly, it was not in the self-interest of the Federal Reserve hierarchy to follow the hypothetical policy [of a monetary rule]. It was therefore a waste of time to try to persuade them to do so."

States Ebeling: "But by the mid 1980s, Friedman had second thoughts about whether government could be trusted ever to follow the necessary restraint to provide this supposedly superior paper money system. He began to regularly quote a sentence from Irving Fisher's 1911 book, *The Purchasing Power of Money*: 'Irredeemable paper money has almost invariably proved a curse to the country employing it.'"

Here, again, thanks to Ebeling, is another quote on this matter from Friedman and his co-author Anna Schwartz from their publication: "Has Government Any Role in Money?"

"The apparently great value to the economy of having a single unit of account linked with an (ultimate) medium of exchange does not mean that government must play any role, or that there need be a single producer of the medium of exchange. And indeed, historically, governments have entered the picture after the event, after the community had settled on a unit of account and private producers had produced media of exchange.... Historically, producers of money have established confidence by promising convertibility into some dominant money, generally specie [e.g., gold or silver]. Many examples can be cited of fairly long-continued and successful producers of private moneys convertible into specie. We do not know, however, of any example of the private production of purely inconvertible fiduciary moneys."

Friedman and Schwartz continued:

"Our own conclusion ... is that leaving monetary and banking arrangements to the market would have produced a more satisfactory outcome than was actually achieved through government involvement."

"Let me emphasize that this note is not a plea for a return to a gold standard.... I regard a return to a gold standard as neither desirable nor feasible – with the one exception that it might become feasible if the doomsday predictions of hyperinflation under our present system should prove correct."

In another publication, "Has Gold Lost Its Monetary Role?" Friedman said, in an almost direct refutation of Frum:

"If you could re-establish a world in which government's budget accounted for 10 percent of the national income, in which *laissez-faire* reigned, in which governments did not interfere with economic activities and in which full employment policies had been relegated to the dustbin, in such a world you might be able to restore a real gold standard. A real honest-to-God gold standard is not feasible because there is essentially no government in the world that is willing to surrender control over its domestic monetary policy."

In his "Real and Pseudo Gold Standards," Friedman explained:

"Under such a real gold standard, private persons or government might go into the business of offering storage facilities, and warehouse receipts might be found more convenient than the gold itself for transactions. If individuals find warehouse certificates for gold more useful than literal gold, private enterprise can certainly provide the service of storing the gold. Why should gold storage and the issuance of warehouse certificates be a nationalized industry? Finally, private persons or governments might issue promises to pay gold either on demand or after a specific time interval which were not warehouse receipts but nevertheless were widely acceptable because of confidence that the promises would be redeemed. Such promises to pay would still not alter the basic character of the gold standard so long as the obligors were not retroactively relieved from fulfilling their promises, and this would be true even if such promises were not fulfilled on time, just as the default of dollar bond issues does not alter the monetary standard. But, of course, promises to pay that were in default or that were expected to be defaulted would not sell at face value, just as bonds in default trade at a discount.... Such a system might, and I believe would, raise grave social problems and foster pressure for government prohibition of or control over the issue of promises to pay gold on demand. But that is beside my present point, which is that it would be a real gold standard."

Let us consider yet another refutation of Frum's position from Friedman's pen: "A real gold standard is thoroughly consistent with [classical] liberal principles and I, for one, am entirely in favor of measures promoting its development."

To conclude. Frum attempts to prove that Congressman Paul is a monetary crank because he differs with Milton Friedman. While it cannot be denied that Dr. Ron Paul and Professor Milton Friedman have some differences on this matter, Frum's contention is nonsense. Paul's critique of the Fed, and support of a free market stateless money system is hardly a "rejection of everything taught by modern economists (such as) Milton Friedman."

Chapter 28. Saving and Investment: A Praxeological Approach

I. Introduction

Science requires, *inter alia*, precision and consistency with respect to its fundamental concepts. One problem of long standing that sets economics apart from the natural sciences is the equivocal and inconsistent use by economists of expressions intended to convey a technical meaning. This paper considers difficulties involved with the concepts and uses of the terms "saving," "investment," and "loanable funds." Because confusion of concepts and terms leads to faulty analysis and conclusions, we are drawn to consideration of: "the" demand for, and supply of, money; the nature interest and interest rates; the relationship of productivity to interest and interest rates; "the" market for loanable funds in contradistinction to "the" market for financial assets; and the connection between forced saving and mal-investment. Some implications for business cycle theory are drawn, especially for problems therewith.

In section II we discuss saving and investment, in an attempt to dispel some of this confusion, and move toward systematizing matters in this regard. We conclude in section III.

II. Saving and Investment

Much confusion in economic theory arises because of an unscientific failure by economists to use words and terms consistently and unambiguously. In the case at hand, we focus on the failure to distinguish between "real" saving and investment and "financial" saving and investment. As soon as one understands leisure to be a form of consumption and exchange a form of production,[646] it is obvious that all one can do as an economic actor is produce or consume. There is no other alternative, though it is possible to produce and consume at the same time, and some people do so not infrequently. But that raises some interesting questions. For example, what does "he saved" or "he invested," or "saving precedes investment," mean?

We begin with saving. It is clear that saving is not consumption. It is, after all, a temporary renunciation of something enjoyable. Therefore it must be production. The real meaning, in this context, of "to save" is "to prepare for the future;" i.e., to arrange for future acts of consumption. Alternatively, saving is the difference between physical production and physical consumption. "To consume," in this context, means to act so as to directly satisfy a want; i.e., consumption is an act intended to directly satisfy a present desire. The standard textbook definition of saving is in terms of foregoing consumption (Samuelson and Nordhaus, 1985., pp. 52 –53;

[646] For an argument that exchange is not a category of action separate from production, and, that therefore, money is a capital good, see: Barnett and Block, 2001.

Mankiw, 2001, pp. 274-275).[647] But, as we have seen, the only way one can forego consumption (act in a way that does not directly satisfy a want) is to *produce*; i.e., the only alternative to consumption is production.

Production is action that is expected to add value; i.e., expected in an ex ante sense to increase human want satisfaction, directly or indirectly. Alternatively, it may be thought of as action that transforms goods from a higher to a lower order. Goods[648] can be categorized as consumers' goods or capital (producers') goods. Consumers' goods are used to directly satisfy wants; capital goods are used in the production of yet other goods, either consumers' or capital. Production, then, consists of producing consumers' services, tangible consumers' goods, capital services, or tangible capital goods.[649]

Production of capital services and tangible capital goods is saving; or, alternatively expressed, one can (attempt to)[650] save by producing capital services and tangible capital goods, and one is saving when one is producing such goods. As with goods, all services are either consumers' services or capital services. The former are intended to directly satisfy a human want; e.g., a haircut, where recipient desires this service for reasons having to do with his role as a consumer, not as a producer. The latter are intended to cooperate in the production of other goods, thereby indirectly satisfying a human want; e.g., the professional services of a petroleum engineer employed by an oil company. But the production of capital services and tangible capital goods is precisely what is referred to as real, in contradistinction to financial, investment. Financial investment consists in exchanging an asset, usually money, for the title to another asset. Therefore, at least insofar as capital services and tangible capital goods are concerned, the act of saving is the act of production

---

[647] It might be argued that not to use up all or a portion of a preexisting stock of goods is to save. However, to fail to do something is not an act and therefore irrelevant to economics. Moreover, that would trivialize the concept, for then any preexisting good would constitute and infinite amount of saving. For example, if one had a can of corn and did not consume it instantly, the can would be continually saved and, therefore, the quantity of saving would be infinite. The stock of preexisting goods constitutes *savings*, and the flow of newly produced goods that are not consumed constitute *saving* and adds to the stock of savings while the using up of preexisting consumers' goods and the physical depreciation of capital goods subtracts from the stock of savings. Net saving which augments savings, then, is saving minus the using up of preexisting capital goods and the physical depreciation of capital goods. And, although saving can never be negative, net saving certainly can be.

[648] Throughout, "goods" also refers to intangibles; i.e., services, and leisure as well as tangibles. Leisure is both a consumption and a(n intangible) consumers' good.

[649] Examples of each are, respectively: a concert; leisure clothes; legal advice in a business matter; and, construction of a factory.

[650] Because all action is forward looking, one can never be sure that the end aimed at will be achieved by the means chosen.

of those goods, which is in turn the act of investment in those goods. This type of saving and investment is referred to as capitalist saving and investment.

But what of the production of consumer services and tangible consumer goods? Here matters are a little more complex. The reason is that all production is forward looking; we produce now to consume in the future, no matter how short the time span between the production and the consumption. This is true even with respect to those acts of production that are also acts of consumption for the producer; i.e., for the producer/consumer. Examples of such "dual" actions are: the professor of economics for whom teaching directly satisfies a want; the physician for whom healing directly satisfies a want; and, the symphony musician for whom performing directly satisfies a want. Of course, in each of these cases the actions are also acts of production of valuable services to the consumers thereof.

Moreover, all tangible consumers' goods are durable to a greater or lesser extent. This leads to an arbitrary, but analytically very useful, distinction. Tangible consumer goods may be categorized as either consumables or durables based on the greater or lesser extent of their useful lives.[651] The arbitrariness arises because durability is a matter of degree, and, therefore, no objective criterion or criteria exist that can determine where the line that separates consumables from durables is to be drawn. It is tempting, because of the term "consumables," to think in terms of criteria related to the physical using up of the good in the process of consumption. However, this also would entail subjectivity as all tangible consumers' goods are, sooner or later, used up in the consumption process.

However, as what is of interest is a goods' ability to satisfy wants in the future, whether or not it could also satisfy them in the present, it would seem that perishability or physical durability is the key criterion. Again, there is no objective way to determine the length of time beyond which a consumers' good's continued existence qualifies it as a durable rather than a consumable. Production of consumables as well as of consumer services is not considered to be preparation for future consumption. Rather, these goods are produced for consumption in the "extended present." Therefore, such production does not constitute an act of saving. Production of consumer durables is, however, preparation for future consumption, and, therefore, is an act of saving. Insofar as durable consumer goods are concerned, the act of saving is the act of production of those goods is also the act of investment in those goods. This type of saving and investment may be referred to as plain saving[652] and investment.

---

[651] Here "useful life" refers to economically-useful life; i.e., the time-span during which it can be used to satisfy, directly or indirectly, human wants.

[652] See on "plain" saving" Mises (1996, 531; http://www.mises.org/humanaction/chap19sec2.asp); Rothbard (1993, 40; http://www.mises.org/rothbard/mes/chap1d.asp)

We have now established that saving and investment are the same thing: production of goods intended to satisfy wants, directly (in the case of plain saving and investment) or indirectly (in the case of capitalist saving and investment); but in either case, they are both intended to satisfy wants primarily in the more distant future, or long run, rather than the extended present, or short run; i.e., "later" rather than "now."

Thus, saving does not precede investment; rather, it is *coincident* with it, consisting in the very same action. However, yet other questions are raised by these answers. Consider only two: what does it mean to save or invest one's money or funds and how then can saving be greater than or less than investment?

Before we can analyze these issues, it is first necessary to come to an understanding of the nature of money as a good. Money comes into existence as the transformation of an existing durable consumers' good or of an existing capital good to money, itself a form of capital good. In either case, part of the stock of savings; i.e., the stocks of capital goods and durable consumers' goods, has been converted from some non-monetary use to monetary use. Therefore an act of saving is necessarily prior to the evolution of money. Fiat money, for all practical purposes, is created ex nihilo (Barnett and Block, 2005B; Hoppe, et. al, 1998).

There are only two (2) types of goods: capital goods and consumers' goods; these two are exhaustive. If this is so it then follows logically that either money is a capital or a consumers' good. Moreover, as we have seen, all that one can do is either produce or consume. Therefore, "trade"[653] is either an act of production or of consumption. But trade, even in the case of the individual for whom the trading process itself is an act of consumption, is also an act of production, Mises and Rothbard to the contrary notwithstanding.[654]

---

[653] "Trade" here refers to all exchanges of rights, barter as well as those involving money. This is to prevent any confusion that might arise because of Mises's (1996, pp. 97-98) use of the term "exchange" to refer to all actions; i.e., every action is an attempt to exchange a less desirable for a more desirable state of affairs.

[654] Rothbard (1993, pp. 60-61) states: "Goods being directly and presently consumed are *present goods*. A *future good* is the present expectation of enjoying a consumers' good at some point in the future. A future good may be a claim on future consumers' goods, or it may be a capital good, which will be transformed into a consumers' good in the future. Since a good is a way station (and nature-given factors are original stations) on the route to consumers' goods, capital goods and nature-given factors are both future goods." He also avers: "In the monetary economy, since money enters into all transactions, the discount of the future good against the present good can, in all cases, be expressed in terms of one good: money. This is so because the money commodity is a present good and because claims to future goods are almost always expressed in terms of future money income" (Rothbard, 1993, p. 298). Therefore, for money to be a present good it must be "directly and presently

Therefore, because money is "the" quintessential trade good; i.e., the medium of exchange *par excellence*, it must be a capital good. Now, as monetary gold (gold in the form of coins or bullion intended to be used as media of exchange) may also satisfy consumers' aesthetic wants, it may be, and is for the relevant consumers, simultaneously, a consumers' good. Nevertheless, though it may be concurrently a consumers' good, it must always and necessarily be a capital good.

Consider, then, what it means to "save" or "invest" one's money. There are two ways to "save" one's money.[655]

---

consumed" in mediating a transaction. This obviously is not the case. For if money is not a present good, it must be a future good, of which there are only two (2) types: claims on future consumers' goods or capital goods. But any asset can be used as a claim on future consumers' goods. That is, the category "claims on future consumers' goods" is so broad as to be almost meaningless. Therefore, as money is not a present good, it is, it must, be a capital good. On this point, see Barnett and Block, 2001.

[655] St. Paul (1 Timothy 6-10) famously said, "For the love of money is the root of all evil..." This is extremely dubious. But as far as economic analysis goes, money is the root of much confusion. The easiest way to see this is to get to the essence of an economic phenomenon. In such cases, we ask if it would/could exist in a barter economy. If so, then money cannot be of the essence of the matter. More important, any definition of the phenomena that involves money is, obviously, inadequate, in that, at best, it is misleading, but usually confusing, thereby causing faulty analysis.

For example, untold time and ink has been squandered developing the theory, and empirical estimates, of "the" demand for, money. However, correct analysis concludes that there is no such thing. Money qua money is one side of every monetary transaction. Therefore, in the market in which X trades for dollars, the price of money is in terms of X/$. Of course, in the market in which Y trades for dollars, the price of money is in terms of Y/$. There is then no "the" demand for money. Rather, in every market in which some good trades for money there is a demand for money; i.e., there are demand*s* for money, not *a* demand for money.

Of course, the foregoing comments apply equally to "the" supply of money. It should be noted that some Austrians, including the present authors, fall into this trap when they are not careful; e.g., when we speak of an increase in "the" supply of money, rather than in the stock of money. That Mises and Rothbard speak in terms of "the" demand for, and supply of, money is proof positive of this problem, especially as Salerno (1993, 133-134) maintains that such analysis is of the essence of monetary economics. Perhaps the beginning of understanding of "money" is the realization it is the only necessarily barter good in a monetary economy, and that as such there is no "the" demand for, or supply of, money.

First, one can refrain from spending it on *anything*. This is referred to as hoarding.[656] Of course, *not spending* is not an action – it is neither production nor consumption. During the time one is abstaining from spending, one is necessarily doing something else. Therefore hoarding is not saving; it is merely the non-action of retaining title to a pre-existing capital good, money.

Second, one can trade one's money for another pre-existing good; e.g., a house or a bond or a share of stock. In this case, the action is trade, a form of production. But, this action does not bring into existence either consumer durables or capital goods; i.e., there is no saving or investment involved. Rather, it "merely" swaps titles to different goods, as the parties to the exchange try to rearrange their portfolios so as to improve their conditions in life. If one offers money to another to entice him to produce a consumer durable or capital good, and the transaction is consummated, there is saving and investment, but it consists in the action of production, not of the trade of money for preexisting goods. The same can be said of the trade of money for newly created financial assets. Neither the creation of financial assets nor the trade of money, therefore, creates durable consumer goods or capital goods; consequently, neither is an act of saving or investment.

III. Conclusion

Austrian economics is based upon a simple theory. Simple in the sense of Occam's Razor, not simplistic: the choices facing the economic actor at any given time are limited to two; praxeology is in effect a binary system. As discussed in the present paper, one may only consume or produce, there is no third alternative. Moreover, production is either for current consumption or it is saving/investment

This, however, is but the tip of the iceberg. The phenomenon runs like a constant refrain throughout the warp and woof of Austrian economics. For example, the only options open to the owner of property are to retain it or release it; he may do the latter by selling it, renting it out, giving it away, but the basic options are only those two. With regard to any two goods A and B

---

[656] The matter of hoarding raises another issue. Except for the virtually instantaneous period of time in which the title to money is transferred from one individual to another, it is never spent on anything. That is, except for those split seconds in which it changes hands, money in wallets and checking accounts is virtually always being "hoarded." What, then, is the real meaning of hoarding? It is a decrease in the average rate at which money is spent; i.e., a decrease in the "velocity of money" of quantity theory fame. In praxeological terms, an individual hoards when he holds onto his money, in value terms; the longer the period of time he keeps it in his cash balances before spending it the greater is his hoarding. It should be noted that a key source of error in Keynes (1936) was his failure to comprehend the difference between the effects of hoarding in commodity-money and fiat-money systems.

or combinations thereof, one may prefer A to B, or B to A. That, contrary to the opinion of the overwhelming majority of economists, is exhaustive of the possibilities. Indifference, a supposed third alternative, is simply not on the menu (for criticism of the viewpoint now being articulated, see Nozick, 1977, Caplan, 1999; for a defense of it see Rothbard, 1993, Block, 1980, 2003B). Why not? Because there is no possible way to *demonstrate* such a choice in actual human action, and the latter is the bedrock of economics from the Austrian perspective. This, of course, is not to deny that the word "indifference" has a perfectly understandable referent, merely that it cannot pass muster as a matter of technical economics.

Similarly, one can only act or not act; demand or supply; engage in labor or leisure; enjoy or renounce; produce or consume; rent or own (borrowing constitutes temporary ownership); possess the rights to a stock or a flow; prefer or set aside; trade or not trade; act in the present to render the future more palatable than it would otherwise have been but for that present act, or not do so; act with regard to the present or the future (the past exists only in our own memories, with or without technological aids such as film, books, etc.)

This binary insight applies to barter and monetary economies, despite the fact that in the real world we typically find an admixture of both. The point is, there is not any third option, completely divorced from either.

When placed in such a context, the thesis of the present paper tends to become, if not more acceptable to non-Austrian economists, at least more comprehensible. It is not a stand-alone contention. Rather, our thesis is embedded in a nexus of similar binary phenomena.

Chapter 29. On Say's Law, Keynes's Money, and Post Keynesians[657]

Abstract

Say's Law maintains that there can never be a superabundance of all goods (if any good were available in greater supply than needed, such as water or air, it would no longer be an economic good at all) and that if there is an excess of some items that are still goods, it will be matched with an insufficiency of others. The reputation of Keynes (1936) was made in part on the basis of a supposed refutation of Say's Law. This paper attempts to probe the irrationality of Keynes' position by examining his concept of money and its relationship to his theory.

I. Introduction

"Men are involuntarily unemployed if, in the event of a small rise in the price of wage-goods relatively to the money-wage, both the aggregate supply of labor willing to work for the current money-wage and the aggregate demand for it [labor] at that wage would be greater than the existing volume of employment" Keynes (1936, 15).

"But the Stock exchange revalues many investments every day and the reevaluations give a frequent opportunity to the individual (though no to the community as a whole) to revise his commitments" Keynes (1936, 151).

"Investments which are thus 'fixed' for the community are made [by existence of a stock market] 'liquid' for the individual" Keynes (1936, 153).

"Of the maxims of orthodox finance none, surely, is more anti-social than the fetish of liquidity...It forgets that there is no such thing as liquidity of investment for the community as a whole" Keynes (1936, 155)

The principle that has come to be known as Say's law is considered to be an essential element of classical economics. Properly understood, there are two aspects to Say's law: 1) there can never be glut of goods in general; 2) there can be a glut of some goods matched by an insufficiency of other goods. Say himself understood this principle to apply to monetary as well as barter economies. It is the case of monetary economies that is relevant for the purposes of this paper.

Say's Law applied to a monetary economy of n goods, $x_1, \ldots, x_{n-1}$, M, where M is the money good. Say (1880) maintains that there can never be a glut of the n goods combined; however, there can be a surplus of any subset of the n goods, in which case there necessarily would be a paucity of the goods in the complementary subset. More simply put, there cannot be too many goods in general, but there can be too many of some goods and not

[657] The authors wish to thank Steve Berger, Lew Rockwell, and the Mises Institute for post Katrina support.

enough of others (Sowell, 1972). In such cases, there is a misallocation of resources. Producers have misjudged consumers' sentiments and produced a suboptimal mix of goods. What is required is a realignment of relative prices such that prices of those goods in excess be decreased relative to the prices of those of which there is a dearth. Of course, that is precisely the way free markets work. The producers of the "glut goods" make actual losses and the producers of "dearth goods" forego potential profits. Their response is to adjust prices altering the structure of prices and reallocating resources more in accord with the desires of consumers. And, it makes no difference if M is the sole good for which there is an insufficiency.

Keynes (1936, 26) misstates Say's Law: "Thus, Say's Law, that the aggregate demand price of output as a whole is equal to the aggregate supply price for all volumes of output, is equivalent to the proposition that there is no obstacle to full employment."[658]

However, Keynes actually agrees with the correct version of Say's Law. What Keynes disagrees with is the adjustment process when the primary "dearth good" is money. According to Keynes, investment – expenditures on new capital goods - are in effect a crapshoot and subject to sudden and large decreases.[659] In such cases there is a rise in liquidity preference; i.e., a boost in the hoarding of money[660] or, in Quantity Theory terms, a fall in the velocity of money.[661]

In section II we discuss Keynes's theory about money and economics; here we offer the building blocks of his system. Section III is devoted to the problems with the foregoing. The burden of sections IV and V are to analyze the views of Lerner and Davidson, respectively, on these issues. In section VI we deal with what might be considered an anomaly: Keynes' concern with money. We conclude in section VII.

---

[658] Keynes provides no cite to Say's works to support his interpretation.

[659] One hears far less of sudden and large increases from this quarter. "Animal spirits," evidently, point in only one direction.

[660] Hoarding of money occurs when the weighted-average period between receipt and expenditure of money increases.

[661] Some authors refer to this, incorrectly, as an increase in the demand for money. This is to misuse the technical term, demand. One may refer to the stock of money at a point in time, but if one wishes to use correctly the term "demand" in reference to money, it must be in the plural form, as it is of the essence of a monetary economy that money trades against all other goods. Therefore, in a specific market, say for good X, there is a supply of good X that constitutes a demand for money and a demand for good X which constitutes a supply of money. As money has no market of its own, but rather trades in every market, there are *demands* for money and *supplies* of money, not a, or the, demand for, and supply of money.

II. On Keynes's Money and Keynes's Economics

There is no doubt as to what Einstein (1920) meant in his General Theory of Relativity. Although physicists do not accept his General Theory as the last word and are still trying to come to a better understanding of reality, yet *they are not arguing about what Einstein meant* 85 years and more after its publication. However, this is not the case with Keynes' 1936 book *The General Theory of Employment, Interest and Money* (hereinafter, GT). Ever since this treatise was published economists have disagreed as to what Keynes said. Moreover, they have also disputed whether he was essentially correct or incorrect, and as to what, if anything in this book is useful or harmful. Thus, some sixty years and more after its publication, *economists are still arguing about what Keynes "really" meant* in his GT. That is a difference between science and pseudoscience. Or, with apologies to Churchill, "The General Theory is a riddle wrapped in a mystery inside an enigma."[662]

Consider the complete title of the GT: "The General Theory of Employment, Interest, and Money." What is the essence of Keynes's theory? Consider the following building blocks:

1. Animal spirits, not rational risk taking

States Garrison (1989,15): "the decision to invest is based, in large part, on the groundless expectations held by the business community, or on animal spirits, to use Keynes's own terminology. Not surprisingly, booms and busts occur with the waxing and waning of business confidence."

2. Liquidity preference

"Social" liquidity can be changed, but only slowly over time; and thus is quite low. It consists in how quickly the real assets; i.e., the capital goods (and durable consumers' goods and, today, we would add, the human capital) of the members of society, can be transformed from their current use to more desirable alternatives. It takes into account the effects of such changes in use on the value of these goods in terms of their ability to satisfy wants directly or indirectly. "Private" liquidity consists in how quickly an individual thinks he can exchange his current stock of assets for other more desirable ones, without loss of value. This, at least in an advanced market society, is usually quite

---

[662] On the clarity of the GT, recall the words of future Nobel Laureate Samuelson (1946): "[Keynes' GT] is a badly written book, poorly organized; any layman who, beguiled by the author's previous reputation, bought the book was cheated of his five shillings. It is not well suited for classroom use. It is arrogant, bad tempered, polemical, and not overly generous in its acknowledgements. It abounds in mares' nests or confusions. Flashes of insight and intuition intersperse tedious algebra. An awkward definition gives way to an unforgettable cadenza. When finally mastered, its analysis is found to be obvious and at the same time new. In short, it is a work of genius." On the quote from Churchill, see http://www.phrases.org.uk/meanings/31000.html

high, but subject to rapid change and thus can become very low. When speaking of individual goods, money is of course the most liquid of all An extremely specialized good with no feasible alternative uses,[663] it is highly liquid, especially in times when there is a relative abundance of it with respect to the then current and expected future demands for its services Alternatively, an extremely specialized good with no feasible alternative uses is highly illiquid, especially in times when there is a relative abundance of it with respect to the then current and expected future demands for its services.[664]

3. A highly unstable demand for investment goods that is also very interest inelastic

When businessman's confidence wanes, so does their demand for new capital goods. The decline in demand for new capital goods is experienced in those industries that produce them and the materials necessary to such production. Workers in these industries are laid-off. Moreover, not only do investors reduce their purchases of new capital goods, they also attempt to sell used ones. Alternatively, they may substitute share sales for this latter. This can occur either if, or because for various reasons, the decline in the value of the used goods is not registered appropriately in the stock market, or because they do not have the necessary authority to liquidate them, and those who do have it do not use it. Thus, in addition to decreased production of new capital goods and concomitant unemployment, the decrease in confidence is manifested by declines in the excess demands for existing shares of stocks; their supplies increase relative to the demands therefor, with concomitant reductions in share prices. Bond prices also fall. Investors anticipate a slowdown in the economy with decreased demand for borrowed funds and, therefore, lower interest rates. Consequently, they step up their purchases of bonds in an attempt to lock in the current rates, and in the process bid up prices and depress bond yields. One outcome of all this is a flight to "liquidity and quality." In the age-old contest between fear and greed, fear reigns, at least temporarily. Investors turn next to short-term securities, especially those perceived as less risky; e.g., short- term Treasuries, and deposits; i.e., money. This is because money is both the most liquid of all goods and also the highest quality, in the sense of lack of default risk. That is, there is an "increase in the demand for money" or, more accurately, an increase in its hoarding.

---

[663] We speak here of fiat currency, not gold. The latter has alternative uses in jewelry, dentistry. Apart from use as wall paper, the former has none.

[664] Although this description might seem to fit money, in fact money is not highly specialized in the sense relevant here. Yes, money is specialized as a medium of exchange, but specialized here refers to a good's abilities to satisfy, directly or indirectly, an individuals' wants. Because money can be used to purchase virtually any good, it can be used to satisfy more wants than any other good. Therefore, in the relevant sense, money is not a highly specialized good.

4. Effects of a change in confidence on liquidity

A decline in confidence makes society more liquid (in the economic sense) in that the *percentage* of total wealth held in liquid form is greater than before. This sounds impossible at the outset. Yes, everyone can *attempt* to become more liquid. But, surely, the entire economy cannot *succeed* in this goal, certainly not in the short term. This result thus comes about not by everyone suddenly producing more liquid goods, but by a reduction in the value of less-liquid preexisting goods as the marginal economic actor attempts to unload them.

If one merely looks at the stock of capital goods including human capital in terms of its capability of producing goods without reference to the value thereof, liquidity appears not to have changed at all. Assume as given the size of the stocks of durable consumer goods and durable capital goods again including human capital, relative to current production thereof. Posit that they have a relatively high degree of specialization in terms of the limited range of goods to the production of which they can be reallocated at a cost that does not exceed the benefit thereof. Then, the degree of "physical liquidity" is relatively low – one might venture to say very low. And it changes very slowly over time no matter how frequently and at what terms its ownership changes, save only in the cases of wars and natural catastrophes.

However, economic liquidity is another matter, as it is concerned with the *values* of the capital goods. Those can change, not only very rapidly, but also by huge amounts, whether gains or losses. And, it is values that are important for economics. That is, a society can greatly increase its economic liquidity in a very short period of time. Unfortunately, it can do so only by becoming poorer: by devaluing its illiquid assets relatively to its liquid assets. Note that the physical liquidity changes hardly at all, which essentially means that society's capacity to produce goods in terms both of the quantity and the mix thereof is unaltered. However, the value of those goods and the goods that produce them decrease, although by varying amounts.

5. The increased hoarding (aka an increase in the demand for money) causes a shortage of money

Concomitant with the increase in demand for money is a decrease in demand for goods. That is, there has been a shift in demand from those goods that are less liquid to those that are more so, especially toward the most liquid of all goods, money. Then:

A. There should be a period of adjustment in which prices adjust to the shortage of money/decrease-in-demand-for-goods by increasing the value of the money (relative to goods); i.e., a general deflation, to bring the prices of goods in line with reduced monetary demands therefor.

B. Even if prices are allowed to so adjust, it takes a considerable period of time as workers resist pay cuts thereby limiting them, the more so if they are unionized; in any case they resist for reasons of "equity." Result: increased unemployment.

C. If wages are not allowed to adjust in a downward direction either because of union power or governmental interference in the market, then, price cuts are virtually ruled out. Result: Again, increased unemployment, but in this case more severe.

6. According to Say's Law, beyond a temporary adjustment period, the shift in demand should not have any effect on the level of resource usage, including labor, but only upon the allocation of resources, including labor, to the production of different goods, with resources shifted away from those goods the demand for which has fallen and to those goods the demand for which has increased.

III. Problems

The problem with the foregoing is not in the nature of the goods experiencing a fall in demand but, rather, in the nature of those experiencing a rise. And this is where the virtually totally neglected part of Keynes (1936, 229-234) having to do with the "essential properties" of money enters.[665]

Keynes' analysis goes something like this. In general, when demand shifts from one group of goods, A, to another group, B, the market will reallocate resources from production of A to B. That is, the classical model (Say's Law) will work despite perhaps minor adjustment "inconveniences." However, if B happens to be money, then all bets are off. The classical model doesn't work. Say's Law becomes inoperable. In any case, the labor freed-up because of the reduced production of A is not required for the manufacture of B, or even of substitutes for it in its essential function as a medium of exchange.

In the view of Keynes (1936, 230-231):

> "The first characteristic which tends toward the above conclusion is the fact that money has, both in the long and in the short period, a zero, or at any rate a very small, elasticity of production, so far as the power of private enterprise is concerned, as distinct from the monetary authority; – elasticity of production[8] meaning, in this context, the response of the quantity of labour applied to producing it to a rise in the quantity of labour a unit of it will command. Money, that is to say, cannot be readily produced; – labour cannot be turned on at will by entrepreneurs to produce money in increasing quantities as its price rises in terms of the wage-unit. In the case of an

[665] The only school of economics which these properties play a role is the Post Keynesian. On this, see the addendum.

inconvertible managed currency this condition is strictly satisfied. But in the case of a gold-standard currency it is also approximately so, in the sense that the maximum proportional addition to the quantity of labour which can be thus employed is very small, except indeed in a country of which gold-mining is the major industry. [Footnote text omitted.]

"The second *differentia* of money is that it has an elasticity of substitution equal, or nearly equal, to zero; which means that as the exchange value of money rises there is no tendency to substitute some other factor for it; – except, perhaps, to some trifling extent, where the money commodity is also used in manufacture or the arts. This follows from the peculiarity of money that its utility is solely derived from its exchange-value, so that the two rise and fall *pari passu,* with the result that as the exchange value of money rises there is no motive or tendency, as in the case of rent-factors, to substitute some other factor for it.

"Thus, not only is it impossible to turn more labour on to producing money when its labour-price rises, but money is a bottomless sink for purchasing power, when the demand for it increases, since there is no value for it at which demand is diverted – as in the case of other rent-factors – so as to slop over into a demand for other things."

It says something about the clarity of Keynes' thought processes and the results thereof that he (Keynes, 1936, 229-230) refers to these very specific qualities as "special characteristics [of the kind of money to which we are accustomed]" and "peculiarities that commonly characterize money as we know it" in Chapter 17: The Essential Properties of Interest and Money, on pages listed in the index under "Money – its essential properties, 222-44, 293," when only a few pages before (Keynes, 1936, 167, n.1) in Chapter 13: The General Theory of the Rate of Interest, he maintains that: "Without disturbance to this definition [of the rate of interest], we can draw the line between "money" and "debts" at whatever point is most convenient for handling a particular problem."

In other words, according to Keynes, rises in the demand for money do not call forth additional labor to produce it. Moreover, this is true whether we are talking about paper money, bank money, or even a commodity money, save for one circumstance. That exception, and one not likely to be of import in the real world: only if the mining of the monetary commodity is a major industry of the relevant country, will there be much scope, if any at all, for additional employment opportunities.

Moreover, as the value of money increases there is no substitution of other goods to satisfy the wants for which it provided. If the price of beef goes up in consequence of increased demand therefor, people tend to substitute other goods; e.g., pork, for it. Therefore, even if there were no possibility of shifting labor to the production of beef, jobs would still open up in the hog industry. But, according to Keynes, this cannot happen with respect to money. It is impossible for other goods to substitute for it. The essence of money is that it is a generally accepted medium of exchange and means of final payment. No other goods serve these functions; had they, they would be money itself now, and before the onset of the liquidity problems. He does allow for this possibility under a gold standard, that there might be some shift of gold from non-monetary to monetary uses, but this would not entail the use of much labor.

Keynes' reasoning re a commodity-money economy is fatally flawed. Suppose, again, that demand shifted from capital goods to liquid assets. In such an economy, even if it had no mineral deposits of the money commodity at all, there would still be no problem, apart from short-run adjustments. For resources, labor most specifically included would be shifted to the production of those goods offering the best opportunity for sale internationally. In other words, the commodity-money need not be produced domestically, it can be imported in *exchange* for other goods that can be produced domestically. Any country can take advantage of this possibility, it being of most importance to those that do not have a significant gold mining industry, or the potential for one. A country need but produce more of those goods in which it has a comparative advantage and export them. If they do so, then, Keynes very much to the contrary, they will not suffer the slings and arrows of the detriments attached to his "liquidity trap." In fact, there will not be one.[666]

It turns out, then, that Say was correct, at least with respect to a commodity-money economy; to wit, if people's demands shift away from other things and to gold, then either the labor unemployed by the shift will, after a short adjustment period, become employed either in the gold mining and processing industries, or in industries that produce for export. There would be no general glut of goods, rather a surplus of some and a shortage of others. This would be dealt with by the market process through price adjustments and consequent factor reallocations.

But what of the case of a fiat money economy? It turns out that Keynes' concept of the liquidity trap is a possibility in a world of inconvertible paper currencies and deposits backed by them. For it is

---

[666] Keynes (1936, 230-231) notes this opportunity: "...whereas if money could be grown like a crop or manufactured like a motor-car, depressions would be avoided or mitigated because, if the price [sic] of other assets was tending to fall in terms of money, more labour would be diverted into the production of money; – as we see to be the case in gold mining countries," and then immediately disparages it, continuing. "though for the world as a whole the maximum diversion in this way is almost negligible." Of course, for "the world as a whole" to be relevant, one would have to assume that the sudden, irrational, failure of nerve, that manifests itself as Keynes' fetish of liquidity, is truly massive – on an international scale.

precisely such monies that have the two characteristics discussed above. Therefore, a decrease in the demand for capital goods that manifested itself, inter alia, as an increase in the demand for fiat money would neither create employment to increase the supply in response thereto – it really does not take much labor to increase the quantity of such monies by any amount – nor would demand shift to other goods to be used as substitute monies for the fiat currencies. So there would be no creation of demand for labor on that account. A Keynesian type liquidity trap is then possible in a fiat currency economy. There can, then, be a general glut of goods in a fiat money economy. If demands shift away from other goods and to the fiat money causing unemployment, the supply of the currency can be increased without increasing the demand for labor. By virtually instantly and at almost zero expense (adding a few zeroes to the currency), the supply of currency can be increased to meet the demand, so that there is no shortage of money to offset the surplus of other goods.

We entertained these notions only arguendo. We now explicitly reject the key assumption that drives Keynes' analysis of this scenario. Keynes' reasoning is correct with respect to the effects a significant shift in demand from capital goods to liquid assets would have in a paper- and/or banknotes-money economy. The flaw, and it applies to commodity-money economy with the same strength, is his assumption about the initial cause of the problem: Keynes assumes that that in a free market economy of profit seeking entrepreneurs/investors/businessmen investment demand is volatile because "the decision to invest is based, in large part, on the groundless expectations held by the business community, or on animal spirits, to use Keynes's own terminology" (Garrison, 1989, 15).[667]

---

[667] To quote Keynes directly: ... it is probable that the actual average results of investments ... have disappointed the hopes that prompted them ... If human nature felt no need temptation to take a chance, no satisfaction (profit apart) in constructing a factory, a railway, amine, or a farm, there might not be much investment as the result of cold calculation. (Keynes, 1936, 150)

"Even apart from the instability due to speculation, there is the instability due to the characteristic of human nature that a large proportion of our positive activities depend on spontaneous optimism rather than mathematical expectations, whether moral or hedonistic or economic. Most, probably, of our decisions to do something positive, the full consequences of which will be drawn out over many days to come, can only be taken as the result of animal spirits - a spontaneous urge to action rather than inaction, and not as the outcome of a weighted average of quantitative benefits multiplied by quantitative probabilities" (Keynes, 1936, 161-162).

"... human decisions affecting the future, whether personal or political or economic, cannot depend on strict mathematical expectation, since the basis for making such calculations does not exist ... it is our innate urge to activity that makes the wheel go around ..." (Keynes, 1936, 162).

However, the fact that an economy does not have commodity money logically implies that it is not entirely a free market economy (Rothbard, 2005; Block, 1999C).[668] Should the government, or the government in conjunction with the banks, increase the supply of money, this could cause a false boom, crisis, and bust (Rothbard, 1963. Mises, 1998; Garrison, 2001). But in that case the cause and course of the bust would be very different from that theorized by Keynes. And, *a fortiori*, policy implications would be very different from those proposed by Keynes and his followers.

We have been employing the arguendo method in a second sense, all throughout this paper. Implicitly we have been assuming the Keynesian collapse of confidence scenario, unless new jobs can be found somewhere to offset those that a gold mining industry would offer, then unemployment is the inevitable result. But to do so would be to ignore that lesson that Hazlitt (1979) offered us: employment can always take care of itself in the free market.[669]

What we want as a society are not jobs, per se, but, rather, the goods and services created though labor. Keynes, in other words, looks at this matter wrong side out. And how does the marketplace create this "miracle" of no involuntary unemployment? Simple. Through adjustments in various wage rates, both with respect to other wage rates and especially with respect to prices. For even if given or specific wage-rates are in their proper relationship with other wage rates, if they are too high relative to prices, unemployment will ensue.[670] If they are "sticky" in a downward direction on a permanent basis, then we have left the realm of economic freedom. But then it is this lacuna, not anything unique about money, that is responsible for our economic plight.

IV. Lerner

Lerner (1952, 184) analyzes Keynes' essential properties of money as follows: "Section III [of Chapter 17 of GT] considers three reasons why *money* may be the culprit." The culprit, in this context is "any asset (e.g., money) whose 'rate of interest' refuses to fall enough, [such that] we will find ourselves without the investment on which prosperity depends" (Lerner, 1952, 182, footnote omitted).

---

[668] It cannot be denied that there are some "free banking" Austrian economists who think that fractional reserve banking could and would exist in a fully laissez faire system, and that it would not be fraudulent under the proper institutional arrangements. For example Selgin, 1988; Selgin and White, 1996; White, 1989. However, in our view this is mistaken. See on this Block and Garschina, 1995; Callahan, 2003; Cochran and Call, 1998; Hoppe, et. al. 1998; Hoppe, 1994B; Hulsmann, 1996, 1998; Rothbard, 1962; Sechrest, 1988, 1993; Shah, 1997; de Soto, 1995, 2001.

[669] Free should be taken here to mean in every way, save for the use of a fiat currency.

[670] If wage rates are too low relative to prices, unemployment will also ensue. However, competition among employers in a free market economy will quickly eliminate such a situation as they would bid up wage rates in order to acquire more employees.

Lerner (1952, 184, reference omitted) continues:

"The marginal efficiency of money refuses to fall because: i) Its elasticity of production is negligible, i.e., it cannot be 'grown like a crop or manufactured like a motor car.' ... This has two consequences. In the first place there is no *direct* increase in investment when there is an increase in demand for money, and in the second place there are no increases in its stock to lower the marginal efficiency of holding it.

"Money is not the only asset that is thus fixed in supply (apartment from government action) ..."

But, this is exactly the point we deal with in the text. Yes, if we are considering a fiat money economy, the elasticity of production of money is zero, and increases in demands for it will not call forth additional labor to produce more of it. Moreover, if such an economy is also characterized by interventionism such that wages, prices, and interest rates are not free to adjust to changes in supplies and demands, then significant unemployment, in terms both of the numbers of people unemployed and the lengths of their periods of unemployment can come into existence. Indeed, these interventions, *not* the zero elasticity of money production with regard to employment, are responsible for the joblessness. However, as we saw above, even with a fiat money; i.e., one with a zero elasticity of production, significant unemployment will not result without interventionism. Moreover, except in the case of a fiat money; i.e., in cases of commodity monies, the elasticity of production will *not* be zero. At least, it will not be zero if we allow for "indirect production." Lerner, supra, says: "there is no *direct* increase in investment." But, for employment and unemployment; i.e., to employers and employees, as a group, it is irrelevant if an increase in investment is direct or indirect.[671] Lerner, then is talking of a fiat money economy; "fixed in supply (apart from government action)." But, in a commodity money economy, the elasticity of production is *not* zero. This holds directly, if there is a significant gold industry, or indirectly, through production of goods for export in exchange for gold.[672]

Unemployment for Lerner, and according to him, Keynes, then, results from a liquidity trap. But liquidity traps are in turn dependent upon money fiat money.

---

[671] This, of course, is not to deny the existence, importantly, of distribution effects; i.e., who benefits more relatively, form a direct v. an indirect increase in investment. But, in terms of the economy as a whole, it is irrelevant.

[672] It would be entirely possible to have significant unemployment in a commodity money economy if it had no gold industry and if there were intervention in export markets such that because of tariffs, etc., they were prevented from exporting, or using their export earnings to import gold. Indeed, this would be by far the most likely outcome.

One might ask why Lerner is included in this article. The reason is, he seems to be the first major economist to focus on Keynes' view on the essential properties of money. It is the position of the present authors that although not a Post Keynesian himself, Lerner was interested in, though critical of, some of the same ideas of Keynes that are central to the Post Keynesians.

V. Davidson

More directly on point is Paul Davidson, undoubtedly the leader of the Post Keynesian movement in the U.S., if not globally.

In a recent article Davidson (1998, 824, emphasis added, reference omitted) states:

"Keynes ... recognized the *need* to 'throw over' these classical axioms. The resulting unemployment model [of Keynes in the GT] has four *fundamental* attributes that are missing from classical models but are relevant to money-using, market oriented economies."

The fourth *fundamental* attribute (Davidson, 1998, 827-828) is:

4. *Money provides liquidity because it possesses two essential elasticity properties* (Keynes, 1936a [The GT], ch. 17, see especially p.241, n.1). First, its elasticity of production is (approximately) zero, i.e., *money does not grow on trees.* Readily producible goods (i.e., things with high elasticities of production), therefore can never fill the liquidity role played by money."

For Keynes (1936, 230, footnote omitted), "elasticity of production mean[s] in this context, the response of the quantity of labour applied to producing it to a rise in the quantity of labour which a unit of it will command."

We include, here, the footnote of Keynes' that Davidson especially wants us to consider; to wit:

"The attribute of liquidity" is by no means independent of the presence of these two characteristics. For it is unlikely that an asset, of which the supply can be easily increased or the desire for which can be easily diverted by a change in relative price, will possess the attribute of "liquidity" in the minds of owners of wealth. Money itself rapidly loses the attribute of "liquidity" if its future supply is expected to undergo sharp changes."

Before going any further, it is interesting to note that these fundamental attributes and the central role they play in Keynes' system are found in chapter 17 of the GT, about which Hansen, perhaps the leading American Keynesian (but by no means a Post Keynesian) of his generation, had this to say (Hansen, 1953, 159): "Immediately after the appearance of the *General Theory* there was a certain fascination about Chap.17, due party no doubt, to its obscurity. Digging in this area, however, soon ceased after it was found that the chapter contained no gold mines."[673] Immediately thereafter, he damns it with faint praise: "Still the discussion (though it certainly could be improved) is not altogether without merit, and some interesting bits can be extracted from it; *yet, in general, not much would have been lost had it never been written.*" So says Hansen, about the chapter in which Keynes explicates his two essential properties of money, which, taken together, Davidson maintains are one of the four fundamental attributes "missing from classical models but [which] are relevant to money-using, market-oriented economies."

Davidson (1998, 827-828) then goes on to discuss Keynes' second essential property of money. This, along with the first, constitutes the fourth fundamental attribute:

"Second the elasticity of substitution between all liquid assets (including money) and the *products of industry* is (approximately) zero. The private sector will not reallocate labor from producing goods to harvesting money from the money tree if people decide to spend less of their income on the products of industry and plan to use the resulting saving to become more liquid; i.e.; by storing the saving in the form of money or other liquid assets and thereby raise the price of nonproducibles [sic] liquid assets relative to producibles. Hahn (1977, p.39) implicitly utilises these elasticity properties when he demonstrates that the existence of any 'nonreproducible asset [i.e., a durable that has a zero elasticity of production] allows for a choice between employment inducing and non-employment inducing demand. But, of course in a monetary economy money is an important nonreproducible asset'. The only necessary condition for the existence of involuntary unemployment equilibrium is that there are 'resting places for saving [in] other than reproducible assets'[18] (Hahn, 1977, p.31), i.e., producibles are not substitutes for money (or liquid assets) for storing value (saving) and therefore the gross substitution axiom is not applicable."

Where to begin? There is enough error in the preceding page and one-half almost to warrant an entire monograph. Consider, first the issue of the elasticity of production. Davidson says money's elasticity of production is zero or "*approximately*" so [our emphasis]. In Keynes' (1936, 230) view money has a "zero, or at any rate a very small, elasticity of production." Moreover, Keynes (136, 241) states that: "For it is unlikely that an asset of which the supply can *easily* be increased or the desire for which can be *easily* diverted by a change in relative price [sic] will possess the attribute of 'liquidity'…" But liquidity is an essential quality of money for Keynes. And, Davidson quotes Hahn: "But in a monetary economy money is an important nonreproducible asset," and then in an aside tells us that a

[673] This is a particularly inelegant metaphor, given the attitudes of Keynesians of all stripes and varieties, toward the yellow metal.

nonreproducible asset "has a zero elasticity of production." It would appear that all of this is an attempt to have your cake and eat it, too.

They maintain that assets are either nonreproducible; i.e., have a: zero [Davidson], or "*approximately*" zero elasticity [Davidson], or "*very small*" [Keynes] elasticity of production, or for which resources cannot be "*easily*" diverted; i.e., a very small [Keynes, again] elasticity of production, or else, by implication it is very large. That is, the implication is that assets are either nonreproducible with a zero elasticity of substitution or they are reproducible with a very high elasticity of production; they seem to rule out the possibility of reproducible assets having an elasticity of production that is neither very small nor very large, but rather of in an intermediate range. However, goods with high elasticities will not do for money for Keynes (1936, 241, n.1): "For, it is unlikely that an asset, of which the supply can be easily increased or the desire for which can be easily diverted by a change I relative price, will possess the attribute of 'liquidity.'" But liquidity is an essential quality of money.

So there you have it – either an asset is "nonreproducible" or nearly so, in which case it can serve as money; or it is readily or easily reproducible, in which case it cannot. And what of a commodity like gold, that is reproducible but not readily or easily? Could it serve as money? Well, according to Keynes, "Yes, but..." Its elasticity of production is so low, save in a country of which it is an important industry, that it is very similar to fiat money in that it cannot be much counted upon to increase the need for employment. If, then, the difference between gold and fiat money is truly negligible (apart from gold producing countries such as Russia and South Africa), then why rely on the barbarous metal for money? Instead, it seems more sensible to use paper and conserve the gold for important uses such as jewelry, etc.

The idea of the zero elasticity of production is to focus our attention on fiat money. The last thing Keynesians of any sect want to be money, or a monetary standard, is gold[674] (that barbarous relic). No, they want the media of exchange to be under the policy control of government – they are, essentially, socialists. But the elasticity of production of gold money is neither zero (nor even approximately so) like fiat money nor is it very high.

---

[674] This is more than passing curious, given that Post Keynesians are hard and fast advocates of fixed exchange rates (Davidson, 1998, 818-821), and the gold standard is the ultimate in fixed exchange rates. In fact, with a true gold money, in contradistinction to a gold standard, exchange rates do not even exist, and, therefore, the issue of fixed exchange rates is moot. Moreover, because gold money eliminates exchange rates, it eliminates any and all uncertainty that arises when they exist. And because it is precisely for the reason that they wish to eliminate uncertainty arising from exchange rate fluctuations that Post Keynesians advocate fixed exchange rates, one would expect that gold would be the ne plus ultra money for them.

Rather, it occupies an intermediate range, one that Keynes and Davidson want to ignore into nonexistence. That is, if the elasticity of production of gold, (directly, or indirectly via production for export markets) is neither so low as to be a sinkhole for liquidity demand nor so high as to make it unsuitable for liquidity purposes, then gold is a viable alternative to fiat money; in fact, because fiat money *is* a sinkhole for liquidity demand, and gold money is not, the latter is the money par excellence.

But there is more to the story. Davidson engages in a non sequitur when he states that: "the elasticity of production of money is (approximately) zero, i.e., *money does not grow on trees*." But, this is exactly backward, or at least it is if the phrase "money does not grow on trees" has its usual meaning. The ordinary language connotation is that if "money grows on trees," it is free; i.e., it is not costly to acquire (in this context, produce) money; if in contrast it "does *not* grow on trees," then it is costly to acquire (produce). But, for money to have a zero elasticity of production, "money must grow on trees;" i.e., it must be able to be produced costlessly; i.e., without employing labor. Davidson's misuse of a metaphor confuses the issue.

And then there is Hahn's: "producibles are not substitutes for money." This runs counter to correct theory; i.e., a good which is producible can be used as money, but will not be if it is so easily producible as to not have much value per unit of weight and/or bulk; i.e., if it is not easily portable.[675] Then there is Hahn's statement: "the only necessary condition for the existence of involuntary unemployment equilibrium is that there are 'resting places for saving [in] other than reproducible assets." But this too is incorrect. Old Masters, rare stamps, etc., as well as paper money and bank deposits are *potential* "resting places for saving;" however, in an economy that also has gold money, their mere existence is not sufficient for the existence of involuntary unemployment; rather, what is required is interventionism, such that wages, prices, and interest rates are not free to adjust to changes in freely offered demands and supplies of goods, including money.

Thus, we see that the Post Keynesians, the only group to take Keynes at his word, both that money is important and what are the essential properties thereof, get it wrong. For that matter, this assessment applies to Keynes, himself.

It also behooves us not to fall into the trap of thinking that if gold were but available in most or all countries (and we could ignore the beneficial effects of international trade which obviate this need in the first place), then its advantage would be that it would create jobs when the demand for money increased. As long as government does not place any obstacles to a fall in

[675] And then there is the exception, even to this, of the stone money of Yap. Of course, this is irrelevant to our discussion.

prices and wages, additional jobs are by no means needed in gold, or, indeed, in any other single industry. Very much to the contrary, Say (1880) was entirely in the right and Keynes (1936) completely in the wrong. Whenever there is unemployment in an industry, wages fall relatively to those in others. And when they do, ceteris paribus, more employment slots open up. If there is still joblessness at any given time, this indicates, only, that wages have not decreased sufficiently. And this phenomenon is totally divorced from the type of money (gold, fiat, whatever) in circulation at the time.

VI. Keynes on money?

The very concept, "Keynes' money," sounds awkward to the modern (economic) ear. After all, it was followers of Keynes who denigrated the public policy implications of money ("pushing on a string")[676] while it was the erstwhile *opponents* of Keynes, the members of the Chicago School, who insisted that "money matters."[677] There are several fallacies and infelicities locked up in these claims; that is, the majority of the economics profession has a tin ear in this regard.

First of all, the word "money" appears in the very title of Keynes (1936). Moreover, several of the chapter headings in this book feature the "m" word. Say what you will about Keynes, and his critics (Hazlitt, 1959, 1960) have had much to say on this score, no one has accused him, let alone made it stick, that he would so grievously and almost fraudulently choose such a misleading title for his work. No, Keynes was interested in money, and thought it important.[678]

Secondly, the Chicago School is by no means an opponent of Keynesianism. Very much to the contrary, at least if one of its leaders, Milton Friedman can be believed, who stated "we are all Keynesians now." Money may indeed "matter" for them, but that cannot gainsay this claim.[679]

It cannot be denied that there is a *difference* between the "monetarist" and non monetarist wings of the Keynesian movement in terms of the importance of money. For the Chicago school Keynesians, "money matters" means that monetary policy is the favored tool of interventionist choice.[680] Money matters, also, for the non Chicago New Keynesians; however, rather than the

---

676 Hoey, 2001; North, 2001, 2004; Piger, 2003

677 Bordo and Schwartz, 2003; Friedman and Schwartz, 1963; Kudlow, 2002; Salerno, 2004A

678 If evidence of this contention other than Keynes' 1936 work is required, his publications of 1913, 1923, 1930A, 1930B will suffice.

679 See on this Block (1999C, fn. 16), Gillis (2003), Samuelson (1967, 210, 1970, 193), Skousen (2001).

680 For a critique of interventionism, of whatever stripe or variety, see Ikeda, 1997; Lavoie, 1982; Mises, 1969; Rothbard, 1970; 1982C

passive, (quantity) rule based policies of the Monetarists, they favor discretionary monetary policies. The Post Keynesians, are also concerned about money, but in a different, or negative way. Production of additional amounts of it cannot be relied upon to solve unemployment in the face of weakened "animal spirits" on the part of entrepreneurs.

Thus, it is a bit over the top for the monetarist Keynesians to claim that the non Chicago Keynesians have no interest in monetary theory, or think money unimportant. For example, it is a staple of their writings that Friedman has "reminded Keynesians that 'money matters.'"[681] While we of course hold no brief for either wing of the Keynesian movement, we must protest.

VII. Conclusion

The problem of Keynes' we discuss in this paper regards hoarding. If entrepreneurs increase their demand to hold money (reduce their rate of investment) to a greater degree than Keynes thinks warranted, he maintains this will lead to unemployment. If people decrease their purchases of an "ordinary" good, and shift their demand to some other similar item, employment losses in the first case will be offset by gains in the second. However, there is one exception for Keynes. When the shift is toward money, it does not enhance employment. Extra zeroes can be added to the currency with very little effort, and analogous steps may be taken in an electronic age, again without requiring any more than trivial extra labor services. Keynes makes an exception for gold mining countries, but rules out the possibility of international trade into his analysis. When this option is taken into account, we realize that a country entirely without a gold mining industry can still increase its employment merely by trading for gold with its own domestic products.

---

[681] See http://cepa.newschool.edu/het/profiles/friedman.htm; http://www.cooperativeindividualism.org/friedmanbio.html; http://www.webenetics.com/hungary/nobel.htm. Search for "reminding Keynesians."

Chapter 30. Reply to Hummel on Austrian Business Cycle Theory

A. Introduction

Hummel (1979) criticized Austrian Business Cycle Theory (ABCT), and it is the intent of the present paper to reply to his criticisms[682], defending this viewpoint against the difficulties he raises with it. This author sees six separate problems with the Austrian or praxeological analysis of the business cycle, and we shall comment on each of them. To wit, following Hummel's outline, we devote section I to the issue of Asymmetry, II to Definitions of the Money Stock, III to Net Investment, IV to Deflation, V to the Constant Rate of Credit Expansion and VI to International Aspects of the ABCT. We conclude in section B. Since Hummel prefaces his remarks with his "fundamental assumption," we shall follow him in that regard in the present introduction.

Hummel (1979, 41) states:

"According to Austrian theory, the boom or cyclical upswing consists of a lengthening of the structure of production induced by credit expansion. The depression or cyclical downturn consists of a shortening of the structure of production until it is back into coordination with consumers' time preferences."[683]

---

[682] Why expend so much time and effort in the present article to react to Hummel (1979), which was, we readily admit, published in an obscure journal, a long time ago? This is because no matter that this author mischaracterizes ABCT, and thus his criticisms of it fall wide of the mark, we are appreciative of the fact that they are serious criticisms. On that ground alone they deserve a serious reply. Then, there is the fact that thought provoking negative assessments of ABCT are few and far between. See for example Tullock (1987, 1989), Wagner (2000), Snippe (1987); for Austrian defenses, see, respectively, Salerno (1989), Block (2001A), and Garrison (1985B, 1987); there is also Cowen's (1997) critique, which has had no reply. This, all by itself, would also be sufficient to justify a reply to Hummel. In sharp contrast, many critiques of ABCT amount to no more than name-calling. For example, Yeager (1986, 378) has this to say about ABCT: it is an "embarrassing excrescence."

[683] Hummel's statements in the text above are fully in keeping with Austrian understanding of ABCT; in contrast, ours are not perfectly congruent. There are really three distinct views of the business cycle now in play, and we do well to distinguish between them all. First is what we will call mainstream Austrianism. This, roughly, is the perspective of Mises (1998), Hayek (1975), Rothbard (1969, 2001) and Garrison (2001). Second is Hummel's view, a critique of the former. Third are the views of the present authors. For the most part, we side with the Austrian mainstream, but not always. In the present instance, although we do not wish to divert our critique of Hummel's paper away from his analysis of this understanding, we note that there is a difference between lengthening (shortening) the structure of production and lengthening (shortening) the period of production. During the credit expansion

What is Hummel's (1979, 41) "fundamental assumption?" It "consists of the observation that, because the boom is a lengthening of the structure of production while a depression is a shortening of it, violent fluctuations in time preferences that generate- similar alterations between lengthening and shortening can theoretically cause a business cycle…. (T)his assumption means that the lengthening of the structure of production that occurs as the result of credit expansion and the lengthening of the structure of production that occurs as a result of a genuine shift in time preferences are basically identical *except* for the fact that the lengthening due to credit expansion must in the future be reversed because it is inconsistent with underlying consumers' tastes."

It cannot be denied that there is an eerie similarity between the two scenarios. Even an otherwise highly accurate outside observer who was not acquainted with the very different causal antecedents between the two of them might well be forgiven for failing to distinguish one from the other. Nevertheless, there is all the world of difference in these two cases. It is, at first approximation, the distinction between a human like marionette, ruled by strings pulled above his head, and a human being, making volitional choices. The similarities, nay, the identities in the movements may fool the unwary, but the first is mere movement of a human look alike creature, and the second is human action.

Consider the following two scenarios. In the first, the government subsidizes (or taxes), initially, only the umbrella industry, and then, secondarily, the sunglass industry alone, and then continually repeats this process. People are led by prices to first purchase more of the one good and less of the other than they otherwise would, and, then, the reverse, in never ending iterations. In the second scenario, the weather is first rainy, and then sunny, in continuously altering patterns. People first buy more umbrellas, and then sunglasses, to suit their tastes that change in response to the weather, and so on. In both cases, let us suppose, the identical acquisitions occur. And, yet, the first scenario, engendered by governmental fiscal policy, is analogous to alterations in credit expansion (and contraction); the second, to "violent fluctuations in time preferences." The first full well deserves the appellation Austrian business cycle. The second does not; it constitutes, merely, the working out of endogenous changes in taste, or time preference, in the case under discussion.

---

initiated boom the period of production might be shortened, not lengthened, and the bust might be characterized by a lengthening, not a shortening, of the period of production. Because the critique in this present paper of Hummel's criticism of mainstream ABCT is from that latter perspective, this does not mean that we are in full accord with standard ABCT; in fact, though we agree with the essence of ABCT as we see it, we disagree with several specific aspects thereof.

Nor is this merely a matter of nomenclature, as important as that is for clarity of analysis. There is more. For with the alterations in taste, whether rainwear vis-à-vis sun gear or a future orientation versus a present one, entrepreneurs (Kirzner, 1973; Mises, 1949) will eventually figure it out; certainly, if this pattern long endures. In very sharp contrast, there is no such expectation regarding the prediction of from which side of the bed the fiscal authorities or, in the case of money, Alan Greenspan, will arise on any given day. That is, there is an element of arbitrariness intrinsically related to government operation that simply does not hold true for market decision-making. The latter is predictable, at least in theory, whereas the former is radically unpredictable (Lachmann, 1976B).

States Hummel (1979, 42):

"If the changes in the structure of production induced by credit expansion are different from changes in the structure of production caused by changes in time preferences in some essential respect other than that they must in the future be reversed, no one has explicitly identified this additional difference." Not so, not so, at least not any more; the issue of predictability in principle has now been explicitly articulated.

It is easy to sell predictability short as a distinction between the two cases, but this would be an error. For, if entrepreneurs can foresee consumer changes in a way that does not apply to fed currency manipulation, they can take steps to reduce or even eliminate its otherwise disruptive qualities. Perhaps, for example, a sufficient supply of both sun wear and rain gear can be planned in advance; when the inevitable (stipulated) changes occur, businessmen can stand ready to supply that which is needed, in a way they cannot do for changes inaugurated by central banking authorities.

Moreover, that the one necessarily will be reversed and the other reversed only with radical fluctuations in the mass of individuals' preferences, especially given the essentially conservative behavior of the mass of people, is far from a trivial matter. That is, the credit/money expansion necessarily creates discoordination between the actions of producers and the preferences of consumers. It leads to misallocations of resources and distortions in the structure of production[684] from the outset; i.e., as soon as the new money that was lent into existence is spent. These misallocations give rise to discoordination between the actions of producers and the preferences of consumers. These are ex ante misallocations/distortions.

---

[684] It also creates distortions in the time structure of consumption, which is analogous to the structure of production. For example, at any one time, there will be an ideal allocation between the following consumer goods: houses that last for hundreds of years, medium enduring cars and refrigerators, and short lived soap and tissue paper. Artificial central bank created alterations in interest rates will play havoc with these allocations, just as they do for producers' goods.

However, if subsequent to them the preferences of consumers should somehow change in precisely such fashion that they align themselves with the altered allocation/structure, neither would there be a crisis nor would there be a bust; i.e., there would not be a cycle[685]. In such a case, what had been ex ante mistakes would prove to be wise decisions ex post. However, that possibility does not in any way challenge the validity of ABCT. Note that absent the subsequent change in preferences: 1) the boom is necessarily self-reversing; 2) necessarily the actions of producers and preferences of consumers were discoordinated; 3) resources were necessarily misallocated; and, 4) the structure of production was necessarily distorted.

Compare that with Hummel's hypothesized violent fluctuations in preferences. If there is no such fluctuation; if, that is, subsequent to the initial change in preferences, there is no further violent change in them, then: 1) the "boom" is not self-reversing; 2) the actions of producers and preferences of consumers are not discoordinated; 3) resources are not misallocated; and 4) the structure of production is not distorted.[686] That is, there are no entrepreneurial mistakes, save for ever present random errors.

Hummel's assumption re violent fluctuations must be just that, fluctuations, swings back and forth. Consider, for example, a situation in which consumers preferences changed to prefer a group of goods, A, relatively more and a group of goods, B, relatively less, and producers responded to this change by reallocating relatively more resources to A and relatively less to B, say from (A_0, B_0) to (A_1, B_1), $A_1 > A_0$, $B_1 < B_0$. If subsequently consumers preferences changed again, but in the same direction – an even greater preference for A relative to B, and producers responded by again reallocating relatively more resources to A and relatively less to B, (A_1, B_1) to (A_2, B_2), where $A_2 > A_1$, $B_2 < B_1$; i.e., by allocating, relatively, yet more resources to A and yet fewer to B. In such a case, then there would be no cycle; rather, the situation would be the same as if there consumers' preferences had changed originally from (A_0, B_0) to (A_2, B_2), $A_2 > A_0$, $B_2 < B_0$, but entrepreneurs' adjustments to the change would be slower; i.e., there would be no cycle, but only what appeared to be slow response to an original change from (A_0, B_0) to (A_2, B_2). Moreover, the misallocated resources

---

[685] Here is the analog to our sun – rain example: the government misallocates resources in terms of these consumer items. But then, accidentally, consumers' tastes change in precisely the direction in which, and to the extent of, the governmental misallocation. If this occurred, then there would be no misallocation at all. Or try this. It is as if someone attempted to murder an innocent man, but instead shot a murderer making his escape.

[686] The latter three of these points abstracts from the random, minor, self-correcting errors made by entrepreneurs.

would not take the form of too many of the type required for the production of A and too few of the type required for the production of B, but rather of too few of the type required for A and too many of the type required for B. That is, the relative additional resources devoted to the production of A would not have been misallocated, nor would the decrease in resources allocated to the production of B be a misallocation, as in the ABCT case; rather the misallocation would be in the form to too few for A and too many for B – the exact opposite of the ABCT case.

Hummel also compares: 1) a situation in which government taxes away money consumers' would have spent on good A and spends it instead on good B, and in which entrepreneurs reallocate resources in line with the changed pattern of demand; with 2) a situation in which consumers shift their expenditures away from A and in favor of B, and in which entrepreneurs reallocate resources in line with the changed patter of demand. He (1979, 42) then maintains that:

"Now, one can say that [in the first situation] the economy is discoordinated with the desires of consumers, that resources spent on the production of B are wasted, and that if the government stops its expropriation, the market will shift back again. One cannot, however, contend that the demand for B manifested by the government with its ill-gotten gains is illusory or that the effect it has on the economy is any different from the effect of [the second situation.]" (Material in brackets supplied by present authors.)

Certainly, from an objective point of view Hummel is correct. However, what is important in economics is the subjective meaning human beings place on that objective reality. It is true that in both situations we would expect to see the same goods produced[687] in the "first round" and subsequent similar reallocations of resources by entrepreneurs from goods necessary to the production of A to those necessary to the production of B. But this ignores the fact that in the real world there are innumerable goods, some of which are neither A nor B, nor used in the production of either.

Moreover, the scenario of tax-induced reallocations is not necessarily self-reversing. As long as the government continued to tax funds that would have been spent on A and spends them instead on B the misdirection of resources will continue. However, that is not true if the misdirection is

---

[687] We abstract from "second order" considerations, such as distribution effects. Even the objective course of production and distribution will necessarily be different. This can be seen by asking, "Who would receive the B purchased by government? Those people will be wealthier than otherwise and the taxpayers poorer. In subsequent periods of time this will lead to different patterns of demand and production than would otherwise have happened in the case where preferences changed in favor of B without a redistribution by government from taxpayers to the "fortunate" recipients of governments' largess in the form of B.

caused by an increase in money/credit. Then, the misdirection is self-reversing because either the government continues to increase money/credit, in which case the situation will inevitably, whether sooner or later, end in a monetary hyperinflation and subsequent collapse, or because at some point before such a catastrophic event occurred the government will stop the money/credit expansion, in which case there will inevitably be a crisis followed by a bust.[688]

I. Asymmetry

Hummel (1979, 42-43) puts forth his challenge to ABCT as follows: "During the boom when the structure of production is lengthened, the capital goods industries (or goods of the higher orders) expand while the consumers' goods industries (or goods of the lower orders) contract. Labor is bid from the consumers' goods industries to capital goods industries. During the depression, when the structure of production is shortened, the reverse takes place. The consumers' goods industries expand, the capital goods industries contract, and labor is bid from the latter to the former. Why are these two processes not symmetrical in their effect? Why is the expansion of the capital goods industries and the contraction of the consumers' goods industries accompanied by *general* prosperity and full employment, while the expansion of the consumers' goods industries and the contraction of the capital goods industries accompanied by *general* depression and unemployment?"

Several responses are in order here. First, in the case of a shift in preferences, the contraction in the consumers' goods industries during the boom is only a *relative* one. In fact, both consumers' goods industries and capital goods industries expand; however the latter increase more than the former. That is, there is not a zero sum substitution of production of capital goods for production of consumers' goods.[689] To the contrary, total production expands. This is made possible by both a more intensive and extensive use of labor and capital goods. Regarding the first, workers put in more hours on the job (overtime), factories put on extra shifts, and offices are used earlier and later than previously. Re the latter, potential workers who

---

[688] It is true that the government can forestall or ameliorate the bust through fiscal and or regulatory wedges, but that is not relevant for this paper. A fiscal wedge is a tax or subsidy that causes a divergence between the prices that would have prevailed in a free market and the actual prices that obtain. A regulatory wedge achieves similar effects by means of, you guessed it, regulations. Such wedges mitigate against the reallocation of resources necessary to alleviate the misallocations that constituted the false boom. The effect is to moderate the intensity of the recession/depression while prolonging it, or in the best of worlds, to "merely" reduce the post recession/depression growth of the economy. For more on wedges, see Barnett and Wood (2002, 2, 4, 6, 9, especially, 24-28).

[689] The only consumers' good that necessarily decreases is leisure.

previously were "idle,"[690] e.g., college students, housewives, and others at leisure become employed, and previously "idle"[691] factories, mines, office buildings, etc., are brought into use. Therefore, in the sense of optimal use of resources, in the boom there is *excess* employment of resources in the market. That is, more resources are used by the market in an artificial boom than in a period of increased capital formation resulting from changed preferences[692]. Similarly, fewer resources are used by the market in a bust than in a period of decreased capital formation resulting from changed preferences. Put another way, if preferences change resources are shifted from production of the less preferred to the more preferred goods, regardless of type, but there is no reason to expect an increase or decrease in the level of resource use, unless the shift in preferences is to or from leisure. In the case of a monetary policy induced change in the allocation of resources, not only are resources initially shifted from the less preferred to the more preferred good; i.e., from non-interest-rate-sensitive goods[693] (NIRSG) to interest-rate-sensitive goods (IRSG), but additional resources are brought into production; when the inevitable crisis and bust occur, not only is the former shift reversed, with resources shifted back, from IRSG to NIRSG, but some resources are withdrawn from production[694].

A second response is that, the worry is depression, not unemployment; as long as there is complete and total wage flexibility, there need not

---

[690] We note that such people are idle only in the sense of not being employed in the market; certainly according to his own values, each was putting his time to its best use, including in some cases non-market labor.

[691] Again, that a resource is idle in the sense of not being physically used in the production process does not mean it was not being put to its most valuable use as determined by its owner(s).

[692] What of the possible objection that this occurs in both scenarios? That is, that more resources are used by the market due to credit expansion, but also because of a decrease in time preferences. We answer as follows: In both cases there will be an increase in production of interest rate sensitive goods. If this takes place as the result of decreased time preference, it will be part and parcel of shift from production of short-term consumers' goods and, perhaps, some reduction in leisure. However, if it is because of an artificial credit expansion, there will be no shift of production from short-term consumers' goods, though there will be a reduction in leisure.

[693] Interest-rate-sensitive goods are those the demand for which is financed in substantial part by credit. See appendix 1 for more on this subject.

[694] It is imperative that we distinguish between two cases: 1) comparison of symmetry between policy (artificially) induced boom and market (naturally) induced shift in preferences from present to future; and, 2) policy induced boom (initiated from "equilibrium" by credit expansion) and policy induced bust (initiated, from "equilibrium" by credit contraction, and not initiated by inevitable crisis at climax of policy induced boom).

be any joblessness at all. Hummel (1979, 43) is quite correct when he asks: "Why is not frictional unemployment equally great in both directions?" It *is* or can be expected to be equally great in both directions; thus, there would be no necessary difference in unemployment in the two scenarios.

However, matters are quite different in three other dimensions.

First, while there is no reason to expect frictional unemployment to be different, that leaves cyclical unemployment which is asymmetric. What Hummel fails to understand is that in the case of a shift to lower time preferences resources are shifted from less interest-elastic to more interest-elastic industries, and vice-versa for the case of a shift to higher time preferences. It is possible that there would be some change in terms of "idle" resources, but there is no reason to expect this to be systematic. However, in the case of an artificial credit expansion, resources are not shifted so much from less interest-elastic industries, but rather from idleness, both to more-interest elastic and to more interest-inelastic industries, and vice-versa in the case of an artificial credit contraction. In terms of labor, this means that the labor force expands in the false boom and contracts in the subsequent bust, in a way it does not in the cases of changed time preferences. It is this difference in labor force participation that gives rise to the asymmetrical unemployment effects.

Second, there is the issue of leisure. When interest rates fall below natural levels due to governmental monetary mismanagement, labor s increased at the expense of leisure, since wage rates in the higher orders of production are bid up. There is no symmetrical effect in the opposite direction when interest rates rise above natural levels due to this source of misallocation.

Third, a movement toward a lower discount rate creates a situation that has rightly been characterized as "9 bricks available, 10 planned for"[695] But this only applies in the first case when the government intervenes into the economy with artificial credit expansion, not the second case of exogenous changes of tastes on the part of market participants.

As to symmetry in ABCT, it is not to be found between the phases of the cycle; i.e., the boom and the bust, but, rather, what symmetry exists is between cycles differentially initiated. Compare the standard Austrian account of the money/credit cycle initiated by new money lent into existence by government, with one that is initiated by existing money borrowed out of existence by the state. In the latter case, as the government sells securities, their prices decline and the yields thereon increase. Moreover, the central banking authorities retire the money so acquired. Then, the rise in interest rates will induce a shift in demand and subsequently production from IRSG

---

[695] This refers to Roger Garrison's "Ivan and the Brickyard." See on this http://www.auburn.edu/- garriro/ivan.ppt

goods to NIRSG. Also, the decrease in the stock of money will cause price deflation. In the interim during which people are adjusting to the reduced stock of money, i.e., before prices fall very much, there will be a decrease in economic activity, along with the shift from IRSG to NIRSG. That is, in addition to the decrease in total economic activity, there will be a relative reduction in the IRSG relative to the NIRSG sector. However, such a decline in the money stock cannot continue indefinitely. If the central bank continues the monetary/price deflation, interest rates will collapse and people will begin to refrain from purchasing all but necessities in anticipation of ever-lower prices, resulting in a crack-up bust[696]. The alternative available to government is to quit borrowing money out of existence before the process ends in the crack-up bust. If this is the path chosen, the bust ends with a crisis as interest rates decline. The catastrophe will give way to a boom / recovery when and as the decline in prices comes to a halt, and the structure of prices, and therefore, that of expected prices and production, is realigned with peoples' preferences.

Compare the two cycles, the one that begins with money being lent into existence, the other with money being borrowed out of existence, both courtesy of governmental intervention. The former begins with an unsustainable, artificial boom that either: 1) ends in a crack-up boom; or 2) ends in a crisis that gives way to a bust and recovery. The latter begins with an unsustainable, artificial bust that either: 1) ends in a crack-up bust; or 2) ends in a crisis that gives way to a boom and recovery.

The asymmetry, both with respect to employment and "the way individuals generally perceive their economic fortunes," between phases of the ABC is caused by an absolute expansion in the boom and an absolute contraction in the bust. That is, not only is there a relative shift from the production of NIRSG to IRSG in the boom, but the total of resources, including, importantly, labor, and thus total production of goods increases. The malinvestment that constitutes forced saving includes not only the unwarranted production of some capital goods (those that are IRSG), but also of those durable consumers' goods that are IRSG, and in recent times, given the ubiquitous availability of credit, even some non-durable consumers' and services that are IRSG[697]. Forced saving implies a misallocative reduction in consumption. The production of durable goods, consumers' as well as capital, is a form of saving. To the extent there is an unwarranted shift in resources from the production of non-durable goods of either type, to durable

[696] Instead of the hyperinflation (and subsequent barter) threatened by government monetary policy in the other direction, here the threat is of direct barter.

[697] Consider the case of paper napkins. When they appear on a table in a restaurant, they are of course a capital good; in the home, a consumer good. However, no matter where they make their presence, they are clearly not IRSGs.

goods of either type, forced saving occurs. Moreover, as there is an improper uneconomic increase in the quantity of labor used in production, leisure, a form of consumption, decreases, and this unwarranted reduction in consumption is an additional source/form of forced saving.

Furthermore, not only is there a relative shift from the production of IRSG to NIRSG in the bust, but the totality of resources, including importantly, labor, falls. Thus the total production of goods decreases.

The malinvestment that constitutes forced saving includes not only the unwarranted production of some capital goods (those that are IRSG)[698], but also of those durable consumers' goods that are IRSG, and in recent times, given the ubiquitous availability of credit, even some non-durable consumers' and services that are IRSG. Forced saving implies a reduction in consumption. The production of durable goods, consumers' as well as capital, is a form of saving. To the extent that there is an unwarranted shift in resources from the production of non-durable goods of either type, to durable goods of either type, forced saving occurs. Moreover, as there is an unwarranted increase in the quantity of labor used in production, leisure, a form of consumption, decreases, and this unwarranted reduction in consumption also is a source/form of source of forced saving.

For Austrians, a necessary element of the business cycle is the "cluster of error" (Rothbard, 1969, 11). Without such a cluster, there can be no ABC. Yet, money creation on the part of the fed certainly qualifies as a cause of such a cluster. Such machinations cause a cluster of errors because they send to entrepreneurs market signals that do not accurately reflect the underlying time preferences of society.

Can a back and forth alteration between high and low time preferences engender a similar cluster of error? There is no reason to believe that this is the case. After all, business can more or less accurately predict, and thus act in accordance with, other "fickle" consumer preferences: rising and falling hemlines in women's dresses, different and continually changing styles in women's shoes. Entrepreneurs, too, have dealt successfully with novelty items such as the pet rock and the hula hoop.[699] Music has come to us in many variations: 78 r.p.m., 45 r.p.m. records, tapes, cassettes, disks, etc. True, there is no back and forth movement in any of these examples (except

---

698 There can be no facile correlation, let alone equation, of durability and higher or lower orders of capital goods, one the one hand, and interest rate sensitivity on the other. Their relationship is a complex one in that durability can appear at any stage. For example, a first order capital good may be an IRSG if it is very durable, and not if not, and the same exact situation applies to higher order capital goods. Paper clips, or cotton balls, for instance, can take part in production at any stage of the structure, and are NIRSG wherever they appear. It is typically the very opposite with steel.

699 Those that have not are entrepreneurs no longer.

for the length of skirt hemlines), but the essence of the issue is not endless repeatability. Rather, it is the question of whether accurate market signals can be generated or not. If they can, there is no cluster of error. If not, there is. And, Hummel has not offered any reasons to suppose that market prices cannot function in the face of change, while it is no less than an unchallenged, even by Hummel, staple of Austrian economics both that credit expansion falsifies market price communication, and that the weeding out process of the marketplace (Hazlitt, 1979) tends to ensure that the challenges of change are not beyond the ability of entrepreneurs.

Finally, let it be noted that the asymmetry is a consequence of the natural imperfections of the real world. If, for every change in the "data," whether individual preferences, technology, stock of resources, every individual's understanding of the economic significance of such events were correct, then they would act so as to adjust all prices. Therefore, all relative prices would fully and accurately reflect the new data. If it were costless to shift resources from one use to another on the basis of the revised structure of production, then there would be continuous correct resource allocations, and there would be symmetry between expansions and contractions. The asymmetry comes about because the world is imperfect and therefore there are such things as contracts, etc., that cause asymmetry in adjustments to changed data. For example, wage contracts are likely to be more flexible in an upward direction than in a downward one. At the extreme, zero is a floor beneath which wages cannot fall, but there is no such limitation in the opposite direction. Wages can conceivably rise without end, but not fall below zero[700].

II. Definitions of the Money Stock

Hummel (1979, 45) starts out this section in a reasonable enough manner: "What is needed is a defining criterion for what constitutes a money substitute, so that this wide spectrum of financial instruments can be clearly divided between those that are money substitutes and those that are credit instruments. The reason a clear dividing line is necessary relates to the various means by which a genuine change in time preferences on the part of consumers can manifest itself." Who, after all, can oppose clarity of definitions, ceteris paribus? But even here there are problems, specifically, those of continua. While it may be *desirable*, and not only from an aesthetic perspective, for the world to be divisible into watertight compartments, such is not always the case. For example, the light spectrum can be broken up into Red, Orange, Yellow, Green, Blue, Indigo and Violet (the familiar Roy G. Biv distinction), they all shade into one another. Just because they do, however, does not mean no useful differences can be drawn. So is the situation between money substitutes and credit instruments.

---

[700] Strictly speaking, we must abstract from the possibility of negative wages in making this claim.

A more important criticism of Hummel's call this distinction is that it is not necessary to ABCT. The key to ABCT is the distinction not between money substitutes and credit instruments but between the allocation of resources in the production and consumption processes. This may also be referred to as the structure of production and consumption as they would be in the presence versus absence of government intervention in the credit markets. Government intervention in credit markets causes, ceteris paribus, interest rates to differ from what they otherwise would be.[701] The usual case is intervention which causes them to be *lower* than otherwise. But in either case, the artificially distorted interest rates affect the demand for IRSG relative to NIRSG. It is the reallocation of resources necessitated by this intervention that constitutes the artificial boom or artificial bust. Resources are not used optimally. Moreover, because such "false" interest rates affect the production of both durable capital and consumers' goods, they affect the structure of production and consumption into the future, such that even after the distortions of the initial phase of the cycle are eliminated they still alter the future course of the economy. This is because the liquidation of the distortions is not, in the vast majority of cases, physical in nature, but rather takes the form of temporary "idleness" followed by revaluation. The physical goods that constitute the distortions are integrated into the structure of production on the basis of their new "correct"[702] valuations. The whole issue of time preference is thus something of a red herring. If interest rates change because of the voluntary actions of individuals then the reallocations of resources, i.e., the alterations in the structure of production, induced thereby are warranted. If, however, interest rates change because of government intervention, resources are misallocated as a consequence. Another red herring, of course, is Hummel's emphasis on money substitutes vis-à-vis credit instruments; as we can see, they have played no role in our analysis of the ABC.

In the view of Hummel (1979, 45-46):

"The dividing line between money substitutes and credit instruments is the margin between cash balances and investment. If this margin is not well defined, it becomes theoretically impossible to distinguish between changes in

---

[701] Examples include: governmental guarantees of repayment of principal which reduce a lender's risk and therefore the interest rate on a loan; differential treatment of interest paid (allowing or not allowing interest paid to be deducted from income for the purpose of calculating taxable income) which, ceteris paribus, results in higher (lower) interest rates, respectively; and, credit market expansions that affect expectations of inflation and, thus, interest rates.

[702] It cannot be denied that these new valuations will only be "correct" in equilibrium, and that the economy never reaches this nirvana like state. But, at least these new evaluations are not systematically altered by governmental monetary mismanagement, and, except for random mistakes, closer, if not much closer, to market clearing valuations.

the stock of money and changes in time preferences brought about by non-neutral shifts in the demand for money relative to investment spending."

Certainly the dividing line between money substitutes and credit instruments is clear. "A medium of exchange which is commonly used as such is called money" (Mises, 1966, 398). A money substitute is a claim to a specific amount of money that can be instantly exchanged for money without expense (Mises, 1996, 432).[703] What Mises omits is that when a money substitute, and a fortiori, money itself, serves as a medium of exchange; i.e., when it is given by a buyer and accepted by a seller in exchange for some good, the transaction is complete – the buyer is under no further obligation with respect to that transaction. For example, when an exchange is effectuated by means of a check drawn on a demand or "checkable" deposit account, once the check clears, the buyer is under no further obligation to the seller. However, had a credit instrument been used instead, the buyer would be under an obligation to redeem, at some time in the future, the credit instrument by payment of money or money substitutes. The margin between money substitutes and credit instruments is, then, well defined.

Moreover, certainly in the modern world, the "dividing line between money substitutes and credit instruments is" *not* "the margin between cash balances and investment," as the amount of consumers' credit is immense.

---

[703] "Claims to a definite amount of money, payable and redeemable on demand, against a debtor about whose solvency and willingness to pay there does not prevail the slightest doubt, render to the individual all the services money can render, provided that all parties with whom he could possibly transact business are perfectly familiar with these essential qualities of the claims concerned: minute to minute maturity as well as undoubted solvency and willingness to pay on the part of the debtor. We may call such claims *money-substitutes*, as they can fully replace money in an individual's or a firm's cash holding. The technical and legal features of the money-substitutes do not concern catallactics. A money-substitute can be embodied either in a banknote or in a demand deposit with a bank subject to check ("checkbook money" or deposit currency), provided the bank is prepared to exchange the note or the deposit daily free of charge against money proper. Token coins are also money-substitutes, provided the owner is in a position to exchange them at need, free of expense and without delay, against money. To achieve this it is not required that the government be bound by law to redeem them. What counts is the fact that these tokens can be really converted free of expense and without delay. If the total amount of token coins issued is kept within reasonable limits, no special provisions on the part of the government are necessary to keep their exchange value at par with their face value. The demand of the public for small change gives everybody the opportunity to exchange them easily against pieces of money. The main thing is that every owner of a money-substitute is perfectly certain that it can, at every instant and free of expense, be exchanged against money" (Mises, 1996, 432-433).

Hummel (1979, 45-46, footnote added) then enters into even more treacherous waters. He states:

"An individual with a money income continuously faces three possible ways of allocating that income. He can spend it on consumers' goods, he can spend it on investment goods, or he can increase (or decrease) his cash balances…. But non-neutral changes in the demand for money can also affect the structure of production. A neutral change in the demand for money would be, say a fall in cash balances that increased equally both consumption and investment spending, thus maintaining the same aggregate consumption-investment ratio.[704] If… cash balances fall primarily by adding to investment spending, this is, in effect, a fall in time preferences. Similarly, if cash balances fall primarily by adding to consumption spending, this represents a rise in time preferences."

There is a fundamental confusion in the foregoing. First, his trichotomy is false. There are more choices than Hummel lists, unless he is lumping all expenditures that are not made for the purchase of *currently* produced consumer' goods[705] into the category of expenditures on investment goods.[706] In addition to the purchases of such goods, an individual can spend his money on used consumers' goods, used capital goods, and more important, on non-money financial assets, including foreign monies that do not function as money in his domestic economy.

Moreover, there is a stock-flow confusion involved here. At the aggregate level cash balances do not fall when purchases, whether of consumers' or capital goods, are made, by A from B; rather A's cash balance falls and B's rises by the exact amount of the decline in A's balance. Cash balances can rise or fall for any one individual, but not for all of those who comprise an economy, since the money must be owned by someone at all times[707].

---

[704] Obviously, in this context "equally" should be taken to mean that the ratio of additional expenditures on consumers' goods to those on investment goods should be equal to the ratio that existed prior to the new expenditures.

[705] We assume that Hummel is not including "used" consumers' goods in his category "consumers' goods," but rather that it refers to "currently" produced consumers' goods. However, even if he does include such expenditures in his category, our point requires only a slight modification; to wit, the deletion as alternatives of those categories he has lumped together.

[706] We assume that his category "investment goods" refers to newly produced capital goods and does not include financial assets.

[707] Suppose Mr. Monte Burns uses a $100 bill to light his cigar. Then, strictly speaking, the statement in the text is incorrect, so we implicitly extract from such money destruction. However, in this case, there would be a tendency for the value of all the money to rise, and this would to some degree compensate for that loss.

Furthermore, to say that an increase in expenditures on investment goods or consumers' goods represents a decrease or increase, respectively, in time preference is to enter the realm of thymology,[708] not praxeology. In praxeology there is only preferring A to B. There are no *rates* of preference, time or other. So just as there is no praxeological meaning to "I prefer the red shirt twice as much as the blue one," there is no meaning to "My rate of time preference is X," whatever X may be; e.g. 10% or even 10% per annum[709].

Time preference is a categorical requisite of human action. No mode of action can be thought of in which satisfaction within a nearer period of the future is not--other things being equal--preferred to that in a later period. The very act of gratifying a desire implies that gratification at the present instant is preferred to that at a later instant. He who consumes a nonperishable good instead of postponing consumption for an indefinite later moment thereby reveals a higher valuation of present satisfaction as compared with later satisfaction. If he were not to prefer satisfaction in a nearer period of the future to that in a remoter period, he would never consume and so satisfy wants. He would always accumulate, he would never consume and enjoy. He would not consume today, but he would not consume tomorrow either, as the morrow would confront him with the same alternative (Mises, 1966, 484).

What is the relevance of this statement, one of the most aesthetically beautiful statements Mises, or anyone else for that matter, ever wrote? The point is this: Mises does not even so much as refer to the "*rate* of time preference" in contradistinction to plain old ordinary "time preference," as mentioned above. In fact, that term never appears in any of his writings, to the best of our knowledge[710].

Time preference is just that, a preference, as Mises, says, for a "satisfaction within a neared period of the future" rather, ceteris paribus, than in a

---

[708] Following Mises (1998), "thymology" herein means the knowledge of human valuations and volitions.

[709] But if people increase the ratio of expenditure on investment goods vis-à-vis consumers' goods, e.g., the triangle gets flatter, is that not equivalent to a lowering of time preference, forget about by how much it gets lowered? Yes, it is equivalent from the perspective of thymology; however, from a *praxeological* point of view, all we observe at any point in time is the choice of A over B (as seen by the actor – all a third party sees, if he sees anything, is the choice of A). The ascription of the choice presumes a motive, and yes we do so through versthehen, but though indeed useful, it is not praxeological. That is, today you choose the combination of consumption and saving/investment (C_0, I_0) and tomorrow you choose (C_1, I_1); who, other than the actor may say that the *value* of $C_0 <$ the *value* of C_1 and the ***value*** of $I_1 >$ the *value* of I_0 (or vice versa)?

[710] A perusal of the electronic version of Mises (1998) fails to reveal this phrase in the entire book (http://www.mises.org/humanaction.asp). Naturally, we can only make this claim with somewhat less confidence regarding all his other publications.

later period. But there is no way to generate a *rate* of time preference from this[711]. Certainly, in this sense, a rate is a ratio, e.g., 10% or 10% per annum. However, there is no way to take a ratio of satisfactions, unless, perhaps we have an objective theory of value and measure satisfactions in, say, utils.[712]

Another difficulty arises with Hummel's tri-part division of goods[713] into consumption, investment, and money. In contrast, regarding goods we hold a binary perspective. In our view, there are only two, not three, types of goods: consumption and investment; for us, money is an investment good, and does not belong in any third category, apart from these two. This is not the time nor the place for a full rehearsal of the arguments in favor of a binary, and opposed to a tertiary distinction. We have done this elsewhere (Barnett and Block, 2008B). Suffice it to say at this point that human action is a binary phenomenon: it admits of two choices, not three: consumption (including leisure) or production; but as every act of production is either an act of saving/investment, all one can do is either consume or save/invest; buy or sell; prefer or set aside. In the present case, either money gives intrinsic satisfaction, or it is an intermediary, a means toward an end. Since it is the latter that commonly motivates people with regard to money, it is a capital good, not an item of consumption[714]. That being the case, the difficulty raised by Hummel becomes obviated.

---

[711] We acknowledge that Hummel is far closer to the Austrian mainstream (if we can be permitted to use such an expression) on this matter than are the present authors.

[712] It is interesting to note that Mises, himself, falls into this trap when he states (1996, 526): "Originary interest is the ratio of value assigned to want satisfaction in the immediate future and the value assigned to want satisfaction in remote periods of the future." Elsewhere, however, he contradicts this erroneous position. Of course, for him value is subjective: "There is no standard of greater or lesser satisfaction other than individual judgments of value, different for various people and for the same people at various times. What makes a man feel uneasy and less uneasy is established by him from the standard of his own will and judgment, from his personal and subjective valuation" (Mises, 1996, 14). And, "There are in the sphere of values and valuations no arithmetical operations; there is no such thing as a calculation of values" (Mises, 1996, 122).

[713] We assume he is here ignoring financial assets.

[714] The best counterexample known to the authors is the case of Scrooge McDuck, of comic book fame. He would enjoy taking baths in money: throwing it up over his head, and letting is cascade down upon him. Thus, for Mr. McDuck and all others of his ilk, money is a consumer good. But people of this sort also use money in the normal way, and when they do so money becomes a capital good. There is nothing intrinsic *within* money that makes it a capital or consumer good; it all depends upon the purposes of the economic actor. But the same can be said for seed corn, or water, etc. There are perverts out there who, presumably, can use these items too, in weird and exotic ways.

That said, Hummel's (1979, 45-46) statement about the "theoretical impossibil[ity] [of] distinguish[ing] between changes in the stock of money and changes in time preferences brought about by non-neutral shifts in the demand for money relative to investment spending" is confusing. What is brought about by non-neutral shifts in the demand for money relative to investment spending is not changes in time; therefore it must be changes in the stock of money that is brought about by such non-neutral shifts. But given stability in the monetary base on the part of the authorities, the stock of money is determined by the public's desired ratio of currency to demand deposits, not by non-neutral shifts in the demand for money. Unless the central government/ bank changes the monetary base and/or the public changes its desired currency to deposit ratio, the money stock will not change regardless of any change in the demand for money, neutral or not. It is changes in preferences that alter these shifts in the demand for money, not the other way around.

Hummel's hypothetical about an economy in which the banks issue time deposits only, and that has no central bank is also problematical.[715] He (1979, 46) then assumes that: "...the quantity of time deposits increases over a period until a banking panic wipes them all out. Such a sequence of events, especially in the absence of a central bank, may not be very likely, but it is at least theoretically conceivable." He has, of course, assumed, implicitly, that the banks are operating on a fractional or, perhaps, zero (0) reserve basis vis-à-vis their time deposits. Let us be clear that time deposits are not money. If, by explicitly positing that banks issue only time deposits, he has implicitly assumed that such deposits are money, then we have to call into question his concept of money, else he really is dealing with an imaginary economy the relevance of which to Austrian theory is nil. Given, then, that time deposits are not money, one wonders how the quantity of time deposits increased. It is one thing for someone with money to put it in a time deposit, it is quite another for someone to borrow funds to place in a time deposit, unless the banks are paying their depositors a higher rate of interest than that which they are charging their borrowers. But if people are not borrowing for the purpose of acquiring time deposits, it is difficult to see how "the quantity of time deposits increases," in contrast to a system in which there are demand deposits, and in which people borrow for the purpose of acquiring such deposits, which serve as media of exchange.

Although Hummel maintains that his scenario "is at least theoretically conceivable," let us see what is necessary for such a conception. First,

[715] Obviously, there must be money in this economy, else what is it that the banks are receiving in return for issuing time deposits? And, as there are no banknotes or demand deposits, this must be one of the following: 1) commodity money; 2) commodity money with100% backed government paper; 3) commodity money with government paper that is not 100% backed; or 4) government paper that has no backing.

because the deposits are time deposits, only those that mature today can be the object of a panic.[716] Now unless all such deposits mature "today," they cannot all be wiped out in a panic at present. Moreover, to the extent that the banks have some actual reserves, only the excess of maturing deposits over the amount of reserves would be "wiped out," and in such a case they would not really be wiped out, as the depositors would still be in the pool with others whose time deposits had not matured that day. Further, the bank would necessarily have some assets, besides its investments, that it could liquidate to pay off depositors as their deposits matured. Additionally, they might be able to raise cash by selling bonds, if their investments were viewed as sound. Deposits would be wiped out only to the extent that maturing deposits exceeded banks' reserves plus cash flow from maturing investments plus cash that could be raised from sales of bonds or other longer term financial assets plus cash that could be raised by sale of the banks other assets.

Only if there are not enough reserves plus maturing sound loans to cover today's maturing deposits will some depositors be left holding the bag. In general, for his scenario to occur, banks would have had to mismatch their maturity dates; i.e., they have to have borrowed short and lent long. Moreover, a sufficient number of banks would have to have done this for there to be a simultaneous run on banks in general, not merely on the relatively few mismanaged banks. Of course, in a free market system, such banks would tend to be eliminated via differential clearings almost as quickly as they come into existence, and, therefore, there would be few if any around at any given time, and almost certainly not enough for a panic. Thus, Hummel has implicitly assumed that banks, as a rule, are mismanaged, in spite of the competitive pressures of the market that eliminate the inefficient.

III. Net Investment

Hummel (1979, 46-47) sets out his challenge in this regard as follows: "Lengthening the structure of production entails positive net investment. Maintaining the structure of production intact at its current length entails zero net investment. Shortening the structure of production entails disinvestments. During depressions, therefore, net investment should be negative. But in U.S. history, the only depression in which measured net investment was actually negative was the Great Depression. In all the others for which data are available, net investment fell but still remained positive. Does this mean that Austrian theory is irrelevant to all but one major depression in U.S. history?"

---

[716] Any deposits not redeemed when they mature must be deposited for a set period of time, else they become demand deposits, of which Hummel assumes there are none. Moreover, if he assumes the minimum maturity period of time deposits to be very short, he has time deposits de jure, but demand deposits de facto. But one imporant characteristic of Austrian theory is that it attempts to deal with substance, not form.

There are several responses that can be made to this challenge.

First, net investment may shorten the structure of production.[717] Consider a situation in which there is no net investment, say an Evenly Rotating Economy. The purpose of net investment would to alter the situation in such fashion that after it is incorporated into the economy and there is once again no net investment, either: 1) the *time* structure, i.e., the period, of production is unchanged and yet there is greater output per unit of inputs than previously, so that from producing and waiting for the same amount of time we obtain more output; or 2) the time structure of production is lengthened and yet there is sufficiently greater output per unit of inputs than previously, so that from producing and waiting for a longer period of time, we get sufficiently more output to make the additional production and waiting time worthwhile; or 3) the time structure of production is *shortened* and yet there is a) at least as much output per unit of inputs than previously, so that from producing and waiting for the shorter period of time we get at least as much output as previously or b) less output than before, but the loss in satisfaction resulting from the reduction in output is less than the gain in satisfaction from the shortened period of production/waiting. Indeed, what would seem to be most desirable would be a net investment that once integrated into the economy and returned to a no net investment situation would *shorten* the period of production to virtually zero. Instantaneous production, after all, is our goal. Producers in such a situation could provide desired goods to consumers virtually the instant they desired them.

Second, if ABCT is relevant only to one depression in U.S. history, as Hummel (1979, 47) asks, or, even to none at all, so be it. Praxeological reasoning cannot be shown to be erroneous just because it is not widely applicable, and truth, not applicability, is surely the criterion on the basis of which Austrianism should be judged.

Third, even if we revise Hummel eliminating his erroneous assertions regarding the relationships among changes in the time structure of production, stages of the cycle, and net investment, to say only that there should be positive net investment during the boom and negative net

---

[717] One can perform a gedanken experiment that is not farfetched involving Robinson Crusoe in which positive net investment results in a shortened structure of production once net investment has returned to zero, and yet output per period is greater than before. Certainly, if it is possible for RC to shorten his period of production; i.e., increase his leisure, and yet be able to produce more consumers' goods per period, societies should be able to do so also. Moreover, one can use he same gedanken experiment to conclude that negative net investment can result in a lengthened structure of production. The biggest problem is defining what one means by the period, or length of the structure, of production. For this radical critique of the usual Austrian assumptions about the triangle, see Barnett and Block, 2006C

investment during the bust, his argument is still problematical. It is quite possible that during the boom measured net investment is positive while real net investment is negative. This is because investments are measured for the purpose of the National Income and Product Accounts (NIPA)[718] at current market value, whereas the very idea of malinvestment carries with it the idea that, at the time of their production, the market value of the capital goods whose production constitutes malinvestment is necessarily overstated. Were it not, the capital goods would not malinvestment. Of course, not all investment during the boom is malinvestment. In fact, there is no way to know at the time, else, again, there would be no malinvestment. It is possible, then, that if measured investment were reduced by the amount of malinvestment in the boom the resulting number might be negative; i.e., there might be actual *disinvestment* during the boom. Similarly, and for similar reasons, it is possible that in the bust measured net investment is negative, while real net investment is positive.

Furthermore, it is only possible to measure correctly "net investment," or, indeed, any other kind of investment, not to mention any other macroeconomic variable, at equilibrium. For it is only at equilibrium that prices reflect economic phenomena accurately. (And even then, the one must assume that the expectations upon which the market clearing actions are based are themselves correct.) However, we never in the real world attain the evenly rotating economy, without which proper assessment cannot be made of net investment. Thus, Hummel's (1979, 47) empirical evidence claims cannot support his position. Moreover, the use of government data on net investment may not be relied upon to make his point, as such data are at best bureaucratic estimates.[719]

Fourth, government statistics on investment seem to be a weak reed on which to label praxeology incorrect. If it can be shown that there were other depressions, and even recessions, which were accompanied by a fall in net investment, this would show the wider applicability of ABCT. But suppose it cannot be shown that depressions and recessions other than that of 1933 were accompanied by disinvestment. If this were true, then we would have to concede that ABCT is of virtually no consequence, save as a theoretical curiosity, because it has no other relevance for the real world; i.e., its applicability would be so severely limited as to make it practically trivial, if theoretically valid. Even under these heroic assumptions, by no means demonstrated by Hummel, there is nothing wrong with practically trivial, but theoretically valid economic analysis. It is, first, valuable for its own sake. Secondly, while impractical at present, it might become rendered less so, or not at all, in future.

---

[718] http://www.bea.doc.gov/bea/an/nipaguid.pdf

[719] See appendix 2 for support of this position.

Hummel (1979, 48) ends this section on the following note: "A depression could be forestalled if the increased real saving that otherwise would have further lengthened the structure of production is sufficient to maintain the malinvestments induced by the credit expansion."

Yes, there is little doubt that, after a depression is created by governmental credit expansion which extends the structure of production further than that amount justified by changing time preferences, *if* time preferences are then subsequently lowered, then the worse effects of the depression can be avoided. But there will still be some resource misallocation compared to the scenario where the time preferences were lowered (or entrepreneurs predicted that they would be, and acted accordingly), and this lead to entrepreneurial lengthening of the structure of production. The differences stem from timing. In Hummel's scenario, there is discoordination, until (and unless!) time preferences propitiously change in the proper direction, and to the precise extent, called for in order to justify the rash acts of the central bank. Improper investment initially takes place, which is only later vindicated by later events; i.e., what was a mistaken allocation of resources ex ante becomes a correct allocation ex post because sometime after the misallocation began, peoples' preferences changed to favor that allocation – a fortuitous happenstance, indeed. In contrast, in the case where there is no government intervention, and consumers lower their time preference rates, followed by (or better yet, anticipated by) proper entrepreneurial behavior, there is no such discoordination[720]

IV. Deflation

In this section Hummel (1979, 48) announces he will discuss "all the additional events other than credit expansion that will, according to a consistent application of Austrian theory, cause a depression. All of them can cause depressions with no previous boom; a few seem to facilitate a trailing boom." In contrast, it is the contention of the present authors that the *only* possible cause of the ABC is governmental central bank (e.g., fed) mismanagement: credit expansion.

a. Capital Consumption

States Hummel (1979, 48): "As time preferences rise, the structure of production will shorten, and a depression will continue until time preferences stabilize. Capital consumption will always involve depression." But this is perilously close to equating depression and disequilibrium. One might as

---

[720] An analogy may shed light on this distinction. Hummel's scenario would be akin to A shooting B to death, attempting to murder him, and it later turning out that B was in the act of attempting a murder of his own against an innocent person, C, and thus A's act was really justified, in that it prevented this other murder. Or, it turns out that B was already dead, shot by someone else, D, right before A did this, and thus A was not guilty of murder, but merely of shooting a dead body.

well claim that every time a person goes on a diet, reducing his consumption of chocolate and increasing his purchase of carrots, there will be a depression in the chocolate industry, and a boom in carrots. In fact, if there is no government intervention, an increase in time preferences will lead to capital consumption; however, that is not synonymous with depression. Instead, resources would be shifted from the production and maintenance of capital goods to the production of consumers' goods. There would, of course, be transition phenomena similar to those that occur anytime there is any sort of change in preferences, or technology for that matter. But this does not equate to a depression. Capital consumption no more always leads to a depression than capital formation always leads to a false boom. As warranted capital formation results in a structure of production more in keeping with individuals' preferences, so also does warranted capital consumption also result in a more harmonious structure of production. And as unwarranted capital formation impairs the structure of production, so also does unwarranted consumption. In the former case, a false boom ends with a crisis that turns into a depression during which prices adjust and resources are reallocated in accord with people's preferences. In the latter case, a depression is followed an expansion in which prices adjust and resources are reallocated in accord with people's preferences.

b. Deflation

Hummel (1979, 48) erroneously equates deflation and credit contraction when he refers to "Deflation or, more precisely, credit contraction" But the two are very different. We have had price deflation, without any government intervention whatsoever, in goods such as television sets, cars, air travel and computers. When these products were first introduced to the market, they were playthings for the rich, luxury items, or were restricted only to large commercial use. But, with innovation, large-scale production, assembly line technologies, and a relatively hands off policy of the state, prices fell and they became accessible to the masses. This occurred, Hummel to the contrary notwithstanding, without any discernable depression.

As to credit contraction, Hummel (1979, 48) states that:

"…it will drive the loan rate of interest above the natural rate. If credit contraction occurs as a secondary feature of a depression already caused by previous credit expansion, it will bring about more shortening of the structure of production than is necessary and aggravate the depression."

That one consequence of the depression phase of an Austrian business cycle may well be a secondary deflation comes as no surprise, having been noted as far back as 1933 by Hayek (1975 [1939] 176). That once the excesses of the boom have been appropriately incorporated into the structure of production through relevant price adjustments and restructuring, the economy returns to its natural growth path is also standard Austrian fare.

Hummel (1979, 48) continues: "If credit contraction occurs with no immediately preceding credit expansion, it will cause a depression with no prior boom." However, the consequences of a credit contraction that begins without a prior credit expansion depend on the nature of the monetary system and the cause of the credit contraction. In a modern monetary economy, interest rates are set in credit markets.[721] Mainstream Austrian theory posits time preference as the sole reason for the existence of interest, though it must admit that other factors affect the rate of interest.[722] If the credit contraction occurs in a system with 100% reserve backing for banknotes and demand deposits and is strictly the result of voluntary action, then it will *not* "drive the loan rate of interest above the natural rate," (Hummel, 1979, 48) nor, for that matter, will it drive the loan rate below the natural rate.[723] Whether the natural rate will increase or decrease depends on the factors that caused the credit contraction in the first place. In fact, a credit contraction can increase or decrease the natural rate of interest, with concomitant increase or decrease, respectively, in the loan, or market, rate, which will adjust to the natural rate with a lag, the length of which will depend on a variety of factors. If the credit contraction occurs because of a decline in the demand for credit not offset by an equal or greater increase in its supply, market rates will *decline* in keeping with the *lower* natural rate. Alternatively, if the contraction occurs because of a decrease in the supply of credit that is not offset by an equal or greater increase in demand, then market rates will rise in keeping with the higher natural rate. However, in both of these cases, the volume of credit would contract.

In either case, the structure of production will be shortened, but his will be in accord with changed time preferences. Resources will be shifted from the production of higher order goods to lower orders, including especially, consumers' goods. There will be no depression. Of course, the reduction in

---

[721] This is not standard Austrian fare in which "the *interest rate is equal to the rate of price spread in the various stages*" (Rothbard, 2001 [1962], 317, emphasis in original). However, in a world of scarcity, instantaneous production, heterogeneous time preferences, and money, where there would be no stages and therefore no price spreads between stages, there would still be interest and interest rates. Let us now invert matters: suppose a situation where there are indeed stages of production (we call this into question in Barnett and Block, A) but no credit market. Would there be an interest rate? Our answer is that there would not be. But what of the price differentials between otherwise homogeneous goods at different stages? These, to be sure would still exist, but they would be "merely" price differentials, not interest rates. Yes, in an ERE world of both credit markets and production stages, there must be an equilibration between the two. But this does not logically imply that the two are indistinguishable. They are: one is an interest rate, the other is not.

[722] For more on this point, see appendix 3.

[723] This is true whether it is a system of commodity or fiat money.

production of capital goods will shift the economy to a lower growth path, but that is a downward change in the trend, not a depression.

However, if the credit contraction is the result of governmental monetary policy, that is a different matter entirely. Then, the contraction would drive the market rate above the natural rate. And, Hummel is correct in maintaining that a depression would ensue, though incorrect when he contends that when consumers' preferences are reasserted a "trailing boom" would follow; actually, it would not be a "boom," but rather an expansion that would return the economy to its natural growth path, as modified by the "injection" and distribution effects of the governmental monetary policy and its effects on the structure of production.

c. Consumption spending

Hummel (1979, 48) makes several mistakes in this section.

First, he states: "If new money, rather then entering the loan market, is spent exclusively on consumption…" But this is a false dichotomy. He conflates two issues: the way new money comes into existence and what the new money is used to purchase. New money is either lent or spent into existence. Austrian cycle theory is typically concerned with the former case, in which the supply of credit is increased depressing interest rates and causing a misallocation of resources in the direction of the higher orders that results in a distorted structure of production. It does not at all address the consequences of new money being spend into existence; i.e., a "pure" inflation, which is one of the bases of Hummel's attack in this section. Moreover, regardless of the way new money comes into existence it may be spend on consumers' goods or on capital goods, or, for that matter, on financial assets on foreign currencies, in turn used to purchase whatever. There is no necessary connection between a pure inflation and purchases of consumers' goods, as Hummel implies.

Second, he takes the position that "war time monetary expansions have been neutral with respect to the structure of production" since they "have not been accompanied by depressions" (1979, 48) and they would have been so accompanied, had these expansions not been neutral in this regard.

The problem, here, is in thinking that government can invest; e.g., that government expenditures can elongate the structure of production. But, as Rothbard (1970, 173) has shown, this is an impossibility. The state may, indeed, spend money on things (airplane factories, steel, rubber) such that if private individuals did so we would have no compunction about labeling them as investment; nevertheless, when *government* does so, it *cannot* be considered investment and *must* be considered consumption (1970, 173). So, contrary to Hummel, the government must of necessity be non-neutral, at least in his terminology. It must *always* create a depression, if we credit Hummel's economic analysis, and combine it with the Rothbardian insight.

Perhaps more important is that wartime governmental policies include fiscal and regulatory, as well as monetary, and, it is virtually impossible in such historical contexts to separate the effects of these different policies, especially since some may reinforce others, while they interfere with yet others. As Austrians, unlike Friedmanites, are wont to say, an economic theory is either correct or it is not, but in either case it cannot be tested empirically (Hoppe, 1988, 1992; Mises, 1957).

The third difficulty is that Hummel (1979, 48) maintains: "If one assumes an underlying progressing economy, then some of the depression effects will be offset by falling time preferences." The implication here seems to be that there is a negative correlation between wealth and time preference rates: the greater (lesser) is the former, the lower (higher) will be the latter. Nor is this, merely, an empirical observation on Hummel's part. His statement is much too definitive to be interpreted in any such manner. Rather, he sees some necessary connection between the two.

This is precisely the error committed by Hoppe (2001), and refuted by Barnett, Block and Salerno (2006). The gist of the latter argument is that there is no praxeological requirement that the income effect of a gain in income or wealth be associated with a fall in time preference rates. Although this may be correct enough as an empirical generalization, there is no logical contradiction implied by supposing that a man gains wealth, and, yet, chooses a higher, not a lower, time preference rate.

V. Constant Rate of Credit Expansion

There are three separate claims in this section that must be dealt with. We do so in order of presentation.

a. According to Hummel (1979, 49): "… nowhere is the outcome of a credit expansion at a steady rate clearly specified. Presumably, since such a policy cannot generate a continuous boom, it must either result in (a) a continuous alternation of booms and depressions or (b) a boom followed by a continuous depression. Much Austrian writing is ambiguous between these two alternatives."

There is good and sufficient reason for this lacuna. It is unlikely in the extreme, and Austrians have had their hands more than full addressing actual events, or, at least likely ones; so much so that they have not devoted precious time resources to all but impossible ones.

If we are to strictly and accurately interpret this statement, and how else are we to react to it, "a credit expansion at a steady rate" means just that, through good times and bad times, through thick and thin, an undeviating sticking to one's guns no matter what the result. In other words, the government announces a credit expansion, of, say, 5% per annum, at a daily rate, and does not deviate from this policy by even an iota, ever. Eventually, this will become fully anticipated, and incorporated into expectations. It does not matter whether this program features a public announcement or not. That will only reduce the time it takes for people to take this situation into account in their planning.[724]

According to what Hummel might classify as "classical ABCT," such a policy would, in the first instance, elongate the structure of production, enticing capitalist entrepreneurs to devote more resources to investment in higher order capital goods, and less to lower order investments and consumers' goods, than would otherwise have been the case. After all, the credit expansion lowers the market rate of interest below the natural rate, fooling, enticing, or inducing businessmen into thinking that profits will be increased by such reallocations of resources.

Wagner (2000) criticized ABCT on the ground that all entrepreneurs would eventually become expert in these insights. That being the case, they would refuse to act so as to elongate the structure of production in response to a credit increase on the ground that it would not be sustainable. But this is erroneous, for several reasons. First, academic economists, let alone entrepreneurs, have at least so far proven impervious to the niceties of ABCT. It will be only in the *very* long run before any such thing is likely to come to pass, on the assumption that knowledge of this perspective definitely and strongly raises profit levels.

However, there is no necessary causal relationship between an understanding of correct (e.g., Austrian) economics, and entrepreneurial success. The two are epistemologically separate. It is akin to expecting a theoretical physicist or mathematician to garner great success in the computer or engineering businesses. Surely, the former cannot be an impediment as far as the latter is concerned, but the one is certainly no guarantee of the other.

Another difficulty is that Wagner (2000) does not properly distinguish between a stock and a flow. Just because the investment in the higher order of production cannot be sustainable in the long run (given that the underlying time preference rates have not been lowered by the credit expansion, which would have made them viable), does not preclude the possibility of getting in and then out, while the getting is good, before the bottom drops out of the higher orders of production.[725] Moreover, there is no necessary reason that investments in higher order goods need go uncompleted, or be abandoned if already completed, when the crisis hits. Certainly those that would not have been made but for the artificially lower market rates of interest deserve the

---

[724] Or, perhaps, increase it depending upon people's experiences with the veracity, or lack thereof, of governmental pronouncements.

[725] For a rejoinder to Wagner (2000), see Block (2001A).

appellation, "malinvestments," and must be liquidated. However, abandonment and mothballing are not the only ways to liquidate such investments. Financial liquidation may do the trick. If the capital value of such investments can be, and is, written down sufficiently, these higher order goods can be integrated into a/the new sustainable structure of production.

Further, there is a relevant difference between Wagner (2000) and Hummel (1979). The former incorporates the real world assumption of a fed free to change policy at a whim. The latter imposes upon this institution the requirement, as we have seen, that credit policy remains entirely unchanged throughout. To compare the two, Wagner has in mind a moving target, Hummel, a stationary one. The problem with Hummel's choices between (a) a continuous alternation of booms and depressions or (b) a boom followed by a continuous depression, is that leaves out a third option: c. an undetermined; better yet, undeterminable, state of economic affairs.

For, on the one hand, given full information as to the stable goal, no rational profit maximizer would be mislead into malinvestents. On the other hand, he is being subsidized into doing so, but only on the assumption that he can get out before the time of the crash, leaving someone else to hold the bag. If we assume full and complete information has been incorporated into *all* decision-making, i.e., that it is *false* that "a sucker is born every minute," then it cannot be denied that no one would bite. On the other hand, people miss not only moving targets, but stationary ones as well. So which is true? One cannot say, given the assumptions provided. It is undetermined. It is akin to dividing a number by zero. The result is not "infinity," rather it is "undefined." Something similar is operating in the present context. Thus the answer to Hummel's question: "a or b," is "neither of those, but rather c," that is, not only is it uncertain, but it is indeterminable.

b. In the view of Hummel (1979, 49): "... a constant rate of increase in credit has the same impact on the structure of production as a once-and-for-all fall in time preferences that moves the consumption-investment ratio to a new stable level."

We are doubtful of this contention. In our view, "a once-and-for-all fall in time preferences that moves the consumption-investment ratio to a new stable level" can indeed lengthen the structure of production, and do so on a stable basis, ceteris paribus. However, "a constant rate of increase in credit" either is not sustainable due to a runaway inflation or, if we can somehow ignore that possibility, is unstable since it does not accord with the underlying time preference rates of the populace, which, we are assuming, have not changed.

c. Hummel's (1979, 49) third claim in this section we wish to deal with is that "Obviously, there must exist *some* rate at which credit expansion will maintain the lengthened structure of production."

It is not readily apparent to us as to why this must be the case. Indeed, based on our foregoing comments, it would appear to be the case that there is no such rate that would accomplish this task. And this is completely apart from *finding* such a rate, assuming that it exists, which would be more of a central planning (Hayek, 1976) problem than anything else. No, our claim is more radical: that it does not exist, indeed, that it *cannot* exist.

As a final point on this issue, it must be noted that that this entire argument of Hummel's is built on a faulty foundation. Consider his (1979, 49) statement: "The reason for this conclusion is that, ceteris paribus, a constant rate of increase in credit has the same impact on the structure of production as a once-and-for-all fall in time preferences that moves the consumption-investment ration to a new stable level." And, "In sum if time preferences and the demand for money remain the same, then a constant rate of credit expansion will maintain an artificially lengthened structure of production. Only if anticipations change time preferences or the demand for money [sic] will the rate of credit expansion have to accelerate" (Hummel, 1979, 50). He seems to recognize that a constant rate of credit expansion leads to inflation. Does he not understand that the experience of inflation causes people to adjust their expectations thereof? And, does he not realize that expectations of inflation lead to decreases in the demand for money; i.e., the famous flight to reals? It seems Hummel has assumed his way to his conclusions, with most unrealistic assumptions. As soon as his assumptions are relaxed in favor of more realistic ones, his argument fails. He assumes a constant rate of credit expansion with no increase in demand for money; i.e., he says "Only if anticipations change time preferences or the demand for money [sic] will the rate of credit expansion have to accelerate(1979, 50)," But that "only if" gives the game away. It is like saying only if massive increases in the supply of money causes prices to increase…" That is, Hummel's assertion is correct only in a world in which credit expansion at a steady rate does *not* cause, via anticipations, changes in time preferences or in the demand for money. To put this more colloquially, Hummel is assuming a 600 pound gorilla that cannot scratch itself, and then deducing the presence of such an incapacitated animal.

VI. International Aspects of the ABCT

Hummel (1997, 50-51) in section calls for further Austrian research in an international environment: "of competing national central banks;" of a "central bank in one nation and a decentralized fractional-reserve banking system in another;" and, of "a central bank in one nation and a commodity, 100 percent reserve standard in another." We join him in wishing that an Austrian analysis of these situations take place.

B. Conclusion

Hummel (1997) offers five challenges to praxeological analysis, and one (set of) requests for further research. We cannot see our way clear to agreeing with him that the former call any basic tenets of Austrianism into question, but we do join with him in wishing for the latter.

Appendix 1

Interest rate sensitive goods (IRSG) are those, as the name implies, he demand for which is relatively highly elastic with respect to a change in the relevant discount rate. Such goods are financed in substantial part by credit because their pecuniary value is sufficiently high to render that occurrence very likely[726]. This concept applies to every type of good: capital goods, consumers' goods, resources, and financial assets. The sensitivity is dependent on time; however, it is not simply the economic life, or, for financial assets, the term to maturity; e.g., for bonds it is their duration. However, such factors as call provisions for bonds and pre-payment provisions for mortgage notes also affect sensitivity. Regarding interest rate sensitivity, the same elements of time relevant for capital goods are also relevant for labor and natural resources. In this regard, it is perhaps best to think of natural resources as circulating capital[727] (although in their pristine state they are not yet truly capital of any sort), and labor as human capital. The analysis infra that deals with capital

---

[726] In a world where credit transactions were successfully prohibited, or never discovered, there would be no such thing as interest rate sensitivity.

[727] Unlike the natural sciences where technical terms are used unambiguously, such terms in economics almost always have multiple meanings. This is true for circulating and fixed capital. The definitions that best fit "triangle" analysis are as follows:

Circulating capital (CC) goods are man-made tangible goods, including finished, but not final, goods (save for inventories of final goods not yet sold), that are in the process of being incorporated into a finished good. For example, iron in the process of being made into steel is CC. If the steel is then in the process of being made into a machine to be used in production, it, as with the iron, is CC. After the machine into which the steel is incorporated is finished the steel is now part of a fixed capital (FC) good. Also, if the steel is then in the process of being made into a consumers' good (CG) it, as with the iron, is CC. After the CG into which the steel is incorporated is finished the steel is now part of a CG. (We note that many definitions of CC include "the wages fund" as a part thereof, where the wages fund is taken as either the consumers' goods used to support the workers during the production process or the funds set aside to pay the workers during the production process.)

Fixed capital (FC) is either man-made tangible goods or human capital used in the production of other goods, tangible or intangible, capital or consumers', which does not become embodied or incorporated in the good being produced. The only way human capital can become incorporated in the good being produced is by accident; e.g., a man's finger gets cut off and mixed with the rest of the ground meat which ends up being eaten in, say, a meat loaf.

goods should then be understood to refer to circulating as well as fixed capital, including its human capital component[728].

The length of time during which the value of an individual capital good is tied up in the production process before its value is realized in the form of sale to the consumer of the consumer good(s) it was used to produce, has two dimensions. We refer to these two dimensions as the "vertical", V, and "horizontal", H, time dimensions. The vertical dimension V is the period of time from the application of the capital good in the production of a specific individual consumer good until that specific individual consumer good is sold to the consumer. The horizontal dimension H is the period of time over which the capital good is expected to enter into the production of successive individual consumer goods. For example, consider a stick of dynamite used on 1/1/2000 to blast free a piece of stone which, after N years of work by a sculptor, ends up as a work of art sold to the connoisseur, on 1/1/2000 + N. It has a vertical time dimension of N years. Note that all of the "work" done by the capital good (the dynamite) was done instantaneously on 1/1/2000, but the value of that work was not realized until 1/1/2000 + N; therefore that value was tied up in the production process for N years.

Now consider a cash register used at the point of sale at a retail store. In this case, the capital good does its "work" with respect to any specific individual consumer good virtually instantaneously, as did the dynamite, but now, unlike in the case of the dynamite, this "work" is tied up in the production of a specific individual consumer good only momentarily; i.e., for the time necessary to consummate the transaction. Thus its vertical time dimension is virtually zero. However, and again unlike the case of the dynamite, which could be used but once, the cash register can be used over and over again in the production process; i.e., in the production of many individual consumer goods. If the cash register is expected to be used for, say, M years, then its horizontal time dimension is M years.

This example has contrasted the extremes; that is, two capital goods, one with a time dimension of (V = N, H = 0), and the other with a time dimension of (V = 0, H = M). Of course, for most capital goods, neither time dimension is zero.

In our terms, the greater is V, the earlier is entry of the capital good into the production process (Austrian theory would say the capital good was of "higher order"), and the greater is H, the more durable is the capital good. Thus, the earlier a capital good enters into the production process and/or the more durable it is, the greater is its composite time dimension (T); i.e., the composite time dimension is: T depends upon both V and H.

---

728 The material which appears in the text immediately below, with minor changes, taken directly from Barnett and Wood, 2002, 29 30, n.12.

In contrast, the horizontal dimension is the durability of a fixed capital good or of a consumers' good.

There are two vertical time dimensions: placement or position, and processing-time remaining or time to completion. The placement aspect has to do with the position of a fixed capital good in the production process; i.e., does it enter early, like a mining machine used to mine iron that will be made into steel that will be embodied in a consumers' good, or does it enter late like a paining machine used to paint the consumers' good shortly before it is sold. The processing-time remaining has to do with the amount of time remaining until a circulating capital good will be embodied in a final good.

For discounting purposes, the only relevant dimension of a circulating capital good that will sooner or later, assuming no errors, be embodied in a consumers' good is processing time. For one that will be embodied in a fixed capital good, the relevant dimensions are processing time, and both placement and durability of the fixed capital good in which it will be embodied. For fixed capital, the only relevant dimensions are placement and durability.

Circulating capital has only the V dimension, processing-time remaining as it is used in only one "vintage"[729] of production, whereas durable fixed capital goods have in addition to the V dimension, placement, the H dimension, as they are used in multiple vintages of production.

The time element is important for consumer goods, also. However, in their case there is only one time dimension, the horizontal (H). That is, as consumer goods are intended to satisfy wants directly, the only time element of concern is their durability. Thus for consumer goods, the composite time dimension is the horizontal dimension.

Rothbard (2001 [1962], 317) maintains[730] that: "It is important to realize that the *interest rate is equal to the rate of price spread in the various stages*" (emphasis in original)." Mises (1998, 521) says essentially the same thing: "As consumers' goods are present goods, while the factors of production are means for the production of future goods, and as present goods are valued higher than future goods of the same kind and quantity, the sum thus apportioned, even in the imaginary construction of the evenly rotating economy, falls behind the present price of the consumers' goods concerned. This difference is the originary interest."[731] This is correct only for circulating capital goods or goods in process; i.e., capital goods whose processing times decrease constantly as they move through the production

[729] A "vintage" of production refers to an individual unit of output produced, or the units of output produced in a relatively short time period; i.e., a year or less.

[730] He elaborates on pages 317-319.

[731] He elaborates on pages 521-529.

process, eventually becoming consumers' goods or finished fixed capital goods. It is not true for fixed capital goods themselves,[732] as even though their present value or current price is equal to their discounted marginal contributions to the value of the consumers' goods to whose production they contribute, nevertheless, the capital goods of the same kind and quantity have the same present value or current price, regardless that they are used in even widely different stages of production. If, then, identical capital goods with identical present values or current prices are used in different stages of production of the same vintage of a particular consumers' good, it is obvious that the contribution of the one that enters into the production process earlier on; i.e., in an earlier stage, must contribute more to the final value of the consumers' good than the other one (Block, 1990C).

For example, a ton of coal is a ton of coal is a ton of coal. It will be purchased on the market for the same price whether it is used in a high, medium or low stage of production, or, for that matter, in consumption. Any other conclusion would lead to an ERE with different prices for the same good.

Appendix 2

The following is taken directly from the U.S. government's own webpages. It does not require more than a casual reading, much less a perusal, to realize how problematic are the official data on the capital stock and changes therein. Of course, this is but part and parcel of the problematic nature of any aggregate economic data.

A Guide to The National Income and Product Accounts (NIPA) (http://www.bea.doc.gov/bea/an/nipaguid.pdf):

During the 1960's [sic]and 1970's [sic], the estimates of capital stock in NIPA were expanded to cover all business and government-owned fixed assets and consumer durable goods. In 1976, in order to provide a more consistent valuation, the estimates of consumption of fixed capital (CFC) were shifted to a current-cost basis from a book-value basis valued at historical cost, which had reflected a mixture of prices for the various years in which the assets were acquired (M2)

Consumption of fixed capital (CFC) (1–26) is the charge for the using up of private and government fixed capital located in the United States. It is defined as the decline in the value of the stock of assets due to wear and tear, obsolescence, accidental damage, and aging. For most types of assets, estimates of CFC are based on geometric depreciation patterns; empirical studies of the prices of used equipment and structures in resale markets have concluded that a geometric pattern of depreciation is appropriate for most

---

[732] In this regard labor may be usefully thought of as human capital, and that a type of fixed capital good.

types of assets.[733] For general government and for nonprofit institutions that primarily serve individuals, CFC is recorded in government consumption expenditures and in PCE [personal consumption expenditures], respectively, as a partial measure of the value of the current services of the fixed assets owned and used by these entities. *Private capital consumption allowances* consist of tax-return-based depreciation charges for corporations and non-farm proprietorships and of historical-cost depreciation (calculated by the BEA [Bureau of Economic Affairs], using a geometric pattern of price declines) for farm proprietorships, rental income of persons, and nonprofit institutions. *Private capital consumption adjustment* is the difference between private capital consumption allowances and private CFC. (M11-12)

The Capital Consumption Adjustment is the difference between private consumption of fixed capital (CFC) and private capital consumption allowances. Private CFC is a charge for the using up of private fixed capital. It is based on studies of prices of used equipment and structures in resale markets. Private capital consumption allowances consist of tax-return-based depreciation charges for corporations and non farm proprietorships and of historical-cost depreciation, calculated by BEA, for farm proprietorships, rental income of persons, and nonprofit institutions.

Net domestic product (NDP). The net market value of the goods and services attributable to labor and property located in the United States; equal to GDP less consumption of fixed capital (CFC). NDP may be viewed as an estimate of sustainable product--the level of consumption that can be maintained while leaving capital assets intact. (http://www.bea.gov/bea/glossary/glossary_n.htm)

Appendix 3

Mises (1996, 524-550) distinguishes the originary from the market rate of interest, both of which exist in the evenly rotating economy (ERE) and in the real world. Originary interest and the originary rate of interest depend solely on time preference,[734] whereas the market rate of interest depends not only on time preference, but also on returns to the lender qua

---

[733] Several asset types use depreciation patterns that are not geometric. For example, computers and peripheral equipment and private autos use actual empirical depreciation profiles, and missiles and nuclear fuel rods use a straight-line pattern. For more information on depreciation patterns, see U.S. Bureau of Economic Analysis, 1999).

[734] In addition to time preference, the other condition necessary for interest – that the credit transaction be in terms of commensurables – would necessarily be met in the ERE as no objective exchange ratio would ever undergo alteration; e.g., there is no risk either of default or of inflation/deflation. Because of the very nature of the ERE, whatever amount of interest pertained to any point in time or time period would continue at every other point in time or time period of equal duration.

entrepreneur for the risks of default and of expected price changes. Because in the ERE there are no risks of default or of inflation or deflation, "There prevails in the whole system only one rate of interest. The rate of interest on loans coincides with the rate of originary interest as manifested in the ratio of prices of present and of future goods" (Mises, 1996, 538). However, this is only a first approximation of the truth. Insofar as the market rates of interest are concerned, whether in the ERE or the real world, the quantum of interest and the rate of interest must also take into account the expenses involved in acquiring the other resources (i.e., other than the money lent), of the creditor, qua entrepreneur; e.g., for a bank, the services of loan officers, office space, etc.[735] Additionally, a measure of profit for the creditor qua entrepreneur must be included, though this element is relevant only in the real world and not in the ERE, as of course no profits could exist in the latter. Moreover, there is no reason to think that "market rates" should include, in addition to originary interest, only returns to the lender qua entrepreneur for risk bearing and a measure of profit. Why should they not incorporate, also, returns to the lender qua entrepreneur from these other sources; e.g., specifically, for his contributions to the realization of gains from *increases* in productivity? Of course this element, also, is irrelevant in the ERE, as there would be no changes in productivity. Furthermore, it should be noted that with regard to profits, the other objective image of a gain from exchange that has been assigned its own name, according to Greaves (1990, 40) Mises recognizes uncertainty re future consumer demand, changes in productivity,[736] the time consuming nature of production, and differences in entrepreneurial foresight.

Fifth, as with all other gains from exchange, the phenomenon of creditors' gains from exchange arises from time preference. As interest is but the objective image of creditors' gains from exchange, interest also and necessarily arises because of time preference; that is, without time preference there would be no credit transactions and therefore, no creditors' gains from exchange or interest.

In the non-ERE situation, one of the factors that can affect the quantum of interest and interest rate[737] of a specific credit transaction is *an*

---

[735] We are indebted to our colleague Michael Saliba for this important point concerning the expenses of the creditor.

[736] "The ceaseless changes in the demand for and supply of the various human and physical factors of production, which constantly create new opportunities *for better adjusting production to anticipated future consume wants*" (Greaves, 1990, 40, emphasis added).

[737] What is the difference between these two things? If A lends B $100 today and B agrees to pay A back $150, the interest is $50, regardless of whether the agreement is to pay him back in one day or 10 years. Obviously, the interest rate is different in these cases though the interest is not.

increase[738] *in* productivity[739]. For example, imagine an entrepreneur willing to offer r% for funds to acquire a set of resources, R, to produce X. He then foresees an opportunity to acquire a set of resources, S, to produce Y, where he expects the use of S to produce Y to be more profitable than the use of R to produce X. In that case he would be willing to offer s% (>r%) in order to acquire the resources, R, thereby bidding up the "price of credit;" i.e., the interest rate. Of course, he would also have to offer a higher prices[740]for the resources in S, in order to bid them away from their current uses. That is, the gains from the increased productivity would be manifested by increased prices for the resources *and* a higher interest rate. However, this latter would be a transitory phenomenon. As other entrepreneurs attempted to earn greater profits by competing to acquire resources of the type in S, or suitable substitutes, and produce Y, or substitutes therefor, more of the gains from the increased productivity would end up redounding to the benefit of the resource owners, in the form of higher prices paid for them, and to the benefit of the purchasers of Y. At the same time, profits would decrease below the level initially earned by the entrepreneur who first perceived and acted on the S/Y opportunity. Consequently, he would not be willing to pay as high an interest rate as he had previously, and, consequently, the interest rate would decrease. Assuming no change in the other relevant data, preeminently time preference, competition over time would bid up the prices of the resources in S, and down the price of Y, so that the entire benefits from the increased productivity come to be received by the relevant resource owners and purchasers of the good. With all of the gains thus absorbed, there would be none left for the entrepreneur in the form of "above normal" profits, nor any to be paid by the entrepreneur to lenders in the form of higher interest rates. As profits fall back to "normal" so also would interest rates decrease to their prior levels. Therefore, as noted above, the effects of productivity increases on interest rates is transitory, lasting only during the adjustment period. Once the market is fully adjusted to such changes the effect on interest rates is eliminated.

---

[738] What about a *decrease* in productivity? The same analysis would hold, mutatis mutandis, again given the absence of ERE conditions.

[739] This sounds suspiciously as if we oppose the pure time preference theory of interest rate determination. We do not. Please persevere, gentle reader, and do not jump to conclusions.

[740] This discussion could be in terms of higher rental rates for the services of the resources instead of higher prices for their outright purchase, or some combination thereof. However, it would make no difference as higher rental rates would result in higher prices, and vice versa.

We see, then, that with an unchanged time preference[741], an entrepreneur is willing to offer a higher rate of interest to borrow funds to acquire resources for invest in a project expected to be more productive than one expected to be less productive, until competition bids away the profit opportunity at which time he is no longer willing to pay the higher rate of interest.

Therefore, though time preference is, and productivity is not, essential to, i.e., a necessary condition for, the existence of interest (Bohm Bawerk, 73-120, 290-308; Mises, 1996, 524-532; Rothbard, 297-301, 313-332) nevertheless changes in productivity can and do (temporarily) affect market rates of interest.

In sum, the originary rate of interest is a pure time preference phenomenon. Therefore, the theory of interest is a pure time preference theory (Bohm Bawerk, 73-120, 290-308; Mises, 1996, 524-532; Rothbard, 297-301, 313-332). However, market rates of interest, whether in the ERE or in the real world are affected by other factors. These include, besides risk, changes in productivity and the expenses incurred in acquiring collaborating factors necessary to the functioning of the credit business. They affect market interest rates in the ERE as well as the real world, whereas others, risks of default and of (unanticipated) inflation or deflation, and entrepreneurial profits are non-existent in the ERE, but are relevant in the real world.

---

[741] It could be argued that becoming aware of the opportunity to use S to produce Y changed the entrepreneurs' time preference; however, to do so would be to trivialize the concept of time preference and, in the process define away the possibility of productivity affecting time preference.

Chapter 31. Going (back) to gold money with no government gold: blood in the streets?[742]

Abstract

Most scenarios for a return to the gold standard rely on matching in some manner or other extant currency and demand (sometimes also time) deposits with the amount of gold in the hands of the government. But, suppose that the federal authorities do not have *any* gold in their coffers. Should we then move back to a gold standard? And, if so, how so?

I. Introduction

There are two types of people who favor a return to the gold standard. First, there are the gold bugs,[743] or gold fetishists. For them, there is something unique, mystical, alluring and magical about this precious metal. It has secret powers that render it indescribably wonderful. They love to clasp gold to their bosoms, to run their fingers through it, in an ecstasy that approaches religious fervor: think Scrooge McDuck wallowing in the yellow metal in his money bin, pouring it all over himself in a sort of "golden shower."

Second, there are those, such as the present authors, who favor the free enterprise system in general, and in the monetary realm in particular. Such commentators have no zeal for gold whatsoever. This commodity is favored solely for historical reasons: whenever people were free to choose,[744] they chose gold.[745] For those who espouse this philosophy, "gold" is merely a short hand synonym for "whichever commodity market participants choose as their means of conducting indirect exchange." Had platinum or zinc been the choice of the economic actors, members of this camp would have been happy to champion that decision. And, if and when we in the future turn away from our present use of fiat currency and embrace once again commodity money, if we voluntarily move toward another of these other options instead of gold, such advocates would be equally satisfied.

---

[742] The authors wish to thank their friends and colleagues in the economics department of Loyola University New Orleans, John Levendis and Dan D'Amico for aid and assistance in the writing of this paper. All errors are of course ours alone.

[743] For the use of "gold bug" in a pejorative manner, see http://en.wikipedia.org/wiki/Gold_bug; http://www.humanevents.com/article.php?id=21358. Milton Friedman engaged in this sort of name calling on many occasions. See for example, Friedman and Friedman, 1998, 194; http://www.mskousen.com/articles/mskousen_friedman.pdf

[744] This is the title of Friedman and Friedman, 1980. These authors favor the right of people to be "free to choose" in many economic and non economic contexts; not, however, unfortunately, when it comes to the choice of the monetary medium.

[745] And, typically, silver or copper for smaller transactions.

There is thus not much at all that these two schools of thought – the gold bugs or perverts, and those who favor liberty in choice of medium of exchange – have in common, critics who conflate the two to the contrary notwithstanding. Yes, it cannot be denied, both favor gold; but for reasons so disparate that it is a reach to even consider them both in the same sentence.

Before we begin our analysis of a return to the gold standard,[746] one further issue must be addressed: at present, it is exceedingly unlikely that any such financial alteration will occur. Advocates of gold for the second reason are typically confused with those who do for the first. As of the time of the present writing, none of the leading candidates for the presidency of the U.S. – McCain, Clinton, Obama – favor free enterprise at all, let alone to the extent necessary to bring about monetary privatization. This question does not even make the top 27 list of those questions commonly queried of economists (Block and Walker, 1988; Frey, et al, 1984). There is absolutely no support for such a transition on the part of any monetary authority, such as the Fed, the World Bank, the WTO, etc.

Why, then, even write about such a quixotic subject?

There are several reasons.

One, through this analytic device light may be shed upon certain issues that would otherwise remain opaque and intractable.

Two, it ill behooves us as a society to remain unprepared for this eventuality, however unlikely it appears at present. After all, other momentous economic events have crept up on us, leaving us with our pants down around our ankles, so to speak, in terms of our ability to deal with them. The 1929 crash, the dissolution of the USSR, the fall of the Berlin Wall: none of them were anticipated; if anyone predicted them, they were ignored by all and sundry. To be forewarned is to be forearmed. Had we been more open to the possibilities of these eventualities, we would likely have been in a better position to deal with them. Karl Marx was laboring in the British Museum writing his treatises long before communism became the economic system of large parts of the world. If he could so long anticipate the installation of a system very different from the one prevailing when he wrote, then so can we with regard to a return to the gold standard.[747]

Three, perhaps monetary dissolution is no so unlikely, despite the views to the contrary of leading financial analysts. The failure of Bear Sterns, the real estate bubble, the plummeting of the once might U.S. dollar, the Herculean and failing efforts of the Fed to deal with these challenges,[748]

---

[746] That is, allow market participants to freely choose their monetary medium

[747] We owe this point to Joe Salerno.

[748] After causing them all in the first place

might well portend and economic crash and a subsequent search for alternative institutional arrangements. One of these might be a return to the gold standard.

Four, if we are to move in the direction of free enterprise, we must determine some procedure or other for divesting the government of its ill attained gold stocks. This is part and parcel of a return to a fully functioning gold standard. A similar, although intellectually less challenging difficulty was faced by Margaret Thatcher when she privatized the large stocks of U.K public (council) housing, and by the denizens of the USSR when they moved away from public ownership of factories, mills, and farms in that country.

With this introduction, we are now ready to discuss a return to the gold standard. In section II we discuss a return to gold with no government holdings to serve as backing. Section III is addresses the scenario where there is a currency break down. We conclude in section IV.

II. A return to gold with no government holdings to serve as backing

Most commentators[749] have focused on matching the gold stocks held by government with the currency in circulation and deposit money,[750] and using these stocks as backing for this fiat money now in circulation. The literature divides at this point into those who advocate 100% gold backed dollars, on the one hand, and, on the other, those who favor fractional reserve banking (FRB). We shall not pursue this well trodden path. Instead, we will take upon ourselves a more daunting challenge: how can we return to (newly enter) a regime of free market money on the assumption that there are *no* reserves at all, not a single ounce, of gold in governmental coffers?[751] That is, we shall assume, arguendo, that there is no longer any government involvement in the money supply; that there is as great a separation between money and state as some would like there to be between church and state. That is, there is no longer a fed, no longer a central bank, no longer legal tender laws.

At this point, several possible scenarios arise. None of them apodictically follow from the above premises; all are contingent.

---

[749] For example, Bagus, Unpublished; de Soto, 2006; Ebeling; Greaves, 1995. Hazlitt, 1965, 1980; Herbener, 2002; Hulsmann, 1998; Kaza, 1996; Laffer and Kadlec, 1981; Leconte, 2003; Mises, 1952, 1981; Mundell, 1981; North, 1986; Paul, 1985; Rader, 1980; Reisman, 1996; Rothbard, 1962, 1994; Sennholz, 1975, 1979, 1985; Siegel, 1984, Vieira, 2002.

[750] This includes currency circulating outside of the U.S. and eurodollar deposits.

[751] Given: 1) the lack of any evidence of a physical audit of the U.S. Government's gold stocks; and, 2) governmental loans of gold to bullion banks that use them for the gold carry trade, there is no way to know whether the U.S Government actually has possession of any gold or if the bullion banks who owe gold to the Government could repay it if the government so demanded.

One of them is the "blood on the streets" possibility. Here, people would riot, due to the fact that their money (currency and checking deposits) would become totally and utterly worthless. Why? Without legal tender laws, it might be supposed, no one would any longer accept this money in discharge of obligations. This may well be so, but it is by no means a necessary result of the working out of our assumptions. The likelihood of this scenario would be weakened if we suppose that there is still a government in existence, that taxes us. Then, even in the absence of legal tender laws, we may suppose that the government would still accept "its" currency[752] for tax payments, and, if so, that private individuals would continue to do so as well.

Now, however, stipulate no government at all.[753] Will the presently used fiat currency continue to circulate? This is unclear, but the tendency in this direction can be strengthened by yet a further assumption: God takes over the money function. We can rely on Him, totally, to do the following: ensure that no expansion of the money stock can occur; that there will be no more creation of currency or check book accounts; the only new money to be printed up would be to replace worn out paper currency. Will people continue to accept this proxy in payment of debts, for purchases, etc? They only will do so if they are sure that others will, in turn, accept this from them, when they wish to expend the monies they have just taken in. That is, they will accept this currency if they believe they will not be left "holding the bag." But what ensures this, in the very specialized context we are now considering? Inertia of course plays a large role in such deliberations. Will it be sufficient? If so, we have a problem. For we will then be on what kind of standard? A paper standard? Not so, not so. For the paper money we use in this way is merely token. Its best alternative use, we may suppose, is as *wall paper*, a low valued use indeed, for $1,000 bills. And yet it is a basic premise of Austrian economics that money necessarily starts out as a valuable commodity. Could some sort of Mengerian regression effect counteract this insight in the present case? That is, given that people are already accustomed to U.S. currency, could this familiarity override the requirement that under a regime of freedom, money must consist of a valuable commodity?

---

[752] With the tie between money and state irretrievably broken, this is no longer as clear as once it was

[753] Here, we buy into the views, at least arguendo, of the anarcho capitalists who claim society would be *less* chaotic than at present. See on this Anderson and Hill, 1979; Benson, 1989, 1990; Cuzan, 1979; Fielding, 1978; Friedman, 1989; Hoppe, 1993, 2001, 2003; Leeson and Stringham, 2005; Long, 2004; Molinari, 1977; Molyneux, 2007; Murphy, 2002, 2005; R. and E. Perkens, 1971; Rothbard, 1973, 1978B, 1982B; Sechrest, 1999; Sneed, 1977; Spooner, 1870; Stringham, 1998-1999; M. and L. Tannehill, 1984, Tinsley, 1998-1999; Wollstein, 1969; Woolridge, 1970.

Then, too, the "riot in the streets" scenario is a per se troubling one on philosophical grounds. For, we are now contemplating a move from a statist FRB fiat currency to one of pure free enterprise in monetary affairs. The riot possibility goes against everything we know about free enterprise. That is, it brings about wealth and prosperity for all reaches of the economy, usually focused particularly on the poorest segments of society. Here, the very opposite would appear to be the case.

It would appear, if we are to make sense of our assumptions, that a significant conversion to the free enterprise philosophy must have occurred to rid ourselves of FRB, the Fed, taxes, governments, etc. And, as a result, the people are so much worse off that they are rioting? If so, we have uncovered for the very first time a true market failure.[754] Perish the thought. We must dig deeper.

On the other hand, there is no apodictic certainty that such a scenario cannot come about under the conditions we are contemplating. We assume then, arguendo, in order to make forward progress in this direction, that there will be no "blood in the streets" consequent upon return to gold as money.

III. Fiat currency break down

Suppose now that there is a break down in the ex fiat currency – present "paper" standard. Some few people refuse to accept this "currency." They demand something of real value to consummate indirect exchange. This spreads. The currency breaks down. How do people engage in indirect exchange? They again resort to gold. Since government has none, the yellow metal must emanate from bullion, coin hoards and melted down jewelry, we may suppose. This has two deleterious effects.

First, there is a tremendous loss of wealth; the entire value of currency and deposits vanishes; this generates the "riot in the street" phenomenon. According to our rough calculations, this loss amounts to $14 trillion, assuming an interest rate of 10%.[755] Nor will this loss be spread out, evenly, amongst all Americans; it will all depend upon how heavily invested they are in currency and deposits.[756]

---

[754] For a critique of the market failure literature, see Cowen, 1988; Hoppe, 2003.

[755] This figure is taken from John Williams' Shadow Government Statistics revised estimate of the seasonally adjusted, monthly average M3 for August, 2008: $13.973 trillion.

[756] An interesting question arises as to the allocation of bank resources amongst depositors. If this were stocks we were discussing, there would at least be the distinction between preferred and common stock to guide us; the former would be paid off first. In the present case there is no such guide. So, how is the allocation to be made? First come first served? Pay off the small (large) depositors first?

Second, there will be a loss that stems from the melting down of jewelry. Before, under the present system, people had a serviceable money,[757] plus bullion, coin hoards and jewelry. Now, they have only the latter. If they want the former, and we assume they do, then they must give up (some of) the latter, in whatever proportions they deem most suitable. But no matter how you slice it, they are worse off.

How can this be? Why should they be impoverished by free market money? Well, to be more accurate, there were losses to be sure (the fiat currency declines in value to zero, loss of gold jewelry), but there are also gains: no more inflation, unemployment, business cycles of the sort associated with fiat currency and FRB.

How, then to reconcile this seemingly irreconcilable situation? Gold, when used as money, serves in a sense as a security blanket, or an insurance policy. It relieves us of the risk of the governmentally created depredations of inflation, unemployment, recessions, depressions, business cycles. Under present institutional arrangements, society has no choice: we *cannot* avail ourselves of this insurance policy. The law prevents this.

Milton Friedman (1962, 40, emphasis added) is correct when he asserts that a gold standard is costly:

"The fundamental defect of a commodity standard (read gold standard) from the point of view of the *society as a whole*, is that it re quires the use of real re sources to add to the stock of money. People must work hard to dig gold out of the ground in South Africa - in order to re bury it in Fort Knox or some similar place. The necessity of using real re sources for the operation of a commodity standard establishes a *strong incentive for people* to find ways to achieve the same result with out employing these resources. If people *will accept* as money pieces of pa per on which is printed 'I promise to pay - units of the commodity standard,' these pieces of paper can perform the same function as the physical pieces of gold or silver, and they require very much less in resources to produce."[758]

If God were in charge of our monetary policy, and maintained fiat currency at optimal levels,[759] we could have our cake and eat it too. We could have a monetary system and also keep our jewelry (and gold teeth). But in

---

[757] Well, a functioning one, one that brought in its train all sorts of economic upheaval: unemployment, business cycles, inflation, etc.

[758] This author goes on to draw the unwarranted *normative* claim from this correct positive statement that society *should* jettison the gold standard and embrace fiat paper money. For a critique of this inference see Block, 1999C.

[759] Barnett and Block (2004) argue that the optimal amount of fiat currency is either zero (society adopts gold or some other free market money), or unchanged from whatever it is at any given time.

the real world, where God is not so involved, where we live on the wrong side of the fence that separates us from the Garden of Eden, we are forced to pay for this insurance policy. The reason things seem to be going to the dogs when we move from the present system to a gold standard in the absence of governmental gold stocks is that we have indeed taken a "hit," a very serious one: we have assumed the absence of all government stocks of gold, and, no matter how we twist and turn, we cannot escape from the implications of that assumption. We must lose the value of this disappeared money, and give up a portion of our jewelry in order once again to be able to use gold as money. The loss stems *not* from the malfunction of markets, nor from anything intrinsic to the gold standard. It emanates from our assumption of a massive loss of governmental gold. First, the government seized private gold; then, just as we are about to take it back, privatize it so as to use it as the basis of extant fiat currency, we "learn" it has all disappeared. It should occasion no surprise that were there a type of neutron bomb that wiped out massive amounts of gold, we would all be the poorer for it.

IV. Summary and conclusion

There is a literature concerned with a return to market money; i.e., gold, given governmental holdings thereof. The issues dealt with therein are how to privatize the government's gold stock in the context of governmental paper currency and deposits of various types redeemable in such currency. The present paper considers the same issues. However, we assume that there are no governmental stocks of gold, a major departure from the extant literature. The most ominous scenario is that there would be "blood in the streets," as people's paper money and deposits became worthless. We examine this scenario and conclude that the "riot in streets," if any occurs, would be a result of a massive redistribution of wealth from those holding paper currency and deposits to those holding gold. This would not be the fault of the free enterprise system, e.g., the use of gold as money; rather, the proper blame would lie with government for banning gold in the first place, and then, second, for (hypothetically) disposing of this confiscated gold.

Chapter 32. Plain Old Inflation vs. Price Inflation

Abstract

It is very important to distinguish between inflation (a boost in the supply of fiat currency) and price inflation (an increase in the price level as measured by a price index). This has important implications for the doctrine of "market failure" as applied to this subject. The claim of the present paper is that Mises was at best confused about this issue and at worst downright mistaken.

Introduction

In the view of many economists, there is a stark difference between the Austrian and the neoclassical schools on the issue of inflation. For the former, this word refers, solely, to government creation of, or additions to, the stock of its fiat currency; e.g., fractional reserve deposits based thereon.[760] For the latter, the only proper use of this word is to connote a rise in the general level of prices, as denoted by a price index, or indices. Further, for the praxeologists, the very rise in price level used by the mainstream to depict inflation, is, instead, called "price inflation." And, how do the majority of economists use this term? They totally eschew it, as indicated by Chart I. That is, they do not at all utilize the term "price inflation," as separate and apart from plain old ordinary "inflation."

Chart 1

	Austrian	Neoclassical
rise in price level induced by market	N A	inflation
rise in price level induced by increases in fiat media of exchange	price inflation	inflation
increase in fiat media of exchange	inflation	N A
increase in commodity money	N A	N A

---

760 This definition is problematical as it excludes increases in private sector fractional reserve deposits and/or banknotes, whether in a situation commodity money or fiat currency. This raises the question: In a system of unregulated private sector banking, with a commodity money and deposits and banknotes only partially backed by the commodity, are increases in such notes and deposits considered by Austrians to be a form of inflation? Perhaps a better definition of inflation is "an increase in media of exchange other than a commodity money that is not fully backed by an increase in such commodity money." Note, however, that this definition means that government is not necessarily involved in inflation, as an increase in fractionally backed deposits or banknotes in a gold-based system in which government is not involved, is considered "inflation" according to this definition.

We attempt to make several points in this paper. First, this understanding[761] is incorrect, at least insofar as Mises may be counted an Austrian, and it would be eccentric not to do so, since he was the greatest contributor to this body of knowledge of his generation. Second, that Rothbard, in contrast, was very clear on this distinction.[762] Third, that the Austrian (e.g., Rothbardian) vision on this matter is very much preferable to the alternative competing view as expressed by Mises and numerous members of the neoclassical Chicago School of thought.

I. Mises' view

Our claim that Mises (1998) conflated "inflation" and "price inflation" stems from the following quote:[763]

"The notions of inflation and deflation are not praxeological concepts.[764] They were not created by economists, but by the mundane speech of the public and of politicians. They implied the popular fallacy that there is such a thing as neutral money or money of stable purchasing power and that sound money should be neutral and stable in purchasing power. From this point of view the term inflation was applied to signify cash-induced changes resulting in a drop in purchasing power, and the term deflation to signify cash-induced changes resulting in a rise in purchasing power" (Mises, 1998, 422; footnote added).

There is a bit of hedging here. Mises contents himself with a mere reportorial role; "inflation was applied." He does not necessarily buy into this notion. On the other hand, anyone familiar with this author knows full well that he rarely if at all absents himself from controversy. If he had any

[761] That there is a stark difference between the Austrian and the neoclassical schools on this issue of inflation.

[762] What is the contribution of this present paper if Rothbard was perfectly sound on this matter? There are several. First, there is a pure matter of antiquarian interest. We maintain that the history of economic thought, despite its relegation to the background in many Ph.D. granting universities, is still an important one for our discipline. It is important that the record be set straight on the contributions of leading economists, such as Mises. Second, to overturn the "view of many economists" that Mises and members of the Chicago School, for example, disagreed upon this issue. In a very important sense, they did not. Third, to underscore the importance of Rothbard's contribution both to the Austrian edifice, and, in this case, toward undermining yet another argument for "market failure."

[763] Throughout, somewhat lengthy quotes are is smaller type; we intersperse our commentary on them in larger type.

[764] In contrast, Rothbard (2001, 942, fn. 131) correctly maintains the very opposite: "As here defined, the terms "inflation" and "deflation" *are* praxeological categories."

criticism of this "mundane speech of the public and of politicians" it is likely, in the extreme that he would have negatively commented upon it.

"However, those applying these terms are not aware of the fact that purchasing power never remains unchanged and that consequently there is always either inflation or deflation. They ignore these necessarily perpetual fluctuations as far as they are only small and inconspicuous, and reserve the use of the terms to big changes in purchasing power. Since the question at what point a change in purchasing power begins to deserve being called big depends on personal relevance judgments, it becomes manifest that inflation and deflation are terms lacking the categorial precision required for praxeological, economic, and catallactic concepts. Their application is appropriate for history and politics. Catallactics is free to resort to them only when applying its theorems to the interpretation of events of economic history and of political programs. Moreover, it is very expedient even in rigid catallactic disquisitions to make use of these two terms whenever no misinterpretation can possibly result and pedantic heaviness of expression can be avoided. But it is necessary never to forget that all that catallactics says with regard to inflation and deflation--i.e., *big* cash-induced changes in purchasing power--is valid also with regard to small changes, although, of course, the consequences of smaller changes are less conspicuous than those of big changes" (Mises, 1998, 423).

Here, Mises writes more clearly. He far less ambiguously buys into the notion that purchasing power changes are either inflationary or deflationary,[765] depending upon their direction.

"The terms inflationism and deflationism, inflationist and deflationist, signify the political programs aiming at inflation and deflation in the sense of big cash-induced changes in purchasing power.

"The semantic revolution which is one of the characteristic features of our day has also changed the traditional connotation of the terms inflation and deflation. What many people today call inflation or deflation is no longer the great increase or decrease in the supply of money, but its inexorable consequences, the general tendency toward a rise or a fall in commodity prices and wage rates. This innovation is by no means harmless. It plays an important role in fomenting the popular tendencies toward inflationism" (Mises, 1998, 423).

So far removed are the claims in the preceding paragraph from what is supposed to be the Austrian point of view on this matter that they might as well have been written by a Milton Friedman. This is just about Mises' clearest rendition of the Chicago monetarist position it is possible to imagine.

---

[765] For an analysis of deflation, see Salerno (2003).

"First of all there is no longer any term available to signify what inflation used to signify. It is impossible to fight a policy which you cannot name. Statesmen and writers no longer have the opportunity of resorting to a terminology accepted and understood by the public when they want to question the expediency of issuing huge amounts of additional money. They must enter into a detailed analysis and description of this policy with full particulars and minute accounts whenever they want to refer to it, and they must repeat this bothersome procedure in every sentence in which they deal with the subject. As this policy has no name, it becomes self-understood and a matter of fact. It goes on luxuriantly" (Mises, 1998, 423).

In this paragraph we discern a bit of ambivalence on Mises' part. With relevance to chart I, it is almost as if Mises is regretting the fact that one of the cells, the one in which NA is in bold type, is empty; i.e. that the economics profession has no way to distinguish between the government "issuing huge amounts of additional money," on the one hand, and, on the other, the price level rising for reasons intrinsic to the market.[766] But the answer is clear: cleave to the "traditional" Austrian distinction between the government boosting the money stock ("inflation") and all other causes of a rise in the price level as measured by a price index ("price inflation," for want of a better phrase.)

"The second mischief is that those engaged in futile and hopeless attempts to fight the inevitable consequences of inflation--the rise in prices--are disguising their endeavors as a fight against inflation. While merely fighting symptoms, they pretend to fight the root causes of the evil. Because they do not comprehend the causal relation between the increase in the quantity of money on the one hand and the rise in prices on the other, they practically make things worse" (Mises, 1998, 423-424).

In this paragraph, in sharp contrast, we interpret Mises as reversing fields. That is, he clearly distinguishes "between the increase in the quantity of money on the one hand and the rise in prices on the other." Indeed, as he correctly sees, there is a "causal relation" between them: the former brings about the latter. But, surely, if this is the case, then we desperately need language that can distinguish the one from the other. Imagine if we had no

[766] For example, an alteration in the demand to hold cash balances. Not only can the price level rise from the (governmental) supply side, it can also do so from the (private) demand side: people wish to reduce their holdings of cash balances. They cannot all do so, together, at least initially, but, if they try, they can succeed. All they need do is spend off those elements of their cash balances they now regard as superfluous. In so doing, they will, ceteris paribus, drive up prices. And this will have the effect of reducing the real value of their cash holdings, thus tending to satisfy their original intent. With regard to such a phenomenon, the Austrians would *not at all* regard this as "inflation." Rather, they would characterize this as "price inflation."

agreed upon verbiage to distinguish between cause and effect in any other area of human endeavor. Coherent thought, let alone incisive analysis, would be all but impossible.

To summarize our comments so far: there is a bit of ambiguity in this Mises quote. At some points, he seems to adopt the erroneous Chicagoite position; at others, he seems to regret this perspective, but sees no way out of the quagmire. And at still other places, he seems almost on the verge of clarity on this issue.

Let us probe further, then, into Mises' oeuvre, and see if we can distill his views from his other writings. Accordingly, we arrive at Mises (1912, 239-241), where he states (emphasis **in bold** added by present authors):

"Observant readers may perhaps be struck by the fact that in this book no precise definition is given of the terms *inflation* and *deflation* (or restriction or contraction); that they are in fact hardly employed at all, and then only in places where nothing in particular depends upon their precision. Only inflationism and deflationism (or restrictionism) are spoken of, and an exact definition is given of the concepts implied by these expressions. Obviously this procedure demands special justification."

"I am by no means in agreement with those unusually influential voices that have been raised against the employment of the expression *inflation* altogether. But I do think that it is an expression that it is possible to do without, and that it would be highly dangerous, on account of a serious difference between its meaning in the pure economic theory of money and banking and its meaning in everyday discussions of currency policy, to make use of it where a sharp scientific precision of the words employed is desirable.

"In theoretical investigation there is only one meaning that can rationally be attached to the expression *inflation:* an increase in the quantity of money (in the broader sense of the term, so as to include fiduciary media as well), that is not offset by a corresponding increase in the need for money (again in the broader sense of the term), so that a fall in the objective exchange value of money must occur. Again, deflation (or restriction, or contraction) signifies a diminution of the quantity of money (in the broader sense) which is not offset by a corresponding diminution of the demand for money (in the broader sense), so that an increase in the objective exchange value of money must occur If we so define these concepts, it follows that either inflation or deflation is constantly going on, for a situation in which the objective exchange value of money did not alter could hardly ever exist for very long. The theoretical value of our definition is not in the least reduced by the fact that we are not able to measure the fluctuations in the objective exchange value of money, or even by the fact that we are not able to discern them at all except when they are large.

"If the variations in the objective exchange value of money that result from these causes are so great that they can no longer remain unobserved, it is usual in discussions of economic policy to speak of inflation and deflation (or restriction, or contraction). Now in these discussions, whose practical significance is extraordinarily great, it would be very little to the purpose to use those precise concepts which alone come up to a strictly scientific standard. It would be ridiculous pedantry to attempt to provide an economist's contribution to the controversy as to whether in this or the other country inflation has occurred since 1914 by saying: "Excuse me, there has probably been inflation throughout the whole world since 1896, although on a small scale." In politics, the question of degree is sometimes the whole point, not, as in theory, the question of principle.

"But once the economist has acknowledged that it is not entirely nonsensical to use the expressions *inflation* and *deflation* to indicate such variations in the quantity of money as evoke *big* changes in the objective exchange value of money, he must renounce the employment of these expressions in pure theory. For the point at which a change in the exchange ratio begins to deserve to be called big is a question for political judgment, not for scientific investigation.

"It is incontrovertible that ideas are bound up with the popular usage of the terms *inflation* and *deflation* that must be combated as altogether inappropriate when they creep into economic investigation. In everyday usage, these expressions are based upon an entirely untenable idea of the stability of the value of money, and often also on conceptions that ascribe to a monetary system in which the quantity of money increases and decreases *pari passu* with the increase and decrease of the quantity of commodities the property of maintaining the value of money stable. Yet however worthy of condemnation this mistake may be, it cannot be denied that the first concern of those who wish to combat popular errors with regard to the causes of the recent tremendous variations in prices should not so much be the dissemination of correct views on the problems of the nature of money in general, as the contradiction of those fundamental errors which, if they continue to be believed, must lead to catastrophic consequences. Those who in the years 1914-24 contested the balance-of-payments theory in Germany in order to oppose the continuation of the policy of inflation may claim the indulgence of their contemporaries and successors if they were not always quite strictly scientific in their use of the word *inflation*. In fact, it is this very indulgence that we are bound to exercise toward the pamphlets and articles dealing with monetary problems that obliges us to refrain from using these misleading expressions in scientific discussion."

In this material, Mises unequivocally uses "inflation" to refer to some increases, not only of fiat media of exchange, but also of commodity money and/or 100% backed banknotes and deposits. And, which are they?

That is, given that Mises uses "inflation" to refer to *some* but not all increases of commodity money, which is which? Why, those "not offset by a corresponding increase in the need for money… so that a fall in the objective exchange value of money must occur." Clearly, Mises here did not restrict "inflation" to mean an increase in fiat media of exchange. Moreover, any increase in such that does not lead to an increase in the general level of prices, is not held to be a case of inflation. This concept of inflation is illustrated in chart 2.

Chart 2

	Offset by an increase in the need for money	Not offset by an increase in the need for money
Increase in fiat media of exchange	not inflation	inflation
Increase in commodity money and/or 100% backed banknotes and deposits	not inflation	inflation

Moreover, Mises remarks (Director, 1952, 3, fn.4): "It passes over in silence the problem of the increase in the quantity of money in circulation and deposits subject to check, the phenomenon that until a few years ago would commonly have been called 'inflation.…' The second group wants to stop inflation by preventing the government from increasing the quantity of money in circulation and bank deposits subject to check."

It is obvious that these usages of "inflation" by Mises do not square with the Austrian concept of inflation as an increase in fiat media of exchange. They are, on the one hand, too broad by including increases in commodity money and/or 100% backed banknotes and deposits, and, on the other, too narrow, excluding increases in fiat money that are offset by increases in the need for money such that there is not a decline in the objective exchange value of money.

II. Rothbard's view

In sharp contrast, Rothbard's (2001, 1022, ft. 131) take on the matter is like a clarion call of rationality: "Inflation is here defined as *any* increase in the money supply greater than an increase in specie…" Further, states Rothbard (2001, 990, fn. 106)

"Inflation, in this work, is explicitly defined to exclude increases in the stock of specie. While these increases have such similar effects as raising the price of goods, they also differ sharply in other effects: (a) simple increases in specie do not constitute an intervention in the free market, penalizing one group and subsidizing another; and (b) they do not lead to the processes of the business cycle."

Why are we so fussy about an issue that might be dismissed by many as merely definitional? There are several reasons, in addition to these two alluded to by Rothbard. Let us number them in continuation with those mentioned immediately above:

(c) linguistic clarity

This, admittedly, does not sound like much. "Clarity, schmarity," is the likely response from some people. Or, perhaps, "Clarity, yes; fussiness, no." But we vociferously claim that while economics may never equal the precision of physics or chemistry,[767] unless we at least make a good faith effort in this direction with our own basic lingua franca, such as "inflation," the competition is over before the game has even begun. Physicists may disagree on many things but not, surely, over the very definitions of phenomenon such as force, energy, and work, etc. Inflation is a counterpart of these. The fact that there is not one common definition, embraced, at least, by all professional economists,[768] of such basic nomenclature as "inflation" is a barrier to clear thought and the development of the dismal science.[769]

(d) "market failure"

However unclear the economics profession as a whole may be about inflation, it is hardly a positive concept in and of itself. Yes, there are those who claim that without it, the economy is headed for hell in a hand basket. But we can speak without fear of contradiction when we say that no one advocates it as intrinsically beneficial, apart from these supposed salutary effects.

However, "inflation," at least in the manner in which Mises sometimes, and non Austrians without exception, use this term, can be caused by pure market activity. To put this into the correct perspective, for Mises [price] "inflation" can stem from the voluntary decisions of private economic actors. All they need do, as we have seen, is decrease the level of their desired cash balances.

---

767 Human purpose, motivations, action are more complicated than the mere movements of atoms or chemicals. On the "physics envy" of many economists, see Prowse (1996).

768 We need not overly concern ourselves about laymen. They use the basic concepts of physics, too, in a manner far different than the professionals. For example, for the physicist, work is the product of force and displacement. No movement, no work. For the average man in the street, holding 20 pound weights at arm's length is "work." Sweat pours down the brow before even a few seconds elapse. For the Austrian economist, strictly speaking, there is no such thing as "indifference" in human action. Yet, we all use this concept in ordinary language. For more on this see Rothbard, (2001, 265, 267).

769 For another way in which economics does not follow the practices of physics to the detriment of clear thought, see Barnett (2003)

If, then, "inflation" can arise from such a source, and it is a "bad," then this constitutes yet another "market failure." And, in turn, when such a phenomenon eventuates, it constitutes a prima facie case for government intervention[770], at least in some quarters. When we realize that such a "case" arises solely from "mere" definitional matters, the argument for language clarification becomes even the more important.

(e) students

We owe it to our students to leave the basic building blocks in a more coherent, rational and systematic way than we found them. There can be few things that are more illogical than the status quo with regard to "inflation." If this present paper can contribute in some small way to bringing about a reform in this regard, it will have served a very useful purpose.

[770] For a critique of this viewpoint, see Cowen (1988).

Chapter 33. Is there *a* market for money, or are there market*s* for money? There ain't no such thing as the supply of or demand for money

Abstract

There are as many markets for money as there are goods and services that trade for money. In the non barter economy, this includes all goods and services. Here, necessarily, there are, plural, markets, for money but not, singular, a market for money, nor the market for money.

I. Introduction

St. Paul (1 Timothy 6-10) famously said, "For the love of money is the root of all evil..." This is extremely dubious. But as far as economic analysis goes, money is the root of much confusion. The easiest way to see this is to get to the essence of an economic phenomenon. In such cases, we ask if the phenomena would/could exist in a barter economy. If so, then money cannot be of the essence of the matter. More important, any definition of the phenomena that involves money is, obviously, inadequate, in that, at best, it is misleading, but usually confusing, thereby causing faulty analysis. For example, untold time and ink has been squandered developing the theory, and empirical estimates, of "the" demand for, money. However, correct analysis concludes that there is no such thing. Money qua money is one side of every monetary transaction. Therefore, in the market in which X trades for dollars, the price of money is in terms of X/$. Of course, in the market in which Y trades for dollars, the price of money is in terms of Y/$. There is then no "the" demand for money. Rather, in every market in which some good trades for money there is a demand for money; i.e., there are demand*s* for money, not *a* demand for money. Of course, the foregoing comments apply equally to "the" supply of money. It should be noted that some Austrians, including the present authors, fall into this trap when they are not careful; e.g., when we speak of an increase in "the" supply of money, rather than in the stock of money.

In section II we outline the thesis of this paper, that there are numerous markets for money, not a single one. Section III is devoted to documenting failures in the economic literature to appreciate this point. We conclude in section IV.

II. Many markets for money

According to Barnett and Block (2005-2006, 205): "Money is the only good that has no (non-trivial) money price. As such there is no market for money. Rather, there are as many markets for money as there are non-money goods that people wish to exchange for money. Thus, in a real sense there is neither a demand for, nor a supply of, money; rather, in each market there is a demand for, and supply of, the non-money good."

This is as good a jumping-off point for us in terms of the thesis of the present paper. We wish to assert the claim that while there are *many* markets for money, as many as there are goods and services people wish to trade for money, there is no *a* or *the* market for money. There logically cannot be any such thing, since money takes part in *every* exchange in the non barter economy.

It might at the outset seem unduly pedantic to insist upon such a careful, even narrow word usage. But if economics is to become a science, one of the requisites for this eventuality is a common and accurate language. If the dismal science is to be truly scientific, it cannot tolerate sloppiness and imprecision.[771]

Literally, if there were to be *a* or *the* market for money, there could be only *one* good or service traded against the monetary medium. Since no one contends any such thing, there can only be plural, market*s* for money.

Consider one possible exception to this general rule. Can we not speak of *the* market for foreign money? For example, someone wants to purchase euros with dollars. Would it violate the thesis of the present paper to refer to *the* market for euros? Perhaps in a world where these were the only two currencies such talk might be reasonable, but in the present one with numerous types of notes, this would clearly be impermissible.

But even here we go too far. For consider another possible exception: contemplate that glorious day when we all use gold money. Gold is the only money; there is no other. Would it make sense to claim that there is now *a* market for money, instead of many such market*s*? Again, no, for gold money would now trade against numerous goods and services, and there would be as many markets for this precious resource as there would be goods and services.

It is possible, even likely, that in a monetary economy in which gold is the monetary commodity, money might consist both of gold coins and bullion. In that case there would be a demand for bullion money in terms of coin money, and vice versa. However, even in that case there would be no *the* demand for and *the* supply of money. Rather, when considering gold-coin money, there would merely be one more demand for such money, along with all the other demands thereof, save in that case in addition to such demands for money (supplies of other goods) there would also be a gold-bullion

[771] We do not object to imprecision in ordinary language. For example, the word "indifferent" has a perfectly clear referent amongst most speakers of the English language. But there is no such thing as indifference in economics, since every time man acts, he chooses one thing, and sets aside another. If he were indifferent, he could never act in such a manner. In like manner, "work" in physics means mass multiplied by distance. In commonplace language, holding weights at arms length entails great work, even though it would not in science since nothing moves any distance at all in this example.

demand for money (supply of gold-bullion money). That is, this would be no different than any other case in which there was more than one money commodity; e.g., silver-coin money, circulating alongside gold-coin money, with the two sometimes exchanging against each other at free-market prices.

Let us consider an objection to our thesis. It might be asserted that there is indeed such a thing as *the* demand for money (in contradistinction to supplies of goods, as we argue) on the basis that in some cases it is specifically the *money* that is the desired object in an exchange; i.e., the reason A enters into an exchange with B is to get *money* from B; therefore A *does* have *a* demand for money. And if we add all such demands from the many As out there, the result is *the* market demand for money.

Superficially, this objection sounds like a refutation of our viewpoint. However, it is problematical from the point of view of standard supply and demand (S&D) analysis. The reason is that if we are to take the object of the market participants' desire as the criterion, than in most every case it is what is being sought, not what is being foregone that is the key. It is true that sometimes the key to an exchange is that A wishes to be rid of some good, x, and will in some cases even, pay to be rid of it. However, that is not the usual case. In a normal situation, A, an automobile dealer, desires to acquire money (for some yet undetermined purpose) and must sell cars to obtain it. The motive is to get ahold of the money, the sale of the car is only the means to this end.

If then, we refer to A's acts as constituting his demand for money, and not his supply of cars, if we are to be consistent we must apply the same "logic" to his exchange partners. That is, the motive of *each* of the Bs to whom he sells his cars is to acquire one or more vehicles, and the parting with money is but the means to that end. Therefore, to be consistent, we must think in terms of their demand(s) for autos, and not their supplies of money. Then, in terms of S&D analysis, we must consider the interactions of A's demand for money with B's demand for cars. That is, we have not S&D analysis, but *D&D* (and this does *not* refer to Dungeons and Dragons) analysis. All of which raises the question of the relevant price. What, pray tell, would an S&D figure look like if the relevant curves were the buyer's demand curve for the good x, and the seller's (of x) demand curve for money? To pose the question is to make the point that for a monetary economy S&D analysis is the analysis of the supply of, and demand for, goods in terms of money prices, not *the* supply of, and *the* demand for, money, in terms of any price or price-like construct such as the PPM.

III. Erroneous claims of a single market for money

Errors abound in the mainstream economic literature on this issue. Unfortunately, they are so legion that the examples appearing below constitute only the tip of the iceberg. Every author who employs a "market for money" in his model makes this mistake, and virtually every macroeconomics text does so. In addition, consider just these few examples (all emphases on *a* or *the* "*market for money* in quotes in this section has been inserted by the present authors):

1. Friedman, D. (1989, 219) mentions "*The market for money*" as a chapter heading.

2. Slok (2000) offers this view: "A market-based monetary policy depends on the existence of *a market for money*..."

3. Friedman, B. (1983, 180) follows the same practice: "*The market for money* and the market for credit" is used to head a section of a chapter.

4. Lutz (2006, 252) likewise entitles his chapter 21: "*The market for money* ..."

Unhappily, even Austrian economists, who are usually more careful scholars about such matters, err on this point. Many fewer of them model the "market for money," but still this error may be found in this literature too. Consider these examples:

1. Garrison (1984, 197) states: "It is argued below that the "market for time" and the "*market for money*" both in their conceptual isolation and in their actual interaction, give rise to all the phenomena that are conventionally regarded as macroeconomic in nature."

2. And again (Garrison, 1984, footnotes deleted): "Though it may be thought unnecessary to argue the centrality of money in macroeconomic theory, it is worthwhile to consider the special sense in which money is an economy wide phenomenon. Monetary theorists have long recognized that "money has no market of its own." It is the obverse of this truth that highlights the macroeconomic character of money. With trivial exceptions every market is *a market for money*. In a modern economy every exchange involves some specific quantity of money. That this fact should be the focus of our attention has been recognized by economists both new and old. There is no denying, of course, that money serves several functions, as listed in any principles text, but the presence of money on one side of each exchange in every market is the special sense in which money is an economy wide phenomenon."

3. In the view of Rothbard (2004, ch. 10, emphasis in bold added by present authors) "Making this distinction, we find that, contrary to Hutt, each individual has *self-sovereignty* over his person and property on the free market. The producer, and the producer alone, decides whether or not he will keep his property (including his own person) idle or sell it on **the market for money**, the results of his production then going to the consumers in exchange for their money. This decision—concerning how much to allocate to the market and how much to withhold—is the decision of the individual producer and of him alone."

4. And again (Rothbard MES, ch. 6, Appendix: Professor Oliver on socioeconomic goals, C. The Attack on Income According to Earnings; http://www.mises.org/rothbard/mes/chap18b.asp): "His goods or services are freely exchanged on *the market for money*."

5. According to Loasby (1998, 81): "This Hayek (1933) attempts to do through the introduction of money, together with *a market for money*."

6. In the opinion of Endres (1991, 79): "Time horizons and associated contractual obligations in *the market for money* credit destined for more permanent productive investment are much longer and substantially different from horizons which normally obtain in the market for consumption loans."

7. Here is a statement from Carilli, Dempster and Rohan (2004, 38): "Thus, in every case where price level rigidity causes a shortage of funds, incentives will lead to the dissipation of that shortage, but in cases where prices and wages adjust quickly, the shortage will be eliminated by the mutual adjustment of quantity supplied and quantity demanded in *the market for money.*"

8. And another one from these authors (2004, 41): "A plausible real world view is that the process of price level (Austrian) and money supply (Monetarist) adjustment will occur, in most instances, simultaneously toward a new price-quantity equilibrium in *the market for money*."

Happily, there is at least one other Austrian economist on record with a correct analysis of this matter. States Ebeling (1975, 6): "There IS no single market for money, and, therefore, no single price. Rather, money exists in a 'state of barter' with every other goods (sic) and service…."

IV. Conclusion

The plethora of neoclassical and some Austrian economists notwithstanding, we maintain that it is erroneous to base one's analysis on a single market for money. No, there are numerous such markets.

Part IV. Political Economy and Libertarianism

Chapter 34. Arm the Coeds

There has been a spate of robberies and sexual assaults aimed at university coeds in uptown New Orleans. According to newspaper reports, a single black man approaches girls walking in the street in pairs at night and then proceeds to rob, confine, and sexually assault them.

The reaction on the part of the police authorities is the usual blather about being "street smart," not carrying a weapon, not resisting, and not venturing out at night. If going unarmed was such great advice, why don't they follow it themselves? Further, why should the *victims* have to pay twice, once in the form of being robbed and raped, and then, again, in the form of having their liberties to walk on the public streets curtailed?

The response from school authorities is, if anything, even worse: holding candlelight vigils, praying, having "take back the night" marches, and organizing teach-ins attempting to indoctrinate the students with the usual leftist feminist and liberal shibboleths, ad nauseam. If these things give university students any comfort, it is a *false* sense of security, which could prove to be their undoing. Quite possibly the assailant joins the very parade set up against him, biting his lip to keep from laughing outright, which might well be the only harm that befalls him from these events. Such tactics might make some people feel good, but they do nothing to address the problem.

In contrast, we offer a five-point program of arming the victims, virtually guaranteed to solve the problem.

1. Take down those signs on campuses announcing they are "gun-free" zones. That is the worst possible message to be sent to potential perpetrators of violence against our community. We might as well post a sign saying, "C'mon in, attackers, we've disarmed ourselves and will be easy prey." This no-gun policy, thank God, does not apply to campus police who can't be everywhere, as is the case with their city counterparts

2. Require that all female students own a pistol or other means of self defense; (e.g., pepper spray or mace, stun gun or other electric shock device) and carry it with them at all times. The women of Kennesaw, Georgia, an affluent northern suburb of Atlanta Georgia, were once plagued by rapists. This town not only allowed, but *required* its citizens to be armed. You'll never guess what happened to the rape rate after this progressive policy was enacted.

The law, however, was compulsory, and, as such, violated the rights of pacifists and other local citizens who might have objected. But this would not at all apply to Loyola, a private institution. This change in policy would have to be "grand-fathered in" so as to avoid contractual violations, but in the future females who do not wish to protect themselves in this way would be perfectly free to attend other universities. They would have no right to be on campus, unless they obey all rules and regulations (in contrast, the citizenry of Kennesaw *did* have a right to remain there, in violation of the law). In the meantime, this enlightened policy could be introduced on a voluntary basis, and encouraged by the administration.

3. Packing a weapon is necessary, but not sufficient. All women at Loyola ought to be required to take a course in gun safety. The last thing we want are accidental shootings. Leftists bruit about statistics on accidents where children are killed with revolvers. But these data are wildly exaggerated by including the shooting deaths of young, teenaged gang-bangers, whose deaths are certainly purposeful.

4. Volleyball, basketball, cross-country, and baseball teams are all well and good, but a sports organization aimed at improving marksmanship would be far more helpful in present circumstances. (When is the last time a Loyola student won an Olympic medal in target shooting? Never, that's when. It is time, it is long past time, for a change.) All students don't have to be sharp shooters. Reasonable accuracy even at 10 to 15 feet will be more than enough to scare off potential rapists. Heck, even the presence of an automatic in a co-ed's hand bag or pocket fully accomplishes this task.

5. When the new student center at Loyola is erected, it should include an indoor shooting range, just as the old field house did. The new rifle and pistol team would practice there, as would every woman student who so wished. The muffled sounds of target practice would alone give pause to all ne'er-do-wells in the neighborhood.

It will undoubtedly be objected against this "modest proposal" that arming young girls will not protect them; that their weapons will be seized by their attackers. Logic, common sense, and vast hordes of empirical evidence give the lie to all such negativism.

Put yourself in the position of a New Orleans mugger and rapist: would you really want to engage in your usual depredations in the uptown area, knowing full well that you could do so on no more than even terms? Not bloody likely. The uptown predator has already come armed; let his victims face him on even terms. As to the facts of the matter, world-class economist John Lott has done a series of studies linking gun ownership with *increased* personal safety.

After this forward-looking policy proves a success in the collegiate uptown area, it could be implemented by private organizations throughout the entire city. Then and only then would the scourge of raping and robbing have a good chance of being vastly decreased throughout our whole community.

Chapter 35. Arm the Coeds, Postscript

Note to the Loyola Community:

On November 30, 2001, Professor William Barnett and I published an Op Ed in the Maroon entitled "Required gun possession the answer to attacks." In it, we suggested that arming and training Loyola co-eds in weapon use (including guns) would be an efficient means toward their protection from a spate of rapes and attacks that had previously occurred.

Professors Julian Wasserman and Marcus Smith replied to our article in their "Campus gun slinging not best solution to crime" (Maroon, January 18, 2002). As well, the Maroon subsequently published numerous letters to the editor, all but one in support of the Wasserman-Smith position, and that one irrelevant to the gun issue.

In February 2002 I tried to publish an Op Ed rejoinder to the Wasserman-Smith article in the Maroon, but it was rejected. Then, I asked that this be published as a letter to the editor. This, too, was declined. Whereupon I offered to publish this reply in the Maroon as a paid advertisement, and this, too, was rebuffed.

The editor of the Maroon for the last academic year (2001-2002) refused to run my reply in any format whatsoever unless I made large cuts to it. He also insisted that I cite original rather than secondary sources, something unprecedented in such venues, and a requirement he did not impose on *any* of the people on the other side of this debate. A similar decision was made by this years' Maroon editor.

I am therefore taking the rather unusual step of sending to the Loyola community my reply to Professors Wasserman and Smith's op ed on guns via this message. My thought was that the students, faculty and staff deserve to see my reaction to the Wasserman-Smith communiqué, and see it in its entirety. What bothered me was not so much Wasserman and Smith's arguments on gun control, although I found what they said on this topic sparse and weak, but rather their resort to slurs, name calling and to the argumentum ad hominem.

In the interim period between then and now, several events not irrelevant to the substantive debate have occurred. Please keep these in mind, as a background to the arguments offered in the attached reply:

1. Louisiana Governor Mike Foster's reaction to a serial killer murdering women in Baton Rouge was the following: "You have the right to get a gun permit," he said on his weekly radio show. "Learn to use it."

2. Second Amendment Sisters, a feminist group which favors self defense for women, has been actively encouraging women to empower themselves in just this manner. Here is a quote from their website: "the Justice Department's annual National Crime Victimization Survey shows that when a woman resists a stranger rape with a gun, the probability of completion was 0.1 percent and of victim injury 0.0 percent, compared to 31 percent and 40 percent, respectively, for all stranger rapes."

3. The U.S. Senate has recently voted that pilots on commercial aircraft allowed to be armed. (See on this http://www.washingtontimes.com/business/20020906-69328962.htm; September 6, 2002; "Senate says yes to arming air pilots.")

4. An interesting debate on this issue has arisen within the black community; for the view that gun control is a racist measure, see http://www.federalobserver.com/archive.php?aid=3312

Here, now, attached, is the material in question, that I was unable to send to the Loyola community in any other way:

Reply to Wasserman and Smith on self-defense for Loyola students; by Walter Block

According to that old legal aphorism, "When the facts are against you, argue the law, when the law is against you, argue the facts, and when both are against you, pound the desk and rant and rave." Professors Julian Wasserman and Marcus Smith ("Campus gun slinging not best solution to crime," Maroon, January 18, 2002) have adopted the latter policy, in their reply to "Required gun possession the answer to attacks" (Maroon, November 30, 2001), that I co-authored with Professor William Barnett.

Both the facts (provided by Dr. John Lott at http://www.tsra.com/LottPage.htm) and the law favor the use of guns and other weaponry in defending against rape, mugging, murder and other crimes of violence, especially on the part of females. And no amount of obfuscation, misdirection, innuendo, name-calling and ad hominem attacks ("sneer," "harangue," "intellectual dishonesty," "rhetorical cowardice," "twaddle," "nuttiness," lack of "courage," "cultism," etc.) should be allowed to hide this elemental truth, as Wasserman and Smith (WS) attempt to do.

Consider these findings:

The National Crime Victimization Report, done by the U.S. Department of Justice, indicates consistently that women who behave passively are 2.5 times more likely to be seriously injured than women who defend themselves with a gun

Civilians use guns defensively to stop about 2 million crimes a year, five times more often than guns are used to commit crimes

In 98% of the cases of defensive gun use, simply brandishing a gun is sufficient to stop a crime

In the U.S., the states with the highest gun ownership rates have by far the lowest violent crime rates. And similarly, over time, states with the largest increases in gun ownership have experienced the biggest drops in violent crime.

A study examining homicide rates across 44 countries found those with the strictest gun control laws also tended to have the highest homicide rates.

In Britain crimes with guns have risen 40% since handguns were banned in 1997

Fortunately, accidental gun deaths among children are rare. With almost 35 million children under the age of 10, 48 children died in 1997 from all accidental gunshots, including five from handguns. With over 80 million adults owning at least one gun, the overwhelming majority of gun owners must be extremely careful or the figures would be much higher.

Only 21 children under age 15 died from accidental handgun deaths in 1996. But about 40 children under the age of 5 drown in 5-gallon water buckets every year, and bathtubs claim 80 lives annually.

Rosie O'Donnell's bodyguards have applied for permits for concealed handguns. She is a leader of the Million Mom March in Washington, which called for the abolition of the 2nd Amendment

The movie "Schindler's List," left out how Schindler, an avid gun collector, stockpiled guns and hand grenades in case the Jews he was protecting needed to defend themselves

Now consider a few of the more egregious errors made by Wasserman and Smith (WS):

1. Barnett and I did not at all "demand" that the administration institute a gun owning policy; rather, we *offered* this as a solution, given that we are presently beleaguered by hoodlums, murderers and rapists. Nor need *every* last person on campus pack heat. There are, after all, conscientious objectors even during wartime. But those signs saying that we are a gun free area ought to be torn down; they function as an invitation to aggressors.

2. Our core argument was not pistol owning, but rather *defense,* which includes, among many other responses, the use of "pepper spray, mace, stun gun or electric shock device." It also features unarmed combat, and we are delighted that Loyola University continues to offer a Rape Aggression Defense Class (Self Defense for Women).

3. WS claim that our suggestions (again, not "demands") are probably "criminally illegal," an unexpected redundancy given the source. These English literature professors urge us to consult La. R.S. 14: 95.2 and R.S. 14: 96.6. (Actually, the correct cite is 95.6, not 96.6). The former specifically exempts "… a firearm contained entirely within a motor vehicle," as does the latter for "A student who possesses a firearm in his dormitory room or while going to or from his vehicle … with permission of the administration." WS might well consult: http://www.legis.state.la.us/tsrs/tsrs.asp?lawbody=RS&title=14&section=95.2 and http://www.legis.state.la.us/tsrs/tsrs.asp?lawbody=RS&title=14&section=95.6. Further, they might consider the Second Amendment to the U.S. Constitution.

4. WS fear for our future enrollments if word gets out that Loyola University New Orleans will act decisively to quell this outbreak of violence that has engulfed us. I, in contrast, am concerned for the safety of our students and other members of the university community. I fear for our future enrollments if we keep our heads in the sand, and do not reply forcefully to these dangers.

5. We are serious about our proposal. It is no exaggeration to say that a civilized order depends upon a stalwart defense, including police and, yes, privately owned weapons. The phrase "modest proposal," has meanings other than the one to which they so intently attach it. This debate will not be settled by literary allusions, but rather by rational argument. Nevertheless, any misunderstanding or injury that may have resulted from the use of that term was unintended and is regrettable. Moreover, WS accused us of making a light of a tragedy, yet that is exactly what they did. The picture of themselves that WS obviously posed for and allowed to grace their article, with them facing back to back holding their hands aloft as if they were going to engage in a duel with index finger pistols, was not unintended; rather, it was obviously intended to be humorous.

6. Nowhere do WS dispute our claim that pistols are a causal agent in reducing criminal depredations; that there is an inverse relationship between the danger perceived by the criminal to himself and the amount of such behavior he will engage in. Indeed, they cannot, for this is only a matter of common sense. Do you think a mugger would rather face an armed or unarmed victim?

7. I fail to see how relying only on the police -- who cannot be everywhere --"recognizes the value of 'the human person.'" Their counsel amounts to turning the other cheek, unilateral disarmament and pacifism. It seems to be consonant with Catholic social tradition but it is not; according to its just war theory: "self-defense against an armed attack is always considered to be a just cause."

8. In attacking Barnett and me for our support of the free enterprise system, WS reveal themselves as ignorant of the fact that this system is responsible, to the extent we have it, for our magnificent standards of living, the envy of most of the rest of the world. In sharp contrast is the Soviet economy, which lead to starvation and economic disarray. Surely, after the economic malfunction of the USSR, and the fall of the Berlin Wall, only those blinded by a dirigiste ideology can still denigrate capitalism.

9. Contrary to our learned friends, we maintain a sharp distinction between human beings and property. It is a matter of no little surprise that they should interpret our defense of human beings against outrageous attacks as a failure to make this distinction. If anyone in this debate has disrespect for human rights it is those who would disarm victims of aggression.

10. If anyone "owes an apology" to rape victims and their families, it is not those who are using the best evidence provided by social science to help empower them. It is, rather, those who commit such dastardly deeds and those who act so as to disarm potential victims.

I have not replied to WS's obscene, irrelevant and monstrous charge that Barnett and I defend slavery, or are making fun of rape victims. Their McCarthyite demand that the Dean of the Business School repudiate our position on self defense is also beneath contempt. If there is anyone deserving of censure from academic authorities it is those who resort to charges of guilt by association and who lower debate from a serious consideration of the issues to that befitting a bar room brawl.

Chapter 36. The Living Wage: What's Wrong?

The latest on the minimum-wage front, brought to us by the academic minions of "social justice," is a private, not a public, effort to raise the pay of low-wage workers. Emanating first from prestigious institutions of higher learning such as Harvard and Yale, this initiative has spread like wildfire to colleges all around the country.

The gist of the program is to raise the wages of janitors and others at the lower end of the pay distribution to $10 or $12 an hour, and to boycott suppliers who do not undertake a similar program. A minimum wage of $5.15, it would appear, might be all well and good, but something twice that amount is necessary if it is to be a "living wage."

It is entirely legitimate for a private university to offer whatever pay scale it wishes and to boycott any businesses whatsoever, for any reason it chooses. However, institutions of higher learning are supposedly distinguished by rational dialogue, and it is in this vein that we wish to register an objection to this unwise policy.

Let us consider several reasons for declining to pay labor more than is necessary to attract a sufficient number of job applicants and for ending discrimination against firms that pay market wages.

Universities attempt to raise funds from the entire business community (among many other constituents). Making invidious comparisons between firms-singling out those that operate under market conditions for implicit condemnation-can hardly be conducive to this end. But this is mere pragmatism, unworthy perhaps of even being considered.

The program will likely not have its intended effect of boosting the wages of low-skilled workers. Suppose the typical university subcontractor pays its unskilled employees $6 an hour and the "social justice" wage is $10. People in this stratum of the labor force would give their eyeteeth for such a position, since it pays 40 percent more than the market says the job is worth. Would not everyone and his uncle making under $10 gladly take up such a job? How will the limited number of spaces be allotted to the vast hordes of people? Would it unduly challenge credulity to think that some of the few selected would be willing to make a side payment to the hiring staff? Or that this might be demanded of applicants? Or that nepotism, favoritism, and other forms of discrimination might arise? After all, if prices are not allowed to allocate labor resources, other criteria will be used.

If you want to give money to poor people, why not just go ahead and do it? Why tie it to their jobs of all things? That is, why conflate charity with an attempt to disrupt the labor market? Universities, at least private ones, are part of the market. Therefore they cannot disrupt it with any voluntary act on their part, even of this sort. But why even try? Why offer extra money to the unskilled in the form of higher salaries when you can use these funds for education or training or anything else under the sun?

People Are Different

The notion of justice underlying the "living wage" is predicated on the philosophy that income differences are unfair. It is patently obvious that in a market-based society, the primary reason some people are wealthy and others very much not so is that they have different initial endowments of intelligence, work ethic, ambition, talents, and entrepreneurial skills, as well as inherited material wealth and even luck. But despite these differences, the market tends to diminish income differences that would otherwise exist. This is because to become rich under free enterprise, you must enrich the lives of many other people; at the apex of the economic pyramid you gain a great deal, but you also drag onto a higher economic plane practically an entire society. (Think of Bill Gates or Henry Ford.) If we all lived on tiny islands as hermits, without economic interaction, some of us would be far wealthier than others. If material differences in wealth are unfair, then are not the very causes thereof, different endowments of human capital, also unfair?

Egalitarianism as a philosophy is dead from the neck up, insofar as even its adherents do not and, indeed, cannot take it seriously. Yet suppose there were a magical machine that could transfer IQ points (or beauty or health or hair follicles or musical ability) from those that have "a lot" to those who have "too little." It would be the rare egalitarian who would follow through on this pernicious philosophy. In contrast, the freedom philosophy requires only that people keep their hands off other people and their property, something far more peaceful and just, and also more readily attainable.

Chapter 37. Voluntary Taxes: Abusive Language and Politicians

In his March 20, 2002 letter to the *Wall Street Journal* "'Tough-Guy' Proposals for Indiana's Budget," that state's Governor Frank O'Bannon calls "for increases in two minor, voluntary taxes – on cigarettes and riverboat admissions."

"Voluntary taxation?" "Voluntary taxation" is an oxymoron if ever there was one; it is similar to "jumbo shrimp," "an important trifle," or "a square circle." "Voluntary taxation" is a downright contradiction in terms, since if there is anything that taxation is not, it is voluntary. The proof is, if you do not pay, your property is forcibly confiscated and/or you go to jail. "Coercive taxation" is a redundancy, because once you comprehend the latter word in this phrase, you know the meaning of the former is a constituent part of that understanding.

This is but one – though a typical one – example of the way politicians abuse the language in attempting to deceive the people about the true nature of their actions.

Does the good governor mean that purchasers of cigarettes/entrants onto riverboats don't have to pay the relevant tax if they don't want to? Or does he mean that they don't have to pay the tax if they don't buy cigarettes/ enter riverboats? It is not likely that he intends the former. If the latter, then, of course, all taxes are voluntary; e.g., one could avoid property taxes on residential property or sales taxes on food merely by going homeless or not buying food, respectively. In the latter case, perhaps one could survive by foraging in dumpsters. Similarly, he might mean that income taxes are really voluntary, in that you can choose not to earn an income, in which case you are not subject to the tax. That is, because voluntary choice determines whether or not a tax applies, the levy in question is not really compulsory.

But if this were true, then robbery would no longer be a crime. A robbery victim could simply choose not to own anything. That, surely, would foil any would be thief. Or, an intended murder victim could be offered the choice of a slow, painful death by torture or administering to himself a dose of a quick painless poison. This would no longer be murder. Instead, utilizing the "logic" of Governor O'Bannon, it would become a (voluntary) suicide.

C'mon, Governor, give us a break! Using the coercive power of government to relieve people of their hard earned wealth is bad enough, but debasing the language (no doubt quality education is a top priority for this servant of the people) in the process only adds insult to injury.

Chapter 38. The Paradox of Coase as a Defender of Free Markets

Coase (1960) is viewed by virtually all economists as a staunch defender of free markets. Part of the reason for this might be the fact that in his other works he did indeed take this position. For example, not only did Coase (1974B) present the claim that lighthouses *had* been privately run, he was *happy* to present it in this manner[772]. And this free enterprise perspective applies, too, to his (1959, 1965, 1966, 1979A, 1979B) analyses of radio frequencies and his (1977) treatment of advertising, to say nothing of his (1955, 1961) analysis of the post office. Further, his (1974A) work was a ringing endorsement of free speech. But this notion that Coase (1960) may be counted as a supporter of the market has not gone unchallenged. Critics of Coase (1960) on these grounds include Block (1977B, 1995, 1996, 2000), Cordato (1989, 1992A, 1998), Krecke (1996), North (1992) and Rothbard (1990)[773]. In the present paper, we challenge this mainstream Coase-as-free-enterpriser view, by considering several cases in point.

In section I we explore why it is that the Coase Theorem is often and mistakenly taken to be a pro-market argument; section II is devoted to making the case that Coase is worse than Pigou in terms of both adherence to free market principles and maximizing wealth; the theme of section III is to analyze the Coasean focus on transaction costs;[774] we conclude in section IV with an analysis of the tort-liability crisis, the intellectual underpinnings of which his writings form a substantial part.

I. The Coase Theorem is often mistakenly taken to be a pro-market argument

"The Problem of Social Cost" (Coase, 1960) is the most cited economics article in history.[775] And what it is so famous for is something that has come to be called "The Coase Theorem." Why the Coase Theorem (Coase, 1960) is taken to be supportive of free markets is a riddle wrapped in an enigma folded into a paradox, with apologies to Winston Churchill.[776] It may be stated as follows: The initial assignment of the rights to a good or resource are irrelevant to the efficient use thereof, provided that the transactions costs are zero, or sufficiently low, and that there are no inhibiting wealth[777] effects.

---

[772] For a rejoinder to this claim, see Van Zandt (1993) and Barnett and Block (2007A).

[773] For defenders of Coase (1960) see Medema (1997), Medema and Samuels (1997), Medema and Zerbe (1997)

[774] That the concept of "transactions costs" is confused, see Barnett, Saliba, and Block (2002).

[775] Shapiro, 1966

[776] Churchill actually said: "I cannot forecast to you the action of Russia. It is a riddle, wrapped in a mystery, inside an enigma."

[777] Block (1977B) criticizes Coase's failure to make this assumption about wealth.

Let us examine this concept. The fundamental idea is that if individual A values the rights to good or resource X more than anyone else, then if A was assigned the rights to X initially, no other individual will be willing to offer A enough for A to part with his rights to X, and therefore, X will be used in its most highly valued use as determined by A. That is, the efficient allocation, i.e., the allocation of X to its most highly valued use, will prevail. Alternatively, if some individual, B, other than A was assigned the rights to X initially, A would be willing to offer B more for the rights to X than anyone else will, and this offer will be sufficient to induce B to transfer voluntarily to A the rights to X. Therefore, in this case also, the efficient allocation of the rights to X, that is, the allocation thereof to A who values X more than anyone else, will occur. There are, however, in this latter case where B is the initial rights owner, two (2) potential flies in the ointment of efficient allocation. First, it is possible that the transactions costs[778] involved in effectuating the transfer of rights from B to A may exceed the expected gain in value from the shift, negating its desirability, in which case the rights are not conveyed from B to A. Second, although A might be willing to offer B sufficient inducement to effectuate the transfer, A may be unable to do so for lack of sufficient wealth. That is, A may be willing but unable[779], under which assumption, also, the rights do not migrate from B to A. Therefore, there are cases in which if the rights are not initially assigned to the one who values them most highly, they will *not* subsequently be transferred to him, in which cases there will be a continuing misallocation of goods/resources; i.e., they will be allocated to sub-optimal uses, and there will be no way for these situations to be corrected through the voluntary actions of the individuals involved. That is, an inefficient allocation of resources will prevail.

The Coase theorem in a nutshell: the pro-market part of his findings is that property rights allow negotiators to take advantage of "special circumstances of time and place" (Hayek, 1948A, p. 80) in ways not available to regulators. (Even if one justifies private property on a natural rights basis, it is nice to know that it makes us wealthier as well.) But this is only in the zero-transaction cost world.

Why is the Coase Theorem assumed to promote free markets?

---

[778] Transactions costs are those involved in effectuating the transfer of rights: the costs of search, bargaining, and enforcement of contracts.

[779] In discussing demand in a first course in economics it is explained to students that for an offer to buy to count as part of the demand for a good or resource, the potential buyer must be "willing *and* able" to deliver that which he offers. Certainly, our offer to pay $1,000,000,000 for, say, Z, does not constitute part of the demand for Z, as we do not have $1,000,000,000.

Mainstream/standard/orthodox/neoclassical economics worships at the shrine of efficiency.[780] That is, free markets are thought to be desirable because, and to the extent that, they yield efficient results, rather than because they are free. Because most of the attention given to the Coase theorem has assumed situations in which zero/low transactions costs are the norm,[781] and because the theorem maintains that in such situations free markets yield efficient allocations of rights, the Coase theorem is thought to promote free markets. That is, because the ultimate social desiderata is

---

[780] The mainstream definition of efficiency leaves something to be desired, to say the least. A situation is said to be efficient (referred to as a Pareto optimum) if there is no possible change in the allocation of rights (the allocation of goods and resources, if you prefer) that could be made that would improve the well being of one or more individuals, without at the same time making at least one individual worse off; alternatively, a change is said to be efficient (referred to as a Pareto superior move) if it makes at least one person better off, without making even one other person worse off.

Thus all voluntary exchanges are efficient. Moreover, if a change were to make A better off, but B worse, it would not be voluntarily entered into by B, and therefore, would not be efficient, save if it would increase A's well being sufficiently for A to be able to, and would, compensate B to the extent that B would willing agree to the change. Such a case would also be one of voluntary exchange. However, mainstream economists use the concept of Kaldor-Hicks efficiency (a.k.a. a *potential* Pareto superior move) to evade the strict voluntariness required by adherence to the conditions for Pareto superior moves. Kaldor-Hicks efficiency merely holds that a move is efficient if the gain to the beneficiary(ies) exceeds the loss to those harmed to such an extent that the former *could* compensate the latter sufficiently to induce them to make the change voluntarily.

However, and here is the problem, the Kaldor-Hicks compensation is only imaginary; it is never paid. That is, a transfer, from B to A, of the rights to X is Kaldor-Hicks efficient if the benefits to A are great enough that A *could* compensate B enough that he would willing make the transfer. Of course, B never gets the compensation, so if the transfer occurs he ends up worse off in reality. Moreover, as A doesn't have to actually compensate B, there is no way to know how much he actually would benefit from the transfer; i.e., he is free to exaggerate the benefits at no cost to himself; if the exaggeration helps him get the rights to X is he is necessarily better off. (This ignores the morality of lying to acquire material gain.) This is unlike a free market situation, in which if he exaggerated the benefits in a legally binding agreement (a contract) to transfer the rights to X, and B accepted, A would be made worse. And, since B will not receive any compensation if the transfer is made, he is free to exaggerate the cost to himself of the transfer in hopes that it will not be made. This, also, is unlike a free market situation, in which if he exaggerated the costs to himself A might not agree to the transfer of rights, in which case B might forego a transaction that would have made him better off. That is, in a free market situation exaggerations create risks for the parties; there is no risk from so doing in situations where the government uses Kaldor-Hicks criteria for assigning/transferring rights.

[781] The issue of "insufficient wealth" is rarely considered. See on this Block (1977B).

efficiency and the Coase theorem maintains that free markets yield efficient results in situations assumed to constitute the vast majority of cases, therefore the Coase theorem is widely seen as a bulwark of freedom/free markets/free enterprise.

But there are difficulties with this position. First, free markets are desirable precisely because, and to the extent that, they are free. That is, they are beneficial, of necessity, no matter what their assumed efficiency (Rothbard, 1979; Block, 1995; Roth, 2002).

Second, the assumption that the vast majority of cases do not involve excessively high transactions costs (and/or wealth constraints), even if true, is not controlling. The reason is that, because efficiency is seen as the overriding goal, one implication of the Coase theorem is that in such cases disputes over rights should be resolved in favor of the one who values them most highly. That is, government should intervene to settle such disputes *and* should do so by transferring them from the original owner to a new owner because the latter values them more highly, even though he was not able to manifest this presumed higher valuation in the market because of the excessively high transactions costs and/or because he was constrained by a lack of wealth.[782]

Third, even if small in number, many of these cases are important to the wider society, and they are always vital to the parties involved.

Fourth, as all costs are subjective, there is no way to determine if they are excessive; i.e., no way to determine if they are the sole reason that a transaction that otherwise would have been consummated was not. And, even if we only consider the objective (i.e., measured in monetary terms) expenses, it is virtually impossible for third parties to put an accurate figure on such expenses.

Fifth, situations in which governmental courts are asked to decide disputes over rights and might apply the Coase theorem do not really involve the initial assignment of rights. Rather, one of the parties owns the rights and

---

[782] Although the theorem itself does not address the issue of the transfer of wealth that accompanies such a transfer of rights, being concerned only with the efficient allocation of rights, such effects are referred to as "distribution" effects and thought to be irrelevant. That is, "society's" total wealth is maximized by the transfer of rights; that the distribution of wealth among the members of society is altered is irrelevant to the theorem, and, implicitly, is not considered important to "society;" of course, it is very important to the individuals involved. Moreover, even when the transfer of wealth is considered and thought worthy of compensation, the approach is to have some disinterested neutral, independent, objective, impartial, unbiased, third-party decide upon the appropriate compensation to the party who has lost his rights. Obviously, such compensation will fall short of the value of the rights to that party, else he would have voluntarily transferred them.

the other party wants to acquire them either for no payment at all or a fee below fair market levels. To transfer rights from one party to another in such cases is not to promote free markets, but rather just the opposite. In such cases, the job of the court is to declare who the owner is, not to make an "initial" assignment of ownership.

Sixth, transactions costs are real costs in that they involve the use of resources to effectuate transfers. Because they are real costs they should be taken into account in determining whether the benefits of a transaction exceed the costs.

Seventh, high transactions costs can not be avoided by removing the decision from the market to the courts, as the very use of governmental courts to resolve disputes over rights resources itself involves the use of resources, which is properly understood as a form of transactions costs. And, as with virtually everything government does we can expect its courts to be inefficient; i.e., using the courts *increases* the transactions costs.

Eighth, the wealth constraint is invalid because of the existence of credit. If A really values X more than B does, but A has not the wherewithal to induce B to part with X, A can resort to credit, borrowing the money. And, it will not do to say that credit markets are less than "perfectly competitive," and consequently A might not be able to borrow the necessary funds. The use of credit markets involves real costs, also. And, of course, "perfect competition" is a fantasy with no counterpart in the real world. It is easy for A to say, "Transfer the rights to X to me because I value them more than B, but unfortunately I have not the funds to induce B to transfer the rights; moreover, I would be willing to borrow the funds but I, a creditworthy specimen, am unable to do so because of imperfections in the credit markets. However, A pays no cost for exaggerating the amount he is willing to borrow and pay to B, knowing he will not be called on to so do as no potential lender will provide him the funds; and, for the same reason, he can exaggerate, at no cost to himself, the rate of interest he would be willing to pay to borrow the funds.

The Coase Theorem is used to provide intellectual cover for a party who wishes to come into possession of another individual's rights without acquiring them through a freely bargained exchange. It constitutes no less than an attempt to use the power of the state to acquire such property without having to pay the fair market value, or, perhaps, anything, to the owner. The rationale involved in this cover is that certain real costs – the transactions costs involved in the market process, the cost of credit (which is, effectively, infinite for uncreditworthy borrowers) and the (transactions) costs involved in the use of the courts – are in some sense artificial and unnecessary to effectuate exchanges, and therefore should be ignored

II. Why Coase Is Worse Than Pigou

This will sound exceedingly surreal, given the view of the economics profession to the contrary, but it is our contention that Pigou had a stronger sense of property rights than Coase!

For Coase, property is only assigned by judges, in the same way a basketball coach assigns Smith to guard Jones. Whoever can use the property under dispute[783] "best" at the moment gets it, but if circumstances change, it will be reassigned. But what are the efficiency effects of insecure property rights?

One need not adopt a natural rights view of private property to see the flaw in Coase's argument. The mere existence of such a position highlights the problem. This holds true so long as there are people who maintain that no gain in "efficiency" measured in whatever sense is sufficient to compensate for rights violations. (If you can't excuse killing someone because it will make you rich, you also can't excuse it because it will make you very, very rich.) Coase has no argument that enables him to isolate the preferences of these people as some inadmissible category of preference amidst the world of other, valid preferences. A Coasean (e.g., Demsetz, 1966, 1967, 1979, 1997)[784] might attempt to "sterilize" Coasean analysis by limiting it to monetary payments as a proxy for efficiency, but this argument begs the question: the ability to make monetary payments depends very much on how the property rights arrangements are or are not altered by legal decree in the first place.

The puzzle: given the fact that Pigou saw himself as an interventionist economist battling a generally pro-market profession and that Coase saw himself as a pro-market economist battling an anti-market profession, how did Coase wind up developing the more anti-market position?

III. Transactions Costs

Why do Coase's pro-market inclinations dramatically attenuate when it comes to solving the problem of externalities? It is our contention that, at least in part, the attenuation is due to Coase's mistaken view that transaction costs are something external to the market process, rather than an integral part of it.

---

[783] Nor should one think that the title to very little property would be disputed in a full Coasean world. For once the word gets out that property under contention goes not to he who can establish historical ownership, but rather to the person who can best claim that in the future his ownership of it is most likely to maximize GDP, then all bets are off. *Every* piece of hitherto private property would be open to continual disputation.

[784] For a critique of Demsetz's views on property rights, see Block (1977B, 1995, 2000)

Coase's approach, in which transaction costs should be eliminated by fiat if possible, implies a world where, before the market process begins, agents already know everything necessary about all transactions in which they might engage. The market process itself is merely one among several possible means of attempting to achieve a "socially optimal" allocation of resources, rather than the only means of approaching such a goal.

We want to point out that there is nothing inherently wrong in an analysis that isolates transactions costs as a particular aspect of economic activity -- just as can be done for marketing costs, sales costs, labor costs, land costs, or, indeed, office supply costs.

A problem arises only when such categories of costs are viewed as somehow external to actual market transactions, so that we could eliminate one category of costs -- clearly a benefit! -- and nevertheless retain the full benefit of a working market.

As Coase sees it, the potential for governmental improvements of market outcomes arises in the case of "high" transaction costs. If, somehow, it is determined that it is merely transaction costs preventing some exchange from occurring, the rules of private property may be suspended and property rights re-shuffled until the "right" outcome, the one that would arise in a world of zero transaction costs, is achieved.

However, contrary to this view, a market transaction is an attempt, on the part of both parties, to improve some unsatisfactory aspect of their current circumstances. If the parties agree to an exchange, it is because they both anticipate that their circumstances after the exchange will be superior to those that would have come to pass had they not exchanged. The cost of the resulting exchange, for either participant, is the value of the most valuable opportunity he sacrificed in order to make the trade. As such, the costs entailed by any action are whatever[785] the participants perceive them costs to be (Buchanan, 1969).

Furthermore, the costs of convincing other actors to respond to one's actions as hoped for are intrinsic to human action itself. As Oakeshott (1975: 45-46) puts it: "Doing… is action in search of a wished-for response from other agents which it may not receive…. And conduct thus recognized is… a transaction between agents in terms of the postulate persuasion."

An offer to buy (or sell) is a performance intended to elicit a response to sell (or buy) on the part of another actor. The performance is an essential part of the market process, since the essence and efficacy of the market springs from the voluntary nature of market transactions. A transaction that

---

785 Explains Herbener, "The price for the existing stock of each consumer good reflects, but is not and cannot be equal to, the subjective value of its marginal unit…" (Herbener, 1997)

would have occurred except for high transaction costs is simply a case in which one or both parties did not persuade the other that the transaction was worthwhile. If a potential party to a transaction is holding out for better terms, that is because he is not yet persuaded that his best course of action is to make a deal at the terms so far offered.

Let us consider a hypothetical case in which organic dairy farmers persuade the legislature that organic milk is much better for "the people" than is non-organic milk. The organic farmers may even be correct in assuming that all consumers would purchase organic milk, if only they fully understood its benefits. However, the organic lobbyists point out, the public is not properly informed of the wonderfulness of such milk. If only the organic dairy farmers had the marketing wherewithal of the non-organic producers, they would have achieved market dominance long ago. But since the legislature is now convinced of the benefits of the organic product, such marketing costs are, the lobbyists contend, an unnecessary expense: it is more "socially efficient" simply to mandate that only the superior, organic milk be sold.

However, if a consumer is not informed about the wonders of organic milk and therefore chooses to buy milk containing antibiotics and so on, then it must be admitted that he really is not informed. For the consumer to change his mind and voluntarily buy organic milk, someone must undertake the cost of educating him as to its advantages. It is only by actually informing him of the benefits and then seeing what he decides that his real preferences are revealed (Rothbard, 1997I).

It is absurd to pretend that the cost of persuasion doesn't exist, and then claim that by forcing everyone to buy organic milk, one has reduced costs. In fact, those costs have simply been imposed upon the unwilling buyers of the organic milk. Since costs are subjective, the costs of being forced to buy a product are whatever the buyer perceives them to be. Under the fiat organic milk regime, many buyers will pay a higher price for this product, without perceiving any compensatory benefit.

Mises recognized that persuasion is an integral part of the market process: "The way in which many contemporary writers deal with various problems--for instance, advertising and marketing--is manifestly a relapse into the crude errors which should have disappeared long ago...."

He continues, "The consumer is not omniscient. He does not know where he can obtain at the cheapest price what he is looking for. Very often he does not even know what kind of commodity or service is suitable to remove most efficaciously the particular uneasiness he wants to remove.... A businessman expends money for advertising if and as far as he expects that the increase in sales resulting will increase the total net proceeds. In this regard there is no difference between the costs of advertising and all other costs of production. An attempt has been made to distinguish between production costs and sales costs. An increase in production costs, it has been said, increases supply, while an increase in sales costs (advertising costs included) increases demand. This is a mistake. All costs of production are expended with the intention of increasing demand."

Anthony de Jasay makes a similar point about "exclusivity," which is also often regarded as a special, avoidable cost: "Nothing is 'excludable' without further ado; for nothing can be sold without the seller incurring costs to exclude from access those who would not pay the price. Exclusion cost is no more avoidable in a good destined to be sold than is the cost of production or transport. Everything is excludable at some cost..." (http://www.mises.org/journals/rae/pdf/rae9_1_5.pdf).

We might make our case by paraphrasing de Jasay: Nothing is exchangeable without further ado; for nothing can be sold without the seller incurring costs in persuading buyers to purchase his wares.

Transaction costs are, in other words, simply another cost of production. In fact, they are a special case of marketing costs, where the marketing effort is being directed not at a broad group of targeted consumers, but at particular, known parties with whom one hopes to transact. If transaction costs are high, it is a sign that at least one of the parties to a potential transaction has not been persuaded that the transaction, on the terms offered, is in his best interest[786].

High transaction costs are not, as is sometimes contended chiefly the result of having to deal with a large number of parties at once. The buyer of commodity wheat does not face high transaction costs, despite possibly having to deal with numerous sellers, because there is little disagreement over how to price the wheat. In such a commodity market, all of the sellers can simply consult The Wall Street Journal and discover at what price wheat was recently being sold. When a polluter faces high transactions costs in negotiating with many property owners for an easement that will allow him to emit soot onto their land, the high transactions costs occur precisely because each of the property owners may have his own, perhaps radically divergent, perception of the value of soot-free property.

A case involving such property-rights issues comes before a Coasean judge only when at least one of the potential parties to a transaction has not succeeded in persuading at least one of the other potential parties that a deal on the terms offered is worth his while. The opinion of the judge, in deciding who has the relevant property rights in such a case, is just one possible

---

786 (Of course, state intervention may create transaction costs that truly are external to the market process. For instance, many of the transaction costs involved in acquiring a mortgage are the result of regulatory requirements, rather than being intrinsic to the transaction itself.)

valuation of a contentious situation. By altering property rights to line up with what he sees as the efficient solution, the Coasean judge is not reducing costs, but is instead imposing them upon whomever he decides the costs ought to be imposed.

It would only be in a world where everyone already knew all of the advantages and disadvantages of every possible transaction that the persuasive performances necessary to elicit voluntary exchanges would be redundant. It is through this process of mutual persuasion that actors both disclose and discover their preferences. There is no conceivable mechanism, absent such a process, by which welfare-maximizing exchange ratios could be discovered (Hayek, 1948A, 1948C, Rothbard, 1997I).

IV. The Liability crisis

To say that we are in the midst of a liability crisis is easy to document. The tobacco awards and the case of the lady who successfully sued McDonalds for selling her hot tea (which she placed in between her legs while driving) are but tips of the veritable iceberg in this regard[787]. Some of these cases are so counter to common sense that they have been made into jokes.

But what, pray tell, do these liability cases have to do with the Coase Theorem? Say what you will about the latter, it cannot fairly be claimed that it is either intrinsically funny, nor, yet, that there is any obvious connection between it and this spate of liability cases mentioned above. In order to see the connection, we shall have to dig deeper.

Let us begin by reviewing Coase (1960) once again. Its essential point is that there are two states of the world, the real one, and an ideal one where there are no transactions costs. In the latter case, says Coase, it does not matter (at least for wealth considerations), when there is property under dispute, which party is awarded it. A bargaining session will ensue after the judge makes any determination, and the commodity will end up in the hands of the person for whom it has the greatest value. In the former case, with high transactions costs, we cannot rely upon any such "market"[788] process. This being the case, it is now the duty of the magistrate to decide in whose hands the good would have ended up in, on the assumption of zero transactions costs (e.g., who "values"[789] it more) and then to make the award on this basis. That

---

[787] See text, below, for more such cases.

[788] Quotation marks are supplied to indicate we do not at all regard this Coasean scenario as related to free markets. That is, free markets are based upon property rights, which are, in turn, dependant upon homesteading and voluntary trade (Nozick, 1974), not upon judges' decisions save as they go to issues of homesteading and/or voluntary exchange.

[789] Note that this is valuation in the abstract as opposed to valuation by revealed preference; i.e., it de facto assumes that transactions costs are not real costs.

is, when property is under dispute, the Coasean rule is to judge in favor of the person whose ownership will maximize total societal wealth[790]. One might well ask with Epstein (1980, 135): "What possible benefits from the rearrangement could outweigh the costs of a compulsory reassignment of property rights?"

But more. Another implication of this analysis involves liability suits. Now the ordinary libertarian (e.g., non Coasean) normative analysis of liability is to rule in favor of the party who is least responsible for the accident in question. The concepts of "blame" and "cause" and "contract" and "fraud" and "justice" figure heavily into this analysis. For example, it is crystal clear that after decades of clearly labeling their product as "dangerous to health,"[791] the cigarette companies, in justice, would have no responsibility whatsoever to those adults who willingly took on this risk. In the free society, the only way that tobacco firms would be responsible for cancer or emphysema contracted by smokers would be if the seller *compelled at gunpoint* such behavior. As for the woman who situated hot tea between her legs, to require the vendor to pay for her injuries reeks to the high heavens of injustice. This was *her* foolish action, not that of McDonalds'. Spilling tea on oneself is the responsibility of the spiller, not the seller. One might as well sue the company that sells Drano or rat poison if a customer swallows either of these products.

But Coase (1960) would have none of this. Not for him any consideration of blame or personal responsibility. Instead, he relies on the concept of "least cost avoider." That is, in liability cases, the Coasean judge is called upon to favor the party who can, at least cost, avoid the accident[792].

Moreover, it ignores the fact that non-market transactions costs are involved when courts are involved; i.e., the court process uses resources to transfer rights just as markets do. And, in many cases the transactions costs involved in using the court process is probably much greater than those involved in using markets. The only reason courts are used in such cases is that one of the parties does not like the outcome that would be reached by voluntary actions; i.e., the market process.

[790] Inevitably, this opens up horrendous problems of interpersonal comparisons of utility. See on this Block (1977B, 1995, 1996, 2000, 2003D, 2006), Cordato (1989, 1992A, 1998), Krecke (1996), North (1992, 2002) and Rothbard (1990). Moreover, even assuming, *arguendo,* the validity of the concept of "societal wealth," the use of courts in such situations does not "maximize societal wealth," as the transactions costs involved in using the court process is ignored.

[791] That there were *forced* to do this by government is unjustified on the basis of caveat emptor; but this issue is in any case outside of our present purview

[792] It is important to consider how "least cost avoider" differs from "least responsible." It is possible to define the least cost avoider as the more responsible party and the higher cost avoider as the less responsible one. This is where the idea of causality enters, and with it strict liability (see Epstein, 1980). We must also

There is a parallel between disputes over property and liability for Coase. In both cases this author eschews the ordinary concerns of law[793] and instead resorts to wealth maximization. In the former case, he favors the party whose ownership of the good in question maximizes wealth. In the latter case, again so as to increase material goods, he tips the scales of justice in the direction of he who can at least cost avoid the accident.

Let us apply this insight to the cases we have been mentioning. Who has more knowledge of the health effects of tobacco? The cigarette companies, or any one individual smoker, or even all customers put together? To ask this question is to answer it. Obviously, the firms in this industry have been able to amass information about their own product that would put in the dark any efforts on the part of consumers to match it. They have a comparative advantage in generating such information. So, who, then, is in a better position, to deal with these threats? Who, in a word, is the "least cost avoider" (Coase, 1960) in this situation? Obviously, the industry. Hence, in a Coasean world, they, not the purchaser, must be found guilty.

Let us now consider a possible objection to this claim: "In a Coasean world the cigarette companies would be liable only if their cost of insuring their "victims" were less than the victims' cost to insure or if their cost to avoid (perhaps by screening potential purchasers for susceptibility to smoking related health problems and not selling to susceptible people – they might have to require on monitored, on-premise, use to avoid illegal transfer *or* by not selling at all; i.e., going out of business) were less than their customers' cost to avoid or insure. It is a safe assumption that the cost to insure for either would be prohibitive. Therefore, on Coasean grounds, the least cost avoider should be held liable. In fact, given all the publicity for at least the last half century (even in the 1940 children called cigarettes "coffin nails;" also there was a song "Smoke! Smoke! Smoke! (That Cigarette) with the same message[794]) it is not clear that the tobacco companies would have

---

consider the concept of least cost insurer. That is, according to Coasean analysis, the responsible party should be either the least cost avoider or the least cost insurer, depending upon which cost is lower. If it is cheaper for the least cost avoider to avoid than for the least cost insurer to insure, then for Coase the least cost avoider should be liable; however, if it is cheaper for the least cost insurer to insure than for the least cost avoider to avoid, than the least cost insurer should be liable.

[793] That is, blame, cause, contract, fraud and justice.

[794] (1947) written by Merle Travis for Tex Williams; the release not only saved Tex Williams' waning career, but also became Capitol Records' first million-seller. Travis later released his own version. These two are the most commonly heard versions. From the New York Times, Oct. 13, 1985:

Country-western songwriter and entertainer Sollie "Tex" Williams, a heavy smoker best known for his tune, "Smoke, Smoke, Smoke That Cigarette," died after a year-long battle with cancer, his daughter said... her father, who was diagnosed a

been held liable if Coase's principles had been properly applied. That is, given the virtual impossibility of being unaware of the health hazards of

---

year ago as having cancer, smoked two packs of cigarettes a day, dropping to about a pack a day before he died. "He tried to quit, but he couldn't," she said.

Smoke! Smoke! Smoke! (That Cigarette)

Now I'm a fellow with a heart of gold
And the ways of a gentleman I've been told
Kind-of-a-guy that wouldn't even harm a flea
But if me and a certain character met
The guy that invented that cigarette
I'd murder that son-of-a gun in the first degree
It ain't cuz I don't smoke 'em myself
and i don't reckon that it'll hinder your health
I smoked 'em all my life and I ain't dead yet
But nicotine slaves are all the same
at a pettin' party or a poker game
Everything gotta stop while they have a cigarette

CHORUS: Smoke, smoke, smoke that cigarette
Puff, puff, puff until you smoke yourself to death.
Tell St. Peter at the Golden Gate that you hate to make him wait,
But you just gotta have another cigarette.

In a game of chance the other night
Old dame fortune was good and right
The kings and queens they kept on comin' around
Aw, I was hittin' em good and bettin' 'em high
But my bluff didn't work on a certain guy
He kept callin' and layin' his money down

See, he'd raise me then I'd raise him
and I'd say to him buddy ya gotta sink or swim
Finally called me but didn't raise the bet!
--Hmmph! I said Aces Full Pal -- I got you!
He said, "I'll pay up in a minute or two
But right now, i just gotta have another cigarette." CHORUS

Now the other night I had a date
with the cutest little gal in any state
A high-bred, uptown, fancy little dame
She said she loved me and it seemd to me
That things were sorta like they oughtta be
So hand in hand we strolled down lovers lane

She was a long way from a chunk of ice
And our pettin' party was goin' real nice
And I got an idea I might have been there yet
So I give her a kiss and a little squeeze
Then she said, "Travis, Excuse me Please
But I just gotta have a cigarette." CHORUS

smoking, it seems that the smokers had the least cost of prevention – all they had to do was stop, or not begin in the first place. Both are relatively easy, witness the number of people who have never smoked and the number who have quit, relative to those who start and do not stop."

The problem with this objection, from our perspective, is that it makes the Coasean theory far too coherent. In our view, there is a thread of incomprehensibility running through this theorem that belies the possibility of any such clear determination, as posited by the objection to our thesis. This is because the Coase theorem relies on the comparison of costs between different people, and this is an inherently subjective issue.

Thus, interpersonal comparisons are tendentious, unscientific and invalid[795]. Thus, it always possible for two Coasean analysts, while both remaining true to the underlying principles of this framework, to reach opposite conclusions. Consider, again, the cigarette case. Our critic claims that, given the widespread knowledge of the dangers of smoking tobacco (it is celebrated in a popular song, even children know this), that its purveyors would not be found liable. It cannot be denied that this is a plausible interpretation of how a Coasean might look at the matter. On the other hand, it is *also* possible to maintain, again within the Coasean framework, the very opposite: that this knowledge did not permeate as fully as possible[796], that even to the extent that it did, still, the vast amount of information garnered by professionals in the industry would put to shame whatever limited knowledge consumers might manage to garner, that there was a lot of "noise" in the system, e.g., customers being confused by advertising for this product, etc.

A similar perspective applies to the hot tea case. Ask yourself, gentle reader, not who is *responsible* for this scalding; instead, thrust yourself into the Coasean world, and query, who is the least cost avoider of accidents of this sort? E.g., who knows more about, who can at less cost generate information concerning, hot tea: a gigantic corporation which brews veritable swimming pools full of this beverage every day, or some little old lady who drinks it once in a while? Again, to ask this question is to answer it: the indictment of McDonalds is implicit once we look at the world through Coasean eye-glasses. Or, at least, this is *one* conclusion that could be reached in this manner. But again, it is possible to disagree, utilizing Coasean "insights." The cost to avoid is not solely dependent on the information

---

795 For support of this contention, see Barnett (1989), Buchanan and Thirlby (1981), Buchanan (1969), Cordato (1989), DiLorenzo (1990A), Garrison (1985A), Gunning (1990), Kirzner (1986), Mises (1949), Rizzo (1979B, 1980), Rothbard (1979, 1993, 1997I).

796 In the real world, if not the one occupied by mainstream economists, the perfectly competitive assumption of full and complete information on the part of all participants does *not* obtain. See on this Hayek, 1948A.

costs. In this case, presuming she was not an idiot (a real leap of faith), this woman knew hot tea can scald, therefore her avoidance cost was the postponement of drinking it until she had completed her trip. McDonald's cost was to make a less desirable (e.g., cooler) product for their millions of daily tea and coffee drinking, non-idiot, customers. Here, then, is the case for arguing that even in a Coasean world, McDonalds should have prevailed in the lawsuit.

We are now ready to apply to other examples our hard earned insights into the Coasean world-view. We shall do so in the form of commentaries about a spate of liability cases now making the rounds of the internet. Here are seven case studies[797], each followed, below, by commentary of the present authors.

1. "January 2000: Kathleen Robertson of Austin Texas was awarded $780,000 by a jury of her peers after breaking her ankle tripping over a toddler who was running amuck inside a furniture store. The owners of the store were understandably surprised at the verdict, considering the misbehaving tyke was Ms. Robertson's son."

A. Coasean comment: The big bad rich furniture store can surely more easily and cheaply figure out a way to rein in rampaging toddlers than can a single distraught mother[798]. Shouldn't they have had a kiddie romper room, so that mothers can shop in peace? For those worried about blameworthiness, the fact that this vendor did *not* offer such a feature ought to be sufficient to condemn them.

On the other hand, to wear our alternative Coasean hat, the very opposite conclusion is *also* compatible with this philosophy. Namely, that who apart from the *mother* of a particular child can know him better, more easily, more cheaply? Surely, the parents of toddlers have far more, better and less expensive information about them than any random furniture store.

B. Libertarian comment: In this one sees how Coaseanism leads easily to central planning and business regulation. Information disparity, and costs of avoiding accidents are completely irrelevant. The inescapable point is that the mother lost control of her own child, and the law should not allow her to make others pay for this difficulty. Had the mischievous tot been responsible for any damage to the furniture, ordinary justice would require that the mother reimburse the store for that as well.

2. "June 1998: A 19 year old Carl Truman of Los Angeles won $74,000 and medical expenses when his neighbor ran his hand over with a

---

[797] This material came to the lead author via the internet; we have not been able to authenticate the veracity of any of these stories. Given this failure of ours, it is best to consider these stories as hypothetical.

[798] This contention might also (or better) be argued on the basis of lower cost to insure.

Honda Accord. Mr. Truman apparently didn't notice someone was at the wheel of the car whose hubcap he was trying to steal."

A. Coasean comment: Who knows more about Honda vehicles? Carl Truman, a relatively "innocent" thief[799], his victim neighbor from whom the aforesaid person was trying to steal a hubcap, or the Honda Corporation? Need we even ask? Surely it is the latter who knows, or who *should know* more about this automobile, its characteristics, its ability to smash hands, etc., than anyone else. What *other* theory, beside that of Coase, apart from sheer lunacy suddenly gripping judges, is sufficient to explain this travesty of justice.

B. Libertarian comment: vehicular knowledge is beside what should be the legal point. The real issue, obvious to anyone not hailing from the planet Mungo, is that the thief should be forced to pay, not only for his own medical expenses, but also for his attempted theft.

3. "October 1998: A Terrence Dickson of Bristol Pennsylvania was exiting a house he finished robbing by way of the garage. He was not able to get the garage door to go up, the automatic door opener was malfunctioning. He couldn't reenter the house because the door connecting the house and garage locked when he pulled it shut. The family was on vacation, so Mr. Dickson found himself locked in the garage for eight days. He existed on a case of Pepsi he found, and large bag of dry dog food. This upset Mr. Dickson, so he sued the home owner's insurance claiming the situation caused him undue mental anguish. The jury agreed to the tune of half a million dollars and change."

A. Coasean comment: Let us construct a hierarchy of blame, based on the Coasean insights related to least cost avoiding of accidents in this case. Obviously, at the top of the heap is the firm that manufactured this malfunctioning automatic door opener. They likely have the deepest pockets, most information about their operation, and should be hit with the biggest penalty. Thus we can see that the jury missed a bet in not attacking those at the top of this particular food chain. Second, is of course the insurance company; second, only to the manufacturer[800] in terms of knowledge about, and therefore responsibility for, the good operation of this implement. Third would be the homeowner, whose duty it is to keep this machinery functioning, so that criminals will not be inconvenienced. A thousand pardons; so that people with even less knowledge about the workings of the garage door, e.g., visitors and guests, will not be victimized. In the absence of the manufacturer and insurer[801], it is the homeowner who

---

[799] See what happens when one eschews morality and yet wishes to discuss theft?

[800] We are now assuming equally deep pockets on the part of both miscreants.

[801] Assuming in effect that both these worthies were visited with the bankruptcy they so richly deserve

should have been made to pay, and pay heavily, for the horrible conditions the "criminal"[802] was forced to endure.

B. Libertarian comment: Deep pocket searches are obviously anathema to justice. The criminal[803] should not only be made to do time for his robbery, he ought to pay for the dog food he ate, the Pepsi he drank, and for a week's rent for occupying that garage. And not just at market prices either. He ought to pay at least double[804], since these were seizures, not purchases.

4. "October 1999: Jerry Williams of Little Rock Arkansas was awarded $14,500 and medical expenses after being bitten on the buttocks by his next door neighbor's beagle. The beagle was on a chain in it's owner's fenced in yard, as was Mr. Williams. The award was less than sought after because the jury felt the dog may have been provoked by Mr. Williams who, at the time, was shooting it repeatedly with a pellet gun."

A. Coasean comment: We are here faced with a plethora of actors, this time human and non human, and, in order to apply the Coasean "insights" to the case, must again construct a hierarchy of blame, responsibility, least cost avoiding and information. Between Mr. Williams, the trespasser, and his neighbor, the trespassee, who had more knowledge about the behavior of the dog? Obviously, the latter. Therefore, it was incumbent upon *him*, not Mr. Williams, to ensure safe conditions on the yard for any and sundry who might choose to while away the hours there. The cruelty toward the animal, while perhaps regrettable, is not pertinent. If the dog were not left unattended in the first place, by the reckless neighbor, the incident would not have occurred.

B. Libertarian comment: The is nonsense on stilts. The so-called "Mr." Williams ought to be made to pay the penalty for animal cruelty (to another person's property) and trespass. The jurors who made this award ought to be sent back to their home planet, Mungo. The judge who allowed it to stand ought to be disbarred. The reasoning behind this declaration is the ordinary commonsensical notion that people ought to be forced to compensate others for their misdeeds, and not be allowed to make them come to their rescue.

---

[802] We use quotation marks to indicate that while we concede he acted improperly, there were others with far more culpability than his, at least from the Coasean perspective.

[803] No quotation marks. For the libertarian, criminals are people who steal legitimately owned private property, and that is not an oxymoron. For a defense of property along these lines see Hoppe (1993), Rothbard (1982A, 1982B), Kinsella (1996A, 1996B, 1997).

[804] For the libertarian thesis that proper libertarian punishment consists of "two teeth for a tooth" plus expenses and compensation for fright, see Rothbard (1982B, p. 94), Block (1999B).

5. "May 2000: A Philadelphia restaurant was ordered to pay Amber Carson of Lancaster Pennsylvania $113,500 after she slipped on a spilled soft drink and broke her coccyx. The beverage was on the floor because Ms. Carson threw it at her boyfriend 30 seconds earlier during an argument."

A. Coasean comment: One might think that the Coasean would say, who better to know the dangers of a spilled drink that the restaurant proprietor? But in this context, the Coasean might well disagree with the ruling. He could argue that as a general principle restaurateurs are indeed lower cost avoiders than patrons, but in this particular case (the woman threw the drink herself, only a half minute had elapsed) placing blame on Miss Carson would actually enhance the GDP.

B. Libertarian comment: Finally, there is agreement with the Coasean conclusion, but certainly not with the reasoning. Miss Carson should not only be held responsible for her own medical bills, but should be made to pay for cleaning of the mess she made on the floor. This is because she was a victim of her own prior action. In ordinary parlance, she "brought it upon herself." To allow her to foist the costs of her own folly on to someone else would be the height of injustice.

6. "December 1997: Kara Walton of Claymont, Delaware successfully sued the owner of a night club in a neighboring city when she fell from the bathroom window to the floor and knocked out her two front teeth. This occurred while Ms. Walton was trying to sneak through the window in the lady's room to avoid paying the $3.50 cover charge. She was awarded $12,000 and dental expenses."

A. Coasean comment: In the ordinary course of events, the night club owner would be more aware of the dangers emanating from his own property than would any of his patrons. The owner in question should have exhibited more care in the present case than he did since it would have been cheaper for him to have done so, than for the customer. The fact that she was in the process of attempting to steal services from him is of no moment, since theft is a normative concept, and the Coaseans are concerned, only, with positive economic analysis.

B. Libertarian comment: This is yet another case where the Coaseans diverge markedly not only from the libertarian, but also from the ordinary man in the street. To actually pay a thief damages, instead of penalizing her from theft is not only non pragmatic (it exacerbates stealing) but also reeks to the heavens with injustice.

7. "And just so you know that cooler heads do occasionally prevail: Kenmore Inc., the makers of Dorothy Johnson's microwave, were found not liable for the death of Mrs. Johnson's poodle after she gave it a bath and attempted to dry it by putting the poor creature in her microwave for, 'just a few minutes, on low.' The case was quickly dismissed."

A. Coasean comment: The logic of the Coasean position forces him to demur from this reasonable legal assessment. For the microwave manufacturers surely know more about their product than those who buy them at retail. Kenmore, to be sure, cannot be expected to have predicted that particular abuse of its product. But their retailers could have done more to obviate such misuse.

B. Libertarian comment: There is nothing "crazier" about Mrs. Johnson's actions regarding her poodle than with putting hot tea between your legs in a moving automobile, and expecting someone else to pay for the negative results of that activity. Mrs. Johnson is no more unreasonable than smokers who sue tobacco companies. The "logic" of these cases, in a negative way to be sure, is impeccable. Once allow these other travesties of injustice into the tent, and there is no stopping point. For the Coasean, Mrs. Johnson must be compensated.

It cannot be denied that there is no smoking gun to be found in the writings of Coase. He nowhere gives his explicit imprimatur to the lunatic decisions we have been considering. But there is a direct implicit, or logical connection between: 1) a refusal to consider the concept of justice[805], and a reliance on wealth maximization and its manifestation re liability, least cost avoidance of, or insurance against, accidents; and, 2) this spate of lunatic court decisions we have been discussing.

---

[805] One searches in vain for even a *mention* of this concept in all of Coase (1960). This would be unremarkable, and unexceptionable, in an essay on positive economics. But whatever Coase (1960) is, and it is many things, it is by no means limited to that concern; rather, it also involves itself not only in what the law *is* (positive law), but also in what the law *should be*! Surely it is an anomaly that "justice" should not be so much as even *mentioned* in a tractate devoted to what the law should be.

Chapter 39. The economic case for laissez faire capitalism[806]

I. Introduction

It is our contention that laissez faire capitalism is the last best hope for justice, prosperity and economic efficiency. We shall attempt to make this case according to the outline that appears above.

By laissez faire capitalism we mean a system based upon private property rights and free markets. This gives rise to two possible scenarios. First, government is strictly limited to protecting the persons and property of its citizens[807]. To this end, it has three separate institutions at its disposal: armies, to protect us from foreign aggressors, police, to do the same regarding domestic hoodlums, and courts, to determine guilt or innocence, and to mediate other disputes[808]. Second, more radically, government does not exist at all, and all of the tasks that supposedly require its participation are accomplished, instead, by private enterprise; this is called anarcho capitalism or libertarian anarchism[809].

II. The case

A. The banking system

1. Offshore banking

Part and parcel of a free enterprise regime are laws that allow unrestricted offshore banking (Gwartney, Lawson and Block, 1996). Moreover, for the protection of the masses of people who cannot make use of this option, real estate used for banking purposes must be legally extra-territorial insofar as financial matters are concerned, much as Churches at one time were havens and sanctuaries. That is to say, regarding financial matters; i.e., dollar denominated notes, bonds, etc., and deposits, the government should have no authority over the transactions that take place on that property. Much as there is political immunity for certain foreign diplomats,

---

[806] The authors wish to thank Guillermo Yeatts for the financial support necessary to write this article. All mistakes and errors, of course, are the responsibility of the authors.

[807] That is, when and only when they are residing in their own country. Government in effect tells them that when they travel abroad, they are on their own, safety wise. The reason for this is that if government A protects its citizen, a, when he is visiting country B, then there is an overlapping sovereignty problem. *Two* governments now claim sole responsibility for one and the same person, a recipe for war.

[808] For the case in behalf of limited government libertarianism, or minarchism, see Boaz (1997), Gwartney and Stroup (1993), Machan (1978, 1982, 1990), Murray (1997), Nozick (1974), Read (1964, 1977).

[809] See (Benson (1989, 1990), Friedman (1989), Hoppe (1993, 2001, 2003), Rothbard (1973, 1982B), Spooner (1870), Stringham (1998-1999), Tannehills (1984), Tinsley (1998-1999), Woolridge (1970).

etc., which immunity runs to the person[810], *and* for certain property that is owned by foreign governments[811], there would financial immunity for non-theft and non-fraudulent financial transactions undertaken on bank-owned property used for banking purposes. Then the government could not freeze accounts or force conversion of deposits. That this is taking place on bank property would be, for financial matters, legally equivalent to occurring on foreign soil.

2. 100% reserve banking

It is at the core of free enterprise policy that fractional reserve banking must be eliminated[812]. Although fractional reserve banking in a dollarized economy would not be as bad as in a domestic currency economy, in either case it is a disaster waiting to happen. In the former case, no fractional reserve bank could withstand a run, something that is not unknown, to say the least, in banking history. Moreover, as the government would not be in a position to serve as lender of last resort, as purchaser of assets at above market prices, or provider of deposit insurance, such banks would fail, which would lead to runs on other such banks and the collapse of the entire system. On the other hand, no matter how good the intentions of the government, runs on fractional reserve banks in a domestic-currency economy would lead the government to "print" money (whether to buy assets at above market prices, to act as a lender of last resort, or to provide deposit insurance) in an attempt to save the financial system. Thus, fractional reserve banking must be eliminated. This may well be the single most important aspect of monetary reform! The elimination of fractional reserve banking, besides ending in one fell swoop all bank runs and hence stabilizing the financial system, would have a second salutary effect: the price of credit would more accurately reflect the true scarcity of loanable funds. This would enhance decision making, providing incentives for increase saving and more careful decisions re the allocation of scarce capital.

Under a regime of economic justice the central bank will be liquidated; we will then shift to 100% reserve commercial/transactions banking. The goal will be to sell any and all domestic assets the central bank has, and pay off its domestic liabilities; i.e., buy financial assets from the banks, starting with their deposits at the central bank.

---

810 Think traffic tickets by UN big shots that they don't have to pay because the City of New York has no personal jurisdiction over the offending person.

811 Think embassies, on the property of which murder can and may be committed without the murderer being subject to U.S. jurisdiction because the property is considered to be foreign soil.

812 For arguments in support of this position see Hoppe, et. al. (1998).

Simultaneously, the banks will be required to hold 100% reserves against *all* of their deposits, time and savings, as well as demand. This would put them out of the financial intermediary business, as they could no longer lend out funds received from any type of deposit made by their customers. New financial intermediaries would spring up to take in time and savings deposits and make loans, but they would not be able to offer demand deposits, else they too would be required to hold 100% reserves against *all* of their deposits. This would reduce the debt obligations of the government, both the direct ones and the indirect ones owed by the central bank to the commercial banks. The requirement for 100% reserves against time and savings deposits will be made *only* at institutions that offer demand deposits. Institutions that do not offer time and savings deposits would not be required by law to maintain any reserves at all. And, they could sell bonds, etc. This would separate the transactions function from the intermediary function; there would be separate institutions for each. Banks would be driven out of the time and savings deposits business because they could no longer offer interest on such deposits, as they could not lend out *any* deposits. No doubt people would cash in their time and savings deposits at commercial banks and open new accounts at the new financial intermediaries. These, given the absence of any reserve requirement, would then be in a position to make loans. Presumably, under this system, any one making excessive or imprudent loans would be disciplined by the market. Moreover, these institutions should be required to publish prominently the amount of their short-term (one-week) liabilities and their cash and short-term (one-week) financial assets in the newspapers.

3. International considerations

In order to attain a free enterprise economy, it is necessary that a country resign from the International Monetary Fund (IMF), World Bank, World Trade Organization (WTO), Inter-American Development Bank (IADB), etc.; i.e., from all such international economic agencies. It will repudiate any debt[813] owed to these agencies, justifying this step on the grounds that these loans should never have been made in the first place, that the country is worse off for having received them, that the conditions placed on the recipient country in order to obtain these loans, or renewals thereof, were detrimental to the economy, and that the true beneficiaries were foreign private sector lenders, who lent funds that should never have been lent, and those at exorbitant rates, expecting to be paid off from the proceeds of loans from the IMF, etc., to the recipient government, if the loans were defaulted upon. That is to say, such nations were the victim of moral hazard because of the IMF, etc., loans. The other beneficiaries were those wealthy domestic citizens who received the private sector loans that would not have been forthcoming save for the expectation of an IMF, etc., bailout if need be.

[813] For support of government debt repudiation, see Rothbard (1992A).

Moral hazard, in the present context, refers to the situation where foreign private sector lenders made loans, at artificially high rates of interest, because of the supposedly high risk, to both the borrowing government and the private sector that would not have been made had not they expected the IMF etc., to cover any loans that turned out badly. That is, interest rates were excessive given the expected lower risk because of expected IMF, etc. bailouts. Had the IMF, etc. not been expected to bail them out of such loans if and when they turned sour, they would not have been made in the first place, or only at higher rates of interest. The people of these countries did not benefit from such loans, the government did. A standard definition of moral hazard is: When an insured party acts less cautiously then he would have had not he been insured. Certainly, that is what some of the foreign private lenders did. Although one normally thinks of the hazard coming at the expense of the insured, in this case it is not the IMF, etc. that suffers, but the taxpayers of both donor and recipient counties.

This plan will have a salutary effect on the rest of the world, because the IMF could no longer [falsely] claim that that none of its loans have gone into default. In fact, many have, de facto, but this international financial institution maintains appearances by rolling such de facto defaulted loans over again and again so that they can make their claim and be correct de jure. A borrowing country's repudiation on principle would blow the whistle on this whole sordid mess and throw the IMF and its practices into the harsh light of the day of financial reality. It might even set an example for other nations, particularly those that have been impoverished by, or at least whose poverty has been exacerbated by the IMF, while their ruling classes have benefitted, often squirreling away the proceeds of such loans in Europe or anywhere else save for their own home countries.

We should not be overly concerned about debt owed to such foreign private sector lenders, because of this moral hazard issue. That money truly owed by the private sector to foreign private lenders will be based on ordinary commercial practices. If a country's bankruptcy laws are not fair to creditors or to debtors, they should be revamped so that the private sector renegotiations are fair. This will also help market participants to reestablish their credibility/credit-worthiness so that future foreign investment is not disrupted. As to government debt owed to foreign private sources, it also should be renegotiated on a fair basis. In any case, the renegotiations would de facto amount to partial defaults, thereby lessening recipient nation's debt service requirements relative to current levels

B. Foreign Trade

1. Unilateralism

Any country wishing to be worthy of the honorific appellation "free enterprise" will make an immediate and unilateral declaration[814] of free trade with all nations in the world[815]. Regional trading blocks are but customs unions; to be sure, they lower trading barriers *between* their relatively few member nations, but typically raise them against all outsiders. The so-called North American Free Trade Association (NAFTA) is but a regional trading bloc; organizations of this sort, too, must be avoided. Instead, under a laissez faire capitalist policy, each country will announce, unilaterally, with no "negotiation"[816] at all, that it stands ready to trade with all of the world's peoples with no barriers standing in the way whatsoever. That is, any items, including tangible goods, services, and real and financial assets may be sold or leased to non-citizens on the same basis as to citizens; no taxes, fees or regulations shall apply to such exports save as they apply domestically or as are required to prevent the import of goods that might contain germs or potentially harmful flora or fauna.

2. Eliminate tariffs

Tariffs are popular with the public since it is widely thought that they protect domestic jobs. Nothing can be further from the truth. Very much to the contrary, the only thing that "protectionism" protects is industrial investment in the home country. If foreigners can produce a good more cheaply than domestic economic actors, it behooves us to allow them to do so in our behalf, and to take advantage of the economies that are thereby afforded us. To refrain from so doing is to decline to avail ourselves of bargains, surely a foolish commercial endeavor. And where will the jobs come from to take the place of those "lost" due to imports? From new firms and even industries set up to supply our trading partners with those things they take from us in return for their exports to our country (foreigners will not for very long export products to us if we fail to reciprocate. Tariffs are an unnecessary burden on the economy.

---

[814] This is a rough description of the policy of the independent country Hong Kong, before being subsumed under the control of communist China. Hong Kong has been characterized as the economically freest country in the world. See on this Gwartney (1996).

[815] And with Mars and Venus too, should potential trading partners ever be discovered there.

[816] Which costs millions of dollars and wastes years.

3. Eliminate both retentions and subsidies for exports

The optimal amount of exports is precisely the amount that comes about as a result of the free decisions of market participants. (The same goes for the optimal amount of imports)[817]. Government should neither seek to reduce exports from their optimal market levels with a retention policy, nor try to increase, by means of subsidies, exports from those levels which would prevail under a system of economic freedom. Rather, a policy of laissez faire ought be put in place, so that the freely made decisions of buyers and sellers can be implemented.

4. Open immigration

Voluntary immigration is a "victimless crime,"[818] and a value added activity. Merely by moving to and taking up residence in a given geographical area, a newcomer necessarily commits no crime against natural law. He is not a trespasser, in that others will rent or sell him a home. In days gone by, a passport was a document introducing a traveler to foreigners. Nowadays, it has become in effect a travel permit, incarcerating those, guilty of no crime, who do not bear the necessary papers. It ill behooves all peoples, many of whom are the children or grand children of immigrants, to deny to today's new entrants what our forefathers were so graciously given. Moreover, by the very fact that they are willing to immigrate they manifest entrepreneurial attitudes that will be of benefit to domestic society. Immigrants tend to be hard working and thrifty; and, given that there will be no welfare system, they cannot be a burden on present members of society.

<u>C. The Domestic Economy</u>

1. Subsidies for businesses

All federal, state and local governmental subsidies for businesses should be eliminated. The function of firms should be the production of want-satisfying products and services, not the seeking of favors, privileges, or subsidies from government. If a firm is unable to provide goods that its customers value sufficiently highly so that they are willing to pay a price that covers the costs, then that business should be allowed to go bankrupt, and make way for other firms that can better satisfy the consumer. When government at any level subsidizes a corporation, it short-circuits this process; it props up firms that waste resources, from the perspective of the ultimate consumer. The phrase,

---

[817] In similar manner, the optimal amount of invention and innovation is not that which emanates from laws that improperly protect intellectual property, such as copyright and patent. Rather, the appropriate level is that which is consistent with no such laws at all. For more on this, see Kinsella (2001).

[818] There has been a ferocious debate within libertarian circles on this very issue. See on this http://www.mises.org/jlsDisplay.asp?action=sort&volume=13 &number=2&submit=View

"welfare bum," properly excoriates those individuals who take advantage of the generous and benevolent, though mistaken, motivations which lie behind the welfare system. But being a "corporate welfare bum, namely a firm made rich because it lives off the travails of the general taxpayer, is, if anything, even worse, in the view of some. For here are *wealthy* people taking advantage of those with less than they have; and, this tends to place capitalism in ill repute, conflating production for consumers with seizure from them[819].

2. Monopolies and other grants of privilege

All monopolies and other grants of privilege in any form whatsoever created by federal, state or local government should be eliminated and no new ones created or granted.

A monopoly is an exclusive grant of privilege to a business concern that protects it from the competition of all others. But competition is the life-blood of the economy. Monopolies are thus a form of economic arteriosclerosis, choking out the health of the market. Adam Smith (1776) wrote a magnificent blueprint for economic efficiency and justice, called "The Wealth of Nations." In it he showed that entrepreneurs in seeking profits are led by an "invisible hand" to do that which is in the best interests of society as a whole. This only works when competition is allowed. Under monopoly, it is not.

Anti-trust and anti-combines legislation, in contrast, must be repealed, root and branch. There is all the world of difference between a firm which gains a large share of the market through cutting costs, attracting customers, making superior offers to consumers, and one protected from the hurly burly of competition by government. The former are not monopolies at all, but rather successful businesses, of which the economy can never have enough. The latter represent the Sovietization of the economy, and must be eliminated, in their entirety.

Other grants of privilege also interfere with free competition and cause the misallocation of society's scarce resources. Many people of lesser means are prevented from putting their labor to its most highly valued use and, therefore, earn lower incomes than need be. For example, the restriction of licenses for cabs, jitneys, buses and other modes of transportation prevent many people from engaging in these activities, when such employment would be the best use of their labor and capital. Under the administration of any system deserving to be described as "laissez faire," anyone could open any kind of business without red tape.

---

[819] We deny that it is any worse for a rich man to steal from a poor one, as in the circumstance described in the text, than for a poor man to rob a rich one. Theft is theft is theft. There is no such thing as a particularly "perverse income transfer," which is sometimes used to describe a tax system in which the rich are benefited at the expense of the poor. The very opposite is *equally* objectionable.

3. Labor

There are two kinds of labor organizations; legitimate ones, and illegitimate ones[820]. The former confine themselves to soliciting voluntary membership; providing education and training so that their members will be more productive; presenting management with legitimate grievances, e.g., abusive foremen, in voluntary meetings; providing various types of insurance of members on a voluntary basis; and organizing peaceful mass walkouts and boycotts of the employers' goods unless their demands are met.

The latter may or may not provide these services, but they do engage in truly nefarious activities: they forcibly preclude the employer from hiring replacement workers. They do so either directly or indirectly. In the first case they employ physical invasion and brute force on their own account; e.g., they beat up those who would take the jobs they spurn, or set up "picket lines," and then commit assault and battery on anyone who would dare cross them, such as customers, suppliers, or "scabs."[821] In the second case they accomplish this goal through legislation that: compels firms to "deal fairly" and negotiate with the union, whether or not the firm considers it to be in its best interest; forces workers to pay dues whether or not they wish to do so; makes it very costly, if not impossible, to fire disruptive union workers; and, requires firms to hire and pay union officials who engage in union business and perform union work on company time and on company property. Just as it is the natural right of workers to choose their employers, and to sever the employment relationship if and when it is no longer satisfactory subject to any contractual agreements they may have entered into freely, so it is the natural right of employers to choose their employees, and to sever, again subject to any voluntarily agreed upon contractual obligations, the employment relationship if and when it proves to be unsatisfactory.

With regard to an illegitimate union, the officials thereof should be prosecuted under the relevant criminal statutes, and, if the criminal behavior continues under a different set of union bosses, that union should be banned outright by law as the essentially criminal organization it is. However, if that is not possible, the second best policy is to control such organizations with a welter of restrictions, prohibiting industry wide negotiation, mandating that several unions represent the workers of any one company, enforcing secret ballots in all elections, barring organized labor from using dues for political purposes, keeping union organizers off company property, prohibiting automatic check offs for union dues, and legalizing "yellow dog" contracts (which allow firms to hire employees subject to the condition that the latter do not join a union, and should be legal in any case).

---

[820] For a free enterprise oriented analysis of organized labor, see Block (1991A).

[821] No appellation deserves to be characterized as "hate speech," and banned on this ground; but if any did, "scab" would certain pass muster in this regard.

As far as legitimate unions are concerned[822], no such restrictions shall apply to them. (Of course, compelled union dues would be illegal regardless of the legitimacy of the union.) They are as righteous as any other private organization, club, charity, or, indeed, business firm. They are akin to the business manager hired by many actors and professional athletes to deal with movie producers or team owners. But once they resort to force or promote legislation that has this effect, then they lose the legal right to be treated as a legitimate organization.

The case for free labor certainly extends to the draft, whether of soldiers or jurors. In many jurisdictions service on a jury is compulsory. This is just as unconscionable as any other kind of forced servitude. A far better system is to actually pay each juror his market wage plus a small bonus to compensate for inconvenience, etc. for their contribution to the social order. As in the case of the army draft, there are always costs to labor. When either soldiers or jurors are forced to take up these occupations, these costs do not disappear; they merely become hidden. But a free society is willing to pay for what it needs; it does not stoop to seizing it.

4. Private retirement security

In the ideal world, people would be entirely free to save for their own retirements and old age. This is the only public policy consistent with true liberty. For if some people are too immature to consider the future when they will no longer be able to work, and do not save for this eventuality during their years of employment, how can they be considered mature enough to govern other aspects of their lives; e.g., deciding to have, and raising children, choosing their political leaders? On the other hand, if they are allowed to govern other aspects of their lives, then the presumption is that they do not need a paternalistic government to dictate to them their saving behavior. Thus the ultimate goal of the economic freedom philosophy is to leave provision of social security fully in private hands.

---

[822] Should any ever be discovered to exist.

However, as an interim step in this direction[823], we pledge the following: those who can prove they will not be a burden on society, either by posting a bond to that effect or investing sufficiently in a recognized pension plan, will not be compelled to take part in a governmentally mandated retirement plan. A mandatory retirement-income system based upon the Chilean program will be initiated. A defined investment system will require workers to put 10% of their incomes into a private sector investment fund. A wide choice of funds will be available; criteria for such funds will be set and any of them, foreign or domestic, that satisfies the criteria will be eligible to mange retirement investments. The Chilean system is far superior to any other extant government plan, and it is in keeping with devolving to the private sector those governmental functions that can be devolved.

5. Private unemployment insurance

One source of unemployment is a result of wages being bid by government above productivity levels. This can be done either directly, via minimum wage legislation, or indirectly, by giving unions special powers, and allowing them to boost wages up to artificially high levels. Another cause of unemployment is central bank mismanagement that creates the business cycle[824]. Any free market oriented policy must undertake not to create unemployment, in either of these two ways, or, indeed, in any other. As a result, there will be little if any need for unemployment insurance. Nonetheless, if there are those who feel a need to be protected in this way from the scourges of unemployment, they are free to seek private insurance policies to this end, in the free society.

6. Health care

Ideally, medical coverage should be economically indistinguishable from any other good or service: e.g., gourmet meals, concerts, etc. That is, individuals should be free to contract with one another for the purchase and sale of these services. There is nothing intrinsically different between medical coverage and the provision of any other highly skilled labor.

---

[823] It is sometimes claimed that plans such as school vouchers are a step in the direction of economic freedom. Whatever may be the case in this regard, allowing people to opt out of social security if they can demonstrate they are unlikely to be a burden on others in their retirement years is more like a tax reduction than a scheme which still involves the government in a field proscribed to it by strict principles of capitalism, such as education. That is, this opting out has an unambiguously positive implication for economic freedom. Take another example. Suppose we are in 1860 in the U.S. and for some reason we are only allowed to free some but not all slaves, say, 10% of them. Would such a step be an unambiguous one in the right direction? Yes, we argue, since some are freed and none are further enslaved, or necessarily have their yokes tightened.

[824] See on this Rothbard (1996B), Garrison (2001), Hayek (1933), Salerno (1989).

This applies to the provision of gourmet meals and concerts, to say nothing of the products provided to us by chemists, biologists, physicists, lawyers, economists, mathematicians, engineers, etc. There is simply no reason why the services of doctors and others in the health care industry, should, by law, be treated any differently from all these other professionals.

Except for one thing. Physicians have succeeded, to a degree these others can only dream of, in restricting entry into their profession. As a result of these guild-like restrictions, doctors typically earn some 5-times more than others, with similar interests in, and abilities to, pursue this vocation, who are denied the opportunity because legal restrictions on entry. For example, Ph.D.s in biology or chemistry typically are paid some 20% of doctors' salaries[825]. When we factor in the fact that medical salaries constitute a large proportion of all spending on health, this alone accounts for a large part of why health care is beyond the pocketbook of many people.

Advocates of dirigisme in medicine have used government, under the guise that health care is in some way different from food, shelter, etc., when it comes to the problem of efficiently allocating scarce resources and therefore normal market processes do not result in optimal allocations of resources to health, to regulate the health care industry ostensibly for the betterment of society, but actually for the betterment of the suppliers of health care.

Thus, the long run ideal solution to this problem is to sweep away these special privileges long enjoyed by physicians and other health care providers. When the price of medical services falls in response, at one fell swoop most of the financial problems of health care will have ended[826].

Some jurisdictions, e.g., Canada, the U.K., Sweden, have attempted to solve the problem of astronomically high health care through socialized medicine. But this "cure" is worse than the "disease." When patients are charged very low or zero fees, they tend to overuse these services. This excessive demand, sometimes called "moral hazard," puts great pressure on available supply. If price cannot ration the shortfall, then long queues come into being. As a result, it is not uncommon for those in need to be placed on waiting lists that stretch on for months and even years[827].

---

[825] See Friedman (1962), Hamowy (1984).

[826] A similar analysis applies to FDA type arrangements that keep medicines off the market as inefficacious. Improper from a free enterprise point of view is any attempt to restrict access to many important medicines, etc., save by those who pay for the privilege of having a doctor give them a prescription. See on this Henderson (2001), Peltzman (1973)

[827] http://www.fraserinstitute.ca; Henderson (2001).

Therefore the health care industry will be unregulated by a freedom-oriented administration. This will reduce the cost of health care and make it more affordable, and because the users will be required to pay the cost, either directly or through payments for private sector programs that provide coverage, they will economize on the use of health care-resources. This should reduce the demand also, further decreasing the cost of care.

What of the poor who cannot afford direct payment or the cost even to enroll in an inexpensive free market health care program? This is the reddest of red herrings. It is an attempt to undermine free market institutions. The same objection could be made against the privatization of *any* industry: shoes, sweaters, sofas. In point of fact, it is the poor who benefit *most* from economic freedom, as attested to the magnificent standards of living enjoyed by those at the *bottom* of the economic pyramid in relatively free countries, compared to those suffered by even the middle of the income distribution in societies which have become enmeshed in dirigisme economies.

Chapter 40. A positive program for laissez faire capitalism[828],[829]

I. Basic philosophy

Our goal is to bring about a more free, and ipso facto a more just, peaceful, and prosperous society. In order to achieve these ends we rely upon private property rights, the rule of law, and individual and cooperative effort.

If the demise of the economic systems of the USSR and Eastern Europe have taught us anything, it is that government is best which governs least. The implication is that it is best to leave to civil society – the market, the church, voluntary associations, businesses – all or virtually all tasks. It is imperative that the laws apply equally to all, and that the rule of law (Hayek, 1960)[830] be relied upon to promote the commonweal. Although coercion is occasionally necessary, force must be kept to an absolute minimum; its utilization has great power, but it always threatens to rend the social fabric.

A properly limited government is at most the *referee* of the economy, not an actual *player*. Can you imagine what chaos would ensue in a soccer match if the referee started to kick the ball into one of the nets, all the while blowing the whistle at athletes who were trying to defend against him? (This is a rough but reasonable depiction of the late and non-lamented Soviet economy)[831]. That, roughly, is what ensues when government takes on the entrepreneurial role.

There is a similar case to be made with regard to production. A properly constituted government[832] does not itself *create* any economic goods. It does produce domestic and foreign defense, and dispute resolution services. What it does not do is manufacture guns, planes, court buildings, etc. Instead, it purchases those things from the private sector firm that offers

---

[828] The authors wish to thank Guillermo Yeatts for the financial support necessary to write this article. All mistakes and errors, of course, are the responsibility of the authors.

[829] Henry Simons (1948) used the title “A Positive Program for Laissez Faire,” for one of the chapters of this book. However, in our view, that was a misnomer in that what he advocated would better be described as the “mixed economy” or “democratic socialism.” (See on this Block, 2002A). Our use of this title can be interpreted as our attempt to rescue the one he used from the charge of fraudulent labeling.

[830] But see Hasnas, 1995, and Rothbard, 1982B, pp. 219-228. See also Barnett, 1998, Barro, 2000, Raz, 1979, Pipes, 2000. For a critique of the latter, see Block, 2002B.

[831] See on this Boettke (1991), Conway (1987), Ebeling (1993), Foss (1995), Gordon (1990), Hoppe (1989C, 1991, 1996), Keizer (1987), Klein (1996), Maltsev (1993), Mises (1981), Rothbard (1997P).

[832] For the argument that the only properly constituted government is no government at all, see Benson (1989, 1990), Friedman (1989), Hoppe (1993, 2001, 2003), Rothbard (1973, 1982B), Spooner (1870), Stringham (1998-1999), Tannehills (1984), Tinsley (1998-1999), Woolridge (1970)

them for the lowest price. Rather, it sets up the rules and regulations, and then defends them against law-breakers, so that *businessmen* can produce the goods and services needed by the economy. A limited government operates as does a catalyst in a chemical experiment. It enables the other chemicals to interact with each other to achieve synergistic effects, yet itself comes out of the process unchanged.

Nor is there is any need for a governmental role in mediating between members of the private sector[833]. The fact that one is thought to be required is evidence of the chaos now operating. An analogous situation occurs with regard to rent controls. Before their advent, there was never any need for a separate landlord tenant court. But rent control has so exacerbated relations between owners and renters[834] that the sheer enormity of the caseload overwhelms ordinary courts. The solution, however, is not to create special and additional judicial bodies, but to eliminate the mischievous law which called them into being in the first place.

II. The Economic Program

A. Money

First, let us be clear that the reason that the monetary system is an issue is because of inflation in general[835], and the particular challenges in this regard now being faced in the world. Second, let us also understand that as long as there are governments in charge of this sector of the economy, no monetary system, regardless of its nature, is a guarantee against inflation, for the government can always use its coercive power to change/revise/override/replace the extant system. Third, let us also acknowledge that the fundamental problem is that politicians always want to spend more money; they are voracious; they are never satisfied. No amount of expenditures, no matter how great, can satisfy them for more than a short while. However, their ability to raise revenues is limited. They can acquire the wherewithal from taxation, but there is a limit to what the people in a more or less free society will pay in taxes; they can acquire the funds through borrowing, but there is an upper bound to what people will lend them; or they can inflate the money supply. The latter is vastly preferable to the bureaucrats in that the average man knows full well the source of taxation and government borrowing; in contrast, the source of inflation – the creation of fiat currency – is far better hidden from his scrutiny. Thus inflation is the by far preferred method of raising funds for these purposes.

---

833 Apart from upholding a proper criminal code (limited to quelling physical invasions) and defending contract and property rights.

834 Baird (1980), Block and Olsen (1981), Block (1993). Grant (1989), Johnson (1982), Salins (1980)

835 See on this Mises (1912), Rothbard (1990A).

The next issue is how to prevent the government from inflating a domestic currency. The best option, albeit the most unlikely to be realized, is to freeze absolutely the supply of domestic currency at its then current level. In this case, the nation's currency value would necessarily be determined in the market, free from any intervention by the government.

B. Infrastructure and social amenities

It is a shibboleth in some quarters that all economic, social, and cultural infrastructure must be provided by government. Ultimately, our goal is to place as much of such infrastructure into private hand as possible. In the short run, the following can be done:

1. Privatization of public conveyances

Privatize subways, trolleys, street-cars, ferries, and other such projects and allow the new owners to charge the customers that use it the full amount necessary to keep these conveyances in operation. That is, these transportation vehicles should be run by private enterprise, without benefit of government subsidies. The same will be done with bridges, highways, railroads airports, docks and wharves, etc., electric and other utilities. To the extent that these amenities are already "private, but regulated," it will be to the betterment of the economy that they be deregulated and competition encouraged.

2. Privatization of social amenities

Privatize museums, libraries, art galleries, symphonies, opera houses, etc. For all too long these amenities have served as the playgrounds for the upper middle classes and the rich. When the poor seek entertainment, they disproportionately patronize amusement parks, bowling alleys and pool halls, bars and saloons where they pay, out of their own pockets, the full amount necessary to fund them. This is exactly as it should be. But why should the rich be subsidized in their diversions?

One advantage of privatization is that competition will be allowed by play its usual salutary role. We have reasonably good pizza, popsicles and porcelain due to the market's automatic weeding out process[836]. Those entrepreneurs who do not do a good job supplying us with such amenities tend to suffer losses. If they do not change the error of their ways, bankruptcy is

---

[836] It cannot be denied that there is a pale carbon copy of a weeding out process that operates in the statist sector of the economy. The ballot box vote plays something of the same role as does the dollar vote in the economy. But the former takes place only every four years; the latter, dozens of times per day. In the ballot box, apart from referenda or plebiscites, one must vote for one candidate or the other. But suppose you like policies 1,3,5,9, etc., of candidate A, and 2,4,6,8, etc., of B. You have no way to make such distinctions. You are forced into a package deal. In contrast, in the market, you can highly focus your dollar vote: for a blue tie, or red suspenders with polka dots, for example.

the inevitable result. In contrast, those firms that do satisfy customers earn profits, with which to expand the base of their operations. With this automatic feedback mechanism, it is no wonder that the private sector is a bastion of efficiency and consumer sovereignty. In very sharp contrast, none of this operates in the government sector of the economy. When government roads, ferries or the post office do not provide a good quality service, they make suffer losses, but they *cannot* go bankrupt, and leave room for better alternatives. Ditto for museums and opera houses. They, too, are "above" the market.

It is for this reason that the post office urges that we not mail packages during the Christmas season. In contrast, FedEx makes no such demands. It is for this reason that it is far safer in Six Flags or Disneyland than in New York City's Central Park or New Orleans' Audubon Park; in private malls rather than on the public streets.

Another advantage of privatization is that with people buying and selling private property, market prices can emerge. Without prices based on supply and demand, the economy flies blind. In the U.S.S.R. and other communist countries, there were no capital markets. Thus, allocating goods in this sector was a hit or miss affair; there could be no rational economic planning. Communism was able to last as long as it did only because of the "Sears and Roebuck" phenomenon: they had access to western prices.

C. Welfare and poverty

The principle of "first, do no harm," commonly attributable to the medical profession, is a valuable one in the present context. It is particularly important as it relates to the lives of the poor, as they have the least margin for survival. Accordingly, this principle informs our policy with regard to the poor: first, do not further impoverish them; their plight is already serious enough, thanks, in large part, to past governmental mismanagement. To this end, we must undertake to eliminate a whole host of programs which have the effect of worsening the position of the poverty stricken: rent controls (which reduce available housing); minimum wages (which lead to unemployment for the unskilled)[837]; agricultural subsidies (which raise food prices for all, but have a pernicious and insidious impact on the poor, as they spend a disproportionate percentage of their limited income on these items); welfare programs themselves (which undermine the family, the last best hope for alleviating poverty)[838]; social security (a weakening of intergenerational family bonds)[839].

[837] For support of this claim see Becker (1995), Sowell (1995), Rothbard (1988), Hazlitt (1979).

[838] Although contentious in some intellectual arenas, e.g., sociology, there is strong evidence available in its support: Anderson, G. (1987), Anderson, M. (1978), Brown (1987), Rothbard (1996A), Tucker (1984).

[839] See Ferrara (1982)

Second, rely upon private charity[840]. This institution has several very important advantages over governmental programs. For one thing, the recipients are made to realize that individual people, on a voluntary basis, gave of their own funds so that the recipient could have a better life. Charity is incompatible with the "welfare rights" doctrine, so inimical to self-improvement. For another, recipients are typically asked, as a condition of receiving charity, that they write to the donor and thank him for his contrib-ution. This buttresses the fact, all the more, that sacrifices have been made in his behalf; it is the rare recipient who, under these conditions, is not inspired to try harder. Then there is the fact that charity is often intermediated by a religious organization, and comes coupled with prayer, expert advice, and/or spiritual training. This, too, tends to be beneficial, in that the recipient, perhaps for the first time in his life, comes into contact with a philosophy that has been of tremendous importance to many people. Finally, private charity is free to distinguish between the deserving poor; i.e., those who are impoverished through no fault of their own, and those who are themselves responsible for their own poverty. The appropriate assistance can then be rendered to those in the former category, while those in the latter can be denied help unless they undertake to change their lives in such ways as to work their way out of poverty.

Third, and most important, society can cure poverty, to the extent, given human nature, that it is humanly possible, by promoting the free enterprise system. It is surely no accident that in countries that rely heavily on markets and property rights, the "poor" own color television sets, telephones, cars, refrigerators and air conditioners[841].

<u>III. Crime and Security:</u>

1. Victimless "crimes"

It is not enough to have a well-motivated and well-paid police force. Their job must be strictly limited to preventing real crimes, with unwilling victims, such as murder, rape and theft, and punishing the perpetrators when these heinous acts do occur. The men in blue must not be called upon to arrest anyone for doing anything that does not constitute a physical invasion (or fraud) against a person or his property. There will be no laws against "crimes" that have willing "victims" for the police to enforce. This means that there will be no laws prohibiting voluntary acts between consenting adults such as prostitution, pornography, gambling, the sale, purchase, and use of addictive drugs, etc. Law enforcement manpower, as with other resources, are far too scarce to be squandered trying to protect "willing

---

[840] Olasky (1992), Hughes (1998).

[841] For the relationship between poverty and economic freedom in an international context, see Gwartney (1996).

victims" when they are needed to protect real sufferers from true criminals. Society must distinguish between the criminal and the immoral. It is not the job of the police to save men's souls; it is their job to protect men's lives, liberties, and property.

2. Freedom of association

We stand foursquare behind the rights of free association. This means that all interaction between people (e.g., adults) shall be on a completely voluntary basis. No one shall be forced to associate with anyone else, nor prevented from so doing.

The total denial of freedom of association is outright slavery. Fortunately, modern society is not faced with such a threat. But if slavery is the complete abnegation of free association, then partial denials of this right amount to no less than partial slavery. And here there are dozens of cases, all of which we must pledge to fight.

Whenever workers are prohibited from organizing together, to urge better wages or working conditions, this is a denial of their basic right of freedom of association[842]. (Of course, when unions attempt to violate the freedom of association of employers and "scabs: to associate with each other, or to force workers to join, then they violate this liberty (see section III E 3).

But what is sauce for the goose is also sauce for the gander: if employees may freely associate with each other for commercial purposes, then so may employers. The may do so in the labor market (to face unions with a united front), in the factor market (to bargain collectively with suppliers) or in the consumer or final goods market (to fix prices). This means that cartels are every bit as much an instance of freedom of association as are labor organizations. This means, also, that anti-trust or anti-combines legislation must be totally eliminated[843]. For what are trusts and "monopolies," other than the amalgamation, on a voluntary basis, of a number of entrepreneurs? (These kinds of contracts should be called "single sellers" or voluntary cartels; the word "monopoly" should be reserved for exclusive grants of privilege by government to operate a business denied to other potential competitors, for example the post office, or in some other way to restrict competition.

---

[842] For the case in behalf of labor organizations along libertarian lines, see Block (1991A).

[843] See on this For an Austrian critique of neoclassical monopoly theory, see Anderson, et. al. (2001), Armentano (1972, 1982, 1991), Armstrong (1982), Block (1977A, 1982, 1994), Boudreaux and DiLorenzo (1992), DiLorenzo (1997), DiLorenzo and High (1988), High (1984-1985), McChesney (1991), Rothbard (1970), Shugart (1987), Smith (1983).

Another implication of the freedom to associate is the right to engage in discrimination on the basis of race, sex, sexual preference, ethnicity, intelligence, sense of humor, musical or athletic ability, hair or eye color or, indeed, anything else under the sun.

Civilized societies pretty much already enjoy all these rights, in the present day, at least as far as personal relations are concerned. That is, the government has not (yet) prohibited discrimination on any of these grounds in friendship patterns, dating, marriage, etc. But these rights must be extended so as to include commercial interactions.

That is, it should be legal for retail shops to pick and choose their range of customers. No longer will they be forced to open their doors to the entire public. This right is presently enjoyed by customers, who are free to avoid stores on the basis of race or ethnicity, etc., and patronize others, also on this basis; we must even up the playing field in this regard, and thus treat *all* people equally, whether they are buyers or sellers.

No longer will firms be forced to hire any specific type of employee; there will be no quotas for hiring females, or members of any particular racial or ethnic group. This right is presently enjoyed only by employees, who are now free to discriminate against employers for any reason they choose. We must also even up the playing field in this regard, and thus treat *all* people equally, whether they are seeking a job or offering one.

Similarly, landlords will not have to rent to people against their will, nor sell their homes or businesses on an "affirmative action" basis. Tenants and homebuyers already have the right to boycott landlords and homeowners, motivated by racial, ethnic or sexual preference considerations. Our policy would do no more than even the balance, giving the same rights to *all* participants in commercial interactions.

It should not be thought that these rules will unduly create poverty for the downtrodden minority groups who are discriminated against by the majority, nor that past discrimination is responsible for the present plight of these groups. If this were so, then Jews and Orientals would be amongst the poorest members of society; instead, they are among the richest[844].

Why is it that discrimination is all but impotent to impoverish the poor? This is because whenever a group is "victimized" by a commercial boycott, either their wages fall, or the prices they must pay for goods rises. But this sets up profit opportunities for entrepreneurs to "exploit" the downtrodden, by either hiring them at these new lower wages, or selling to them at these now higher prices. This, in turn, tends to undermine the initial deleterious wage and price changes. As more and more opportunistic profit seekers hire more minority group members, to "take advantage" of their

---

[844] Sowell (1975, 1981, 1983, 1994)

plight, wages rise again, up toward pre discrimination levels. And as more and more "greedy" merchants sell to the discriminated against groups, the prices they must pay tends to fall[845], again obviating the economic effects of the original discrimination.

No. The reason people are poor is because: their God-given mental and/or physical capabilities are low; they are indolent; they are imprudent, and do not invest in their own human capital; and/or, the government short circuits the market which, as we have seen, is their benefactor, their only real hope for help in improving their condition, save for private charity, itself working where possible to assist them to function in the market. It has little or nothing to do with whether they are minority group members.

IV. Environmental issues

1. Introduction

Our environmental policy will be based on "free market environmentalism."[846] This is the doctrine which states that ecological problems are the result *not* of private property rights being upheld and respected, but of the *absence* of such a legal regime; that the solution for these challenges is *not* increased governmental ownership of environmental amenities, nor, yet, greater control over such private holdings by governments, but rather enhancement of private property rights, preeminently including punishment for trespass.

2. Air pollution

Air pollution is nothing more than a name for property rights violations; to wit, trespassing smoke particles. The law is clear if Jones dumps his garbage onto the property of Smith, Jones is clearly guilty of trespass. But, if Jones first incinerates his garbage, and then sends it wafting, through the air, onto Smith's property, lungs, laundry, the law has all too often ignored this violation of property rights[847]. (But suppose Jones had been operating a factory, feedlot or airport long before Smith arrived on the scene with his property purchase, and had been polluting the air with dust particles, smells and noise, respectively. Would Smith have a case in law

---

[845] Of course, if there are higher crime rates in poorer areas, and, typically, there are (see Levin, 1997), these additional costs will tend to be reflected in prices higher than they otherwise would be.

[846] This is *not* an oxymoron. For evidence on this claim, see Anderson and Hill, 1981; Anderson and Leal, 1991; Block, 1990A, 1991B, 1998B; Block and Whitehead, 1999; Block and Yeatts, 1999-2000; DiLorenzo, 1990B; Hill and Meiners, 1998; Hoppe, 1993; Horwitz, 1977; McGee, 1992, 1993; McGee and Block, 1994; Moore, 1991; Rothbard, 1982A; Stroup and Goodman, et. al. 1991; Stroup and Baden, 1982; Whitehead and Block, 2000.

[847] Anderson, 1989.

against Jones? Not at all. This is called "coming to the nuisance," and should be thrown out of court on the ground that Jones had first homesteaded the property rights to "pollute" the air around him. In contrast, if Smith purchased a home in a dangerous neighborhood where Jones' gang engaged in mass robbery, then Smith would have a case at law against Jones, since the latter has no right to steal the property of others, but he does have a right to homestead unowned property by "polluting" it.)

The solution to the problem of pollution consists not of government edicts concerning CAFÉ mileage standards for automobiles, nor subsidies for alternative energy sources (e.g., windmills, etc.) but rather of environmental forensics: chemically analyzing dust particles, determining their source, and them imposing heavy penalties on the perpetrators.

3. Forests

No private owner of a forest who hopes to earn a profit and survive in business, will engage in clear cutting without replanting. When, and to the extent that these ravages of the environment have occurred, those responsible have been either public authorities, or private concerns operating on governmentally owned land (where the commercial incentives toward stewardship operate in the very opposite manner.) Our policy for managing the forests thus consists of privatizing them, and allowing the "magic of the market" to protect these treasured resources.

4. Sanitation

All solid waste management facilities will be privatized. Socialized garbage dumps do not generate market prices, and without them it is impossible to rationalize this sector of the economy. Consider the issue of whether plastic or paper bags are more environmentally friendly, and suppose that the latter is the case, as has been argued by the "greens."[848] If so, then the combination of the price of paper bags, based upon free market trees, and the disposal cost, based upon private disposal will be less than combined price of plastic bags, based upon petroleum prices, and presumably higher, burial cost for plastic than for paper bags, that would be charged a private disposal company. This, in turn, will lead people, as if by Adam Smith's (1776) "invisible hand" to prefer more paper, and less plastic. Nor will the economic effects stop here. Packagers, too, will find they can enhance profits by saving their customers disposal fees. It is in this way that the entire problem will tend to disappear, but only when and if markets are allowed to fully operate.

5. Species extinction

The reason cows, chickens, dogs, cats and pigs have not come within a million miles of risking extinction is because they are all privately owned.

---

[848] They should be called the "watermelons": green on the outside, red on the inside.

Their owners have an economic incentive to protect them, even to see to it that their numbers are increased, for that is the way they can best maximize profits. In sharp contrast, the elephant, the rhino, the deer, the buffalo have all in recent years been endangered, save for those the rights to which have been privatized. This is *not* due to the fact that profits cannot be made by exploiting these animal resources. Very much to the contrary, the latter animals are also very valuable to humans; in fact, in those cases where the rights have been privatized, these animals have generated incomes for their owners. The real explanation is that laws have, almost always, prevented private property ownership of them. Thus, our policy will be to rescind all legislation prohibiting the ownership of *any* non-human species. This is our last best hope for protecting them from extinction.

6. Mineral and other non-renewable resources

The critical economic issue with respect to non-renewable resources is the optimum rate of extraction/depletion/use. Because their tenures in office are uncertain, politicians in republics/representative democracies have the incentive to exploit such resources at an uneconomically rapid rate in order to acquire and use the revenues therefrom while they are in office rather than leaving such revenues for their successors. That is, the present discounted value of such resources, given the social rate of time preference, is not maximized. This has had serious consequences. For example, overrapid recovery from an oil reservoir can result in reducing the pressure therein to such an extent that oil that could have been recovered economically had not depletion been so fast becomes uneconomical to recover and therefore remains in the ground, unexploited and unable to serve man. A private owner of mineral resources, on the other hand has precisely the incentive to maximize the present value thereof. Moreover, if, as with the politicians, the owner's personal rate of time preference is less than the social rate as manifested by market rates of interest, he will have every incentive to sell the resources to someone who values them more highly and will exploit them more rapidly. Therefore, our policy consists of privatizing natural resources and, as with forests, allowing the "magic of the market" to protect these treasured resources.

Chapter 41. Rejoinder to Critics of Laissez-Faire Capitalism

In Block and Barnett (2005) we make the case that the best way to promote peace and prosperity, to protect the environment and fight poverty is to rein in government to the greatest extent possible. Each of our critics (Batten and Szilagyi (2005), Higgins (2005), and Jonker (2005), challenges this thesis, and we consider them in the order they appear in the Journal.

Batten and Szilagyi exhibit confusion about Mises' views on limited government vis-à-vis anarcho capitalism. They (2005, 43) claim he takes a position "opposing taxes" and sees "none at all" as the proper role for government. Not so; Mises saw a very limited, but important role for the state. These authors maintain that we favor a "stateless social order." But this is difficult to reconcile with our statement (2005, 32) that "coercion is occasionally necessary."[849]

We object to their claim that "a powerful corporation may impose..." In the completely free society, firms can only have moral and economic power (ability to buy and sell, build, etc.) but not the political power necessary to "impose." Even now, Microsoft, Wal-Mart, etc., have no ability to control others against their will at all; they have only great wealth, for as long, that is, as they continue to satisfy customers. Otherwise, they would go the way of the Nash Automobile Company, United Shoe Manufacturers and Texaco, Pan American World Airways and Braniff International Airways. (http://www.bankruptcydata.com/Research/15_Largest.htm). The only politically "powerful corporations" at loose at present are those that are given special favors from the state; under laissez faire, there would be no such thing.

Batten and Szilagyi (2005, 44) claim that "markets are rarely, if ever, efficient." Compared to what, we should like to know? To government? No one who has lived through Katrina and her aftermath could make any such statement. Similarly, the "recent corporate scandals involving Worldcom and Enron" are eloquent testimony to the *health* of markets. Where are these companies now? Nowhere! The same, unfortunately, cannot be said for governments that waste and steal thousands of times more money than those pikers. Moreover, when we hear the phrase "stakeholders" we reach to check our wallets. Customers, neighbors, suppliers, employees, etc., simply have no rights to dispose of property they do not own. Suppose we claimed to be "stakeholders" in the houses or automobiles now owned by Batten and Szilagyi. Such talk is an affront to a civilized order.

---

[849] The first mentioned author of the present article greatly regrets this language, as he, indeed, favors a completely stateless society. But Batten and Szilagyi (2005, 43) still err in attributing this position to Block and Barnett (2005).

Our critics (2005, 44) make much of the fact that "transactions costs, differences in tax treatment…, product illiquidity and an inability to arbitrage between similar products all provide explanations for the fact that markets are rarely, if ever, efficient." Again, we ask for the first, third and fourth of these, compared to what? The state? It cannot be denied that these so called market "failures" provide profit opportunities for those entrepreneurs who successfully address them. What more can be done? As for the second, this, surely, is a logical howler, since it is the government, not the market, that engages in taxation. Transactions are real costs in the sense that they involve the use of resources. To ignore them is to ignore reality and shift decisions where they are high to governmental decision makers, who can ignore them. These authors could as easily have mentioned the "hold-out problem." We see what happens when the government gets involved to solve that type of "problem." Perhaps they have not heard of the Kelo case (Block, 2006) and the Lost Liberty Hotel project?

It is more than passing curious that these authors highlight Beach and O'Driscoll (2005, 45). They do so in criticism of the fact that in this paper of ours we focus only on "the single factor (property) rights" (Batten and Szilagyi, 2005, 45), instead of engaging in a multi factor analysis. But, not every paper can deal with every issue. Batten and Szilagyi, further, do not seem to realize that one of the present authors has written a similar book on freedom indices (Gwartney, et. al, 1996) even though this was cited in Block and Barnett (2005, 40). Batten and Szilagyi, (2005, 47) criticize us on the ground that "those countries with interventionistic government … all have the highest individual incomes." First, this is contradicted by Gwartney, et. al, 1996. Second, even was this the case, which it is not, this would be *despite* government interventionism, not because of it.

Higgens (2005, 51) starts off by citing the *Economist*'s (1994) claim that "income inequality has increased the most … where free-market policies have been developed and implemented the most vigorously." Time series data, unless they are of long duration, are relatively unimportant; the relationship between economic freedom and income inequality will, of course, fluctuate. Of greater moment is cross sectional analysis, and here, it is clear, that there is a negative relationship between the two variables (Gwartney, et al. 2000, 17). That is, markets promote income *equality*. In addition to the empirical evidence buttressing this claim, it is important to understand *why* this should be so: because it is apodictically necessary that *all trades* be mutually beneficial, at least in the *ex ante* sense, since they are voluntary. Since free enterprise consists of no more and no less than all such commercial interactions (buying, selling, hiring, etc.), it should not be the occasion of surprise that markets would tend to reduce income inequality. Yes, Bill Gates made a bundle, but in doing so he *enriched* all of his many customers. The market is a positive sum game. In contrast, when a politician or bureaucrat prospers, he does so at the *expense* of the long suffering taxpayer, as this is a coercive, zero sum game. The greatest disparities between the privileged and the masses arise in dictatorships in which there are no secure property rights. In those societies the only equality is among the impoverished masses.

Higgens also talks about "trust." And properly so. But where is this crucial element of civilization more likely to prosper? In a society based on mutual agreed upon interaction, or in one based on coercive relationships? To ask this question is to answer it. A similar analysis applies to association. If it is free, if people are not forced to associate with others against their will, social cooperation and trust will be supported. If it is forced, as, for example, through "affirmative action," it will be undermined (Sowell, 1982).

Jonker (2005, 54) asks: Why does our piece "evoke such ferocious emotions?" One answer is, "speak for yourself." Speaking for ourselves, while we sharply disagree with people such as Galbraith, Keynes, Rawls, Marx and their ilk, some of us manage to restrain our "ferocious emotions." Another answer is, sociobiology or evolutionary psychology. For eons our species lived in very small groups. There, explicit or direct cooperation was the only kind that could occur. We are thus "hard wired" to accept charity, "kindness and goodness." But we now live in a society with billions of people. Here, the only possibility for human cooperation is implicit or indirect; that is, through markets. The invisible hand of Adam Smith eschews "kindness and goodness" and substitutes for these qualities selfishness and greed, at least in the market, narrowly construed. Of course, businessmen, in their role as private citizens, can and do give generously to charity. When they do so as a corporation, for other than defensive purposes (to ward off regulations aimed at them) they are doing so with other people's money. That is called theft. We assume that they do not own 100% of the corporation nor that there are but a few shareholders and all agree. Nor does it apply to partnerships where the partners agree. But some of us, those who are not sophisticated in economics, are appalled at the prospect that commerce should be largely motivated by self interest.

Jonker (2005, 54) takes it as a given that modern "complexity" requires some sort of central planning, or at least a spurning of the simple free enterprise system. He errs in thinking that "going back" to a prior system of laws and institutions is "outmoded if not dangerous." It all depends upon the specifics of the case. Society has not continuously progressed; there have been fits and starts. Do we not want to "go back" to the time of Mozart, Beethoven and Bach? Must we necessarily prefer atonal and rap "music" just because these things came later in time? Is Jackson Pollock really to be preferred to Rembrandt? Attack Adam Smith's ideal of limited government if you will, but it is highly problematic to do so merely because this system occurred centuries ago.

Chapter 42. Time deposits, dimensions and fraud

Abstract

We stipulate, arguendo, that fractional reserve demand deposit banking is per se fraudulent. We ask whether or not time deposit banking can also be illicit, and answer in the positive, if there is a mismatch between the time dimensions of deposits and loans. To wit, if an intermediary borrows short and lends long.

I. Introduction

The purpose of this paper is to explore the ethical and economic status of mismatched time deposit lending and borrowing.[850] It arises, of course, with respect to fractional-reserve-demand deposits. One problem that has interested us for some time is the continuum problem with respect to such deposits. Suppose we accept, arguendo, that fractional-reserve-demand deposits should be illegal, but that fractional-reserve-time deposits should be legal. Then, it would be against the law for a bank or other financial institution to accept a demand deposit and turn around and lend it out; but it would not be for it to accept a time deposit for, say, six months and turn around and lend those funds out. The continuum problem arises when we ask whether it is OK to take in a time deposit for say, one month, and lend it out? Of course, But, how about one week? one day? one hour? one minute? one second? That is, just how instantaneous does "instantly" have to be for the purpose of determining whether a transfer of funds to a bank constitutes a demand or a time deposit?

The real issue for economics does not lie with the length of the time period between the deposit and when it must be repaid; i.e., the time length of the time between that at which X received the deposit and that at which X is obligated to return the funds. Consider the case where A deposits funds with X, where X is obligated to return the funds, not instantly (whatever that may mean) on demand beginning at the moment of deposit, but, say, instantly on demand at any time commencing, say, one minute after the moment of deposit. Is such an account a demand or a time deposit?

That question is irrelevant for economics. In contrast, the relevant question for economics is: What may X do with the funds that have been deposited with it? The answer is really quite simple: X may lend A's deposits out for any period of time such that the term of the loan ends no later then the earliest moment at which X is legally obligated to return the funds to A. Thus, with a true demand deposit X may not lend the funds at all. However, with six-month deposit made on 1/1/2008; i.e., a deposit that

[850] Of course, this also raises the issue of whether fractional-reserve banking should be illegal.

X is not legally obligated to redeem before 6/30/2008, X may lend the funds out for a period ending no later then 6/30/2008.

Specifically, is it proper (for a bank or any other such institution) to borrow short and lend long? That is, suppose A lends B $100 for a year, B turns around and lends that $100 to C, but not for a single year; rather, for two years. Before we can confront that issue, let us consider a bit of background.

We take it as a given for the purposes of this paper that fractional reserve demand deposits are illegitimate, could not survive in the free economy and are economically destructive.[851] Let us briefly review each of these claims.

First, fractional reserve demand deposits are illicit because they involve the creation of more property titles than there is property in existence. For example, right now, in a small town, there are 1,000 cars, we may suppose. There are also *precisely* 1,000 titles to these automobiles. All is well. But if someone were to print up an additional 100 property titles for these items, for which there are no additional vehicles, and tried to circulate them, that is, by seizing control of someone else's property with them, this would clearly be recognized as the fraud that it is. It would not matter at all whether this was done "contractually" or not; for there is something more basic than mere voluntary agreement: the laws of logic and reality. If there were 1,100 titles for only 1,000 cars, 100 of those autos would have not one but two owners. Nor would these 100 cases consist of partial ownership, where two people are partners, and own 50% each of a vehicle. No, they would constitute cases where two individuals *each* own 100% of the automobile, an utter impossibility. This is like a surface that is all red and all blue in the same respect at the same time. It is for this reason that a "contract" whereby the party of the first part agrees to confer on the party of the second part, for an agreed upon fee, a "square circle" would be considered an invalid agreement. There is no such thing as a square circle, and the laws of logic prevent "one" from ever coming into existence.

Similarly, we may suppose that in the same small town there are now 1,000 ounces of gold money, and, also, the identical number of titles to these gold ounces, namely, 1,000. The same analysis applies. If someone prints up an additional 100 titles to gold ounces of money, there is fraud afoot, there is something logically amiss, no matter who or how many people agree to this act. For, with these additional titles to 100 ounces of gold that do not exist, there is now an "over ownership" of property. Two people, not one person,

---

[851] For material in support of this contention, see Block and Garschina, 1996; Hoppe, et. al. 1998; Hoppe, 1994B; Hulsmann, 1996, 1998, 2000B, 2000C; Rothbard, 1962; de Soto, 1995, 1998A, 2001. For the opposing viewpoint: Sechrest, 1987, 1989A, 1989B, 1991A, 1991B, 1993, 2007; Selgin, 1994, 1998, 2007a, 2007b, 2007c; Selgin and White, 1996; White, 1992, 1995, 1999.

own each and every ounce of this excess money, an utter impossibility. This we take it is a praxeological claim, not open to empirical refutation.

Because it is fractional reserve banking that is being considered, we ask how the additional titles come into existence. The answer, of course, is that individuals pay money into a demand deposit. Some portion of these deposits is kept "in reserve" and the remainder is lent, in the process creating additional demand deposits; i.e., the new (excess) ownership titles are lent into existence. The cause of the problem is that the bank had no right to make such loans, because it did not have the relevant elements of ownership of the deposited funds. That is, it had title to the funds only for period for which it had borrowed them, so it only had the right to lend these monies for a period ending no later then the time at which it had to repay the loan by which it acquired the funds it lent.

Second, fractional reserve banking for demand deposits could not long endure in the free enterprise system where property rights and the niceties of bankruptcy law are respected, save for the possibility (probability?) that they might be able to exist with very high reserve ratios, say 98% or more, but this is an empirical question. For fractional reserve banks (FRBs) would be immediately subject to negative clearing house accounts by 100% reserve banks demanding immediate payment for their paper and/or demand deposits. And, since failure to immediately make good on any and all demand deposits outstanding against a ban constitutes bankruptcy, and, since bankruptcy in turn is grounds for immediate dissolution of a company guilty of so egregious behavior, the prognostication for such companies is not a positive one.

Again, it must be noted that this is an empirical, not a praxeological claim. That is, there is always the possibility that, for reasons that need not concern us in detail,[852] the 100% banks would not call for the immediate payment of all demand deposits and notes issued by the FRBs. If so, immediate bankruptcy would not be the necessary result.[853] Moreover, the differential clearing rate need not necessarily favor the 100% bank, as it

---

[852] The issue turns on whether or not the transactions costs of "attacking" the 99% fractional reserve bank through adverse clearing house balances, are more or less than the benefits of eliminating a competitor.

[853] The second mentioned author of the present article maintains that in equilibrium, e.g., in the evenly rotating economy, FRB could not exist, assuming profit seeking behavior on the part of the 100% reserve banks. The first mentioned author demurs because he finds the concept of equilibrium in economics, in any of its guises including the ERE, unscientific.

would depend on the relative sizes of the different banks extant, and the actual patterns of money transfers among their depositors.[854]

Third, FRB is economically destructive in that it is the causal antecedent of the Austrian Business Cycle (ABC).[855] FRB leads to an increase in the money stock, compared to what it would have been in the absence of this institution; given that this new money enters is lent into existence, it drives risk-adjusted, interest rates down below the level that would otherwise have obtained. This, in turn, encourages and rewards businesses and households that borrow and spend the new funds before the price inflation that is the inevitable consequence of the increase in the stock of money occurs. In general, this involves investing in the most interest-rate-sensitive sectors of the economy and purchasing interest-rate -sensitive consumers' goods, which are incompatible with the unchanged time preferences of the economic actors. When these misallocations can no longer be sustained, there is a crisis that initiates a cleansing depression, undoing the mal effects of FRB induced monetary/credit expansion.

With this as a background, we are now ready to explore the thesis of the present paper: that not only is fractional reserve banking for demand deposits fraudulent, but so also can time deposit banking be fraudulent, when there is a mismatch in the time dimension between the bank's borrowing and lending, such that it borrows short and lends long.

In section II we explore the legitimacy of time-dimension-mismatched lending and borrowing. We conclude in section III.

II. Mismatched time deposits

Suppose B borrows $100 from A for a year, and then lends that $100 to C, but not for a single year; rather, for *two* years. Is this a legitimate market transaction? At first blush, it is not: the time dimensions[856] do not match. B the banker is lending the $100 to C for a period of time, two years, that he, B, has no proper control over. A lent B these funds to be sure, but only for *one* year, not two. It is as if A lends B a book for a year, and B lends that book to C for *two* years. B simply has no right to lend to C what he does

---

[854] For example, suppose that Bank A, (a 100% reserve bank) had demand deposits of 100 ounces of gold and Bank B, (a 98% reserve bank) had 50. If Bank B's depositors only did business with other customers of Bank B, but some of Bank A's customers bought things from customers of Bank B, it would be Bank A, the 100% reserve bank, that would lose its gold to Bank B, the 98% reserve bank.

[855] On Austrian Business Cycle Theory (ABCT) see: Barnett and Block, 2005, 2006; Block, 2001A; Block and Garschina, 1996; Carilli and Dempster, 2001; Garrison, 1994, 2001, 2004; Garrison and Bellante, 1988; Hayek, 1931; Mises, 1998; Rothbard, 1975, 1993

[856] For the importance of dimensions in economic analysis see Barnett, 2004.

not have in his proper possession. A entrusted B with the book for one year, and B goes off and confers on C something he was not initially given by A.[857] And what is true for books is also the case for money.[858]

But the defense is not without an answer of its own. Suppose the following. At the outset of our little tableau, A lends $100 to B for a year. B lends this "same" $100 to C, for two years, as before. Now the first year is up, and A wants his $100 back from B.[859] B, of course, cannot demand this money back from C, for it is not due for an entire additional twelve months, until the end of year two, and at present it is only the end of year one. Whereupon B goes out into the market and borrows $100 from D, for a year. He gives this $100 to A, absolving himself of any problem with the latter.

Now the end of year two arrives. C's $100 is now due to B. B takes these funds and turns them over to D, acquitting himself of any difficulty with D. Case closed: B owes no one anything. Assuming appropriate interest rate arrangements, B has earned profits sufficient to maintain himself in business. Where is the rights violation, the defender of borrowing short and lending long asks?

In this case, there is still that little matter of over determination of property titles, precisely the shortcoming of FRB. Consider the situation during the first year of our little scenario. There are not one but *two* people with a valid claim for that $100 at the end of the first year. First of all there is A; he lent the $100 to B for only one year, and has a legitimate claim on this money at the end of the year. And then there is C who was told by B that these monies are not due back until the end of year two. There is thus a logical incompatibility in this scenario, similar to the one that emanates from FRB.[860]

---

[857] We abstract from the possible difficulty that A does not want B to lend anything to C, for any amount of time. We assume that B may lend to C what was entrusted to him by A; the *only* issue revolves around the time dimension.

[858] Dissimilar to cases of loans of books, lawnmowers, etc., which are not, in general, fungible goods, and which require, therefore, the return of the exact item lent, money is a fungible good, and therefore unless it is specified in the loan contract that the identical pieces of money must be returned -- a term not to be found in real world contracts -- a loan of money may be repaid with any equal amount of money.

[859] Plus interest, of course, but we ignore this complication.

[860] What of the possible objection to our thesis that the futures market would also have to be banned if we are correct? There, too, the man who sells in a futures market promises to do something that he does not have it in his power to do, at least at the present time. This objection fails, for there is a relevant difference between the two cases: the person who borrows short and lends long does something he has no right to do, whereas in the futures market both buyers and sellers are only promising to do something in the future, but what they promise is something they have every right to do, and therefore they have every right to promise to do so

III. Conclusion

Fractional reserve demand deposits are not the only fraudulent banking practice. Also to be added to this list are time deposits, where the bank borrows short but lends long. This practice, borrowing short and lending long, is engaged in by others than commercial banks; e.g., investment banks. Of course, investment banks do not issue deposits, time or demand, when they borrow short. In fact, the reason for the Bear Stearns collapse and bailout was the inability of this firm to roll over or refinance its short-term debt when the credit markets seized-up.[861]

Because it could not roll over its short-term debt, Bear Stearns would have had to pay it off as it came due. In turn this would have required BS to liquidate assets immediately in order to acquire the necessary funds. Many of these assets were derivatives of various kinds with thin markets, at best, or no markets at all. Moreover, the quality of many of those assets had turned out to be significantly lower then supposed because the underlying securities included subprime-mortgage notes. Therefore, they would have had to have been liquidated in a fire sale. That BS had a liquidity problem was obvious to all involved. But mere liquidity problems can be overcome in various ways. The more serious difficulty was that the fire sales were expected to reveal that BS was actually bankrupt. That is, the revenues from the fire sales were expected to be so low that BS's liabilities exceeded its assets and it had negative equity, aka insolvency.[862]

But it is most unlikely that the bankruptcy of BS would have been a sufficient cause to for the Fed and the treasury to get involved, even though this process undoubtedly would have been long, acrimonious, and expensive, as the various claimants fought over whatever value was thought to remain.[863] Rather, as they themselves stated, the reason for the intervention was fear of systemic risk in the financial system; i.e., they feared a breakdown of the financial system that would have spread to the "real" economy. The cause of their concern was that the sale of BS's assets at very low prices would have

---

[861] For more on this episode, see Reisman, 2008; Shostak, 2008

[862] Thus the hue and cry among some that the haircut BS's shareholders took under the governmentally-arranged bailout was not short enough – their heads should have been completely shaved.

[863] Economic losses are generated when resources are misallocated. However, if it were apparent that a use of resources was a misallocation, such use would never be undertaken. So, mistakes are made, but they only come to light later when they manifest themselves as financial losses. Bankruptcy proceedings are one method of distributing, ex post facto, the losses among the various relevant parties.

negatively affected other financial institutions because of mark-to-market rules.[864]

These distress prices would have set benchmarks that other firms would have had to use in pricing their assets, requiring them to write down the value of their own assets. In turn, this would have eroded their capital, thereby threatening or destroying their capital adequacy. Moreover, because the credit markets were seizing up, these other firms, too, would have been unable to roll over their short-term debt. With the short-term debt markets frozen and without the ability to borrow long term[865] the only alternatives would have been to raise capital by selling equity or to reduce the need for capital by selling assets. It is true that some major firms did sell equity stakes to sovereign wealth funds, but the cost to the stockholders of the dilution of their share of the remaining assets was very high, and in the cases of preferred stock, the interest rates and other terms were very high. This meant that the FRS and the UST expected massive, fire sales of assets that would have resulted in a financial meltdown that would have then have led to such a widespread collapse of credit markets that non-financial businesses would have been unable to fund operations, much less property, plant, and equipment. That is, the FRS and UST feared that if BS were not bailed out it would collapse, inducing a breakdown of the entire financial system and concomitant crash of the "real" economy. These fears of the FRS and the UST led to their efforts to force an orderly sale of Bear Stearns to JPMorgan Chase; i.e., a bail out of BS, with all that implies for the too-big-too-fail approach to governmental policy and attendant moral hazard in the guise of the greater-fool approach to investing, the greater fools being the taxpayers.[866]

---

[864] Mark-to market rules require that the value of a financial asset be recorded on the books at the current market price for that, or similar, instruments. If no market exists, then (computer) models are used to concoct a price.

[865] Who would have lent capital to them long-term in such circumstances?

[866] It would take us too far afield to argue for the laissez-faire public policy in this case. The interested reader may consult Rothbard (1975), for the argument that bail outs, subsidies to business, etc., are *never* justified, either on an economic or ethical basis.

References

1 Kings 17: 8-16. 1976. Good New Bible. New York: American Bible Society.

Abel, Andrew B., and Ben S. Bernanke. 1992. Macroeconomics. Reading, MA: Addison Wesley.

Abrams, M. A. 1934. Money, and a Changing Civilization. London: The Bodley Head

Aghion, Philippe, Roman Frydman, Joseph Stiglitz, Michael Woodford, eds. 2003. Knowledge, Information, and Expectations in Modern Macroeconomics: In Honor of Edmund S. Phelps. Princeton: Princeton University Press

Alesina, Alberto and Beatrice Weder. 2002. "Do Corrupt Governments Receive Less Foreign Aid?" American Economic Review, September, vol. 92, 1126-1137

American Jurisprudence 2d, Vol. 17

Anderson, Gary M. 1987. "Welfare Programs in the Rent Seeking Society," Southern Economic Journal, 54: 377-386

Anderson, Martin. 1978. Welfare: The Political Economy of Welfare Reform in the United States, Stanford: Hoover Institution

Anderson, Martin. 1989. The Christian Science Monitor, 4 January, p. 19

Anderson, Terry and Hill, P.J. 1979. "An American Experiment in Anarcho-Capitalism: The Not So Wild, Wild West," Journal of Libertarian Studies, 3: 9-29

Anderson, Terry L. and Hill, Peter J. 1981. "Property Rights as a Common Pool Resource," Bureaucracy vs. Environment: The Environmental Costs of Bureaucratic Governance, John
Baden and Richard L. Stroup, eds., Ann Arbor: University of Michigan Press

Anderson, Terry L., and Leal, Donald R. 1991. Free Market Environmentalism, San Francisco: Pacific Research Institute

Anderson, William L. 2003. "Pounding Square Pegs into Round Holes: Another Look at the Neoclassical Theory of Predatory Pricing." The Quarterly Journal of Austrian Economics. 6(1): 23-40.

Anderson, William, Walter Block, Thomas J. DiLorenzo, Ilana Mercer, Leon Snyman and Christopher Westley. 2001. "The Microsoft Corporation in Collision with Antitrust Law," The Journal of Social, Political and Economic Studies, Vol. 26, No. 1, Winter, pp. 287-302

Armentano, Dominick T. 1972. The Myths of Antitrust, New Rochelle, N.Y.: Arlington House

Armentano, Dominick T. 1982. Antitrust and Monopoly: Anatomy of a Policy Failure, New York, Wiley.

Armentano, Dominick T. 1991. Antitrust Policy: The Case for Repeal. Washington, D.C.: The Cato Institute.

Armstrong, Donald. 1982. Competition versus Monopoly: Combines Policy in Perspective, Vancouver: The Fraser Institute.

Arnold, Roger A. 2001. Macroeconomics. 5th ed. Cincinnati: South-Western College Publishing.

Arnott, Richard J., and Mintz, Jack M. 1987. Rent Control: The International Experience, Kingston, Ontario: John Deutsch Institute

Arrow, K. J. 1969. The Organization of Economic Activity: Issues Pertinent to the Choice of Market Versus Nonmarket Allocation in U.S. Congress, Joint Economic Committee, Subcommittee on Economy in Government, 91st Congress, 1st Session, The Analysis and Evaluation of Public Expenditures: the PPB System. 1, at 47, 58.

Bagus, Philip. Unpublished. "Monetary Reform and Deflation – A Critique of Mises, Rothbard, Huerta de Soto and Sennholz."

Baird, Charles. 1980. Rent Control: The Perennial Folly, Washington D.C.: The Cato Institute

Barnett, Randy E. 1998. The Structure of Liberty: Justice and the Rule of Law. Oxford, England: Oxford University Press.

Barnett, William II. 1989. "Subjective Cost Revisited," Review of Austrian Economics, Vol. 3, pp. 137-138

Barnett, William II. 2003. "The Modern Theory of Consumer Behavior: Ordinal or Cardinal?" The Quarterly Journal of Austrian Economics. 6 (1): 41 – 65. http://www.qjae.org/journals/qjae/pdf/qjae6_1_3.pdf

Barnett, William II. 2004. "Dimensions and Economics: Some Problems." Quarterly Journal of Austrian Economics. Spring. Vol. 7, No. 1, pp. 95-104; http://www.mises.org/journals/qjae/pdf/qjae7_1_10.pdf

Barnett, William. Unpublished. "Contra Caplan's Economic Methodology"

Barnett, William II and Walter Block. 2004. "On the Optimum Quantity of Money," *Quarterly Journal of Austrian Economics*, Vol. 7, No. 1, pp. 39-52

Barnett, William II and Walter Block. 2005A. "Professor Tullock on Austrian Business Cycle Theory," Advances in Austrian Economics, Vol. 8, pp. 431-443

Barnett, William II, and Walter Block. 2005B. "Money: Capital Good, Consumers' Good, or (Media of) Exchange Good?" Review of Austrian Economics. 18 (2): 179-194

Barnett, William II, and Walter Block. 2005-2006. "Mises, Rothbard and Salerno on Costs." Corporate Ownership & Control, Winter, Vol. 3, No. 2, pp. 203-205

Barnett, William II and Walter Block. 2006A. "On Gallaway and Vedder on Stabilization Policy" Quarterly Journal of Austrian Economics. Vol. 9, No. 1, spring, pp. 57-81

Barnett, William II, and Walter Block. 2006B. "Rothbard on V shaped average and
total cost curves." *Quarterly Journal of Austrian Economics*, Vol. 9, No. 3, Fall, pp. 61-66; http://mises.org/journals/qjae/pdf/qjae9_3_4.pdf

Barnett, William II and Walter Block. 2006C. "On Hayekian Triangles." *Procesos De Mercado: Revista Europea De Economia Politica*; Vol. III, No. 2, Fall, pp. 39-141; http://tinyurl.com/2zkvj7; http://mises.org/journals/scholar/block18.pdf

Barnett, William II and Walter Block. 2007A. "Coase and Van Zandt on Lighthouses," *Public Finance Review*, Vol. 35, No. 6, November, pp. 710-733

Barnett, William II and Walter Block. 2007B. "Saving and Investment: A Praxeological Approach." *New Perspectives on Political Economy*, Vol. 3, No. 2, pp. 129 – 138

Barnett, William II and Walter Block. 2008. "Economic Singularism." *Research in the History of Economic Thought & Methodology*. Vol. 26-A, pp. 15–30

Barnett, William II and Walter E. Block. 2008A. "Plain Old Inflation vs. Price Inflation" *Franklin Business & Law Journal;* Issue 3, pp. 139; http://www.franklinpublishing.net/franklinbusinesslaw.html

Barnett, William II and Walter E. Block. 2008B. "On Hummel on Austrian Business Cycle Theory." *Reason Papers* Vol. 30, Fall, pp. 59-90; http://www.reasonpapers.com/pdf/30/rp_30_4.pdf

Barnett, William II and Walter E. Block. 2009A. "Coase and Bertrand on Lighthouses," *Public Choice*; 140(1–2):1–13, http://dx.doi.org/10.1007/s11127-008-9375-x

Barnett, William II and Walter E. Block. 2009B. "Is there a market for money, or are there markets for money? There ain't no such thing as the Supply of or the Demand for Money." *Laissez-Faire*, No. 30-31, pp. 18-22, March-September; http://fce.ufm.edu/publicaciones/laissezfaire/

Barnett, William II, Walter Block and Michael Saliba. 2005. "Perfect Competition: A Case of 'Market-Failure,'" *Corporate Ownership & Control*. Vol. 2, No. 4, summer, pp. 70-75

Barnett, William II, and Jerry W. Dauterive. Unpublished A. "Rent-seeking from a Property Rights Perspective."

Barnett, William II, and Jerry W. Dauterive. Unpublished B. "Differential Effects of Rent Seeking."

Barnett, William II, Jerry Dauterive and Walter E. Block. 2008. "Subsidy is Worse than Tax" *Icfai University Journal of Public Finance*, Vol. VI, No. 4, November, pp. 62-71

Barnett, William II, Jerry W. Dauterive, and E. White. 1985. "A Taxonomy of Government Intervention." Journal of The Southwestern Society of Economists. 12 (1): 127-130.

Barnett, W. II, and Michael T. Saliba. Unpublished A. Traditional Marginal Cost: Conceptual Problems and Some Implications.

Barnett, William II, and Michael Saliba. Unpublished B. "Neoclassical Theory and the Inconsistent Application of Subjectivism."

Barnett, William II, and J. Stuart Wood. 2002. "Business Cycle Theory and Stagflation." Proceedings of the 8th Annual Austrian Scholars Conference. http://www.mises.org/asc/2002/asc8-barnett.pdf

Barro, Robert J. 2000. "Rule of Law, Democracy, and Economic Performance." In Gerald P. O'Driscoll, Jr., Kim R. Holmes and Melanie Kirkpatrick, eds. 2000 Index of Economic Freedom. Washington: The Heritage Foundation and Dow Jones & Company, Inc.: 31-49.

Barro, Robert, and Xavier Sal-i-Martin. 1998. "Economic Growth." The MIT Press

Barrowclough, Diane. 1999. "Lighthouses, Television and the Theory of Public Goods," Keynes, Post-Keynesianism and Political Economy: Essays in Honor of Geoff Harcourt, edited by Peter K. Kriesler and Claudio Sardoni, Rutledge

Batemarco, Robert. 1985. "Positive Economics and Praxeology: The Clash of Prediction and Explanation," Atlantic Economic Journal, July, 13(2), pp. 31-27.

Batten, Jonathan A and Peter G. Szilagyi. 2005. "Response to Block and Barnett, 'A Positive Programme for Laissez -Faire Capitalism," The Journal of Corporate Citizenship, Issue 19, Autumn, pp. 43-50

Bauer, Peter T. 1981. Equality, the Third World, and Economic Delusion, Cambridge: Harvard University Press

Bauer, Peter T. 1982. "Ecclesiastical Economics is Envy Exalted," This World, No. 1, Winter/Spring, pp. 56-69.

Bauer, Peter T. 1984. Reality and Rhetoric: Studies in the Economics of Development, Cambridge Mass., Harvard University Press.

Bauer, Peter T. 1991. The Development Frontier: Essays in Applied Economics. Harvester Wheatsheaf

Bauer, Peter T. and Basil S. Yamey. 1957. The Economics of Under-developed Countries, The University of Chicago Press, Chicago, Il.

Baumol, H., William J. Baumol and A. Rubinstein. 1990. "On the Economics of the Performing Arts in the U.S.S.R. and the U.S.A.: A Preliminary Comparison of the Data." New York City: C.V. Starr Center for Applied Economics.

Baumol, William J. and William G. Bowen. 1965. "On the Performing Arts: the anatomy of their economic problems." American Economic Review.

Baumol, William J. and William G. Bowen. 1966. Performing Arts: The Economic Dilemma. New York City: The Twentieth Century Fund

Beach, William and Gerry P. O'Driscoll, Jr. 2005. "Explaining the Factors of the Index of Economic Freedom," in M.A. Miles, E.J. Feulner and M.A. O'Grady, eds., The Heritage Foundation/Wall Street Journal Index of Economic Freedom. New York: Heritage Books; www.heritage.org/research/features/index/index.cfm.

Becker, Gary S. 1995. "It's Simple: Hike the Minimum Wage, and You Put People Out of Work," Business Week, March 6.

Bellante, Don, and Roger W. Garrison. 1988. "Phillips Curves And Hayekian Triangles: Two Perspectives on Monetary Dynamics." History of Political Economy. 20 no. 2, Summer, pp. 207-234; http://www.auburn.edu/~garriro/fm3bellante.htm.

Benson, Bruce L. 1989. Enforcement of Private Property Rights in Primitive Societies: Law Without Government," The Journal of Libertarian Studies, Vol. IX, No. 1, Winter, pp. 1-26

Benson, Bruce L. 1990. The Enterprise of Law: Justice Without the State. San Francisco: Pacific Research Institute for Public Policy.

Bernanke, Ben S. 2002. "Deflation: Making Sure 'It' Doesn't Happen Here." Remarks before the National Economists Club, Washington, D.C., November 21; http://www.Federalreserve.gov/boarddocs/speeches/2002/20021121/default.htm

Bertrand, Elodie. 2006. "The Coasean Analysis of Lighthouse Financing: Myths and Realities," Cambridge Journal of Economics 30:389-402

Block, Walter. 1973. "A Comment on 'The Extraordinary Claim of Praxeology' by Professor Gutierrez," Theory and Decision, June, 3(4), pp.377-387.

Block, Walter. 1977a. "Austrian Monopoly Theory -- a Critique," The Journal of Libertarian Studies, Vol. I, No. 4, Fall, pp. 271-279

Block, Walter. 1977B. "Coase and Demsetz on Private Property Rights," The Journal of Libertarian Studies, Vol. I, No. 2, Spring, pp. 111-115.

Block, Walter. 1978A. "The Negative Rate of Interest: Toward a Taxonomic Critique." The Journal of Libertarian Studies. 2 (2): 121-124.

Block, Walter. 1978B. "Abortion, Woman and Fetus: Rights in Conflict?" Reason, April, pp. 18-25.

Block, Walter. 1980. "On Robert Nozick's 'On Austrian Methodology'." Inquiry. Vol. 23, No. 4, Fall, pp. 397-444

Block, Walter. 1981. "The Negative Impact of Government Policies on the Built Environment," International Journal of Housing Science, Vol. 5, No. 2, Spring, pp. 131-140

Block, Walter. 1982. Amending the Combines Investigation Act, Vancouver: Fraser Institute

Block, Walter. 1983. "Public Goods and Externalities: The Case of Roads," The Journal of Libertarian Studies: An Interdisciplinary Review, Vol. VII, No. 1, Spring, pp. 1-34;

Block, Walter. 1986. "A Comment on 'Towards an Economic Theory of Methodology' by Professor Gerard Radnitzky," Methodology and Science, Vol.XIX, No.2, pp.148-152

Block, Walter. 1988. "Fractional Reserve Banking," Man, Economy and Liberty: Essays in Honor of Murray N. Rothbard, Walter Block and Llewellyn Rockwell, eds., Washington, D.C. The Mises Institute , 1988, pp.24-31;

Block, Walter. 1989A. "Ludwig von Mises and The 100% Gold Standard," The Meaning of Ludwig von Mises, Llewellyn Rockwell, ed., New York, Lexington Books

Block, Walter. 1989B. "The Justification of Taxation in the Public Finance Literature: An Unorthodox View." Journal of Public Finance and Public Choice. 3 (Fall): 141-158.

Block, Walter, ed. 1990A. Economics and the Environment: A Reconciliation, Vancouver: The Fraser Institute

Block, Walter. 1990B. "Earning Happiness Through Homesteading Unowned Land: a comment on 'Buying Misery with Federal Land' by Richard Stroup," Journal of Social Political and Economic Studies, Vol. 15, No. 2, Summer, pp. 237-253.

Block, Walter. 1990C. "The Discounted Marginal Value Product - Marginal Value Product Controversy: A Note," Review of Austrian Economics, Vol. IV, pp. 199-207

Block, Walter. 1991A. "Labor Relations, Unions and Collective Bargaining: A Political Economic Analysis," Journal of Social Political and Economic Studies, Vol. 16, No. 4, Winter, pp. 477-507.

Block, Walter. 1991B. "Dumping on the Economy: Why Artificial Prices Encourage Waste," Journal of Pricing Management, Vol. 14, No. 2, Spring, 21-26.

Block, Walter. 1991C[1976]. Defending the Undefendable. New York: Fox and Wilkes.

Block, Walter. 1992. "Socialist Psychology: Values and Motivations," Cultural Dynamics, Vol. V, No. 3, pp. 260-286

Block, Walter. 1993. "Canadian Public Finance Texts Cannot Justify Government Taxation: A Critique of Auld & Miller; Musgrave, Musgrave & Bird; McCready; and Wolf." Canadian Public Administration. 36 (2): No. 2: 225-262.

Block, Walter. 1994. "Total Repeal of Anti-trust Legislation: A Critique of Bork, Brozen and Posner, Review of Austrian Economics, Vol. 8, No. 1, pp. 35-70.

Block, Walter. E. 1995. Ethics, Efficiency, Coasean Property Rights and Psychic Income: A Reply to Demsetz, Review of Austrian Economics, Vol. 8, No. 2, 1995, pp. 61-125

Block, Walter E. 1996. O.J.'s Defense: A Reductio Ad Absurdum of the Economics of Ronald Coase and Richard Posner, European Journal of Law and Economics, Vol. 3, pp. 265-286

Block, Walter. 1997. "Tobacco Advertising," International Journal of Value Based Management, Vol. 10, No. 3, pp. 221-235, May

Block, Walter. 1998A. "Taxes and the Structure of Production." Journal of Public Finance and Public Choice. 17 (2-3): 145-159.

Block, Walter. 1998B. "Environmentalism and Freedom: The Case for Private Property Rights," Journal of Business Ethics, Vol. 17, No. 6, December, pp. 1887-1899

Block, Walter. 1999A. "Austrian Theorizing, Recalling the Foundations: Reply to Caplan," Quarterly Journal of Austrian Economics, Vol. 2, No. 4, winter, pp. 21-39

Block, Walter. 1999B. "Market Inalienability Once Again: Reply to Radin," Thomas Jefferson Law Journal, Vol. 22, No. 1, Fall, pp. 37-88

Block, Walter. 1999C. "The Gold Standard: A Critique of Friedman, Mundell, Hayek, Greenspan," Managerial Finance, Vol. 25, No. 5, pp. 15-33

Block, Walter. 2000. Private Property Rights, Erroneous Interpretations, Morality and Economics: Reply to Demsetz," Quarterly Journal of Austrian Economics, Vol. 3, No. 1, Spring, pp. 63-78

Block, Walter. 2001A. "Yes, We Have No Chaff: A Reply to Wagner's "Austrian Business Cycle Theory: Saving the Wheat While Discarding the Chaff," Quarterly Journal of Austrian Economics, Vol. 4, No. 1, Spring, pp. 63-73

Block, Walter. 2001B. "Stem Cell Research: The Libertarian Compromise"; September 3; http://www.lewrockwell.com/block/block5.html

Block, Walter. 2002a. "Henry Simons Is Not A Supporter of Free Enterprise," Journal of Libertarian Studies. 16 (4): 3-36

Block, Walter. 2002B. Review of Pipes, Richard, Property and Freedom: The story of how through the centuries private ownership has promoted liberty and the rule of law, New York: Knopf, 2000, in The Quarterly Journal of Austrian Economics, Vol. 5, No. 1, Spring, pp. 97-101

Block, Walter. 2002C. "A critique of the legal and philosophical case for rent control," *Journal of Business Ethics,* Vol. 40, pp. 75-90

Block, Walter. 2002-2003. "Berman on Blackmail: Taking Motives Fervently," Florida State University Business Review, Vol. 3, No. 1, pp. 57-114

Block, Walter. 2003A. "Libertarianism vs. Objectivism; A Response to Peter Schwartz," Reason Papers, Vol. 26, Summer, pp. 39-62

Block, Walter. 2003B. "Realism: Austrian vs. Neoclassical Economics, Reply to Caplan," Quarterly Journal of Austrian Economics, Vol. 6, No. 3, Fall, pp. 63-76

Block, Walter. 2003C. "National Defense and the Theory of Externalities, Public Goods and Clubs." The Myth of National Defense: Essays on the Theory and History of Security Production, Hoppe, Hans-Hermann, ed., Auburn: Mises Institute, pp. 301-334

Block, Walter. 2003D. "Private property rights, economic freedom, and Professor Coase: A Critique of Friedman, McCloskey, Medema and Zorn," *Harvard Journal of Law and Public Policy*, Vol. 26, No. 3, Summer, pp. 923-951

Block, Walter. 2004A. Austrian Law and Economics: The Contributions of Adolf Reinach and Murray Rothbard, Quarterly Journal of Austrian Economics, Vol. 7, No. 4, Winter, pp. 69-85

Block, Walter. 2004B. "Reply to Frank van Dun's 'Natural Law and the Jurisprudence of Freedom,'" Journal of Libertarian Studies. Vol. 18, No. 2, Spring, pp. 65-72.

Block, Walter. 2004C. "Libertarianism, Positive Obligations and Property Abandonment: Children's Rights," International Journal of Social Economics; Vol. 31, No. 3, pp 275-286

Block, Walter. 2006. "Coase and *Kelo*: Ominous Parallels and Reply to Lott on Rothbard on Coase," *Whittier Law Review*, Vol. 27, No. 4, pp. 997-1022

Block, Walter. 2007. "Reply to Caplan on Austrian Economic Methodology" Corporate Ownership & Control, Vol. 4, No. 2, November, pp. 312-319.

Block, Walter and William Barnett II. 2005. "A Positive Programme for Laissez -Faire Capitalism," The Journal of Corporate Citizenship, Issue 19, Autumn, pp. 31-42;

Block, Walter, William Barnett II and Gene Callahan. 2005. "The Paradox of Coase as a Defender of Free Markets," NYU Journal of Law & Liberty, Vol. 1, No. 3, pp. 1075-1095

Block, Walter, William Barnett II and Joseph Salerno. 2006. "Relationship between wealth or income and time preference is empirical, not apodictic: critique of Rothbard and Hoppe," *Review of Austrian Economics,* Vol. 19, No. 2, pp. 69-80

Block, Walter, William Barnett II and Stuart Wood. 2002. "Austrian Economics, Neoclassical Economics, Marketing and Finance," Quarterly Journal of Austrian Economics, Summer, Vol. V, No. 2, pp. 51-66

Block, Walter and Paul Cwik. 2007. "Teaching Business Ethics: A Classificationist Approach" Business Ethics: A European Review. Vol. 16, No. 2 April, pp. 98-107; http://www.blackwell-synergy.com/toc/beer/16/2

Block, Walter and Tom DiLorenzo. 2000. "Is Voluntary Government Possible? A Critique of Constitutional Economics," Journal of Institutional and Theoretical Economics, Vol. 156, No. 4, December, pp. 567-582

Block, Walter and Tom DiLorenzo. 2001. "The Calculus of Consent Revisited," Public Finance and Management, Vol. 1, No. 3

Block, Walter and Kenneth Garschina. 1996. "Hayek, Business Cycles and Fractional Reserve Banking: Continuing the De-Homogenization Process," Review of Austrian Economics, Vol. 9, No. 1, pp. 77-94

Block, Walter, and Llewellyn H. Rockwell, eds. 1988. Man, Economy and Liberty: Essays in Honor of Murray N. Rothbard. Auburn University, The Mises Institute.

Block, Walter and Michael A. Walker. 1988. "Entropy in the Canadian Economics Profession: Sampling Consensus on the Major Issues," Canadian Public Policy, Vol. XIV. No. 2, June, pp. 137-150.

Block, Walter, Christopher Westley and Alex Padilla. Forthcoming. "Internal vs. external explanations: a new perspective on the history of economic thought," *Procesos De Mercado: Revista Europea De Economia Politica*

Block, Walter and Roy Whitehead. 1999. "The Unintended Consequences of Environmental Justice," Forensic Science International, Vol. 100, Nos. 1 and 2, March, pp. 57-67

Block, Walter and Roy Whitehead. 2005. "Compromising the Uncompromisable: A Private Property Rights Approach to Resolving the Abortion Controversy," Appalachian Law Review, 4 (2) 1-45

Block, Walter and Guillermo Yeatts. 1999-2000. "The Economics and Ethics of Land Reform: A Critique of the Pontifical Council for Justice and Peace's 'Toward a Better Distribution of Land: The Challenge of Agrarian Reform,'" Journal of Natural Resources and Environmental Law, Vol. 15, No. 1, pp. 37-69

Boaz, David. 1997. Libertarianism: A Primer, New York: Free Press

Boettke, Peter J. 1990. The Political Economy of Soviet Socialism: The Formative Years, 1918-1928, Boston: Kluwer

Boettke, Peter J. 1991. "The Austrian Critique and the Demise of Socialism: The Soviet Case," in Austrian Economics: Perspectives on the Past and Prospects for the Future. Vol. 17, Richard M. Ebeling, ed., Hillsdale, MI: Hillsdale College Press, pp. 181-232.

Boettke, Peter J. 1993. Why Perestroika Failed: The Politics and Economics of Socialist Transformation, London: Routledge

Boettke, Peter J., ed. 1994A. The Collapse of Development Planning, New York: New York University Press

Boettke, Peter J. 1994B. "The Reform Trap in Politics and Economics in the Former Communist Economies," Journal des Economistes et des Etudes Humaines, V, Nos. 2/3, June/September, 267-293

Boettke, Peter J. 2002. "Information and Knowledge: Austrian Economics in Search of its Uniqueness." Review of Austrian Economics, 15 (4), 263-274.

Boettke, Peter J., and Anderson, Gary. 1993. "Perestroika and Public Choice: the economics of autocratic succession in a rent seeking society," Public Choice, 75, no. 2, February, 101-118

Boettke, Peter J., and Anderson Gary. 1997. "Soviet Venality: The USSR as a Mercantilist State, Public Choice

Boettke, Peter J. and David L. Prychitko, eds. 1994. The Market Process: Essays in Contemporary Austrian Economics. Brookfield, VT: Edward Elgar

Bohm-Bawerk, E. von. 1959 [1884]. Capital and Interest. Vol. 2, Positive Theory of Capital. Translated by G.D. Huncke and Hans F. Sennholz. Libertarian Press; http://www.mises.org/store/product1.asp?SID=2&Product_ID=19

Böhm-Bawerk, Eugen von. 1890. "The Historical vs. the Deductive Method in Political Economy," Annals of the American Academy of Political and Social Science, vol. 1

Böhm-Bawerk, Eugen von. 1994. Classics in Austrian Economics, Volume 1: The Founding Era, Israel M. Kirzner, ed., London: William Pickering, pp. 108-129;

Bordo, Michael D. and Anna J. Schwartz. 2003. "IS-LM and Monetarism." Speech given at Duke University, April 25; http://econweb.rutgers.edu/bordo/ISLM.pdf

Bork, Robert H. 1978. The Antitrust Paradox: A Policy at War with Itself. New York, Basic Books.

Bostaph, Samuel. 1976. Epistemological Foundations of Methodological Conflict in Economics: The Case of the Nineteenth Century Methodenstreit. Unpublished Ph.D. dissertation, Southern Illinois University at Carbondale.

Bostaph, Samuel. 1978. "The Methodological Debate between Carl Menger and the German Historicists," Atlantic Economy Journal, 6(3);

Boudreaux, Donald J., and DiLorenzo, Thomas J. 1992. "The Protectionist Roots of Antitrust," Review of Austrian Economics, Vol. 6, No. 2, pp. 81-96

Boulding, Kenneth. [1941] (1966). Economic Analysis. Vol. II, Macroeconomics. 4th ed.

Boyes, William, and Michael Melvin. 2002. Macroeconomics. 5th ed. Boston: Houghton Mifflin Co.

Bradley, Robert L., Jr. Unpublished ms. Political Capitalism: Insull, Enron & Beyond. Institute for Energy Research

Brietzke, Paul. 2001. "Securitisation and Bankruptcy in Indonesia: Theme and Variations", Global Jurist Topics: Vol. 1: No. 1, Article 5.

Brown, Arnold. 1987. "The Shadow Side of Affluence: The Welfare System and the Welfare of the Needy," Fraser Forum, October.

Brozen, Yale. 1982. Concentration, Mergers, and Public Policy. Macmillan.

Brubaker, Earl R. 1975. "Free Ride, Free Revelation, or Golden Rule?" Journal of Law and Economics, Vol. 18, No. 1, April, pp. 147-161

Buchanan, J. M. 1969. Cost and Choice: An Inquiry into Economic Theory, Chicago: Markham

Buchanan, James M. 1975. The Limits of Liberty: Between Anarchy and Leviathan, Chicago: University of Chicago Press.

Buchanan, James M. 2000. The demand and supply of public goods. Indianapolis, IN: Liberty Fund

Buchanan, J. M. and G.F. Thirlby. 1981. L.S.E. Essays on Cost, New York: New York University Press.

Buchanan, J. M. and G. Tullock. 1962 [1971]. The Calculus of Consent. Ann Arbor: University of Michigan Press.

Butos, William and Roger Koppl. 1997. "The varieties of subjectivism: Keynes, Hayek on expectations." History of Political Economy, 29 (2), pp. 327-359.

Butos, William N. 2001. "Garrison and the 'Keynes Problem.' The Quarterly Journal of Austrian Economics. Vol. 4, No. 3, pp. 5-16.

Callahan, Gene. 2002. Economics for Real People. Auburn, AL: Ludwig von Mises Institute.

Callahan, Gene. 2003. The Libertarian Case Against Fractional-Reserve Banking, Anti-State.com, July 22

Canaan, Edwin. 1921. "Application of the Theoretical Apparatus of Supply and Demand to Units of Currency." Economic Journal. 31: 453-461.

Caplan, Bryan. 1999. "The Austrian Search for Realistic Foundations." Southern Economic Journal, April, Vol. 65, No. 4, pp. 823-838

Caplan, Bryan. 2001. "Probability, Common Sense, and Realism: A Reply to Huelsmann and Block." Quarterly Journal of Austrian Economics. Vol. 2, No. 4, summer, pp. 69-86; http://www.mises.org/journals/qjae/pdf/qjae4_2_6.pdf

Caplan, Bryan, 2003. "Probability and the Synthetic A Priori: A Reply to Block," Quarterly Journal of Austrian Economics Vol. 6, No. 3, Fall, pp. 77-83

Card, David, and Alan B. Krueger. 1994. "Minimum Wages and Employment: A Case Study of the Fast-Food Industry in New Jersey and Pennsylvania," American Economic Review, Vol. 84, No. 4, September, pp. 772-793

Carilli, Anthony M. and Gregory M. Dempster. 2001. "Expectations in Austrian Business Cycle Theory: An Application of the Prisoner's Dilemma." Review of Austrian Economics. Vol. 14, No. 4, pp. 319-330; http://www.gmu.edu/rae/archives/VOL14_4_2001/4_carilli&dempster.pdf

Carilli, Anthony M., Gregory M. Dempster, and J. Rory Rohan. 2004. "Monetary reform from a comparative-theoretical perspective." The Quarterly Journal of Austrian Economics. vol. 7, no. 3, Fall, pp. 29-44

Case, Karl E., and Ray C. Fair. 2002. Principles of Economics. 6th ed. Upper Saddle River, N.J.: Prentice Hall.

Castle, Eugene W. 1957. The great giveaway; the realities of foreign aid, Chicago, H. Regnery Co.

Chafuen, Alejandro A. 1986. Christians for Freedom: Late Scholastic Economics, San Francisco: Ignatius Press

Cheung, Steven N.S. 1983. "The Contractual Nature of the Firm," Journal of Law and Economics, 26:1-21

Chodorov, Frank. 1962. "Taxation Is Robbery" [From Out of Step: The Autobiography of an Individualist, by Frank Chodorov; The Devin-Adair Company, New York, 1962, pp. 216–239]; http://www.mises.org/etexts/taxrob.asp

Coase, Ronald, H. 1937. "The Nature of the Firm," Economica, November, Vol. 4, pp. 386-406

Coase, Ronald. 1955. The Postal Monopoly in Great Britain: An Historical Survey, in Economic Essays in Commemoration of the Dundee School of Economics, 1931-55 25-37 (J. K. Eastham ed., W. Culross, Dundee School of Economics, Dundee).

Coase, Ronald. 1959. The Federal Communications Commission, 2 Journal of Law and Economics 1-40.

Coase, Ronald, H. 1960. "The Problem of Social Cost," Journal of Law and Economics, October, Vol. 3, pp. 1-44.

Coase, Ronald. 1961. The British Post Office and the Messenger Companies, 4 Journal of Law and Economics 12-65

Coase, Ronald. 1965. Evaluation of Public Policy Relating to Radio and Television Broadcasting: Social and Economic Issues, 41 Land Economics 161-167.

Coase, Ronald. 1966. The Economics of Broadcasting and Government Policy, 56 American Economic Review, Papers and Proceedings 440.

Coase, Ronald. 1974a. The Market for Goods and the Market for Ideas, 64 American Economic Review, Papers and Proceedings 384.

Coase, Ronald H. 1977. "Advertising in Free Speech," Journal of Legal Studies, 6:1-34

Coase, Ronald. 1979A. Payola in Radio and Television Broadcasting, 22 Journal of Law and Economics 269-328.

Coase, Ronald. 1979B. Should the Federal Communications Commission Be Abolished?, in Regulation, Economics, and the Law 41 (Bernard H. Siegan ed., Lexington Books, Lexington MA, 1979B) (with Nicholas Johnson).

Coase, R. H. 1988 [1974b]. "The Lighthouse in Economics." The Firm, The Market, and The Law. Chicago: Univ. of Chicago Press, 187-213, reprinted from: The Journal of Law and Economics. 17(2): 357-376.

Cobin, John. 1998. "Abortion Policy and the Market." Journal of Interdisciplinary Studies, vol. XV, no. 1/2.

Cochran, John P. 2004. "Capital, Monetary Calculation, and the Trade Cycle." The Quarterly Journal of Austrian Economics. Vol. 7, No. 1, Spring, pp. 17-25; http://www.mises.org/journals/qjae/pdf/qjae7_1_2.pdf

Cochran, John P. & Call, Steven T. 1998. "The Role of Fractional-Reserve Banking and Financial Intermediation in the Money Supply Process: Keynes and the Austrians," The Quarterly Review of Austrian Economics, Fall, 1.3, pp. 29-40;

Cochran, John P. and Fred Glahe. 1999. The Hayek-Keynes Debates: Lessons for Current Business Cycle Research, Lewiston, New York: Edwin Mellen Press

Cohen, A. J., and G. C. Harcourt. 2003. "Whatever Happened to the Cambridge Capital Theory Controversies?" Journal of Economic Perspectives. 17 (1): 199-214.

Colander, David C. 1998. Macroeconomics 3rd ed. Boston: Irwin, McGraw-Hill.

Conway, David. 1987. A Farewell to Marx: An Outline and Appraisal of His Theories, Middlesex, England: Penguin Books.

Copeland, Peter and Keith Parsons. 2004. "Toward a Postmodern Paleontology?" Academic Questions. Spring, Vol. 17, No. 2, pp. 6-17

Cordato, Roy E. 1989. "Subjective Value, Time Passage, and the Economics of Harmful Effects," Hamline Law Review, Vol. 12, No. 2, Spring, pp. 229-244.

Cordato, Roy E. 1992A. "Knowledge Problems and the Problem of Social Cost" *Journal of the History of Economic Thought*, vol.14, Fall, pp. 209-224.

Cordato, R. E. 1992B. Welfare Economics and Externalities in an Open-Ended Universe: A Modern Austrian Perspective, Boston: Kluwer

Cordato, Roy. 1998. "Time Passage and the Economics of Coming to the Nuisance: Reassessing the Coasean Perspective," Campbell Law Review, vol. 20, No. 2, Spring, pp. 273-292

Cowen, Tyler, ed. 1988. The Theory of Market Failure: A Critical Examination, Fairfax, VA: George Mason University Press

Cowen, Tyler. 1997. Risk and Business Cycles: New and Old Austrian Perspectives. London: Routledge.

Cowen, Tyler. 1998. In Praise of Commercial Culture. Harvard University Press

Cragg, J.G. 1974. "Rent Control Report" commissioned by British Columbia Rentalsman, mimeo

Cubeddu, Raimondo. 1993. The Philosophy of the Austrian School. New York: Routledge, pp. 1-108;

Cuzan, Alfred G. 1979. "Do We Ever Really Get Out of Anarchy?," The Journal of Libertarian Studies, Vol. 3, No. 2, Summer, pp. 151-158

D'Amico, D. J. 2008. Who's to blame for all the heartache?: A response to anti-capitalistic mentalities after Katrina. The International Journal of Social Economics. Vol. 35, No. 8, pp. 590-602.

Dauterive, Jerry W, and Mike Sibley. 1990. "Ownership Structure and Board Independence Among Small Firms," paper presented at the Annual Meeting of the Financial Management Association, Orlando, October

Davidson, Paul. 1998. "Post Keynesian Employment Analysis and the Macroeconomics of OECD Unemployment." The Economic Journal. 108 (448): 817-831.

De Jasay, Anthony. 1989. Social Contract, Free Ride: A Study of the Public Goods Problem. Oxford University Press

De Jasay, Antony. 1996. "Hayek: Some missing pieces." *The Review of Austrian Economics* Vol. 9, No .1: 107-118; http://www.mises.org/journals/rae/pdf/rae9_1_5.pdf

de Molinari, Gustave. 1977. The Production of Security, New York: Center for Libertarian Studies

de Soto, Jesús Huerta. 1995. "A Critical Analysis of Central Banks and Fractional-Reserve Free Banking from the Austrian Perspective," Review of Austrian Economics, 8(2), pp. 25-38.

de Soto, Jesús Huerta. 1996. "New Light on the Prehistory of the Theory of Banking and the School of Salamanca." *The Review of Austrian Economics*, Vol. 9, No. 2, pages 59-81; http://mises.org/journals/rae/pdf/RAE9_2_4.pdf

de Soto, Jesus Huerta. 1998A. "A Critical Note on Fractional-Reserve Free Banking," The Quarterly Journal of Austrian Economics, Winter, 1.4, 25-49.

de Soto, Jesus Huerta. 1998B. "The Ongoing Methodenstreit of the Austrian School," Journal des Economistes et des Etudes Humaines, March, 8:1, pp. 75-113;

de Soto, Jesus Huerta. 2001. "A Critical Note on Fractional Reserve Free Banking," The Quarterly Journal of Austrian Economics, Vol. 1, No. 4, Fall, pp. 34, 35

de Soto, Jesus Huerta. 2006. Money, Bank Credit, and Economic Cycles, translated by Melinda A. Stroup, ch. 9; Auburn, AL: Ludwig von Mises Institute; http://www.mises.org/books/desoto.pdf

Demsetz, Harold. 1966. "Some Aspects of Property Rights," Journal of Law and Economics, Vol. IX, October

Demsetz, Harold. 1979. "Ethics and Efficiency in Property Rights Systems," in Time, Uncertainty and Disequilibrium: Explorations of Austrian Themes, Mario Rizzo, ed., Lexington Mass.: D.C. Heath and Co.

Demsetz, Harold. 1997. "Block's Erroneous Interpretations," Review of Austrian Economics, Vol. 10, No. 2, pp. 101-109

DiLorenzo, Thomas J. 1990A. "The Subjectivist Roots of James Buchanan's Economics," The Review of Austrian Economics, Vol. 4, pp. 180-195

DiLorenzo, Thomas. 1990B. "Does Capitalism Cause Pollution?," St. Louis, Washington University: Center for the Study of American Business, Contemporary Issues Series 38.

DiLorenzo, Thomas J. 1997. "The Myth of Natural Monopoly," Review of Austrian Economics, Vol. 9, No. 2, pp. 43-58

DiLorenzo, Thomas J. 2002. "The Futility of Bureaucracy." The Free Market. August, Vol. 20, No. 7; http://www.mises.org/freemarket_detail.asp?control=409&sortorder=articledate

DiLorenzo, Tom and Walter Block. 2001. "Constitutional Economics and the Calculus of Consent," The Journal of Libertarian Studies, Vol. 15, No. 3, Summer, pp. 37-56; http://www.mises.org/journals/jls/15_3/15_3_2.pdf

DiLorenzo, Tom and Jack High. 1988. "Antitrust and Competition, Historically Considered," Economic Inquiry, July.

Director, Aaron., ed. 1952. Defense, Controls, and Inflation. University of Chicago Press.

Dirmeyer, Jenny. 2008. The futile fight against (human) nature: A public choice analysis of the US Army Corps of Engineers – special focus on Hurricane Katrina. The International Journal of Social Economics. Vol. 35, No. 8, pp. 627-638

Dornbusch, Rudiger, and Stanley Fischer. 1987. Macroeconomics. 4th ed. New York: McGraw Hill.

Downs, Anthony. 1988. Residential Rent Controls: An Evaluation, Washington: The Urban Land Institute

Druckerman, Pamela. 2001. "Argentina's President Aims to Rally Public Around Pledges Key to IMF Bailout Deal," Wall Street Journal, August 24.

Durbin, E. F. M. 1933 [1934]. Purchasing Power & Trade Depression: A Critique of Under-Consumption" Theories. London: Jonathan Cape.

Durbin, E. F. M. 1935. The Problem of Credit Policy. London: Chapman & Hall

Eatewell, et al, ed. 1987. The New Palgrave: A Dictionary of Economics. New York: Macmillan.

Ebeling, Richard M. 1974. "Austrian Economics On The Rise." Vol. VI, No. 10, October, pp. 3-6. The Libertarian Forum. http://www.mises.org/journals/lf/1974/1974_10.pdf

Ebeling, Richard M. 1975. "The Second Austrian Conference." The Libertarian Forum, Vol. III, No. 7, July, pp. 4-8. http://www.mises.org/journals/lf/1975/1975_07.pdf

Ebeling, Richard M., ed. 1991. Austrian Economics: A Reader. Hillsdale College Press.

Ebeling, Richard. 1992. "Introduction." In Richard Ebeling, ed. The Global Failure of Socialism. Hillsdale, MI: Hillsdale College Press, pp. 6-8.

Ebeling, Richard M. 1993. "Economic Calculation Under Socialism: Ludwig von Mises and His Predecessors," in Jeffrey Herbener, ed., The Meaning of Ludwig von Mises, Norwell, MA: Kluwer Academic Press. pp. 56-101.

Ebeling, Richard M. compiler. 1996. The Austrian Theory of the Trade Cycle and Other Essays. Auburn, AL: Ludwig von Mises Institute.

Ebeling, Richard M., ed. 2000. "Selected Writings of Ludwig von Mises," Vol. 3: 'The Political Economy of International Reform and Reconstruction,' (Indianapolis, IN: Liberty Fund) Ch 6: "A Non-Inflationary Proposal for Postwar Monetary Reconstruction," pp. 71-118

Egger, John. 1979. "The Austrian Method," in New Directions in Austrian Economics, Louis Spadaro, ed., Kansas City: Sheed Andrews and McMeel, pp. 19-39;

Einstein, Albert. 1920. Relativity: The Special and General Theory. trans. Lawson, R. W. New York: Henry L. Holt.

Ekelund, Robert B, Jr. and Shawn Ritenour. 1999. "An Exploration of the Beckerian Theory of Time Costs: Symphony Concert Demand." The American Journal of Economics and Sociology, October; http://www.findarticles.com/p/articles/mi_m0254/is_4_58/ai_58496764

Endres, A. M. 1991. "Austrian Capital and Interest theory: Wieser's Contribution and the Menger Tradition." Review of Austrian Economics Vol. 5, No. 1, pp. 67-90

Epstein, Richard A. 1980. A Theory of Strict Liability." San Francisco: Cato Institute.
errata: http://www.mises.org/journals/qjae/pdf/qjae2_4_9.pdf

Faber, M. 1979. Introduction to Modern Austrian Capital Theory. New York: Springer – Verlag.

Faber, M. ed. 1986. Studies in Austrian Capital Theory, Investment and Time. New York: Springer – Verlag.

Farmer, Roger E. 2002. Macroeconomics. 2nd ed., Cincinnati: South-Western College Publishing.

Ferguson, Niall, ed. 1999. Virtual History: Alternatives and Counterfactuals. New York: Basic Books.

Ferguson, Niall. 2000. The Pity of War: Explaining World War I. New York, NY: Basic Books

Ferrara, Peter J. 1982. Social Security: Averting the Crisis, Washington DC: Cato Institute

Fetter, Frank A. 1977. Capital, Interest and Rent: Essays in the Theory of Distribution. Ed. by Rothbard, Murray N. Kansas City: Sheed, Andrews and McMeel.

Fielding, Karl T. 1978. "The role of personal justice in anarcho-capitalism," The Journal of Libertarian Studies, Vol. 2, No. 3, Fall, pp. 239-242

Foldvary, Fred. 2003. "The Lighthouse as a Private-Sector Collective Good," The Half-Life of Policy Rationales: How New Technology Affects Old Policy Issues; Fred Foldvary and Daniel Klein eds. Washington D.C.: Cato Institute

Foss, Nicolai Juul. 1994. "The Theory of the Firm: The Austrians as Precursors and Critics of Contemporary Theory," Review of Austrian Economics, Vol. 7, No. 1, pp. 31-65;

Foss, Nicolai Juul. 1995. "Information and the Market Economy: A Note on a Common Marxist Fallacy," Review of Austrian Economics, 8(2), pp. 127-136.

Fox, Glenn, 1992, "The Pricing of Environmental Goods: A Praxeological Critique of Contingent Valuation," Cultural Dynamics, Vol. V, No. 3, pp. 245-259

Frey, Bruno S., Werner W. Pommerehne, Friedrich Schneider and Guy Gilbert. 1984. "Consensus and Dissension Among Economists: An Empirical Inquiry, American Economic Review, December, 74:5:986-94;

Friedman, Benjamin M. 1983. "The Roles of Money and Credit in Macroeconomic Analysis." Macroeconomics, Prices, and Quantities: Essays in Memory of Arthur M. Okun; James Tobin, ed. Washington D.C.: Brookings Institution

Friedman, David. 1989. The Machinery of Freedom: Guide to a Radical Capitalism, La Salle, IL: Open Court, 2nd ed.; http://www.daviddfriedman.com/Libertarian/Machinery_of_Freedom/MofF_Chapter_41.html

Friedman, Milton. 1953. "The Methodology of Positive Economics." Essays in positive economics, Chicago: University of Chicago Press, pp. 3-43

Friedman, Milton. 1962. Capitalism and Freedom, Chicago: University of Chicago Press.

Friedman, Milton. 1968. "The Role of Monetary Policy." American Economic Review. 58 (1): 1-17

Friedman, Milton. 1969. "The Optimum Quantity of Money." In The Optimum Quantity of Money and Other Essays. Aldine: 1-50.

Friedman, Milton. 1992. Money Mischief: Episodes in Monetary History. Harcourt Brace Jovanovich, Pub.

Friedman, Milton and Rose D. Friedman. 1980. Free to Choose, New York: Harcourt, Brace, Jovanovich.

Friedman, Milton and Rose D. Friedman. 1998. Two Lucky People, Chicago: University of Chicago Press

Friedman, Milton and Anna J. Schwartz. 1963. A Monetary History of the U.S., 1867-1960, New York: National Bureau of Economic Research.

Friedman, Milton and Anna J. Schwartz. 1965. The Great Contraction: 1929-1933. Princeton: Princeton University Press.

Friedman, Milton vs. Walter Block. 2006. "Fanatical, Not Reasonable: A Short Correspondence Between Walter Block and Milton Friedman." *Journal of Libertarian Studies*, Vol. 20, No. 3, Summer, pp. 61–80

Froyen, Richard T. 1999. Macroeconomics: Theories and Policies. 6th ed. Upper Saddle River, N.J.: Prentice Hall.

Fullerton, Don. 1982. "On the Possibility of an Inverse Relationship Between Tax Rates and Government Revenues." Journal of Public Economics. 18: 3-22.

Gaitskell, Hugh T. N. 1933. "Four Monetary Heretics" in G. D. H. Cole, ed., What Everybody Wants to Know About Money. New York: Alfred A. Knopf

Gallaway, Lowell, and Richard K. Vedder. 1987 "Wages, Prices, and Employment: Von Mises and the Progressives." Review of Austrian Economics. 1: 33-80.

Gallaway, Lowell, and Richard Vedder. 1997 [1993]. Out of Work: Unemployment and Government in Twentieth-Century America. Updated ed. The Independent Institute.

Gallaway, Lowell, and Richard Vedder. 2000. "The Fraud of Macroeconomic Stabilization." Quarterly Journal of Austrian Economics. 3(3):19-33.

Gallaway, Lowell, and Vedder, Richard. 2006. "How Big Is the Austrian Tent? A Reply to Barnett and Block." The Quarterly Journal of Austrian Economics. Vol. 9, No. 3, fall, 67-69

Garrison, Roger W. 1978. "Austrian Macroeconomics: A Diagrammatical Exposition," New Directions in Austrian Economics, ed. Louis M. Spadaro, Kansas City: Sheed Andrews and McMeel

Garrison, Roger. 1979A. "Comment: Waiting in Vienna." In Rizzo, Mario J., ed., Time, Uncertainly, and Disequilibrium. Lexington, MA: Lexington Books, pp. 215-226.

Garrison, Roger. 1979B. "In Defense of the Misesian Theory of Interest." Journal of Libertarian Studies. 3 (2): 141-150.

Garrison, Roger. 1982. "Austrian Economics as the Middle Ground: Comment on Loasby," in: Market Process, and Austrian Economics: Essays in Honor of Ludwig von Mises, Kirzner, Israel M., ed., Lexington MA: Lexington Books, pp. 131-138

Garrison, Roger W. 1984. "Time and Money: The Universals of Macroeconomic Theorizing." Journal of Macroeconomics. vol. 6, no. 2, pp. 197-213; http://www.auburn.edu/~garriro/b6time.htm

Garrison, Roger. 1985A. "A Subjectivist Theory of a Capital Using Economy," in O'Driscoll, Gerald P. and Rizzo, Mario, The Economics of Time and Ignorance, Oxford: Basil Blackwell,

Garrison, Roger. 1985B. "Intertemporal coordination and the invisible hand: an Austrian perspective on the Keynesian vision." History of Political Economy, 17: 309-21.

Garrison, Roger. 1987. "Full employment and intertemporal coordination: a rejoinder." History of Political Economy, 19(2): 335-41.

Garrison, Roger. 1988. "Professor Rothbard and the Theory of Interest." In Block, Walter, and Llewellyn H. Rockwell, eds., Man, Economy and Liberty: Essays in Honor of Murray N. Rothbard. Auburn University, The Mises Institute, pp. 44-55.

Garrison, Roger W. 1989. "The Austrian Theory of the Business Cycle In the Light of Modern Macroeconomics." Review of Austrian Economics. 3(1): pp. 3-29.

Garrison, Roger. 1993. "Mises and His Methods," in The Meaning of Ludwig von Mises, Jeffrey M. Herbener ed., Auburn, AL: Ludwig von Mises Institute; Boston, MA: Kluwer, pp. 102-117;

Garrison, Roger W. 1994. "Hayekian Triangles and Beyond," in Jack Birner and Rudy van Zijp, eds., Hayek, Coordination and Evolution: His Legacy in Philosophy, Politics, Economics, and the History of Ideas. London: Routledge

Garrison, Roger W. 1995. "Keynes Was a Keynesian," Review of Austrian Economics, Vol. 9, No. 1, pp. 165-172

Garrison, Roger W. 1996. "The Austrian Theory: A Summary." In Ebeling, R. M., compiler. 1996. The Austrian Theory of the Trade Cycle and Other Essays. Auburn, AL: Ludwig von Mises Institute.

Garrison, Roger W. 2001. Time and Money: The Macroeconomics of Capital Structure. New York: Routledge.

Garrison, Roger W. 2004. "Overconsumption and Forced Saving in the Mises-Hayek Theory of the Business Cycle, History of Political Economy, vol. 36, no. 2 (Summer), pp. 323-349.

Garrison, Roger W. 2005. "The Austrian School." Modern Macroeconomics: Its Origins, Development and Current State. Snowdon, Brian and Howard R. Vane, Cheltenham, U.K.: Edward Elgar, pp. 474-516.

Garrison, Roger W. and Don Bellante. 1988. "Phillips Curves and Hayekian Triangles: Two Perspectives on Monetary Dynamics," History of Political Economy, vol. 20,

Gillis, Malcolm. 2003. "Economics and The Chicago School: Yesterday, Today and Tomorrow. March 18. Rice University; http://www.professor.rice.edu/professor/031820031.asp?SnID=325297287

Gordon, David. 1986. Hermeneutics versus Austrian Economics, Monograph, Auburn, AL: Ludwig von Mises Institute

Gordon, David. 1990. Resurrecting Marx: The Analytical Marxists on Freedom, Exploitation, and Justice, New Brunswick, NJ: Transaction.

Gordon, David. 1993A. "Ludwig von Mises and the Philosophy of History," in The Meaning of Ludwig von Mises, Jeffrey M. Herbener ed., Auburn, AL: Ludwig von Mises Institute; Boston, MA: Kluwer, pp. 118-133;

Gordon, David. 1993B. "The Philosophical Contributions of Ludwig von Mises," Review of Austrian Economics, 7(1), pp. 95-106;

Gordon, David. 2000. An Introduction to Economic Reasoning, Auburn, Alabama: Mises Institute

Gordon, David. 2003. "Epistemological Problems of Economics"; http://www.mises.org/studyguide.aspx?action=author&Id=64

Gordon, Robert J. 1993. Macroeconomics. 6th ed. New York, N.Y.: HarperCollins.

Gottheil, Fred. 2002. Principles of Macroeconomics. 3rd ed. Cincinnati: South-Western College Publishing.

Graff, Delia and Timothy Williamson, eds. 2002. Vagueness. Aldershot: Ashgate

Grant, R.W. 1989. Rent Control and the War Against the Poor, Manhattan Beach: Quandary House

Greaves, Bettina Bien. 1995. "How to Return to the Gold Standard." The Freeman: Ideas on Liberty; Vol. 45, No. 11, November; http://www.fee.org/publications/the-freeman/article.asp?aid=4848

Greaves, Percy L. Jr. 1974. Mises Made Easier: A Glossary for Ludwig von Mises's Human Action, Dobbs Ferry, New York: Free Market Books. http://www.mises.org/easier/easier.asp

Gregory, Anthony and Walter Block. 2007. "On Immigration: Reply to Hoppe." *Journal of Libertarian Studies*, vol. 21, No. 3, Fall, pp. 25-42; http://mises.org/journals/jls/21_3/21_3_2.pdf

Gunning, J. Patrick. 1986. "The Methodology of Austrian Economics and Its Relevance to Institutionalism" American Journal of Economics and Sociology, January, pp. 79-89;

Gunning, J. Patrick. 1988. "Professor Caldwell on Ludwig von Mises' Methodology," Review of Austrian Economics, Vol. 3.

Gunning, J. Patrick. 1990. The New Subjectivist Revolution: An Elucidation and Extension of Ludwig von Mises's Contribution to Economic Theory, Savage, MD: Rowan and Littlefield.

Gwartney, James, Robert Lawson and Walter Block. 1996. Economic Freedom of the World, 1975-1995, Vancouver, B.C.: The Fraser Institute

Gwartney, James, Robert Lawson and Dexter Samida. 2000. 2000 Annual Report: Economic Freedom of the World, Vancouver, B.C.: The Fraser Institute

Gwartney, James D., and Richard L. Stroup. 1993. What Everyone Should Know about Economics and Prosperity. Vancouver, B.C.: The Fraser Institute.

Hahn, F. H. 1977. "Keynesian Economics and General Equilibrium Theory." In: Harcourt, G. C. ed. The Microfoundations of Macroeconomics.

Hall, Thomas E., and David Ferguson. 1998. The Great Depression: An International Disaster of Perverse Economic Policies. The University of Michigan Press.

Hamowy, Ronald 1984. Canadian Medicine: A Study in Restricted Entry, Vancouver: The Fraser Institute

Hansen, Alvin H. 1953. A Guide to Keynes. McGraw-Hill.

Hansen, Alvin. H. 1964. Business Cycles and National Income. Exp. ed. W.W. Norton &Co., Inc.

Harcourt, G. C. 1970. Some Cambridge Controversies in the Theory of Capital. Cambridge University Press.

Harcourt, G. C. ed. 1977. The Microfoundations of Macroeconomics. Macmillan.

Hasnas, John. 1995. "The Myth of the Rule of Law," Wisconsin Law Review, 1

Hayek, Friedrich A. 1931. Prices and Production. London: Routledge.

Hayek, Friedrich A. 1934A. "Capital and Industrial Fluctuations." Econometrica, Vol. 2, No. 2, April, pp. 152-167.

Hayek, Friedrich A. 1934B. "On the Relationship Between Investment and Output." The Economic Journal, Vol. 44, No. 174, June, pp. 207-231.

Hayek, Friedrich A. 1935. Prices and Production. 2nd ed. London: Routledge

Hayek, Friedrich A. 1937. "Economics and Knowledge." Economica, pp. 33-54

Hayek, F.A. 1945. "Time-Preference and Productivity: A Reconsideration." Economica. Vol. 12, No. 45, February, pp. 22-25

Hayek, Friedrich A. 1948A[1945]. "The Use of Knowledge in Society," Individualism and Economic Order, Chicago: University of Chicago Press.

Hayek, F. A. 1948B. "The Conditions of Equilibrium between the Production of Consumers' Goods and the Production of Producers' Goods." In The Essence of Hayek.

Hayek, F.A. 1948C. "Socialist Calculation I, II, & III," Individualism and Economic Order, Chicago: University of Chicago Press

Hayek, F.A. 1954. Capitalism and the Historians, ed., (essays by T.S. Ashton, L.M. Hacker, W.H. Hutt, B. de Jouvenel), The University of Chicago Press, Chicago

Hayek, Friedrich A. 1955. The Counter-Revolution of Science, Glencoe, IL: The Free Press, pp. 13-43;

Hayek, Friedrich A. 1960. The Constitution of Liberty, Henry Regnery Company, Chicago

Hayek, Friedrich A. 1966 [1933]. Monetary Theory and the Trade Cycle, New York, Kelley

Hayek, Friedrich A. 1967. "The Non Sequitur of the 'Dependence Effect.'" In Hayek, F.A., Studies in Philosophy, Politics and Economics. New York, Simon and Schuster.

Hayek, Friedrich A. 1972. A Tiger by the Tail. London: Institute of Economic Affairs.

Hayek, F. A. 1975 [1939]. The Present State and Immediate Prospects of the Study of Industrial Fluctuations. In Hayek, F. A. 1975 [1939]. Profits, Interest, and Investment. Augustus M. Kelley. Translated from Der Stand und die nächste Zukunft der Konjunktur forschung, Festschrift für Arthur Spiethoff, Munich 1933.

Hayek, F.A. 1975 [1941]. Pure Theory of Capital. University of Chicago Press.

Hayek, Friedrich A. 1978A. The Denationalisation of Money, 2nd ed., London: Institute of Economic Affairs

Hayek, Friedrich, A. 1978B. "New Confusion about 'Planning.'" January, Morgan Guaranty Survey, pp. 4-13.

Hayek, F. A. 1979. The Counter-Revolution of Science: Studies on the Abuse of Reason. 2d ed., Liberty Press, Indianapolis.

Hayek, Friedrich A. 1995. Contra Keynes and Cambridge: Essays, Correspondence. Chicago: University of Chicago Press

Hazlitt, Henry. 1959. The Failure of the "New Economics, New York: Van Nostrand

Hazlitt, Henry. 1965. "Back to Gold?" The Freeman: Ideas on Liberty, Vol. 15, No. 10, October; http://www.fee.org/publications/the-freeman/article.asp?aid=7670

Hazlitt, Henry. 1979. "Economics in One Lesson." New York: Arlington House Publishers

Hazlitt, Henry. 1980. "How to Return to Gold?" The Freeman: Ideas on Liberty, Vol. 30, No. 9, September; http://www.fee.org/publications/the-freeman/article.asp?aid=458

Hazlitt, Henry, ed. 1983[1960]. The Critics of Keynesian Economics New York: New York University Press

Heinrich, David J. 2004. "Notes on 'Epistemological Problems of Economics' by David Gordon." June 8; http://blog.mises.org/blog/archives/2004_06.asp

Helfferich, Karl. 1923. Das Geld, 6th ed. Leipzig. (1924. Money. London). Cited in Mises (1980, 96).

Henderson, David R. 2001. The Joy of Freedom: An Economist's Odyssey, Financial Times Prentice Hall.

Herbener, Jeffrey M. 1991. "Ludwig von Mises and the Austrian School of Economics." Review of Austrian Economics, Vol. 5, No. 2, pp. 33-50; http://www.mises.org/journals/rae/pdf/rae5_2_2.pdf

Herbener, Jeffrey M., ed. 1992. The Meaning of Ludwig von Mises: Contributions in Economics, Sociology, Epistemology and Political Philosophy. Auburn: Ludwig von Mises Institute.

Herbener, Jeffrey M. 1997. "The Pareto Rule and Welfare Economics" The Review of Austrian Economics 10(1): 79-106.)

Herbener, Jeffrey M. 2002. "After the Age of Inflation: Austrian Proposals for Monetary Reform," The Quarterly Journal of Austrian Economics, Vol. 5, No. 4, Winter: 5-19.

Higgins, Colin. 2005. "Response to Block and Barnett, 'A Positive Programme for Laissez -Faire Capitalism," The Journal of Corporate Citizenship, Issue 19, Autumn, pp. 51-52;

Higgs, Robert. 1992. "Wartime Prosperity? A Reassessment of the U.S. Economy in the 1940s." Journal of Economic History. 52 (March): 41 – 60.

Higgs, Robert. 1995. "The Myth of 'Failed' Policies." The Free Market. June. Vol. 13, No. 6. http://www.mises.org/freemarket_detail.asp?control=239&sortorder=articledate

Higgs, Robert. 1997. "Regime Uncertainty: Why the Great Depression Lasted So Long and Why Prosperity Resumed after the War." The Independent Review. 1(4): 561-590.

High, Jack. 1984-1985. "Bork's Paradox: Static vs Dynamic Efficiency in Antitrust Analysis," Comtemporary Policy Issues, Vol. 3, pp. 21-34;

Hill, Peter J., and Meiners, Roger E., eds. 1998. Who Owns the Environment? New York: Rowman and Littlefield

Hoey, Richard B. 2001. "Pushing on a string? The State of the Debate"; http://www.mellon.com/news/stateofthedebate/SD3.pdf

Holcombe, Randall. 1995. Economic Models and Methodology. Westport, CT: Greenwood

Hoppe, Hans-Hermann. 1988. Praxeology and Economic Science. Auburn, Al.: Mises Institute, Auburn University.

Hoppe, Hans-Hermann. 1989A. "Fallacies of the Public Goods Theory and the Production of Security," The Journal of Libertarian Studies, Vol. IX, No. 1, Winter, pp. 27-46; http://www.mises.org/journals/jls/9_1/9_1_2.pdf

Hoppe, Hans-Hermann. 1989B. "In Defense of Extreme Rationalism: Thoughts on Donald McClosky's The Rhetoric of Economics," Review of Austrian Economics, 3, pp. 179-214.

Hoppe, Hans-Hermann. 1989C. A Theory of Socialism and Capitalism, Boston, MA: Kluwer Academic Publishers.

Hoppe, Hans-Hermann. 1989D. "Capitalist Production and the Problem of Monopoly," A Theory of Socialism and Capitalism: Economics, Politics and Ethics, Boston: Dordrecht, pp. 167-186

Hoppe, Hans-Hermann. 1990. "Banking, Nation States, and International Politics: A Sociological Reconstruction of the Present Economic Order," Review of Austrian Economics, 4, pp. 55-87;

Hoppe, Hans-Hermann. 1991. "De-Socialization in a United Germany," Review of Austrian Economics, 5(2), pp. 77-106.

Hoppe, Hans-Hermann. 1992. "On Praxeology and the Praxeological Foundation of Epistemology and Ethics." Herbener, J., ed. The Meaning of Ludwig von Mises. Boston: Dordrecht

Hoppe, Hans-Hermann. 1993. The Economics and Ethics of Private Property: Studies in Political Economy and Philosophy. Boston: Kluwer

Hoppe, Hans-Hermann. 1994A. "Austrian Rationalism in the Age of the Decline of Positivism," in Austrian Economics: Perspectives on the Past and Prospects for the Future, Vol. 17, Richard M. Ebeling, ed., Hillsdale, MI: Hillsdale College Press, pp. 59-96.

Hoppe, Hans-Hermann. 1994B. "How is Fiat Money Possible? or, The Devolution of Money and Credit," Review of Austrian Economics, 7(2), pp. 49-74.

Hoppe, Hans-Hermann. 1995 [1988]. Economic Science and the Austrian Method. Auburn, AL: Ludwig von Mises Institute; previously published in shorter version as Praxeology and Economic Science, Auburn, AL: Ludwig von Mises Institute, 1988; http://www.mises.org/esandtam/pfe3.asp

Hoppe, Hans-Hermann. 1996. "Socialism: A Property or Knowledge Problem?" Review of Austrian Economics, 9(1), pp. 147-154.

Hoppe, Hans-Hermann. 2001. Democracy The God That Failed: The Economics and Politics of Monarchy, Democracy, and Natural Order. Rutgers University, N.J.: Transaction Publishers.

Hoppe, Hans-Hermann, ed. 2003. "National Defense and the Theory of Externalities, Public Goods and Clubs." The Myth of National Defense: Essays on the Theory and History of Security Production, Hoppe, Hans-Hermann, ed., Auburn: Mises Institute

Hoppe, Hans Hermann. 2005. "Must Austrians Embrace Indifference?," Quarterly Journal of Austrian Economics, Vol. 8, No. 4, Winter, pp. 87-91; http://www.mises.org/journals/qjae/pdf/qjae8_4_6.pdf

Hoppe, Hans-Hermann. 2007. "The Misesian Case Against Keynes." March 31; http://www.mises.org/story/2492

Hoppe, Hans-Hermann and Walter Block. 2002. "Property and Exploitation," International Journal of Value-Based Management, Vol. 15, No. 3, pp. 225-236; http://www.mises.org/etexts/propertyexploitation.pdf

Hoppe, Hans-Hermann, with Guido Hulsmann and Walter Block. 1998. "Against Fiduciary Media," Quarterly Journal of Austrian Economics, Vol. 1, No. 1, pp. 19-50, http://www.mises.org/journals/qjae/pdf/qjae1_1_2.pdf

Horwitz, Morton J. 1977. The Transformation of American Law: 1780-1860, Cambridge: Harvard University Press

Horwitz, Steven. 2005. "Monetary Disequilibrium Theory and Austrian Macroeconomics: Further Thoughts on a Synthesis." In Roger Koppl, ed., Money, Markets, and Method: Essays in Honor of Leland B. Yeager. London: Routledge.

HR 29, First Session, 106Th Congress. http://thomas.loc.gov/cgi-bin/query/z?c106:h.r.29.ih:

Huang, H., and J. Whalley. 2003. "The Use of Literature Based Elasticity Estimates in Calibrated Models of Trade-Wage Decompositions: A Calibmetric Approach"; http://www.ssc.uwo.ca/economics/newsletter/misc/2003/Huang_WhalleyOct20.pdf

Hughes, Arthur Middleton. 1997. "The Recession of 1990: An Austrian Explanation," The Review of Austrian Economics, Vol. 10, No. 1

Hughes, Mark. 1988. "Review of Walter W. Powell, ed., The Nonprofit Sector: A Research Handbook, New Haven: Yale University Press, 1987," in The Philanthropist, Vol. 7, No. 4, Summer, pp. 61-65

Hughes, Mark. 1989. "Unmasking the Two-Tier Tax-Credit Scheme." The Philanthropist 8 (2): 16-31.

Hughes, Mark. 1990. "Counterpoint: A Response to Bennett and DiLorenzo, The Philanthropist, Vol. 9, No. 3, Fall, pp. 43-56.

Hulsmann, Jorg Guido. 1996. "Free Banking and the Free Bankers." Review of Austrian Economics. Vol. 9, No. 1. pp. 3-53; http://www.mises.org/journals/rae/pdf/rae9_1_1.pdf

Hulsmann, Jorg Guido. 1998. "Free Banking Fractional Reserves: Reply to Pascal Salin." *Review of Austrian Economics*, Vol. 1, No. 3; 67-71; http://www.mises.org/journals/qjae/pdf/qjae1_3_8.pdf

Hülsmann, Jörg Guido. 1999. "Economic Science and Neoclassicism." Quarterly Journal of Austrian Economics, Vol. 2 Num. 4, pp. 1-20; http://www.mises.org/journals/qjae/pdf/qjae2_4_1.pdf

Hulsmann, Jorg Guido. 2000A. "A Realist Approach to Equilibrium Analysis." Quarterly Journal of Austrian Economics. Vol. 3, No. 4, Winter, pp. 3-51; http://www.mises.org/journals/qjae/pdf/qjae3_4_1.pdf

Hulsmann, Jorg Guido. 2000B. "Banks Cannot Create Money", The Independent Review: A Journal of Political Economy, vol. 5, no. 1, summer, pp. 101—110; http://www.independent.org/pdf/tir/tir_05_1_hulsman.pdf

Hülsmann, Jörg Guido. 2000C. "Economic Principles and Monetary Institutions": Review Essay of Lawrence H. White's The Theory of Monetary Institutions; Journal des Economistes et des Etudes Humaines; Volume 10, Numbéro 2/3, Juin/Septembre, pp. 421-441

Hulsmann, Jorg Guido. 2003. "Facts and Counterfactuals in Economic Law." The Journal of Libertarian Studies. Vol. 17, Num. 1, pp. 57-102; http://www.mises.org/journals/jls/17_1/17_1_3.pdf

Hummel, Jeffrey R. 1979. "Problems with Austrian Business Cycle Theory," Reason Papers, No. 5, Winter, 41-53. http://www.reasonpapers.com/pdf/05/rp_5_4.pdf

Hummel, Jeffrey. 1990. "National Goods vs. Public Goods: Defense, Disarmament and Free Riders," The Review of Austrian Economics, Vol. IV, pp. 88-122; http://www.mises.org/journals/rae/pdf/rae4_1_4.pdf

Hutt, William H. 1940. "The Concept of Consumers' Sovereignty." Economic Journal. March: 66-77.

Hutt, William. 1956. "The Yield from Money Held." In On Freedom and Free Enterprise, ed. Mary Sennholz. Van Nostrand Co., Inc., pp. 196-216.

Hutt, William H. 1979. The Keynesian Episode Indianapolis: Liberty Press.

Ikeda, Sanford. 1997. Dynamics of the Mixed Economy: Toward a Theory of Interventionism London and New York: Routledge.

Interview of Hans Hoppe by Emrah Akkurt. 2004. Turkey-Association for Liberal Thinking. Special issue of the economic journal Piyasa on socialism; http://www.mises.org/fullstory.asp?control=1455; accessed on 4/6/04

Jansen, Dennis W., Charles D. Delorme and Robert B. Ekelund, Jr. 1994. Intermediate Macroeconomics. St. Paul: West Publishing.

JEL Classification System: http://www.aeaweb.org/journal/jel_class_system.htm

Jevons, William Stanley. 1965 [1871]. The Theory of Political Economy, 3d ed. London, New York, Macmillan and Co.

Johnson, M. Bruce, ed. 1982. Resolving the Housing Crisis: Government Policy, Decontrol, and the Public Interest, San Francisco: The Pacific Institute

Jonker, Jan. 2005. "The Invisible Hand Revisited: Some Personal Reflections on Block and Barnett, 'A Positive Programme for Laissez -Faire Capitalism," The Journal of Corporate Citizenship, Issue 19, Autumn, pp. 53-54

Kaul, Inge, Isabelle Grunberg, and Marc Stern, eds. 1999. Global Public Goods: International Cooperation in the 21st Century. Oxford University Press.

Kaza, Greg. 1996. "Is There a Case for the Gold Standard?" The Intercollegiate Review
http://www.mmisi.org/ir/32_01/kaza.pdf

Keizer, William. 1987. "Two Forgotten Articles by Ludwig von Mises on the Rationality of Socialist Economic Calculation," Review of Austrian Economics, 1, pp. 109-122.

Keynes, John Maynard. 1913. Indian Currency and Finance. Reprinted in Keynes, Collected Writings, vol. 1.

Keynes, John Maynard. 1923. Tract on Monetary Reform. Reprinted in Keynes, Collected Writings, vol. 4.

Keynes John Maynard. 1930A. A Treatise on Money. Vol. 1: The Pure Theory of Money. 1930. Reprinted in Keynes, Collected Writings, vol. 5.

Keynes John Maynard. 1930B. A Treatise on Money. Vol. 2: The Applied Theory of Money. 1930. Reprinted in Keynes, Collected Writings, vol. 6.

Keynes, J. M. 1936. General Theory of Money, Interest and Money. New York: Harcourt, Brace.

Kinsella, Stephan. 1995. "Legislation and the Discovery of Law in a Free Society." Journal of Libertarian Studies. 11 (2): 132-181.

Kinsella, Stephan. 1996A. "Punishment and Proportionality: The Estoppel Approach," Journal of Libertarian Studies, Vol. 12, No. 1, Spring, pp. 51-73;

Kinsella, Stephan. 1996B. "New Rationalist Directions in Libertarian Rights Theory," Journal of Libertarian Studies, Vol. 12, No. 2, Spring, pp. 313-326;

Kinsella, Stephan. 1997. "A Libertarian Theory of Punishment and Rights," Loyola of Los Angeles Law Review, Vol. 30, pp. 607-645;

Kinsella, N. Stephan. 1998. "Knowledge, Calculation, Conflict, and Law," book review of The Structure of Liberty: Justice and the Rule of Law by Randy E. Barnett , New York: Oxford University (Clarendon Press); Quarterly Journal of Austrian Economics. Vol. 2, No. 4, pp. 49-71; http://www.mises.org/journals/qjae/pdf/Qjae2_4_4.pdf

Kinsella, N. Stephan. 2001. "Against Intellectual Property." Journal of Libertarian Studies 15 (2): 1-53; http://www.stephankinsella.com/publications/against_ip_jls.pdf

Kinsella, N. Stephan. 2003. "Reply to Palmer." August 18; http:blog.lewrockwell.com/lewrw/archives/001240.html

Kinsella, N. Stephan. 2005. "Palmer Lies about Involuntary Unemployment" July 10; http://ancapistan.typepad.com/the_palmer_periscope/2005/07/palmer_lies_abo.html

Kirzner, Israel M. 1963. Market Theory and the Price System, Princeton N.J.: D. Van Nostrand

Kirzner, Israel M. 1973. Competition and Entrepreneurship. Chicago: University of Chicago Press.

Kirzner, Israel. 1975. The Economic Point of View: An Essay in the History of Economic Thought, Kansas City: Sheed and Ward

Kirzner, Israel M. 1976A. "On the Austrian Method in Economics," The Foundations of Modern Austrian Economics, Edwin G. Dolan, ed. Kansas City: Sheed and Ward, pp. 40-51;

Kirzner, Israel M. 1976B. "Austrian Definitions of the Money Supply." The Foundations of Modern Austrian Economics, Edwin G. Dolan, ed. Kansas City: Sheed and Ward

Kirzner, Israel M. 1976C. The Economic Point of View. Kansas City: Sheed and Ward

Kirzner, Israel M. 1979. Perception, Opportunity and Profit, Chicago: University of Chicago Press

Kirzner, Israel M., ed. 1982. Method, Process, and Austrian Economics: Essays in Honor of Ludwig von Mises Lexington, MA: Lexington Books.

Kirzner, Israel M. 1985. Discovery and the Capitalist Process, Chicago: University of Chicago Press

Kirzner, Israel, ed. 1986. Subjectivism, Intelligibility and Economic Understanding, New York: New York University Press

Kirzner, Israel M. 1989. Discovery, Capitalism and Distributive Justice, Oxford: Basil Blackwell,

Kirzner, Israel M. 1993. "The Pure Time-Preference Theory of Interest." In Herbener, Jeffrey M., ed., The Meaning of Ludwig von Mises: Contributions in Economics, Sociology, Epistemology and Political Philosophy. Auburn: Ludwig von Mises Institute, pp. 166-192.

Klein, Daniel B. 2006. "A Plea to Retire the term 'Austrian' and Replace it with 'Spontaneous Order'"; http://economics.gmu.edu/pboettke/workshop/Spring_06/Plea_to_Retire_Austrian.doc

Klein, Peter G. 1996. "Economic Calculation and the Limits of Organization" Review of Austrian Economics, 9(2), pp 3- 28.

Klein, Peter G. 1999. "Entrepreneurship and Corporate Governance," Quarterly Journal of Austrian Economics, Vol. 2, No. 2, pp. 19-49.

Knies, Karl. 1885. Geld und Kredit. Bd. I. Berlin: Weidmann. Cited in Mises (1980, 96).

Krecke, E. 1996. Law and the Market Order: An Austrian Critique of the Economic Analysis of Law, Journal des Economistes et des Etudes Humaines 7(1), March, pp.19-37;

Kudlow, Larry. 2002. "Milton's on the money: The Fed should tune in to Friedman." National Review On Line. October 4; http://www.nationalreview.com/kudlow/kudlow100402.asp

Kuznetsov, Yuri. 1990. "Fiat Money as an Administrative Good," The Review of Austrian Economics, Vol. 10, No. 2, pp. 111-114; Mises, Ludwig von. "Money," in Money, Method, and the Market Process, Richard M. Ebeling, ed. Boston, MA: Kluwer Academic Publishers, pp. 55-112

LaBletta, Nicole and Walter Block. 1999. "The Restoration of the American Dream: A Case for Abolishing Welfare," Humanomics, Vol. 15, No 4, pp. 55-65

Lachmann, Ludwig M. 1956. Capital and Its Structure. London: London School of Economics and Political Science.

Lachmann, Ludwig. 1969. "Methodological Individualism and the Market Economy." In: Erich Striessler, ed Roads to Freedom: Essays in Honour of Friedrich A. von Hayek. London: Routledge & Kegan Paul.

Lachmann, Ludwig M. 1976A. "On the Central Concept of Austrian Economics: Market Process," in Foundations of Modern Austrian Economics, ed., Edwin G. Dolan, Kansas City: Sheed & Ward

Lachmann, Ludwig. 1976B. "From Mises to Shackle: An Essay on Austrian Economics and the Kaleidic Society." Journal of Economic Literature. 14(10): 54-62.

Lachmann, Ludwig. 1977. Capital, Expectations and the Market Process, Kansas City: Sheed, Andrews and McMeel

Laffer, Arthur, and Charles Kadlec. 1981. "The Point of Linking the Dollar to Gold." Wall Street Journal, October 13.

Landsburg, Steve. 2001. Price Theory and Applications. South-Western College Pub; 5th edition

Lankford, K. 1999. "How Does FDIC Insurance Work?"; http://banking.yahoo.com/q0728.html

Lavoie, Don. 1981. "A Critique of the Standard Account of the Socialist Calculation Debate," The Journal of Libertarian Studies, Vol. V, No. 1, Winter, pp. 41-88.

Lavoie, Don. 1982. "The Development of the Misesian Theory of Interventionism" in Method, Process and Austrian Economics: Essays in Honor of Ludwig von Mises, Israel Kirzner, ed. Lexington, MA: D.C. Heath and Company; pp. 169-183.

Leconte, Pierre. 2003. La tragédie monétaire, 2nd ed., Paris: François-Xavier de Guibert

Leeson, P. T. 2007. "An-arrgh-chy: The Law and Economics of Pirate Organization," Journal of Political Economy, Vol. 115, No. 6, pp. 1049-1094

Leeson, Peter T., and Edward P. Stringham. 2005. "Is Government Inevitable? Comment on Holcombe's Analysis." Independent Review. Vol. 9, No. 4, Spring, 543-549.

Lerner, Abba P. 1952. "The Essential Properties of Interest and Money." The Quarterly Journal of Economics. 66 (2): 172-193.

Levin, Michael. 1997. Why Race Matters: Race Differences and What They Mean, New York: Praeger

Lewin, Peter. 1997. "Rothbard and Mises on Interest: An Exercise in Theoretical Purity." Journal of the History of Economic Thought. Spring: 141-159. http//www.utdallas.edu/~plewin/ptpt.pdf.

Lewin, Peter and Steven E. Phelan. 1999. Firms, Strategies, and Resources: Contributions from Austrian Economics, Quarterly Journal of Austrian Economics, Vol. 2, No. 2, pp. 3-18;

Margolis, Stephen E. and Stan Liebowitz. 1999. Winners, Losers & Microsoft: Competition and Antitrust in High Technology. Independent Institute

Loasby, Brian J. 1998. "Coordination Failure: economic theory in the 1930s." Historical Perspectives on Macroeconomics: Sixty years after the General Theory. Philippe Fontaine and Albert Jolink, eds. London: Routledge.

Locke, John. 1948. An Essay Concerning the True Origin, Extent and End of Civil Government, in E. Barker, ed., Social Contract, New York: Oxford University Press, pp. 17-18.

Loeber, Thomas S. 1961. Foreign aid: our tragic experiment, New York: Norton

Long, Roderick T. 1993. "Abortion, Abandonment, and Positive Rights: The Limits of Compulsory Altruism," Social Philosophy and Policy vol. 10 no.1 (Winter)

Long, Roderick. 2004. "Libertarian Anarchism: Responses to Ten Objections" http://www.lewrockwell.com/long/long11.html

Lutz, Friedrich A. 2006. The theory of interest. 2nd ed. London: Aldine

Macfie, Alec L. 1934. Theories of the Trade Cycle. London: Macmillan

Machan, Tibor. 1978. "Against nonlibertarian natural rights," The Journal of Libertarian Studies, Vol. 2, No. 3, Fall, pp. 233-238

Machan, Tibor, ed. 1982. The Libertarian Reader, Totowa, N.J.: Rowman and Littlefield

Machan, Tibor. 1990. Capitalism and Individualism. New York: St. Martin's Press.

Machlup, Fritz. 1967. "Theories of the Firm: Marginalist, Behavioral, Managerial," American Economic Review, 57:1-33

Machovec, F.M. 1995. Perfect Competition and the Transformation of Economics. New York: Routledge, 12.

Maltsev, Yuri N. 1993. Requiem for Marx. Auburn, AL: Ludwig von Mises Institute.

Mankiw, N. G. 2001. Principles of Macroeconomics. 2nd ed. Harcourt College Publishers.

McChesney, Fred. 1991. "Antitrust and Regulation: Chicago's Contradictory Views," Cato Journal, Vol. 10.

McConnell, Campbell R and Stanley L. Brue. 2002. Economics: Principles, Problems and Policies. 15th ed. Boston: Irwin, McGraw-Hill.

McDonald, Forrest. 1962. Insull. Chicago: University of Chicago Press

McElroy, Wendy. 2001. "The Chilling Effect," Liberty, December, pp. 37-39.

McElroy, Wendy. 2005. "Will Science Trump Politics in Resolving Abortion Debate? September 22. http://lewrockwell.com/mcelroy/mcelroy91.html

McGee, Robert W. 1992. "Should Superfund Be Wasted? The Case to Trash the Comprehensive Environmental Response, Compensation and Liability Act of 1980 (CERCLA)," Glendale Law Review, Vol. 11, Nos. 1-2, 1992, 120-142.

McGee, Robert W. 1993. "Superfund: It' Time for Repeal After a Decade of Failure," UCLA Journal of Environmental Law and Policy, 12:1, pp. 165-182.

McGee, Robert, and Block, Walter. 1994. "Pollution Trading Permits as a Form of Market Socialism, and the Search for a Real Market Solution to Environmental Pollution," Fordham University Law and Environmental Journal, Vol. VI, No. 1, Fall, pp. 51-77

McNeill, Desmond. 1981. The contradictions of foreign aid, London : Croom Helm.

Medema, Steven G. 1997. "The Trial of Homo Economicus: What Law and Economics Tells Us about the Development of Economic Imperialism," New Economics and Its History: History of Political Economy Annual Supplement 29: 122-42.

Medema, Steven G., and Samuels, Warren J. 1997. "Ronald Coase on Economic Policy Analysis: Framework and Implications," in Steven G. Medema, ed., Coasean Economics: Law and Economics and the New Institutional Economics. Boston: Kluwer Academic Publishers, pp. 161-183.

Medema, Steven G., and Zerbe, Jr. Richard O. 1997. "Ronald Coase, the British Tradition, and the Future of Economic Method," in Steven G. Medema, ed., Coasean Economics: Law and Economics and the New Institutional Economics. Boston: Kluwer Academic Publishers, 209-238.

Menger, Carl. 1950[1871]. Principles of Economics. Editors and translators, James Dingwall and Bert F. Hoselitz, Glencoe, IL: Free Press; http://www.mises.org/etexts/menger/principles.asp

Menger, Carl. 1960. "Toward a Systematic Classification of the Economic Sciences," in Essay in European Economic Thought, Louise Sommer, ed. Princeton, NJ: Van Nostand, pp. 1-38; and Israel M. Kirzner, Classics in Austrian Economics, London: William Pickering, 1994, pp. 2-32;

Menger, Carl. 1980 [1923]. Grundsätze der Volkswirtschafyslehre. 2nd ed. Vienna. Cited in Mises, 95.

Menger, Carl. 1981. Problems of Economics and Sociology, James Dingwall and Bert F. Hoselitz, trans. and an Introduction by Friedrich A. Hayek, New York: New York University Press, 1981. Also published under Investigations into the Method of the Social Sciences, Francis J. Nock, trans., New York: New York University Press, 1985;

Mill, John Stuart. 1965. Principles of Political Economy. J.M. Robson, ed. The Collected Works of John Stuart Mill, Vol. 3

Miller, Roger Leroy and David Van Hoose. 2001. Macroeconomics: Theories, Policies and International Applications. 2nd ed. Cincinnati: South-Western College Publishing.

Mises, Ludwig. 1952. Epilogue to The Theory of Money and Credit, "The United States' Return to a Sound Currency."

Mises, Ludwig von. 1957. Theory and History, New Haven: Yale University Press http://www.mises.org/th.asp

Mises, Ludwig von. 1969. Omnipotent Government, New Rochelle, N.Y.: Arlington House

Mises, Ludwig von. 1971 [1912]. The Theory of Money and Credit. Foundation for Economic Education.

Mises, Ludwig von. 1972. The Anticapitalist Mentality, South Holland, IL: Libertarian Press

Mises, Ludwig von. 1975[1933]. "Economic Calculation in the Socialist Commonwealth," in Hayek, F.A., ed., Collectivist Economic Planning, Clifton, N.J.: Kelley

Mises, Ludwig von. 1976. Epistemological Problems in Economics, New York: New York University Press

Mises, L. von. 1977. A Critique of Interventionism, New Rochelle, N.Y.: Arlington House; http://www.mises.org/etexts/mises/interventionism/contents.asp

Mises, Ludwig von. 1978A. On the Manipulation of Money and Credit, Dobbs Ferry, NY: Free Market Books; http://www.mises.org/manipulation/section2.asp

Mises, Ludwig von. 1978B. The Ultimate Foundation of Economic Science, Kansas City: Sheed Andrews and McMeel; Rizzo, Mario, "Praxeology and Econometrics: A Critique of Positivist Economics," in New Directions in Austrian Economics, Louis Spardo, ed. Kansas City: Sheed Andrews and McMeel, 1979, pp. 40-56;

Mises, L. von. 1980 [1971, 1912]. The Theory of Money and Credit. Indianapolis: Liberty Classics.

Mises, Ludwig von. 1981 [1969]. Socialism, Indianapolis: LibertyPress/LibertyClassics.

Mises, Ludwig von. 1983[1981, 1971, 1953, 1912].. The Theory of Money and Credit, Indianapolis: LibertyPress/LibertyClassics

Mises, Ludwig von. 1985. Theory and History: An Interpretation of Social and Economic Evoluation, Auburn, AL: Ludwig von Mises Institute

Mises, Ludwig von. 1990A. "The Treatment of 'Irrationality' in the Social Sciences," Money, Method, and the Market Process, Richard M. Ebeling, ed., Boston, MA: Kluwer Academic Publishers, pp. 16-36;

Mises, Ludwig von. 1990B. "Epistemological Relativism in the Sciences of Human Action," in Money, Method, and the Market Process, Richard M. Ebeling, ed., Boston, MA: Kluwer Academic Publishers, pp. 37-54

Mises, L. von. 1990C [1932]. "The Position of Money among Economic Goods." In R. M. Ebeling, ed. Money, Method, and the Market Process." Kluwer academic Publishers.

Mises, Ludwig von. 1998 [1949, 1963, 1966, 1996]. Human Action, Scholars' Edition. Auburn: Mises Institute. http://www.mises.org/humanaction.asp

Moakley, Joe (D – MA) 1999. http://www.house.gov/rules/rules_moak03.htm

Molyneux, Stefan. 2007. "Stateless Dictatorships: How a Free Society Prevents the Re-emergence of a Government" June 27; http://www.lewrockwell.com/molyneux/molyneux37.html

Moore, Thomas Gale. 1991. Central Planning USA-Style: The Case Against Corporate Average Fuel Economy (CAFE) Standards. Stanford: Hoover Institution

Muhammad, Marie. 1999. "Indonesia: From Uncertainty to Certainty." Conference on Crisis & Credit: Restructuring Asia's Financial Sector. http://www.asiasociety.org/speeches/muhammad.html

Mundell, Robert. 1981. "Gold Would Serve into the 21st Century." Wall Street Journal, September 30.

Murphy, Robert P. 2002. Chaos Theory: Two Essays on Market Anarchy. New York: RJ Communications LLC.

Murphy, Robert P. 2003. "An Austrian in Grad School: Confronting the Mainstream." July 28. http://www.mises.org/story/1285

Murphy, Robert. 2005. "But Wouldn't Warlords Take Over? July, 7. http://www.mises.org/story/1855

Murray, Charles. 1984. Losing Ground: American Social Policy from 1950 to 1980, New York: Basic Books

Murray, Charles. 1997. What It Means to be a Libertarian, New York: Broadway Books
New York: Harper and Row.

North, Gary. 1986. Honest Money: Biblical Principles of Money and Banking, chaps 11-13

North, Gary. 1990. Tools of Dominion: The Case Laws of Exodus, Tyler, TX: Institute for Christian Economics.

North, Gary. 1992. The Coase Theorem, Tyler, TX: The Institute for Christian Economics

North, Gary. 2001. "Pushing on a string?" December 27; http://www.lewrockwell.com/north/north75.html

North, Gary. 2002. Undermining Property Rights: Coase and Becker, The Journal of Libertarian Studies: An Interdisciplinary Review, Vol. 16, No. 4, Fall, pp. 75-100; http://www.mises.org/journals/jls/16_4/16_4_5.pdf

North, Gary. 2004. "Sitting on a string?" January 15; http://www.lewrockwell.com/north/north242.html

Nozick, Robert. 1974. Anarchy, State and Utopia. New York: Basic Books.

Nozick, Robert. 1977. "On Austrian methodology," Synthese 36, pp. 353-392

Oakeshott, M. 1975. *On Human Conduct.* Oxford, England: Oxford University Press.
O'Driscoll, Gerald P. 1977. Economics as a Coordination Problem: The Contributions of Friedrich A. Hayek, Kansas City: Sheed, Andrews and McMeel.

OED 1: http://dictionary.oed.com/cgi/entry/00299035

OED 2: http://dictionary.oed.com/cgi/entry/00299033

Olasky, Marvin. 1992. The Tragedy of American Compassion, Chicago: Regnery Gateway.

Olson, Charles B. 1979. "Law in Anarchy." The Libertarian Forum. November-December, 4; http://64.233.167.104/u/Mises?q=cache:gFT18_ZusWoJ:www.mises.org/journals/lf/1979/1979_11-12.pdf+two+teeth+for+a+tooth&hl=en&ie=UTF-8

Osterfeld, David. 1989. "Anarchism and the Public Goods Issue: Law, Courts and the Police," The Journal of Libertarian Studies, Vol. 9, No. 1, Winter, pp. 47-68; http://www.mises.org/journals/jls/9_1/9_1_3.pdf

Osterfeld, David. 1992. Prosperity versus planning: how government stifles economic growth, New York: Oxford University Press; Oxford: Blackwell Oxford: Blackwell

Pamini, Paolo. 2002. "Behavioral Finance and Monetary Policy." Masters' Thesis. University of Zurich.

Pashigian, B. Peter. 1998. Price Theory and Applications, Irwin McGraw-Hill

Pasour, Jr., E.C., 1981, "The Free Rider as a Basis for Government Intervention," The Journal of Libertarian Studies, Vol. V, No. 4, Fall, pp. 453-464; http://www.mises.org/journals/jls/5_4/5_4_6.pdf

Paul, Ron. 1985. "The Political and Economic Agenda for a Real Gold Standard," delivered at the Mises Institute's 1985 conference on the gold standard; final chapter in The Gold Standard: Perspectives in the Austrian School: http://www.mises.org/books/goldstandard.pdf; http://www.mises.org/story/2826

Peacock, Alan. 1979. "The Limitations of Public Goods Theory: The Lighthouse Revisited," The Economic Analysis of Public Goods Theory and Related Themes, Martin Robertson, ed., Oxford Press

Pellengahr, I. 1986A. "Austrians Versus Austrians I: A Subjectivist View of Interest." In Faber, M. ed., Studies in Austrian Capital Theory, Investment and Time. New York: Springer – Verlag, pp. 60-77.

Pellengahr, I. 1986B. "Austrians Versus Austrians II: Functionalist Versus Essentialist Theories of Interest." In Faber, M. ed., Studies in Austrian Capital Theory, Investment and Time. New York: Springer – Verlag, pp. 78-96.

Pellengahr, I. 1996. The Austrian Subjective Theory of Interest: An Investigation into the History of Thought. Frankfurt: Peter Lang.

Peltzman, Sam. 1973. "An Evaluation of Consumer Protection Legislation: The 1962 Drug Amendments." Journal of Political Economy. Sept.-Oct. p.1049-91.

Perkins, Richard and Ernestine Perkens. 1971. Precondition for Peace and Prosperity: Rational Anarchy. Ontario: Phibbs Printing World

Phelps, E.S., A.A. Alchian, C. C. Holt, et. al., eds. 1970. Microeconomic Foundations of Employment and Inflation Theory, New York: Norton

Piger, Jeremy. 2003. "Pushing on a string." Monetary Trends. The Federal Reserve Bank of St. Louis; http://research.stlouisfed.org/publications/mt/20030301/cover.pdf

Pipes, Richard. 2000. Property and Freedom: The story of how through the centuries private ownership has promoted liberty and the rule of law, New York: Knopf

Posner, Richard. 1976. Antitrust Law: an Economic Perspective. University of Chicago Press.

Posner, Richard A. 1992. Economic Analysis of Law, fourth ed., Boston: Little Brown.

Powell, Jim. 2005. Wilson's War: How Woodrow Wilson's Great Blunder Led to Hitler, Lenin, Stalin, and World War II. Crown Forum

Prowse, Michael. 1996. "Austrian Economics and the Public Mind" The Austrian Economics Newsletter Spring. Vol. 16, No. 1 http://www.mises.org/journals/aen/Aen_sp96.asp?printFriendly=Yes

Rader, Randall R. 1980. "Remonetizing Gold, Again." The Freeman: Ideas on Liberty. Vol. 30, No. 8, September; http://www.fee.org/publications/the-freeman/article.asp?aid=461

Rashid, Salim, and Abdus Samad. 1996. "Portfolio Management of the Free Banks of Illinois: An Examination of Historical Allegations," Review of Austrian Economics, 9(1), pp. 55-76

Rawls, John. 1971. A Theory of Justice, Cambridge: Harvard University Press

Raz, Joseph. 1979. "The Rule of Law and its Virtues." In Robert L. Cunningham, ed. Liberty and the Rule of Law. College Station, Texas: Texas A&M University Press: 3-21.

Read, Leonard, E. 1964. Anything That's Peaceful. Irvington-on-Hudson, N.Y.: Foundation for Economic Education.

Read, Leonard, E. 1977. Awake for Freedom's Sake, Irvington-on-Hudson, N.Y.: Foundation for Economic Education

Reisman, George. 1996. Capitalism. Ottawa, Il.: Jameson Books

Reisman, George. 2008. "Our Financial House of Cards," March 25; http://www.mises.org/story/2926

Riddell, Roger. 1987. Foreign aid reconsidered, Baltimore : Johns Hopkins University Press.

Ringer, Fritz K. 1969. The German Inflation of 1923. New York: Oxford University Press.

Rizzo, Mario. 1979A. "Praxeology and Econometrics: A Critique of Positivist Economics," New Directions in Austrian Economics, Louis Spadaro, ed., Kansas City: Sheed Andrews and McMeel, pp. 40-56

Rizzo, Mario J. 1979B. "Uncertainty, Subjectivity, and the Economic Analysis of Law", in Mario J. Rizzo (ed.), Time, Uncertaintly, and Disequilibrium, Lexington, MA: Lexington Books, pp. 71-90

Rizzo, Mario J. 1980. "The Mirage of Efficiency", Hofstra Law Review, Vol 8, pp. 641-658

Robbins, Lionel. An Essay on the Nature and Significance of Economic Science, London: Macmillan, 1932;

Rockwell, Llewellyn H., Jr. 1995. Why Austrian Economics Matters. Auburn AL: The Mises Institute; http://www.mises.org/etexts/why_ae.asp

Rockwell, Llewellyn H. 2003. "Deflation: Hurrah!" The Free Market. Auburn, AL: The Ludwig von Mises Institute, Vol. 23, No. 8, August. http://www.mises.org/freemarket_detail.asp?control=451&sortorder=articledate

Rockwell, Jr., Llewellyn H. 2006. "The French Employment Fiasco" April 11; http://www.mises.org/story/2113

Rogge, Benjamin A. 1979. Can Capitalism Survive? Indianapolis: Liberty Fund

Roscher, Wilhelm. 1906. System der Volkswirtschaf. Ed. Pöhlmann, 24th ed. Vol. Stuttgart. Cited in Mises (1980, 96).

Roth, Timothy P. 2002. Getting Welfare Economics Right. Edward Elgar.

Rothbard, Murray N. 1951A. "Praxeology: Reply to Mr. Schuller." American Economic Review, December

Rothbard, Murray N. 1951B. "Mises's Human Action: Comment." American Economic Review, March

Rothbard, M.N. 1956. "Toward a Reconstruction of Utility and Welfare Economics." In Sennholz, M. ed. On Freedom and Free Enterprise: Essays in Honor of Ludwig von Mises. Princeton, NJ: D. Van Nostrand, 1956, pp.252-253.

Rothbard, Murray N. 1957. "In Defense of Extreme Apriorism," Southern Economic Journal, January, 23(1), pp. 314-320.

Rothbard, Murray N. 1958. "A Hard Look At Foreign Aid." Review of Foreign Aid Reexamined, by H. Schoeck and J. Wiggins (eds.). National Review, November 8, pp. 313-314.

Rothbard, Murray N. 1959. "Challenge to Keynes." Review of The Failure of the New Economics, National Review, August 15, pp. 279-280.

Rothbard, Murray N. 1960. "One-Two Punch." Review of The Critics of Keynesian Economics, by H. Hazlitt (ed.). National Review, December 3, pp. 350-351.

Rothbard, Murray N. 1969. Economic Depressions: Causes and Cures. Lansing, MI: Constitutional Alliance, Inc., March 5. National Issues Series of Politics, Vol. IV, No. 8.

Rothbard, Murray N. 1970. Power and Market: Government and the Economy. Menlo Park Cal.: Institute for Humane Studies

Rothbard, Murray N. 1973. "Praxeology and the Method of Economics," Phenomenology and the Social Sciences, M. Natanson, ed., Evanston, IL: Northwestern University Press, vol. 2, p. 311 342; and Austrian Economics: A Reader Vol. 18, Richard M. Ebeling, ed., Hillsdale, MI.: Hillsdale College Press, 1991, pp. 55-91.

Rothbard, M. 1975 [1963]. America's Great Depression. Kansas City: Sheed Andrews and Ward. http://www.mises.org/rothbard/agd.pdf

Rothbard, Murray N. 1976A. "Praxeology: The Methodology of Austrian Economics," in The Foundations of Modern Austrian Economics. Edwin G. Dolan, ed., Kansas City: Sheed and Ward, pp. 19-39.

Rothbard, Murray N. 1976B. "Deflation Reconsidered." P. Corbin and M. Sabrin (eds.), Geographical Aspects of Inflationary Processes, Vol. I. Pleasantville, NY: Redgrave Publishing

Rothbard, Murray N. 1976C. "Ludwig von Mises and Economic Calculation Under Socialism," Moss, Laurence S., ed., The Economics of Ludwig von Mises, Kansas City: Sheed & Ward, pp. 67-77

Rothbard, Murray N. 1977A [1970]. Power and Market: Government and the Economy. Kansas City: Sheed Andrews and McMeel.

Rothbard, Murray N., ed. 1977B. Capital, Interest and Rent: Essays in the Theory of Distribution Kansas City: Sheed, Andrews and McMeel.

Rothbard, Murray N. 1977C. "Introduction." In Fetter, Frank A., Capital, Interest and Rent: Essays in the Theory of Distribution. Kansas City: Sheed, Andrews and McMeel.

Rothbard, Murray N. 1978A. "Society Without a State." J. R. Pennock and J. W. Chapman (eds.), *Anarchism*: Nomos XIX. New York: New York University Press, pp. 191-207. Originally appeared in *The Libertarian Forum*, January 1975, pp. 3-7. Reprinted in T. R. Machan, *The Libertarian Reader*. Totowa, NJ: Rowman and Littlefield, 1982, pp. 53-63.

Rothbard, Murray N. 1978B [1973]. For a New Liberty, Macmillan, New York; http://www.mises.org/rothbard/ethics/ethics.asp

Rothbard, Murray N. 1979. "Comment: The Myth of Efficiency", in Mario J. Rizzo, ed., Time, Uncertaintly, and Disequilibrium, Lexington, MA: Lexington Books: pp. 91-96

Rothbard, Murray N. 1981. "Forward: to Mises' Theory of Money and Credit." Indianapolis: LibertyFund Edition; http://www.mises.org/Rothbardintros/ThofM&C.asp

Rothbard, M. N. 1982A. Law, Property Rights, and Air Pollution, Cato Journal, Vol. 2, No. 1, Spring; reprinted in Economics and the Environment: A Reconciliation, Walter Block, ed., Vancouver: The Fraser Institute, 1990, pp. 233-279. http://www.mises.org/rothbard/lawproperty.pdf

Rothbard, Murray N. 1982B. The Ethics of Liberty, Humanities Press, Atlantic Highlands, N.J.

Rothbard, Murray N. 1982C. "Interventionism: Comment on Lavoie." I. Kirzner (ed.), *Method, Process, and Austrian Economics*. Lexington, MA: Lexington Books, pp. 185-188.

Rothbard, M. N. 1983A [1975, 1963]. America's Great Depression. 4th ed. New York: Richardson and Snyder; http://www.mises.org/rothbard/agd.pdf

Rothbard, Murray N. 1983B. The Mystery of Banking. New York. Richardson and Snyder, Dutton

Rothbard, Murray N. 1983C. "Should Abortion Be a Crime? The Abortion Question Once More." Libertarian Vanguard, August, pp. 4-5, 8.

Rothbard, Murray N. 1984A. "The Federal Reserve as a Cartelization Device: the Early Years, 1913-1930," in Money in Crisis: the Federal Reserve, the Economy, and Monetary Reform, Barry N. Siegel, ed., Cambridge, MA: Ballinger Publishing, pp. 89-136

Rothbard, Murray N. 1984B. "Eric Mack and the Anarchist Case for War" Libertarian Forum, Vol. 18, Nos. 5-6, May-June, p. 6.

Rothbard, Murray N. 1985A. "Airport Congestion: A Case of Market Failure?" The Free Market. Auburn, AL: The Ludwig von Mises Institute, January, pp. 5-4.

Rothbard, Murray N. 1985B. "The Case for a Genuine Gold Dollar," The Gold Standard: An Austrian Perspective; Llewellyn H. Rockwell, Jr. (ed.). Lexington: Lexington Books; Auburn, AL: Ludwig von Mises Institute, 1992, pp. 1-18;

Rothbard, Murray N. 1987. "Time Preference." In: The New Palgrave: A Dictionary of Economics. New York: Macmillan, as reprinted in Ebeling, R. M., ed., 1991. Austrian Economics: A Reader. Hillsdale College Press, pp. 414-422.

Rothbard, Murray N. 1988. "Outlawing Jobs: The Minimum Wage, Once More." The Free Market. Auburn, AL: The Ludwig von Mises Institute, December, 1, 7-8.

Rothbard, Murray N. 1989A. "The Other Side of the Coin: Free Banking in Chile," Austrian Economics Newsletter, Winter, pp. 1-3

Rothbard, Murray N. 1989B. "Public Choice: A Misshapen Tool." Liberty, May, pp. 20-21.

Rothbard, Murray N. 1990[1963]. What Has Government Done to Our Money? Auburn, AL: The Ludwig von Mises Institute.

Rothbard, Murray N. 1991A. "The End of Socialism and the Calculation Debate Revisited," Review of Austrian Economics, 5(2), pp. 51-70.

Rothbard, Murray N. 1991B. "Deflation, Free or Compulsory." The Free Market. Auburn, AL: The Ludwig von Mises Institute, April, pp. 1, 3-4.

Rothbard, Murray N. 1992A. "Repudiating the National Debt." Chronicles, June, pp. 49-52.

Rothbard, Murray N. 1992B. "Aurophobia: or, Free Banking on What Standard?" Review of Austrian Economics, 6(1), pp. 97-108;

Rothbard, M. N. 1993 [1962, 1970]. Man, Economy, and State. Ludwig von Mises Institute.

Rothbard, M. N. 1994. The Case Against the Fed. Auburn, AL: Ludwig von Mises Institute

Rothbard, Murray N. 1995. Classical Economics: An Austrian Perspective on the History of Economic Thought. Vol. 1 Hants, England: Edward Elgar.

Rothbard, Murray N. 1996A. "Origins of the Welfare State in America," The Journal of Libertarian Studies, Vol. 12, No. 2, Fall, pp. 193-230

Rothbard, Murray N. 1996B. "Economic Depressions: Their Cause and Cure." The Austrian Theory of the Trade Cycle and Other Essays. Auburn, AL: The Ludwig von Mises Institute, pp. 37-64.

Rothbard, Murray N. 1997A. The Logic of Action One: Method, Money, and the Austrian School. Glos, UK: Edward Elgar Publishing Ltd.

Rothbard, Murray N. 1997B. "The Mantle of Science," in The Logic of Action One. Murray N. Rothbard, ed., UK: Edward Elgar Publishing Limited, pp. 3-23

Rothbard, Murray N. 1997C. "What is the Proper Way to Study Man?,"in The Logic of Action One. Murray N. Rothbard, ed., UK: Edward Elgar Publishing Limited, pp. 24-27

Rothbard, Murray N. 1997D. "Praxeology as the Method of the Social Sciences," in The Logic of Action One. Murray N. Rothbard, ed., UK: Edward Elgar Publishing Limited, pp. 28-57.

Rothbard, Murray N. 1997E. "Praxeology: The Methodology of Austrian Economics," in The Logic of Action One. Murray N. Rothbard, ed., UK: Edward Elgar Publishing Limited pp.58-77

Rothbard, Murray N. 1997F. "Praxeology, Value Judgments, and Public Policy," in The Logic of Action One. Murray N. Rothbard, ed., UK: Edward Elgar Publishing Limited, pp.78-99

Rothbard, Murray N. 1997G.j.d. "In Defense of 'Extreme Apriorism'," in The Logic of Action
One. Murray N. Rothbard, ed., UK: Edward Elgar Publishing Limited, pp. 100-108.

Rothbard, Murray N. 1997H [1992]. "The Present State of Austrian Economics." Working Paper from the Ludwig von Mises Institute, November. Reprinted in The Logic of Action One: Method, Money, and the Austrian School. Glos, UK: Edward Elgar Publishing Ltd., pp. 111-172. Reprinted in Journal des Economistes et des Etudes Humaines, Vol. 6, No. 1 (March 1995), pp. 43-89.

Rothbard. Murray N. 1997IJc [1956]. "Toward a Reconstruction of Utility and Welfare Economics." reprinted in The Logic of Action One Lyme, NH: Edward Elgar. pp. 211-254; http://www.mises.org/rothbard/toward.pdf

Rothbard, Murray N. 1997JIL[1976]. "The Austrian Theory of Money." E. G. Dolan (ed.), *The Foundations of Modern Austrian Economics*. Kansas City: Sheed & Ward, Inc., pp. 160-184. Reprinted in *The Logic of Action One: Method, Money, and the Austrian School*. Glos, UK: Edward Elgar Publishing Ltd., 1997, pp. 297-320.

Rothbard, Murray N. 1997Km. "Money, the State, and Modern Mercantilism," The Logic of Action One UK: Edward Elgar Publishing Limited, pp. 321-336

Rothbard, Murray N. 1997L[1978]. "Austrian Definitions of the Supply of Money." Louis Spadaro (ed.), *New Directions in Austrian Economics*. Kansas City: Sheed Andrews and McMeel, Inc., pp. 143-156. Reprinted in *The Logic of Action One: Method, Money, and the Austrian School*. Glos, UK: Edward Elgar Publishing Ltd., 1997, pp. 337-349.

Rothbard, Murray N. 1997Mn. "Gold vs Fluctuating Fiat Exchange Rates," The Logic of Action One UK: Edward Elgar Publishing Limited, pp.350-363

Rothbard, Murray N. 1997No [1962]. "The Case for a 100 Percent Gold Dollar," In Search of a Monetary Constitution, Leland B. Yeager, ed., Cambridge, MA: Harvard University Press, pp. 94-136, and Auburn, AL: Ludwig von Mises Institute, 1991. See also "The Logic of Action One," pp. 364-384.

Rothbard, Murray N. 1997O p[1971]. "Lange, Mises and Praxeology: The Retreat from Marxism." Toward Liberty. Vol. II, Menlo Park, CA: Institute for Humane Studies, pp. 307-321. Reprinted in The Logic of Action One: Method, Money, and the Austrian School. Glos, UK: Edward Elgar Publishing Ltd., 1997, pp. 384-396.

Rothbard, Murray N. 1997Pq [1991]. "The End of Socialism and the Calculation Debate Revisited." The Review of Austrian Economics, Vol. 5, No. 2, pp. 51-76. Reprinted in The Logic of Action One: Method, Money, and the Austrian School. Glos, UK: Edward Elgar Publishing Ltd., 1997, pp. 408-437; http://www.mises.org/journals/rae/pdf/rae5_2_3.pdf

Rothbard, Murray N. 1997Qr. The Logic of Action Two: Applications and Criticism from the Austrian School, Vol. II, Cheltenham, UK: Edward Elgar

Rothbard, Murray N. 1997Rs. "Buchanan and Tullock's The Calculus of Consent." The Logic of Action Two: Applications and Criticism from the Austrian School. Glos, UK: Edward Elgar Publishing Ltd., pp. 269-274.

Rothbard, Murray N. 1997St[1988]. "The Myth of Free Banking in Scotland," Review of Austrian Economics, 2, pp. 229-246; see also in The Logic of Action Two pp. 311-330

Rothbard, Murray N. 1998[1982] The Ethics of Liberty, Humanities Press, Atlantic Highlands, N.J., http://www.mises.org/rothbard/ethics/ethics.asp

Rothbard, Murray N. 2004 [2001, 1993, 1970, 1962]. Man, Economy, and State with Power and the Market. Scholar's Edition. Auburn: The Mises Institute. http://www.mises.org/rothbard/mespm.pdf

Rothbard, Murray N. 2005. What Has Government Done to Our Money and The Case for a 100 Percent Gold Dollar. Auburn, AL: The Mises Institute

Rothbard, Murray N. n.d. Economic Depressions: Causes and Cure. Lansing, MI: Constitutional Alliance. Alternative title: Depressions: Their Cause and Cure.

Rozeff, Michael S. 2005. "Original Appropriation and Its Critics." September 1.
http://www.lewrockwell.com/rozeff/rozeff18.html

Sainsbury, Mark and Timothy Williamson. 1997. "Sorites," in R. Hale and C. Wright, eds., Blackwell Companion to the Philosophy of Language. Oxford: Blackwell.

Salerno, Joseph T. 1982. "The 100 Percent Gold Standard: A Proposal for Monetary Reform," in Supply-Side Economics, Richard Fink, ed., Frederick, MD: University Publications of American

Salerno, Joseph T. 1987. "Gold Standards: True and False," in The Search for Stable Money, James A. Dorn and Anna J. Schwartz, Chicago: University of Chicago Press, pp. 241-256;

Salerno, Joseph T. 1989. "Comment on Tullock's 'Why Austrians Are Wrong About Depressions," Review of Austrian Economics, Vol. 3, pp. 141-145 http://www.mises.org/journals/rae/pdf/rae3_1_11.pdf

Salerno, Joseph T. 1990A. "Ludwig von Mises as Social Rationalist," Review of Austrian Economics, Vol. 4, pp. 26-54; http://www.mises.org/journals/rae/pdf/rae4_1_2.pdf

Salerno, Joseph T. 1990B. "Postscript: Why a Socialist Economy is 'Impossible'," in Ludwig von Mises, Economic Calculation in the Socialist Commonwealth, Auburn, AL: Ludwig von Mises Institute, pp. 51-71.

Salerno, Joseph T. 1992. "The Development of Keynes's Economics: From Marshall to Millenialism," Review of Austrian Economics, Vol. 6, No. 1, pp. 3-64

Salerno, Joseph T. 1993. "Mises and Hayek Dehomogenized," Review of Austrian Economics, Vol. 6, No. 2, pp. 113-146; http://www.mises.org/journals/rae/pdf/rae6_2_5.pdf

Salerno, Joseph, T. 1994. "Ludwig von Mises's Monetary Theory in Light of Modern Monetary Thought," Review of Austrian Economics, Vol. 8, No. 1, pp. 71-115.

Salerno, Joseph. 1995. "A Final Word: Calculation, Knowledge and Appraisement," Review of Austrian Economics, Vol. 9, No. 1, pp. 141-142; http://www.mises.org/journals/rae/pdf/rae9_1_8.pdf

Salerno, Joseph. 2001. "Does the Concept of Secular Growth Have a Place in Capital-Based Macroeconomics," The Quarterly Journal of Austrian Economics, Vol. 4, No. 3, Fall

Salerno, Joseph. 2003. "An Austrian Taxonomy of Deflation – With Applications to the U.S." The Quarterly Journal of Economics. 6 (4): 81-109. http://www.mises.org/journals/qjae/pdf/qjae6_4_8.pdf

Salerno, Joseph. 2004A. "Money matters no more?" June 29; http://www.mises.org/fullstory.aspx?control=1550&id=74

Salerno, Joseph. 2004B. Deflation and Depression: Where's the Link? October 5. http://www.mises.org/fullstory.aspx?control=1583

Salins, Peter D. 1980. The Ecology of Housing Destruction: Economic Effects of Public Intervention in the Housing Market, New York: New York University Press.

Samuelson, P. A. 1946. "Lord Keynes and the General Theory." Econometrica. July. Reprinted in: Harris, Seymour, ed. The New Economics. Alfred A. Knopf (1948)

Samuelson, Paul A. 1954. "The Pure Theory of Public Expenditures," Review of Economics and Statistics, 36(4): 350-356

Samuelson, Paul A. 1955. "Diagrammatic Exposition of a Theory of Public Expenditure," Review of Economics and Statistics, 37(4):350-356

Samuelson, Paul A. 1958. "Aspects of Public Expenditure Theories," Review of Economics and Statistics, 40(4):332-33

Samuelson, Paul A. 1964. Economics, 6th ed. New York: McGraw Hill

Samuelson, Paul A. 1970[1967]. Economics. 7th ed. New York: McGraw-Hill

Samuelson, P. A. and W. D. Nordhaus. 1985. Economics. 12th ed. McGraw-Hill Book Co.

Saulnier, Raymond J. 1938. Contemporary Monetary Theory. New York: Columbia University Press. Part III, pp. 213-300.

Say, Jean-Baptiste. 1971 [1880]. A Treatise on Political Economy: or the Production, Distribution and Consumption of Wealth. Translated by C.R. Prinsep and Clement C. Biddle. New York: Augustus M. Kelley

Schmidtchen, Dieter. 1993. "Time, Uncertainty, and Subjectivism: Giving More Body to Law and Economics", International Review of Law and Economics, 13: 61-84

Schmidtz, David. 1991. The Limits of Government: An Essay on the Public Goods Argument, Boulder Co: Westview Press

Scholliers, Peter. 1989. Real wages in 19th and 20th century Europe: historical and comparative perspectives. New York: Berg, St. Martin's Press; http://www.worldcatlibraries.org/wcpa/ow/f7604190d73460f9a19afeb4da09e526.html

Schumpeter, J. A. 1954. History of Economic Analysis. Oxford University Press.

Sechrest, Larry. 1987. "White's Free Banking Thesis: A Case of Mistaken Identity," Review of Austrian Economics, November, Vol. II, 247-57.

Sechrest, Larry J. 1988. "White's Free-Banking Thesis: A Case of Mistaken Identity," Review of Austrian Economics, 2, pp. 247-258.

Sechrest, Larry. 1989A. Review of George Selgin's The Theory of Free Banking, Journal of Economics, Vol. XV, 196-98.

Sechrest, Larry. 1989B. "Free Banking vs. Central Banking: A Geometrical Analysis," South African Journal of Economic and Management Sciences, November, Vol. II, 83-97.

Sechrest, Larry. 1991a. "Free Banking in Scotland: A Dissenting View," Cato Journal, Winter, Vol. 10, No. 3, 799-808.

Sechrest, Larry. 1991b. "Banking, Central and Free", pages 145-51, Magill's Survey of Social Science: Economics, Salem Press.

Sechrest, Larry. 1993. Free Banking: Theory, History, and a Laissez-Faire Model, Westport, Connecticut: Quorum Books

Sechrest, Larry J. 1999. Rand, anarchy, and taxes. The Journal of Ayn Rand Studies 1, no. 1, Fall: 87–105.

Sechrest, Larry J. 2003. "Privateering and National Defense: Naval Warfare for Private Profit." In Hoppe, Hans-Hermann, ed., The Myth of National Defense: Essays on the Theory and History of Security Production. Auburn, AL: The Ludwig von Mises Institute, pp. 239-274

Sechrest, Larry. 2004. "Public Goods and Private Solutions in Maritime History." The Quarterly Journal of Austrian Economics. Vol. 7, No. 2. Summer, 3-27; http://www.mises.org/journals/qjae/pdf/qjae7_2_1.pdf

Sechrest, Larry. 2007. "Free Banking Basics," The Free Radical, July/August, Vol. 76, 40-41.
Selgin, G.A. 1988a. "Praxeology and Understanding: An Analysis of the Controversy in Austrian Economics." Review of Austrian Economics. Vol. 2, pp. 19-58; and Praxeology and Understanding, Auburn, AL: Ludwig von Mises Institute, 1990.

Selgin, George A. 1988b. The Theory of Free Banking: Money Supply Under Competitive Note Issue, Totowa, N.J.: Rowman and Littlefield.

Selgin, George. 1994. "Free Banking and Monetary Control." Economic Journal 104: 1449-59.

Selgin, George. 1998. The Theory of Free Banking: Money Supply under Competitive Note Issue. Totowa, New Jersey: Rowman & Littlefield

Selgin, George. 2007a. "Is fractional-reserve banking inflationary?" January 23. *Free Market News Network;* http://www.fmnn.com/Analysis/241/6794/banking.asp?nid=6794&wid=241

Selgin, George. 2007b. "Notes on free banking: fractional reserves and economic development, part I" February 14. Free Market News Network; http://www.fmnn.com/Analysis/241/6939/notes.asp?nid=6939&wid=241

Selgin, George. 2007c. "Notes on free banking: fractional reserves and economic development, part II" February 15. Free Market News Network; http://www.fmnn.com/Analysis/241/6949/notes.asp?nid=6949&wid=241

Selgin, George A., and White, Lawrence H., 1996, "In Defense of Fiduciary Media - or, We are Not Devo(lutionists), We are Misesians!," Review of Austrian Economics, Vol. 9, No. 2, pp. 83-107; http://mises.org/journals/rae/pdf/rae9_2_5.pdf

Sennholz, Hans, ed. 1975. The Lustre of Gold. Westport, CT Greenwood Press, part IV

Sennholz, Hans. 1979. Age of Inflation, Western Islands; chap. VI

Sennholz, Hans. 1985. Money and Freedom, Spring Mills, Penn.: Libertarian Press, ch. 8

Sexton, Robert L. 2002. Exploring Macroeconomics. 2nd ed. Cincinnati: South-Western College Publishing.

Shah, Parth. 1997. "The Option Clause in Free-Banking Theory and History: A Reappraisal," The Review of Austrian Economics, Vol. 10, No. 2, pp. 1-26
Shapiro, Fred R. 1966. "The Most Cited Law Review Articles Revisited." 71 Chi.-Kent L. Rev, 751, 767

Shostak, Frank. 2003. "The Myth of Price Stability." August 26; http://www.mises.org/fullstory.aspx?control=1303

Shostak, Frank. 2004. "The Myth of Shock-Free Monetary Policy." September 5. http://www.mises.org/fullstory.aspx?control=1561

Shostak, Frank. 2008. "The Fed's New Tricks Are Creating Disaster," March 18; http://www.mises.org/story/2922

Shoup, Carl S. 1969. Public Finance. Chicago: Aldine

Shugart II, William F. 1987. "Don't Revise the Clayton Act, Scrap It!" Cato Journal. 6 (3): 925-932

Siegel, Barry, ed. 1984. Money in Crisis: The Federal Reserve, The Economy, and Monetary Reform. San Francisco: Pacific Institute.

Simons, Henry. 1936. "Rules vs. Authority in Monetary Policy," Journal of Political Economy, Vol. XLIV;

Simpson, Barry Dean, and Scott A. Kjar. Unpublished. "Israel Kirzner's Didactic Rediscovered."

Skousen, Mark. 1990. The Structure of Production, New York: New York University Press

Skousen, Mark. 1991. Economics, Homewood, IL: Irwin

Skousen, Mark, ed. 1992. Dissent on Keynes, A Critical Appraisal of Economics. New York: Praeger

Skousen, Mark. 1998. The 100 Percent Gold Standard: Economics of a Pure-Money Commodity, Lanham, MD: University Press of America, 1977. And Economics of a Pure Gold Standard. Auburn, AL: Ludwig von Mises Institute

Skousen, Mark. 2001. "The Perseverance of Paul Samuelson's Economics." Forecasts & Strategies. February 1; http://www.mskousen.com/Books/Articles/perserverance.html

Slok, Torsten. 2000. "Can Monetary Policy Be Effective During Transition?: Lessons from Mongolia." Finance & Development. Vol. 37, No. 3, September, International Monetary Fund; http://www.internationalmonetaryfund.com/external/pubs/ft/fandd/2000/09/slok.htm

Slutsky, E. 1927. "The Summation of Random Causes as the Source of Cyclic Processes." Problems of Economic Conditions. Moscow: Conjuncture Institute. 3 (1).

Slutsky, E. 1937. "The Summation of Random Causes as the Source of Cyclic Processes." Econometrica. 5: 105-146.

Smiley, Gene. 1987. "Some Austrian Perspectives on Keynesian Fiscal Policy and the Recovery in the Thirties," Review of Austrian Economics, Vol. 1, pp. 145-179

Smith, Adam. 1979 [1776]. An Inquiry into the Nature and Causes of the Wealth of Nations, Indianapolis, IN: Liberty Fund

Smith, Barry. 1990. "The Question of Apriorism," Austrian Economics Newsletter, Fall

Smith, Barry. 1994. "The Philosophy of Austrian Economics," Review of Austrian Economics, 7(2), pp. 127-132;

Smith, Barry. 1996. "In Defense of Extreme (Fallibilistic) Apriorism," Journal of Libertarian Studies, 12, pp.179-192;

Smith, Jr., Fred L. 1983. "Why not Abolish Antitrust?" Regulation. Jan-Feb, 23

Sneed, John D., 1977, "Order without law: where will anarchists keep the madmen?," The Journal of Libertarian Studies, Vol. 1, No. 2, Spring, pp. 117-124

Snippe, J. 1987. Intertemporal coordination and the economics of Keynes: comment on Garrison." History of Political Economy. 19(2): 329-334.

Snowdon, Brian, Howard Vane and Peter Wynarczyk, eds. 1994. A Modern Guide to Macroeconomics: An Introduction to Competing Schools of Thought. Cheltanham, UK: Edward Elgar.

Sorensen, Roy. 2001.Vagueness and Contradiction. Oxford: Clarendon Press.
Sowell, Thomas. 1972. Say's Law: An Historical Analysis. Princeton, N.J.: Princeton University Press.

Sowell, Thomas. 1975. Race and Economics. New York: Longman

Sowell, Thomas. 1981. Ethnic America. New York: Basic Books.

Sowell, Thomas. 1982. "Weber and Bakke and the presuppositions of 'Affirmative Action,'" Discrimination, Affirmative Action and Equal Opportunity, Walter Block and Michael Walker, eds., Vancouver: The Fraser Institute, pp. 37-63

Sowell, Thomas. 1983. The Economics and Politics of Race: An International Perspective. New York, Morrow.

Sowell, Thomas. 1994. Race and Culture: A World View. New York: Basic Books

Sowell, Thomas. 1995. "Repealing the Law of Gravity," Forbes, May 22.

Spooner, Lysander. 1966 [1870]. No Treason: The Constitution of No Authority and A Letter to Thomas F. Bayard, Larkspur, Colorado: Rampart College;
http://www.lysanderspooner.org/notreason.htm

Spulber, Daniel F, ed. 2002. Famous Fables of Economics, Myths of Market Failures, Blackwell.

Stalebrink, Odd J. 2004. "The Hayek and Mises Controversy: Bridging Differences." Quarterly Journal of Austrian Economics, Vol. 7, No. 1, Spring, pp. 27-38

Stigler, G. J. 1957. "Perfect Competition, Historically Contemplated." JPE: 65 (Feb.) reprinted in Stigler, G. J. 1965. Essays in the History of Economics. Chicago: Univ. of Chicago Press

Stigler, George J. 1961. "The Economics of Information," Journal of Political Economy 69, June

Stigler, George. 1962 [1942]. The Theory of Price. New York: Macmillan.

Stigler, G. J. 1965. "Perfect Competition, Historically Contemplated." in Essays in the History of Economics. Chicago: Univ. of Chicago Press, pp. 266-267. Originally pub.: 1957. JPE: 65 (February).
Stigler, George. 1968. The Organization of Industry. Richard D. Irwin.

Strigl, Richard von. (1934)[2000]. Capital & Production. Auburn, AL: The Mises Institute

Stringham, Edward. 1998-1999. "Justice Without Government," Journal of Libertarian Studies, Vol. 14, No. 1, Winter, pp. 53-77

Stringham, Edward. 2001. "Kaldor-Hicks Efficiency and the Problem of Central Planning." Quarterly Journal of Austrian Economics. 4 (2): 41-50. http://www.qjae.org/journals/qjae/pdf/qjae4_2_3.pdf

Stringham E. P. and Nicholas A. Snow. 2008. The broken trailer fallacy: Seeing the unseen effects of government policies in Post-Katrina New Orleans. The International Journal of Social Economics. Vol. 35, No.7; pp. 480-489

Stroup, Richard L., and Baden, John A. 1982. "Endowment Areas: A Clearing in the Policy Wilderness," Cato Journal, 2 Winter, pp. 691-708

Stroup, Richard L., and John C. Goodman, et. al. 1991. Progressive Environmentalism: A Pro-Human, Pro-Science, Pro-Free Enterprise Agenda for Change, Dallas, TX: National Center for Policy Analysis, Task Force Report

Swire, P. P. 1992. "Bank Insolvency Law Now That It Matters Again." Duke Law Journal. 42 (December): 469. http://www.acs.ohio state.edu/units/law/swire1/psduke.htm

Tannehill, Morris and Linda Tannehill. 1984 [1970]. The Market for Liberty, New York: Laissez Faire Books

Taussig, Frank W. 1896. Wages and Capital. New York: Augustus M. Kelley

Taylor, A.J.P. 1972. The First World War. London: Perigee Trade

Taylor, A.J.P. 1996. The Origins of the Second World War. New York, NY: Simon & Schuster

Taylor, A.J.P. 2001. Private Property, Public Interest, and the Role of the State in Nineteenth-century Britain: The Case of Lighthouses. The Historical Journal. 44 (3): 749-771.

Telser, Lester. 1987. A Theory of Efficient Cooperation and Competition. Cambridge University Press.

The Concise Encyclopedia of Economics. http://www.econlib.org/library/Enc/bios/Jevons.html

The Economist. 1994. "For Richer, For Poorer," November.

Thies, Clifford F., ed. 1996. The Contributions of Murray Rothbard to Monetary Economics. Winchester, VA: Durell Institute of Monetary Science;

Thirlby, G.F. 1981. "The Subjective Theory of Value and Accounting Cost," Buchanan, James M. and G.F. Thirlby, eds., L.S.E. Essays on Cost, New York: New York University Press, pp. 135-162.

Thornton, Mark. 2002. "Corruption and Foreign Aid." November 19. http://www.mises.org/fullstory.aspx?control=1093

Tinsley, Patrick. 1998-1999. "With Liberty and Justice for All: A Case for Private Police," Journal of Libertarian Studies, Vol. 14, No. 1, Winter, pp. 95-100

Tucker, Irvin. 2003. Macroeconomics for Today. 3rd ed. Cincinnati: South-Western College Publishing.

Tucker, Jeffrey. 1997. "The Marshall Plan Myth." The Free Market. September, Vol. 15, No. 9; http://www.mises.org/freemarket_detail.asp?control=120&sortorder=articledate

Tucker, William. 1984. "Black Family Agonistes," The American Spectator, July, pp. 14-17.

Tucker, William. 1990. The Excluded Americans: Homelessness and Housing Policies, Washington D.C., Regnery Gateway

Tullock, Gordon. 1987. "Why the Austrians Are Wrong About Depressions." Review of Austrian Economics 2: 73-78. http://www.mises.org/journals/rae/pdf/rae2_1_4.pdf

Tullock, Gordon. 1989. "Reply to Comment by Joseph T. Salerno." Review of Austrian Economics 3: 147-49.
http://www.mises.org/journals/rae/pdf/rae3_1_12.pdf
U.S. Bureau of Economic Analysis, Fixed Reproducible Tangible Wealth in the United States, 1925–94, Washington, DC: U.S. Government Printing Office, August 1999;
http://www.bea.gov/bea/regional/definitions/nextpage.cfm?key=Capital%20consumption%20adjustment%20(CCAdj)

Van den Hauwe, Ludwig. 2000. "Hayek-Keynes Debate, The: Lessons for Current Business Cycle Research" The Quarterly Journal of Austrian Economics vol. 3, no. 2: pp. 63-79

Van Dun, Frank. Unpublished. "Bayesianism and Austrian Apriorism." http://allserv.rug.ac.be/~frvandun/Texts/Articles/Bayesianism-Austrian.pdf

Van Zandt, David E. 1993. "The Lessons of the Lighthouse: 'Government' or 'Private' Provision of Goods." Journal of Legal Studies, Vo. XXII, January, pp. 47-72.

Vance, Laurence M. 2007. "Real Tax Reform." April 16; http://www.mises.org/story/2552

Vance, Laurence M. 2006. "The Fraudulent Tax" October 9; http://www.mises.org/story/2327

Vance, Laurence M. 2000. "The Foreign Aid Debacle." The Free Market. December, Vol. 18, No. 12;
http://www.mises.org/freemarket_detail.asp?control=334&sortorder=articledate

Varian, Hal R. 1993. "Markets for public goods?" Critical Review. Vol. 17, No. 4, pp. 539-557

Varzi, Achille. 2003. "Cut-offs and their Neighbors," J. C. Beall, ed., Liars and Heaps: New Essays on Paradox. Oxford: Oxford University Press.

Vedder, Richard and Lowell Gallaway. 1997 [1993]. Out of Work: Unemployment and Government in Twentieth-Century America. Updated ed. The Independent Institute.

Vieira, Edwin. 2002. Pieces of Eight, 2nd ed., Fredericksburg, VA: Sheridan

Vihanto, Martti. 1988. The Austrian Theory of Free Monetary Institutions, Turku, Finland: Turku School of Economics

Vuk, Vedran. 2008. Taking advantage of disaster: misrepresentation of housing shortage for political gain. The International Journal of Social Economics. Vol. 35, No. 8, pp. 603-614.

Wagner, Richard E. 1999. "Austrian Cycle Theory: Saving the Wheat while Discarding the Chaff." Review of Austrian Economics. 12 (1) 65-80; 2000. reprinted, Festschrift for James Buchanan: http://www.gmu.edu/jbc/fest/files/wagner.htm

Walras, Leon. 1874. Principe d'une theorie mathematique de l'echange. Memoire lu a l'Academie des sciences morales et politiques (Seances des 16 et 23 aout 1873) Paris, Guillaumin,

Walton, Douglas N. 1992. Slippery Slope Arguments. Oxford: Clarendon Press.

Wertes. Vienna. Cited in Mises (1980, 95).

White, Larry. 1977. "T Shirt with Hayekian Structure of Production Triangle on it."

White, Lawrence H. 1984. Methodology of the Austrian School Economists. Auburn, AL: Ludwig von Mises Institute

White, Lawrence H. 1989. Competition and Currency, New York: New York University Press

White, Lawrence H. 1992. Competition and Currency: Essays on Free Banking and Money. New York: New York University Press

White, Lawrence H. 1995. Free Banking in Britain: Theory, Experience, and Debate, 1800-1845, 2nd ed. London: Institute of Economic Affairs

White, Lawrence H. 1999. The Theory of Monetary Institutions. Oxford: Basil Blackwell

Whitehead, Roy and Walter Block. 2000. "Environmental Justice Risks in the Petroleum Industry," William and Mary Environmental Law and Policy Review, Vol. 24, No. 1, Winter, pp. 67-88

Whitehead, Roy and Walter Block. 2003. "Taking the assets of the criminal to compensate victims of violence: a legal and philosophical approach," Wayne State University Law School Journal of Law in Society Vol. 5, No. 1, Fall, pp. 229-254
Wicksell, Knut. 1934. Lectures on Political Economy. George Routledge and Sons, Ltd.

Wicksell, Knut. 1969. Selected Papers on Economic Theory. New York: Augustus M. Kelley.

Wien-Claudi, Franz. 1936. Austrian Theories of Capital, Interest, and The Trade-Cycle. London: Stanley Nott Ltd.

Wieser, Friedrich. von. 1884. Über den Ursprung und die Hauptgesetze deswirtschaftlichen

Williamson, O. E. 1985. The Economic Institutions of Capitalism. The Free Press.

Williamson, O. E. 2000. "The New Institutional Economics: Taking Stock, Looking Ahead," Journal of Economic Literature, 38, September, pp. 595-613;

Witt, Marco de. 1991. "On The Misesian Epistemology," Hallinnon Tutkimus: The Special Issue of the Austrian Theory. vol. 4, pp. 300-305;

Wollstein, Jarret B. 1969. "Society Without Coercion." Society Without Government. New York: Arno Press

Woods, Thomas E. Jr. 2005. The Church and the Market: A Catholic Defense of the Free Economy Rowman and Littlefield

Woolridge, William C. 1970. Uncle Sam the Monopoly Man, New Rochelle, N.Y.: Arlington House

Yeager, Leland B. 1986. "The Significance of Monetary Disequilibrium." Cato Journal. 6 (2): 369-99

Young, Andrew T. 2005. "Reallocating labor to initiate changes in capital structures: Hayek revisited." *Economics Letters*. Vol. 89, No. 3, pp. 275-282; http://ideas.repec.org/a/eee/ecolet/v89y2005i3p275-282.html

INDEX

INDEX

INDEX

INDEX

INDEX

INDEX

INDEX

INDEX

INDEX

INDEX

INDEX

INDEX